k_I Weighted average cost of capital for a project

k^* Cost of equity capital if all equity financed

L Parent's target debt ratio

LC   Local currency

L/C   Letter of credit

LDC   Less-developed country

LIBOR   London interbank offer rate

MNC   Multinational corporation

NPV   Net present value

OFDI   Office of Foreign Direct Investment

P Put option premium

P/E   Price-earnings ratio on a share of stock

PPP   Purchasing power parity

r Effective yield on a bond

r_h Home currency interest rate

r_f Foreign currency interest rate

r_{us} U.S. interest rate

r_L Local currency interest rate

R_f Risk-free rate of return

R_m Required return on the market

S Current spot rate

S_i Interest subsidy in period i

SDR   Special drawing right

t (a) Tax rate or (b) Time, when used as a subscript

t_a Foreign affiliate tax rate

T_i Tax savings in period i associated with using debt financing

X_i Home currency cash flow in period i

FOUNDATIONS OF MULTINATIONAL FINANCIAL MANAGEMENT

FIFTH EDITION

Alan C. Shapiro

UNIVERSITY OF SOUTHERN CALIFORNIA

WILEY

JOHN WILEY & SONS, INC.

Publisher	Susan Elbe
Acquisitions Editor	Leslie Kraham
Marketing Manager	Charity Robey
Production Editor	Sandra Russell
Designer	Harold Nolan
Managing Editor	Kevin Dodds
Associate Editor	Cindy Rhoads
Cover Designer	Benjamin Reece
Production Management Services	Leyh Publishing, LLC

This book was typeset in 10.5/12 Berkeley by Leyh Publishing, LLC, and printed and bound by RR Donnelley-Willard. The cover was printed by Phoenix Color.

This book is printed on acid-free paper. ∞

U.S. ISBN: 0-471-56337-4
WIE ISBN: 0-471-66117-1

Printed in the United States of America.

10   9   8   7   6   5   4   3   2   1

BRIEF CONTENTS

CONTENTS

PART III   FOREIGN EXCHANGE RISK MANAGEMENT

PART IV   FINANCING THE MULTINATIONAL CORPORATION

PART VI   MULTINATIONAL WORKING CAPITAL MANAGEMENT

APPROACH

The basic thrust of this fifth edition of *Foundations of Multinational Financial Management* is to provide a conceptual framework within which the key financial decisions of the multinational firm can be analyzed. As in the sixth edition of *Multinational Financial Management*, my more comprehensive book on this topic, the approach is to treat international financial management as a natural and logical extension of the principles learned in the foundations course in financial management. Thus, it builds on and extends the valuation framework provided by domestic corporate finance to account for dimensions unique to international finance.

Foundations focuses on decision making in an international context. Analytical techniques help translate the often vague rules of thumb used by international financial executives into specific decision criteria. The book offers a variety of real-life examples, both numerical and institutional, that demonstrate the use of financial analysis and reasoning in solving international financial problems. These examples have been culled from the thousands of illustrations of corporate practice that I have collected over the years from business periodicals and my consulting practice. By scattering the best of these examples throughout the text, students can see the value of examining decision problems with the aid of a solid theoretical foundation. Seemingly disparate facts and events can then be interpreted as specific manifestations of more general financial principles.

All the traditional areas of corporate finance are explored, including working capital management, capital budgeting, cost of capital, and financial structure. However, this is done from the perspective of a multinational corporation, concentrating on those decision elements that are rarely, if ever, encountered by purely domestic firms. These elements include multiple currencies with frequent exchange rate changes and varying rates of inflation, differing tax systems, multiple money markets, exchange controls, segmented capital markets, and political risks such as nationalization or expropriation. Throughout the book, I have tried to demystify and simplify multinational financial management by showing that its basic principles rest on the same foundation as does corporate finance.

The emphasis throughout this book is on taking advantage of being multinational. Too often companies focus on the threats and risks inherent in venturing abroad rather than on the opportunities that are available to multinational firms. These opportunities include the ability to obtain a greater degree of international diversification than security purchases alone can provide as well as the ability to arbitrage between imperfect capital markets, thereby obtaining funds at a lower cost than could a purely domestic firm.

AUDIENCE

Foundations of Multinational Financial Management, as suggested earlier, is a shorter version of my other text, *Multinational Financial Management* (MFM). It emphasizes broad concepts and practices rather than extensive quantitative material. Compared to *MFM*, *Foundations* reduces the range and complexity of the subject matter covered. Although *Foundations* is intended primarily for an undergraduate audience, it is suitable for use in master's level courses where there is not enough time to cover the full range of topics dealt with in *MFM* or where the students do not have the necessary preparation for using *MFM*. It is also suitable for use in bank management and other executive development programs.

FEATURES

Foundations of Multinational Financial Management presumes a knowledge of basic corporate finance, economics, and algebra. However, it does not assume prior knowledge of international economics or international finance, and it is, therefore, self-contained in that respect. For those who are not familiar with *Multinational Financial Management*, here are some of the distinctive features that have led to its widespread adoption. These features have been incorporated and enhanced in *Foundations*.

- Extensive discussion of the basic concepts of absolute and comparative advantage as well as some insight into the gains and income redistributions associated with free trade and the consequences of barriers to trade (Appendix 1A: The Origins and Consequences of International Trade)
- Role of expectations in determining exchange rates (Chapter 2)
- Extensive discussion of the Mexican currency crisis in 1994–1995 (Chapter 2)
- Discussion of currency boards and the role of central bank credibility in the context of the dramatic changes made recently in Argentina and New Zealand (Chapter 2)
- Analysis of the September 1992 and August 1993 European currency crises (Chapter 3)
- Discussion of monetary union, optimum currency areas, and the causes and consequences of the introduction of the euro (Chapter 3)
- Extensive discussion of the causes and consequences of the Asian and other emerging market currency crises in 1997–1998 (Chapters 1, 2, and 3)
- Integrated discussion of the five key parity relationships in international finance and how they can be used to forecast exchange rates (Chapter 4)
- Discussion of recent research on biases in the forward exchange rate and possible causes, including the peso problem (Chapter 4)
- Discussion on linking currency forecasts to specific decision rules (Chapter 4)
- Use of the balance-of-payments framework to assess the economic links among nations (Chapter 5)
- Demonstration of double-entry bookkeeping in balance-of-payments accounting (Chapter 5)
- Discussion of country risk analysis for both companies and banks, along with an analysis of the dramatic changes taking place throughout Latin America, Eastern Europe, and China and their implications for economic growth (Chapter 6)
- Comprehensive discussion of the foreign exchange market and its institutions and mechanisms, including electronic trading (Chapter 7)
- Understanding of currency futures and options contracts (Chapter 8), and their use in exchange risk management (Chapter 10)
- Presentation on how to compute gains, losses, and maintenance margins on a futures contract (Chapter 8)
- Discussion of currency spreads and knockout (or barrier) options (Chapter 8)
- Use of interest rate and currency swaps to manage foreign exchange and interest rate risk (Chapter 9)
- Discussion of fixed-for-fixed and fixed-for-floating currency interest rate swaps (Chapter 9)

- Discussion of interest-rate risk management techniques, including forward rate agreements, forward forwards, and Eurodollar futures (Chapter 9)
- Discussion and comparison of the three basic types of exposure–accounting exposure, transaction exposure, and operating exposure (Chapter 10)
- Extended discussion on the design of a hedging strategy (Chapter 10)
- Discussion of managing the risk management function, including lessons learned from some highly publicized cases of derivatives-related losses (Chapter 10)
- Use of currency risk sharing in international contracts (Chapter 10)
- Comparison of hedging alternatives when there are transaction costs (Chapter 10)
- Discussion of cross-hedging using a simple regression analysis (Chapter 10)
- Discussion of how to structure and use currency collars (or range forwards) and currency cylinders to hedge exchange risk (Chapter 10)
- Identification of the economic, as opposed to accounting, aspects of foreign exchange risk (Chapter 11)
- Development of marketing and production strategies to cope with exchange risk (Chapter 11)
- Analysis of how Japanese firms have coped with the appreciation of the yen (Chapter 11)
- Discussion of the functions, consequences, and globalization of financial markets and the links between national and international capital markets (Chapter 12)
- Discussion of the external medium- and long-term financing options available to the multinational corporation (Chapter 12)
- Discussion of international differences in corporate governance and the economic consequences of those differences (Chapter 12)
- Discussion of project financing (Chapter 12)
- Discussion of the Eurocurrency and Eurobond markets (Chapter 13)
- Discussion of how to calculate the effective costs of Eurocurrency loans and Eurocommercial paper and all-in costs of Eurobonds (Chapter 13)
- Evaluation of foreign currency-denominated debt (Chapter 14)
- Extended discussion of calculating the cost of capital for multinational companies (Chapter 14)
- Design of a global financing strategy (Chapter 14)
- Discussion of alternative approaches to estimating the cost of capital for foreign operations (Chapter 14)
- Understanding of the nature and consequences of international portfolio investment (Chapter 15)
- Discussion of the home bias in international portfolio investing and the effects of hedging on the efficient frontier for internationally diversified portfolios (Chapter 15)
- Analysis of exchange risk associated with foreign portfolio investments (Chapter 15)
- Development of global strategies of MNCs (Chapter 16)
- Assessment of the true profitability of a foreign operation (Chapter 17)
- Valuation of the growth options often associated with foreign investments (Chapter 17)

- Role of countertrade in financing international trade (Chapter 18)
- Calculation of the cost of acceptance financing and factoring (Chapter 18)
- Costs and benefits of managing interaffiliate fund flows on a global basis (Chapter 20)
- Discussion of new transfer pricing issues and "earnings-stripping" charges involving foreign company operations in the United States (Chapter 20)
- Integration of tax management with financial management based on recent tax law changes (Chapter 20)

CHANGES TO THE FIFTH EDITION

Overall, the book has been updated and shortened. Specific changes that have been made to the fifth edition of *Foundations of Multinational Financial Management* include the following:

- Part I remains as before, Environment of International Financial Management. The other sections of the book have been rearranged. A new Part II, titled Foreign Exchange and Derivative Markets, has been added. Foreign Exchange Risk Management, which was previously Part II, is now Part III. The organization of the remaining parts has been changed as well. Previously, the sequence was Part III (Working Capital Management), Part IV (Financing Foreign Operations), and Part V (Foreign Investment Analysis); it is now Part IV (Financing Foreign Operations), Part V (Foreign Investment Analysis), and Part VI (Working Capital Management). The aim is to deal with the financing subject matter, including the cost of capital, prior to discussing the investment decision.

- Part I now includes one new chapter. This addition is Chapter 4, which was previously Chapter 8, Parity Conditions in International Finance and Currency Forecasting. The aim is to bring this key chapter up front, right after the discussion of exchange rate determination and the international monetary system in Chapters 2 and 3, respectively. Further, the previous Chapter 5, Country Risk Analysis, which sheds light on key economic and political factors affecting the economic health of nations, is now Chapter 6.

- Part I also contains a new case, "Will Argentina Devalue Its Peso?," that deals with the factors that would enter into a forecast of peso devaluation.

- The section on interest-rate parity theory has been transferred from Chapter 7 (The Foreign Exchange Market) to Chapter 4 (Parity Conditions in International Finance) where it provides the link between the spot and forward exchange markets and money markets.

- The old Chapter 13, on currency and interest rate swaps, has been updated and shifted to Part II, where it is now titled Swaps and Interest Rate Derivatives.

- Old Chapters 9 and 10 have been combined into a new Chapter 10, Measuring and Managing Translation and Transaction Exposure.

- Former Chapter 15 (International Financing and International Financial Markets) has been split into two separate chapters, Chapter 12 (International Financing and National Financial Markets) and Chapter 13 (The Euromarkets).

- Part VI has a new case, "Xerox Miscopies Foreign Interest Rate Data," that explores the problems Xerox has had in recording revenues from foreign affiliates and valuing their lease receivables.

At the same time that the book has been updated, reorganized, and shortened, new material has been added, including the following:

- Many new solved numerical problems in the body of the chapters to illustrate the application of the various concepts and techniques presented in the text, along with new end-of-chapter problems.
- Addition of mini-cases in many chapters that feature a short case with a series of questions for students to answer.
- Much more discussion of China, its new role in the world economy and its various economic policies, such as its weak yuan exchange rate policy (see Chapters 1, 2, 3, and 6).

The book also contains many new charts and illustrations of corporate practice that are designed to highlight specific techniques or teaching points. Again, the emphasis is on reinforcing and making more relevant the concepts developed in the body of each chapter. To make the text more suitable as a teaching vehicle, I have added numerous questions and problems at the end of each chapter, most of which are based on up-to-date information and real-life situations.

PEDAGOGY

The pedagogical thrust of the book is greatly enhanced by including the following learning and teaching aids:

1. Focus on Corporate Practice. Throughout the text, numerous real-world examples and vignettes provide actual applications of financial concepts and theories. They show students that the issues, tools, and techniques discussed in the book are being applied to day-to-day financial decision making.

2. Extensive Use of Examples and Illustrations. Numerous short illustrations and examples of specific concepts and techniques are scattered throughout the body of most chapters.

3. Lengthier Illustrations of Corporate Practice. Seven longer illustrations of actual company practices appear at the end of key chapters and are designed to demonstrate different aspects of international financial management.

4. Problems and Discussion Questions. There are hundreds of realistic end-of-chapter questions and problems that offer practice in applying the concepts and theories being taught. Many of these questions and problems relate to actual situations and companies.

5. Chapter Learning Objectives. Each chapter opens with a statement of its action-oriented learning objectives. This statement enhances learning by previewing and guiding the reader's understanding of the materials that will be encountered in the chapter.

6. Key Terms. The introduction to each chapter also contains a list of key terms. Placing these terms at the beginning of the chapter gives readers added preparation for what is to come.

7. Key Concepts. Most pages contain one or two key ideas in the margins next to the point where these ideas appear in the text. Highlighting these key ideas serves as an effective study and review tool for students.

8. Mini-cases. Most chapters now have at least one mini-case that briefly presents a situation that illustrates an important concept in that chapter and then has a series of questions to test student understanding of that concept.

9. Each chapter has a section called "Internet Resources and Exercises" that contains a set of relevant Web sites for that chapter and several exercises that use those Web sites to address various issues that arise in the chapter.

10. Glossary. The back of the book contains a Glossary that defines all the key terms appearing in the text.

11. Supplements. A complete set of ancillary materials is available for adopters of *Foundations* to supplement the text. These include:

   - An Instructor's Manual containing detailed solutions to the end-of-chapter questions and problems and tips for teaching each chapter.

   - A Test Bank prepared by Joseph Greco of California State University-Fullerton containing over 160 additional questions and problems suitable for use in multiple-choice exams.

   - A Study Guide written by Professor Andrea L. DeMaskey of Villanova University is available. The Study Guide contains detailed chapter outlines and a number of solved questions and problems.

   - A Companion Web site containing Lecture Outline PowerPoint Presentations for each chapter prepared by Joseph Greco of California State University-Fullerton and electronic Word files for the printed supplements for instructors.

THANKS

I have been greatly aided in developing *Foundations of Multinational Financial Management* by the helpful suggestions of the following reviewers: Richard Ajayi, University of Central Florida; Robert Aubey, University of Wisconsin; James Baker, Kent State University; W. Brian Barrett, University of Miami; Donald T. Buck, Southern Connecticut State University; Deanne Butchey, Florida International University; C. Edward Chang, Southwest Missouri State University; Mitch Charkiewicz, Central Connecticut State University; Jay Choi, Temple University; Robert C. Duvic, University of Texas–Austin; Imad Elhaj, University of Louisville; Mel Jameson, University of Nevada-Las Vegas; Janice Wickstead Jadlow, Oklahoma State University; Steve Johnson, University of Texas at El Paso; Boyden C. Lee, New Mexico State University; Marc Lars Lipson, Boston University; Richard K. Lyons, University of California–Berkeley; Dileep Mehta, Georgia State University; Margaret Moore, Franklin University; Yoon S. Park, George Washington University; William Pugh, Auburn University; Bruce Seifert, Old Dominion University; Helen K. Simon, Florida International University; Jay Sultan, Bentley College; Paul J. Swanson, Jr., University of Cincinnati; Kishore Tandon, Baruch College (C.U.N.Y.); and Steve Wyatt, University of Cincinnati.

My family, especially my wife, Diane, as well as my mother and three brothers, have provided me (once again) with continual support and encouragement during the writing of this book. I appreciate the (usual) cheerfulness with which Diane and my children, Thomas and Kathryn, endured the many hours I spent writing the fifth edition of this text.

A.C.S.
Pacific Palisades

PART I
ENVIRONMENT OF INTERNATIONAL FINANCIAL MANAGEMENT

INTRODUCTION: MULTINATIONAL ENTERPRISE AND MULTINATIONAL FINANCIAL MANAGEMENT

What is prudence in the conduct of every private family can scarce be folly in that of a great kingdom. If a foreign country can supply us with a commodity cheaper than we ourselves can make it, better buy it of them with some part of the produce of our own industry employed in a way in which we have some advantage.

Adam Smith (1776)

CHAPTER LEARNING OBJECTIVES

- To understand the nature and benefits of globalization
- To explain why multinational corporations are the key players in international economic competition today
- To classify the three historical types of multinational corporations (MNCs) and explain their motivations for international expansion
- To explain why managers of MNCs need to exploit rapidly changing global economic conditions and why political policy makers must also be concerned with the same changing conditions
- To identify the advantages of being multinational, including the benefits of international diversification
- To describe the general importance of financial economics to multinational financial management and the particular importance of the concepts of arbitrage, market efficiency, capital asset pricing, and total risk
- To characterize the global financial marketplace and explain why MNC managers must be alert to capital market imperfections and asymmetries in tax regulations

KEY TERMS

absolute advantage	international diversification
arbitrage	internationalization
arbitrage pricing theory	investment decision
capital asset pricing model	investment flows
capital market imperfections	market efficiency
comparative advantage doctrine	multinational corporation (MNC)
efficient market	reverse foreign investment
financial economics	risk arbitrage
financing decision	systematic (nondiversifiable) risk
foreign direct investment	tax arbitrage
global economy	terms of trade
global manager	total risk
globalization	unsystematic (diversifiable) risk

A key theme of this book is that companies today operate within a global marketplace and can ignore this fact only at their peril. The internationalization of finance and commerce has been brought about by the great advances in transportation, communications, and information-processing technology. This development introduces a dramatic new commercial reality—the global market for standardized consumer and industrial products on a previously unimagined scale. It places primary emphasis on the one great thing all markets have in common—the overwhelming desire for dependable, world class products at aggressively low prices. The international integration of markets also introduces the global competitor, making firms insecure even in their home markets.

The transformation of the world economy has dramatic implications for business. American management, for example, is learning that the United States can no longer be viewed as a huge economy that does a bit of business with secondary economies around the world. Rather, the United States is merely one economy, albeit a very large one, that is part of an extremely competitive, integrated world economic system. To succeed, U.S. companies need great flexibility; they must be able to change corporate policies quickly as the world market creates new opportunities and challenges. Big Steel, which was virtually the antithesis of this modern model of business practice, paid the price for failing to adjust to the transformation of the world economy. Similarly, non-U.S. companies are finding that they must increasingly turn to foreign markets to source capital and technology and sell their products.

Today's financial reality is that money knows no national boundary. The dollar has become the world's central currency, with billions switched at the flick of an electronic blip from one global corporation to another, from one central bank to another. The international mobility of capital has benefited firms by giving them more financial options, while at the same time complicating the job of the chief financial officer by increasing its complexity.

Because we operate in an integrated world economy, all students of finance should have an international orientation. Thus, a key aim of this book is to help you bring to bear on key business decisions a global perspective, manifested by questions such as, Where in the *world* should we locate our plants? Which *global* market segments should we seek to penetrate? Where in the *world* should we raise our financing? This international perspective is best captured in the following quotation from an ad for J.P. Morgan, the large, successful New York bank (known as J.P. Morgan Chase & Co. since its December 2000 merger with Chase Manhattan): "J.P. Morgan is an international firm with a very important American business."

Companies today operate within a competitive and integrated world economy.

An international orientation is critical for success in today's global economy.

1.1 THE RISE OF THE MULTINATIONAL CORPORATION

Despite its increasing importance today, international business activity is not new. The transfer of goods and services across national borders has been taking place for thousands of years, antedating even Joseph's advice to the rulers of Egypt to establish that nation as the granary of the Middle East. Since the end of World War II, however, international business has undergone a revolution out of which has emerged one of the most important economic phenomena of the latter half of the twentieth century: the multinational corporation.

A **multinational corporation** (MNC) is a company engaged in producing and selling goods or services in more than one country. It ordinarily consists of a parent company located in the home country and at least five or six foreign subsidiaries, typically with a high degree of strategic interaction among the units. Some MNCs have upward of 100 foreign subsidiaries scattered around the world. The United Nations estimates that at least 35,000 companies around the world can be classified as multinational.

The rise of the multinational corporation was not anticipated by the classical theory of international trade.

Based in part on the development of modern communications and transportation technologies, the rise of the multinational corporation was unanticipated by the classical theory of international trade as first developed by Adam Smith and David Ricardo. According to this theory, which rests on the doctrine of **comparative advantage,** each nation should specialize in the production and export of those goods that it can produce with highest relative efficiency and import those goods that other nations can produce relatively more efficiently.

Underlying this theory is the assumption that goods and services can move internationally but factors of production, such as capital, labor, and land, are relatively immobile. Furthermore, the theory deals only with trade in commodities—that is, undifferentiated products; it ignores the roles of uncertainty, economies of scale, transportation costs, and technology in international trade; and it is static rather than dynamic. For all these defects, however, it is a valuable theory, and it still provides a well-reasoned theoretical foundation for free-trade arguments (see Appendix 1A). But the growth of the MNC can be understood only by relaxing the traditional assumptions of classical trade theory.

Classical trade theory implicitly assumes that countries differ enough in terms of resource endowments and economic skills for those differences to be at the center of any analysis of corporate competitiveness. Differences among individual corporate strategies are considered to be of only secondary importance; a company's citizenship is the key determinant of international success in the world of Adam Smith and David Ricardo.

Differences among corporations are more important today than differences among countries.

This theory, however, is increasingly irrelevant to the analysis of businesses in the countries currently at the core of the world economy—the United States, Japan, the nations of Western Europe, and, to an increasing extent, the most successful East Asian countries. Within this advanced and highly integrated core economy, differences among corporations are becoming more important than aggregate differences among countries. Furthermore, the increasing capacity of even small companies to operate in a global perspective makes the old analytical framework even more obsolete.

Not only are the "core nations" more homogeneous than before in terms of living standards, lifestyles, and economic organization, but their factors of production tend to move more rapidly in search of higher returns. Natural resources have lost much of their previous role in national specialization as advanced, knowledge-intensive societies move rapidly into the age of artificial materials and genetic engineering. Capital moves around the world in massive amounts at the speed of light; increasingly, corporations raise capital simultaneously in several major markets. Labor skills in these countries no longer can be considered fundamentally different; many of the students enrolled in American graduate schools are foreign, while training has become a key dimension of many joint ventures between international corporations. Technology and "know-how" are also rapidly becoming a global pool, with companies like General Electric, Morgan Stanley, Electronic Data Systems, Cisco Systems, McKinsey & Co., and IBM outsourcing software writing, accounting, engineering, and other skilled services to countries like India and China. Thanks to the massive development of the means to communicate, duplicate, store, and reproduce information, companies can now trade internationally what has historically been untradeable—education, skill, and dedication.

Against this background, the ability of corporations of all sizes to use these globally available factors of production is a far bigger factor in international competitiveness than broad macroeconomic differences among countries. Contrary to the postulates of Smith and Ricardo, the very existence of the multinational enterprise is based on the international mobility of certain factors of production. Capital raised in London on the Eurodollar market may be used by a Swiss-based pharmaceutical firm to finance the acquisition of German equipment by a subsidiary in Brazil. A single Barbie doll is made in ten countries—designed in California, with parts and clothing from Japan, China, Hong Kong, Malaysia, Indonesia, Korea, Italy, and Taiwan, and assembled in Mexico—and sold in 144 countries. Information technology also makes it possible for worker skills to flow with little regard to borders. In the semiconductor industry, the leading companies typically locate their design facilities in high-tech corridors in the United States, Japan, and Europe. Finished designs are transported quickly by computer networks to manufacturing plants in countries with more advantageous cost structures. In effect, the traditional world economy in which products are exported has been replaced by one in which value is added in several different countries.

U.S. companies have some significant competitive advantages.

The value added in a particular country—product development, design, production, assembly, or marketing—depends on differences in labor costs and unique national attributes or skills. Although trade in goods, capital, and services and the ability to shift production act to limit these differences in costs and skills among nations, differences nonetheless remain based on cultural predilections, historical accidents, and government policies. Each of these factors can affect the nature of the competitive advantages enjoyed by different nations and their companies. For example, at the moment, the United States has some significant competitive advantages. For one thing, individualism and entrepreneurship—characteristics that are deeply ingrained in the American spirit—are increasingly a source of competitive advantage as the creation of value becomes more knowledge-intensive. When inventiveness and entrepreneurship are combined with abundant risk capital, superior graduate education, and an inflow of foreign brainpower, it is not surprising that U.S. companies—from Boston to Austin, from Silicon Alley to Silicon Valley—dominate world markets in software, biotechnology, Internet-related business, microprocessors, aerospace, and entertainment. Also, U.S. firms are moving rapidly forward to construct an information superhighway and related multimedia technology, whereas their European and Japanese rivals face continued regulatory and bureaucratic roadblocks.

Recent experiences also have given the United States a significant competitive advantage. During the 1980s and 1990s, fundamental political, technological, regulatory, and economic forces radically changed the global competitive environment. A brief listing of some of these forces would include the following:

- Massive deregulation
- The collapse of Communism
- The sale of hundreds of billions of dollars of state-owned firms around the world in massive privatizations designed to shrink the public sector
- The revolution in information technologies
- The rise in the market for corporate control with its waves of takeovers, mergers, and leveraged buyouts
- The jettisoning of statist policies and their replacement by free-market policies in Third World nations
- The unprecedented number of nations submitting themselves to the exacting rigors and standards of the global marketplace

The new global economic environment is characterized by brutal price and service competition.

These forces have combined to usher in an era of brutal price and service competition. The United States is further along than other nations in adapting to this new world economic order, largely because its more open economy has forced its firms to confront rather than hide from competitors. Facing vicious competition at home and abroad, U.S. companies—including such corporate landmarks as IBM, General Motors, Walt Disney, Xerox, American Express, Coca-Cola, and Kodak—have been restructuring and investing heavily in new technologies and marketing strategies to boost productivity and expand their markets. In addition, the United States has gone further than any other industrialized country in deregulating its financial services, telecommunications, airlines, and trucking industries. The result: Even traditionally sheltered U.S. industries have become far more competitive in recent years, and so has the U.S. workforce. The heightened competitiveness of U.S. firms has, in turn, compelled European and Japanese rivals to undergo a similar process of restructuring and renewal.

> *China has become a global competitor in the past decade.*

Perhaps the most dramatic change in the international economy over the past decade is the rise of China as a global competitor. From 1978, when Deng Xiaoping launched his country's economic reform program, to 2003, China's gross domestic product rose by over 700 percent, the most rapid growth rate of any country in the world during this two-decade-plus period. Since 1991, China has attracted the largest amount of foreign investment among developing countries each year, with annual foreign investment by the late 1990s exceeding $50 billion. In 2002, China became the world's number one destination for **foreign direct investment** (FDI), which is the acquisition abroad of companies, property, or physical assets such as plant and equipment, attracting $52.7 billion in FDI flows. About 400 out of the world's 500 largest companies have now invested in China. The transformation of China from an insular nation to the world's low-cost site for labor-intensive manufacturing has had enormous effects on everything from Mexico's competitiveness as an export platform to the cost of furniture and computers in the United States to the value of the dollar to the number of U.S. manufacturing jobs.

> *The multinational corporation acquires and allocates resources on a globally coordinated basis to maximize group performance.*

The prime transmitter of competitive forces in this global economy is the multinational corporation. For example, 84 percent of China's exports in the year ending June 2003 were by foreign companies manufacturing in China. What differentiates the multinational enterprise from other firms engaged in international business is the globally coordinated allocation of resources by a single centralized management. Multinational corporations make decisions about market-entry strategy; ownership of foreign operations; and production, marketing, and financial activities with an eye to what is best for the corporation as a whole. The true multinational corporation emphasizes group performance rather than the performance of its individual parts.

MINI-CASE   *General Electric Globalizes Its Medical Systems Business*

One of General Electric's key growth initiatives is to globalize its business. According to its Web site, "Globalization no longer refers only to selling goods and services in global markets. Today's most valuable innovations and solutions are envisioned, designed, built and offered on a global scale."[1]

A critical element of General Electric's global strategy is to be first or second in the world in a business or to exit that business. For example, in 1987, GE swapped its RCA consumer electronics division for Thomson CGR, the medical equipment business of Thomson SA of France, to strengthen its own medical unit. Together with GE Medical Systems Asia (GEMSA) in Japan, CGR makes GE number one in the world market for X-ray, CAT scan, magnetic resonance, ultrasound, and other diagnostic imaging devices, ahead of Siemens (Germany), Philips (Netherlands), and Toshiba (Japan).

General Electric's production is also globalized, with each unit exclusively responsible for equipment in which it is the volume leader. Hence, GE Medical Systems (GEMS) now makes the high end of its CAT scanners and magnetic resonance equipment near Milwaukee (its headquarters) and the low end in Japan. The middle market is supplied by GE Medical Systems S.A. (France). Engineering skills pass horizontally from the

---

[1] savelives.gecareers.com/abtus_growth.html.

United States to Japan to France and back again. Each subsidiary supplies the marketing skills to its own home market.

The core of GEMS's global strategy is to "provide high value global products and services, created by global talent, for global customers."[2] As part of this strategy, "GE Medical Systems focuses on growth through globalization by aggressively searching out and attracting talent in the 150 countries in which we do business worldwide."[3]

GEMS also grows by acquiring companies overseas in order to "broaden our ability to provide product and service solutions to our customers worldwide. Through several key acquisitions, we've strengthened our position in our existing markets, and entered new and exciting markets."[4] For example, in April 2003, GE announced that it would acquire Instrumentarium, a Finnish medical technology company, for $2.1 billion. According to the press release, "The combination of Instrumentarium and GE offerings will further enable GE Medical Systems to support healthcare customers with a broad range of anesthesia monitoring and delivery, critical care, infant care and diagnostic imaging solutions and help ensure the highest quality of care."[5]

Recently, in line with GE's decision to shift its corporate center of gravity from the industrialized world to the emerging markets of Asia and Latin America, Medical Systems has set up joint ventures in India and China to make low-end CAT scanners and various ultrasound devices for sale in their local markets. These machines were developed in Japan with GEMS's 75 percent joint venture GE Yokogawa Medical Systems, but the design work was turned over to India's vast pool of inexpensive engineers through its joint venture WIPRO GE Medical Systems (India). At the same time, engineers in India and China are developing low-cost products to serve markets in Asia, Latin America, and the United States, where there is a demand from a cost-conscious medical community for cheaper machines. In 2002, for example, GEMS derived almost $1 billion in revenue from sales to China.

Although it still pursues geographic market expansion, GE's **globalization** drive now focuses on taking advantage of its global reach to find less expensive materials and intellectual capital abroad. In material procurement, GE bought $4.8 billion in materials and components abroad in 2000, up from $3.1 billion in 1999 and $1.5 billion in 1997, producing annual savings in excess of $1 billion. On the human capital side, General Electric has established research and development (R&D) centers in India and Bangladesh for its Plastics, Aircraft Engine, and Medical Systems divisions. In 2001 alone, GE hired about 1,000 Indian scientists and engineers. By sourcing intellect globally, GE now has three times the engineering capacity for the same cost. For Medical Systems, the ability to produce in low-cost countries has meant bringing to market a low-priced CAT scanner for $200,000 (most sell for $700,000–$1 million) and still earn a 30 percent operating margin.

QUESTIONS

1. What advantages does General Electric seek to attain from its international business activities?
2. What actions is it taking to gain these advantages from its international activities?
3. What risks does GE face in its foreign operations?
4. What profit opportunities for GE can arise out of those risks?

---

[2] Ibid.
[3] Ibid.
[4] Ibid.
[5] www.gemedicalsystems.com/company/acquisitions/index.html.

Evolution of the Multinational Corporation

Every year, *Fortune* publishes a list of the most admired U.S. corporations. Year in and year out, most of these firms are largely multinational in philosophy and operations. In contrast, the least admired tend to be national firms with much smaller proportions of assets, sales, or profits derived from foreign operations. Although multinationality and economic efficiency do not necessarily go hand in hand, international business is clearly of great importance to a growing number of U.S. and non-U.S. firms. The list of large American firms that receive 50 percent or more of their revenues and profits from abroad and that have a sizable fraction of their assets abroad reads like a corporate *Who's Who*: Motorola, Gillette, Dow Chemical, Colgate-Palmolive, McDonald's, and Hewlett-Packard. In 2000, Apple Computer and Pfizer earned more than 90 percent and 100 percent, respectively, of their profits overseas.

Industries differ greatly in the extent to which foreign operations are of importance to them. For example, oil companies and banks are far more heavily involved overseas than are tobacco companies and automakers. Even within industries, companies differ markedly in their commitment to international business. For example, in 2000, ExxonMobil had 69 percent of its sales, 63 percent of its assets, and 60 percent of its profits abroad. The corresponding figures for Chevron were 45 percent, 53 percent, and 52 percent. Similarly, General Motors generated 61 percent of its income overseas, in contrast to a loss on overseas operations for Ford. These and other examples of the importance of foreign operations to U.S. business are shown in Exhibit 1.1.

EXHIBIT 1.1 • SELECTED LARGE U.S. MULTINATIONALS

	Foreign Revenue ($ billions)	Foreign Revenue (% of total)	Net Profit ($ billions)	Net Profit (% of total)	Foreign Assets ($ billions)	Foreign Assets (% of total)
ExxonMobil	143.0	69%	10.2	60%	56.7	63%
Ford	51.2	30%	−0.6	NA	19.9	43%
IBM	51.2	58%	3.9	48%	14.3	40%
General Motors	48.2	26%	2.9	61%	12.6	36%
Chevron	31.4	45%	2.7	52%	27.1	53%
Hewlett-Packard	27.2	56%	2.2	61%	2.2	50%
Procter & Gamble	19.9	50%	1.5	42%	17.0	50%
Intel	19.8	59%	3.6	34%	3.9	26%
Motorola	19.7	53%	1.6	74%	16.8	40%
Dow Chemical	14.1	62%	1.1	73%	4.2	46%
Coca-Cola	12.4	61%	0.8	36%	5.5	37%
Pfizer	11.6	39%	3.9	106%	5.7	47%
McDonald's	9.0	63%	1.2	62%	12.8	59%
3M	8.8	53M	0.9	47%	2.1	37%
Colgate-Palmolive	6.6	71%	0.7	69%	3.2	67%
Gillette	5.5	60%	0.5	56%	1.8	52%
HJ Heinz	4.6	49%	0.5	58%	2.1	43%
Nike	4.0	44%	0.3	55%	0.7	43%
Apple Computer	3.8	48%	1.0	93%	0.6	13%
Avon Products	3.8	67%	0.3	69%	1.6	56%

Source: Forbes, June 30, 2001.

The degree of internationalization of the American economy is often surprising. For example, analysts estimate that about 60 percent of the U.S. film industry's revenues came from foreign markets in 1997. The film industry illustrates other dimensions of internationalization as well, many of which are reflected in *Total Recall,* a film that was made by a Hungarian-born producer and a Dutch director, starred an Austrian-born leading man (now governor of California) and a Canadian villain, was shot in Mexico, and was distributed by a Hollywood studio owned by a Japanese firm.

Exhibit 1.2 provides further evidence of the growing internationalization of American business. It shows that overseas investment by U.S. firms and U.S. investment by foreign firms are in the hundreds of billions of dollars each year. The stock of **foreign direct investment** by U.S. companies, which is the acquisition abroad of companies, property, or physical assets such as plant and equipment, reached $1.52 trillion in 2002, while direct investment by foreign companies in the United States exceeded $1.34 trillion that year. Worldwide, the stock of FDI reached $6.8 trillion in 2001, as shown in Exhibit 1.3. Moreover, these investments have grown steadily over time, facilitated by a combination of factors: falling regulatory barriers to overseas investment; rapidly declining telecommunications and transport costs; and freer domestic and international capital markets in which vast sums of money can be raised, companies can be bought, and currency and other risks can be hedged. These factors have made it easier for companies to invest abroad, to do so more cheaply, and to experience less risk than ever before. A brief taxonomy of the MNC and its evolution is given in the sections that follow.

Foreign direct investment, which is the acquisition abroad of operating assets, has grown dramatically in the past twenty years.

EXHIBIT 1.2 • ANNUAL U.S. FOREIGN DIRECT INVESTMENT INFLOWS AND OUTFLOWS: 1960–2002

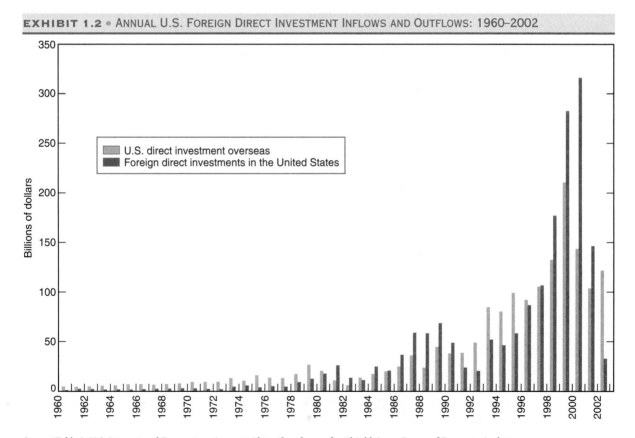

Source: "Table 1, U.S. International Transactions Accounts," http://bea.doc.gov/bea/di/table1.exe, Bureau of Economic Analysis, U.S. Department of Commerce.

EXHIBIT 1.3 • THE STOCK OF WORLDWIDE FOREIGN DIRECT INVESTMENT: 1980–2001

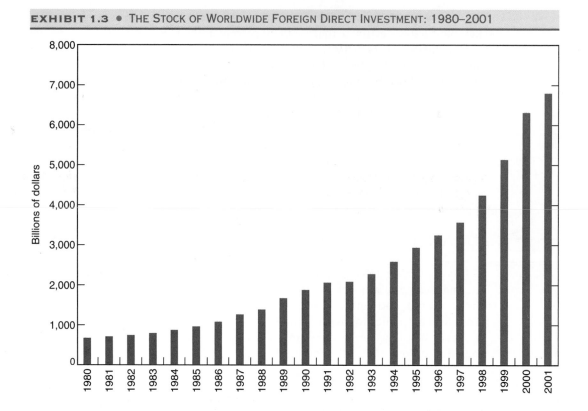

_____

The three basic types of multinational firms are raw materials seekers, market seekers, and cost minimizers.

Raw-Materials Seekers   Raw-materials seekers were the earliest multinationals, the villains of international business. They are the firms—the British, Dutch, and French East India Companies, the Hudson's Bay Trading Company, and the Union Miniere Haut-Katanga—that first grew under the protective mantle of the British, Dutch, French, and Belgian colonial empires. Their aim was to exploit the raw materials that could be found overseas. The modern-day counterparts of these firms, the multinational oil and mining companies, were the first to make large foreign investments, beginning in the early years of the twentieth century. Hence, large oil companies such as British Petroleum and Standard Oil, which went where the dinosaurs died, were among the first true multinationals. Hard-mineral companies such as International Nickel, Anaconda Copper, and Kennecott Copper were also early investors abroad.

Market Seekers   The market seeker is the archetype of the modern multinational firm that goes overseas to produce and sell in foreign markets. Examples include IBM, Volkswagen, and Unilever. Similarly, branded consumer-products companies such as Nestlé, Levi Strauss, McDonald's, Procter & Gamble, and Coca-Cola have been operating abroad for decades and maintain vast manufacturing, marketing, and distribution networks from which they derive substantial sales and income.

    Although there are some early examples of market-seeking MNCs (for example, Colt Firearms, Singer, Coca-Cola, N.V. Philips, and Imperial Chemicals), the bulk of foreign direct investment took place after World War II. This investment was primarily a one-way flow—from the United States to Western Europe—until the early 1960s. At that point, the phenomenon of **reverse foreign investment** began, primarily with Western European firms acquiring U.S. firms. More recently, Japanese firms have begun investing in the United States and Western Europe, largely in response to perceived or actual restrictions on their exports to these markets.

Cost Minimizers   Cost minimizer is a fairly recent category of fi͟
internationally. These firms seek out and invest in lower cost produc͟
(for example, China, Taiwan, and Ireland) to remain cost-competitive͟
abroad. Many of these firms are in the electronics industry. Exampl͟
Instruments, Intel, and Seagate Technology. Increasingly, companies are o͟
ices overseas, not just manufacturing work. For example, as of 2002,͟
employees in India to handle accounting, claims processing, customer ser\ ͟ ͟ ..credit
evaluation and research. Similarly, companies such as AOL (customer service), American
Express (finance and customer service), and British Airways (accounting) have set up call
centers and are shifting work to countries such as India, Jamaica, Hungary, Morocco, and
the Philippines for savings of up to 60 percent.

A Behavioral Definition of the Multinational Corporation

Regardless of its underlying reasons for global expansion, the true multinational corporation is characterized more by its state of mind than by the size and worldwide dispersion of
its assets. Rather than confine its search to domestic plant sites, the multinational firm asks,
Where in the world should we build that plant? Similarly, multinational marketing management seeks global, not domestic, market segments to penetrate, and multinational financial
management does not limit its search for capital or investment opportunities to any single
national financial market. Hence, the essential element that distinguishes the true multinational is its commitment to seeking out, undertaking, and integrating manufacturing, marketing, R&D, and financing opportunities on a global, not domestic, basis. For example,
IBM's superconductivity project was pioneered in Switzerland by a German scientist and a
Swiss scientist who shared a Nobel Prize in physics for their work on the project.

> The true multina-
> tional treats the
> world as its oyster.

Necessary complements to the integration of worldwide operations are flexibility,
adaptability, and speed. Indeed, speed has become one of the critical competitive weapons in
the fight for world market share. The ability to develop, make, and distribute products or
services quickly enables companies to capture customers who demand constant innovation
and rapid, flexible response. Exhibit 1.4 illustrates the combination of globally integrated
activities and rapid response times of Limited Brands, a Columbus, Ohio–based family of
seven clothing chains (including The Limited and Victoria's Secret) with 4,000 retail outlets.

> Successful multina-
> tionals focus on their
> key value-creating
> skills.

Another critical aspect of competitiveness in this new world is focus. *Focus* means
figuring out and building on what a company does best. This process typically involves
divesting unrelated business activities and seeking attractive investment opportunities in
the core business.

ILLUSTRATION • *ARCO Chemical Develops a Worldwide Strategy*

In the 1980s, ARCO Chemical shed its less successful product lines. At one point, revenue shrank from $3.5 billion annually to $1.5 billion. But by stripping down to its most
competitive lines of business, ARCO could better respond to the global political and economic events constantly buffeting it. Around the world, it now can take advantage of its
technological edge within its narrow niche—mostly intermediate chemicals and fuel
additives. This strategy has paid off: By 1992, more than 40 percent of ARCO's $3 billion
in sales were made abroad, and it now makes about half of its new investment outside
the United States. It also claims half the global market for the chemicals it sells.

ARCO Chemical went global because it had to. The company's engineering resins
are sold to the auto industry. In the past, that meant selling exclusively to Detroit's Big
Three in the U.S. market. Today, ARCO Chemical sells to Nissan, Toyota, Honda, Peugeot,
Renault, and Volkswagen in Japan, the United States, and Europe. It also deals with Ford

and General Motors in the United States and Europe. ARCO must be able to deliver a product anywhere in the world or lose the business.

Global operations also have meant, however, that ARCO Chemical faces increasingly stiff competition from abroad in addition to its traditional U.S. competitors such as Dow Chemical. European companies have expanded operations in America, and Japanese competitors also began to attack ARCO Chemical's business lines. For example, in 1990 Japan's Asahi Glass began a fierce price-cutting campaign in both Asia and Europe on products in which ARCO Chemical is strong.

In response, ARCO set up production facilities around the world and entered into joint ventures and strategic alliances. It counterattacked Asahi Glass by trying to steal one of Asahi's biggest customers in Japan. ARCO's joint venture partner, Sumitomo Chemical, supplied competitive intelligence, and its knowledge of the Japanese market was instrumental in launching the counterattack.

In July 1998, ARCO Chemical was acquired by Lyondell Petrochemical. This acquisition was driven by Lyondell's desire to expand into high-growth global markets for ARCO's products as well as the opportunity to gain significant integration benefits with Equistar Chemicals, LP, a joint venture among Lyondell, Millennium Chemicals, and Occidental Petroleum Corporation. According to Lyondell's 1998 Annual Report:

> ARCO Chemical was a perfect fit with Lyondell's core businesses. Among the benefits: substantial integration for propylene and other raw materials provided by Equistar and Lyondell; a global infrastructure providing a platform for future growth; and leading positions in high growth markets for chemicals and synthetics. The acquisition provides us with a business that has less cyclical earnings and cash flows.
>
> Consolidation is a positive trend that will continue to enhance the efficiency of the industry by allowing companies to spread overhead, distribution and research and development costs over a larger asset base. It will result in increased globalization and competition, which benefits both customers and investors. Lyondell will continue to be a leader in driving these changes. The acquired business provides significant strategic benefits to Lyondell, including:
>
> • A preeminent, global market position in propylene oxide and derivatives, driven by an advantaged technology position
>
> • Vertical integration with propylene, ethylene, and benzene produced by Equistar as well as integration with methanol produced by Lyondel
>
> • Reduced cyclicality of Lyondell's earnings through a broadened product mix in markets that are less cyclical than olefins and polymers
>
> • A platform for future domestic and international growth with a worldwide infrastructure of manufacturing facilities and service centers

In this world-oriented corporation, a person's passport is not the criterion for promotion. Nor is a firm's citizenship a critical determinant of its success. Success depends on a new breed of businessperson: the **global manager.**

The Global Manager

Today's managers must think globally and be able to anticipate and respond quickly to constant change.

In a world in which change is the rule and not the exception, the key to international competitiveness is the ability of management to adjust to change and volatility at an ever faster rate. In the words of General Electric Chairman Jack Welch, "I'm not here to predict the world. I'm here to be sure I've got a company that is strong enough to respond to whatever happens."[6]

---

[6] Quoted in Ronald Henkoff, "How to Plan for 1995," *Fortune*, December 31, 1990, p. 70.

EXHIBIT 1.4 • HOW THE LIMITED CUTS THE FASHION CYCLE TO 60 DAYS

From point-of-sale computers, daily reports on what is selling well flow into headquarters of The Limited in Columbus, Ohio.

To restock, the company sends orders by satellite to plants in the U.S., Hong Kong, South Korea, Singapore, and Sri Lanka.

The goods are hustled back to Columbus from Hong Kong aboard a chartered Boeing 747 that makes four flights a week.

At a highly automated distribution center in Columbus, apparel is sorted, priced, and prepared for shipment—all within 48 hours.

By truck and plane, the apparel moves out to The Limited's 3,200 stores, including Express and Victoria's Secret outlets.

Within 60 days of the order, the apparel goes on sale. Most competitors still place orders six months or more in advance.

Source: Fortune. September 26, 1988, p. 56. Chart by Renee Klein, *Fortune,* © 1988 Time, Inc. Reprinted with permission by *Fortune* magazine.

The rapid pace of change means that new global managers need detailed knowledge of their operations. Global managers must know how to make the products, where the raw materials and parts come from, how they get there, the alternatives, where the funds come from, and what their changing relative values do to the bottom line. They must also understand the political and economic choices facing key nations and how those choices will affect the outcomes of their decisions.

In making decisions for the global company, managers search their array of plants in various nations for the most cost-effective mix of supplies, components, transport, and funds. All this is done with the constant awareness that the options change and the choices must be made again and again.

Constant change presents both risks and opportunities to today's global managers.

The problem of constant change disturbs some managers. It always has. But today's global managers have to anticipate it, understand it, deal with it, and turn it to their company's advantage. The payoff to thinking globally is a quality of decision making that enhances the firm's prospects for survival, growth, and profitability in the evolving world economy.

1.2 THE INTERNATIONALIZATION OF BUSINESS AND FINANCE

The existence of global competition and global markets for goods, services, and capital is a fundamental economic reality that has altered the behavior of companies and governments worldwide. For example, Tandon Corp., a major California-based supplier of disk drives for microcomputers, cut its U.S. work force by 39 percent and transferred production overseas in an effort to achieve "cost effectiveness in an

Globalization has
forced companies to
change their key
business decisions.

extremely competitive marketplace."[7] As the president of Tandon put it, "We can wait for the Japanese to put us out of business or we can be cost-effective."[8] Increasingly, companies are bringing an international perspective to bear on their key production, marketing, technology, and financial decisions. This international perspective is exemplified by the following statement in General Electric's 1999 Annual Report (p. 2), which explains why globalization is one of its key initiatives:

> *Globalization evolved from a drive to export, to the establishment of global plants for local consumption, and then to global sourcing of products and services. Today, we are moving into its final stages—drawing upon intellectual capital from all over the world—from metallurgists in Prague, to software engineers in Asia, to product designers in Budapest, Monterrey, Tokyo, Paris and other places around the globe. … Our objective is to be the "global employer of choice," and we are striving to create the exciting career opportunities for local leaders all over the world that will make this objective a reality. This initiative has taken us to within reach of one of our biggest and longest-running dreams—a truly global GE.*

Yet despite the many advantages of operating in a world economy, many powerful interest groups feel threatened by globalization and have fought it desperately.

Political and Labor Union Concerns about Global Competition

Global competition
leads to winners and
losers.

Politicians and labor leaders, unlike corporate leaders, usually take a more parochial view of globalization. Many instinctively denounce local corporations that invest abroad as job "exporters," even though most welcome foreign investors in their own countries as job creators. However, many U.S. citizens today view the current tide of American asset sales to foreign companies as a dangerous assault on U.S. sovereignty.[9] They are unaware, for example, that foreign-owned companies account for more than 20 percent of industrial production in Germany and more than 50 percent in Canada, and neither of those countries appears to have experienced the slightest loss of sovereignty. Regardless of their views, however, the global rationalization of production will continue, as it is driven by global competition. The end result will be higher living standards brought about by improvements in worker productivity and private sector efficiency.

Despite the common view that U.S. direct investment abroad comes at the expense of U.S. exports and jobs, the evidence clearly shows the opposite. By enabling MNCs to expand their toeholds in foreign markets, such investments tend to increase U.S. exports of components and services and create more and higher-paying jobs in the United States. Ford and IBM, for example, would be generating less U.S.-based employment today had they not been able earlier to invest abroad—both by outsourcing the production of parts to low-wage countries such as Mexico and by establishing assembly plants and R&D centers in Europe and Japan.

Similarly, the argument that poor countries drain jobs from rich countries and depress wages for all—a major theme of 1999's "Battle in Seattle" over reductions in trade barriers sponsored by the World Trade Organization (WTO)—is demonstrably false. The fact is that as poor countries prosper, they buy more of the advanced goods produced by the richer countries that support higher-paying jobs. Indeed, the growth in trade and **investment flows** since the end of World War II has raised the wealth and

---

[7] "Tandon to Reduce U.S. Work Force, Concentrate Abroad," *Wall Street Journal*, March 1984, p. 22.

[8] Ibid.

[9] The importance of foreign investment in the United States is indicated by a few facts: four of America's six major music labels are now foreign-owned; Goodyear is the last major American-owned tire manufacturer; Japanese auto companies are now able to build more than two million cars a year in their U.S. plants, over 15 percent of the total in a typical sales year; four of Hollywood's largest film companies are foreign-owned; and in July 1995, Zenith, the last of the twenty-one companies manufacturing televisions in the United States that was American-owned, was purchased by the South Korean firm LG Group.

living standards of developed countries while lifting hundreds of millions of people around the world out of abject poverty. China and the Asian tigers are the most obvious examples of this phenomenon. According to then President Ernesto Zedillo of Mexico, "Every case where a poor nation has significantly overcome poverty has been achieved while engaging in production for export and opening itself to the influx of foreign goods, investment, and technology; that is, by participating in globalization."[10] Moreover, by generating growth and introducing values like accountability, openness, and competition, globalization has been a powerful force for spreading democracy and freedom in places as diverse as Mexico, Korea, and Poland.

Opponents of free trade and globalization also claim that competition by Third World countries for jobs and investment by multinational corporations encourages a "race to the bottom" in environmental and labor standards. However, this concern ignores the fact that the surest way to promote higher environmental standards for a country is to raise its wealth. The economic growth stimulated by expanded trade and capital flows will help developing countries to better afford the cleaner environment their wealthier citizens will now demand. Similarly, although protestors claim that Nike and other apparel makers contract out work to foreign "sweatshops" where underpaid workers toil in unhealthful conditions, conditions in factories where Nike goods are made are, comparatively speaking, progressive for their countries. Statistics that show very low employee turnover in such factories indicate that workers do not have better prospects. Moreover, although employees of U.S. affiliates in developing countries are paid much less than equivalent U.S. employees, they are paid significantly more than the average local wage. The evidence is clear that the surest way to improve the lives of the many desperately poor workers in developing countries is to pursue market-opening reforms that further globalization and facilitate wealth creation. Conversely, as North Korea shows, economic isolation is the fast track to poverty, disease, poor working conditions, environmental degradation, and despair. As such, protectionist governments in the West victimize the Third World entrepreneurs and their employees who have begun to make a better life for themselves by selling their goods in Western markets.

The moral basis for free trade was spelled out by President George W. Bush in May 2001:

> *Open trade is not just an economic opportunity, it is a moral imperative. Trade creates jobs for the unemployed. When we negotiate for open markets, we are providing new hope for the world's poor. And when we promote open trade, we are promoting political freedom. Societies that are open to commerce across their borders will open to democracy within their borders, not always immediately, and not always smoothly, but in good time.*

The growing irrelevance of borders for corporations will force policy makers to rethink old approaches to regulation. For example, corporate mergers that once would have been barred as anticompetitive might make sense if the true measure of a company's market share is global rather than national.

International economic integration also reduces the freedom of governments to determine their own economic policy. If a government tries to raise tax rates on business, for example, it is increasingly easy for business to shift production abroad. Similarly, nations that fail to invest in their physical and intellectual infrastructure—roads, bridges, R&D, education—will likely lose entrepreneurs and jobs to nations that do invest. Capital—both financial and intellectual—will go where it is wanted and stay where it is well treated. In short, economic integration is forcing governments, as well as companies, to compete. For example, after America's 1986 tax reform that slashed

[10] Quoted in Mortimer B. Zuckerman, "A Bit of Straight Talk," *U.S. News and World Report,* July 3, 2000, p. 60.

Capital markets are quick to reward sound economic policies while punishing economic mismanagement.

income tax rates, virtually every other nation in the world followed suit. In a world of porous borders, governments found it difficult to ignore what worked. Similarly, big U.S. mutual funds are wielding increasing clout in developing nations, particularly in Latin America and Asia. In essence, the funds are trying to do overseas what they are already doing domestically: pressure management (in this case governments) to adopt policies that will maximize returns. The carrot is more money; the stick is capital flight. Simply put, the globalization of trade and finance has created an unforgiving environment that penalizes economic mismanagement and allots capital and jobs to the nations delivering the highest risk-adjusted returns. As markets become more efficient, they are quicker to reward sound economic policy—and swifter to punish the profligate. Their judgments are harsh and cannot be appealed.

ILLUSTRATION   *The Asian Tigers Fall Prey to World Financial Markets*

For years, the nations of East Asia were held up as economic icons. Their typical blend of high savings and investment rates, autocratic political systems, export-oriented businesses, restricted domestic markets, government-directed capital allocation, and controlled financial systems were hailed as the ideal recipe for strong economic growth, particularly for developing nations. However, by the summer of 1997, the financial markets became disenchanted with this region, beginning with Thailand. Waves of currency selling left the Thai baht down 40 percent and the stock market down 50 percent. Thailand essentially went bankrupt. Its government fell and the International Monetary Fund (IMF) put together a $17 billion bailout package, conditioned on austerity measures. What the financial markets had seen that others had not was the rot at the core of Thailand's economy. Thais had run up huge debts, mostly in dollars, and were depending on the stability of the baht to repay these loans. Worse, Thai banks, urged on by the country's corrupt political leadership, were shoveling loans into money-losing ventures that were controlled by political cronies. As long as the money kept coming, Thailand's statistics on investment and growth looked good, but the result was a financially troubled economy that could not generate the income necessary to repay its loans.

Investors then turned to other East Asian economies and saw similar flaws there. One by one, the dominoes fell, from Bangkok to Kuala Lumpur, Jakarta to Manila, Singapore to Taipei, Seoul to Hong Kong. The Asian tigers were humbled as previously stable currencies were crushed (see Exhibit 1.5A), local stock markets crashed (see Exhibit 1.5B), interest rates soared, banking systems tottered, economies contracted, bankruptcies spread, and governments were destabilized. The international bailout for the region grew to over $150 billion, crowned by $60 billion for South Korea, as the United States and other developed nations poured in funds for fear that the events in East Asia would spin out of control, threatening the world financial system with ruin and leading to a global recession. How to stave off such crises? The answer is financial markets that are open and transparent, leading to investment decisions that are based on sound economic principles rather than cronyism or political considerations.

What is the bright side of the awesome power wielded by the global financial markets? Simply this: These markets bring economic sanity even to nations run by corrupt elites. Global markets have no tolerance for regimes that suppress enterprise, reward cronies, or squander resources on ego-building but economically dubious, grandiose projects. Indeed, although Asian business still has a long way to go, the forced restructuring that had already occurred resulted by the summer of 2000, three years later, in a dramatic recovery of the Asian economies.

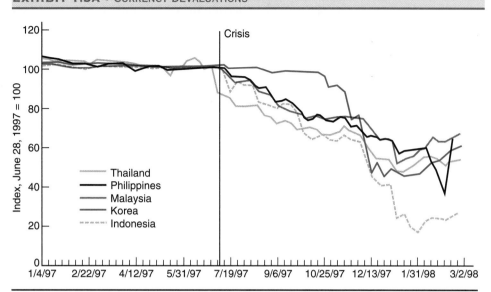

EXHIBIT 1.5A • CURRENCY DEVALUATIONS

Source: Southwest Economy, March/April 1998, Federal Reserve Bank of Dallas.

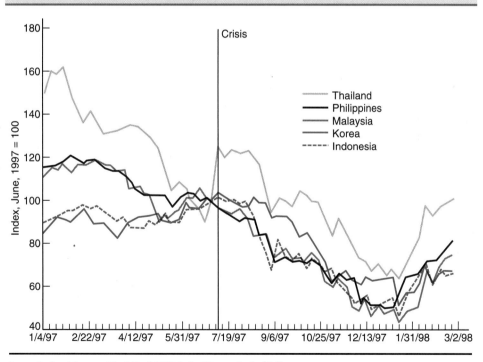

EXHIBIT 1.5B • STOCK MARKET DROP

Source: Southwest Economy, March/April 1998, Federal Reserve Bank of Dallas.

Paradoxically, however, even as people are disturbed at the thought of their government losing control of events, they have lost faith in government's ability to solve many of their problems. One result has been the collapse of Communism in Eastern Europe and the spread of free-market economics in developed and developing countries alike. Rejecting the statist policies of the past, they are shrinking, closing, pruning, or privatizing state-owned industries and subjecting their economies to the rigors of foreign competition. In response to these changes, developing countries in 1996, just prior to the Asian currency crisis, received over $240 billion in new foreign investment. Five years earlier, by contrast, they were exporting savings, as they paid service costs on their large foreign debts and as local capital fled hyperinflation and confiscatory tax and regulatory regimes. These dramatic shifts in policy—and the rewards they have brought to their initiators—have further strengthened the power of markets to set prices and priorities around the world.

Consequences of Global Competition

Foreign competition disrupts established industries and limits worker compensation.

The stresses caused by global competition have stirred up protectionists and given rise to new concerns about the consequences of free trade. For example, the sudden entry of three billion people from low-wage countries such as China, Mexico, Russia, and India into the global marketplace is provoking anxiety among workers in the old industrial countries about their living standards. As the accompanying illustration of the U.S. auto industry indicates, companies and unions are quite rational in fearing the effects of foreign competition. It disrupts established industry patterns, and it limits the wages and benefits of workers by giving more choice to consumers. The U.S.-Canada trade agreement, which ended tariff barriers by 2000, has caused major disruption to Canada's manufacturing industry. Plants are closing, mergers are proliferating, and both domestic and multinational companies are adjusting their operations to the new continental market. Similarly, the North American Free Trade Agreement (NAFTA), which created a giant free-trade area from the Yukon to the Yucatán, has forced formerly sheltered companies, especially in Mexico, to cut costs and change their way of doing business. It led U.S. companies to shift production both into and out of Mexico, while confronting American and Canadian workers with a new pool of lower-priced (but also less productive) labor.

ILLUSTRATION *Japanese Competition Affects the U.S. Auto Industry*

Until recently, Japanese competition steadily eroded the influence of the Big Three U.S. automakers in the auto industry. During the 1980s, Japanese auto companies raised their U.S. market share 8 points, to 28 percent, versus 65 percent for Detroit and 5 percent for Europe.

The tough Japanese competition was a big factor in the sales and profit crunch that hit the Big Three. General Motors, Ford, and Chrysler responded by shutting down U.S. plants and by curbing labor costs. Thus, Japanese competition has limited the wages and benefits that United Auto Workers (UAW) union members can earn, as well as the prices that U.S. companies can charge for their cars. Both unions and companies understand that in this competitive environment, raising wages and car prices leads to fewer sales and fewer jobs. One solution, which allows both the Big Three and the UAW to avoid making hard choices—sales volume versus profit margin, and jobs versus wages and benefits—is political: Limit Japanese competition through quotas, tariffs, and other protectionist devices, and thereby control its effects on the U.S. auto industry. Unfortunately, American consumers get stuck with the tab for this apparent free lunch in the form of higher car prices and less choice.

The best argument against protectionism, however, is long-term competitiveness. It was, after all, cutthroat competition from the Japanese that forced Detroit to get its act together. The Big Three swept away layers of unneeded management, raised productivity, and dramatically increased the quality of their cars and trucks. They also shifted their focus toward the part of the business in which the Japanese did not have strong products but which just happened to be America's hottest and fastest growing automotive segment—light trucks, which includes pickups, minivans, and sport-utility vehicles. Combined with a strong yen and higher Japanese prices, these changes helped Detroit pick up three percentage points of market share in 1992 and 1993 alone, mostly at the expense of Japanese nameplates. By 1994, the Japanese share of the U.S. auto market, which peaked at 29 percent in 1991, had fallen to 25 percent.

The inescapable fact is that Japanese automakers forced Detroit to make better cars at better prices. Handicapping the Japanese could not possibly have had the same effect.

The trend is toward greater integration of national economies.

So it is all the more encouraging that political leaders keep trying to stretch borders. The world's long march toward a **global economy** accelerated considerably in the past decade as the U.S.-Canada-Mexico free-trade pact, the European Community's drive to create a truly common market, and China's entrance into the WTO proceeded as planned. The greater integration of national economies is likely to continue despite the stresses it causes as politicians worldwide increasingly come to realize that they either must accept this integration or watch their respective nations fall behind.

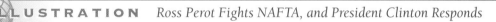

ILLUSTRATION   *Ross Perot Fights NAFTA, and President Clinton Responds*

In November 1993, the North American Free Trade Agreement (NAFTA) was signed into law but not before it stirred spirited opposition among unions and politicians. The best-known critic of NAFTA was Ross Perot, the billionaire Texan who launched a multimillion-dollar campaign against the free-trade treaty. He claimed that if NAFTA were ratified, the United States would hear a "giant sucking sound" as businesses rushed to Mexico to take advantage of its lower wages, putting nearly six million U.S. jobs at risk.

This argument ignores the economic theory of trade as well as its reality. If it is true that American factory workers are paid about eight times as much as their Mexican counterparts, it is also true that they are about eight times as productive. As Mexican workers become more productive, their pay will rise proportionately. This prediction is borne out by recent economic history. Like critics of NAFTA in 1993, many in 1986 feared a giant sucking sound from south of another border—the Pyrenees. Spain, with wages less than half those of its northern neighbors, and Portugal, with wages about a fifth Europe's norm, were about to join the European Community. Opponents said their low wages would drag down wages or take away jobs from French and German workers.

What happened? Job creation in France and Germany exceeded job creation in Spain and Portugal. More important, workers got to trade up to better jobs because opening trade allows all countries to specialize where their advantage is greatest. Specialization raises incomes. It is the reason all parties benefit from trade. Again the evidence bears this assertion out: by 1993, French and German wages had doubled; Spanish and Portuguese wages increased slightly faster. Put simply, countries do not grow richer at each other's expense. If allowed to trade freely, they grow richer together—each supplying the other with products, markets, and the spur of competition.

After numerous appeals by NAFTA supporters that he speak out in favor of the treaty, President Bill Clinton finally responded. On September 14, 1993, he gave the following eloquent argument for open borders and open markets:

> *I want to say to my fellow Americans, when you live in a time of change, the only way to recover your security and to broaden your horizons is to adapt to the change, to embrace it, to move forward. Nothing we do in this great capital can change the fact that factories or information can flash across the world, that people can move money around in the blink of an eye. Nothing can change the fact that technology can be adopted, once created, by people all across the world and then rapidly adapted in new and different ways by people who have a little different take on the way that technology works.*

For two decades, the winds of global competition have made these things clear to any American with eyes to see. The only way we can recover the fortunes of the middle class in this country so that people who work harder and smarter can at least prosper more, the only way we can pass on the American dream of the past 40 years to our children and their children for the next 40 is to adapt to the changes that are occurring.

In a fundamental sense, this debate about NAFTA is a debate about whether we will embrace these changes and create the jobs of tomorrow or try to resist these changes, hoping we can preserve the economic structures of yesterday. I tell you, my fellow Americans, that if we learn anything from the collapse of the Berlin Wall and the fall of the governments in Eastern Europe, even a totally controlled society cannot resist the winds of change that economics and technology and information flow have imposed in this world of ours. That is not an option. Our only realistic option is to embrace these changes and create the jobs of tomorrow.

Based in large part on the existence of NAFTA, total trade (exports plus imports) with Mexico rose from $81.5 billion in 1993 to $232.1 billion in 2002.

M I N I - C A S E   *Democrats Turn Protectionist*

In the fall of 1993, President Clinton was lobbying hard for passage of NAFTA but facing tough opposition from Ross Perot among others. To help get out the administration's message and build congressional and popular support, Vice President Al Gore agreed to go on CNN's "Larry King Live" to debate—and discredit—the Texas billionaire. During the debate, Al Gore talked about the critical importance of NAFTA to the future of the United States. "This is a major choice for our country of historic proportions," Gore said. "Sometimes we do something right; the creation of NATO, the Louisiana Purchase, Thomas Jefferson did the right thing there, the purchase of Alaska. These were all extremely controversial choices, but they made a difference for our country. This is such a choice." Elaborating, Gore then said, "This is a choice between the politics of fear and the politics of hope. It's a choice between the past and the future." The reviews for Gore's performance were solid, with most observers agreeing that he won the debate.

Seven years later, however, when Al Gore was running in the Democratic presidential primary against Senator Bill Bradley, he and his supporters hammered Bradley for the latter's support of NAFTA (while neglecting his own role in NAFTA's passage). A story in *The New York Times* helped to explain Gore's conversion:

Many officials from the powerful industrial unions in Illinois, Michigan, Missouri, Ohio, Pennsylvania and Wisconsin—the auto workers, the steelworkers and the machinists— say that if Gore hopes to motivate union activists to campaign for him and union members to vote for him in primaries and in the general election, he must address labor's concerns on manufacturing and the related subject of trade. "It's one thing for the vice president to get the AFL-CIO's endorsement, and it's quite another to mobilize our members," said George Becker, president of the United Steelworkers of America. Becker met with Gore last week to press him on trade and manufacturing. "I have one overall goal in life," Becker said, "and that is to reverse the trend of de-industrializing America and to stop these insane trade laws that force our manufacturers to compete against impossible odds."

In 2003, virtually all the Democratic presidential hopefuls came out strongly against free trade, thereby reversing the position the Democratic Party had taken while Bill Clinton was president. Howard Dean, John Kerry, John Edwards, and Wesley Clark abandoned their past positions on trade and joined Richard Gephardt, a longtime critic of free trade and favorite of labor unions, in resisting efforts to lower trade barriers with Mexico and other nations in South America and Asia. Of the top-tier Democratic presidential candidates, only Joseph Lieberman continued to push the Clinton emphasis on forging trade agreements. "We cannot put a wall around America," he said.

QUESTIONS

1. What might explain the candidates' and Democratic Party's reversal of position on free trade? Which voting constituencies would be most likely to reject free trade? Why?

2. What leverage do the trade unions have in persuading Al Gore and other Democratic candidates to pay attention to their anti-free-trade position? Explain why these particular unions might be particularly powerful.

3. What trade-offs do Al Gore and other Democrats face in accommodating labor? Explain.

4. How can U.S. manufacturers compete with foreign producers? Are they doomed, as suggested by the president of the United Steelworkers of America? Explain.

5. Are the unions and their members right to be concerned about the effects of free-trade policies? What are these effects that they are concerned about? Who would be helped and who would be hurt if the unions got their way on trade? Explain.

1.3 MULTINATIONAL FINANCIAL MANAGEMENT: THEORY AND PRACTICE

The objective of multinational financial management is to maximize shareholder wealth.

Although all functional areas can benefit from a global perspective, this book concentrates on developing financial policies that are appropriate for the multinational firm. The main objective of multinational financial management is to maximize shareholder wealth as measured by share price. This means making financing and investment decisions that add as much value as possible to the firm. It also means that companies must manage effectively the assets under their control. The focus on shareholder value stems from the fact that shareholders are the legal owners of the firm and management has a fiduciary obligation to act in their best interests. Although other stakeholders in the company do have rights, these are not coequal with the shareholders' rights. Shareholders provide the risk capital that cushions the claims of alternative stakeholders. Allowing alternative stakeholders coequal control over capital supplied by others is equivalent to allowing one group to risk someone else's capital. This undoubtedly would impair future equity formation and produce numerous other inefficiencies.

A more compelling reason for focusing on creating shareholder wealth is that those companies that do not are likely to be prime takeover targets and candidates for a forced corporate restructuring. Conversely, maximizing shareholder value provides the best defense against a hostile takeover: a high stock price. Companies that build shareholder value also find it easier to attract equity capital. Equity capital is especially critical for companies that operate in a riskier environment and for companies that are seeking to grow.

Maximizing shareholder wealth maximizes the economic interests of all stakeholders over time.

Last, but not least, shareholders are not the only beneficiaries of corporate success. By forcing managers to evaluate business strategies based on prospective cash flows, the shareholder value approach favors strategies that enhance a company's cash-flow generating ability—which is good for everyone, not just shareholders. Companies that create value have more money to distribute to all stakeholders, not just shareholders. Put another way, you have to create wealth before you can distribute it. Thus, there is no inherent economic conflict between shareholders and stakeholders. Indeed, most financial economists believe that maximizing shareholder value is not merely the best way, it is the *only* way to maximize the economic interests of *all* stakeholders over time.

Although an institution as complex as the multinational corporation cannot be said to have a single, unambiguous will, the principle of shareholder wealth maximization provides a rational guide to financial decision making. However, other financial goals that reflect the relative autonomy of management and external pressures also are examined here.

Criticisms of the Multinational Corporation

Critics of the MNC liken its behavior to that of an octopus with tentacles extended, squeezing the nations of the world to satisfy the apparently insatiable appetite of its center. Its defenders claim that only by linking activities globally can world output be maximized. According to this view, greater profits from overseas activities are the just reward for providing the world with new products, technologies, and know-how.

Critics of the MNC claim it expropriates wealth from its host nations.

This book's focus is on multinational financial management, so it does not directly address this controversy. It concentrates instead on the development of analytical approaches to deal with the major environmental problems and decisions involving overseas investment and financing. In carrying out these financial policies, however, conflicts between corporations and nation-states will inevitably arise.

A classic case is that of General Motors–Holden's Ltd. The General Motors (GM) wholly owned Australian affiliate was founded in 1926 with an initial equity investment of A\$3.5 million. The earnings were reinvested until 1954, at which time the first dividend, for A\$9.2 million, was paid to the parent company in Detroit. This amount seemed reasonable to GM management, considering the twenty-eight years of forgoing dividends, but the Australian press and politicians denounced a dividend equal to more than 260 percent of GM's original equity investment as economic exploitation and imperialism.[11]

More recently, Brazil, facing one of its periodic balance-of-payments crises, chose to impose stringent controls on the removal of profits by MNCs, thereby affecting the financial operations of such firms as Volkswagen and Scott Paper. In addition, companies operating in countries as diverse as Canada and Chile, Italy and India, and the United States and Uruguay have faced various political risks, including price controls and confiscation of local operations. This book examines modifying financial policies to align better with national objectives in an effort to reduce such risks and minimize the costs of the adjustments.

This text also considers the links between financial management and other functional areas. After all, the analysis of investment projects is dependent on sales forecasts and cost estimates, and the dispersal of production and marketing activities affects a firm's ability to flow funds internationally as well as its vulnerability to expropriation.

Functions of Financial Management

Financial management is traditionally separated into two basic functions: the acquisition of funds and the investment of those funds. The first function, also known as the **financing decision**, involves generating funds from internal sources or from sources external to the firm at the lowest long-run cost possible. The **investment decision** is concerned with the allocation of funds over time in such a way that shareholder wealth is maximized. Many of the concerns and activities of multinational financial management, however, cannot be categorized so neatly.

Financial management involves the acquisition of funds and the investment of those funds.

Internal corporate fund flows such as loan repayments often are undertaken to access funds that are already owned, at least in theory, by the MNC itself. Other flows, such as dividend payments, may take place to reduce taxes or currency risk. Capital structure and other financing decisions frequently are motivated by a desire to reduce investment risks as well as financing costs. Furthermore, exchange risk management involves both the financing

---

[11] Reported in, among other places, Sidney M. Robbins and Robert B. Stobaugh, *Money in the Multinational Enterprise* (New York: Basic Books, 1973), p. 59.

decision and the investment decision. Throughout this book, therefore, the interaction between financing and investment decisions is stressed because the right combination of these decisions is the key to maximizing the value of the firm to its shareholders.

Theme of This Book

Financial executives of MNCs face added political and economic risks, as well as more complex tax laws and multiple money markets.

Financial executives in multinational corporations face many factors that have no domestic counterparts. These factors include exchange and inflation risks; international differences in tax rates; multiple money markets, often with limited access; currency controls; and political risks, such as sudden or creeping expropriation.

When companies consider the unique characteristics of multinational financial management, they understandably emphasize the additional political and economic risks faced when going abroad. But a broader perspective is necessary if firms are to take advantage of being multinational.

Benefits of global operations include international diversification, access to new information, and enhanced bargaining power with unions and governments.

The ability to move people, money, and material on a global basis enables the multinational corporation to be more than the sum of its parts. By having operations in different countries, the MNC can access segmented capital markets to lower its overall cost of capital, shift profits to lower its taxes, and take advantage of **international diversification** of markets and production sites to reduce the riskiness of its earnings. Multinationals have taken the old adage "don't put all your eggs in one basket" to its logical conclusion.

Operating globally confers other advantages as well: It increases the bargaining power of multinational firms when they negotiate investment agreements and operating conditions with foreign governments and labor unions; it gives MNCs continuous access to information on the newest process technologies available overseas and the latest research and development activities of their foreign competitors; and it helps them diversify their funding sources by giving them expanded access to the world's capital markets.

ILLUSTRATION   *General Electric Discusses the Risks and Benefits of Globalization*

In its 1999 Annual Report, General Electric explains the pluses and minuses of its global activities, as follows:

> *The activities of GE and GECS [GE Capital Services] span all global regions and primarily encompass manufacturing for local and export markets, import and sale of products produced in other regions, leasing of aircraft, sourcing for GE plants domiciled in other global regions and provision of financial services within these regional economies. Thus, when countries or regions experience currency and/or economic stress, GE may have increased exposure to certain risks but also may have new profit opportunities. Potential increased risks include, among other things, higher receivables delinquencies and bad debts, delays or cancellation of sales and orders principally related to power and aircraft equipment, higher local currency financing costs and a slowdown in established financial services activities. New profit opportunities include, among other things, lower costs of goods sourced from countries with weakened currencies, more opportunities for lower cost outsourcing, expansion of industrial and financial services activities through purchases of companies or assets at reduced prices and lower U.S. debt financing costs.*

In summary, this book emphasizes the many opportunities associated with being multinational without neglecting the corresponding risks. To properly analyze and balance these international risks and rewards, we must use the lessons to be learned from domestic corporate finance.

Relationship to Domestic Financial Management

Financial economics, which focuses on the behavior of financial markets, contains valuable insights for international financial managers.

In recent years, an abundance of new research has been conducted in the area of international corporate finance. The major thrust of this work has been to apply the methodology and logic of financial economics to the study of key international financial decisions. Critical problem areas, such as foreign exchange risk management and foreign investment analysis, have benefited from the insights provided by **financial economics**—a discipline that emphasizes the use of economic analysis to understand the basic workings of financial markets, particularly the measurement and pricing of risk and the intertemporal allocation of funds.

By focusing on the behavior of financial markets and their participants rather than on how to solve specific problems, we can derive fundamental principles of valuation and develop from them superior approaches to financial management, much as a better understanding of the basic laws of physics leads to better-designed and better-functioning products. We also can better gauge the validity of existing approaches to financial decision making by seeing whether their underlying assumptions are consistent with our knowledge of financial markets and valuation principles.

Three basic concepts provide the foundation for the study of international finance: arbitrage, market efficiency, and capital asset pricing.

Three concepts arising in financial economics have proved to be of particular importance in developing a theoretical foundation for international corporate finance: arbitrage, market efficiency, and capital asset pricing. Throughout the remainder of the book, we rely on these concepts, which are briefly described in the next sections.

Arbitrage   **Arbitrage** traditionally has been defined as the purchase of assets or commodities on one market for immediate resale on another in order to profit from a price discrepancy. In recent years, however, arbitrage has been used to describe a broader range of activities. **Tax arbitrage**, for example, involves the shifting of gains or losses from one tax jurisdiction to another to profit from differences in tax rates. In a broader context, **risk arbitrage**, or speculation, describes the process that leads to equality of risk-adjusted returns on different securities, unless market imperfections that hinder this adjustment process exist.

The concept of arbitrage is of particular importance in international finance because so many of the relationships between domestic and international financial markets, exchange rates, interest rates, and inflation rates depend on arbitrage for their existence. In fact, it is the process of arbitrage that ensures **market efficiency**.

Market Efficiency   An **efficient market** is one in which the prices of traded securities readily incorporate new information. Numerous studies of U.S. and foreign capital markets have shown that traded securities are correctly priced in that trading rules based on past prices or publicly available information cannot consistently lead to profits (after adjusting for transaction costs) in excess of those due solely to risk taking.

The predictive power of markets lies in their ability to collect in one place a mass of individual judgments from around the world. These judgments are based on current information. If the trend of future policies changes, people will revise their expectations, and prices will change to incorporate the new information.

To say that markets are efficient, however, is not to say that they never blunder. Swept up in enthusiasms or urged on by governments, investors appear to succumb periodically to herd behavior and go to excess, culminating in a financial crisis. In the 1980s, for example, an international banking crisis developed as a result of overly optimistic lending to developing nations, and in the 1990s the Asian crisis was associated with overly optimistic lending to the rapidly growing Asian tigers. To date, these crises have been resolved, albeit with much pain. Between crisis and resolution, however, is always uncharted territory, with the ever-present potential of panic feeding on itself and spreading from one nation to another, leading to global instability and recession. What we can say about markets, however, is that they are self-correcting; unlike governments, when investors spot problems, their instinct is to withdraw funds, not add more. At the same time, if a nation's economic fundamentals are basically sound, investors will eventually recognize that and their capital will return.

Capital Asset Pricing   *Capital asset pricing* refers to the way in which securities are valued in line with their anticipated risks and returns. Because risk is such an integral element of international financial decisions, this book briefly summarizes the results of more than four decades of study on the pricing of risk in capital markets. The outcome of this research has been to posit a specific relationship between risk (measured by return variability) and required asset returns, now formalized in the **capital asset pricing model** (CAPM) and the more general **arbitrage price theory** (APT).

Both the CAPM and the APT assume that the total variability of an asset's returns can be attributed to two sources: (1) marketwide influences that affect all assets to some extent, such as the state of the economy, and (2) other risks that are specific to a given firm, such as a strike. The former type of risk is usually termed **systematic**, or **nondiversifiable**, **risk**, and the latter, **unsystematic**, or **diversifiable**, **risk**. Unsystematic risk is largely irrelevant to the highly diversified holder of securities because the effects of such disturbances cancel out, on average, in the portfolio. On the other hand, no matter how well diversified a stock portfolio is, systematic risk, by definition, cannot be eliminated, and thus the investor must be compensated for bearing this risk. This distinction between systematic risk and unsystematic risk provides the theoretical foundation for the study of risk in the multinational corporation and is referred to throughout the book.

The Importance of Total Risk

Although the message of the CAPM and the APT is that only the systematic component of risk will be rewarded with a risk premium, this does not mean that **total risk**—the combination of systematic and unsystematic risk—is unimportant to the value of the firm. In addition to the effect of systematic risk on the appropriate discount rate, total risk may have a negative impact on the firm's *expected* cash flows.[12]

The inverse relation between risk and expected cash flows arises because financial distress, which is most likely to occur for firms with high total risk, can impose costs on customers, suppliers, and employees and thereby affect their willingness to commit themselves to relationships with the firm. For example, potential customers will be nervous about purchasing a product they might have difficulty getting serviced if the firm goes out of business. Similarly, a firm struggling to survive is unlikely to find suppliers willing to provide it with specially developed products or services, except at a higher-than-usual price. The uncertainty created by volatile earnings and cash flows also may hinder management's ability to take a long view of the firm's prospects and make the most of its opportunities.

In summary, total risk is likely to affect a firm's value adversely by leading to lower sales and higher costs. Consequently, any action taken by a firm that decreases its total risk will improve its sales and cost outlooks, thereby increasing its expected cash flows.

These considerations justify the range of corporate hedging activities that multinational firms engage in to reduce total risk. This text focuses on those risks that appear to be more international than national in nature, including inflation risk, exchange risk, and

---

[12] The effect of total risk is discussed in Alan C. Shapiro and Sheridan Titman, "An Integrated Approach to Corporate Risk Management," *Midland Corporate Finance Journal*, Summer 1985, pp. 41–56.

political risk. As we will see, however, appearances can be deceiving, because these risks also affect firms that do business in only one country. Moreover, international diversification may actually allow firms to reduce the total risk they face. Much of the general market risk facing a company is related to the cyclical nature of the domestic economy of the home country. Operating in several nations whose economic cycles are not perfectly in phase should reduce the variability of the firm's earnings. Thus, even though the risk of operating in any one foreign country may be greater than the risk of operating in the United States (or other home country), diversification can eliminate much of that risk.

What is true for companies is also true for investors. International diversification can reduce the riskiness of an investment portfolio because national financial markets tend to move somewhat independently of each other. Investors today have options to invest internationally that did not exist in the past. They can invest in multinational firms, foreign stocks and bonds, securities of foreign firms issued domestically, and mutual funds that hold portfolios of foreign stocks and bonds.

International diversification can reduce investment risk.

The Global Financial Marketplace

Market efficiency has been greatly facilitated by the marriage of computers and telecommunications. The resulting electronic infrastructure melds the world into one global market for ideas, data, and capital, all moving at almost the speed of light to any part of the planet. Today there are more than 200,000 computer terminals in hundreds of trading rooms, in dozens of nations, that light up to display an unending flow of news. Only about two minutes elapse between the time a president, a prime minister, or a central banker makes a statement and the time traders buy or sell currency, stocks, and bonds according to their evaluation of that policy's effect on the market.

Financial markets continually judge each nation's economic policies.

The result is a continuing global referendum on a nation's economic policies, which is the final determinant of the value of its currency. Just as we learn from television the winner of a presidential election weeks before the electoral college even assembles, so, too, do we learn instantly from the foreign exchange market what the world thinks of our announced economic policies even before they are implemented. In a way, the financial market is a form of economic free speech. Although many politicians do not like what it is saying, the market presents judgments that are clear-eyed and hard-nosed. It knows that there are no miracle drugs that can replace sound fiscal and monetary policies. Thus, cosmetic political fixes will exacerbate, not alleviate, a falling currency.

The Role of the Financial Executive in an Efficient Market

The basic insight into financial management that we can gain from recent empirical research in financial economics is the following: *Attempts to increase the value of a firm by purely financial measures or accounting manipulations are unlikely to succeed unless there are capital market imperfections or asymmetries in tax regulations.*

Financial managers can create value by taking advantage of capital market imperfections and tax asymmetries.

Rather than downgrading the role of the financial executive, the net result of these research findings has been to focus attention on those areas and circumstances in which financial decisions can have a measurable impact. The key areas are capital budgeting, working capital management, and tax management. The circumstances to be aware of include **capital market imperfections**, caused primarily by government regulations, and asymmetries in the tax treatment of different types and sources of revenues and costs.

The value of good financial management is enhanced in the international arena because of the much greater likelihood of market imperfections and multiple tax rates. In addition, the greater complexity of international operations is likely to increase the payoffs from a knowledgeable and sophisticated approach to internationalizing the traditional areas of financial management.

1.4 OUTLINE OF THE BOOK

This book is divided into six parts.

- Part I: Environment of International Financial Management
- Part II: Foreign Exchange and Derivatives Markets
- Part III: Foreign Exchange Risk Management
- Part IV: Financing the Multinational Corporation
- Part V: Foreign Investment Analysis
- Part VI: Multinational Working Capital Management

The following sections briefly discuss these parts and their chapters.

Environment of International Financial Management

Part I examines the environment in which international financial decisions are made. Chapter 2 discusses the basic factors that affect currency values. It also explains the basics of central bank intervention in foreign exchange markets, including the economic and political motivations for such intervention. Chapter 3 describes the international monetary system and shows how the choice of system affects the determination of exchange rates. Chapter 4 is a crucial chapter because it introduces five key equilibrium relationships— among inflation rates, interest rates, and exchange rates—in international finance that form the basis for much of the analysis in the remainder of the text. Chapter 5 analyzes the balance of payments and the links between national economies, while Chapter 6 discusses the subject of country risk analysis, the assessment of the potential risks and rewards associated with making investments and doing business in a country—a topic of great concern these days.

Foreign Exchange and Derivatives Markets

Part II explores the foreign exchange and derivative markets used by multinational corporations to manage their currency and interest rate risks. Chapter 7 describes the foreign exchange market and how it functions. Foreign currency futures and options contracts are discussed in Chapter 8. Chapter 9 analyzes interest rate and currency swaps and interest rate forwards and futures and how these derivatives can be used to manage risk.

Foreign Exchange Risk Management

Part III discusses foreign exchange risk management, a traditional area of concern that is receiving even more attention today. Chapter 10 discusses the likely impact that an exchange rate change will have on a firm (its exposure) from an accounting perspective and then analyzes the costs and benefits of alternative financial techniques to hedge against those exchange risks. Chapter 11 examines exposure from an economic perspective and presents marketing, logistic, and financial policies to cope with the competitive consequences of currency changes. As part of the analysis of economic exposure, the relationship between inflation and currency changes and its implications for corporate cash flows is recognized.

Financing the Multinational Corporation

Part IV focuses on laying out and evaluating the medium- and long-term financing options facing the multinational firm, then developing a financial package that is tailored to the firm's specific operating environment. Chapter 12 describes the alternative external, medium- and long-term debt financing options available to the multinational corporation. Chapter 13 discusses the international capital markets—namely, the Eurocurrency and Eurobond markets. Chapter 14 seeks to determine the cost-of-capital figure(s) that MNCs should use in evaluating foreign investments, given the funding sources actually employed.

Foreign Investment Analysis

Part V analyzes the foreign investment decision process. Chapter 15 begins by discussing the nature and consequences of international portfolio investing—the purchase of foreign stocks and bonds. In Chapter 16, the strategy of foreign direct investment is discussed, including an analysis of the motivations for going abroad and those factors that have contributed to business success overseas. Chapter 17 presents techniques for evaluating foreign investment proposals, emphasizing how to adjust cash flows for the various political and economic risks encountered abroad, such as inflation, currency fluctuations, and expropriations. It also discusses how companies can manage political risks by appropriately structuring the initial investment and making suitable modifications to subsequent operating decisions.

Multinational Working Capital Management

Part VI examines working capital management in the multinational corporation. The subject of trade financing is covered in Chapter 18. Chapter 19 discusses current asset management in the MNC, including the management of cash, inventory, and receivables. It also deals with current liability management, presenting the alternative short-term financing techniques available and showing how to evaluate their relative costs. Chapter 20 describes the mechanisms available to the MNC to shift funds and profits among its various units, while considering the tax and other consequences of these maneuvers. The aim of these maneuvers is to create an integrated global financial planning system.

QUESTIONS

1. a. What are the various categories of multinational firms?
   b. What is the motivation for international expansion of firms within each category?

2. a. How does foreign competition limit the prices that domestic companies can charge and the wages and benefits that workers can demand?
   b. What political solutions can help companies and unions avoid the limitations imposed by foreign competition?
   c. Who pays for these political solutions? Explain.

3. a. What was ARCO Chemical's rationale for globalizing?
   b. What advantages has ARCO Chemical realized from its global operations?

4. a. What factors appear to underlie the Asian currency crisis?
   b. What lessons can we learn from the Asian currency crisis?

   c. What is an efficient market?

5. a. What is the capital asset pricing model?
   b. What is the basic message of the CAPM?
   c. How might a multinational firm use the CAPM?

6. A memorandum by Labor Secretary Robert Reich to President Bill Clinton suggested that the government penalize U.S. companies that invest overseas rather than at home. According to Reich, this kind of investment hurts exports and destroys well-paying jobs. Comment on this argument.

7. Are multinational firms riskier than purely domestic firms? What data would you need to address this question?

8. Is there any reason to believe that MNCs may be less risky than purely domestic firms? Explain.

9. In what ways do financial markets grade government economic policies?

INTERNET RESOURCES

www.wto.org Web site of the World Trade Organization (WTO). Contains news, information, and statistics on international trade.

www.worldbank.org Web site of the World Bank. Contains economic and demographic data on 206 countries (organized in "Country At-A-Glance" tables), various economic forecasts, and links to a number of other data sources.

www.bea.doc.gov Web site of the Bureau of Economic Analysis (BEA). Contains data and articles on U.S. international trade, capital flows, and other international economic matters.

www.wsj.com Web site of *The Wall Street Journal*, the foremost business newspaper in the United States. Contains domestic and international business news.

www.ft.com Web site of *Financial Times*, the foremost international business newspaper, published in London. Contains a wealth of international financial news and data.

www.economist.com Web site of *The Economist*. Contains stories on the economic and political situations of countries and international business developments, along with various national and international economic and financial data.

www.oecd.org Web site of the Organisation for Economic Cooperation and Development (OECD). Contains news, analyses, and data on international finance and economics.

fisher.osu.edu/fin/fdf/osudata.htm Web site run by the Finance Department of Ohio State University. Contains a detailed listing of and links to many different Web sites related to finance and economics.

www.census.gov/ipc/www/idbnew.html Contains the International Data Base (IDB), which is a computerized data bank with statistical tables of demographic, and socioeconomic data for 227 countries and areas of the world.

www.dismal.com Covers over sixty-five economic releases from over fifteen countries. Also contains numerous stories dealing with international finance and economics.

www.reportgallery.com Web site that contains links to annual reports of over 2,200 companies, many of which are multinationals.

INTERNET EXERCISES

1. Who are the major trading partners of the United States? Which countries are the top five exporters to the United States? Which countries are the top five importers of U.S. goods? Good references are the WTO site and the BEA site.

2. Who are the major recipients of U.S. overseas investment? Which countries are the major sources of foreign investment in the United States? A good reference is the BEA site.

3. Go to the Web sites of companies such as the ones listed below and examine their international business activity. For example, what importance do these companies appear to place on international business? What percentage of sales revenues, assets, and income do these companies derive from their foreign operations? What percentage of their sales and income comes from exports? Is their foreign activity increasing or decreasing? How many countries and continents do these companies operate on? Which countries are listed as locations of the company's foreign subsidiaries? What is the headquarters country of each company? Much of this information can be gleaned from the annual reports of the companies, which can be found at www.reportgallery.com.

Ford Motor Company
Walt Disney Company
General Electric
DaimlerChrysler
Philips Electronics
Unilever
IBM
Sony
Nestlé
Microsoft
Coca-Cola
ExxonMobil

4. Based on your review of the *Economist*, the *Wall Street Journal*, and *Financial Times*, which countries appear to be giving foreign investors concerns? What are these concerns?

APPENDIX 1A

THE ORIGINS AND CONSEQUENCES OF INTERNATIONAL TRADE

Underlying the theory of international trade is the doctrine of comparative advantage. This doctrine rests on certain assumptions:

1. Exporters sell undifferentiated (commodity) goods and services to unrelated importers.
2. Factors of production cannot move freely across countries. Instead, trade takes place in the goods and services produced by these factors of production.

As noted at the beginning of Chapter 1, the doctrine of comparative advantage also ignores the roles of uncertainty, economies of scale, and technology in international trade; and it is static rather than dynamic. Nonetheless, this theory helps to explain why nations trade with each other, and it forms the basis for assessing the consequences of international trade policies.

To illustrate the main features of the doctrine of comparative advantage and to distinguish this concept from that of absolute advantage, suppose the United States and the United Kingdom produce the same two products, wheat and coal, according to the following production schedules, where the units referred to are units of production (labor, capital, land, and technology).[1] The first schedule shows how many units it costs to produce each ton:

	Wheat	*Coal*
U.S.	2 units/ton	1 unit/ton
U.K.	3 units/ton	4 units/ton

These figures show clearly that the United States has an **absolute advantage** in both mining coal and growing wheat. That is, in using fewer units of production per ton produced, the United States is more efficient than the United Kingdom in producing both coal and wheat. However, although the United Kingdom is at an absolute disadvantage in both products, it has a **comparative advantage** in producing wheat. Put another way, the United Kingdom's absolute disadvantage is less in growing wheat than in mining coal. This lesser disadvantage can be seen by redoing the production figures above to reflect the output per unit of production for both countries:

	Wheat	*Coal*
U.S.	0.5 tons/unit	1 ton/unit
U.K.	0.33 tons/unit	0.25 ton/unit

Productivity for the United States relative to the United Kingdom in coal is 4:1 (1/0.25), whereas it is "only" 1.5:1 (0.5/0.33) in wheat.

In order to induce the production of both wheat and coal prior to the introduction of trade, the profitability of producing both commodities must be identical. This condition is satisfied only when the return per unit of production is the same for both wheat and coal in each country. Hence, prior to the introduction of trade between the two countries, the exchange rate between wheat and coal in the United States and the United Kingdom must be as follows:

U.S. 1 ton wheat = 2 tons coal
U.K. 1 ton wheat = 0.75 tons coal

---

[1] The traditional theory of international trade ignores the role of technology in differentiating products, but it leaves open the possibility of different production technologies to produce commodities.

THE GAINS FROM TRADE

Based on the relative prices of wheat and coal in both countries, there will be obvious gains to trade. By switching production units from wheat to coal, the United States can produce coal and trade with the United Kingdom for more wheat than those same production units can produce at home. Similarly, by specializing in growing wheat and trading for coal, the United Kingdom can consume more coal than if it mined its own. This example demonstrates that trade will be beneficial even if one nation (the United States here) has an absolute advantage in everything. As long as the degree of absolute advantage varies across products, even the nation with an across-the-board absolute disadvantage will have a comparative advantage in making and exporting some goods and services.

The gains from trade for each country depend on exactly where the exchange rate between wheat and coal ends up following the introduction of trade. This exchange rate, which is known as the **terms of trade**, depends on the relative supplies and demands for wheat and coal in each country. However, any exchange rate between 0.75 and 2.0 tons of coal per ton of wheat will still lead to trade because trading at that exchange rate will allow both countries to improve their ability to consume. By illustration, suppose the terms of trade end up at 1:1—that is, one ton of wheat equals one ton of coal.

Each unit of production in the United States can now provide its owner with either 1 ton of coal to consume or 1 ton of wheat or some combination of the two. By producing coal and trading for wheat, each production unit in the United States now enables its owner to consume twice as much wheat as before. Similarly, by switching from mining coal to growing wheat and trading for coal, each production unit in the United Kingdom will enable its owner to consume 0.33 tons of coal, 33 percent (0.33/0.25 = 133%) more than before.

SPECIALIZED FACTORS OF PRODUCTION

So far, we have assumed that the factors of production are unspecialized. That is, they can easily be switched between the production of wheat and coal. However, suppose that some factors such as labor and capital are specialized (that is, relatively more efficient) in terms of producing one commodity rather than the other. In that case, the prices of the factors of production that specialize in the commodity that is exported (coal in the United States, wheat in the United Kingdom) will gain because of greater demand once trade begins, whereas those factors that specialize in the commodity that is now imported (wheat in the United States, coal in the United Kingdom) will lose because of lower demand. This conclusion is based on the economic fact that the demand for factors of

production is derived from the demand for the goods those factors produce.

The gains and losses to the specialized factors of production will depend on the magnitude of the price shifts after the introduction of trade. To take an extreme case, suppose the terms of trade become 1 ton of wheat equals 1.95 tons of coal. At this exchange rate, trade is still beneficial for both countries but far more so for the United Kingdom than the United States. The disparity in the gains from trade can be seen as follows: By producing coal and trading it for wheat, the United States can now consume approximately 2.5 percent more wheat than before per ton of coal.[2] On the other hand, the United Kingdom gains enormously. Each unit of wheat traded for coal will now provide 1.95 tons of coal, a 160 percent (1.95/0.75 − 1) increase relative to the earlier ratio.

These gains are all to the good. However, with specialization comes costs. In the United States, the labor and capital that specialized in growing wheat will be hurt. If they continue to grow wheat (which may make sense because they cannot easily be switched to mining coal), they will suffer an approximate 2.5 percent loss of income because the wheat they produce now will buy about 2.5 percent less coal than before (1.95 tons instead of 2 tons). At the same time, U.S. labor and capital that specializes in mining coal will be able to buy about 2.5 percent more wheat. Although gains and losses for specialized U.S. factors of production exist, they are relatively small. The same cannot be said for U.K. gains and losses.

As we saw earlier, U.K. labor and capital that specialize in growing wheat will be able to buy 160 percent more coal than before, a dramatic boost in purchasing power. Conversely, those factors that specialize in mining coal will see their wheat purchasing power plummet, from 1.33 (4/3) tons of coal before trade to 0.5128 (1/1.95) tons of wheat now. These figures translate into a drop of about 61 percent (0.5128/1.33 = 39%) in wheat purchasing power.

This example illustrates a general principle of international trade: *The greater the gains from trade for a country overall, the greater the cost of trade to those factors of production that specialize in producing the commodity that is now imported.* The reason is that in order for trade to make sense, imports must be less expensive than the competing domestic products. The less expensive these imports are, the greater will be the gains from trade. By the same token, however, less expensive imports drive down the prices of competing domestic products, thereby reducing the value of those factors of production that specialize in their manufacture.

It is this redistribution of income—from factors specializing in producing the competing domestic products to consumers of those products—that leads to demands for protection from imports. However, protection is a double-edged sword. These points are illustrated by the experience of the U.S. auto industry.

---

[2] With trade, the United States can now consume 1/1.95 = 0.5128 tons of wheat per ton of coal, which is 2.56 percent more wheat than the 0.5 tons it could previously consume (0.5128/0.50 = 1.0256).

As discussed in the chapter, the onslaught of Japanese cars in the U.S. market drove down the price and quantity of cars sold by American manufacturers, reducing their return on capital and forcing them to be much tougher in negotiating with the United Auto Workers. The end result was better and less expensive cars for Americans but lower profits for Detroit automakers, lower wages and benefits for U.S. autoworkers, and fewer jobs in the U.S. auto industry.

The U.S. auto industry responded to the Japanese competition by demanding, and receiving, protection in the form of a quota on Japanese auto imports. The Japanese response to the quota—which allowed them to raise their prices (why cut prices when you can't sell more cars anyway?) and increase their profit margins—was to focus on making and selling higher quality cars in the U.S. market (as these carried higher profit margins) and shifting substantial production to the United States. In the end, protection did not help U.S. automakers nearly as much as improving the quality of their cars and reducing their manufacturing costs. Indeed, to the extent that protection helped delay the needed changes while boosting Japanese automaker profits (thereby giving them more capital to invest), it may well have hurt the U.S. auto industry.

MONETARY PRICES AND EXCHANGE RATES

So far, we have talked about prices of goods in terms of each other. To introduce monetary prices into the example we have been analyzing, suppose that before the opening of trade between the two nations, each production unit costs $30 in the United States and £10 in the United Kingdom. In this case, the prices of wheat and coal in the two countries will be as follows:

	Wheat	Coal
U.S.	$60/ton	$30/ton
U.K.	£30/ton	£40/ton

These prices are determined by taking the number of required production units and multiplying them by the price per unit.

Following the introduction of trade, assume the same 1:1 terms of trade as before and that the cost of a unit of production remains the same. The prices of wheat and coal in each country will settle at the following, assuming that the exported goods maintain their prices and the prices of the goods imported adjust to these prices so as to preserve the 1:1 terms of trade:

	Wheat	Coal
U.S.	$30/ton	$30/ton
U.K.	£30/ton	£30/ton

These prices present a potential problem in that there will be equilibrium at these prices only if the exchange rate is $1 = £1. Suppose, however, that before the introduction of trade, the exchange rate is £1 = $3. In this case, dollar-equivalent prices in both countries will begin as follows:

	Wheat	Coal
U.S.	$60/ton	$30/ton
U.K.	$90/ton	$120/ton

This is clearly a disequilibrium situation. Once trade begins at these initial prices, the British will demand both U.S. wheat and coal, whereas Americans will demand no British coal or wheat. Money will be flowing in one direction only (from the United Kingdom to the United States to pay for these goods), and goods will flow only in the opposite direction. The United Kingdom will run a massive trade deficit, matched exactly by the U.S. trade surplus. Factors of production in the United Kingdom will be idle (because there is no demand for the goods they can produce) whereas U.S. factors of production will experience an enormous increase in demand for their services.

This is the nightmare scenario for those concerned with the effects of free trade: One country will sell everything to the other country and demand nothing in return (save money), leading to prosperity for the exporting nation and massive unemployment and depression in the importing country. However, such worries ignore the way markets work.

Absent government interference, a set of forces will swing into play simultaneously. The British demand for dollars (to buy U.S. coal and wheat) will boost the value of the dollar, making U.S. products more expensive to the British and British goods less expensive to Americans. At the same time, the jump in demand for U.S. factors of production will raise their prices and hence the cost of producing U.S. coal and wheat. The rise in cost will force a rise in the dollar price of U.S. wheat and coal. Conversely, the lack of demand for U.K. factors of production will drive down their price and hence the pound cost of producing British coal and wheat. The net result of these adjustments in the pound:dollar exchange rate and the cost of factors of production in both countries is to make British products more attractive to consumers and U.S. products less competitive. This process will continue until both countries can find their comparative advantage and the terms of trade between coal and wheat are equal in both countries (say, at 1:1).

TARIFFS

Introducing tariffs (taxes) on imported goods will distort the prices at which trade takes place and will reduce the quantity of goods traded. In effect, tariffs introduce a wedge between the prices paid by domestic customers and the prices received by the exporter, reducing the incentive of both to trade. To see this, suppose Mexican tomatoes are sold in the United States at a price of $0.30 per pound. If the United States imposes a tariff of, say, $0.15 per pound on Mexican tomatoes, then Mexican tomatoes will have to sell for $0.45 per pound to provide Mexican producers with the same pretariff profits on their tomato exports to the United States. However, it is likely that at this price, some Americans will forgo Mexican tomatoes and either substitute U.S. tomatoes or do without tomatoes in their salads. More likely, competition will preclude Mexican tomato growers from raising their price to $0.45 per pound. Suppose, instead, that the price of Mexican tomatoes, including the tariff, settles at $0.35 per pound. At this price, the Mexican tomato growers will receive only $0.20 per pound, reducing their incentive to ship tomatoes to the American market. At the same time, the higher price paid by American customers will reduce their demand for Mexican tomatoes. The result will be fewer Mexican tomatoes sold in the U.S. market. Such a result will benefit American tomato growers (who now face less competition and can thereby raise their prices) and farmworkers (who can now raise their wages without driving their employers out of business) while harming U.S. consumers of tomatoes (including purchasers of Campbell's tomato soup, Ragu spaghetti sauce, Progresso ravioli, and Heinz ketchup).

Ultimately, the effects of free trade are beneficial for an economy because it promotes increased competition among producers. This leads to lower prices for consumers, greater productivity and rising wages for workers, and higher living standards for the country overall.

Questions

1. In a satirical petition on behalf of French candlemakers, Frederic Bastiat, a French economist, called attention to cheap competition from afar: sunlight. A law requiring the shuttering of windows during the day, he suggested, would benefit not only candlemakers but "everything connected with lighting" and the country as a whole. He explained: "As long as you exclude, as you do, iron, corn, foreign fabrics, in proportion as their prices approximate to zero, what inconsistency it would be to admit the light of the sun, the price of which is already at zero during the entire day!"
   a. Is there a logical flaw in Bastiat's satirical argument?
   b. Do Japanese automakers prefer a tariff or a quota on their U.S. auto exports? Why? Is there likely to be consensus among the Japanese carmakers on this point? Might there be any Japanese automakers who would prefer U.S. trade restrictions? Why? Who are they?
   c. What characteristics of the U.S. auto industry have helped it gain protection? Why does protectionism persist despite the obvious gains to society from free trade?

2. Review the arguments both pro and con on NAFTA. What is the empirical evidence so far?

3. Given the resources available to them, countries A and B can produce the following combinations of steel and corn.

Country A		Country B	
Steel (tons)	Corn (bushels)	Steel (tons)	Corn (bushels)
36	0	54	0
30	3	45	9
24	6	36	18
18	9	27	27
15	12	18	36
6	15	9	45
0	18	0	54

a. Do you expect trade to take place between countries A and B? Why?
b. Which country will export steel? Which will export corn? Explain.

THE DETERMINATION OF EXCHANGE RATES

Experience shows that neither a state nor a bank ever have had the unrestricted power of issuing paper money without abusing that power.

David Ricardo (1817)

CHAPTER LEARNING OBJECTIVES

- To explain the concept of an equilibrium exchange rate
- To identify the basic factors affecting exchange rates in a floating exchange rate system
- To calculate the amount of currency appreciation or depreciation associated with a given exchange rate change
- To describe the motives and different forms and consequences of central bank intervention in the foreign exchange market
- To explain how and why expectations affect exchange rates

KEY TERMS

appreciation
ask rate
asset market model
bid rate
central bank
currency board
depreciation
devaluation
dollarization
equilibrium exchange rate
exchange rate
fiat money
floating currency
foreign exchange market intervention
forward rate

freely floating exchange rate
liquidity
monetary base
monetize the deficit
moral hazard
nominal exchange rate
open-market operation
pegged currency
real (inflation-adjusted) exchange rate
reference currency
revaluation
seigniorage
spot rate
sterilization
unsterilized intervention

conomic activity is globally unified today to an unprecedented degree. Changes in one nation's economy are rapidly transmitted to that nation's trading partners. These fluctuations in economic activity are reflected, almost immediately, in fluctuations in currency values. Consequently, multinational corporations, with their integrated cross-border production and marketing operations, continually face devaluation or revaluation worries somewhere in the world. The purpose of this chapter and the next one is to provide an understanding of what an exchange rate is and why it might change. Such an understanding is basic to dealing with currency risk.

This chapter first describes what an exchange rate is and how it is determined in a **freely floating exchange rate** regime—that is, in the absence of government intervention. The chapter next discusses the role of expectations in exchange rate determination. It also examines the different forms and consequences of central bank intervention in the foreign exchange market. Chapter 3 describes the political aspects of currency determination under alternative exchange rate systems and presents a brief history of the international monetary system.

Before proceeding further, here are definitions of several terms commonly used to describe currency changes. Technically, a **devaluation** refers to a decrease in the stated par value of a **pegged currency**, one whose value is set by the government; an increase in par value is known as a **revaluation**. By contrast, a **floating currency**—one whose value is set primarily by market forces—is said to **depreciate** if it loses value and to **appreciate** if it gains value. However, discussions in this book will use the terms *devaluation* and *depreciation,* and *revaluation* and *appreciation,* interchangeably.

2.1 SETTING THE EQUILIBRIUM SPOT EXCHANGE RATE

An exchange rate, which can be for spot or forward delivery, is the price of one country's currency in terms of another currency.

An **exchange rate** is, simply, the price of one nation's currency in terms of another currency, often termed the **reference currency**. For example, the yen/dollar exchange rate is just the number of yen that one dollar will buy. If a dollar will buy 100 yen, the exchange rate would be expressed as ¥100/$ and the yen would be the reference currency. Equivalently, the dollar/yen exchange rate is the number of dollars one yen will buy. Continuing the previous example, the exchange rate would be $0.01/¥ (1/100) and the dollar would now be the reference currency.

Exchange rates can be for spot or forward delivery. A **spot rate** is the price at which currencies are traded for immediate delivery, or in two days in the interbank market. A **forward rate** is the price at which foreign exchange is quoted for delivery at a specified future date.

To understand how exchange rates are set, it helps to recognize that they are market-clearing prices that equilibrate supplies and demands in foreign exchange markets. The determinants of currency supplies and demands are first discussed with the aid of a two-currency model featuring the U.S. dollar and the euro, the official currency of the twelve countries that participate in the European Monetary Union (EMU). The members of EMU are often known collectively as Euroland, the term used here. Later, the various currency influences in a multicurrency world will be studied more closely.

Demand for a Currency

The demand for the euro in the foreign exchange market (which in this two-currency model is equivalent to the supply of dollars) derives from the American demand for Euroland goods and services and euro-denominated financial assets. Euroland prices are set in euros, so in order for Americans to pay for their Euroland purchases they must first exchange their dollars for euros. That is, they will demand euros.

An increase in the euro's dollar value is equivalent to an increase in the dollar price of Euroland products. This higher dollar price normally will reduce the U.S. demand for Euroland goods, services, and assets. Conversely, as the dollar value of the euro falls,

The demand for a foreign currency derives from the demand for that country's goods, services, and assets.

Americans will demand more euros to buy the less-expensive Euroland products, resulting in a downward-sloping demand curve for euros. As the dollar cost of the euro (the exchange rate) falls, Americans will tend to buy more Euroland goods and so will demand more euros.

Supply of a Currency

Similarly, the supply of euros (which for the model is equivalent to the demand for dollars) is based on Euroland demand for U.S. goods and services and dollar-denominated financial assets. In order for Euroland residents to pay for their U.S. purchases, they must first acquire dollars. As the dollar value of the euro increases, thereby lowering the euro cost of U.S. goods, the increased Euroland demand for U.S. goods will cause an increase in the Euroland demand for dollars and, hence, an increase in the amount of euros supplied.[1]

In Exhibit 2.1, e is the spot exchange rate (dollar value of one euro, that is, €1 = \$$e$), and Q is the quantity of euros supplied and demanded. Since the euro is expressed in terms of dollars, the dollar is the reference currency. The euro supply (S) and demand (D) curves intersect at e_0, the **equilibrium exchange rate**. The foreign exchange market is said to be in equilibrium at e_0 because both the demand for euros and the supply of euros at this price is Q_0.

Before continuing, it should be noted that the notion of a single exchange rate is a convenient fiction. In reality, exchange rates—both spot rates and forward rates—are quoted in pairs, with a dealer (usually a bank foreign exchange trader) standing willing to buy foreign exchange at the **bid rate** or to sell foreign exchange at the **ask rate**. As might be expected, the bid rate is always less than the ask rate, enabling dealers to profit from the spread between the bid and ask rates by buying low and selling high. Chapter 7 describes the mechanics of the foreign exchange market in great detail.

Factors that Affect the Equilibrium Exchange Rate

As the supply and demand schedules for a currency change over time, the equilibrium exchange will also change. Some of the factors that influence currency supply and demand are inflation rates, interest rates, economic growth, and political and economic risks. Section 2.2 shows how expectations about these factors also exert a powerful influence on currency supplies and demands and, hence, on exchange rates.

Relative Inflation Rates   Suppose that the supply of dollars increases relative to its demand. This excess growth in the money supply will cause inflation in the United States,

EXHIBIT 2.1 ● EQUILIBRIUM EXCHANGE RATES

Dollar price of one euro (€1 = \$$e$)

Quantity of euros

---

[1] This statement holds provided the price elasticity of Euroland demand, E, is greater than 1. In general, $E = -(\Delta Q/Q)/(\Delta P/P)$, where Q is the quantity of goods demanded, P is the price, and ΔQ is the change in quantity demanded for a change in price, ΔP. If $E > 1$, then total spending goes up when price declines.

which means that U.S. prices will begin to rise relative to prices of goods and services in Euroland. Euroland consumers are likely to buy fewer U.S. products and begin switching to Euroland substitutes, leading to a decrease in the amount of euros supplied at every exchange rate. The result is a leftward shift in the euro supply curve to S' as shown in Exhibit 2.2. Similarly, higher prices in the United States will lead American consumers to substitute Euroland imports for U.S. products, resulting in an increase in the demand for euros as depicted by D'. In effect, both Americans and residents of Euroland are searching for the best deals worldwide and will switch their purchases accordingly as the prices of U.S. goods change relative to prices in Euroland. Hence, a higher rate of inflation in the United States than in Euroland will simultaneously increase Euroland exports to the United States and reduce U.S. exports to Euroland.

Inflation causes a nation's currency to depreciate.

A new equilibrium rate $e_1 > e_0$ results. In other words, a higher rate of inflation in the United States than in Europe will lead to a depreciation of the dollar relative to the euro or, equivalently, to an appreciation of the euro relative to the dollar. In general, a nation running a relatively high rate of inflation will find its currency declining in value relative to the currencies of countries with lower inflation rates. This relationship will be formalized in Chapter 4 as purchasing power parity (PPP).

Relative Interest Rates   Interest rate differentials will also affect the equilibrium exchange rate. A rise in U.S. interest rates relative to Euroland rates, all else being equal, will cause investors in both nations to switch from euro- to dollar-denominated securities to take advantage of the higher dollar rates. The net result will be depreciation of the euro in the absence of government intervention.

Higher real interest rates cause a nation's currency to appreciate.

It should be noted that the interest rates discussed here are real interest rates. The **real interest rate** equals the nominal or actual interest rate minus the rate of inflation. The distinction between nominal and real interest rates is critical in international finance and will be discussed at length in Chapter 4. If the increase in U.S. interest rates relative to Euroland rates just reflects higher U.S. inflation, the predicted result will be a weaker dollar. Only an increase in the real U.S. interest rate relative to the real Euroland rate will result in an appreciating dollar.

Relative Economic Growth Rates   Similarly, a nation with strong economic growth will attract investment capital seeking to acquire domestic assets. The demand for domestic assets, in turn, results in an increased demand for the domestic currency and a stronger currency, other things being equal. Empirical evidence supports the hypothesis that economic growth should lead to a stronger currency. Conversely, nations with poor growth prospects will see an exodus of capital and weaker currencies.

Strong economic growth and low political risk strengthen a nation's currency.

EXHIBIT 2.2 • IMPACT OF U.S. INFLATION ON THE EQUILIBRIUM EXCHANGE RATE

Political and Economic Risk Other factors that can influence exchange rates include political and economic risks. Investors prefer to hold lesser amounts of riskier assets; thus, low-risk currencies—those associated with more politically and economically stable nations—are more highly valued than high-risk currencies.

ILLUSTRATION   *The Ruble Is Rubble*

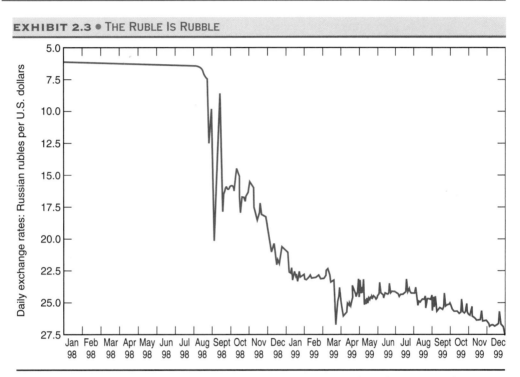

EXHIBIT 2.3 • THE RUBLE IS RUBBLE

Source: Pacific Exchange Rate Service, pacific.commerce.ubc.ca/xr/plot.html, © 2000 by Prof. Werner Antweiler, University of British Columbia, Vancouver BC, Canada. Time period shown in diagram: 1/Jan/1998–31/Dec/1999.

From the breakup of the former Soviet Union in 1991 on, the Russian government had difficulty managing its finances. By spending more than it was collecting in revenues, Russia faced persistent budget deficits financed by issuing short-term treasury bills and printing rubles. By late 1997, the combination of rapidly increasing debt issuance and falling commodity prices (a major source of Russia's revenue and foreign exchange comes from exports of oil, timber, gold, and other commodities) increased investors' doubts that Russia would be able to service its growing debt burden, including $160 billion in foreign debt. Sensing blood, speculators launched a series of attacks against the Russian ruble. The Russian government responded by repeatedly raising interest rates, which eventually reached 150 percent by the middle of May 1998. To help support the ruble, the International Monetary Fund (IMF) put together a $23 billion financial package, contingent on Russia implementing an adjustment program that stressed boosting tax revenues. When the Russian parliament balked at the tax collection measures, the IMF withheld its funds. Despite the high interest rates it was paying, the government had difficulty persuading investors to roll over their short-term government debt. The stock market sank to new lows, interest rates remained high, and investors began transferring money out of Russia.

Facing accelerating capital flight and mounting domestic problems, the Russian government announced a radical policy shift on August 17, 1998. The key measures included abandonment of its currency supports, suspension of trading in treasury bills combined with a mandatory restructuring of government debt, and a 90-day moratorium on the repayment of corporate and bank debt to foreign creditors (that is, default). In response, the Russian ruble plunged in value (see Exhibit 2.3). Rather than dealing with the root causes of the financial crisis, the government reverted to previously discarded administrative measures. It imposed extensive controls on the foreign exchange market, increasingly financed its debt by printing more rubles, and forced exporters to surrender 75 percent of their export earnings. The crisis and the government's subsequent actions resulted in a steep rise in inflation and a deep recession in Russia, causing a continuing sharp decline in the ruble's value shown in Exhibit 2.3.

Calculating Exchange Rate Changes

Depending on the current value of the euro relative to the dollar, the amount of euro appreciation or depreciation is computed as the fractional increase or decrease in the dollar value of the euro. For example, if the €/$ exchange rate goes from €1 = $0.93 to €1 = $1.09, the euro is said to have appreciated by the change in its dollar value, which is (1.09 – 0.93)/0.93 = 17.20%.

The general formula by which we can calculate the euro's appreciation or depreciation against the dollar is as follows:

$$\frac{\text{Amount of euro appreciation}}{\text{(depreciation)}} = \frac{\text{New dollar value of euro} - \text{Old dollar value of euro}}{\text{Old dollar value of euro}}$$

$$= \frac{e_1 - e_0}{e_0} \tag{2.1}$$

Substituting in the numbers from the previous example (with e_0 = $0.93 and e_1 = $1.09) yields the 17.20 percent euro appreciation.

Alternatively, we can calculate the change in the euro value of the dollar. We can do this by recognizing that if e equals the dollar value of a euro (dollars per euro), then the euro value of a dollar (euros per dollar) must be the reciprocal, or $1/e$. For example, if the euro is worth $0.93, then the dollar must be worth €1.08 (1/0.93). The change in the euro value of the dollar between time 0 and time 1 equals $1/e_1 - 1/e_0$. In percentage terms, the dollar is said to have depreciated (appreciated) against the euro by the fractional decrease (increase) in the euro value of the dollar:

Dollar depreciation is the flip side of euro appreciation.

$$\frac{\text{Amount of dollar depreciation}}{\text{(appreciation)}} = \frac{\text{New euro value of dollar} - \text{Old euro value of dollar}}{\text{Old euro value of dollar}}$$

$$= \frac{1/e_1 - 1/e_0}{1/e_0} = \frac{e_0 - e_1}{e_1} \tag{2.2}$$

Employing Equation 2.2, we can find the increase in the euro exchange rate from $0.93 to $1.09 to be equivalent to a dollar depreciation of 14.68 percent [(0.93 – 1.09)/1.09 = –0.1468]. (Why don't the two exchange rate changes equal each other?)[2]

---

[2] The reason the euro appreciation is unequal to the amount of dollar depreciation depends on the fact that the value of one currency is the inverse of the value of the other one. Hence, the percentage change in currency value differs because the base off which the change is measured differs.

ILLUSTRATION   *Calculating Yen Appreciation against the Dollar*

During 2002, the yen went from $0.0074074 to $0.0084746. By how much did the yen appreciate against the dollar?

Solution. Using Equation 2.1, the yen has appreciated against the dollar by an amount equal to $(0.0084746 - 0.0074074)/0.0074074 = 14.41\%$.

By how much has the dollar depreciated against the yen?

Solution. An exchange rate of ¥1 = $0.0074074 translates into an exchange rate of $1 = ¥135 ($1/0.0074074 = 135$). Similarly, the exchange rate of ¥1 = $0.0084746 is equivalent to an exchange rate of $1 = ¥118. Using Equation 2.2, the dollar has depreciated against the yen by an amount equal to $(118 - 135)/135 = -12.59\%$.

ILLUSTRATION   *Calculating Dollar Appreciation against the Thai Baht*

On July 2, 1997, the Thai baht fell 17 percent against the U.S. dollar. By how much has the dollar appreciated against the baht?

Solution. If e_0 is the initial dollar value of the baht and e_1 is the post-devaluation exchange rate, then we know from Equation 2.1 that $(e_1 - e_0)/e_0 = -17\%$. Solving for e_1 in terms of e_0 yields $e_1 = 0.83e_0$. From Equation 2.2, we know that the dollar's appreciation against the baht equals $(e_0 - e_1)/e_1 = (e_0 - 0.83e_0)/0.83e_0 = 0.17/.83 = 20.48\%$.

ILLUSTRATION   *Calculating Yugoslav Dinar Devaluation against the Dollar*

April 1, 1998, was an ill-fated date in Yugoslavia. On that day, the government devalued the Yugoslav dinar, setting its new rate at 10.92 dinar to the dollar, from 6.0 dinar previously. By how much has the dinar devalued against the dollar?

Solution. The devaluation lowered the dinar's dollar value from $0.1667 (1/6) to $0.0916 (1/10.92). According to Equation 2.1, the dinar has devalued by $(0.0916 - 0.1667)/0.1667 = -45\%$.

By how much has the dollar appreciated against the dinar?

Solution. Applying Equation 2.2, the dollar has appreciated against the dinar by an amount equal to $(10.92 - 6)/6 = 82\%$.

ILLUSTRATION   *Calculating Afghani Appreciation against the Pakistani Rupee*

The afghani, Afghanistan's currency, has a perverse tendency to go up whenever sitting governments fall. So as soon as commentators labeled Osama bin Laden the prime suspect in the September 11 World Trade Center attack, currency traders figured the Taliban would become a target of the United States, bringing prospects of a new government and, perhaps, economic development—and a rise in the afghani's value. So it has. Under the Taliban, the exchange rate—quoted as the number of Pakistani rupees it takes to buy 100,000 afghanis—fell to around 85 rupees. September 11 galvanized the market. By mid-November 2001, military gains by the Northern Alliance opposition pushed the exchange rate up to 165. By how much has the afghani appreciated against the rupee?

Solution. Applying Equation 2.1, the afghani has appreciated against the rupee by an amount equal to $(165 - 85)/85 = 94\%$.

Similarly, between September 11 and mid-November, the dollar went from 78,000 to 34,000. By how much did the dollar depreciate against the afghani during this two-month period?

Solution. According to Equation 2.2, the dollar depreciated during this period by an amount equal to $(34,000 - 78,000)/78,000 = -56\%$. Equivalently, the afghani appreciated against the dollar by 129 percent $([1/34,000] - [1/78,000])/(1/78,000)$.

2.2 EXPECTATIONS AND THE ASSET MARKET MODEL OF EXCHANGE RATES

Although currency values are affected by current events and current supply and demand flows in the foreign exchange market, they also depend on expectations—or forecasts—about future exchange rate movements. And exchange rate forecasts, as we will see in Chapter 4, are influenced by every conceivable economic, political, and social factor.

The role of expectations in determining exchange rates depends on the fact that currencies are financial assets and that an exchange rate is simply the relative price of two financial assets—one country's currency in terms of another's. Thus, currency prices are determined in the same manner that the prices of assets such as stocks, bonds, gold, or real estate are determined. Unlike the prices of services or products with short storage lives, asset prices are influenced comparatively little by current events. Rather, they are determined by people's willingness to hold the existing quantities of assets, which in turn depends on their expectations of the future worth of these assets. Thus, for example, frost in Florida can bump up the price of oranges, but it should have little impact on the price of the citrus groves producing the oranges; instead, longer-term expectations of the demand and supply of oranges govern the values of these groves.

> Since currencies are long-lived assets, foreign exchange rates are strongly influenced by expectations of future economic, political, and social factors.

Similarly, the value today of a given currency, say, the dollar, depends on whether or not—and how strongly—people still want the amount of dollars and dollar-denominated assets they held yesterday. According to this view—known as the **asset market model** of exchange rate determination—the exchange rate between two currencies represents the price that just balances the relative supplies of, and demands for, assets denominated in those currencies. Consequently, shifts in preferences can lead to massive shifts in currency values.

> Higher risk-adjusted returns on U.S. assets in the 1990s boosted the value of the dollar.

For example, during the 1990s, the Cold War ended and the United States became the sole global power. Following a brief recession, the U.S. economy innovated and grew rapidly while Japan and Europe largely stagnated. Capital was attracted to the United States by the strength of its economy, the high after-tax real rate of return, and the favorable political climate—conditions superior to those attainable elsewhere. Foreigners found the United States to be a safer and more rewarding place in which to invest than elsewhere, so they added many more U.S. assets to their portfolios. In response, the dollar soared in value against other currencies.

> Exchange rates are forward looking.

The desire to hold a currency today depends critically on expectations of the factors that can affect the currency's future value; therefore, what matters is not only what is happening today but what markets expect will happen in the future. Thus, currency values are forward looking; they are set by investor expectations of their issuing countries' future economic prospects rather than by contemporaneous events alone. Moreover, in a world of high capital mobility, the difference between having the right policies and the wrong ones has never been greater. This point is illustrated by the Asian currency crisis of 1997.

During the second half of 1997, and beginning in Thailand, currencies and stock markets plunged across East Asia, while hundreds of banks, builders, and manufacturers went bankrupt. The Thai baht, Indonesian rupiah, Malaysian ringgit, Philippine peso, and South Korean won depreciated by 40 percent to 80 percent apiece. All this happened despite the fact that Asia's fundamentals looked good: low inflation, balanced budgets, well-run central banks, high domestic savings, strong export industries, a large and growing middle class, a vibrant entrepreneurial class, and industrious, well-trained, and often well-educated workforces paid relatively low wages. But investors were looking past these positives to signs of impending trouble. What they saw was that many East Asian economies were locked on a course that was unsustainable, characterized by large trade deficits, huge short-term foreign debts, overvalued currencies, and financial systems that were rotten at their core. Each of these ingredients played a role in the crisis and its spread from one country to another.

LOSS OF EXPORT COMPETITIVENESS

To begin, most East Asian countries depend on exports as their engines of growth and development. Along with Japan, the United States is the most important market for these exports. Partly because of this, many of them had tied their currencies to the dollar. This tie served them well until 1995, promoting low inflation and currency stability. It also boosted exports at the expense of Japan as the dollar fell against the yen, forcing Japanese companies to shift production to East Asia to cope with the strong yen. Currency stability also led East Asian banks and companies to finance themselves with dollars, yen, and Deutsche marks—some $275 billion worth, much of it short term—because dollar and other foreign currency loans carried lower interest rates than did their domestic currencies. The party ended in 1995, when the dollar began recovering against the yen and other currencies. By mid-1997, the dollar had risen by over 50 percent against the yen and by 20 percent against the German mark. Dollar appreciation alone would have made East Asia's exports less price competitive. But their competitiveness problem was greatly exacerbated by the fact that during this period, the Chinese yuan depreciated by about 25 percent against the dollar.[3] China exported similar products, so the yuan devaluation raised China's export competitiveness at East Asia's expense. The loss of export competitiveness slowed down Asian growth and caused utilization rates—and profits—on huge investments in production capacity to plunge. It also gave the Asian central banks a mutual incentive to devalue their currencies. According to one theory, recognizing these altered incentives, speculators attacked the East Asian currencies almost simultaneously and forced a round of devaluations.[4]

MORAL HAZARD AND CRONY CAPITALISM

Another theory suggests that **moral hazard**—the tendency to incur risks that one is protected against—lies at the heart of Asia's financial problems. Specifically, most Asian banks and finance companies operated with implicit or explicit government guarantees. For example, the South Korean government directed the banking system to lend massively to

---

[3] For a discussion of the role that the Chinese yuan devaluation played in the Asian crisis, see Kenneth Kasa, "Export Competition and Contagious Currency Crises," *Economic Letter,* Federal Reserve Bank of San Francisco, January 16, 1998.

[4] See C. Hu and Kenneth Kasa, "A Dynamic Model of Export Competition, Policy Coordination, and Simultaneous Currency Collapse," working paper, Federal Reserve Bank of San Francisco, 1997.

companies and industries that it viewed as economically strategic, with little regard for their profitability. When combined with poor regulation, these guarantees distorted investment decisions, encouraging financial institutions to fund risky projects in the expectation that the banks would enjoy any profits, while sticking the government with any losses. (These same perverse incentives underlie the savings and loan fiasco in the United States during the 1980s.) In Asia's case, the problem was compounded by the crony capitalism that is pervasive throughout the region, with lending decisions often dictated more by political and family ties than by economic reality. Billions of dollars in easy-money loans were made to family and friends of the well-connected. Without market discipline or risk-based bank lending, the result was overinvestment—financed by vast quantities of debt—and inflated prices of assets in short supply, such as land.[5]

This financial bubble persists as long as the government guarantee is maintained. The inevitable glut of real estate and excess production capacity leads to large amounts of nonperforming loans and widespread loan defaults. When reality strikes, and investors realize that the government doesn't have the resources to bail out everyone, asset values plummet and the bubble is burst. The decline in asset values triggers further loan defaults, causing a loss of the confidence on which economic activity depends. Investors also worry that the government will try to inflate its way out of its difficulty. The result is a self-reinforcing downward spiral and capital flight. As foreign investors refuse to renew loans and begin to sell off shares of overvalued local companies, capital flight accelerates and the local currency falls, increasing the cost of servicing foreign debts. Local firms and banks scramble to buy foreign exchange before the currency falls further, putting even more downward pressure on the exchange rate. This story explains why stock prices and currency values declined together and why Asian financial institutions were especially hard hit. Moreover, this process is likely to be contagious, as investors search for other countries with similar characteristics. When such a country is found, everyone rushes for the exit simultaneously and another bubble is burst, another currency is sunk.

The standard approach of staving off currency devaluation is to raise interest rates, thereby making it more attractive to hold the local currency and increasing capital inflows. However, this approach was problematic for Asian central banks. Raising interest rates boosted the cost of funds to banks and made it more difficult for borrowers to service their debts, thereby further crippling an already sick financial sector. Higher interest rates also lowered real estate values, which served as collateral for many of these loans, and pushed even more loans into default. Thus, Asian central banks found their hands were tied and investors recognized that.

THE BUBBLE BURSTS

These two stories—loss of export competitiveness and moral hazard in lending combined with crony capitalism—combine to explain the severity of the Asian crisis. Appreciation of the dollar and depreciation of the yen and yuan slowed down Asian economic growth and hurt corporate profits. These factors turned ill-conceived and overleveraged investments in property developments and industrial complexes into financial disasters. The Asian financial crisis then was touched off when local investors began dumping their own currencies for dollars and foreign lenders refused to renew their loans. It was aggravated by politicians, such as in Malaysia and South Korea, who preferred to blame foreigners for their problems rather than seek structural reforms of their economies. Both foreign and domestic investors, already spooked by the currency crisis, lost yet more confidence in these nations and dumped more of their currencies and stocks, driving them to record lows.

---

[5] This explanation for the Asian crisis is set forth in Paul Krugman, "What Happened to Asia?" MIT working paper, 1998.

This synthesized story is consistent with the experience of Taiwan, which is a net exporter of capital and whose savings are largely invested by private capitalists without government direction or guarantees. Taiwanese businesses also are financed far less by debt than by equity. In contrast to its Asian competitors, Taiwan suffered minimally during 1997, with the Taiwan dollar (NT$) down by a modest 15 percent (to counteract its loss of export competitiveness to China and Japan) and its stock market actually up by 17 percent in NT$ terms.

"The way out," said Confucius, "is through the door." The clear exit strategy for East Asian countries was to restructure their ailing financial systems by shutting down or selling off failing banks (for example, to healthy foreign banks) and disposing of the collateral (real estate and industrial properties) underlying their bad loans. Although the restructuring has not gone as far as it needs to, the result so far is fewer but stronger and better-capitalized banks and restructured and consolidated industries and a continuation of East Asia's strong historical growth record. However, progress has been slow in reforming bankruptcy laws, a critical element of reform. Simply put, governments must step aside and allow those who borrow too much or lend too foolishly to fail. Ending government guarantees and politically motivated lending will transform Asia's financial sector and force cleaner and more transparent financial transactions. The result will be better investment decisions—decisions driven by market forces rather than personal connections or government whim—and healthier economies that attract capital for the right reasons.

The Nature of Money and Currency Values

Money provides liquidity and purchasing power.

To understand the factors that affect currency values, it helps to examine the special character of money. To begin, money has value because people are willing to accept it in exchange for goods and services. The value of money, therefore, depends on its purchasing power. Money also provides **liquidity**—that is, you can readily exchange it for goods or other assets, thereby facilitating economic transactions. Thus, money represents both a *store of value* and a *store of liquidity*. The demand for money, therefore, depends on money's ability to maintain its value and on the level of economic activity. Hence, the lower the expected inflation rate, the more money people will demand. Similarly, higher economic growth means more transactions and a greater demand for money to pay bills.

The demand for money is also affected by the demand for assets denominated in that currency. The higher the expected real return and the lower the riskiness of a country's assets, the greater is the demand for its currency to buy those assets. In addition, as people who prefer assets denominated in that currency (usually residents of the country) accumulate wealth, the value of the currency rises.

The demand for money depends on its usefulness as a store of value, as well as on the demand for assets denominated in that currency.

Because the exchange rate reflects the relative demands for two moneys, factors that increase the demand for the home currency should also increase the price of home currency on the foreign exchange market. In summary, the economic factors that affect a currency's foreign exchange value include its usefulness as a store of value, determined by its expected rate of inflation; the demand for liquidity, determined by the volume of transactions in that currency; and the demand for assets denominated in that currency, determined by the risk-return pattern on investment in that nation's economy and by the wealth of its residents. The first factor depends primarily on the country's future monetary policy, whereas the latter two factors depend largely on expected economic growth and political and economic stability. All three factors ultimately depend on the soundness of the nation's economic policies. The sounder these policies, the more valuable the nation's currency will be; conversely, the more uncertain a nation's future economic and political course, the riskier its assets will be, and the more depressed and volatile its currency's value.

Sound economic policies strengthen a nation's currency.

ILLUSTRATION   *The Peso Problem*

On December 20, 1994, Mexico devalued its peso by 12.7 percent. Two days later, the government was forced to let the peso float freely, whereupon it quickly fell an additional 15 percent. By March 1995, the peso had fallen over 25 percent more, a total of over 50 percent altogether (see Exhibit 2.4). Even President Clinton's dramatic rescue package involving $52 billion in loans and loan guarantees from the United States and various international financial institutions could only halt the freefall temporarily. The story of the peso's travails illustrates the importance of credibility in establishing currency values. This credibility depends, in part, on the degree of consistency between the government's exchange rate policy and its other macroeconomic objectives.

Until the devaluation, Mexico had a system under which the peso was allowed to fluctuate within a narrow band against the dollar. Pegging the peso to the dollar helped stabilize Mexico's economy against hyperinflation. The credibility of this exchange rate regime depended on people believing that Banco de Mexico (Mexico's central bank) would defend the currency to keep it within this band. As long as investors had confidence in the country's economic future, this policy worked well. However, that confidence was shaken during 1994 by an armed uprising in the state of Chiapas, assassinations of leading Mexican politicians (including the front-running presidential candidate), and high-level political resignations. Another source of concern was the enormous trade deficit, which was about 8 percent of gross domestic product (GDP) for 1994.

The trade deficit jeopardized future growth because, to attract the dollars needed to finance this deficit, the government had to keep interest rates high, especially because interest rates were rising in the United States and around the world. Foreign investors began to bet that this situation was unsustainable, that in order to continue to finance the deficit Mexico would have to raise interest rates so much that it would damage its economy. Such a rise was unlikely given the political difficulties the government was already facing. At the same time, under pressure from an administration facing a tough election, the central bank permitted a monetary expansion of more than 20 percent during 1994, leading to fears of rising inflation. Sensing that something had to give, many investors ran for the exits, draining Banco de Mexico's dollar reserves.

Here is where Mexico made a fundamental error. The central bank did not allow the supply of pesos to fall, even though the various political shocks—and the economic uncertainties they created—reduced the demand for pesos. As investors sold pesos to Banco de Mexico for dollars, reducing the supply of pesos to the level actually demanded,

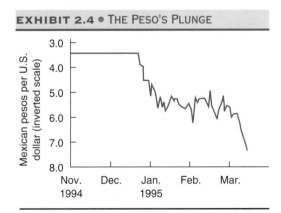

EXHIBIT 2.4 ● THE PESO'S PLUNGE

Source: Wall Street Journal. March 10, 1995. p. A3. Reprinted by permission. © 1995 Dow Jones & Company, Inc. All rights reserved worldwide.

the central bank—fearing that a reduced supply of pesos would cause interest rates to rise (a politically costly step)—put these pesos back into circulation by buying an offsetting amount of government notes and bonds from the public (a process known as **sterilization**; see Section 2.3). The result was a continuing excess supply of pesos that the central bank kept buying up with its shrinking dollar reserves. Despite this inherent conflict between Mexico's monetary policy and its exchange rate policy, many investors trusted the government's adamant promise to maintain the peso's link with the dollar.

Mexico's devaluation, therefore, represented an enormous gamble that foreign investors would not lose confidence in the country's financial markets. The payoff was swift and bloody: The Mexican stock market plunged 11 percent and interest rates soared as investors demanded higher returns for the new risk in peso securities. At the same time, investors rushed to cash in their pesos, causing Banco de Mexico to lose half its dollar reserves in one day. The next day, the government caved in and floated the peso. It also announced a tightened monetary policy to bolster the peso's value, along with a package of market-oriented structural reforms to enhance Mexican competitiveness and restore investor confidence. Despite the soundness of these new policies, they were too late; the government's loss of credibility was so great that the peso's fall continued until the U.S. rescue plan. Simply put, with the devaluation, Mexico sacrificed its most valuable financial asset—market confidence.

Mexico's peso problem quickly translated into faltering investor confidence in other countries that, like Mexico, suffer from political turmoil and are dependent on foreign investors to finance their deficits—including Canada, Italy, and other Latin American nations viewed as having overvalued currencies.

Central Bank Reputations and Currency Values

As the example of Mexico indicates, another critical determinant of currency values is central bank behavior. A **central bank** is the nation's official monetary authority; its job is to use the instruments of monetary policy, including the sole power to create money, to achieve one or more of the following objectives: price stability, low interest rates, or a target currency value. As such, the central bank affects the risk associated with holding money. This risk is inextricably linked to the nature of a **fiat money**, which is nonconvertible paper money. Until 1971, every major currency was linked to a commodity. Today no major currency is linked to a commodity. With a commodity base, usually gold, there was a stable, long-term anchor to the price level. Prices varied a great deal in the short term, but they eventually returned to where they had been.

Expectations of central bank behavior affect currency values.

With a fiat money, there is no anchor to the price level—that is, there is no standard of value that investors can use to find out what the currency's future value might be. Instead, a currency's value is largely determined by the central bank through its control of the money supply. If the central bank creates too much money, inflation will occur and the value of money will fall. *Expectations* of central bank behavior also will affect exchange rates today; a currency will decline if people *think* the central bank will expand the money supply in the future.

Viewed this way, money becomes a brand-name product whose value is backed by the reputation of the central bank that issues it. And just as reputations among automobiles vary—from Mercedes-Benz to Yugo—so currencies come backed by a range of quality reputations—from the dollar, Swiss franc, and Japanese yen on the high side to the Mexican peso, Thai baht, and Russian ruble on the low side. Underlying these reputations is trust in the willingness of the central bank to maintain price stability.

The high-quality currencies are those expected to maintain their purchasing power because they are issued by reputable central banks. A reputable central bank is one that the markets trust to do the right thing, and not merely the politically expedient thing,

The value of a currency is affected by the reputation of the central bank that issues it.

when it comes to monetary policy. This trust, in turn, comes from history: Reputable banks, like the Bundesbank (Germany's central bank prior to the European Monetary Union), have developed their credibility by having done hard, cruel, and painful things for years in order to fight inflation. In contrast, the low-quality currencies are those that bear little assurance that their purchasing power will be maintained. As in the car market, high-quality currencies sell at a premium, and low-quality currencies sell at a discount (relative to their values based on economic fundamentals alone). That is, investors demand a risk premium to hold a riskier currency, whereas safer currencies will be worth more than their economic fundamentals would indicate.

Uncertainty over a nation's monetary policy can depress the value of its currency.

Price Stability and Central Bank Independence   Because good reputations are slow to build and quick to disappear, many economists recommend that central banks adopt rules for price stability that are verifiable, unambiguous, and enforceable—along with the independence and accountability necessary to realize this goal.[6] Focus is also important. A central bank whose responsibilities are limited to price stability is more likely to achieve this goal. For example, the Bundesbank—a model for many economists—managed to maintain such a low rate of German inflation because of its statutory commitment to price stability, a legacy of Germany's bitter memories of hyperinflation in the 1920s, which peaked at *200 billion percent* in 1923. Absent such rules, the natural accountability of central banks to government becomes an avenue for political influence. For example, even though the U.S. Federal Reserve is an independent central bank, its legal responsibility to pursue both full employment and price stability (aims that conflict in the short term) can hinder its effectiveness in fighting inflation. The greater scope for political influence in central banks that do not have a clear mandate to pursue price stability will, in turn, add to the perception of inflation risk.

This perception stems from the fact that government officials and other critics routinely exhort the central bank to follow "easier" monetary policies, by which they mean boosting the money supply to lower interest rates. These exhortations arise because many people believe (1) that the central bank can trade off a higher rate of inflation for more economic growth, and (2) that the central bank determines the rate of interest independently of the rate of inflation and other economic conditions. Despite the questionable merits of these beliefs, central banks—particularly those that are not independent—often respond to these demands by expanding the money supply.

Central banks that lack independence are also often forced to **monetize the deficit**, which means financing the public-sector deficit by buying government debt with newly created money. Whether monetary expansion stems from economic stimulus or deficit financing, it inevitably leads to higher inflation and a devalued currency.

Independent central banks tend to follow sound money policies.

The idea that central bank independence can help establish a credible monetary policy is being put into practice today, as countries that have been plagued with high inflation rates are enacting legislation to reshape their conduct of monetary policy. For example, New Zealand, England, Mexico, Canada, Chile, and Bolivia all have passed laws that mandate an explicit inflation goal or that give their central banks more independence.

ILLUSTRATION   *Inflation Dies Down Under*

In Germany and Switzerland, long seen as bastions of sound money, inflation rose during the early 1990s. However, Australia and New Zealand, so often afflicted by high inflation, boasted the lowest rates among the nations comprising the Organization for Economic Cooperation and Development (OECD), which consists of all the industrialized nations in the world (see Exhibit 2.5).

---

[6] See, for example, W. Lee Hoskins, "A European System of Central Banks: Observations from Abroad," *Economic Commentary,* Federal Reserve Bank of Cleveland, November 15, 1990.

The cure was simple: restrict the supply of Australian and New Zealand dollars. To increase the likelihood that it would stick to its guns, the Reserve Bank of New Zealand was made fully independent in 1990 and its governor, Donald Brash, was held accountable for cutting inflation to zero to 2 percent by December 1993. Failure carried a high personal cost: He would lose his job. Exhibit 2.5 shows why Mr. Brash kept his job; by 1993, inflation had fallen to 1.3 percent, and it has since then held at about 2 percent. At the same time, growth has averaged a rapid 4 percent a year.

The job of New Zealand's central banker was made easier by the government's decision to dismantle one of the OECD's most taxed, regulated, protectionist, and comprehensive welfare states and transform it into one of the most free-market oriented. By slashing welfare programs and stimulating economic growth through its market reforms and tax and tariff cuts, the government converted its traditionally large budget deficit into a budget surplus and ended the need to print money to finance it. To ensure continued fiscal sobriety, in 1994 parliament passed the Fiscal Responsibility Act, which mandates budgetary balance over the business cycle.

EXHIBIT 2.5 ● INFLATION DIES DOWN UNDER

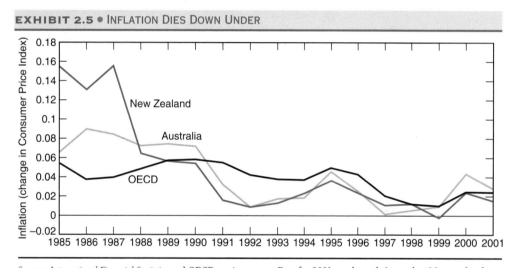

Sources: International Financial Statistics and OECD, various years. Data for 2001 are through September 30 annualized.

Currency Boards   Some countries, like Argentina, have gone even further and established what is in effect a currency board. Under a **currency board** system, there is no central bank. Instead, the currency board issues notes and coins that are convertible on demand and at a fixed rate into a foreign reserve currency. As reserves, the currency board holds high-quality, interest-bearing securities denominated in the reserve currency. Its reserves are equal to 100 percent, or slightly more, of its notes and coins in circulation. The board has no discretionary monetary policy. Instead, market forces alone determine the money supply.

Over the past 150 years, more than 70 countries (mainly former British colonies) have had currency boards. As long as they kept their boards, all of those countries had the same rate of inflation as the country issuing the reserve currency and successfully maintained convertibility at a fixed exchange rate into the reserve currency; no board has ever devalued its currency against its anchor currency. Currency boards are successfully operating today in Estonia, Hong Kong, and Lithuania. Argentina dropped its currency board in January 2002.

In addition to promoting price stability, a currency board also compels government to follow a responsible fiscal (spending and tax) policy. If the budget is not balanced, the government must persuade the private sector to lend to it; it no longer has the option of forcing the central bank to monetize the deficit. By establishing a monetary authority that is independent

Currency boards promote sound money policies.

of the government and is committed to a conservative monetary policy, currency boards are likely to promote confidence in a country's currency. Such confidence is especially valuable for emerging economies with a past history of profligate monetary and fiscal policy.

 ILLUSTRATION   *Argentina Reforms Its Currency*

Argentina, once the world's seventh-largest economy, has long been considered one of Latin America's worst basket cases. Starting with Juan Peron, who was first elected president in 1946, and for decades after, profligate government spending financed by a compliant central bank that printed money to cover the chronic budget deficits had triggered a vicious cycle of inflation and devaluation. High taxes and excessive controls compounded Argentina's woes and led to an overregulated, arthritic economy. However, in 1991, after the country had suffered nearly fifty years of economic mismanagement, President Carlos Menem and his fourth Minister of Economy, Domingo Cavallo, launched the Convertibility Act. (The first Minister of Economy, Miguel Roig, took one look at the economy and died of a heart attack six days into the job.) This act made the austral (the Argentine currency) fully convertible at a fixed rate of 10,000 australs to the dollar, and by law the monetary supply had to be 100 percent backed by gold and foreign currency reserves, mostly dollars. This link to gold and the dollar imposed a straitjacket on monetary policy. If, for example, the central bank had to sell dollars to support the currency, the money supply automatically shrank. Better still, the government could no longer print money to finance a budget deficit. In January 1992, the government knocked four zeros off the austral and renamed it the peso, worth exactly $1.

By effectively locking Argentina into the U.S. monetary system, the Convertibility Act had remarkable success in restoring confidence in the peso and providing an anchor for inflation expectations. Inflation fell from more than 2,300 percent in 1990 to 170 percent in 1991 and 4 percent in 1994 (see Exhibit 2.6). By 1997, the inflation rate was 0.4 percent, among the lowest in the world. Argentine capital transferred overseas to escape Argentina's hyperinflation began to come home. It spurred rapid economic growth and led to a rock-solid currency. In response to the good economic news, stock prices quintupled, in dollar terms, during the first year of the plan. And the price of Argentina's foreign debt rose from 13 percent of its face value in 1990 to 45 percent in 1992.

EXHIBIT 2.6 • ARGENTINA ENDS HYPERINFLATION

Source: International Financial Statistics, various issues. Data for 2001 are estimated.

The likelihood that the Convertibility Act marked a permanent change in Argentina and would not be revoked at a later date—an important consideration for investors—was increased by the other economic actions the Argentine government took to reinforce its commitment to price stability and economic growth: it deregulated its economy, sold off money-losing state-owned businesses to the private sector, cut taxes and red tape, opened its capital markets, and lowered barriers to trade. In September 1994, the Argentine government announced a sweeping privatization plan designed to sell off all remaining state-owned enterprises—including the national mint, the postal service, and the country's main airports.

Since then, however, the Argentine economy suffered from a series of external shocks and internal problems. External shocks included falling prices for its agricultural commodities, the Mexican peso crisis in late 1994, the Asian currency crisis of 1997, and the Russian and Brazilian financial crises of 1998–1999. The financial shocks led investors to reassess the risk of emerging markets and to withdraw their capital from Argentina as well as the countries in crisis. The devaluation of the Brazilian *real* in early 1999—which increased the cost of Argentine goods in Brazil and reduced the cost of Brazilian goods to Argentines—hurt Argentina because of the strong trade ties between the two countries. Similarly, the strong appreciation of the dollar in the late 1990s made Argentina's products less competitive, both at home and abroad, against those of its trading partners whose currencies were not tied to the dollar.

Internal problems revolved around rigid labor laws that make it costly to lay off Argentine workers and excessive spending by the Argentine government. In a decade that saw GDP rise 50 percent, public spending rose 90 percent. Initially, the growth in government spending was funded by privatization proceeds. When privatization proceeds ran out, the government turned to tax increases and heavy borrowing. The result was massive fiscal deficits, a rising debt burden, high unemployment, economic stagnation, and a restive population.

On June 14, 2001, Domingo Cavallo, the treasury secretary for a new Argentine president, announced a dramatic change in policy to stimulate Argentina's slumping economy, then in its fourth year of recession. Henceforth, the peso exchange rate for exporters and importers would be an average of a dollar and a euro, that is, P1 = $0.50 + €0.50. With the euro then trading at about $0.85, exporters would now receive around 8 percent more pesos for the dollars they exchanged and importers would have to pay around 8 percent more for the dollars they bought. Financial markets panicked, fearing that this change was but a prelude to abandonment of the currency board. In response, Mr. Cavallo said that his new policy just amounted to a subsidy for exporters and a surcharge on imports and not an attempt to devalue the peso.

Over the next six months, Argentina's bold currency experiment unraveled amidst political and economic chaos brought about by the failure of Argentine politicians to rein in spending and to reform the country's labor laws. During the two-week period ending January 1, 2002, Argentina had five different presidents and suspended payments on its $132 billion in public debt, the largest sovereign debt default in history. On January 6, 2002, President Eduardo Duhalde announced that he would end Argentina's decade-long currency board system. The collapse of the currency board had devastating consequences. Over the next week, the Argentine peso plunged by 50 percent against the dollar. By year's end, the peso had depreciated 70 percent, the government had imposed a draconian banking freeze that sparked violent rioting, and a severe economic contraction took the Argentine economy back to 1993 levels. In effect, forced to choose between the economic liberalization and fiscal discipline that was necessary to save its currency board and the failed economic policies of Peronism, Argentina ultimately chose the latter and wound up with a disaster.

The downside of a currency board is that a run on the currency forces a sharp contraction in the money supply and a jump in interest rates. High interest rates slow economic activity, increase bankruptcies, and batter real estate and financial markets. For example, Hong Kong's currency board weathered the Asian storm and delivered a stable currency but at the expense of high interest rates (300 percent at one point in October 1997), plummeting stock and real estate markets, and deflation. Short of breaking the Hong Kong dollar's peg to the U.S. dollar, the government can nothing about deflation. Instead of being able to ease monetary policy and cut interest rates during a downturn, Hong Kong must allow wages and prices to decline and wait for the global economy to recover and boost demand for the city's goods and services. Argentina, on the other hand, abandoned its currency board in an attempt to deal with its recession.

One lesson from Argentina's failed currency board experiment is that exchange rate arrangements are no substitute for good macroeconomic policy. The latter takes discipline and a willingness to say no to special interests. The peso and its currency board collapsed once domestic and foreign investors determined that Argentina's fiscal policies were unsound, unlikely to improve, and incompatible with the maintenance of a fixed exchange rate. Another lesson is that a nation cannot be forced to maintain a currency arrangement that has outlived its usefulness. As such, no fixed exchange rate system, no matter how strong it appears, is completely sound and credible.

Dollarization   The ultimate commitment to monetary credibility and a currency good as the dollar is **dollarization**—the complete replacement of the local currency with the U.S. dollar. The desirability of dollarization depends on whether monetary discipline is easier to maintain by abandoning the local currency altogether than under a system in which the local currency circulates but is backed by the dollar. The experience of Panama with dollarization is instructive. Dollarization began in Panama 100 years ago, in 1904. Annual inflation has averaged 1.7 percent for the past thirty years, lower than in the United States; there is no local currency risk; and thirty-year mortgages are readily available. These are unusual conditions for a developing country, and they stem from dollarization. The downside of dollarization is the loss of **seigniorage**, the central bank's profit on the currency it prints. However, this loss is acceptable if the alternative is monetary chaos.

That is what Ecuador decided recently. Ecuador's new government—faced with a plunging currency, accelerating capital flight, a bankrupt banking system, huge budget deficits, in default to foreign creditors, and with its economy in a nosedive—unveiled an economic reform package on January 9, 2000. The centerpiece of that program was the planned replacement of the currency it had used for the past 116 years, the sucre, with the U.S. dollar. As Exhibit 2.7 demonstrates, the announcement of dollarization was enough, by itself, to stabilize the foreign exchange market. The next day, the sucre traded at the new official level of 25,000 per dollar. It remained there, despite nationwide strikes and two changes of government, until September 9, 2000, when Ecuador officially replaced the sucre with the dollar. During the period leading up to that date, some capital returned to Ecuador and the economy began to grow again.

Dollarization by itself, of course, is no guarantee of economic success. It can provide price stability, but like a currency board it is not a substitute for sound economic policies. Even the United States, which by definition is dollarized, has its economic ups and downs. To achieve stable economic growth, what is needed are the types of political and economic reforms discussed in Chapter 6. But what dollarization can do is to provide the macroeconomic stability that will enhance the impact of these reforms.

EXHIBIT 2.7 ● DOLLARIZATION STABILIZES THE SUCRE

Source: Pacific Exchange Rate Service, pacific.commerce.ubc.ca/xr/plot.html, © 2000 by Prof. Werner Antweiler, University of British Columbia, Vancouver BC, Canada. Time period shown in diagram: 1 Jan 1999–9 Sep 2000.

2.3 THE FUNDAMENTALS OF CENTRAL BANK INTERVENTION

The exchange rate is one of the most important prices in a country because it links the domestic economy and the rest-of-world economy. As such, it affects relative national competitiveness.

How Real Exchange Rates Affect Relative Competitiveness

We already have seen the link between exchange rate changes and relative inflation rates. The important point for now is that an appreciation of the exchange rate beyond that necessary to offset the inflation differential between two countries raises the price of domestic goods relative to the price of foreign goods. This rise in the **real** or **inflation-adjusted exchange rate**—measured as the **nominal** (or actual) **exchange rate** adjusted for changes in relative price levels—proves to be a mixed blessing. For example, the rise in the value of the U.S. dollar from 1980 to 1985 translated directly into a reduction in the dollar prices of imported goods and raw materials. As a result, the prices of imports and of products that compete with imports began to ease. This development contributed significantly to the slowing of U.S. inflation in the early 1980s.

A rise in the real or inflation-adjusted exchange rates causes the price of foreign goods to fall relative to the price of domestic goods.

However, the rising dollar had some distinctly negative consequences for the U.S. economy as well. Declining dollar prices of imports had their counterpart in the increasing foreign currency prices of U.S. products sold abroad. As a result, American exports became less competitive in world markets, and American-made import substitutes became less competitive in the United States. Domestic sales of traded goods declined, generating unemployment in the traded-goods sector and inducing a shift in resources from the traded- to the nontraded-goods sector of the economy.

Alternatively, home currency depreciation results in a more competitive traded-goods sector, stimulating domestic employment and inducing a shift in resources from

A strong dollar hurts U.S. exports, while giving consumers access to cheaper foreign products; a weak dollar helps U.S. exports but hurts American consumers.

the nontraded- to the traded-goods sector. The bad part is that currency weakness also results in higher prices for imported goods and services, eroding living standards and worsening domestic inflation.

From its peak in mid-1985, the U.S. dollar fell by more than 50 percent during the next few years, enabling Americans to experience the joys and sorrows of both a strong and a weak currency in less than a decade. The weak dollar made U.S. companies more competitive worldwide; at the same time, it lowered the living standards of Americans who enjoyed consuming foreign goods and services. The dollar hit a low point in 1995 and then began to strengthen, largely based on the substantial success that the United States had in taming inflation and the budget deficit and in generating strong economic growth. Exhibit 2.8 charts the value of the U.S. dollar from 1970 to 2001. Despite its substantial rise in the late 1990s, and more recent decline, the dollar is still below its level achieved back in 1970.

Foreign Exchange Market Intervention

Depending on their economic goals, some governments will prefer an overvalued domestic currency, whereas others will prefer an undervalued currency. Still others just want a correctly valued currency, but economic policy makers may feel that the rate set by the market is irrational; that is, they feel they can better judge the correct exchange rate than the marketplace can. The tradeoffs faced by governments in terms of their exchange rate objectives are illustrated by the example of China's yuan.

EXHIBIT 2.8 • Tracking the Value of the Dollar: 1970–2001

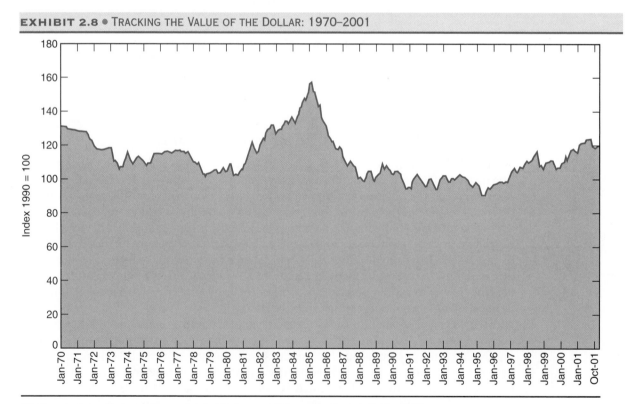

J.P. Morgan narrow effective exchange rate index. Data are monthly averages, through October 2001.

Source: J.P. Morgan, www2.jpmorgan.com/MarketDataInd/Forex/currIndex.html.

MINI-CASE   *A Yen for Yuan*

On September 2, 2003, U.S. Treasury Secretary John Snow traveled to Beijing to lobby his Chinese counterparts to revalue what is widely regarded as an undervalued yuan. In the eyes of U.S. manufacturers and labor unions, a cheap yuan gives China's exports an unfair price advantage and is accelerating the movement of manufacturing jobs to China. One evidence of this problem is the widening U.S. trade deficit with China, which reached $130 billion in 2002. Similarly, Japan, South Korea, and many European and other nations are pushing for China to abandon its fixed exchange rate because a weak U.S. dollar, which automatically lowered the yuan against other currencies, was making already-inexpensive Chinese goods unfairly cheap on global markets, hurting their own exports.

China rejected calls for it to revalue its currency and said it would maintain the stability of the yuan. Since 1996, China has fixed its exchange rate at 8.28 yuan to the dollar. In the past year, the dollar has depreciated significantly against the euro, giving Chinese companies a competitive advantage against European manufacturers. A massive rise in China's foreign exchange reserves in recent years (reserves rose 21 percent in the first half of 2003 to reach $346.5 billion as of June 30, 2003) is evidence that the Chinese government has been holding its currency down artificially. Politicians and business people in the United States and elsewhere have been calling for the yuan to be revalued, which it almost certainly would in a free market. (Economists estimate that the yuan is currently undervalued by 20 percent to 30 percent against the dollar.)

The Chinese government is resisting the clamor for yuan revaluation because of the serious problems it faces. China is often referred to as a "bicycle economy," meaning that it needs to keep moving forward just to avoid falling down. As the country becomes more market-oriented, its money-losing state-owned enterprises must lay off millions of workers. Only flourishing businesses can absorb this surplus labor. The Chinese government is concerned that allowing the yuan to appreciate would stifle the competitiveness of its exports and result in millions of unemployed and disgruntled Chinese wandering the countryside, threatening the stability of its regime. It also justified a weak yuan as a means of fighting the threat of deflation.

Nonetheless, keeping China's currency peg is not risk free. Foreign currency inflows are rising as investors, many of whom are ordinary Chinese bringing overseas capital back home, bet that China will be forced to revalue its yuan. They are betting on the yuan by purchasing Chinese stocks, real estate, and treasury bonds. To maintain its fixed exchange rate, the Bank of China must sell yuan to buy up all these foreign currency inflows. This intervention boosts China's foreign exchange reserves, but at the expense of a surging yuan money supply, which rose 21 percent in the first half of 2003 alone. For a time, a rising domestic money supply seemed an appropriate response to an economy that appeared to be on the verge of deflation. More recently, however, rapid money supply growth threatens inflation, and has led to roaring asset prices, including fears of a speculative bubble in real estate, and excessive bank lending. The latter is particularly problematic as Chinese banks are estimated to already have at least $500 billion in nonperforming loans to bankrupt state companies and unprofitable property developers.

Another risk in pursuing a cheap currency policy is the possibility of stirring protectionist measures in its trading partners. For example, ailing U.S. textile makers are lobbying the Bush administration for emergency quotas on Chinese textiles imports, while other manufacturers are seeking trade sanctions if Beijing won't allow the yuan to rise. Similarly, European government officials have spoken of retaliatory trade measures to force a revalued yuan.

QUESTIONS

1. Why is China trying to hold down the value of the yuan? What evidence suggests that China is indeed pursuing a weak currency policy?
2. What benefits does China expect to realize from a weak currency policy?
3. What policy tool is China using to maintain the yuan at an artificially low level? Are there any potential problems with using this policy tool? What might China do to counter these problems?
4. Does an undervalued yuan impose any costs on the Chinese economy? If so, what are they?
5. Suppose the Chinese government were to cease its foreign exchange market intervention and the yuan climbed to five to the dollar. What would be the percentage gain to a dollar investor?
6. Currently, the yuan is not a convertible currency, meaning that Chinese individuals are not permitted to exchange their yuan for dollars to invest abroad. Moreover, companies operating in China must convert all their foreign exchange earnings into yuan. Suppose China were to relax these currency controls and restraints on capital outflows. What would happen to the pressure on the yuan to revalue? Explain.

Most governments are tempted to intervene in the foreign exchange market to pursue their economic goals.

No matter what category they fall in, most governments will be tempted to intervene in the foreign exchange market to move the exchange rate to the level consistent with their goals or beliefs. **Foreign exchange market intervention** refers to official purchases and sales of foreign exchange that nations undertake through their central banks to influence their currencies.

For example, review Section 2.1 and suppose the United States and Euroland decide to maintain the old exchange rate e_0 in the face of the new equilibrium rate e_1. According to Exhibit 2.2, the result will be an excess demand for euros equal to $Q_3 - Q_2$; this euro shortage is the same as an excess supply of $(Q_3 - Q_2)e_0$ dollars. Either the Federal Reserve (the American central bank), or the European Central Bank (the central bank for Euroland), or both will then have to intervene in the market to supply this additional quantity of euros (to buy up the excess supply of dollars). Absent some change, the United States will face a perpetual balance-of-payments deficit equal to $(Q_3 - Q_2)e_0$ dollars, which is the dollar value of the Euroland balance-of-payments surplus of $(Q_3 - Q_2)$ euros.

Central banks intervene in the foreign exchange market by buying or selling foreign currencies.

Mechanics of Intervention   Although the mechanics of central bank intervention vary, the general purpose of each variant is basically the same: to increase the market demand for one currency by increasing the market supply of another. To see how this purpose can be accomplished, suppose in the previous example that the European Central Bank (ECB) wants to reduce the value of the euro from e_1 to its previous equilibrium value of e_0. To do so, the ECB must sell an additional $(Q_3 - Q_2)$ euros in the foreign exchange market, thereby eliminating the shortage of euros that would otherwise exist at e_0. This sale of euros (which involves the purchase of an equivalent amount of dollars) will also eliminate the excess supply of $(Q_3 - Q_2)e_0$ dollars that now exists at e_0. The simultaneous sale of euros and purchase of dollars will balance the supply and demand for euros (and dollars) at e_0.

If the Fed also wants to raise the value of the dollar, it will buy dollars with euros. Regardless of whether the Fed or the ECB initiates this foreign exchange operation, the net result is the same: The U.S. money supply will fall, and Euroland's money supply will rise.

In March 2003, the Swiss National Bank cut short-term interest rates effectively to zero in an attempt to revive its sinking economy. Once interest rates hit zero, the Swiss central bank had no room to trim rates further to stimulate economic growth and fight deflation. As a substitute for lower interest rates to fight recession and deflation, the Swiss National Bank began weakening its currency (see Exhibit 2.9) by selling Swiss francs in the foreign exchange market. A weakened Swiss franc increases the competitiveness of Swiss exports—45 percent of the country's total output of goods and services—by making them relatively less expensive in foreign markets.

EXHIBIT 2.9 • FALLING FRANC

Having already cut interest rates to zero, the Swiss National Bank is now fighting deflation and recession by weakening the franc. Below, the target band for the three-month deposit rate along with the exchange rate.

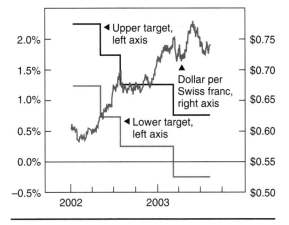

Sources: Thomson Datastream and *Wall Street Journal,* August 11, 2003. p. A2.

Sterilized versus Unsterilized Intervention   The two examples just discussed are instances of **unsterilized intervention**; that is, the monetary authorities have not insulated their domestic money supplies from the foreign exchange transactions. In both cases, the U.S. money supply will fall, and the Euroland money supply will rise. As noted earlier, an increase (decrease) in the supply of money, all other things held constant, will result in more (less) inflation. Thus, the foreign exchange market intervention will not only change the exchange rate, it will also increase Euroland inflation, while reducing U.S. inflation. Recall that it was the jump in the U.S. money supply that caused this inflation. These money supply changes will also affect interest rates in both countries.

> Sterilization neutralizes the effects of foreign exchange market intervention.

To neutralize these effects, the Fed and/or the ECB can *sterilize* the impact of their foreign exchange market intervention on the domestic money supply through an **open-market operation,** which is just the sale or purchase of Treasury securities. For example, the purchase of U.S. Treasury bills by the Fed supplies reserves to the banking system and increases the U.S. money supply. After the open-market operation, therefore, the public will hold more cash and bank deposits and fewer Treasury securities. If the Fed buys enough T-bills, the U.S. money supply will return to its preintervention level. Similarly, the ECB could neutralize the impact of intervention on the Euroland money supply by subtracting reserves from its banking system through sales of euro-denominated securities.

For example, during a three-month period in 2003 alone, the Bank of China issued 250 billion yuan in short-term notes to commercial banks to sterilize the yuan created by its foreign exchange market intervention. The Bank of China also sought to mop up excess liquidity by raising its reserve requirements for financial institutions, forcing banks to keep more money on deposit with it and make fewer loans.

The net result of sterilization should be a rise or fall in the country's foreign exchange reserves but no change in the domestic money supply. These effects are shown in Exhibit 2.10a, which displays a steep decline in Mexico's international reserves during 1994 while its money supply, measured by its **monetary base** (currency in circulation plus bank reserves), followed its usual growth path with its usual seasonal variations. As mentioned earlier, Banco de Mexico sterilized its purchases of pesos by buying back government securities. Conversely, Argentina's currency board precluded its ability to sterilize changes in foreign exchange reserves, forcing changes in Argentina's monetary base to closely match changes in its dollar reserves, as can be seen in Exhibit 2.10b.

The Effects of Foreign Exchange Market Intervention

Foreign exchange intervention to control currency values tends to be either ineffectual or irresponsible.

The basic problem with central bank intervention is that it is likely to be either ineffectual or irresponsible. Because sterilized intervention entails a substitution of foreign currency–denominated securities for domestic currency securities,[7] the exchange rate will be permanently affected only if investors view domestic and foreign securities as being imperfect substitutes. If this is the case, then the exchange rate and relative interest rates must change to induce investors to hold the new portfolio of securities.

If investors consider these securities to be perfect substitutes, however, then no change in the exchange rate or interest rates will be necessary to convince investors to hold this portfolio. In this case, sterilized intervention is ineffectual. This conclusion is

EXHIBIT 2.10 • MEXICO AND ARGENTINA FOLLOW DIFFERENT MONETARY POLICIES

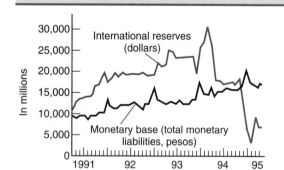

NOTE: End-of-month figures, except latest value plotted April 12, 1995

(a) International Reserves and Monetary Base in Mexico

NOTE: End-of-month figures, except latest value plotted April 11, 1995

(b) International Reserves and Monetary Base in Argentina

Source: Wall Street Journal, May 1, 1995, p. A14. Reprinted by permission. © 1995 Dow Jones & Company, Inc. All rights reserved worldwide.

---

[7] Central banks typically hold their foreign exchange reserves in the form of foreign currency bonds. Sterilized intervention, therefore, involves selling off some of the central bank's foreign currency bonds and replacing them with domestic currency ones. Following the intervention, the public will hold more foreign currency bonds and fewer domestic currency bonds.

consistent with the experiences of Mexico as well as those of the United States and other industrial nations in their intervention policies. For example, Exhibit 2.11 shows that a sequence of eight large currency interventions by the Clinton administration between 1993 and 2000 had little effect on the value of the dollar or its direction; exchange rates appear to have been moved largely by basic market forces. Similarly, Mexico ran through about $25 billion in reserves in 1994, and Asian nations ran through more than $100 billion in reserves in 1997 to no avail.

Sterilized intervention could affect exchange rates by conveying information or by altering market expectations. It does this by signaling a change in monetary policy to the market, not by changing market fundamentals, so its influence is transitory.

On the other hand, unsterilized intervention can have a lasting effect on exchange rates, but insidiously—by creating inflation in some nations and deflation in others. In the example presented above, Euroland would wind up with a permanent (and inflationary) increase in its money supply, and the United States would end up with a deflationary decrease in its money supply. If the resulting increase in Euroland inflation and decrease in U.S. inflation were sufficiently large, the exchange rate would remain at e_0 without the need for further government intervention. But it is the money supply changes, and not the intervention by itself, that affect the exchange rate. Moreover, moving the nominal exchange rate from e_1 to e_0 should not affect the real exchange rate because the change in inflation rates offsets the nominal exchange rate change.

If forcing a currency below its equilibrium level causes inflation, it follows that devaluation cannot be much use as a means of restoring competitiveness. A devaluation improves competitiveness only to the extent that it does not cause higher inflation. If the devaluation causes domestic wages and prices to rise, any gain in competitiveness is quickly eroded. For example, Mexico's 1994 peso devaluation led to a burst of inflation, driving the peso still lower and evoking fears of a continuing inflation-devaluation cycle.

EXHIBIT 2.11 ● THE VISIBLE HAND

The Clinton administration's currency-market interventions, shown with J.P. Morgan's index of the U.S. dollar against eighteen major currencies.

Note: Episodes typically involved more than one sale or purchase of dollars over days or weeks.

Sources: WSJ Market Data Group, Jeffrey A. Frankel, *Wall Street Journal,* July 23, 2002, p. A2.

ILLUSTRATION   *Britain Pegs the Pound to the Mark*

In early 1987, Nigel Lawson, Britain's Chancellor of the Exchequer, began pegging the pound sterling against the Deutsche mark. Unfortunately, his exchange rate target greatly undervalued the pound. In order to prevent sterling from rising against the DM, he had to massively intervene in the foreign exchange market, by selling pounds to buy marks. The resulting explosion in the British money supply reignited the inflation that Prime Minister Margaret Thatcher had spent so long subduing. With high inflation, the pound fell against the mark and British interest rates surged. The combination of high inflation and high interest rates led first to Mr. Lawson's resignation in October 1989 and then to Mrs. Thatcher's resignation a year later, in November 1990.

Surprise central bank intervention can impact the foreign exchange market temporarily.

Of course, when the world's central banks execute a coordinated surprise attack, the impact on the market can be dramatic—for a short period. Early in the morning on February 27, 1985, for example, Western European central bankers began telephoning banks in London, Frankfurt, Milan, and other financial centers to order the sale of hundreds of millions of dollars; the action—joined a few hours later by the Federal Reserve in New York—panicked the markets and drove the dollar down by 5 percent that day.

But keeping the market off balance requires credible repetitions. Shortly after the February 27 blitzkrieg, the dollar was back on the rise. The Fed intervened again, but it was not until clear signs of a U.S. economic slowdown emerged that the dollar turned down in March.

2.4 SUMMARY AND CONCLUSIONS

This chapter studied the process of determining exchange rates under a floating exchange rate system. We saw that in the absence of government intervention, exchange rates respond to the forces of supply and demand, which in turn are dependent on relative inflation rates, interest rates, and GDP growth rates. Monetary policy is crucial here. If the central bank expands the money supply at a faster rate than the growth in money demand, the purchasing power of money declines both at home (inflation) and abroad (currency depreciation). In addition, the healthier the economy is, the stronger the currency is likely to be. Exchange rates also are crucially affected by expectations of future currency changes, which depend on forecasts of future economic and political conditions.

In order to achieve certain economic or political objectives, governments often intervene in the currency markets to affect the exchange rate. Although the mechanics of such interventions vary, the general purpose of each variant is basically the same: to increase the market demand for one currency by increasing the market supply of another. Alternatively, the government can control the exchange rate directly by setting a price for its currency and then restricting access to the foreign exchange market.

A critical factor that helps explain the volatility of exchange rates is that with a fiat money there is no anchor to a currency's value, nothing around which beliefs can coalesce. In this situation, where people are unsure of what to expect, any new piece of information can dramatically alter their beliefs. Thus, if the underlying domestic economic policies are unstable, exchange rates will be volatile as traders react to new information.

QUESTIONS

1. Describe how these three typical transactions should affect present and future exchange rates:

   a. Joseph E. Seagram & Sons imports a year's supply of French champagne. Payment in French francs is due immediately.

   b. MCI sells a new stock issue to Alcatel, the French telecommunications company. Payment in dollars is due immediately.

   c. Korean Airlines buys five Boeing 747s. As part of the deal, Boeing arranges a loan to KAL for the purchase amount from the U.S. Export–Import Bank. The loan is to be paid back over the next seven years with a two-year grace period.

2. The maintenance of money's value is said to depend on the monetary authorities. What might the monetary authorities do to a currency that would cause its value to drop?

3. For each of the following six scenarios, state whether the value of the dollar will appreciate, depreciate, or remain the same relative to the Japanese yen. Explain each answer. Assume that exchange rates are free to vary and that other factors are held constant.

   a. The growth rate of national income is higher in the United States than in Japan.

   b. Inflation is higher in the United States than in Japan.

   c. Prices in Japan and the United States are rising at the same rate.

   d. Real interest rates in the United States rise relative to real rates in Japan.

   e. The United States imposes new restrictions on the ability of foreigners to buy American companies and real estate.

   f. U.S. wages rise relative to Japanese wages, while American productivity falls behind Japanese productivity.

4. The Fed adopts an easier monetary policy. How is this likely to affect the value of the dollar and U.S. interest rates?

5. Comment on the following headline from the *New York Times*. "Germany Raises Interest Rate, and Value of Dollar Declines" (October 10, 1997).

6. In the 1995 election for the French presidency, the Socialist candidate, Lionel Jospin, vowed to halt all privatizations, raise taxes on business, spend heavily on job creation, and cut the workweek without a matching pay cut. At the time Mr. Jospin made this vow, he was running neck-and-neck with the conservative Prime Minister Jacques Chirac, who espoused free-market policies.

   a. How do you think the French franc responded to Mr. Jospin's remarks?

   b. Mr. Chirac won the election. What was the franc's likely reaction?

7. On November 28, 1990, Federal Reserve Chairman Alan Greenspan told the House Banking Committee that despite possible benefits to the U.S. trade balance, "a weaker dollar also is a cause for concern." This statement departed from what appeared to be an attitude of benign neglect by U.S. monetary officials toward the dollar's depreciation. He also rejected the notion that the Fed should aggressively ease monetary policy, as some Treasury officials had been urging. At the same time, Mr. Greenspan did not mention foreign exchange market intervention to support the dollar's value.

   a. What was the likely reaction of the foreign exchange market to Mr. Greenspan's statements? Explain.

   b. Can Mr. Greenspan support the value of the U.S. dollar without intervening in the foreign exchange market? If so, how?

8. Many Asian governments have attempted to promote their export competitiveness by holding down the values of their currencies through foreign exchange market intervention.

   a. What is the likely impact of this policy on Asian foreign exchange reserves? On Asian inflation? On Asian export competitiveness? On Asian living standards?

   b. Some Asian countries have attempted to sterilize their foreign exchange market intervention by selling bonds. What are the likely consequences of sterilization on interest rates? On exchange rates in the longer term? On export competitiveness?

9. As mentioned in the chapter, Hong Kong has a currency board that fixes the exchange rate between the U.S. and H.K. dollars.

   a. What is the likely consequence of a large capital inflow for the rate of inflation in Hong Kong? For the competitiveness of Hong Kong business? Explain.

   b. Given a large capital inflow, what would happen to the value of the Hong Kong dollar if it were allowed to freely float? What would be the effect on the competitiveness of Hong Kong business? Explain.

   c. Given a large capital inflow, will Hong Kong business be more or less competitive under a currency board or with a freely floating currency? Explain.

10. In 1994, an influx of drug money to Colombia coincided with a sharp increase in its export earnings from coffee and oil.

    a. What was the likely impact of these factors on the value of the Colombian peso and the competitiveness of Colombia's legal exports? Explain.

    b. In 1996, Colombia's president, facing charges of involvement in his country's drug cartel, sought to boost his domestic popularity by pursuing more expansionary monetary policies. Standing in the way was Colombia's independent central bank—Banco de la Republica. In response, the president and his supporters discussed the possibility of returning central bank control to the executive branch. Describe the likely economic consequences of ending Banco de la Republica's independence.

PROBLEMS

1. On August 8, 2000, Zimbabwe changed the value of the Zim dollar from Z$38/U.S.$ to Z$50/U.S.$.

   a. What was the original U.S. dollar value of the Zim dollar? What is the new U.S. dollar value of the Zim dollar?

   b. By what percent has the Zim dollar devalued (revalued) relative to the U.S. dollar?

   c. By what percent has the U.S. dollar appreciated (depreciated) relative to the Zim dollar?

2. In 1995, one dollar bought ¥80. In 2000, it bought about ¥110.

   a. What was the dollar value of the yen in 1995? What was the yen's dollar value in 2000?

   b. By what percent has the yen fallen in value between 1995 and 2000?

   c. By what percent has the dollar risen in value between 1995 and 2000?

3. On February 1, the euro is worth $0.8984. By May 1, it has moved to $0.9457.

   a. By what percent has the euro appreciated or depreciated against the dollar during this three-month period?

   b. By what percent has the dollar appreciated or depreciated against the euro during this period?

4. In early August 2002 (the exact date is a state secret), North Korea reduced the official value of the won from $0.465 to $0.0067. The black market value of the won at that time was $0.005.

   a. By what percent did the won devalue?

   b. Following the initial devaluation, what further percentage devaluation would be necessary for the won to equal its black market value?

5. On Friday, September 13, 1992, the lira was worth DM 0.0013065. Over the weekend, the lira devalued against the DM to DM 0.0012613.

   a. By how much had the lira devalued against the DM?

   b. By how much had the DM appreciated against the lira?

   c. Suppose Italy borrowed DM 4 billion, which it sold to prop up the lira. What were the Bank of Italy's lira losses on this currency intervention?

   d. Suppose Germany spent DM 24 billion in an attempt to defend the lira. What were the Bundesbank's DM losses on this currency intervention?

6. At the time Argentina launched its new exchange rate scheme, the euro was trading at $0.85. Exporters and importers would be able to convert between dollars and pesos at an exchange rate that was an average of the dollar and the euro exchange rates, that is, P1 = $0.50 + €0.50.

   a. How many pesos would an exporter receive for one dollar under the new system?

   b. How many dollars would an importer receive for one peso under the new system?

BIBLIOGRAPHY

Frenkel, Jacob A., and Harry G. Johnson, eds. *The Economics of Exchange Rates.* Reading, Mass.: Addison-Wesley, 1978.

Levich, Richard M. "Empirical Studies of Exchange Rates: Price Behavior, Rate Determination and Market Efficiency." In *Handbook of International Economics*, vol. II. Ronald W. Jones and Peter B. Kenen, eds. Netherlands: Elsevier B.V., 1985, pp. 980–1040.

Marrinan, Jane. "Exchange Rate Determination: Sorting Out Theory and Evidence." *New England Economic Review*, November/December 1989, pp. 39–51.

INTERNET RESOURCES

pacific.commerce.ubc.ca/xr/plot.html Contains current and historical foreign exchange rate data for all currencies that you can download into preformatted time series charts.

www.ny.frb.org Web site of the Federal Reserve Bank of New York. Contains information on U.S. interventions in the foreign exchange market.

www.bis.org/cbanks.htm Web site of the Bank for International Settlements (BIS) that takes you directly to links with the various central banks of the world.

www.bis.org/review/index.htm Contains a collection of articles and speeches by senior central bankers.

www2.jpmorgan.com/MarketDataInd/Forex/currIndex.html Web site of J.P. Morgan that contains historical data on real and nominal foreign exchange rate indexes going back to 1970.

research.stlouisfed.org/fred2/ Web site of the Federal Reserve Bank of St. Louis that takes you directly to current and historical foreign exchange rate data that you can download into spreadsheets.

www.federalreserve.gov/releases/H10/hist/ Web site of the Federal Reserve Bank that takes you directly to historical foreign exchange rate data that you can download into spreadsheets.

patriot.net/~bernkopf/ Contains links to central banks and ministries of finance and economics worldwide and to multilateral financial institutions such as the IMF, BIS, World Bank, and OECD. It also contains histories of central banks.

INTERNET EXERCISES

1. Plot the nominal and real values of the dollar over the past ten years using the J.P. Morgan data.

2. How closely correlated are changes in the real and nominal values of the dollar over this period? That is, do the real and nominal exchange rates tend to move together?

3. By how much has the dollar changed in real terms over this period?

4. By how much has the dollar changed in nominal terms over this period?

5. Plot the following exchange rates over the past five years: dollar/yen, dollar/euro, and dollar/pound. Are these exchange rates closely correlated with each other? You can use foreign exchange data from the Federal Reserve for this assignment.

6. Based on your review of several recent currency interventions, what reasons were given by the monetary authorities for these interventions? How much money was expended during these interventions? You can find stories of these interventions by searching the Web site of the Federal Reserve Bank of New York and the Web sites of other central banks linked through the BIS Web site.

7. Based on your review of the *Economist*, the *Wall Street Journal*, and *Financial Times*, which countries are having currency problems? What are the causes of those currency problems?

THE INTERNATIONAL MONETARY SYSTEM

The monetary and economic disorders of the past fifteen years ... are a reaction to a world monetary system that has no historical precedent. We have been sailing on uncharted waters and it has been taking time to learn the safest routes.

Milton Friedman
Winner of Nobel Prize in Economics

CHAPTER LEARNING OBJECTIVES

- To distinguish between a free float, a managed float, a target-zone arrangement, and a fixed-rate system of exchange rate determination
- To describe how equilibrium in the foreign exchange market is achieved under alternative exchange rate systems, including a gold standard
- To identify the three categories of central bank intervention under a managed float
- To describe the purposes, operation, and consequences of the European Monetary System
- To describe the origins, purposes, and consequences of the European Monetary Union and the euro
- To identify the four alternatives to devaluation under a system of fixed exchange rates
- To explain the political realities that underlie government intervention in the foreign exchange market
- To describe the history and consequences of the gold standard
- To explain why the postwar international monetary system broke down
- To describe the origins of and proposed mechanisms to deal with the various emerging market currency crises that have occurred during the past decade

KEY TERMS

austerity
Bank for International Settlements (BIS)
"beggar-thy-neighbor" devaluation
Bretton Woods Agreement
Bretton Woods system
clean float
Common Market
conditionality
dirty float
euro
European Central Bank
European Currency Unit (ECU)
European Community (EC)
European Monetary System (EMS)
European Monetary Union (EMU)

exchange-rate mechanism (ERM)
fiat money
fixed-rate system
free float
G-5 nations
G-7 nations
gold standard
International Bank for Reconstruction and Development (World Bank)
International Monetary Fund (IMF)
international monetary system
lender of last resort
Louvre Accord
Maastricht criteria
Maastricht Treaty

managed float	price-specie-flow mechanism
monetary union	privatization
moral hazard	seigniorage
optimum currency area	Smithsonian Agreement
par value	Special Drawing Right (SDR)
Plaza Agreement	target-zone arrangement

Over the past four decades, increasing currency volatility has subjected the earnings and asset values of multinational corporations, banks, and cross-border investors to large and unpredictable fluctuations in value. These currency problems have been exacerbated by the breakdown of the postwar international monetary system established at the Bretton Woods Conference in 1944. The main features of the **Bretton Woods system** were the relatively fixed exchange rates of individual currencies in terms of the U.S. dollar and the convertibility of the dollar into gold for foreign official institutions. These fixed exchange rates were supposed to reduce the riskiness of international transactions, thus promoting growth in world trade.

However, in 1971 the Bretton Woods system fell victim to the international monetary turmoil it was designed to avoid. It was replaced by the present regime of rapidly fluctuating exchange rates, resulting in major problems and opportunities for multinational corporations. The purpose of this chapter is to help managers, both financial and nonfinancial, understand what the international monetary system is and how the choice of system affects currency values. It also provides a historical background of the international monetary system to enable managers to gain perspective when trying to interpret the likely consequences of new policy moves in the area of international finance. After all, although the types of government foreign-exchange policies may at times appear to be limitless, they are all variations on a common theme.

3.1 ALTERNATIVE EXCHANGE RATE SYSTEMS

The basic market mechanisms for establishing exchange rates include the free float, managed float, target-zone arrangement, and fixed-rate system.

The **international monetary system** refers primarily to the set of policies, institutions, practices, regulations, and mechanisms that determine the rate at which one currency is exchanged for another. This section considers five market mechanisms for establishing exchange rates: free float, managed float, target-zone arrangement, fixed-rate system, and the current hybrid system.

As we shall see, each of these mechanisms has costs and benefits associated with it. Nations prefer economic stability and often equate this objective with a stable exchange rate. However, fixing an exchange rate often leads to currency crises if the nation attempts to follow a monetary policy that is inconsistent with that fixed rate. At the same time, a nation may decide to fix its exchange rate in order to limit the scope of monetary policy, as in the case of currency boards described in Chapter 2. On the other hand, economic shocks can be absorbed more easily when exchange rates are allowed to float freely, but freely floating exchange rates may exhibit excessive volatility, which hurts trade and stifles economic growth. The choice of a particular exchange rate mechanism depends on the relative importance that a given nation at a given point in time places on the trade-offs associated with these different systems.

Free Float

We already have seen that free-market exchange rates are determined by the interaction of currency supplies and demands. The supply-and-demand schedules, in turn, are influenced by price level changes, interest differentials, and economic growth. In a **free float,** as these economic parameters change—for example, because of new government policies or acts of nature—market participants will adjust their current and expected future currency needs. In the two-currency example in Chapter 2 featuring the U.S. dollar and the euro, the shifts in the euro supply-and-demand schedules will, in turn, lead to new equilibrium positions. Over time, the exchange rate will fluctuate randomly as market participants assess and react to new information, much as security and commodity prices in other financial markets respond to news. These shifts and oscillations are illustrated in Exhibits 3.1 and 3.2A for the dollar/euro exchange rate; D_t and S_t are the hypothetical euro demand and supply curves, respectively, for period t. Exhibit 3.2B shows how the dollar/euro exchange rate actually changed during a seven-day period in August 2001. Such a system of freely floating exchange rates is usually referred to as a **clean float**.

Managed Float

Not surprisingly, few countries have been able to long resist the temptation to intervene actively in the foreign exchange market in order to reduce the economic uncertainty associated with a clean float. The fear is that too abrupt a change in the value of a nation's currency could imperil its export industries (if the currency appreciates) or lead to a higher rate of inflation (if the currency depreciates). Moreover, the experience with floating rates has not been encouraging. Instead of reducing economic volatility, as they were supposed

EXHIBIT 3.1 • SUPPLY AND DEMAND CURVE SHIFTS

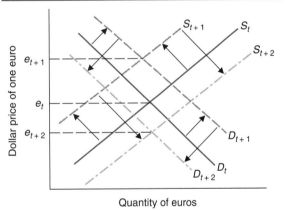

EXHIBIT 3.2A • FLUCTUATING EXCHANGE RATES

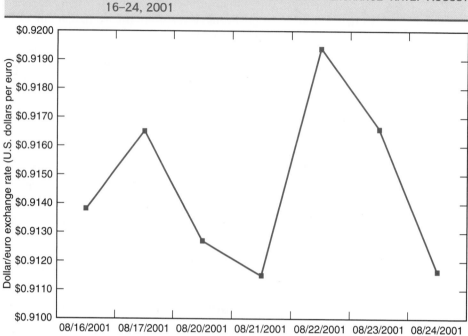

EXHIBIT 3.2B • ACTUAL CHANGES IN THE DOLLAR/EURO EXCHANGE RATE: AUGUST 16–24, 2001

to do, floating exchange rates appear to have increased it. Exchange rate uncertainty also reduces economic efficiency by acting as a tax on trade and foreign investment. Therefore, most countries with floating currencies have attempted, through central bank intervention, to smooth out exchange rate fluctuations. Such a system of managed exchange rates, called a **managed float**, is also known as a **dirty float**.

Managed floats fall into three distinct categories of central bank intervention. The approaches, which vary in their reliance on market forces, are as follows:

Managed floats vary in their reliance on market forces.

1. *Smoothing out daily fluctuations.* Governments following this route attempt only to preserve an orderly pattern of exchange rate changes. They occasionally enter the market on the buy or sell side to ease the transition from one rate to another, rather than resist fundamental market forces; the smoother transition tends to bring about longer-term currency appreciation or depreciation. One variant of this approach is the "crawling peg" system used in some countries, such as Poland, Russia, and Brazil. Under a crawling peg, the local currency depreciates against a reference currency or currency basket on a regular, controlled basis. For example, the Brazilian *real* and Russian ruble are allowed to depreciate monthly by about 0.6 percent and 0.5 percent, respectively, against the dollar. Similarly, the Polish zloty depreciates by 1 percent a month against a basket of currencies.

2. *"Leaning against the wind."* This approach is an intermediate policy designed to moderate or prevent abrupt short- and medium-term fluctuations brought about by random events whose effects are expected to be only temporary. The rationale for this policy—which is primarily aimed at delaying, rather than resisting, fundamental exchange rate adjustments—is that government intervention can reduce for exporters and importers the uncertainty caused by disruptive exchange rate changes. It is questionable, however, whether governments are more capable than private forecasters of distinguishing between fundamental and temporary (irrational) values.

3. *Unofficial pegging*. This strategy evokes memories of a fixed-rate system. It involves resisting, for reasons clearly unrelated to exchange market forces, any fundamental upward or downward exchange rate movements. Thus, Japan historically has resisted revaluation of the yen for fear of its consequences for Japanese exports. With unofficial pegging, however, there is no publicly announced government commitment to a given exchange rate level.

Target-Zone Arrangement

Many economists and policy makers have argued that the industrialized countries could minimize exchange rate volatility and enhance economic stability if the United States, Germany, and Japan linked their currencies in a target-zone system. Under a **target-zone arrangement**, countries adjust their national economic policies to maintain their exchange rates within a specific margin around agreed-upon, fixed central exchange rates. Such a system existed for the major European currencies participating in the European Monetary System and was the precursor to the euro, which is discussed later in this chapter.

A target-zone arrangement allows exchange rates for member currencies to vary within a narrow band.

Fixed-Rate System

Under a **fixed-rate system**, such as the Bretton Woods system, governments are committed to maintaining target exchange rates. Each central bank actively buys or sells its currency in the foreign exchange market whenever its exchange rate threatens to deviate from its stated **par value** by more than an agreed-on percentage. The resulting coordination of monetary policy ensures that all member nations have the same inflation rate. Put another way, for a fixed-rate system to work, each member must accept the group's joint inflation rate as its own. A corollary is that monetary policy must become subordinate to exchange rate policy. In the extreme case, those who fix their exchange rate via a currency board system surrender all control of monetary policy. The money supply is determined solely by people's willingness to hold the domestic currency.

A fixed-rate system requires its members to coordinate their monetary policies so as to maintain target exchange rates.

With or without a currency board system, there is always a rate of monetary growth (it could be negative) that will maintain an exchange rate at its target level. If it involves monetary tightening, however, maintaining the fixed exchange rate could mean a high interest rate and a resultant slowdown in economic growth and job creation.

Under the Bretton Woods system, whenever the commitment to the official rate became untenable, it was abruptly changed and a new rate was announced publicly. Currency devaluation or revaluation, however, was usually the last in a string of temporizing alternatives for solving a persistent balance-of-payments deficit or surplus. These alternatives, which are related only in their lack of success, included foreign borrowing to finance the balance-of-payments deficit, wage and price controls, import restrictions, and exchange controls. The last have become a way of life in many developing countries. Nations with overvalued currencies often ration foreign exchange, whereas countries facing revaluation (an infrequent situation) may restrict capital inflows.

In effect, government controls supersede the allocative function of the foreign exchange market. The most drastic situation occurs when all foreign exchange earnings must be surrendered to the central bank, which, in turn, apportions these funds to users on the basis of government priorities. The buying and selling rates need not be equal, nor need they be uniform across all transaction categories. Exhibit 3.3 lists the most frequently used currency control measures. These controls are a major source of market imperfection, providing opportunities as well as risks for multinational corporations.

Currency controls are an important alternative to devaluation in a fixed-rate system.

Austerity brought about by a combination of reduced government expenditures and increased taxes can be a permanent substitute for devaluation. By reducing the nation's budget deficit, austerity will lessen the need to monetize the deficit. Lowering the rate of

---

EXHIBIT 3.3 • TYPICAL CURRENCY CONTROL MEASURES

- Restriction or prohibition of certain remittance categories such as dividends or royalties
- Ceilings on direct foreign investment outflows (e.g., the elaborate U.S. Office of Foreign Direct Investment controls in effect 1968–1975)
- Controls on overseas portfolio investments
- Import restrictions
- Required surrender of hard-currency export receipts to central bank
- Limitations on prepayments for imports
- Requirements to deposit in interest-free accounts with central bank, for a specified time, some percentage of the value of imports and/or remittances
- Foreign borrowings restricted to a minimum or maximum maturity
- Ceilings on granting of credit to foreign firms
- Imposition of taxes and limitations on foreign-owned bank deposits
- Multiple exchange rates for buying and selling foreign currencies, depending on category of goods or services each transaction falls into

---

money supply growth, in turn, will bring about a lower rate of domestic inflation (disinflation). Disinflation will strengthen the currency's value, ending the threat of devaluation. However, disinflation often leads to a short-run increase in unemployment, a cost of austerity that politicians today generally consider to be unacceptable.

The Current System of Exchange Rate Determination

The current international monetary system is a hybrid, with major currencies floating on a managed basis, some currencies freely floating, and other currencies moving in and out of various types of pegged exchange rate relationships. Exhibit 3.4 presents a currency map that describes some of the various zones and blocs linking the world's currencies as of December 31, 2001.

3.2 A BRIEF HISTORY OF THE INTERNATIONAL MONETARY SYSTEM

The desirable properties of gold have led it to play an important role historically in the international monetary system.

Almost from the dawn of history, gold has been used as a medium of exchange because of its desirable properties. It is durable, storable, portable, easily recognized, divisible, and easily standardized. Another valuable attribute of gold is that short-run changes in its stock are limited by high production costs, making it costly for governments to manipulate. Most important, because gold is a commodity money, it ensures a long-run tendency toward price stability. The reason is that the purchasing power of an ounce of gold, or what it will buy in terms of all other goods and services, will tend toward equality with its long-run cost of production.

For these reasons, most major currencies, until fairly recently, were on a gold standard, which defined their relative values or exchange rates. The **gold standard** essentially involved a commitment by the participating countries to fix the prices of their domestic currencies in terms of a specified amount of gold. The countries maintained these prices by being willing to buy or sell gold to anyone at that price. For example, from 1821 to 1914, Great Britain maintained a fixed price of gold at £4.2474 per ounce. The United States, during the 1834–1933 period, maintained the price of gold at $20.67 per ounce (with the exception of the Greenback period from 1861–1878). Thus, over the period 1834–1914 (with the exception of 1861–1878), the dollar:pound exchange rate, referred to as the par exchange rate, was perfectly determined at

EXHIBIT 3.4 • EXCHANGE RATE ARRANGEMENTS (AS OF DECEMBER 31, 2001)

	Another Currency as Legal Tender	*CFA Franc Zone*[1]	*Euro Zone*	*ECCU*[2]
Exchange arrangements with no separate legal tender (40)	Ecuador (U.S.) dollar El Salvador (U.S. dollar) Kirbati (Australian dollar) Marshall Islands (U.S. dollar) Micronesia (U.S. dollar) Palau (U.S. dollar) Panama (U.S. dollar) San Marino (euro)	Benin Burkima Faso Cameroon Central African Republic Chad Congo Cote d'Ivoire Equatorial Guinea Gabon Mali Niger Senegal Togo	Austria Belgium Finland France Germany Greece Ireland Italy Luxembourg Netherlands Portugal Spain	Antigua & Barbuda Domenica Grenada St. Kits & Nevis St. Lucia St. Vincent & the Grenadines
Currency board arrangement (8)	Argentina (U.S. dollar) Bosnia and Herzegovinia (euro)	Brunei Darussalam (Singapore dollar) Bulgaria (euro) Djibouti (U.S. dollar)	Estonia (euro) Hong Kong (U.S. dollar) Lithuania (U.S. dollar)	

(Continues)

[1] All countries use the CFA franc, with 665.957 CFA francs = 1 euro.
[2] The ECCU (Eastern Carribean Currency Union) countries use the East Carribean dollar (EC$), which is fixed to the U.S. dollar at the rate of EC$2.67 = U.S.$1.00.
Source: International Financial Statistics, International Monetary Fund, April 2003, pp. 2–3.

$$\frac{\$20.67/ounce\ of\ gold}{£4.2474/ounce\ of\ gold} = \$4.8665/£1$$

The gold standard created a remarkable record of price stability.

The value of gold relative to other goods and services does not change much over long periods of time, so the monetary discipline imposed by a gold standard should ensure long-run price stability for both individual countries and groups of countries. Indeed, there was remarkable long-run price stability in the period before World War I, during which most countries were on a gold standard. As Exhibit 3.5 shows, price levels at the start of World War I were roughly the same as they had been in the late 1700s before the Napoleonic Wars began.

This record is all the more remarkable when contrasted with the post–World War II inflationary experience of the industrialized nations of Europe and North America. As shown in Exhibit 3.6, 1995 price levels in all these nations were several times as high as they were in 1950. Even in Germany, the value of the currency in 1995 was only one-quarter of its 1950 level, whereas the comparable magnitude was less than one-tenth for France, Italy, and the United Kingdom. Although there were no episodes of extremely rapid inflation, price levels rose steadily and substantially.

The Classical Gold Standard

A gold standard is often considered an anachronism in our modern, high-tech world because of its needless expense; on the most basic level, it means digging up gold in one

EXHIBIT 3.4 • EXCHANGE RATE ARRANGEMENTS (AS OF MARCH 31, 2003) (CONTINUED)

	Against a Single Currency		*Against a Composite*
Other conventional fixed peg arrangements (including de facto peg arrangements under managed floating) (40)	Aruba	Malaysia	Botswana
	Bahamas	Maldives	Fiji
	Bahrain	Namibia	Kuwait
	Bangladesh	Nepal	Latvia
	Barbados	Netherlands Antilles	Libya
	Belize	Oman	Malta
	Bhutan	Qatar	Morocco
	Cape Verde	Saudi Arabia	Samoa
	China, P.R.	Sudan	Seychelles
	Comoros	Suriname	Vanuatu
	Iran	Swaziland	
	Jordan	Syria	
	Lebanon	Turkmenistan	
	Lesotho	United Arab Emirates	
	Macedonia	Zimbabwe	

	Within a Cooperative Arrangement		*Other Band*
Pegged exchange rates within horizontal bands (5)	Denmark		Cyprus
			Egypt
			Hungary
			Tonga

Crawling pegs (4)	Bolivia	Nicaragua	
	Costa Rica	Solomon Islands	

EXHIBIT 3.5 • WHOLESALE PRICE INDICES: PRE–WORLD WAR I

Year	Belgium	Britain	France	Germany	United States
1776	na	101	na	na	84
1793	na	120	na	98	100
1800	na	186	155	135	127
1825	na	139	126	76	101
1850	83	91	96	71	82
1875	100	121	111	100	80
1900	87	86	85	90	80
1913	100	100	100	100	100

corner of the globe for burial in another corner. Nonetheless, until recently, discontent with the current monetary system, which produced more than two decades of worldwide inflation and widely fluctuating exchange rates, prompted interest in a return to some form of a gold standard. (This interest has abated somewhat with the current low inflation environment.)

To put it bluntly, calls for a new gold standard reflect a fundamental distrust of government's willingness to maintain the integrity of fiat money. **Fiat money** is nonconvertible paper money backed only by faith that the monetary authorities will not cheat (by

EXHIBIT 3.6 • CONSUMER PRICE INDICES (CPI): POST–WORLD WAR II

Nation	*CPI, 1950*	*CPI, 1995*	*Loss of Purchasing Power during Period (%)*
Belgium	100	578	82.7%
France	100	1,294	92.3%
Germany	100	388	74.2%
Italy	100	2,163	95.4%
Netherlands	100	603	83.4%
United Kingdom	100	1,617	93.8%
United States	100	622	83.9%

Calls for a new gold standard derive from governmental abuses of fiat money.

issuing more money). This faith has been tempered by hard experience; the 100 percent profit margin on issuing new fiat money has proved to be an irresistible temptation for most governments.

By contrast, the net profit margin on issuing more money under a gold standard is zero. The government must acquire more gold before it can issue more money, and the government's cost of acquiring the extra gold equals the value of the money it issues. Thus, expansion of the money supply is constrained by the available supply of gold. This fact is crucial in understanding how a gold standard works.

The price-specie-flow mechanism equalized prices across nations and brought international payments into balance.

Under the classical gold standard, disturbances in the price level in one country would be wholly or partly offset by an automatic balance-of-payments adjustment mechanism called the **price-specie-flow mechanism**. (*Specie* refers to gold coins.) To see how this adjustment mechanism worked to equalize prices among countries and automatically bring international payments back in balance, consider the example that is illustrated in Exhibit 3.7.

EXHIBIT 3.7 • THE PRICE-SPECIE-FLOW MECHANISM

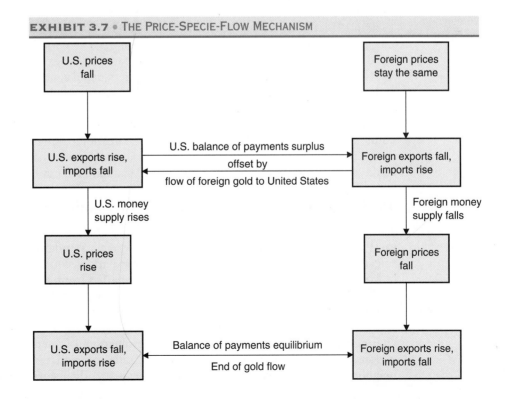

Suppose a technological advance increases productivity in the non-gold-producing sector of the U.S. economy. This productivity will lower the price of other goods and services relative to the price of gold, and the U.S. price level will decline. The fall in U.S. prices will result in lower prices of U.S. exports; export prices will decline relative to import prices (determined largely by supply and demand in the rest of the world). Consequently, foreigners will demand more U.S. exports, and Americans will buy fewer imports.

Starting from a position of equilibrium in its international payments, the United States will now run a balance-of-payments surplus. The difference will be made up by a flow of gold into the United States. The gold inflow will increase the U.S. money supply (under a gold standard, more gold means more money in circulation), reversing the initial decline in prices. At the same time, the other countries will experience gold outflows, reducing their money supplies (less gold, less money in circulation) and, thus, their price levels. In final equilibrium, price levels in all countries will be slightly lower than they were before because of the increase in the worldwide supply of other goods and services relative to the supply of gold. Exchange rates will remain fixed.

Thus, the operation of the price-specie-flow mechanism tended to keep prices in line for those countries that were on the gold standard. As long as the world was on a gold standard, all adjustments were automatic, and although many undesirable things might have happened under a gold standard, lasting inflation was not one of them.

Gold does have a cost, however—the opportunity cost associated with mining and storing it. By the late 1990s, with inflation on the wane worldwide, the value of gold as an inflation hedge had declined. Central banks also began selling their gold reserves and replacing them with U.S. Treasury bonds, which, unlike gold, pay interest. The reduced demand for gold has lowered its price and its usefulness as a monetary asset.

How the Classical Gold Standard Worked in Practice: 1821–1914

The period during which the classical gold standard prevailed was a remarkable period in world economic history.

In 1821, after the Napoleonic Wars and their associated inflation, England returned to the gold standard. From 1821 to 1880, more and more countries joined the gold standard. By 1880, most nations of the world were on some form of gold standard. The period from 1880 to 1914, during which the classical gold standard prevailed in its most pristine form, was a remarkable period in world economic history. The period was characterized by a rapid expansion of virtually free international trade, stable exchange rates and prices, a free flow of labor and capital across political borders, rapid economic growth, and, in general, world peace. Advocates of the gold standard harken back to this period as illustrating the standard's value.

Opponents of a rigid gold standard, in contrast, point to some less-than-idyllic economic conditions during this period: a major depression during the 1890s, a severe economic contraction in 1907, and repeated recessions. Whether these sharp ups and downs could have been prevented under a fiat money standard cannot be known.

The Gold Exchange Standard and Its Aftermath: 1925–1944

The gold standard broke down during World War I and was briefly reinstated from 1925 to 1931 as the Gold Exchange Standard. Under this standard, the United States and England could hold only gold reserves, but other nations could hold both gold and dollars or pounds as reserves. In 1931, England departed from gold in the face of massive gold and capital flows, owing to an unrealistic exchange rate, and the Gold Exchange Standard was finished.

Competitive Devaluations After the devaluation of sterling, twenty-five other nations devalued their currencies to maintain trade competitiveness. These "**beggar-thy-neighbor**" devaluations, in which nations cheapened their currencies to increase their exports at others' expense and to reduce imports, led to a trade war. Many economists and policy makers believed that the protectionist exchange rate and trade policies fueled the global depression of the 1930s.

"Beggar-thy-neigh-bor" devaluations during the Great Depression led to trade wars.

Bretton Woods Conference and the Postwar Monetary System   To avoid such destructive economic policies in the future, the Allied nations agreed to a new postwar monetary system at a conference held in Bretton Woods, New Hampshire, in 1944. The conference also created two new institutions—the **International Monetary Fund (IMF)** and the **International Bank for Reconstruction and Development (World Bank)**—to implement the new system and to promote international financial stability. The IMF was created to promote monetary stability, whereas the World Bank was set up to lend money to countries so they could rebuild their infrastructure that had been destroyed during the war.

IMF rescues of imprudent countries and careless investors may encourage risky behavior.

Role of the IMF   Both agencies have seen their roles evolve over time. The IMF now oversees exchange rate policies in member countries (currently totaling 182 nations) and advises developing countries about how to turn their economies around. In the process, it has become the **lender of last resort** to countries that get into serious financial trouble. It is currently exploring new ways to monitor the financial health of member nations so as to prevent another Mexico-like surprise. Despite these efforts, the IMF was blindsided by the Asian crisis and wound up leading a $118 billion attempt to shore up Asian financial systems. It was also blindsided by the Russian crisis a year later. Critics argue that by bailing out careless lenders and imprudent nations, IMF rescues make it too easy for governments to persist with bad policies and for investors to ignore the risks these policies create. In the long run, by removing from governments and investors the prospect of failure—which underlies the market discipline that encourages sound policies—these rescues magnify the problem of moral hazard and so make imprudent policies more likely to recur.[1] **Moral hazard** refers here to the perverse incentives created for international lenders and borrowers by IMF bailouts. Anticipating further IMF bailouts, investors underestimate the risks of lending to governments who persist in irresponsible policies.

In theory, the IMF makes short-term loans conditional on the borrower's implementation of policy changes that will allow it to achieve self-sustaining economic growth. This is the doctrine of **conditionality**. However, a review of the evidence suggests that the IMF creates long-term dependency. For example, forty-one countries have been receiving IMF credit for ten to twenty years, thirty-two countries have been borrowing from the IMF for between twenty and thirty years, and eleven nations have been relying on IMF loans for more than thirty years. This evidence explains why IMF conditionality has little credibility.

Role of the World Bank   The World Bank is looking to expand its lending to developing countries and to provide more loan guarantees for businesses entering new developing markets. But here too is controversy. Specifically, critics claim that World Bank financing allows projects and policies to avoid being subject to the scrutiny of financial markets and permits governments to delay enacting the changes necessary to make their countries more attractive to private investors.

Role of the Bank for International Settlements   Another key institution is the **Bank for International Settlements (BIS)**, which acts as the central bank for the industrial countries' central banks. The BIS helps central banks manage and invest their foreign exchange reserves, and, in cooperation with the IMF and the World Bank, helps the central banks of developing countries, mostly in Latin America and Eastern Europe. The BIS also holds deposits of central banks so that reserves are readily available.

---

[1] As economist Allan H. Meltzer puts it, "Capitalism without failure is like religion without sin. It doesn't work. Bankruptcies and losses concentrate the mind on prudent behavior."

Unfortunately, despite Bretton Woods, competitive devaluations have not disappeared. According to the *Wall Street Journal* (June 6, 2003, p. B12), "A war of competitive currency devaluations is rattling the $1.2 trillion-a-day global foreign exchange market. ... The aim of the devaluing governments: to steal growth and markets from others, while simultaneously exporting their problems, which in this case is the threat of deflation."

Currency analysts argue that the environment in 2003—of slow growth and the threat of deflation—has encouraged countries such as Japan, China, and the United States to pursue a weak currency policy. For example, analysts believe that the Bush administration is looking for a falling dollar to boost U.S. exports, lift economic growth, battle deflationary pressure, push the Europeans to cut interest rates, and force Japan to overhaul its stagnant economy.

The weapons in this war include policy shifts, foreign exchange market intervention, and interest rates. For example, the foreign exchange market widely views the Bush administration as having abandoned the long-standing strong-dollar policy and welcoming a weaker dollar. Japan has tried to keep its currency from rising against the dollar by selling a record ¥3.98 billion ($33.4 billion) in May 2003 alone. A strong yen hurts Japanese exports and growth and aggravates deflationary tendencies. On the other hand, if Japan succeeds in pushing down the yen sufficiently, South Korea and Taiwan could try to devalue their currencies to remain competitive.

China, meanwhile, has stuck with an undervalued yuan to bolster its economy. Another currency analyst attributed Canada's growth over the past decade to an undervalued Canadian dollar: "They've been the beggar-thy-neighbor success story."[2] On June 5, 2003, the European Central Bank entered the competitive devaluation fray by cutting the euro interest rate by a half percentage point. Over the past year, the euro had appreciated by 27 percent against the dollar, making European business less profitable and less competitive and hurting European growth.

The ultimate fear: an ongoing round of competitive devaluations that degenerates into the same kind of pre–Bretton Woods protectionist free-for-all that brought on the Great Depression.

The Bretton Woods System: 1946–1971

The Bretton Woods system returned the world to a gold standard.

Under the **Bretton Woods Agreement**, implemented in 1946, each government pledged to maintain a fixed, or pegged, exchange rate for its currency vis-à-vis the dollar or gold. As one ounce of gold was set equal to $35, fixing a currency's gold price was equivalent to setting its exchange rate relative to the dollar. For example, the Deutsche mark was set equal to 1/140 of an ounce of gold, meaning it was worth $0.25 ($35/140). The exchange rate was allowed to fluctuate only within 1 percent of its stated par value (usually less in practice).

The fixed exchange rates were maintained by official intervention in the foreign exchange markets. The intervention took the form of purchases and sales of dollars by foreign central banks against their own currencies whenever the supply-and-demand conditions in the market caused rates to deviate from the agreed-on par values. The IMF stood ready to provide the necessary foreign exchange to member nations defending

[2] Michael R. Sesit, "Currency Conflict Shakes Market," *Wall Street Journal*, June 6, 2003, B12.

their currencies against pressure resulting from temporary factors.[3] Any dollars acquired by the monetary authorities in the process of such intervention could then be exchanged for gold at the U.S. Treasury, at a fixed price of $35 per ounce.

These technical aspects of the system had important practical implications for all trading nations participating in it. In principle, the stability of exchange rates removed a great deal of uncertainty from international trade and investment transactions, thus promoting their growth for the benefit of all the participants. Also, in theory, the functioning of the system imposed a degree of discipline on the participating nations' economic policies.

Nations that failed to maintain price stability experienced balance-of-payments deficits.

For example, a country that followed policies leading to a higher rate of inflation than that experienced by its trading partners would experience a balance-of-payments deficit as its goods became more expensive, reducing its exports and increasing its imports. The necessary consequences of the deficit would be an increase in the supply of the deficit country's currency on the foreign exchange markets. The excess supply would depress the exchange value of that country's currency, forcing its authorities to intervene. The country would be obligated to "buy" with its reserves the excess supply of its own currency, effectively reducing the domestic money supply. Moreover, as the country's reserves were gradually depleted through intervention, the authorities would be forced, sooner or later, to change economic policies to eliminate the source of the reserve-draining deficit. The reduction in the money supply and the adoption of restrictive policies would reduce the country's inflation, thus bringing it in line with the rest of the world.

In practice, however, governments perceived large political costs accompanying any exchange rate changes. Most governments also were unwilling to coordinate their monetary policies, even though this coordination was necessary to maintain existing currency values.

Periodic foreign exchange crises arose when governments failed to make necessary adjustments to their economic policies.

The reluctance of governments to change currency values or to make the necessary economic adjustments to ratify the current values of their currencies led to periodic foreign exchange crises. Dramatic battles between the central banks and the foreign exchange markets ensued. Those battles invariably were won by the markets. However, because devaluation or revaluation was used only as a last resort, exchange rate changes were infrequent and large.

In fact, Bretton Woods was a fixed exchange-rate system in name only. Of 21 major industrial countries, only the United States and Japan had no change in par value during the period 1946–1971. Of the twenty-one countries, twelve devalued their currencies more than 30 percent against the dollar, four had revaluations, and four were floating their currencies by mid-1971 when the system collapsed. The deathblow for the system came on August 15, 1971, when President Richard Nixon, convinced that the "run" on the dollar was reaching alarming proportions, abruptly ordered U.S. authorities to terminate convertibility even for central banks. At the same time, he devalued the dollar to deal with America's emerging trade deficit.

The fixed exchange-rate system collapsed along with the dissolution of the gold standard. There are two related reasons for the collapse of the Bretton Woods system. First, inflation reared its ugly head in the United States. In the mid-1960s, the Johnson administration financed the escalating war in Vietnam and its equally expensive Great Society programs by, in effect, printing money instead of raising taxes. This lack of monetary discipline made it difficult for the United States to maintain the price of gold at $35 an ounce.

---

[3] The IMF supplemented its foreign exchange reserves by creating a new reserve asset, the **Special Drawing Right** or **SDR**. The SDR serves as the IMF's unit of account. It is a currency basket whose value is the weighted average of the currencies of five nations (United States, Germany, France, Japan, and Great Britain; the euro is the currency used for France and Germany). The weights, which are based on the relative importance of each country in international trade, are updated periodically.

The Bretton Woods system broke down because the United States issued too many dollars.

Second, the fixed exchange-rate system collapsed because some countries—primarily West Germany, Japan, and Switzerland—refused to accept the inflation that a fixed exchange rate with the dollar would have imposed on them. Thus, the dollar depreciated sharply relative to the currencies of those three countries.

The Post–Bretton Woods System: 1971 to the Present

In December 1971, under the **Smithsonian Agreement**, the dollar was devalued to 1/38 of an ounce of gold, and other currencies were revalued by agreed-on amounts vis-à-vis the dollar. After months of such last-ditch efforts to set new fixed rates, the world officially turned to floating exchange rates in 1973.

OPEC and the Oil Crisis of 1973–1974
October 1973 marked the beginning of successful efforts by the Organization of Petroleum Exporting Countries (OPEC) to raise the price of oil. By 1974, oil prices had quadrupled. Nations responded in various ways to the vast shift of resources to the oil-exporting countries. Some nations, such as the United States, tried to offset the effect of higher energy bills by boosting spending, pursuing expansionary monetary policies, and controlling the price of oil. The result was high inflation, economic dislocation, and a misallocation of resources without bringing about the real economic growth that was desired. Other nations, such as Japan, allowed the price of oil to rise to its market level and followed more prudent monetary policies.

The first group of nations experienced balance-of-payments deficits because their governments kept intervening in the foreign exchange market to maintain overvalued currencies; the second group of nations, along with the OPEC nations, wound up with balance-of-payments surpluses. These surpluses were recycled to debtor nations, setting the stage for the international debt crisis of the 1980s.

U.S. Dollar Crisis of 1977–1978
During 1977–1978, the value of the dollar plummeted, and U.S. balance-of-payments difficulties were exacerbated as the Carter Administration pursued an expansionary monetary policy that was significantly out of line with other strong currencies. The turnaround in the dollar's fortunes can be dated to October 6, 1979, when the Fed (under its new chairman, Paul Volcker) announced a major change in its conduct of monetary policy. From here on, in order to curb inflation, it would focus its efforts on stabilizing the money supply, even if that meant more volatile interest rates. Before this date, the Fed had attempted to stabilize interest rates, indirectly causing the money supply to be highly variable.

The dollar's ups and downs during the past twenty-five years can be traced largely to changes in U.S. economic policy.

The Rising Dollar: 1980–1985
This shift had its desired effect on both the inflation rate and the value of the U.S. dollar. During President Ronald Reagan's first term in office (1981–1984), inflation plummeted and the dollar rebounded extraordinarily. This rebound has been attributed to vigorous economic expansion in the United States and to high real interest rates (owing largely to strong U.S. economic growth) that combined to attract capital from around the world.

The Sinking Dollar: 1985–1987
The dollar peaked in March 1985 and then began a long downhill slide. The slide is largely attributable to changes in government policy and the slowdown in U.S. economic growth relative to growth in the rest of the world.

By September 1985, the dollar had fallen about 15 percent from its March high, but this decline was considered inadequate to dent the growing U.S. trade deficit. In late September of 1985, representatives of the Group of Five, or **G-5 nations** (the

United States, France, Japan, Great Britain, and West Germany), met at the Plaza Hotel in New York City. The outcome was the **Plaza Agreement,** a coordinated program designed to force down the dollar against other major currencies and thereby improve American competitiveness.

The policy to bring down the value of the dollar worked too well. The dollar slid so fast during 1986 that the central banks of Japan, West Germany, and Britain reversed their policies and began buying dollars to stem the dollar's decline. Believing that the dollar had declined enough and in fact showed signs of "overshooting" its equilibrium level, representatives of the United States, Japan, West Germany, France, Britain, Canada, and Italy— also known as the Group of Seven, or **G-7 nations**—met again in February 1987 and agreed to an ambitious plan to slow the dollar's fall. The **Louvre Accord,** named for the Paris landmark where it was negotiated, called for the G-7 nations to support the falling dollar by pegging exchange rates within a narrow, undisclosed range, while they also moved to bring their economic policies into line.

> The Louvre Accord called for the G-7 nations to support the falling dollar.

As always, however, it proved much easier to talk about coordinating policy than to change it. The hoped-for economic cooperation faded, and the dollar continued to fall (see Exhibit 3.8).

Recent History: 1988–2003 Beginning in early 1988, the U.S. dollar rallied somewhat and then maintained its strength against most currencies through 1989. It fell sharply again in 1990 but then stayed basically flat in 1991 and 1992, while posting sharp intrayear swings. The dollar began falling again in 1993, particularly against the yen and DM, and it fell throughout most of 1994 and 1995 before rallying again in 1996. The dollar continued its upward direction through December 2001 owing to the sustained strength of the U.S. economy. Even after the U.S. economy began to slow in late 2000, it still looked strong compared to those its major trading partners. However, in 2002, the sluggishness of the U.S. economy and low U.S. interest rates, combined with the fear of war in Iraq (and later the actual war) and concerns over large U.S. trade and budget deficits, resulted in a significant decline in the value of the dollar relative to the euro and other currencies. The dollar's future course is unpredictable given the absence of an anchor for its value.

> International policy coordination has proven easier in theory than in practice.

EXHIBIT 3.8 • EFFECTS OF GOVERNMENT ACTIONS AND STATEMENTS ON THE VALUE OF THE 1987 DOLLAR

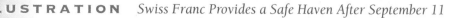

ILLUSTRATION *Swiss Franc Provides a Safe Haven After September 11*

Following the terrorist attacks on the World Trade Center and the Pentagon, the Swiss franc soared in value as investors sought a safe haven no longer provided by the United States. The Swiss franc rose still further after Afghanistan's Taliban leaders declared a holy war against the United States and the United States faced a bio-terrorism threat from anthrax (see Exhibit 3.9). However, the ensuing war in Afghanistan and military successes there, combined with renewed prospects for a U.S. recovery, brought a reminder of American strength—and a stronger dollar. As the Swiss franc lost some of its luster, it fell toward its pre–September 11 value.

EXHIBIT 3.9 • THE SWISS FRANC RISES AND THEN FALLS IN THE AFTERMATH OF SEPTEMBER 11, 2001

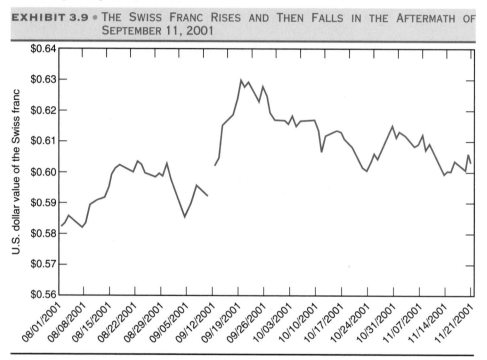

Source: U.S. Federal Reserve System. Rates are noon buying rates in New York City for cable transfers. Data for 9/11/01 are missing owing to the shutdown of financial trading in New York City following the destruction of the World Trade Center.

Assessment of the Floating-Rate System

Floating rates have not stabilized real exchange rates as proponents had claimed would happen.

At the time floating rates were adopted in 1973, proponents said that the new system would reduce economic volatility and facilitate free trade. In particular, floating exchange rates would offset international differences in inflation rates so that trade, wages, employment, and output would not have to adjust. High-inflation countries would see their currencies depreciate, allowing their firms to stay competitive without having to cut wages or employment. At the same time, currency appreciation would not place firms in low-inflation countries at a competitive disadvantage. Real exchange rates would stabilize, even if permitted to float in principle, because the underlying conditions affecting trade and the relative productivity of capital would change only gradually; and if countries would coordinate their monetary policies to achieve a convergence of inflation rates, then nominal exchange rates would also stabilize.

Currency Volatility Has Increased The experience to date, however, is disappointing. The dollar's ups and downs have had little to do with actual inflation and a lot to do with expectations of future government policies and economic conditions. Put another way, real exchange rate volatility has increased, not decreased, since floating began. This instability reflects, in part, nonmonetary (or real) shocks to the world economy, such as changing oil prices and shifting competitiveness among countries, but these real shocks were not obviously greater during the 1980s or 1990s than they were in earlier periods. Instead, uncertainty over future government policies has increased.

Given this evidence, a number of economists and others have called for a return to fixed exchange rates. To the extent that fixed exchange rates more tightly constrain the types of monetary and other policies governments can pursue, this approach should make expectations less volatile and, hence, promote exchange rate stability.

As uncertainty over future government policies has increased, so has exchange rate volatility.

Requirements for Currency Stability   Although history offers no convincing model for a system that will lead to long-term exchange rate stability among major currencies, it does point to two basic requirements. First, the system must be credible. If the market expects an exchange rate to be changed, the battle to keep it fixed is already lost. Second, the system must have price stability built into its very core. Without price stability, the system will not be credible. Recall that under a fixed-rate system, each member must accept the group's inflation rate as its own. Only a zero rate of inflation will be mutually acceptable. If the inflation rate is much above zero, prudent governments will defect from the system.

Even with tightly coordinated monetary policies, freely floating exchange rates would still exhibit some volatility because of real economic shocks. However, this volatility is not necessarily a bad thing because it could make adjustment to these shocks easier. For example, it has been argued that flexible exchange rates permitted the United States to cope with the buildup in defense spending in the early 1980s and the later slowdown in defense spending. Increased U.S. defense spending expanded aggregate U.S. demand and shifted output toward defense. The stronger dollar attracted imports and thereby helped satisfy the civilian demand. As the United States cut back on defense spending, the weakening dollar helped boost U.S. exports, making up for some of the decline in defense spending. To the extent that this argument is correct, the dollar's movements helped buffer the effects of defense spending shifts on American living standards.

Freely floating exchanges facilitates adjustment to economic shocks.

Individual countries can peg their currencies to the dollar or other benchmark currency. However, the Asian and other crises demonstrate that the only credible system for such pegging is a currency board or dollarization. Every other system is too subject to political manipulation and can be too easily abandoned. Even a currency board can come unglued, as we saw in the case of Argentina, if the government pursues sufficiently wrong-headed economic policies.

An alternative system for a fixed-rate system is monetary union. Under **monetary union**, individual countries replace their local currencies with a common currency. An example of monetary union is the United States, with all fifty states sharing the same dollar. In a far-reaching experiment, Europe embarked on monetary union in 1999, following its experiences with the European Monetary System.

3.3 THE EUROPEAN MONETARY SYSTEM AND MONETARY UNION

The purpose of the European Monetary System was to promote monetary stability in the European Community.

The **European Monetary System (EMS)** began operating in March 1979. Its purpose was to foster monetary stability in the **European Community (EC)**, also known as the **Common Market**. As part of this system, the members established the European Currency Unit, which played a central role in the functioning of the EMS. The **European Currency Unit (ECU)** was a composite currency consisting of fixed amounts of the twelve European Community member currencies. The quantity of each country's currency in the ECU reflects that country's relative economic strength in the European Community. The ECU functioned as a unit of account, a means of settlement, and a reserve asset for the members of the EMS.

The Exchange Rate Mechanism

At the heart of the system was an **exchange rate mechanism (ERM)**, which allowed each member of the EMS to determine a mutually agreed-on central exchange rate for its currency; each rate was denominated in currency units per ECU. These central rates attempted to establish equilibrium exchange values, but members could seek adjustments to the central rates.

Each member of the EMS had to determine a central exchange rate for its currency.

Central rates established a grid of bilateral cross-exchange rates between the currencies. Nations participating in the ERM pledged to keep their currencies within a 15 percent margin on either side of these central cross-exchange rates (±2.25 percent for the DM/guilder cross rate). The upper and lower intervention levels for each currency pair were found by applying the appropriate margin to their central cross-exchange rate.

The exchange between two currencies could fluctuate within a band around their central cross-exchange rate.

The original intervention limits were set at 2.25 percent above and below the central cross rates (Spain and Britain had 6 percent margins) but were later increased. Despite good intentions, the ERM came unglued in a series of speculative attacks that began in 1992. By mid-1993, the EMS had slipped into a two-tiered system. One tier consisted of a core group of currencies tightly anchored by the DM. That tier included the Dutch guilder, the French, Belgian, and Luxembourg francs, and at times the Danish krone. The other tier consisted of weaker currencies such as those of Spain, Portugal, Britain, Italy, and Ireland.

Lessons from the European Monetary System

A review of the European Monetary System and its history provides valuable insights into the operation of a target-zone system and illustrates the problems that such mechanisms are likely to encounter. Perhaps the most important lesson the EMS illustrates is that the exchange rate stability afforded by any target-zone arrangement requires a coordination of economic policy objectives and practices. Nations should achieve convergence of those economic variables that directly affect exchange rates—variables such as fiscal deficits, monetary growth rates, and real economic growth differentials.

Maintenance of fixed-rate system or target-zone arrangement requires close coordination of macroeconomic policy.

Although the system helped keep its member currencies in a remarkably narrow zone of stability between 1987 and 1992, it had a history of ups and downs. By January 12, 1987, when the last realignment before September 1992 occurred, the values of the EMS currencies had been realigned twelve times despite heavy central bank intervention. Relative to their positions in March 1979, the Deutsche mark and the Dutch guilder soared, while the French franc and the Italian lira nose-dived. Between 1979 and 1988, the franc devalued relative to the DM by more than 50 percent.

The reason for the past failure of the European Monetary System to provide the currency stability it promised is straightforward: Germany's economic policy makers, responding to an electorate hypersensitive to inflation, put a premium on price stability; in contrast, the French pursued a more expansive monetary policy in response to high domestic unemployment. Neither country was willing to permit exchange rate considerations to override political priorities.

EMS member states allowed political priorities to dominate exchange rate considerations.

The experience of the EMS also demonstrates once again that foreign exchange market intervention not supported by a change in a nation's monetary policy has only a limited influence on exchange rates. For example, the heavy intervention before the EMS realignment on January 12, 1987, was generally not accompanied by changes in national monetary policies. West Germany, in particular, made only small adjustments to monetary policy in response to its increasingly undervalued currency. Consequently, the intervention failed to contain speculation that the DM would revalue, and a realignment became unavoidable.

The Currency Crisis of September 1992

The same attempt to maintain increasingly misaligned exchange rates in the EMS occurred again in 1992. And once again, the system broke down—in September 1992.

The currency crisis of September 1992 stemmed from misaligned exchange rates.

The Catalyst   The catalyst for the September currency crisis was the Bundesbank's decision to tighten monetary policy and force up German interest rates both to battle inflationary pressures associated with the spiraling costs of bailing out the former East Germany and to attract the inflows of foreign capital needed to finance the resulting German budget deficit. To defend their currency parities with the DM, the other member countries had to match the high interest rates in Germany (see Exhibit 3.10). The deflationary effects of high interest rates were accompanied by a prolonged economic slump and even higher unemployment rates in Britain, France, Italy, Spain, and most other EMS members.

As the costs of maintaining exchange rate stability rose, the markets began betting that some countries with weaker economies would devalue their currencies or withdraw them from the ERM altogether rather than maintain painfully high interest rates at a time of rising unemployment.

The threat of a currency realignment forced European governments to raise their interest rates.

The High Cost of Intervention   To combat speculative attacks on their currencies, nations had to raise their interest rates dramatically: 15 percent in Britain and Italy, 13.75 percent in Spain, 13 percent in France, and an extraordinary *500 percent* in Sweden. They also intervened aggressively in the foreign exchange markets. British, French, Italian, Spanish, and Swedish central banks together spent the equivalent of roughly $100 billion trying to prop up their currencies, with the Bank of England reported to have spent $15 billion to $20 billion in just one day to support the pound. The Bundesbank spent another $50 billion in DM to support the ERM. All to no avail.

On September 14, the central banks capitulated but not before losing an estimated $4 billion to $6 billion in their mostly futile attempt to maintain the ERM. Despite these costly efforts, Britain and Italy were forced to drop out of the ERM, and Spain, Portugal, and Ireland devalued their currencies within the ERM. In addition, Sweden, Norway, and Finland were forced to abandon their currencies' unofficial links to the ERM.

The Exchange Rate Mechanism Is Abandoned in August 1993

The final straw was the currency crisis of August 1993, which actually was touched off on July 29, 1993, when the Bundesbank left its key lending rate, the discount rate,

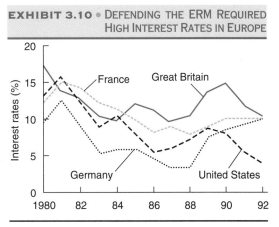

EXHIBIT 3.10 • DEFENDING THE ERM REQUIRED HIGH INTEREST RATES IN EUROPE

Source: Data from OECD and Federal Reserve.
September 30, 1992.

unchanged. Traders and investors had been expecting the Bundesbank to cut the discount rate to relieve pressure on the French franc and other weak currencies within the ERM. As had happened the year before, however, the Bundesbank largely disregarded the pleas of its ERM partners and concentrated on reining in 4.3 percent German inflation and its fast-growing money supply. Given the way the ERM worked, and the central role played by the Deutsche mark, other countries could not both lower interest rates and keep their currencies within their ERM bands unless Germany did so.

The Catalyst   The French franc was the main focus of the ERM struggle. With high real interest rates, recession, and unemployment running at a post–World War II high of 11.6 percent, speculators doubted that France had the willpower to stay with the Bundesbank's tight monetary policy and keep its interest rates high, much less raise them to defend the franc. Speculators reacted logically: They dumped the French franc and other European currencies and bought DM, gambling that economic pressures, such as rising unemployment and deepening recession, would prevent these countries from keeping their interest rates well above those in Germany. In other words, speculators bet—rightly, as it turned out—that domestic priorities would ultimately win out despite governments' pledges to the contrary.

> Speculators bet—correctly—that domestic priorities would win out over government pledges to the contrary.

Governments Surrender to the Market   Despite heavy foreign exchange market intervention (the Bundesbank alone spent $35 billion trying to prop up the franc), the devastating assault by speculators on the ERM forced the franc to its ERM floor. Other European central banks also intervened heavily to support the Danish krone, Spanish peseta, Portuguese escudo, and Belgian franc, which came under heavy attack as well.

It was all to no avail, however. Without capital controls or a credible commitment to move to a single currency in the near future, speculators could easily take advantage of a one-sided bet. The result was massive capital flows that overwhelmed the central banks' ability to stabilize exchange rates. Over the weekend of July 31–August 1, the EC finance ministers agreed essentially to abandon the defense of each other's currencies, and the European Monetary System became a floating-rate system in all but name only.

A Postmortem on the EMS   The currency turmoil of 1992–1993 showed once again that a genuinely stable European Monetary System, and eventually a single currency, requires the political will to direct fiscal and monetary policies at that European goal and not at purely national ones. In showing that they lacked that will, European governments proved once again that allowing words to run ahead of actions is a recipe for failure.

On the other hand, despite its problems, the EMS did achieve some significant success. By improving monetary policy coordination among its member states, the EMS succeeded in narrowing inflation differentials in Europe. In 1980, the gap between the highest inflation rate (Italy's 21.2 percent) and the lowest (West Germany's 5.2 percent) was 16 percentage points. By 1990 the gap had narrowed to less than 4 percentage points. The narrowing of inflation rates, in turn, reduced exchange rate volatility until 1992. Indeed, from January 1987 to September 1992, currencies remained fixed. Moreover, Germany's importance to the European economy and the Bundesbank's unwillingness to compromise its monetary policy forced other members of the EMS to adjust their monetary policies to more closely mimic Germany's low-inflation policy. As a result, inflation rates tended to converge toward Germany's lower rate (see Exhibit 3.11).

> The EMS succeeded in lowering inflation in Europe.

To summarize, the EMS was based on Germany's continuing ability to deliver low inflation rates and low real interest rates. As long as Germany lived up to its end of the bargain, the benefits to other EMS members of following the Bundesbank's policies would exceed the costs. But once the German government broke that compact by running huge and inflationary deficits, the costs to most members of following a Bundesbank monetary

EXHIBIT 3.11 • THE EUROPEAN MONETARY SYSTEM FORCES CONVERGENCE TOWARD GERMANY'S INFLATION RATE

| The EMS could not escape from market forces. | policy designed to counter the effects of the government's fiscal policies exceeded the benefits. Put another way, the existing exchange rates became unrealistic given what would have been required of the various members to maintain those exchange rates. In the end, there was no real escape from market forces. |

European Monetary Union

Many politicians and commentators pointed to the turmoil in the EMS as increasing the need for the European Community to move toward **monetary union**. This view prevailed and was formalized in the **Maastricht Treaty**. Under this treaty, the EC nations would establish a single central bank with the sole power to issue a single European currency called the **euro** as of January 1, 1999. On that date, conversion rates would be locked in for member currencies, and the euro would became a currency, although euro coins and bills would not be available until 2002. All went as planned. Francs, marks, guilders, schillings, lira, and other member currencies were phased out until, on January 1, 2002, the euro replaced them all.

The Maastricht Treaty set tough economic policy standards for joining the European Monetary Union.

Maastricht Convergence Criteria In order to join the **European Monetary Union (EMU)**, European nations were supposed to meet tough standards on inflation, currency stability, and deficit spending. According to these standards, known as the **Maastricht criteria**, government debt could be no more than 60 percent of gross domestic product (GDP), the government budget deficit could not exceed 3 percent of GDP, the inflation rate could not be more than 1.5 percentage points above the average rate of Europe's three lowest-inflation nations, and long-term interest rates could not be more than 2 percentage points higher than the average interest rate in the three lowest-inflation nations. It should be noted that most countries, including Germany, fudged some of their figures through one-time maneuvers (redefining government debt or selling off government assets) or fudged the criteria (Italy's debt/GDP ratio was 121 percent) in order to qualify. Nonetheless, on May 2, 1998, the European parliament formally approved the historic decision to launch the euro with 11 founder nations—Germany, France, Italy, Spain, the Netherlands, Belgium, Finland, Portugal, Austria, Ireland, and Luxembourg. Britain, Sweden, and Denmark opted out of the launch. On January 1, 2001, Greece became the twelfth country to join the eurozone when it was finally able to meet the economic convergence criteria. Britain is currently debating whether to join EMU and retire the pound sterling.

Launch of the Euro As planned, on January 1, 1999, the eleven founding member countries of the European Monetary Union surrendered their monetary autonomy to the new **European Central Bank** and gave up their right to create money; only the European Central

Bank is now able to do so. Governments can issue bonds denominated in euros, just as individual American states can issue dollar bonds. However, like California or New York, member nations are unable to print the currency needed to service their debts. Instead, they can attract investors only by convincing them they have the financial ability (through taxes and other revenues) to generate the euros to repay their debts. The conversion rates between the individual national currencies and the euro are presented in Exhibit 3.12.

EMU and the European Welfare State   The truth is that monetary union is as much about reining in the expensive European welfare state and its costly regulations as it is about currency stability. Because of high taxes, generous social welfare and jobless benefits, and costly labor market regulations—all of which reduce incentives to work, save, invest, and create jobs—and diminished competitiveness—fostered by onerous regulations on business as well as state subsidies and government protection to ailing industries—job growth has been stagnant throughout Western Europe for three decades. (Western Europe failed to create a single net new job from 1973 to 1994, a period in which the United States generated 38 million net new jobs.) As a result, the European unemployment rate in the late 1990s was averaging about 12 percent (in contrast to less than 5 percent for the United States). However, although crucial for strong and sustained economic growth, limiting the modern welfare state is politically risky; too many people live off the state.

> The European Monetary Union was designed to limit the expensive European welfare state and its costly regulations as well as to promote currency stability.

Enter the Maastricht Treaty. European governments could blame the strict Maastricht criteria they had to meet to enter the EMU for the need to take the hard steps that most economists believe are necessary for ending economic stagnation: curbing social-welfare expenditures, including overly generous pension, unemployment, and health-care benefits and costly job creation programs; reducing costly regulations on business; increasing labor market flexibility (primarily by lowering the cost to companies of hiring and firing workers and relaxing collective bargaining rules); cutting personal, corporate, and payroll taxes (the latter exceed 42 percent of gross wages in Germany), and selling off state-owned enterprises (a process known as **privatization**). Thus, the greatest benefit from monetary union likely will be the long-term economic gains that come from the fiscal discipline required for entry. If, however, Europe does not take this opportunity to reform its economic policies, the costs of monetary union will be high because member nations no longer will be able to use currency or interest rate adjustments to compensate for the pervasive labor market rigidities and expensive welfare programs that characterize the modern European economy.

EXHIBIT 3.12 • CONVERSION RATES FOR THE EURO

	Currency Symbol	*1 euro =*
Austrian schilling	ATS	13.7603
Belgian franc	BEF	40.3399
Dutch guilder	NLG	2.20371
Finnish markka	FIM	5.94573
French franc	FRF	6.55957
Greek drachma	GRD	340.75
German mark	DEM	1.95583
Irish punt	IEP	0.787564
Italian lira	ITL	1936.27
Luxembourg franc	LUF	40.3399
Portuguese escudo	PTE	200.482
Spanish peseta	ESP	166.386

ILLUSTRATION   *Sweden Rejects the Euro*

On September 14, 2003, Swedish voters soundly rejected a proposal to adopt the euro and kept the krona, despite the overwhelming support of the nation's business and political establishment and a last-minute wave of sympathy following the stabbing death of the country's popular and pro-euro foreign minister, Anna Lindh. A critical reason for the defeat: fears that adhering to the budget rules necessary to become a member of EMU would force Sweden to become more competitive and cut taxes. That, in turn, would compel Sweden to slash its generous and expensive cradle-to-grave social welfare system. Moreover, when Swedish voters went to the polls, the Swedish economy was stronger than the Euroland economy, its budget was in surplus (in contrast to large Euroland deficits), and unemployment was well below the Euroland average. The European Central Bank was criticized for keeping interest rates too high for too long, stifling growth, and Euroland cooperation on fiscal policy was in disarray (with the rules for budget deficits under the Maastricht criteria flouted by France and Germany). The perception that Sweden was conducting economic policy more intelligently than Euroland and with superior results made joining EMU less appealing as well.

Fortunately, Europe has begun to enact structural changes such as tax cuts and pension reforms to stimulate growth. For example, France, Germany, and Portugal have enacted cuts in personal and corporate taxes. In addition, Germany is starting to revamp its costly retirement, health-care, and welfare systems and modify its rigid labor laws, while France and Italy are attempting to overhaul their expensive pension systems. Nonetheless, there is strong resistance to these necessary changes.

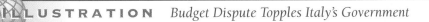

ILLUSTRATION   *Budget Dispute Topples Italy's Government*

In October 1997, Italian Prime Minister Romani Prodi, a Socialist, resigned after his allies in the Communist Party refused to tolerate welfare cuts the government said were vital to enable Italy to stay within the strict budgetary constraints necessary for its entry into the European Monetary Union. The fall of Prodi's seventeen-month-old government ended Italy's first leftist-dominated government since the end of World War II. Although the Communist Party backed down after a national outcry, and Prodi's government was reconstituted, this episode reveals the difficulties European governments faced in getting their citizens to accept painful budget cuts to conform to the Maastricht criteria.

Monetary union has reduced currency conversion costs and the risk of currency fluctuations.

Consequences of EMU   Although the full impact of the euro has yet to be felt, its effects have already been profound. Business clearly benefits from EMU through lower cross-border currency conversion costs. For example, Philips, the giant Dutch electronics company, estimates that a single European currency saves it $300 million a year in currency transaction costs. Overall, the EC Commission estimates that prior to the euro, businesses in Europe spent $13 billion a year converting money from one EC currency to another. Ordinary citizens also bore some substantial currency conversion costs. A tourist who left Paris with 1,000 francs and visited the other eleven EC countries, exchanging her money for the local currency in each country but not spending any of it, would have found herself with fewer than 500 francs when she returned to Paris. Multinational firms also find corporate planning, pricing, and invoicing easier with a common currency.

Adoption of a common currency benefits the European economy in other ways as well. It eliminates the risk of currency fluctuations and facilitates cross-border price comparisons. Lower risk and improved price transparency encourage the flow of trade and investments among member countries and should bring about greater integration of Europe's capital, labor, and commodity markets and a more efficient allocation of resources within the region as a whole. Increased trade, in turn, has intensified Europe-wide competition in goods and services and spurred a wave of corporate restructurings and mergers and acquisitions.

Moreover, monetary union—such as exists among the fifty states of the United States, where the exchange rate between states is immutably set at 1—provides the ultimate in coordination of monetary policy. Inflation rates under monetary union converges, but not in the same way as in the EMS. The common inflation rate is decided by the monetary policy of the European Central Bank. It would tend to reflect the average preferences of the people running the bank, rather than giving automatic weight to the most anti-inflationary nation as in the current system. Thus, for the European Monetary Union to be an improvement over the past state of affairs, the new European Central Bank must be as averse to inflation as Europe's previous de facto central bank—the Bundesbank.

To ensure the European Monetary Union's inflation-fighting success, the new central bankers must be granted true independence along with a statutory duty to devote monetary policy to keeping the price level stable.

Even now, after being in existence for several years, independence of the European Central Bank is an unsettled issue. Germans, who favor a strong, fiercely independent ECB modeled on the Bundesbank, fear the French will politicize it by using it to push job-creation and other schemes requiring an expansionist (and, hence, inflationary) monetary policy. Many French see the Germans as favoring price stability over compassion for the unemployed. This dispute points out a hard reality: The ECB will find it difficult to be tough on inflation without the benefit of a uniformly prudent fiscal policy across all its member states.

Another important issue in forming a monetary union is that of who gets the benefits of **seigniorage**—the profit to the central bank from money creation. In other words, who gets to spend the proceeds from printing money? In the United States, the answer is the federal government. In the case of Europe, however, this issue has not been resolved.

An unspoken reason for strong business support for the European Monetary Union is to boost growth by breaking the lock hold of government and unions on European economies. As described earlier, meeting the Maastricht criteria—particularly the one dealing with the reduced budget deficit—was expected to help diminish the role of the state in Europe and its tax-financed cradle-to-grave benefits. Many economists believe that only by cutting back on government and its generous—and increasingly unaffordable—social welfare programs and costly business and labor market regulations can the stagnant economies of Western Europe start to grow again and create jobs.

Performance of the Euro   The euro was born in optimism given the size and economic potential of the European Union (see Exhibit 3.13). However, reality set in quickly. Although many commentators felt the euro would soon replace the U.S. dollar as the world's de facto currency, Exhibit 3.14 shows that until 2002 the euro mostly fell against the dollar. The euro's decline during this period has been attributed to the continued robustness of the U.S. economy combined with the slowness of many European countries in performing the necessary restructuring of their economies that the euro was supposed to initiate. As one currency analyst said, "The U.S. economy is considered flexible, dynamic and productive; that contrasts with a view of Europe as a region burdened with high taxes, labor and product rigidities and bloated bureaucracies."[4]

Following the terrorist attacks on the United States on September 11, the euro rose briefly as the United States looked to be a relatively riskier place to invest in. But the euro soon reversed course again as it became clear that Euroland's economic environment was

---

EMU will be successful at fighting inflation only if the European Central Bank is granted independence and the mandate to maintain price stability.

Central banks profit from money creation.

---

[4] Michael R. Sesit, "The Dollar Crash That Hasn't Happened," *Wall Street Journal*, July 6, 2001, p. A6.

EXHIBIT 3.13 • COMPARATIVE STATISTICS FOR THE EMU COUNTRIES

	Euro 11[1]	*United States*	*Japan*
Population	290 million	267 million	127 million
GDP	$8.2 trillion	$8.6 trillion	$3.4 trillion
Share of world GDP	19%	20%	8%
Share of world trade	19%	17%	8%
Stock market capitalization	$3.6 trillion	$9.5 trillion	$2.0 trillion

Source: Wall Street Journal, September 28, 1998, R4.
[1]Represents the initial 11 nations in the European Monetary Union.

EXHIBIT 3.14 • THE EURO RIDES A ROLLER COASTER

Note: Rates are noon buying rates in New York City for cable transfers. Data for 9-11-01 are missing owing to the shutdown of financial trading in New York City following the destruction of the World Trade Center.

Source: U.S. Federal Reserve System.

worse than earlier thought and investors became more optimistic about U.S. economic growth reviving. Beginning in 2002, however, continuing sluggish U.S. growth and aggressive Fed lowering of U.S. interest rates, combined with higher yields on euro-denominated securities and signs of structural reform in European economies, led to a dramatic rise in the value of the euro.

The euro has likely risen more than it otherwise would because it must shoulder a disproportionate share of the dollar's decline. The reason is that—as we have already seen—several U.S. trading partners, such as China and Japan, have resisted a rise in their currencies. In the interlocking world of foreign exchange, if the yuan cannot appreciate against the dollar, then other currencies, and especially the euro, have to compensate by appreciating even more to make up for the fixed yuan. Suppose, for example, that the dollar must decline by 10 percent to reach its appropriate trade-weighted value. If the yuan

The euro had risen further against the dollar because China and Japan have resisted appreciation of their currencies.

remains pegged to the dollar, then other currencies must rise by more than 10 percent against the dollar to achieve overall balance.

M I N I - C A S E   *The Euro Reacts to New Information*

According to an article in the *Wall Street Journal* (October 8, 1999), "The European Central Bank left interest rates unchanged but made clear it is seriously considering tightening monetary policy. … The euro initially fell slightly on the ECB's announcement around mid-day that it would hold its key refinancing rate steady at 2.5%. But it rebounded as [ECB President Wim] Duisenberg reinforced expectations that a rate rise is in the works." In the same story, the *Wall Street Journal* reported that "the Bank of England didn't elaborate on its decision to leave its key repo rate unchanged at 5.25%." At the same time, "sterling remains strong, which reduces the threat of imported inflation as well as continuing to pressure U.K. manufacturers. That could work against higher interest rates, which could send sterling even higher."

QUESTIONS

1. Explain the differing initial and subsequent reactions of the euro to news about the European Central Bank's monetary policy.

2. How does a strong pound reduce the threat of imported inflation and work against higher interest rates?

3. Which U.K. manufacturers are likely to be pressured by a strong pound?

4. Why might higher pound interest rates send sterling even higher?

5. What tools are available to the European Central Bank and the Bank of England to manage their monetary policies?

Optimum Currency Area

Monetary union can impose high costs if wages and prices are inflexible.

Most discussion of a European monetary union has highlighted its benefits, such as eliminating currency uncertainty and lowering the costs of doing business. The potential costs of currency integration have been overlooked. In particular, as the discussion of U.S. military spending shifts indicated, it may sometimes pay to be able to change the value of one currency relative to another. Suppose, for example, that the worldwide demand for French goods falls sharply. To cope with such a drop in demand, France must make its goods less expensive and attract new industries to replace its shrinking old ones. The quickest way to do this is to reduce French wages, thereby making its workers more competitive. But this reduction is unlikely to be accomplished quickly. Eventually, high unemployment might persuade French workers to accept lower pay. But in the interim, the social and economic costs of reducing wages by, say, 10 percent will be high. In contrast, a 10 percent depreciation of the franc would achieve the same thing quickly and relatively painlessly.

Conversely, a worldwide surge in demand for French goods could give rise to French inflation, unless France allowed the franc to appreciate. In other words, currency changes can substitute for periodic bouts of inflation and deflation caused by various economic shocks. Once France has entered monetary union, it no longer has the option of changing its exchange rate to cope with these shocks. This option would have been valuable to the ERM, which instead came unglued because of the huge economic shock to its fixed parities brought about by the absorption of East Germany into the German economy.

Taking this logic to its extreme would imply that not only should each nation have its own currency, but so should each region within a nation. Why not a southern California dollar, or indeed a Los Angeles dollar? The answer is that having separate currencies brings costs as well as benefits.

The more currencies there are, the higher the costs of doing business and the more currency risk exists. Both factors impair the functions of money as a medium of exchange and a store of value, so maintaining more currencies acts as a barrier to international trade and investment, even as it reduces vulnerability to economic shocks.

According to the theory of the **optimum currency area**, this trade-off becomes less and less favorable as the size of the economic unit shrinks. So how large is the optimum currency area? No one knows. But some economists argue that Europe might be better off with four or five regional currencies than with only one.[5] Similarly, some have argued that the United States, too, might do better with several regional currencies to cushion shocks such as those that afflicted the Midwest and the Southwest during the 1980s and the Northeast and California in the 1990s. Nonetheless, the experience with floating exchange rates since the early 1970s will likely give pause to anyone seriously thinking of pushing that idea further. That experience suggests that exchange rate changes can add to economic volatility as well as absorb it. At the same time, economic flexibility—especially of labor markets—is critical to reducing the costs associated with currency union. This flexibility can be attained only through further deregulation, privatization, freer trade, labor market and social welfare reform, and a reduction in economic controls, state subsidies, and business regulations. Absent these changes, especially to reduce the rigidities of Europe's labor market, the European Monetary Union will intensify economic shocks because its effects can no longer be mitigated by exchange rate adjustments.

> An optimum currency area trades off the lower transaction costs associated with a single currency against its greater vulnerability to economic shocks.

3.4 EMERGING MARKET CURRENCY CRISES

> The 1990s saw a number of currency crises in emerging markets.

As we saw in the last chapter, the decade of the 1990s was punctuated by a series of currency crises in emerging markets. First was the Mexican crisis in 1994–1995. That was followed by the Asian crisis two years later in 1997, then the Russian crisis of 1998, and the Brazilian crisis of 1998–1999.

Transmission Mechanisms

The problem with these currency crises is that they tend to be contagious, spreading from one nation to another. There are two principal routes of contagion: trade links and the financial system.

Trade Links   Contagion can spread from one emerging market to another through their trade links. For example, when Argentina is in crisis, it imports less from Brazil, its principal trading partner. As Brazil's economy begins to contract, its currency will likely weaken. Before long, the contagion will spread from Brazil to its other emerging market trade partners.

Financial System   The second and more important transmission mechanism is through the financial system. As we saw in the case of the Asian currency crisis, trouble in one emerging market often can serve as a "wake-up call" to investors who seek to exit other countries with similar risky characteristics. For example, Argentina's problems,

---

[5] See, for example, Geoffrey M. B. Tootell, "Central Bank Flexibility and the Drawbacks to Currency Unification," *New England Economic Review,* May–June 1990, pp. 3–18; and Paul Krugman, "A Europe-Wide Currency Makes No Economic Sense," *Los Angeles Times,* August 5, 1990, p. D2.

which stem from its large budget deficit, focused investor attention on Brazil's unresolved fiscal problems. Financial contagion can also occur because investors who are leveraged up start selling assets in other countries to make up for their initial losses. Investors may also become more risk averse and seek to rebalance their portfolios by selling off a portion of all their risky assets.

Debt Policy   Crisis-prone countries tend to have one thing in common that promotes contagion: They issue too much short-term debt that is closely linked to the U.S. dollar. When times are good, confident investors gladly buy short-term emerging market bonds and roll them over when they come due. However, when the bad times come and currencies tumble, the cost of repaying dollar-linked bonds soars, savvy investors rush for the exits, and governments find their debt-raising capacity vanishes overnight. Things quickly spiral out of control.

Origins of Emerging Market Crises

The sequence of currency crises has prompted policy makers to seek ways to deal with them. Many of their crisis-fighting proposals involve increasing the International Monetary Fund's funding and giving it and possibly new international agencies the power to guide global financial markets. However, these proposals could exacerbate the two principal sources of these crises.

IMF intervention in emerging market crises could exacerbate the problem of moral hazard.

Moral Hazard   A number of economists believe that by bailing out first Mexico and then the Asian countries, the IMF actually helped fuel these crises by creating a moral hazard in lending behavior. Specifically, economists like Milton Friedman and Allan Meltzer argue that the Mexican bailout encouraged investors to lend more money on less stringent terms to the Asian countries than they would have otherwise because of their belief that the IMF would bail them out if trouble hit. The $118 billion Asian bailout by the IMF ($57 billion for South Korea alone) reinforced the view of foreign investors that they were operating with an implicit guarantee from the IMF, which led to the Russian currency crisis and then the Brazilian crisis. At the same time, the provision of an IMF safety net gives recipient governments less incentive to adopt responsible fiscal and monetary policies.

In the case of the Brazilian *real* crisis, most observers had believed for a long time that the currency was overvalued (see Case I.4). When speculators attacked the *real* in the wake of the Asian currency crisis, the IMF tried to prevent a crisis by providing $41 billion in November 1998 to boost Brazil's reserves in return for Brazil's promise to reduce its budget deficit. That strategy broke down, however, when Brazil failed to deliver on promised fiscal reforms and investor confidence collapsed. On January 15, 1999, Brazil floated its currency and began implementing reforms. Arguably, without the IMF bailout package, Brazil would have been forced to act on its fiscal reforms sooner. IMF conditionality once again failed to work.

The emerging market currency crises stemmed from a failure to resolve conflicting monetary and exchange-rate policy objectives.

Fundamental Policy Conflict   Underlying the emerging market currency crises is a fundamental conflict among policy objectives that the target nations have failed to resolve and that IMF assistance has only allowed them to drag out. These three objectives are a fixed exchange rate, independent domestic monetary policy, and free capital movement. As we saw in Chapter 2, any two of these objectives are possible; all three are not. Speculators recognized that the attempts by Mexico, Indonesia, Thailand, South Korea, Brazil, Russia, and other countries to achieve these three objectives simultaneously were unsustainable and attacked their currencies, resulting in the inevitable breakdowns in their systems.

Policy Proposals for Dealing with Emerging Market Crises

There are three possible ways to avoid these financial crises. One is to impose currency controls, another is to permit currencies to float freely, and the third is to permanently fix the exchange rate by dollarizing, adopting a common currency as the participants in EMU have done, or establishing a currency board.

Financial crises can be avoided by imposing currency controls, allowing currencies to freely float, or permanently fixing the exchange rate.

Currency Controls   Some economists have advocated abandoning free capital movement, as Malaysia has done, as a means of insulating a nation's currency from speculative attacks. However, open capital markets improve economic welfare by channeling savings to where they are most productive. Moreover, most developing nations need foreign capital and the know-how, discipline, and more efficient resource allocation that come with it. Finally, the long history of currency controls should provide no comfort to its advocates. Currency controls have inevitably led to corruption and government misallocation of foreign exchange, hardly prescriptions for healthy growth.

Freely Floating Currency   With a freely floating currency, the exchange rate is set by the interplay of supply and demand. As Milton Friedman points out, with a floating exchange rate, there never has been a foreign exchange crisis. The reason is simple: The floating rate absorbs the pressures that would otherwise build up in countries that try to peg the exchange rate while simultaneously pursuing an independent monetary policy. For example, the Asian currency crisis did not spill over to Australia and New Zealand because the latter countries had floating exchange rates.

Permanently Fixed Exchange Rate   Through dollarization, establishment of a currency board, or monetary union, a nation can fix its exchange rate permanently. The key to this system's viability is the surrender of monetary independence to a single central bank: the European Central Bank for the countries using the euro and the Federal Reserve for countries like Ecuador and Panama that have dollarized. The Federal Reserve is also the de facto central bank for countries such as Argentina (until 2002) and Hong Kong that have dollar-based currency boards. It is this loss of monetary independence that is the fundamental difference between a truly fixed-rate and a pegged-rate system such as existed under Bretton Woods. In a truly fixed-rate system, the money supply adjusts to the balance of payments. If there is a balance-of-payments deficit, the supply of currency falls; with a surplus, it rises. With a pegged-rate system, on the other hand, governments can avoid—at least temporarily—allowing their money supply to adjust to a balance-of-payments deficit by borrowing from abroad or running down their foreign exchange reserves to maintain the pegged rate. With a persistent deficit, however, fueled by excessive growth of the money supply, an explosion is inevitable.

Adherence to either a truly fixed exchange rate or a floating exchange rate will help avert foreign exchange crises. Which mechanism is superior depends on a variety of factors. For example, if a country has a major trading partner with a long history of a stable monetary policy, then tying the domestic currency to the partner's currency would probably be a good choice. In any event, the choice of either system will eliminate the need for the IMF or other international agency to intervene in or usurp the market.

Better Information   Little noticed in the discussion of emerging market crises is that financial market collapses in Argentina and Turkey in 2001 were not particularly contagious. For example, debt-rating agencies elevated Mexican bonds to investment grade right in the middle of the Argentine debacle. Similarly, Brazilian and Russian bond prices soared from investor perceptions that their economies were improving. A natural conclusions is that information about emerging markets is improving, allowing investors to distinguish good ones from the bad. Taking this experience to its logical conclusion suggests that the best way to reduce financial market contagion in the future is to develop and disseminate better information about emerging market policies and their consequences. This course of action is exactly what one would expect free markets to undertake on their own, without the need for government intervention.

That being said, contagion can still be a problem when a crisis in one country forces portfolio managers to sell assets in other emerging countries. For example, a sell-off of Brazilian assets in early 2002, sparked by the rise of leftist Brazilian presidential candidate Lula da Silva, meant that some money managers had to sell their holdings in other emerging markets to meet margin calls or redemptions resulting from Brazil. Similarly, contagion can result from investors demanding higher risk premiums for bearing emerging market risk.

3.5 SUMMARY AND CONCLUSIONS

This chapter examined the process of exchange rate determination under five market mechanisms: free float, managed float, target-zone system, fixed-rate system, and the current hybrid system. In the last four systems, governments intervene in the currency markets in various ways to affect the exchange rate.

Regardless of the form of intervention, however, fixed rates do not remain fixed for long. Neither do floating rates. The basic reason that exchange rates do not remain fixed in either a fixed- or floating-rate system is that governments subordinate exchange rate considerations to domestic political considerations.

We saw that the gold standard is a specific type of fixed exchange-rate system, one that requires participating countries to maintain the value of their currencies in terms of gold. Calls for a new gold standard reflect a fundamental lack of trust that monetary authorities will desist from tampering with the integrity of fiat money.

Finally, we concluded that intervention to maintain a disequilibrium rate is generally ineffective or injurious when pursued over lengthy periods of time. Seldom have policy makers been able to outsmart, for any extended period, the collective judgment of currency buyers and sellers. The current volatile market environment, which is a consequence of unstable U.S. and world financial conditions, cannot be arbitrarily directed by government officials for long.

Examining the U.S. experience since the abandonment of fixed rates, we found that free-market forces did correctly reflect economic realities thereafter. The dollar's value dropped sharply between 1973 and 1980 when the United States experienced high inflation and weakened economic conditions. Beginning in 1981, the dollar's value rose when American policies dramatically changed under the leadership of the Federal Reserve and a new president, but fell when foreign economies strengthened relative to the U.S. economy. Nonetheless, the resulting shifts in U.S. cost competitiveness have led many to question the current international monetary system.

The principal alternative to the current system of floating currencies with its economic volatility is a fixed exchange-rate system. History offers no entirely convincing model for how such a system should be constructed, but it does point to two requirements. To succeed in reducing economic volatility, a system of fixed exchange rates must be credible, and it must have price stability built into its very fabric. Otherwise, the market's expectations of exchange rate changes combined with an unsatisfactory rate of inflation will lead to periodic battles among central banks and between central banks and the financial markets. The recent experiences of the European Monetary System point to the costs associated with the maintenance of exchange rates at unrealistic levels. These experiences also point out that, in the end, there is no real escape from market forces. Most European nations have responded to this reality by forming a monetary union and adopting the euro as their common currency. Some developing nations have gone further and abandoned their currencies altogether by dollarizing, either explicitly or implicitly through a currency board.

A final lesson learned is that one must have realistic expectations of a currency system. In particular, no currency system can achieve what many politicians seem to expect of it—a way to keep all the benefits of economic policy for their own nation while passing along the costs to foreigners (who do not vote) or to future generations (who do not vote yet). The recent series of emerging market crises points to the futility of this exercise.

QUESTIONS

1. a. What are the five basic mechanisms for establishing exchange rates?
   b. How does each work?
   c. What costs and benefits are associated with each mechanism?
   d. Have exchange rate movements under the current system of managed floating been excessive? Explain.

2. Find a recent example of a nation's foreign exchange market intervention and note what the government's justification was. Does this justification make economic sense?

3. Gold has been called "the ultimate burglar alarm." Explain what this expression means.

4. Suppose nations attempt to pursue independent monetary and fiscal policies. How will exchange rates behave?

5. The experiences of fixed exchange-rate systems and target-zone arrangements have not been entirely satisfactory.
   a. What lessons can economists draw from the breakdown of the Bretton Woods system?
   b. What lessons can economists draw from the exchange rate experiences of the European Monetary System?

6. How did the European Monetary System limit the economic ability of each member nation to set its interest rate to be different from Germany's?

7. Historically, Spain has had high inflation and has seen its peseta continuously depreciate. In 1989, however, Spain joined the EMS and pegged the peseta to the DM. According to a Spanish banker, EMS membership means that "the government has less capability to manage the currency but, on the other hand, the people are more trusting of the currency for that reason."
   a. What underlies the peseta's historical weakness?
   b. Comment on the banker's statement.
   c. What are the likely consequences of EMS membership on the Spanish public's willingness to save and invest?

8. In discussing the European Monetary Union, a recent government report stressed a need to make the central bank accountable to the "democratic process." What are the likely consequences for price stability and exchange rate stability in the EMS if the "Eurofed" becomes accountable to the "democratic process"?

9. In 2003, Chancellor of the Exchequer Gordon Brown called for a national debate on whether Britain should join the European Monetary Union. Discuss the pros and cons for Britain of joining EMU.

10. Comment on the following statement: "With monetary union, the era of protection for European firms and workers has come to an end."

PROBLEMS

1. During the currency crisis of September 1992, the Bank of England borrowed DM 33 billion from the Bundesbank when a pound was worth DM 2.78, or $1.912. It sold these DM in the foreign exchange market for pounds in a futile attempt to prevent a devaluation of the pound. It repaid these DM at the post-crisis rate of DM 2.50:£1. By then, the dollar:pound exchange rate was $1.782:£1.
   a. By what percentage had the pound sterling devalued in the interim against the Deutsche mark? Against the dollar?
   b. What was the cost of intervention to the Bank of England in pounds? In dollars?

2. Suppose the central rates within the ERM for the French franc and DM were FF 6.90403:ECU 1 and DM 2.05853:ECU 1, respectively.
   a. What was the cross-exchange rate between the franc and the mark?
   b. Under the original 2.25 percent margin on either side of the central rate, what were the approximate upper and lower intervention limits for France and Germany?

   c. Under the revised 15 percent margin on either side of the central rate, what were the approximate upper and lower intervention limits for France and Germany?

3. A Dutch company exporting to France had FF 3 million due in 90 days. Suppose that the spot exchange rate was FF 1 = DFl 0.3291.
   a. Under the exchange rate mechanism, and assuming central rates of FF 6.45863/ECU and DFl 2.16979/ECU, what was the central cross-exchange rate between the two currencies?
   b. Based on the answer to part a, what was the most the Dutch company could lose on its French franc receivable, assuming that France and the Netherlands stuck to the ERM with a 15 percent band on either side of their central cross rate?
   c. Redo part b, assuming the band was narrowed to 2.25 percent.
   d. Redo part b, assuming you know nothing about the spot cross-exchange rate.

4. Panama adopted the U.S. dollar as its official paper money in 1904. Currently, $400 million to $500

million in U.S. dollars is circulating in Panama. If interest rates on U.S. Treasury securities are 7 percent, what is the value of the seigniorage that Panama is forgoing by using the U.S. dollar instead of its own-issue money?

5. By some estimates, $185 billion to $260 billion in currency is held outside the United States.

a. What is the value to the United States of the seigniorage associated with these overseas dollars? Assume that dollar interest rates are about 6 percent.

b. Who in the United States realizes this seigniorage?

BIBLIOGRAPHY

Bordo, Michael David. "The Classical Gold Standard: Some Lessons for Today." *Federal Reserve Bank of St. Louis Review,* May 1981, pp. 2–17.

Coombs, Charles A. *The Arena of International Finance.* New York: John Wiley & Sons, 1976.

Friedman, Milton, and Robert V. Roosa. "Free versus Fixed Exchange Rates: A Debate." *Journal of Portfolio Management,* Spring 1977, pp. 68–73.

Mundell, Robert A. "A Theory of Optimum Currency Areas." *American Economic Review,* September 1961, pp. 657–663.

INTERNET RESOURCES

www.imf.org/external/fin.htm Web site of the International Monetary Fund (IMF) that links to information on the IMF, SDRs, exchange rates, position of each country in the IMF, and lending arrangements with member nations.

www.imf.org/external/about.htm IMF Web site that discusses the role of the IMF as well as a number of other topics, including debt relief for poor countries and reforming the international monetary system to cope with financial crises.

www.ex.ac.uk/~RDavies/arian/llyfr.html Contains a detailed history of money from ancient times to the present.

www.ecb.int Web site of the European Central Bank (ECB). Contains press releases and publications put out by the ECB along with exchange rate data and other euro area-related economic and financial statistics.

europa.eu.int Web site of the European Union (EU). Contains news, information, and statistics on the EU and its member nations and the euro.

www.sysmod.com/eurofaq.htm Contains answers to frequently asked questions about the euro and EMU as well as links to related Web sites.

INTERNET EXERCISES

1. Plot the dollar value of the euro since its inception. How has the euro fared in the past year?

2. What explanations have been given for the decline of the euro in the first three years of its existence?

3. What are the objectives of the ECB? What policy trade-offs does the ECB have to consider?

4. According to the IMF, what are its main purposes?

5. What proposals have been made by the IMF to reduce the incidence and severity of international financial crises?

PARITY CONDITIONS IN INTERNATIONAL FINANCE AND CURRENCY FORECASTING

It is not for its own sake that men desire money, but for the sake of what they can purchase with it.

Adam Smith (1776)

CHAPTER LEARNING OBJECTIVES

- To describe the meaning of "the law of one price" and its importance to the study of international finance
- To explain how arbitrage links goods prices and asset returns internationally
- To list and describe the five key theoretical relationships among spot exchange rates, forward exchange rates, inflation rates, and interest rates that result from international arbitrage activities
- To differentiate between the real and nominal exchange rate and the real and nominal interest rate
- To list and describe the four requirements for successful currency forecasting
- To identify a five-stage procedure for forecasting exchange rates in a fixed-rate system
- To describe how to forecast exchange rates in a floating-rate system using the predictions already embodied in interest and forward rates
- To describe the meaning and likelihood of forecasting success in both fixed-rate and floating-rate systems

KEY TERMS

arbitrage
black-market exchange rate
capital market integration
capital market segmentation
charting
covered interest arbitrage
covered interest differential
currency forecasting
Fisher effect (FE)
forward discount
forward premium
fundamental analysis
inflation differential
interest rate differential
interest rate parity

international Fisher effect (IFE)
law of one price
market-based forecasts
model-based forecasts
nominal exchange rate
nominal interest rate
parity conditions
peso problem
purchasing power parity (PPP)
real exchange rate
real interest rate
technical analysis
trend analysis
unbiased forward rate (UFR)
unbiased predictor

On the basis of the flows of goods and capital discussed in Chapter 2, this chapter presents a simple yet elegant set of equilibrium relationships that should apply to product prices, interest rates, and spot and forward exchange rates if markets are not impeded. These relationships, or **parity conditions**, provide the foundation for much of the remainder of this text; they should be clearly understood before you proceed further. The final section of this chapter examines the usefulness of a number of models and methodologies in profitably forecasting currency changes under both fixed-rate and floating-rate systems.

4.1 ARBITRAGE AND THE LAW OF ONE PRICE

Arbitrage is one of the most important concepts in all of finance. It is ordinarily defined as the simultaneous purchase and sale of the same assets or commodities on different markets to profit from price discrepancies. The concept of arbitrage is of particular importance in international finance because so many of the relationships between domestic and international financial markets, exchange rates, interest rates, and inflation rates depend on arbitrage for their existence. Indeed, by linking markets together, arbitrage underlies the globalization of markets.

One of the central ideas of international finance stems from arbitrage: In competitive markets, characterized by numerous buyers and sellers having low-cost access to information, exchange-adjusted prices of identical tradable goods and financial assets must be within transaction costs of equality worldwide. This idea, referred to as the **law of one price**, is enforced by international arbitrageurs who follow the profit-guaranteeing dictum of "buy low, sell high" and prevent all but trivial deviations from equality. Similarly, in the absence of market imperfections, risk-adjusted expected returns on financial assets in different markets should be equal.

> The law of one price says that exchange-adjusted prices of identical tradeable goods and assets must be within transactions costs of equality worldwide.

Five key theoretical economic relationships, which are depicted in Exhibit 4.1, result from these arbitrage activities:

- Purchasing power parity (PPP)
- Fisher effect (FE)
- International Fisher effect (IFE)
- Interest rate parity (IRP)
- Forward rates as unbiased predictors of future spot rates (UFR)

The framework of Exhibit 4.1 emphasizes the links among prices, spot exchange rates, interest rates, and forward exchange rates. Before proceeding, some terminology is in order. Specifically, a foreign currency is said to be at a **forward discount** if the forward rate expressed in dollars is below the spot rate, whereas a **forward premium** exists if the forward rate is above the spot rate. The forward discount or premium is expressed in annualized percentage terms as follows:

$$\text{Forward premium or discount} = \frac{\text{Forward rate} - \text{Spot rate}}{\text{Spot rate}} \times \frac{360}{\text{Forward contract number of days}} \tag{4.1}$$

where the exchange rate is stated in domestic currency units per unit of foreign currency.

According to the diagram in Exhibit 4.1, if inflation in, say, Mexico is expected to exceed inflation in the United States by 3 percent for the coming year, then the

---

EXHIBIT 4.1 • FIVE KEY THEORETICAL RELATIONSHIPS AMONG SPOT RATES, FORWARD RATES, INFLATION RATES, AND INTEREST RATES

Expected percentage change of spot rate of foreign currency −3%

UFR   IFE

PPP

Forward discount or premium on foreign currency −3%

IRP

Interest rate differential +3%

FE

Expected inflation rate differential +3%

Note: UFR = Forward rates as unbiased predictors of future spot rates
PPP = Purchasing power parity
IFE = International Fisher effect
FE = Fisher effect
IRP = Interest rate parity

Mexican peso should decline in value by about 3 percent relative to the dollar. By the same token, the one-year forward Mexican peso should sell at a 3 percent discount relative to the U.S. dollar. Similarly, one-year interest rates in Mexico should be about 3 percent higher than one-year interest rates on securities of comparable risk in the United States.

The common denominator of these parity conditions is the adjustment of the various rates and prices to inflation. According to modern monetary theory, inflation is the logical outcome of an expansion of the money supply in excess of real output growth. Although this view of the origin of inflation is not universally subscribed to, it has a solid microeconomic foundation. In particular, it is a basic precept of price theory that as the supply of one commodity increases relative to supplies of all other commodities, the price of the first commodity must decline relative to the prices of other commodities. Thus, for example, a bumper crop of corn should cause corn's value in exchange—its exchange rate—to decline. Similarly, as the supply of money increases relative to the supply of goods and services, the purchasing power of money—the exchange rate between money and goods—must decline.

The mechanism that brings this adjustment about is simple and direct. Suppose, for example, that the supply of U.S. dollars exceeds the amount that individuals desire to hold. In order to reduce their excess holdings of money, individuals increase their spending on goods, services, and securities, causing U.S. prices to rise. Moreover, as we saw in Chapter 2, this price inflation will cause the value of the dollar to decline.

The adverse consequences of an expansionary monetary policy and the benefits of *a stable monetary policy*—one that leads to stable prices and is not subject to sharp expansions or contractions—are both illustrated in "Bolivia Ends Its Hyperinflation."

Money supply growth, inflation, interest rates, and exchange rates are linked to each other through arbitrage.

ILLUSTRATION   *Bolivia Ends Its Hyperinflation*

In the spring of 1985, Bolivia's inflation rate was running at 101,000 percent a year, one of the highest rates in history. At the time, Bolivian government revenues covered less than 15 percent of its spending, with most of the rest being paid for by printing new pesos. Inflation threatened the very fabric of society. Prices changed by the minute, and people literally carried money around in suitcases. Currency, which was printed abroad, was the third-largest import in 1984. The two-inch stack of money needed to buy a chocolate bar far outweighed the candy. The government eventually solved the stacks-of-money problem by issuing notes in denominations of one million, two million, and ten million pesos. But its failure to solve the inflation problem led to its replacement by a new government that announced an anti-inflation program on August 29, 1985. The program had two basic thrusts: Cut spending, and shut down the printing presses. To cut spending, the new government adopted the simple rule that it would not spend more than it received. Each day the finance minister signed checks only up to the value of the revenues the Treasury had received that day—regardless of the spending that had been budgeted. By October, the monthly inflation rate had fallen below zero, from more than 60 percent in August (see Exhibit 4.2). Economists consider this performance to be a singular verification of basic monetary theory.

EXHIBIT 4.2 • BOLIVIA ENDS ITS HYPERINFLATION IN 1985 BY SHUTTING DOWN THE PRINTING PRESSES

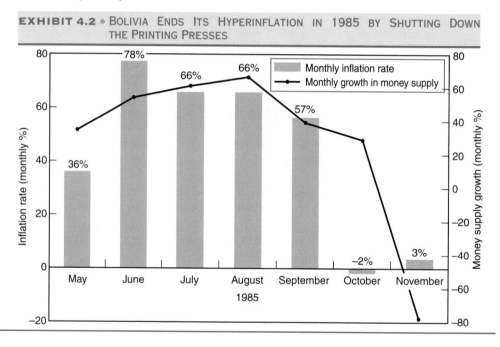

A further link in the chain relating money-supply growth, inflation, interest rates, and exchange rates is the notion that money is neutral. That is, money should have no impact on real variables. Thus, for example, a 10 percent increase in the supply of money relative to the demand for money should cause prices to rise by 10 percent. This view has important implications for international finance. Specifically, although a change in the quantity of money will affect prices and exchange rates, this change should not affect the rate at which domestic goods are exchanged for foreign goods or the rate at which goods today are exchanged for goods in the future. These ideas are formalized as purchasing power parity and the Fisher effect, respectively. We will examine them here briefly and then in greater detail in the next two sections.

The international analogue to inflation is home currency depreciation relative to foreign currencies. The analogy derives from the observation that inflation involves a change in the exchange rate between the home currency and domestic goods, whereas home currency depreciation—a decline in the foreign currency value of the home currency—results in a change in the exchange rate between the home currency and foreign goods.

That inflation and currency depreciation are related is no accident. Excess money-supply growth, through its impact on the rate of aggregate spending, affects the demand for goods produced abroad as well as goods produced domestically. In turn, the domestic demand for foreign currencies changes, and, consequently, the foreign exchange value of the domestic currency changes. Thus, the rate of domestic inflation and changes in the exchange rate are jointly determined by the rate of domestic money growth relative to the growth of the amount that people—domestic and foreign—want to hold.

If international arbitrage enforces the law of one price, then the exchange rate between the home currency and domestic goods must equal the exchange rate between the home currency and foreign goods. In other words, a unit of home currency (HC) should have the same purchasing power worldwide. Thus, if a dollar buys a pound of bread in the United States, it should also buy a pound of bread in Great Britain. For this to happen, the foreign exchange rate must change by (approximately) the difference between the domestic and foreign rates of inflation. This relationship is called **purchasing power parity (PPP)**.

Similarly, the **nominal interest rate**, the price quoted on lending and borrowing transactions, determines the exchange rate between current and future dollars (or any other currency). For example, an interest rate of 10 percent on a one-year loan means that one dollar today is being exchanged for 1.1 dollars a year from now. But what really matters, according to the **Fisher effect (FE)**, is the exchange rate between current and future purchasing power, as measured by the real interest rate. Simply put, the lender is concerned with how many more goods can be obtained in the future by forgoing consumption today, whereas the borrower wants to know how much future consumption must be sacrificed to obtain more goods today. This condition is the case regardless of whether the borrower and lender are located in the same or different countries. As a result, if the exchange rate between current and future goods—the **real interest rate**—varies from one country to the next, arbitrage between domestic and foreign capital markets, in the form of international capital flows, should occur. These flows will tend to equalize real interest rates across countries. By looking more closely at these and related parity conditions, we can see how they can be formalized and used for management purposes.

Inflation and currency depreciation are jointly determined by domestic money supply growth relative to money demand growth.

International arbitrage enforces the law of one price.

4.2 PURCHASING POWER PARITY

Purchasing power parity is widely used by central banks to determine equilibrium exchange rates and by companies to forecast currency movements.

Purchasing power parity (PPP) has been widely used by central banks as a guide to establishing new par values for their currencies when the old ones were clearly in disequilibrium. From a management standpoint, purchasing power parity is often used to forecast future exchange rates, for purposes ranging from deciding on the currency denomination of long-term debt issues to determining in which countries to build plants.

In its *absolute* version, purchasing power parity states that price levels should be equal worldwide when expressed in a common currency. In other words, a unit of home currency (HC) should have the same purchasing power around the world. This theory is just an application of the law of one price to national price levels rather than to individual prices. (That is, it rests on the assumption that free trade will equalize the price of any good in all countries; otherwise, arbitrage opportunities would exist.) However, absolute PPP ignores the effects on free trade of transportation costs, tariffs, quotas and other restrictions, and product differentiation.

The Big Mac index illustrates the law of one price and absolute purchasing power parity. It is calculated by comparing the prices of Big Macs worldwide (they are produced in more than 100 countries). The Big Mac PPP, put together by *The Economist,* is the exchange rate that would leave hamburgers costing the same overseas as in the United States. By comparing Big Mac PPPs with actual exchange rates, which is done in Exhibit 4.3, we can see whether a currency is over- or undervalued by this standard.

For example, a Big Mac in Britain cost £1.99 on April 22, 2003. Dividing this price through by its U.S. price of $2.71 implies a PPP exchange rate of £0.73/$:

$$\frac{£1.99}{$2.71} = £0.73/$$$

EXHIBIT 4.3 • THE BIG MAC HAMBURGER STANDARD

	Big Mac prices		Implied PPP* Exchange Rate (LC/$)	Actual LC/$ Exchange Rate 04/22/03	Under (–)/Over (+) Valuation** Against the Dollar, %
	In Local Currency (LC)	In Dollars			
United States[a]	2.71	2.71	—	—	—
Argentina	Peso4.10	1.43	1.52	2.88	−47
Australia	A$3.00	1.86	1.11	1.61	−31
Brazil	Real4.55	1.48	1.68	3.07	−45
Britain	£1.99	3.14	0.73	0.63	+16
Canada	C$3.20	2.21	1.18	1.45	−18
Chile	Peso1,400	1.95	515	716	−28
China	Yuan9.90	1.20	3.67	8.28	−56
Denmark	DKr27.75	4.10	10.26	6.78	+51
Euro area	€2.71	2.97	1.21	1.10	+10
Hong Kong	HK$11.50	1.47	4.23	7.80	−46
Hungary	Forint490	2.18	180	224	−20
Indonesia	Rupiah16,100	1.84	5,934	8,740	−32
Japan	¥262	2.19	96.97	120	−19
Malaysia	M$5.04	1.33	1.86	3.80	−51
Mexico	Peso23.00	2.18	8.47	10.53	−20
New Zealand	NZ$3.95	2.21	1.45	1.78	−18
Poland	Zloty6.30	1.62	2.33	3.89	−40
Russia	Ruble41.00	1.32	15.15	31.1	−51
Singapore	S$3.30	1.86	1.22	1.78	−31
South Africa	Rand13.95	1.84	5.13	7.56	−32
South Korea	Won3,300	2.71	1,220	1,220	0
Sweden	SKr30.00	3.60	11.08	8.34	+33
Switzerland	SFr6.30	4.59	2.32	1.37	+69
Taiwan	NT$70.00	2.01	25.81	34.8	−26
Thailand	Baht59.0	1.38	21.74	42.7	−49

* Purchasing-power parity: local currency price divided by dollar price in the United States.
** Under/over valuation: (implied PPP rate − actual exchange rate)/implied PPP rate.
[a] Average of New York, Chicago, San Francisco, and Atlanta prices.
Source: McDonald's.

The actual exchange rate on that date was £0.63. By this measure, the pound was 16 percent overvalued on April 22, 2003:

$$\frac{£0.73 - £0.63}{£0.63} = +16\%$$

Alternatively, with a dollar PPP of Y3.65/$ (Y9.90/$2.71), the Chinese yuan appeared to be undervalued by 56 percent [(Y3.65/Y8.80) − 1 = −56%].

The Big Mac standard is somewhat misleading because you are buying not just the hamburger but the location. Included in the price of a Big Mac is the cost of real estate, local taxes, and local services, which differ worldwide and are not traded goods. When the items being compared contain a bundle of traded and nontraded goods and services, as in the case of a Big Mac, it should not be surprising that absolute PPP and the law of one price fail to hold.

The *relative* version of purchasing power parity, which is used more commonly now, states that the exchange rate between the home currency and any foreign currency will adjust to reflect changes in the price levels of the two countries. For example, if inflation is 5 percent in the United States and 1 percent in Japan, then the dollar value of the Japanese yen must rise by about 4 percent to equalize the dollar price of goods in the two countries.

Relative PPP says that exchange rates should change to offset differences in inflation rates.	

Formally, if i_h and i_f are the rates of inflation for the home country and the foreign country, respectively; e_0 is the dollar (HC) value of one unit of foreign currency at the beginning of the period; and e_1 is the spot exchange rate in period 1, then

$$\frac{e_1}{e_0} = \frac{1 + i_h}{1 + i_f} \qquad (4.2)$$

If Equation 4.2 holds, then

$$e_1 = e_0 \times \frac{1 + i_h}{1 + i_f} \qquad (4.3)$$

The value of e_1 appearing in Equation 4.3 is known as the *PPP rate*. For example, if the United States and Euroland are running annual inflation rates of 5 percent and 3 percent, respectively, and the spot rate is €1 = $1.07, then according to Equation 4.3 the PPP rate for the euro in one year should be

$$e_3 = 1.07 \times \frac{1.05}{1.03} = \$1.0908$$

If purchasing power parity is expected to hold, then $1.0908/€ is the best prediction for the euro spot rate in one year.

ILLUSTRATION   *Calculating the PPP Rate for the Swiss Franc*

Suppose the current U.S. price level is at 112 and the Swiss price level is at 107, relative to base price levels of 100. If the initial value of the Swiss franc was $0.58, then according to PPP, the dollar value of the franc should have risen to approximately $0.6071 [0.58 × (112/107)], an appreciation of 4.67 percent. On the other hand, if the Swiss price level now equals 119, then the franc should have depreciated by about 5.88 percent, to $0.5459 [0.58 × (112/119)].

Purchasing power parity is often represented by the following approximation of Equation 4.3:[1]

$$\frac{e_1 - e_0}{e_0} = i_h - i_f \qquad (4.4)$$

That is, the exchange rate change during a period should equal the **inflation differential** for that same time period. In effect, PPP says that *currencies with high rates of inflation should devalue relative to currencies with lower rates of inflation.*

Equation 4.4 is illustrated in Exhibit 4.4. The vertical axis measures the percentage currency change, and the horizontal axis shows the inflation differential. Equilibrium is reached on the parity line, which contains all those points at which these two differentials are equal. At point A, for example, the 3 percent inflation differential is just offset by the 3 percent appreciation of the foreign currency relative to the home currency. Point B, on the other hand, depicts a situation of disequilibrium, where the inflation differential of 3 percent is greater than the appreciation of 1 percent in the HC value of the foreign currency.

Purchasing power parity says that currencies with high rates of inflation should depreciate relative to currencies with lower rates of inflation.

The Lesson of Purchasing Power Parity

Purchasing power parity bears an important message: Just as the price of goods in one year cannot be meaningfully compared with the price of goods in another year without adjusting for interim inflation, so exchange rate changes may indicate nothing more than the reality that countries have different inflation rates. In fact, according to PPP, exchange rate movements should just cancel out changes in the foreign price level rela-

EXHIBIT 4.4 • PURCHASING POWER PARITY

---

[1] Dividing both sides of Equation 4.3 by e_0 and then subtracting 1 from both sides yields

$$\frac{e_1 - e_0}{e_0} = \frac{i_h - i_f}{1 + i_f}$$

Equation 4.4 follows if i_f is relatively small.

tive to the domestic price level. These offsetting movements should have no effects on the relative competitive positions of domestic firms and their foreign competitors. Thus, changes in the **nominal exchange rate**—that is, the actual exchange rate—may be of little significance in determining the true effects of currency changes on a firm and a nation. In terms of currency changes affecting relative competitiveness, therefore, the focus must be not on nominal exchange rate changes but instead on changes in the real purchasing power of one currency relative to another. Here we consider the concept of the real exchange rate.

The **real exchange rate** is the nominal exchange rate adjusted for changes in the relative purchasing power of each currency since some base period. In technical terms, the real exchange rate at time 1 (dollars or HC per unit of foreign currency), e_1', relative to the base period (specified as time 0) is defined as

Only changes in the real exchange rate will affect the relative competitive positions of domestic firms and their foreign competitors.

$$e_t' = e_t \times \frac{P_f}{P_h} \tag{8.5}$$

where P_f is the foreign price level and P_h the home price level at time 1, both indexed to 100 at time 0.

By indexing these price levels to 100 as of the base period, their ratio reflects the change in the relative purchasing power of these currencies since time 0. Note that increases in the foreign price level and foreign currency depreciation have offsetting effects on the real exchange rate. Similarly, home price-level increases and foreign currency appreciation offset each other.

An alternative—and equivalent—way to represent the real exchange rate is to directly reflect the change in relative purchasing powers of these currencies by adjusting the nominal exchange rate for inflation in both countries between time 0 and time 1, as follows:

$$e_t' = e_t \times \frac{1 + i_f}{1 + i_h} \tag{4.6}$$

where the various parameters are the same as those defined previously.

Nominal exchange rate changes offset by differences in inflation rates leave the real exchange rate unchanged.

If changes in the nominal exchange rate are fully offset by changes in the relative price levels between the two countries, then the real exchange rate remains unchanged. (Note that the real exchange rate in the base period is just the nominal rate e_0.) Specifically, if PPP holds, then we can substitute the value of e_1 from Equation 4.2 into Equation 4.6. Making this substitution yields $e_1' = e_0$; that is, the real exchange rate remains constant at e_0. Alternatively, a change in the real exchange rate is equivalent to a deviation from PPP.

ILLUSTRATION   *Calculating the Real Exchange Rate for the Japanese Yen*

Between 1980 and 1995, the ¥/$ exchange rate moved from ¥226.63/$ to ¥93.96. During this same fifteen-year period, the consumer price index (CPI) in Japan rose from 91.0 to 119.2 and the U.S. CPI rose from 82.4 to 152.4.

1. If PPP had held over this period, what would the ¥/$ exchange rate have been in 1995?

   Solution. According to Equation 4.2, in 1995, the ¥/$ exchange rate should have been ¥160.51/$:

$$\text{¥/\$ PPP rate} = 226.63 \times \frac{(119.2/91.0)}{(152.4/82.4)} = \text{¥}160.51/\$$$

In working this problem, note that Equation 4.3 was inverted because we are expressing the exchange rate in ¥/$ terms rather than $/¥ terms. Note too that the ratio of CPIs is equal to the cumulative price-level increase. Comparing the PPP rate of ¥160.51/$ to the actual rate of ¥93.96/$, we can see that the yen has appreciated more than PPP would suggest.

2. What happened to the real value of the yen in terms of dollars during this period?

Solution. To estimate the real value of the yen, we convert the exchange rate from ¥/$ terms to $/¥ terms and apply Equation 4.5 (using the yen quoted in ¥/$ terms would yield us the real value of the U.S. dollar in terms of yen):[2]

$$e_t' = e_t \frac{P_f}{P_h} = \frac{1}{93.96} \times \frac{(119.2/91.0)}{(152.4/82.4)} = \$0.007538/\text{¥}$$

To interpret this real exchange rate and see how it changed since 1980, we compare it to the real exchange rate in 1980, which just equals the nominal rate at that time of 1/226.63 = $0.004412/¥ (because the real and nominal rates are equal in the base period). This comparison reveals that during the 15-year period 1980–1995, the yen appreciated in real terms by (0.007538 − 0.004412)/0.004412 = 71%. This dramatic appreciation in the inflation-adjusted value of the Japanese yen put enormous competitive pressure on Japanese exporters as the dollar prices of their goods rose far more than the U.S. rate of inflation would justify.

Deviations from purchasing power parity cause real exchange rate changes and, hence, currency risk.

The distinction between the nominal exchange rate and the real exchange rate has important implications for foreign exchange risk measurement and management. As we will see in Chapter 11, if the real exchange rate remains constant (i.e., if purchasing power parity holds), currency gains or losses from nominal exchange rate changes will generally be offset over time by the effects of differences in relative rates of inflation, thereby reducing the net impact of nominal devaluations and revaluations. Deviations from purchasing power parity, however, will lead to real exchange gains and losses. In the case of Japanese exporters, the real appreciation of the yen forced them to cut costs and develop new products less subject to pricing pressures. We will discuss their responses in more detail in Chapter 11.

Empirical Evidence

The strictest version of purchasing power parity—that all goods and financial assets obey the law of one price—is demonstrably false. The risks and costs of shipping goods internationally, as well as government-erected barriers to trade and capital flows, are at times high enough to cause exchange-adjusted prices to systematically differ between countries. On the other hand, there is clearly a relationship between relative inflation rates and changes in exchange rates. In particular, over time, as shown in Exhibit 4.5, those currencies with the largest relative decline (gain) in purchasing power saw the sharpest erosion (appreciation) in their foreign exchange values.

---

[2] Dividing both current price levels by their base levels effectively indexes each to 100 as of the base period.

EXHIBIT 4.5 • PURCHASING POWER PARITY EMPIRICAL DATA, 1980–2000

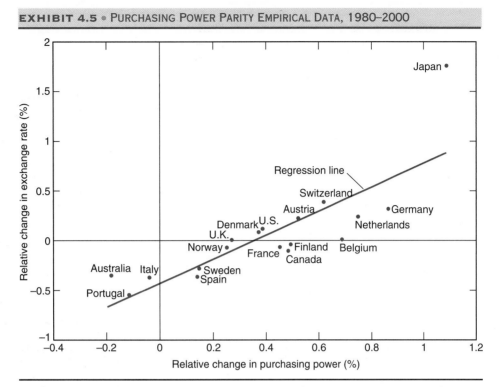

Relative change in purchasing power is calculated as the amount of inflation above or below the average for the 17 OECD countries.

Relative change in the exchange rate is computed as the amount of currency change above or below the average.

PPP holds up well in the long run, but not so well over shorter time periods.	The general conclusion from empirical studies of PPP is that the theory holds up well in the long run, but not as well over shorter time periods.[3] The difference between the short-run and long-run effects can be seen in Exhibit 4.6, which compares the actual dollar exchange rate for 12 countries with their PPP rates. Despite substantial short-run deviations from purchasing power parity, currencies have a distinct tendency to move toward their PPP-predicted rates. Another way to view this evidence is that, despite fluctuations, the real exchange rate tends to revert back to its predicted value of e_0. That is, if $e_1' > e_0$, then the real exchange rate should fall over time towards e_0, whereas if $e_1' < e_0$, the real exchange rate should rise over time towards e_0. Additional support for the existence of mean-reverting behavior of real exchange rates is provided by data spanning two centuries on the dollar-sterling and French franc-sterling real exchange rates.[4] Mean reversion has important implications for currency risk management, which will be explored in Chapter 11.
PPP measures are distorted by non-traded goods and relative price changes.	A common explanation for the failure of PPP to hold is that goods prices are sticky, leading to short-term violations of the law of one price. Adjustment to PPP eventually occurs, but it does so with a lag. An alternative explanation for the failure of most tests to support PPP in the short run is that these tests ignore the problems caused by the combination of differently constructed price indices, relative price changes, and nontraded goods and services. Despite these problems, most tests of relative PPP as a long-term theory of exchange rate determination seem to support its validity.

[3] Perhaps the best known of these studies is Henry J. Gailliot, "Purchasing Power Parity as an Explanation of Long-Term Changes in Exchange Rates," *Journal of Money, Credit, and Banking*, August 1971, pp. 348–357.

[4] See James R. Lothian and Mark P. Taylor, "Real Exchange Rate Behavior: The Recent Float from the Perspective of the Past Two Centuries," *Journal of Political Economy*, June 1996.

EXHIBIT 4.6 • PURCHASING POWER PARITY AND ACTUAL EXCHANGE RATES

In summary, despite often lengthy departures from PPP, there is a clear correspondence between relative inflation rates and changes in the nominal exchange rate. However, for reasons that have nothing necessarily to do with market disequilibrium, the correspondence is not perfect.

4.3 THE FISHER EFFECT

Real interest rates, not nominal rates, are what matter to borrowers and lenders.

The interest rates that are quoted in the financial press are nominal rates. That is, they are expressed as the rate of exchange between current and future dollars. For example, a nominal interest rate of 8 percent on a one-year loan means that $1.08 must be repaid in one year for $1.00 loaned today. But what really matters to both parties to a loan agreement is the real interest rate, the rate at which current goods are being converted into future goods.

Looked at one way, the real rate of interest is the net increase in wealth that people expect to achieve when they save and invest their current income. Alternatively, it can be viewed as the added future consumption promised by a corporate borrower to a lender in return for the latter's deferring current consumption. From the company's standpoint, this exchange is worthwhile as long as it can find suitably productive investments.

The Fisher effect says that borrowers and lenders factor expected inflation into interest rates.

However, because virtually all financial contracts are stated in nominal terms, the real interest rate must be adjusted to reflect expected inflation. The **Fisher effect** states that the nominal interest rate r is made up of two components: (1) a real required rate of return a and (2) an inflation premium equal to the expected amount of inflation i. Formally, the Fisher effect is

$$1 + \text{Nominal rate} = (1 + \text{Real rate})\ (1 + \text{Expected inflation rate})$$

$$1 + r = (1 + a)\ (1 + i)$$

or

$$r = a + i + ai \qquad (4.7)$$

Equation 4.7 is often approximated by the equation $r = a + i$.

The Fisher equation says, for example, that if the required real return is 3 percent and expected inflation is 10 percent, then the nominal interest rate will be about 13 percent (13.3 percent, to be exact). The logic behind this result is that $1 next year will have the purchasing power of $0.90 in terms of today's dollars. Thus, the borrower must pay the lender $0.103 to compensate for the erosion in the purchasing power of the $1.03 in principal and interest payments, in addition to the $0.03 necessary to provide a 3 percent real return.

 ILLUSTRATION   *Brazilians Shun Negative Real Interest Rates on Savings*

In 1981, the Brazilian government spent $10 million on an advertising campaign to help boost national savings, which dropped sharply in 1980. According to the *Wall Street Journal* (January 12, 1981, p. 23), the decline in savings occurred "because the pre-fixed rates on savings deposits and treasury bills for 1980 were far below the rate of inflation, currently 110 percent." Clearly, the Brazilians were not interested in investing money at interest rates less than the inflation rate.

Real interest rates tend to be equalized across countries.

The generalized version of the Fisher effect asserts that real returns are equalized across countries through arbitrage—that is, $a_h = a_f$, where the subscripts h and f refer to home and foreign real rates, respectively. If expected real returns were higher in one currency than another, capital would flow from the second to the first currency. This process of arbitrage would continue, in the absence of government intervention, until expected real returns were equalized.

In equilibrium, then, with no government interference, it should follow that the nominal **interest rate differential** will approximately equal the anticipated inflation differential between the two currencies, or

$$r_h - r_f = i_h - i_f \qquad (4.8)$$

where r_h and r_f are the nominal home and foreign currency interest rates, respectively. The exact form of this relationship is expressed by Equation 4.9:[5]

$$\frac{1 + r_h}{1 + r_f} = \frac{1 + i_h}{1 + i_f} \qquad (4.9)$$

---

[5] Equation 4.9 can be converted into Equation 4.8 by subtracting 1 from both sides and assuming that r_f and i_f are relatively small.

In effect, the generalized version of the Fisher effect says that *currencies with high rates of inflation should bear higher interest rates than currencies with lower rates of inflation.*

For example, if inflation rates in the United States and the United Kingdom are 4 percent and 7 percent, respectively, the Fisher effect says that nominal interest rates should be about 3 percent higher in the United Kingdom than in the United States. A graph of Equation 4.8 is shown in Exhibit 4.7. The horizontal axis shows the expected difference in inflation rates between the home country and the foreign country, and the vertical axis shows the interest differential between the two countries for the same time period. The parity line shows all points for which $r_h - r_f = i_h - i_f$.

Point C, for example, is a position of equilibrium because the 2 percent higher rate of inflation in the foreign country ($i_h - i_f = -2\%$) is just offset by the 2 percent lower HC interest rate ($r_h - r_f = -2\%$). At point D, however, where the real rate of return in the home country is 1 percent lower than in the foreign country (an inflation differential of 2 percent versus an interest differential of 3 percent), funds should flow from the home country to the foreign country to take advantage of the real differential. This flow will continue until expected real returns are again equal.

Empirical Evidence

Exhibit 4.8 illustrates the relationship between interest rates and inflation rates for thirty-two countries as of November 2000. It is evident from the graph that nations with higher inflation rates generally have higher interest rates. Thus, the empirical evidence is consistent with the hypothesis that most of the variation in nominal interest rates across countries can be attributed to differences in inflationary expectations.

The proposition that expected real returns are equal between countries cannot be tested directly. However, many observers believe it unlikely that significant real interest differentials could long survive in the increasingly internationalized capital markets. Most market participants agree that arbitrage, via the huge pool of liquid capital that operates in international markets these days, is forcing pretax real interest rates to converge across all the major nations.

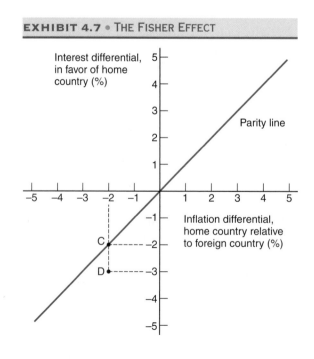

EXHIBIT 4.7 ● THE FISHER EFFECT

EXHIBIT 4.8 • FISHER EFFECT: NOMINAL INTEREST RATE VERSUS INFLATION RATE FOR THIRTY-TWO DEVELOPED AND DEVELOPING COUNTRIES AS OF NOVEMBER 2000

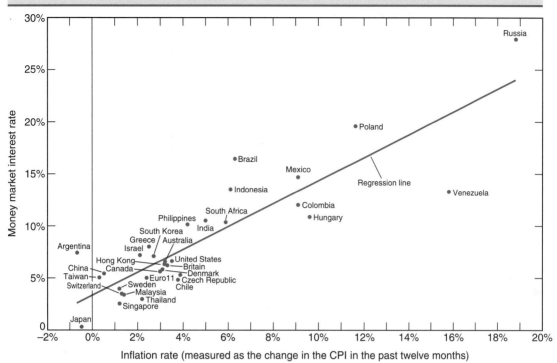

Inflation rate (measured as the change in the CPI in the past twelve months)

<table>
<tr><td>Segmented capital markets can lead real interest rates to differ across countries.</td></tr>
</table>

To the extent that arbitrage is permitted to operate unhindered, capital markets are integrated worldwide. **Capital market integration** means that real interest rates are determined by the global supply and global demand for funds. This is in contrast to **capital market segmentation**, where real interest rates are determined by local credit conditions. The difference between capital market segmentation and capital market integration is depicted in Exhibit 4.9. With a segmented capital market, the real interest rate in the United States, a_{us}, is based on the national demand D_{us} and national supply S_{us} of credit. Conversely, the real rate in the rest of the world, a_{rw}, is based on the rest-of-world supply S_{rw} and demand D_{rw}. In this example, the U.S. real rate is higher than the real rate outside the United States, or $a_{us} > a_{rw}$.

Once the U.S. market opens up, the U.S. real interest rate falls (and the rest-of-world rate rises) to the new world rate a_w, which is determined by the world supply S_w (= S_{us} +

EXHIBIT 4.9 • THE DISTINCTION BETWEEN CAPITAL MARKET INTEGRATION AND CAPITAL MARKET SEGMENTATION

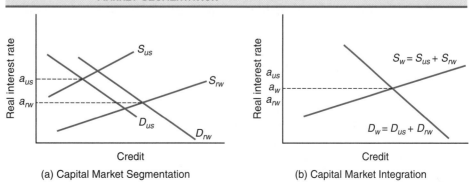

(a) Capital Market Segmentation

(b) Capital Market Integration

S_{rw}) and world demand D_w (= D_{us} + D_{rw}) for credit. The mechanism whereby equilibrium is brought about is a capital inflow to the United States. It is this same capital flow that drives up the real interest rate outside the United States.[6]

As shown by Exhibit 4.9, in an integrated capital market, the domestic real interest rate depends on what is happening outside as well as inside the United States. For example, a rise in the demand for capital by German companies to finance investments in Eastern Europe will raise the real interest rate in the United States as well as in Germany. Similarly, a rise in the U.S. savings rate, other things being equal, will lower the real cost of capital both in the United States and in the rest of the world. Conversely, a fall in U.S. inflation will lower the nominal U.S. interest rate (the Fisher effect), while leaving unchanged real interest rates worldwide.

Capital market integration has homogenized markets around the world, eroding much—though not all—of the real interest rate differentials between comparable domestic and offshore securities, and strengthening the link between assets that are denominated in different currencies but carry similar credit risks.[7] To the extent that real interest differentials do exist, they must be due to either currency risk or some form of political risk.

A real interest rate differential could exist without being arbitraged away if investors strongly preferred to hold domestic assets in order to avoid currency risk, even if the expected real return on foreign assets were higher. The evidence on this point is somewhat mixed. The data indicate a tendency toward convergence in real interest rates internationally, indicating that arbitrage does occur, but real rates still appear to differ from each other.[8] Moreover, the estimated currency risk premium appears to be highly variable and unpredictable, leading to extended periods of apparent differences in real interest rates between nations.[9]

These differences are displayed in Exhibit 4.10, which compares real interest rates (measured as the nominal interest rate minus the past year's inflation rate as a surrogate for the expected inflation rate) as of November 2000 versus nominal rates for the same thirty-two countries shown in Exhibit 4.8. According to this exhibit, countries with higher nominal interest rates (implying higher expected inflation and greater currency risk) tend to have higher real interest rates, resulting in large real rate differentials among some countries.

In addition to currency and inflation risk, real interest rate differentials in a closely integrated world economy can stem from countries pursuing sharply differing tax policies or imposing regulatory barriers to the free flow of capital.

In many developing countries, however, currency controls and other government policies impose political risk on foreign investors. In effect, political risk can drive a wedge between the returns available to domestic investors and those available to foreign investors. For example, if political risk in Brazil causes foreign investors to demand a 7 percent higher interest rate than they demand elsewhere, then foreign investors would consider a 10 percent expected real return in Brazil to be equivalent to a 3 percent expected real return in the United States. Hence, real interest rates in developing countries can exceed those in developed countries without presenting attractive arbitrage opportunities to foreign investors. The combination of a relative shortage of capital and high political risk in most developing countries is likely to

Capital markets are becoming increasingly integrated worldwide.

Political risk and currency risk can cause real interest rates to differ across countries.

Real interest rates tend to be higher in developing countries.

---

[6] The net gain from the transfer of capital equals the higher returns on the capital imported to the United States less the lower returns foregone in the rest of the world. Returns on capital must be higher in the United States prior to the capital inflow because the demand for capital depends on the expected return on capital. Thus, a higher real interest rate indicates a higher real return on capital.

[7] An offshore security is one denominated in the home currency but issued abroad. They are generally referred to as Eurosecurities.

[8] See, for example, Frederick S. Mishkin, "Are Real Interest Rates Equal across Countries? An International Investigation of Parity Conditions," *Journal of Finance,* December 1984, pp. 1345–1357. He finds that, although capital markets may be integrated, real interest rates appear to differ across countries because of currency risk. His findings are consistent with those of Baghar Modjtahedi, "Dynamics of Real Interest Rate Differentials: An Empirical Investigation," *European Economic Review* 32, no. 6 (1988): 1191–1211.

[9] Adrian Throop, "International Financial Market Integration and Linkages of National Interest Rates," *Federal Reserve Bank of San Francisco Economic Review,* no. 3 (1994): 3–18, found that exchange risk caused persistent real interest rate differentials among developed nations for the years 1981–1993.

EXHIBIT 4.10 • REAL INTEREST RATE VERSUS NOMINAL INTEREST RATE FOR THIRTY-TWO DEVELOPED AND DEVELOPING COUNTRIES AS OF NOVEMBER 2000

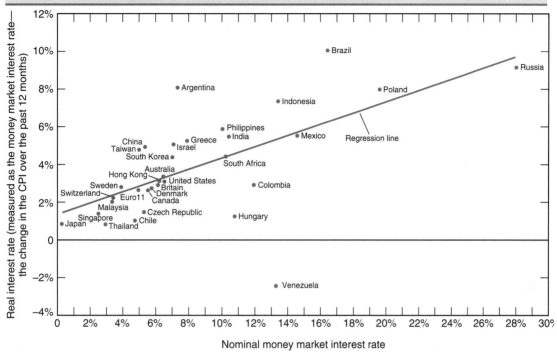

cause real interest rates in these countries to exceed real interest rates in the developed countries. Indeed, the countries in Exhibit 4.10 with the highest real rates of interest are all developing countries.

International capital markets impose discipline on nations engaged in economic mismanagement.

Investors' tolerance of economic mismanagement in developed nations also has fallen dramatically, as financial deregulation, abolition of foreign exchange controls, and the process of global portfolio diversification have swollen the volume of international capital flows. With modern technology enabling investors to move capital from one market to another at low cost and almost instantaneously, the pressure on central banks to seem to "do the right thing" is intense. Conversely, those nations that must attract a disproportionate amount of global capital to finance their national debts and that have no credible policies to deal with their problems in a noninflationary way will be forced to pay a rising risk premium. "Canada's High Real Interest Rate Comes Down" provides a good example of both these trends.

ILLUSTRATION   *Canada's High Real Interest Rate Comes Down*

In early 1995, the Canadian dollar slipped to an eight-and-a-half-year low against the U.S. dollar. At the same time, with Canada's inflation rate under 1 percent and its ten-year government bonds yielding 9.3 percent (about 1.5 percentage points more than ten-year U.S. Treasury bonds), Canada had the highest real long-term interest rates in the world. The weak Canadian dollar and high real interest rates stemmed from the same source—a lack of confidence in Canada's longer-term inflation prospects.

Canada had a large current-account deficit, driven by large budget deficits, political uncertainty, and other structural problems that led to investor worries that the current low rate of inflation was only temporary. The persistently high budget deficits, in turn, reflected big spending on generous social-welfare programs and overly rigid labor markets, along with a lack of political will to attack these problems. At the same time, investors feared that the government would rely more on tax increases than on spending cuts to reduce the deficit. Further increases in the already high Canadian tax rates would likely drive more of the economy underground and aggravate capital flight. Investors were concerned that if higher tax rates did not reduce the deficit, and the government would not cut spending, Canada might be tempted at some point to monetize its deficits, reigniting inflation.

Adding fuel to these fears was the resignation of John Crow, the highly respected head of the Bank of Canada, Canada's central bank, and a strong advocate of price stability. Some analysts contended he was forced out by government officials who opposed his tough low-inflation targets. His successor as head of the Bank of Canada followed a relatively lax monetary policy. Investors responded to these worries by driving down the value of the Canadian dollar and by demanding higher interest rates. In the background was the ever-present fear that Quebec separatists would manage to secede from Canada.

By late 1995, Quebec's separatists had lost their referendum for independence, the federal and provincial governments began slashing their budget deficits and planned even bigger cuts in the future, and Canada's largest province, Ontario, announced large tax cuts as well. Perceived political risk declined, and investors began focusing on Canada's low inflation rate. As a result of these favorable trends, the Canadian dollar strengthened and, in early 1996, short-term Canadian interest rates fell below U.S. rates, after having stayed above U.S. rates for more than a decade. But the yield on ten-year Canadian government bonds stayed about 1 percentage point above that on U.S. Treasuries. With continued low inflation, however, by late 1997, Canada paid about 0.5 percentage points *less* for 10-year money than the United States.

Before we move to the next parity condition, a caveat is in order. We must keep in mind that there are numerous interest differentials just as there are many different interest rates in a market. The rate on bank deposits, for instance, will not be identical to that on Treasury bills. In computation of an interest differential, therefore, the securities on which this differential is based must be of identical risk characteristics save for currency risk. Otherwise, there is the danger of comparing apples with oranges (or at least temple oranges with navel oranges).

Underlying all financial transactions are exchanges of goods today for goods in the future.

Adding Up Capital Markets Internationally   Central to understanding how we can add yen and euro and dollar capital markets together is to recognize that money is only a veil: All financial transactions, no matter how complex, ultimately involve exchanges of goods today for goods in the future. As we will see in Chapter 5, you supply credit (capital) when you consume less than you produce; you demand credit when you consume more than you produce. Thus, the supply of credit can be thought of as the excess supply of goods and the demand for credit as the excess demand for goods. When we add up the capital markets around the world, we are adding up the excess demands for goods and the excess supplies of goods. A car is still a car, whether it is valued in yen or dollars.

4.4 THE INTERNATIONAL FISHER EFFECT

The key to understanding the impact of relative changes in nominal interest rates among countries on the foreign exchange value of a nation's currency is to recall the implications of PPP and the generalized Fisher effect. PPP implies that exchange rates will move to offset changes in inflation rate differentials. Thus, a rise in the U.S. inflation rate relative to those of other countries will be associated with a fall in the dollar's value. It will also be associated with a rise in the U.S. interest rate relative to foreign interest rates. Combine these two conditions and the result is the **international Fisher effect (IFE)**:

$$\frac{1 + r_h}{1 + r_f} = \frac{\bar{e}_1}{e_0} \tag{4.10}$$

Here $\bar{e}_1$ is the expected exchange rate in period 1.

According to Equation 4.10, the expected return from investing at home, $1 + r_h$, should equal the expected HC return from investing abroad, $(1 + r_f)\bar{e}_1/e_0$. As discussed in the previous section, however, despite the intuitive appeal of equal expected returns, domestic and foreign expected returns might not equilibrate if the element of currency risk restrained the process of international arbitrage.

The expected HC returns from investing at home and abroad should be equal.

ILLUSTRATION   *Using the IFE to Forecast U.S.$ and SFr Rates*

In July, the one-year interest rate is 4 percent on Swiss francs and 13 percent on U.S. dollars.

1. If the current exchange rate is SFr 1 = $0.63, what is the expected future exchange rate in one year?

   Solution. According to the international Fisher effect, the spot exchange rate expected in one year equals 0.63 × 1.13/1.04 = $0.6845.

2. If a change in expectations regarding future U.S. inflation causes the expected future spot rate to rise to $0.70, what should happen to the U.S. interest rate?

   Solution. If r_{us} is the unknown U.S. interest rate, and the Swiss interest rate stays at 4 percent (because there has been no change in expectations of Swiss inflation), then according to the international Fisher effect, 0.70/0.63 = (1 + r_{us})/1.04, or r_{us} = 15.56%.

If r_f is relatively small, Equation 4.11 provides a reasonable approximation to the international Fisher effect:[10]

$$r_h - r_f = \frac{\bar{e}_1 - e_0}{e_0} \tag{4.11}$$

The international Fisher effect says that currencies with low interest rates are expected to appreciate relative to currencies with high interest rates.

In effect, the IFE says that *currencies with low interest rates are expected to appreciate relative to currencies with high interest rates.*

A graph of Equation 4.11 is shown in Exhibit 4.11. The vertical axis shows the expected change in the home currency value of the foreign currency, and the horizontal axis shows the interest differential between the two countries for the same time period. The parity line shows all points for which $r_h - r_f = (\bar{e}_1 - e_0)/e_0$.

Point E is a position of equilibrium because it lies on the parity line, with the 4 percent interest differential in favor of the home country just offset by the anticipated 4 percent appreciation in the HC value of the foreign currency. Point F, however, illustrates a

---

[10] Subtracting 1 from both sides of Equation 4.10 yields

$$\frac{\bar{e}_1 - e_0}{e_0} = \frac{r_h - r_f}{1 + r_f}$$

Equation 4.11 follows if r_f is relatively small.

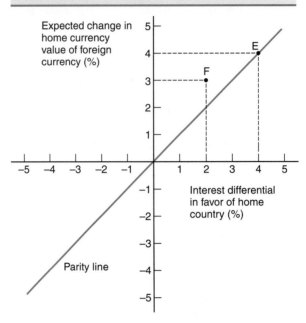

EXHIBIT 4.11 • INTERNATIONAL FISHER EFFECT

situation of disequilibrium. If the foreign currency is expected to appreciate by 3 percent in terms of the HC, but the interest differential in favor of the home country is only 2 percent, then funds would flow from the home to the foreign country to take advantage of the higher exchange-adjusted returns there. This capital flow will continue until exchange-adjusted returns are equal in the two nations.

 Essentially what the IFE says is that arbitrage between financial markets—in the form of international capital flows—should ensure that the interest differential between any two countries is an **unbiased predictor** of the future change in the spot rate of exchange. This condition does not mean, however, that the interest differential is an especially accurate predictor; it just means that prediction errors tend to cancel out over time. Moreover, an implicit assumption that underlies IFE is that investors view foreign and domestic assets as perfect substitutes. To the extent that this condition is violated (see the discussion on the Fisher effect) and investors require a risk premium (in the form of a higher expected real return) to hold foreign assets, IFE will not hold exactly.

International capital flows bring about consistency between currency forecasts and interest rates.

Empirical Evidence

Empirical evidence indicates that currencies with high (low) interest rates tend to depreciate (appreciate).

As predicted, there is a clear tendency for currencies with high interest rates (for example, Mexico and Brazil) to depreciate and those with low interest rates (for example, Japan and Switzerland) to appreciate. The ability of interest differentials to anticipate currency changes is also supported by several empirical studies that indicate the long-run tendency for these differentials to offset exchange rate changes.[11] The international Fisher effect also appears to hold even in the short run in the case of nations facing very rapid rates of inflation. Thus, at any given time, currencies bearing higher nominal interest rates can reasonably be expected to depreciate relative to currencies bearing lower interest rates.

[11] See, for example, Ian H. Giddy and Gunter Dufey, "The Random Behavior of Flexible Exchange Rates," *Journal of International Business Studies*, Spring 1975, pp. 1–32; and Robert A. Aliber and Clyde P. Stickney, "Accounting Measures of Foreign Exchange Exposure: The Long and Short of It," *The Accounting Review*, January 1975, pp. 44–57.

Despite this apparently convincing evidence for the international Fisher effect, a large body of empirical evidence now indicates that the IFE does not hold up very well in the short run for nations with low to moderate rates of inflation.[12] One possible explanation for this result relies on the existence of a time-varying exchange risk premium. However, this explanation for the failure of the IFE to hold in the short run has been challenged by empirical evidence indicating that the currency risk premium, to the extent it exists, is very small.[13]

A more plausible explanation for the IFE's failure in the short run relies on the nature of the Fisher effect. According to the Fisher effect, changes in the nominal interest differential can be due to changes in either the real interest differential or relative inflationary expectations. These two possibilities have opposite effects on currency values. For example, suppose that the nominal interest differential widens in favor of the United States. If this spread is due to a rise in the real interest rate in the United States relative to that of other countries, the value of the dollar will rise. Alternatively, if the change in the nominal interest differential is caused by an increase in inflationary expectations for the United States, the dollar's value will drop.

> The effect on exchange rates of a change in interest rates depends on whether that change is real or is due to a change in expected inflation.

The key to understanding short-run changes in the value of the dollar or other currency, then, is to distinguish changes in nominal interest rate differentials that are caused by changes in real interest rate differentials from those caused by changes in relative inflation expectations. Historically, changes in the nominal interest differential have been dominated, at times, by changes in the real interest differential; at other times, they have been dominated by changes in relative inflation expectations. Consequently, there is no stable, predictable relationship between changes in the nominal interest differential and exchange rate changes.

4.5 INTEREST RATE PARITY THEORY

Spot and forward rates are closely linked to each other and to interest rates in different currencies through the medium of arbitrage. Specifically, the movement of funds between two currencies to take advantage of interest rate differentials is a major determinant of the spread between forward and spot rates. In fact, the forward discount or premium is closely related to the interest differential between the two currencies.

According to *interest rate parity* (IRP) theory, the currency of the country with a lower interest rate should be at a forward premium in terms of the currency of the country with the higher rate. More specifically, in an efficient market with no transaction costs, the interest differential should be (approximately) equal to the forward differential. When this condition is met, the forward rate is said to be at **interest rate parity**, and equilibrium prevails in the money markets.

> Covered interest arbitrage forces interest rates on different currencies to be at parity with each other.

Interest parity ensures that the return on a hedged (or "covered") foreign investment will just equal the domestic interest rate on investments of identical risk, thereby eliminating the possibility of having a money machine. When this condition holds, the **covered interest differential**—the difference between the domestic interest rate and the hedged foreign rate—is zero. To illustrate this condition, suppose an investor with $1,000,000 to invest for 90 days is trying to decide between investing in U.S. dollars at 8 percent per annum (2 percent for 90 days) or in euros at 6 percent per annum (1.5 percent for 90 days). The current spot rate is €1.13110/$, and the 90-day forward rate is €1.1256/$. Exhibit 4.12 shows that regardless of the investor's currency choice, his

---

[12] Much of this research is summarized in Kenneth A. Froot, "Short Rates and Expected Asset Returns," NBER Working Paper No. 3247, January 1990.

[13] See, for example, Kenneth A. Froot and Jeffrey A. Frankel, "Forward Discount Bias: Is It an Exchange Risk Premium?" *Quarterly Journal of Economics,* February 1989, pp. 139–161.

EXHIBIT 4.12 ● **AN EXAMPLE OF INTEREST RATE PARITY**

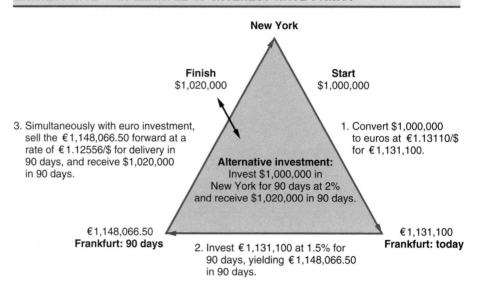

hedged return will be identical. Specifically, $1,000,000 invested in dollars for 90 days will yield $1,000,000 × 1.02 = $1,020,000. Alternatively, if the investor chooses to invest in euros on a hedged basis, he will

1. Convert the $1,000,000 to euros at the spot rate of €1.1311/$. This yields €1,131,100 available for investment.

2. Invest the principal of €1,131,100 at 1.5 percent for 90 days. At the end of 90 days, the investor will have €1,148,066.50.

3. Simultaneously with the other transactions, sell the €1,148,066.50 in principal plus interest forward at a rate of €1.12556/$ for delivery in 90 days. This transaction will yield €1,148,066.50/1.12556 = $1,020,000 in 90 days.

Covered interest differentials tend to disappear through the process known as covered interest arbitrage.

If the covered interest differential between two money markets is nonzero, there is an arbitrage incentive to move money from one market to the other. This movement of money to take advantage of a covered interest differential is known as **covered interest arbitrage**.

ILLUSTRATION   *Covered Interest Arbitrage between London and New York*

Suppose the interest rate on pounds sterling is 12 percent in London, and the interest rate on a comparable dollar investment in New York is 7 percent. The pound spot rate is $1.75, and the one-year forward rate is $1.68. These rates imply a forward discount on sterling of 4 percent [(1.68 − 1.75)/1.75] and a covered yield on sterling approximately equal to 8 percent (12% − 4%). Because there is a covered interest differential in favor of London, funds will flow from New York to London.

To illustrate the profits associated with covered interest arbitrage, we will assume that the borrowing and lending rates are identical and the bid-ask spread in the spot and forward markets is zero. Here are the steps the arbitrageur can take to profit from the discrepancy in rates based on a $1 million transaction. Specifically, as shown in Exhibit 4.13, the arbitrageur will

1. Borrow $1,000,000 in New York at an interest rate of 7 percent. This means that at the end of one year, the arbitrageur must repay principal plus interest of $1,070,000.

2. Immediately convert the $1,000,000 to pounds at the spot rate of £1 = $1.75. This yields £571,428.57 available for investment.

3. Invest the principal of £571,428.57 in London at 12 percent for one year. At the end of the year, the arbitrageur will have £640,000.

4. Simultaneously with the other transactions, sell the £640,000 in principal plus interest forward at a rate of £1 = $1.68 for delivery in one year. This transaction will yield $1,075,200 next year.

5. At the end of the year, collect the £640,000, deliver it to the bank's foreign exchange department in return for $1,075,200, and use $1,070,000 to repay the loan. The arbitrageur will earn $5,200 on this set of transactions.

EXHIBIT 4.13 • **AN EXAMPLE OF COVERED INTEREST ARBITRAGE**

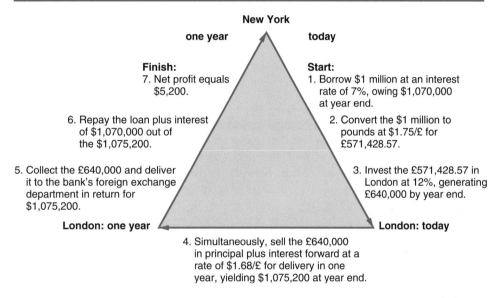

The transactions associated with covered interest arbitrage will affect prices in both the money and foreign exchange markets. In the previous example, as pounds are bought spot and sold forward, boosting the spot rate and lowering the forward rate, the forward discount will tend to widen. Simultaneously, as money flows from New York, interest rates there will tend to increase; at the same time, the inflow of funds to London will depress interest rates there. The process of covered interest arbitrage will continue until interest parity is achieved, unless there is government interference.

If this process is interfered with, covered interest differentials between national money markets will not be arbitraged away. Interference often occurs because many governments regulate and restrict flows of capital across their borders. Moreover, just the risk of controls will be sufficient to yield prolonged deviations from interest rate parity.

The relationship between the spot and forward rates and interest rates in a free market can be shown graphically, as in Exhibit 4.14. Plotted on the vertical axis is the interest differential in favor of the home country. The horizontal axis plots the percentage forward discount (negative) or premium (positive) on the foreign currency relative to the home currency. The interest parity line joins those points for which the forward exchange rate is in equilibrium with the interest differential. For example, if the interest differential

Government intervention can cause persistent covered interest differentials.

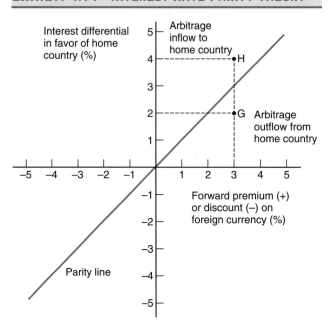

EXHIBIT 4.14 • INTEREST RATE PARITY THEORY

in favor of the foreign country is 2 percent, the currency of that country must be selling at a 2 percent forward discount for equilibrium to exist.

Point G indicates a situation of disequilibrium. Here, the interest differential is 2 percent, whereas the forward premium on the foreign currency is 3 percent. The transfer of funds abroad with exchange risks covered will yield an additional 1 percent annually. At point H, the forward premium remains at 3 percent, but the interest differential increases to 4 percent. Now reversing the flow of funds becomes profitable. The 4 percent higher interest rate more than makes up for the 3 percent loss on the forward exchange transaction, leading to a 1 percent increase in the interest yield.

In reality, the interest parity line is a band because transaction costs, arising from the spread on spot and forward contracts and brokerage fees on security purchases and sales, cause effective yields to be lower than nominal yields. For example, if transaction costs are 0.75 percent, a covered yield differential of only 0.5 percent will not be sufficient to induce a flow of funds. For interest arbitrage to occur, the covered differential must exceed the transaction costs involved.

The covered interest arbitrage relationship can be stated formally. Let e_0 be the current spot rate (dollar value of one unit of foreign currency) and f_1 the end-of-period forward rate. If r_h and r_f are the prevailing interest rates in New York and, say, London, respectively, then one dollar invested in New York will yield $1 + r_h$ at the end of the period; the same dollar invested in London will be worth $(1 + r_f)f_1/e_0$ dollars at maturity. This latter result can be seen as follows: One dollar will convert into $1/e_0$ pounds that, when invested at r_f, will yield $(1 + r_f)/e_0$ pounds at the end of the period. By selling the proceeds forward today, this amount will be worth $(1 + r_f)f_1/e_0$ dollars when the investment matures.

Funds will flow from New York to London if and only if

$$1 + r_h < \frac{(1 + r_f)\, f_1}{e_0}$$

Interest rate parity holds when the interest differential is approximately equal to the forward differential.

Conversely, funds will flow from London to New York if and only if

$$1 + r_h > \frac{(1 + r_f)f_1}{e_0}$$

Interest rate parity holds when there are no covered interest arbitrage opportunities. On the basis of the previous discussion, this no-arbitrage condition can be stated as follows:

$$\frac{1 + r_h}{1 + r_f} = \frac{f_1}{e_0} \tag{4.12}$$

ILLUSTRATION   *Using Interest Rate Parity to Calculate the $/¥ Forward Rate*

The interest rate in the United States is 10 percent; in Japan, the comparable rate is 7 percent. The spot rate for the yen is $0.003800. If interest rate parity holds, what is the 90-day forward rate?

Solution. According to IRP, the 90-day forward rate on the yen, f_{90}, should be $0.003828:

$$f_{90} = \$0.003800 \times \frac{1 + (0.10/4)}{1 + (0.07/4)} = \$0.003828$$

In other words, the 90-day forward Japanese yen should be selling at an annualized premium of about 2.95 percent [$4 \times (0.003828 - 0.003800)/0.0038$].

Interest rate parity is often approximated by Equation 4.13:[14]

$$r_h - r_f = \frac{f_1 - e_0}{e_0} \tag{4.13}$$

In effect, interest rate parity says that *high interest rates on a currency are offset by forward discounts and that low interest rates are offset by forward premiums.*

ILLUSTRATION   *Computing the Covered Interest Differential When Transaction Costs Exist*

Suppose the annualized interest rate on 180-day dollar deposits is 6 7/16 – 5/16%, meaning that dollars can be borrowed at 6 7/16 percent (the ask rate) and lent at 6 5/16 percent (the bid rate). At the same time, the annualized interest rate on 180-day Thai baht deposits is 9 3/8 – 1/8%. Spot and 180-day forward quotes on Thai baht are B 31.5107 – 46/$ (bid of B 31.5107 and ask of B 31.5146) and B 32.1027 – 87/$, respectively. Is there an arbitrage opportunity? Compute the profit using B 10,000,000.

Solution. The only way to determine whether an arbitrage opportunity exists is to examine the two possibilities: Borrow dollars and lend Thai baht or borrow baht and lend dollars, both on a hedged basis. The key is to ensure that you are using the correct bid or ask interest and exchange rates. In this case, it turns out that there is an arbitrage

---

[14] Subtracting 1 from both sides of Equation 4.12 yields $(f_1 - e_0)/e_0 = (r_h - r_f)/(1 + r_f)$. Equation 4.13 follows if r_f is relatively small.

opportunity from borrowing Thai baht and lending dollars. The specific steps to implement this arbitrage are as follows:

1. Borrow B 10,000,000 at the ask rate of 9 3/8 percent for 180 days. This interest rate translates into a 180-day rate of 0.09375/2 = 4.6875%, requiring repayment of B 10,468,750 in principal plus interest at the end of 180 days.

2. Immediately convert the B 10,000,000 to dollars at the spot ask rate of B 31.5146/$ (the baht cost of buying dollars spot). This yields $317,313.25 ($10,000,000/31.5146) available for investment.

3. Invest the principal of $317,313.25 at 0.063125/2 = 3.15625% for 180 days. In six months, this investment will have grown to $327,328.44 ($317,313.25 × 1.0315625).

4. Simultaneously with the other transactions, sell the $327,328.44 in principal plus interest forward at the bid rate of B 32.1027 (the rate at which dollars can be converted into baht) for delivery in 180 days. This transaction will yield B 10,508,126.86 in 180 days.

5. At the end of six months, collect the $327,328.44, deliver it to the bank's foreign exchange department in return for B 10,508,126.86, and use B 10,468,750 of the proceeds to repay the loan. The gain on this set of transactions is B 39,376.86.

High (low) interest rates on a currency are offset by forward discounts (premiums).

Deviations from interest rate parity tend to be small and short-lived.

Transaction costs in the form of bid-ask spreads make the computations more difficult, but the principle is the same: Compute the covered interest differential to see whether there is an arbitrage opportunity.

Empirical Evidence

Interest rate parity is one of the best-documented relationships in international finance. In fact, in the Eurocurrency markets, the forward rate is calculated from the interest differential between the two currencies using the no-arbitrage condition. Deviations from interest parity do occur between national capital markets, however, owing to capital controls (or the threat of them), the imposition of taxes on interest payments to foreigners, and transaction costs. However, as we can see in Exhibit 4.15, these deviations tend to be small and short-lived.

4.6 THE RELATIONSHIP BETWEEN THE FORWARD RATE AND THE FUTURE SPOT RATE

Our current understanding of the workings of the foreign exchange market suggests that, in the absence of government intervention in the market, both the spot rate and the forward rate are influenced heavily by current expectations of future events. The two rates move in tandem, with the link between them based on interest differentials. New information, such as a change in interest rate differentials, is reflected almost immediately in both spot and forward rates.

Suppose a depreciation of the pound sterling is anticipated. Recipients of sterling will begin selling sterling forward, and sterling-area dollar earners will slow their sales of dollars in the forward market. These actions will tend to depress the price of forward sterling. At the same time, banks will probably try to even out their long (net purchaser)

EXHIBIT 4.15 • **UNCOVERED AND COVERED INTEREST RATE DIFFERENTIALS (U.S. $ VERSUS OTHER CURRENCIES)**

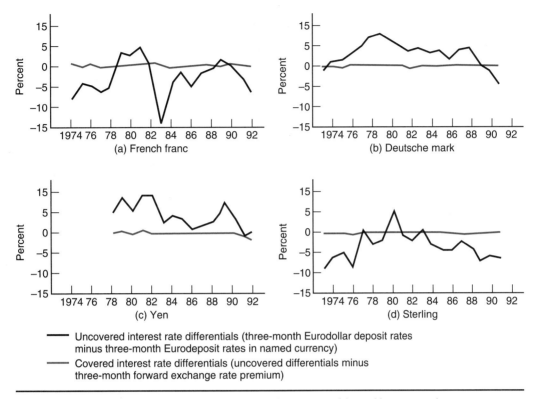

Uncovered interest rate differentials (three-month Eurodollar deposit rates minus three-month Eurodeposit rates in named currency)

Covered interest rate differentials (uncovered differentials minus three-month forward exchange rate premium)

Source: Data from DRI, IMF, and Datastream International reported in "A Survey of the World Economy," *The Economist,* September 19, 1992, p. 23. © 1993 The Economist Newspaper Group, Inc. Used with permission.

positions in forward sterling by selling sterling spot. In addition, sterling-area recipients of dollars will tend to delay converting dollars into sterling, and earners of sterling will speed up their collection and conversion of sterling. In this way, pressure from the forward market is transmitted to the spot market, and vice versa.

> The forward rate should reflect the expected future spot rate on the date of settlement.

Ignoring risk for the moment, equilibrium is achieved only when the forward differential equals the expected change in the exchange rate. At this point, there is no longer any incentive to buy or sell the currency forward. This condition is illustrated in Exhibit 4.16. The vertical axis measures the expected change in the home currency value of the foreign currency, and the horizontal axis shows the forward discount or premium on the foreign currency. Parity prevails at point I, for example, where the expected foreign currency depreciation of 2 percent is just matched by the 2 percent forward discount on the foreign currency. Point J, however, is a position of disequilibrium because the expected 4 percent depreciation of the foreign currency exceeds the 3 percent forward discount on the foreign currency. We would, therefore, expect to see speculators selling the foreign currency forward for home currency, taking a 3 percent discount in the expectation of covering their commitment with 4 percent fewer units of HC.

A formal statement of the **unbiased forward rate (UFR)** is that the forward rate should reflect the expected future spot rate on the date of settlement of the forward contract:

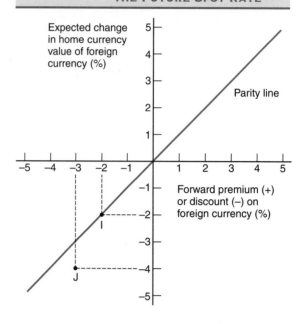

EXHIBIT 4.16 • **RELATIONSHIP BETWEEN THE FORWARD RATE AND THE FUTURE SPOT RATE**

ILLUSTRATION   *Using UFR to Forecast the Future $/€ Spot Rate*

If the 90-day forward rate is €1 = $0.8987, what is the expected value of the euro in 90 days?

Solution. Arbitrage should ensure that the market expects the spot value of the euro in 90 days to be about $0.8987.

$$f_1 = \bar{e}_1 \tag{4.14}$$

where $\bar{e}_1$ is the expected future exchange rate at time 1 (units of home currency per unit of foreign currency) and f_1 is the forward rate for settlement at time 1.

Equation 4.14 can be transformed into the equation reflected in the parity line appearing in Exhibit 4.16, which is that the forward differential equals the expected change in the exchange rate, by subtracting 1 (e_0/e_0) from both sides, where e_0 is the current spot rate (HC per unit of foreign currency):[15]

$$\frac{f_1 - e_0}{e_0} = \frac{\bar{e}_1 - e_0}{e_0} \tag{4.15}$$

If the forward rate includes a currency risk premium, then the forward rate will not equal the expected future spot rate.

Market efficiency requires that people process information and form reasonable expectations; it does not require that $f_1 = \bar{e}_1$. Market efficiency allows for the possibility that risk-averse investors will demand a risk premium on forward contracts, much the same as they demand compensation for bearing the risk of investing in stocks. In this case, the forward rate will not reflect exclusively the expectation of the future spot rate.

---

[15] Note that this condition can be derived through a combination of the international Fisher effect and interest parity theory. Specifically, interest rate parity says that the interest differential equals the forward differential, whereas the IFE says that the interest differential equals the expected change in the spot rate. Things equal to the same thing are equal to each other, so the forward differential will equal the expected exchange rate change if both interest rate parity and the IFE hold.

The principal argument against the existence of a risk premium is that currency risk is largely diversifiable. If foreign exchange risk can be diversified away, no risk premium need be paid for holding a forward contract; the forward rate and expected future spot rate will be approximately equal. Ultimately, therefore, the unbiased nature of forward rates is an empirical, and not a theoretical, issue.

Empirical Evidence

A number of studies have examined the relation between forward rates and future spot rates.[16] Of course, it would be unrealistic to expect a perfect correlation between forward and future spot rates because the future spot rate will be influenced by events, such as an oil crisis, that can be forecast only imperfectly, if at all.

Forward rates tend to be unbiased, though inaccurate, predictors of future spot rates.

Nonetheless, the general conclusion from early studies was that forward rates are unbiased predictors of future spot rates. But more recent studies, using more powerful econometric techniques, argue that the forward rate is a biased predictor, probably because of a risk premium.[17] However, the premium appears to change signs—being positive at some times and negative at other times—and averages near zero. This result, which casts doubt on the risk premium story, should not be surprising given that testing the unbiased nature of the forward rate is equivalent to testing the international Fisher effect (assuming covered interest parity holds).

In effect, we wind up with the same conclusions: Over time, currencies bearing a forward discount (higher interest rate) depreciate relative to currencies with a forward premium (lower interest rate). That is, on average, the forward rate is unbiased. On the other hand, at any point in time, the forward rate appears to be a biased predictor of the future spot rate. More specifically, the evidence indicates that one can profit on average by buying currencies selling at a forward discount (that is, currencies whose interest rate is relatively high) and selling currencies trading at a forward premium (that is, currencies whose interest rate is relatively low). Nonetheless, research also suggests that this evidence of forward market inefficiency may be difficult to profit from on a risk-adjusted basis. One reason is the existence of what is known as the peso problem.

The peso problem can invalidate statistical inferences based on data from periods in which anticipated events did not materialize.

The **peso problem** refers to the possibility that during the time period studied, investors anticipated significant events that did not materialize, thereby invalidating statistical inferences based on data drawn from that period. The term derives from the experience of Mexico during the period 1955–1975. During this entire period, the peso was fixed at a rate of $0.125, yet continually sold at a forward discount because investors anticipated a large peso devaluation. This devaluation eventually occurred in 1976, thereby validating the prediction embedded in the forward rate (and relative interest rates). However, those who limited their analysis on the relation between forward and future spot rates to data drawn only from the 1955–1975 period would have falsely concluded that the forward rate was a biased predictor of the future spot rate.

In their comprehensive survey of the research on bias in forward rates, Froot and Thaler conclude, "Whether or not there is really money to be made based on the apparent inefficiency of foreign exchange markets, it is worth emphasizing that the risk-return trade-off for a single currency is not very attractive. ... Although much of the risk in these [single currency] strategies may be diversifiable in principle, more complex diversified strategies may be much more costly, unreliable, or difficult to execute."[18] This evidence

[16] See, for example, Giddy and Dufey, "The Random Behavior of Flexible Exchange Rates," and Bradford Cornell, "Spot Rates, Forward Rates, and Market Efficiency," *Journal of Financial Economics*, January 1977, pp. 55–65.

[17] See, for example, Lars P. Hansen and Robert J. Hodrick, "Forward Rates as Optimal Predictions of Future Spot Rates," *Journal of Political Economy*, October 1980, pp. 829–853.

[18] Kenneth A. Froot and Richard H. Thaler, "Anomalies: Foreign Exchange," *Journal of Economic Perspectives*, Summer 1990, pp. 179–192.

of bias suggests that the selective use of forward contracts—sell forward if the currency is at a forward premium and buy it forward if it is selling at a discount—may increase expected profits but at the expense of higher risk.

4.7 CURRENCY FORECASTING

Forecasting exchange rates has become an occupational hazard for financial executives of multinational corporations. The potential for periodic—and unpredictable—government intervention makes currency forecasting all the more difficult. But this difficulty has not dampened the enthusiasm for currency forecasts or the willingness of economists and others to supply them. Unfortunately, however, enthusiasm and willingness are not sufficient conditions for success.

Requirements for Successful Currency Forecasting

Currency forecasting can lead to consistent profits only if the forecaster meets at least one of the following four criteria.[19] The successful forecaster

- Has exclusive use of a superior forecasting model
- Has consistent access to information before other investors
- Exploits small, temporary deviations from equilibrium
- Can predict the nature of government intervention in the foreign exchange market

Successful currency forecasting is most likely when governments are willing to spend money to achieve noneconomic objectives.

The first two conditions are self-correcting. Successful forecasting breeds imitators, while early access to information is unlikely to be sustained in the highly informed world of international finance. The third situation is how foreign exchange traders actually earn their living, but deviations from equilibrium are not likely to last long. The fourth situation is the one worth searching out. Countries that insist on managing their exchange rates and are willing to take losses to achieve their target rates present speculators with potentially profitable opportunities. Simply put, consistently profitable predictions are possible in the long run only if it is not necessary to outguess the market to win.

As a general rule, in a fixed-rate system, the forecaster must focus on the governmental decision-making structure because the decision to devalue or revalue at a given time is clearly political. Under the Bretton Woods system, for example, many speculators did quite well by "stepping into the shoes of the key decision makers" to forecast their likely behavior. The basic forecasting methodology in a fixed-rate system, therefore, involves first ascertaining the pressure on a currency to devalue or revalue, and then determining how long the nation's political leaders can, and will, persist with this particular level of disequilibrium. Exhibit 4.17 depicts a five-step procedure for performing this analysis. In the case of a floating-rate system, where government intervention is sporadic or nonexistent, currency prognosticators have the choice of using either market- or model-based forecasts, neither of which guarantees success.

Market-Based Forecasts

Interest rates and forward rates contain implicit currency forecasts.

So far, we have identified several equilibrium relationships that should exist between exchange rates and interest rates. The empirical evidence on these relationships implies that, in general, the financial markets of developed countries efficiently incorporate expected currency changes in the cost of money and forward exchange. This means that currency forecasts can be obtained by extracting the predictions already embodied in interest and forward rates.

---

[19] These criteria were suggested by Giddy and Dufey, "The Random Behavior of Flexible Exchange Rates."

EXHIBIT 4.17 ● FORCASTING IN A FIXED-RATE SYSTEM

Forward Rates   **Market-based forecasts** of exchange rate changes can be derived most simply from current forward rates. Specifically, f_1—the forward rate for one period from now—will usually suffice for an unbiased estimate of the spot rate as of that date. In other words, f_1 should equal $\bar{e}_1$, where $\bar{e}_1$ is the expected future spot rate.

Interest Rates   Although forward rates provide simple and easy-to-use currency fore-casts, their forecasting horizon is limited to about one year because of the general absence of longer-term forward contracts. Interest rate differentials can be used to supply exchange rate predictions beyond one year. For example, suppose five-year interest rates on dollars and euros are 6 percent and 5 percent, respectively. If the current spot rate for the euro is $0.90 and the (unknown) value of the euro in five years is e_5, then $1.00 invested today in euros will be worth $(1.05)^5 e_5 / 0.90$ dollars at the end of five years; if invested in the dollar security, it will be worth $(1.06)^5$ in five years. The market's forecast of e_5 can be found by assuming that investors demand equal returns on dollar and euro securities, or

$$\frac{(1.05)^5 e_5}{0.90} = (1.06)^5$$

Thus, the five-year euro spot rate implied by the relative interest rates is $e_5 = \$0.9437$ $(0.90 \times 1.06^5 / 1.05^5)$.

Model-Based Forecasts

The two principal model-based approaches to currency prediction are known as funda-mental analysis and technical analysis. Each approach has its advocates and detractors.

Fundamental Analysis   **Fundamental analysis** is the most common approach to generat-ing **model-based forecasts** of future exchange rates. It relies on painstaking examination of the macroeconomic variables and policies that are likely to influence a currency's prospects. The variables examined include relative inflation and interest rates, national income growth, and changes in money supplies. The interpretation of these variables and their implications for future exchange rates depend on the analyst's model of exchange rate determination.

The simplest form of fundamental analysis involves the use of PPP. We have previ-ously seen the value of PPP in explaining exchange rate changes. Its application in cur-rency forecasting is straightforward.

 ILLUSTRATION   *Using PPP to Forecast the South African Rand's Future Spot Rate*

The U.S. inflation rate is expected to average about 4 percent annually, and the South African rate of inflation is expected to average about 9 percent annually. If the current spot rate for the rand is $0.008, what is the expected spot rate in two years?

Solution. According to PPP (Equation 4.3), the expected spot rate for the rand in two years is $\$0.008 \times (1.04/1.09)^2 = \$0.00728$.

Most analysts use more complicated forecasting models whose analysis usually cen-ters on how the different macroeconomic variables are likely to affect the demand and supply for a given foreign currency. The currency's future value is then determined by esti-mating the exchange rate at which supply just equals demand—when any current-account imbalance is just matched by a net capital flow.

Forecasting based on fundamental analysis has inherent difficulties. First, you must be able to select the right fundamentals; then you must be able to forecast them—itself a problematic task (think about forecasting interest rates); finally, your forecasts of the fun-damentals must differ from those of the market. Otherwise, the exchange rate will have already discounted the anticipated change in the fundamentals. Another difficulty that forecasters face is the variability in the lag between when changes in fundamentals are forecast to occur and when they actually affect the exchange rate.

Despite these difficulties, Robert Cumby developed a sophisticated regression model—incorporating forward premiums along with real variables such as relative inflation rates and current-account balances—that yielded predictable return differentials (between investing in uncovered foreign deposits and domestic deposits) on the order of 10 percent to 30 percent per annum.[20]

Technical Analysis   **Technical analysis** is the antithesis of fundamental analysis in that it focuses exclusively on past price and volume movements—while totally ignoring economic and political factors—to forecast currency winners and losers. Success depends on whether technical analysts can discover price patterns that repeat themselves and are, therefore, useful for forecasting.

> Technical analysis
> depends on finding
> recurring patterns in
> exchange rate move-
> ments to forecast
> currency
> movements.

There are two primary methods of technical analysis: **charting** and **trend analysis**. Chartists examine bar charts or use more sophisticated computer-based extrapolation techniques to find recurring price patterns. They then issue buy or sell recommendations if prices diverge from their past pattern. Trend-following systems seek to identify price trends via various mathematical computations.

Model Evaluation

> Currency forecasting
> models rely on
> either fundamental
> analysis or technical
> analysis.

The possibility that either fundamental or technical analysis can be used to profitably forecast exchange rates is inconsistent with the efficient market hypothesis, which says that current exchange rates reflect all publicly available information. Because markets are forward-looking, exchange rates will fluctuate randomly as market participants assess and then react to new information, much as security and commodity prices in other asset markets respond to news. Thus, exchange rate movements are unpredictable; otherwise, it would be possible to earn arbitrage profits. Such profits could not persist in a market—such as the foreign exchange market—that is characterized by free entry and exit and an almost unlimited amount of money, time, and energy that participants are willing to commit in pursuit of profit opportunities.

In addition to the theoretical doubts surrounding forecasting models, a variety of statistical and technical assumptions underlying these models have been called into question as well. For all practical purposes, however, the quality of a currency forecasting model must be viewed in relative terms. That is, a model can be said to be "good" if it is better than alternative means of forecasting currency values. Ultimately, a currency forecasting model is "good" only to the extent that its predictions will lead to better decisions.

Certainly interest differentials and/or forward rates provide low-cost alternative forecasts of future exchange rates. At a minimum, any currency forecasting model should be able to consistently outperform the market's estimates of currency changes. In other words, one relevant question is whether *profitable* decisions can be made in the forward and/or money markets by using any of these models.

Currency forecasters charge for their services, so researchers periodically evaluate the performance of these services to determine whether the forecasts are worth their cost. The evaluation criteria generally fall into two categories: accuracy and correctness. The accuracy measure focuses on the deviations between the actual and the forecasted rates, and the correctness measure examines whether or not the forecast predicts the right direction of the change in exchange rates.

> Currency forecasts
> should be linked to
> economic decisions
> to see whether prof-
> itable forecasts are
> possible.

An accurate forecast may not be correct in predicting the direction of change, and a correct forecast may not be very accurate. The two criteria are sometimes in conflict. Which of these two criteria should be used in evaluation depends on how the forecasts are to be used.

An analysis of forecasting errors—the difference between the forecast and actual exchange rate—will tell us little about the profit-making potential of econometric forecasts. Instead, we need to link these forecasts to actual decisions and then calculate the

---

[20] Robert Cumby, "Is It Risk? Deviations from Uncovered Interest Parity," *Journal of Monetary Economics*, September 1988, pp. 279–300.

resulting profits or losses. For example, if the forecasts are to be used to decide whether or not to hedge with forward contracts, the relative predictive abilities of the forecasting services can be evaluated by using the following decision rule:

$$\text{If } f_1 > \bar{e}_1 \text{, sell forward.}$$
$$\text{If } f_1 < \bar{e}_1 \text{, buy forward.}$$

where f_1 is the forward rate and e_1 is the forecasted spot rate at the forward contract's settlement date. In other words, if the forecasted rate is below the forward rate, the currency should be sold forward; if the forecasted rate is above the forward rate, the currency should be bought forward.

The percentage profit (loss) realized from this strategy equals $100[(f_1 - e_1)/e_1]$ when $f_1 > e_1$, and equals $100[(e_1 - f_1)/e_1]$ when $f_1 < \bar{e}_1$, where e_1 is the *actual* spot rate being forecasted.

ILLUSTRATION   *The Distinction Between an Accurate Forecast and a Profitable Forecast*

Suppose that the ¥/$ spot rate is currently ¥110/$. A 90-day forecast puts the exchange rate at ¥102/$; the 90-day forward rate is ¥109/$. According to our decision rule, we should buy the yen forward. If we buy $1 million worth of yen forward and the actual rate turns out to be ¥108/$, then our decision will yield a profit of $9,259 [(109,000,000 − 108,000,000)/108]. In contrast, if the forecasted value of the yen had been ¥111/$, we would have sold yen forward and lost $9,259. Thus, an accurate forecast, off by less than 3 percent (3/108), leads to a loss; and a less accurate forecast, off by almost 6 percent (6/108), leads to a profitable decision.

When deciding on a new investment or planning a revised pricing strategy, however, the most critical attribute of a forecasting model is its accuracy. In the latter case, the second forecast would be judged superior.

> There is some evidence that currency forecasting can lead to consistently profitable decisions, but this evidence may be misleading.

Despite the theoretical skepticism over successful currency forecasting, a study of fourteen forecast advisory services by Richard Levich indicates that the profits associated with using several of these forecasts seem too good to be explained by chance.[21] Of course, if the forward rate contains a risk premium, these returns will have to be adjusted for the risks borne by speculators. It is also questionable whether currency forecasters would continue selling their information rather than act on it themselves if they truly believed it could yield excess risk-adjusted returns. That being said, it is hard to attribute expected return differentials of up to 30 percent annually (Cumby's results) to currency risk when the estimated equity risk premium on the U.S. stock exchange is only about 8 percent for a riskier investment.

Of course, if you take a particular data sample and run every possible regression, you are likely to find some apparently profitable forecasting model. But that does not mean it is a reliable guide to the future. To control for this tendency to "data mine," you must do *out-of-sample forecasting.* That is, you must see if your model forecasts well enough to be profitable in time periods not included in the original data sample. Hence, the profitable findings of Cumby and others may stem from the fact that their results are based on the in-sample performance of their regressions. That is, they used the same data sample both to estimate their model and to check its forecasting ability. Indeed, Richard Meese and Kenneth Rogoff concluded that sophisticated models of exchange rate determination make

[21] Richard M. Levich, "The Use and Analysis of Foreign Exchange Forecasts: Current Issues and Evidence," paper presented at the Euromoney Treasury Consultancy Program, New York, September 4–5, 1980.

poor forecasts.[22] Their conclusion is similar to that of Jeffrey Frankel, who—after reviewing the research on currency forecasting—stated that

> *the proportion of exchange rate changes that are forecastable in any manner—by the forward discount, interest rate differential, survey data, or models based on macroeconomic fundamentals—appears to be not just low, but almost zero.*[23]

Frankel's judgment is consistent with the existence of an efficient market in which excess risk-adjusted returns have a half-life measured in minutes, if not seconds.

Forecasting Controlled Exchange Rates

Black-market exchange rates are a useful indicator of future changes in controlled currencies.

A major problem in currency forecasting is that the widespread existence of exchange controls, as well as restrictions on imports and capital flows, often masks the true pressures on a currency to devalue. In such situations, forward markets and capital markets are invariably nonexistent or subject to such stringent controls that interest and forward differentials are of little practical use in providing market-based forecasts of exchange rate changes. An alternative forecasting approach in such a controlled environment is to use **black-market exchange rates** as useful indicators of devaluation pressure on the nation's currency.

The black-market rate tends to be a good indicator of where the official rate is likely to go if the monetary authorities give in to market pressure. It seems to be most accurate in forecasting the official rate one month ahead and is progressively less accurate as a forecaster of the future official rate for longer time periods.[24]

4.8 SUMMARY AND CONCLUSIONS

In this chapter, we examined five relationships, or parity conditions, that should apply to spot rates, inflation rates, and interest rates in different currencies: purchasing power parity (PPP), the Fisher effect (FE), the international Fisher effect (IFE), interest rate parity (IRP) theory, and the forward rate as an unbiased forecast of the future spot rate (UFR). These parity conditions follow from the law of one price, the notion that in the absence of market imperfections, arbitrage ensures that exchange-adjusted prices of identical traded goods and financial assets are within transaction costs worldwide.

The technical description of these five equilibrium relationships is summarized as follows:

- Purchasing power parity

$$\frac{e_1}{e_0} = \frac{1 + i_h}{1 + i_f}$$

where

e_1 = the home currency value of the foreign currency at time 1

e_0 = the home currency value of the foreign currency at time 0

i_h = the domestic inflation rate

i_f = the foreign inflation rate

[22] Richard A. Meese and Kenneth Rogoff, "Empirical Exchange Rate Models of the Seventies: Do They Fit Out of Sample?" *Journal of International Economics 14*, no. 1/2 (1983): 3–24.

[23] Jeffrey Frankel, "Flexible Exchange Rates: Experience Versus Theory," *Journal of Portfolio Management*, Winter 1989, pp. 45–54.

[24] See, for example, Ian Giddy, "Black Market Exchange Rates as a Forecasting Tool," Working Paper, Columbia University, May 1978.

- Fisher effect

$$1 + r = (1 + a)(1 + i)$$

where

r = the nominal rate of interest
a = the real rate of interest
i = the rate of expected inflation

- Generalized version of Fisher effect

$$\frac{1 + r_h}{1 + r_f} = \frac{1 + i_h}{1 + i_f}$$

where

r_h = the home currency interest rate
r_f = the foreign currency interest rate

- International Fisher effect

$$\frac{1 + r_h}{1 + r_f} = \frac{\bar{e}_1}{e_0}$$

where

$\bar{e}_1$ = the expected home currency value of the foreign currency at time 1

- Interest rate parity

$$\frac{1 + r_h}{1 + r_f} = \frac{f_1}{e_0}$$

where

f_1 = the forward rate at time 0 for delivery of one unit of foreign currency at time 1

- Forward rate as an unbiased predictor of the future spot rate

$$f_1 = \bar{e}_1$$

Despite the mathematical precision with which these parity conditions are expressed, they are only approximations of reality. A variety of factors can lead to significant and prolonged deviations from parity. For example, both currency risk and inflation risk may cause real interest rates to differ across countries. Similarly, various shocks can cause the real exchange rate—defined as the nominal, or actual, exchange rate adjusted for changes in the relative purchasing power of each currency since some base period—to change over time. Moreover, the short-run relation between changes in the nominal interest differential and changes in the exchange rate is not so easily determined. The lack of definiteness in this relation stems from the differing effects on exchange rates of purely nominal interest rate changes and real interest rate changes.

We examined the concept of the real exchange rate in more detail as well. The real exchange rate at time 1, e_1', incorporates both the nominal exchange rate between two currencies and the inflation rates in both countries. It is defined as follows:

- Real exchange rate

$$e_1' = e_t \frac{P_f}{P_h}$$

where

P_f = the foreign price level at time 1 indexed to 100 at time 0

P_h = the home price level at time 1 indexed to 100 at time 0

We then analyzed a series of forecasting models that purport to outperform the market's own forecasts of future exchange rates as embodied in interest and forward differentials. We concluded that the foreign exchange market is no different from any other financial market in its susceptibility to profitable predictions.

Those who have inside information about events that will affect the value of a currency or a security should benefit handsomely. Those who do not have this access will have to trust either to luck or to the existence of a market imperfection, such as government intervention, to assure themselves of above-average, risk-adjusted profits. Given the widespread availability of information and the many knowledgeable participants in the foreign exchange market, only the latter situation—government manipulation of exchange rates—holds the promise of superior risk-adjusted returns from currency forecasting. When governments spend money to control exchange rates, this money flows into the hands of private participants who bet against the government. The trick is to predict government actions.

QUESTIONS

1. a. What is purchasing power parity?
   b. What are some reasons for deviations from purchasing power parity?
   c. Under what circumstances can purchasing power parity be applied?

2. One proposal to stabilize the international monetary system involves setting exchange rates at their purchasing power parity rates. Once exchange rates were correctly aligned (according to PPP), each nation would adjust its monetary policy so as to maintain them. What problems might arise from using the PPP rate as a guide to the equilibrium exchange rate?

3. Suppose the dollar/rupiah rate is fixed but Indonesian prices are rising faster than U.S. prices. Is the Indonesian rupiah appreciating or depreciating in real terms?

4. Comment on the following statement. "It makes sense to borrow during times of high inflation because you can repay the loan in cheaper dollars."

5. Which is likely to be higher, a 150 percent ruble return in Russia or a 15 percent dollar return in the United States?

6. The interest rate in England is 12 percent; in Switzerland it is 5 percent. What are possible reasons for this interest rate differential? What is the most likely reason?

7. Over the period 1982–1988, Peru and Chile stand out as countries whose interest rates were not consistent with their inflation experience. Specifically, Peru's inflation and interest rates averaged about 125 percent and 8 percent, respectively, over this period, whereas Chile's inflation and interest rates averaged about 22 percent and 38 percent, respectively.
   a. How would you characterize the real interest rates of Peru and Chile (e.g., close to zero, highly positive, highly negative)?
   b. What might account for Peru's low interest rate relative to its high inflation rate? What are the likely consequences of this low interest rate?
   c. What might account for Chile's high interest rate relative to its inflation rate? What are the likely consequences of this high interest rate?
   d. During this same period, Peru had a small interest differential and yet a large average exchange rate change. How would you reconcile this experience with the international Fisher effect and with your answer to Part b?

8. Over the period 1982–1988, a number of countries (e.g., Pakistan, Hungary, Venezuela) had a small or negative interest rate differential and a large average annual depreciation against the dollar. How would you explain these data? Can you reconcile these data with the international Fisher effect?

9. What factors might lead to persistent covered interest arbitrage opportunities among countries?

10. In early 1989, Japanese interest rates were about 4 percentage points below U.S. rates. The wide difference between Japanese and U.S. interest rates prompted some U.S. real estate developers to borrow in yen to finance their projects. Comment on this strategy.

11. Recently, Japanese and German interest rates rose while U.S. rates fell. At the same time, the yen and euro fell against the U.S. dollar. What might explain the divergent trends in interest rates?

12. In late December 1990, one-year German Treasury bills yielded 9.1 percent, whereas one-year U.S. Treasury bills yielded 6.9 percent. At the same time, the inflation rate during 1990 was 6.3 percent in the United States, double the German rate of 3.1 percent.
    a. Are these inflation and interest rates consistent with the Fisher effect?
    b. What might explain this difference in interest rates between the United States and Germany?

13. The spot rate on the euro is $1.09, and the 180-day forward rate is $1.11. What are possible reasons for the difference between the two rates?

14. German government bonds, or Bunds, currently are paying higher interest rates than comparable U.S. Treasury bonds. Suppose the ECB eases the money supply to drive down interest rates. How is an American investor in Bunds likely to fare?

15. In 1993 and early 1994, Turkish banks borrowed abroad at relatively low interest rates to fund their lending at home. The banks earned high profits because rampant inflation in Turkey forced up domestic interest rates. At the same time, Turkey's central bank was intervening in the foreign exchange market to maintain the value of the Turkish lira. Comment on the Turkish banks' funding strategy.

PROBLEMS

1. From base price levels of 100 in 2000, Japanese and U.S. price levels in 2003 stood at 102 and 106, respectively.
   a. If the 2000 $:¥ exchange rate was $0.007692, what should the exchange rate be in 2003?
   b. In fact, the exchange rate in 2003 was ¥ 1 = $0.008696. What might account for the discrepancy? (Price levels were measured using the consumer price index.)

2. Two countries, the United States and England, produce only one good, wheat. Suppose the price of wheat is $3.25 in the United States and is £1.35 in England.
   a. According to the law of one price, what should the $:£ spot exchange rate be?
   b. Suppose the price of wheat over the next year is expected to rise to $3.50 in the United States and to £1.60 in England. What should the one-year $:£ forward rate be?
   c. If the U.S. government imposes a tariff of $0.50 per bushel on wheat imported from England, what is the maximum possible change in the spot exchange rate that could occur?

3. If expected inflation is 100 percent and the real required return is 5 percent, what should the nominal interest rate be according to the Fisher effect?

4. In early 1996, the short-term interest rate in France was 3.7 percent, and forecast French inflation was 1.8 percent. At the same time, the short-term German interest rate was 2.6 percent and forecast German inflation was 1.6 percent.
   a. Based on these figures, what were the real interest rates in France and Germany?
   b. To what would you attribute any discrepancy in real rates between France and Germany?

5. In July, the one-year interest rate is 12 percent on British pounds and 9 percent on U.S. dollars.
   a. If the current exchange rate is $1.63:£1, what is the expected future exchange rate in one year?
   b. Suppose a change in expectations regarding future U.S. inflation causes the expected future spot rate to decline to $1.52:£1. What should happen to the U.S. interest rate?

6. Suppose that in Japan the interest rate is 8 percent and inflation is expected to be 3 percent. Meanwhile, the expected inflation rate in France is 12 percent, and the English interest rate is 14 percent. To the nearest whole number, what is the best estimate of the one-year forward exchange premium (discount) at which the pound will be selling relative to the euro?

7. Chase Econometrics has just published projected inflation rates for the United States and Germany for the next five years. U.S. inflation is expected to be 10 percent per year, and German inflation is expected to be 4 percent per year.
   a. If the current exchange rate is $0.95/€, forecast the exchange rates for the next five years.
   b. Suppose that U.S. inflation over the next five years turns out to average 3.2 percent, German inflation averages 1.5 percent, and the exchange rate in five years is $0.99/€. What has happened to the real value of the euro over this five-year period?

8. During 1995, the Mexican peso exchange rate rose from Mex$5.33/U.S.$ to Mex$7.64/U.S.$. At the same time, U.S. inflation was approximately 3 percent in contrast to Mexican inflation of about 48.7 percent.
   a. By how much did the nominal value of the peso change during 1995?
   b. By how much did the real value of the peso change over this period?

9. Suppose three-year deposit rates on Eurodollars and Eurofrancs (Swiss) are 12 percent and 7 percent, respectively. If the current spot rate for the Swiss franc

is $0.3985, what is the spot rate implied by these interest rates for the franc three years from now?

10. Assume that the interest rate is 16 percent on pounds sterling and 7 percent on euros. At the same time, inflation is running at an annual rate of 3 percent in Germany and 9 percent in England.

   a. If the euro is selling at a one-year forward premium of 10 percent against the pound, is there an arbitrage opportunity? Explain.

   b. What is the real interest rate in Germany? in England?

   c. Suppose that during the year the exchange rate changes from €1.8:£1 to €1.77:£1. What are the real costs to a German company of borrowing pounds? Contrast this cost to its real cost of borrowing euros.

   d. What are the real costs to a British firm of borrowing euros? Contrast this cost to its real cost of borrowing pounds.

11. Suppose the Eurosterling rate is 15 percent and the Eurodollar rate is 11.5 percent. What is the forward premium on the dollar? Explain.

12. Suppose the spot rates for the euro, pound sterling, and Swiss franc are $0.92, $1.13, and $0.38, respectively. The associated 90-day interest rates (annualized) are 8 percent, 16 percent, and 4 percent; the U.S. 90-day rate (annualized) is 12 percent. What is the 90-day forward rate on an ACU (ACU 1 = €1 + £1 + SFr 1) if interest parity holds?

13. Suppose that three-month interest rates (annualized) in Japan and the United States are 7 percent and 9 percent, respectively. If the spot rate is ¥142:$1 and the 90-day forward rate is ¥139:$1,

   a. Where would you invest?

   b. Where would you borrow?

14. Here are some prices in the international money markets:

Spot rate	= $0.95: €
Forward rate (one year)	= $0.97: €
Interest rate (€)	= 7% per year
Interest rate ($)	= 9% per year

   a. Assuming no transaction costs or taxes exist, do covered arbitrage profits exist in this situation? Describe the flows.

   b. Suppose now that transaction costs in the foreign exchange market equal 0.25 percent per transaction. Do unexploited covered arbitrage profit opportunities still exist?

   c. Suppose no transaction costs exist. Let the capital gains tax on currency profits equal 25 percent and the ordinary income tax on interest income equal 50 percent. In this situation, do covered arbitrage profits exist? How large are they? Describe the transactions required to exploit these profits.

15. Suppose today's exchange rate is $1.05/€. The six-month interest rates on dollars and euros are 6 percent and 3 percent, respectively. The six-month forward rate is $1.0478. A foreign exchange advisory service has predicted that the euro will appreciate to $1.0790 within six months.

   a. How would you use forward contracts to profit in the above situation?

   b. How would you use money-market instruments (borrowing and lending) to profit?

   c. Which alternatives (forward contracts or money market instruments) would you prefer? Why?

BIBLIOGRAPHY

Aliber, Robert A., and Clyde P. Stickney. "Accounting Measures of Foreign Exchange Exposure: The Long and Short of It." *The Accounting Review,* January 1975, pp. 44–57.

Cornell, Bradford Cornell. "Spot Rates, Forward Rates, and Market Efficiency," *Journal of Financial Economics,* January 1977, pp. 55–65.

Dufey, Gunter, and Ian H. Giddy. "Forecasting Exchange Rates in a Floating World." *Euromoney,* November 1975, pp. 28–35.

_____. *The International Money Market.* Englewood Cliffs, N.J.: Prentice Hall, 1978.

Frankel, Jeffrey. "Flexible Exchange Rates: Experience Versus Theory," *Journal of Portfolio Management,* Winter 1989, pp. 45–54.

Froot, Kenneth A., and Jeffrey A. Frankel. "Forward Discount Bias: Is It an Exchange Risk Premium?" *Quarterly Journal of Economics,* February 1989, pp. 139–161.

Froot, Kenneth A., and Richard H. Thaler. "Anomalies: Foreign Exchange." *Journal of Economic Perspectives,* Summer 1990, pp. 179–192.

Gailliot, Henry J. "Purchasing Power Parity as an Explanation of Long-Term Changes in Exchange Rates." *Journal of Money, Credit, and Banking,* August 1971, pp. 348–357.

Giddy, Ian H. "An Integrated Theory of Exchange Rate Equilibrium." *Journal of Financial and Quantitative Analysis,* December 1976, pp. 883–892.

_____. "Black Market Exchange Rates as a Forecasting Tool," Working Paper, Columbia University, May 1978.

Giddy, Ian H., and Gunter Dufey. "The Random Behavior of Flexible Exchange Rates," *Journal of International Business Studies,* Spring 1975, pp. 1–32.

Hansen, Lars P. and Robert J. Hodrick. "Forward Rates as Optimal Predictions of Future Spot Rates," *Journal of Political Economy,* October 1980, pp. 829–853.

Levich, Richard M. "Analyzing the Accuracy of Foreign Exchange Advisory Services: Theory and Evidence." In *Exchange Risk and Exposure,* Richard Levich and Clas Wihlborg, eds. Lexington, Mass.: D.C. Heath, 1980.

Lothian, James R., and Mark P. Taylor. "Real Exchange Rate Behavior: The Recent Float from the Perspective of the Past Two Centuries," *Journal of Political Economy,* June 1996.

Mishkin, Frederick S. "Are Real Interest Rates Equal across Countries? An International Investigation of Parity Conditions." *Journal of Finance,* December 1984, pp. 1345–1357.

Modjtahedi, Baghar. "Dynamics of Real Interest Rate Differentials: An Empirical Investigation." *European Economic Review 32,* no. 6, 1988, pp. 1191–1211.

Officer, Lawrence H. "The Purchasing-Power-Parity Theory of Exchange Rates: A Review Article." *IMF Staff Papers,* March 1976, pp. 1–60.

Shapiro, Alan C. "What Does Purchasing Power Parity Mean?" *Journal of International Money and Finance,* December 1983, pp. 295–318.

Strongin, Steve. "International Credit Market Connections." *Economic Perspectives,* July/August 1990, pp. 2–10.

Throop, Adrian. "International Financial Market Integration and Linkages of National Interest Rates." *Federal Reserve Bank of San Francisco Economic Review,* no. 3, 1994, pp. 3–18.

INTERNET RESOURCES

www.oecd.org/topicstatsportal/0,2647,en_2825_495691_1_1_1_1_1,00.html Contains data on PPP exchange rates for the OECD countries going back to 1970. The PPP exchange rate data are presented in a spreadsheet that can be saved.

www.oanda.com Contains current exchange rates along with currency forecasts and news.

mwprices.ft.com/custom/ft-com/html-marketsDataTools.asp Web site of the *Financial Times* that contains data on short-term Eurocurrency interest rates for the U.S. dollar, euro, Swiss franc, yen, pound, and several other currencies. This Web site also links to worldwide exchange rate data.

INTERNET EXERCISES

1. Using data from the OECD, compare the most recent PPP exchange rates for the pound, yen, and euro with their nominal exchange rates. What differences do you observe? What accounts for these differences?

2. Using OECD data, plot the PPP exchange rates for the pound, yen, Mexican peso, and Korean won. Have these PPP exchange gone up or down over time? What accounts for the changes in these PPP exchange rate over time?

3. Find the 90-day interest rates from the *Financial Times* Web site for the dollar, yen, euro, and pound. Are the yield differentials on these currencies consistent with the forward rates reported in the *Wall Street Journal*? What might account for any differences?

4. Examine forecasts from www.oanda.com for the pound, yen, and euro.

    a. Which of these currencies are forecast to appreciate and which to depreciate?

    b. Compare these forecasts to the forward rates for the same maturity. Are the predicted exchange rates greater or less than the corresponding forward rates?

    c, Compare these forecasts to the actual exchange rates. How accurate were these forecasts?

    d. If you had followed these forecasts (by buying forward when the forecasted exchange rate exceeded the forward rate and selling forward when it was below the forward rate), would you have made or lost money?

5. How have forward premiums and discounts relative to the dollar changed over annual intervals during the past five years for the Japanese yen, British pound, and euro? Use beginning-of-year data.

THE BALANCE OF PAYMENTS AND INTERNATIONAL ECONOMIC LINKAGES

I had a trade deficit in 1986 because I took a vacation in France. I didn't worry about it; I enjoyed it.

Herbert Stein
Chairman of the Council of Economic
Advisors under Presidents Nixon and Ford

We have almost a crisis in trade and this is the year Congress will try to turn it around with trade legislation.

Lloyd Bentsen
Former U.S. Senator from Texas

Despite all the cries for protectionism to cure the trade deficit, protectionism will not lower the trade deficit.

Phil Gramm
Former U.S. Senator from Texas

CHAPTER LEARNING OBJECTIVES

- To distinguish between the current account, the capital account, and the official reserves account and describe the links among these accounts
- To calculate a nation's balance-of-payments accounts from data on its international transactions
- To identify the links between domestic economic behavior and the international flows of goods and capital and to describe how these links are reflected in the various balance-of-payments accounts

KEY TERMS

balance of payments	net liquidity balance
basic balance	official reserves account
capital account	official reserve transactions balance
current account	portfolio investment
direct investment	real investment
macroeconomic accounting identities	reserve assets
national expenditure	statistical discrepancy
national income	trade deficit
national product	unilateral transfers
net international wealth	

Akey theme of this book, as noted, is that companies today operate within a global marketplace, and they can ignore this fact only at their peril. In line with that theme, the purpose of this chapter is to present the financial and real linkages between the domestic and world economies and examine how these linkages affect business viability. The chapter identifies the basic forces underlying the flows of goods, services, and capital between countries and relates these flows to key political, economic, and cultural factors.

Politicians and the business press realize the importance of these trade and capital flows. They pay attention to the balance of payments, on which these flows are recorded, and to the massive and continuing U.S. trade deficits. As we saw in Chapter 2, government foreign exchange policies are often geared toward dealing with balance-of-payments problems. However, as indicated by the three quotations that opened the chapter, many people disagree on the nature of the trade deficit problem and its solution. In the process of studying the balance of payments in this chapter, we will sort out some of these issues.

5.1 BALANCE-OF-PAYMENTS CATEGORIES

The balance of payments summarizes a nation's international economic transactions.

The **balance of payments** is an accounting statement that summarizes all the economic transactions between residents of the home country and residents of all other countries. Balance-of-payments statistics are published quarterly in the United States by the Commerce Department and include such transactions as trade in goods and services, transfer payments, loans, and short- and long-term investments. The statistics are followed closely by bankers and businesspeople, economists, and foreign exchange traders; the publication affects the value of the home currency if these figures are more, or less, favorable than anticipated.

Currency inflows are recorded as *credits,* and outflows are recorded as *debits.* Credits show up with a plus sign, and debits have a minus sign. There are three major balance-of-payments categories:

- **Current account,** which records flows of goods, services, and transfers
- **Capital account,** which shows public and private investment and lending activities
- **Official reserves account,** which measures changes in holdings of gold and foreign currencies—**reserve assets**—by official monetary institutions

Exports of goods and services are credits; imports of goods and services are debits. Interest and dividends are treated as services because they represent payment for the use of capital. Capital inflows appear as credits because the nation is selling (exporting) to foreigners valuable assets—buildings, land, stock, bonds, and other financial claims—and receiving cash in return. Capital outflows show up as debits because they represent purchases (imports) of foreign assets. The increase in a nation's official reserves also shows up as a debit item because the purchase of gold and other reserve assets is equivalent to importing these assets.

Balance of payments accounting is based on double-entry bookkeeping.

The balance-of-payments statement is based on double-entry bookkeeping; every economic transaction recorded as a credit brings about an equal and offsetting debit entry, and vice versa. According to accounting convention, a source of funds (either a decrease in assets or an increase in liabilities) is a credit, and a use of funds (either an increase in assets or a decrease in liabilities or net worth) is a debit. Suppose a U.S. company exports machine tools to Switzerland at a price of 2,000,000 Swiss francs (SFr). At the current exchange rate of SFr 1 = $0.75, this order is worth $1,500,000. The Swiss importer pays for the order with a check drawn on its Swiss bank account. A credit is recorded for the increase in U.S. exports (a reduction in U.S. goods—a source of funds), and because the exporter has acquired a Swiss franc deposit (an increase in a foreign asset—a use of funds), a debit is recorded to reflect a private capital outflow:

	Debit	Credit
U.S. exports		$1,500,000
Private foreign assets	$1,500,000	

Suppose the U.S. company decides to sell the Swiss francs it received to the Federal Reserve for dollars. In this case, a private asset would have been converted into an official (government) liability. This transaction would show up as a credit to the private asset account (as it is a source of funds) and a debit to the official assets account (as it is a use of funds):

	Debit	Credit
Private assets		$1,500,000
Official assets	$1,500,000	

Similarly, if a German sells a painting to a U.S. resident for $1,000,000, with payment made by issuing a check drawn on a U.S. bank, a debit is recorded to indicate an increase in assets (the painting) by U.S. residents, which is a use of funds, and a credit is recorded to reflect an increase in liabilities (payment for the painting) to a foreigner, which is a source of funds:

	Debit	Credit
Private liabilities to foreigners		$1,000,000
U.S. imports	$1,000,000	

In the case of **unilateral transfers**, which are gifts and grants overseas, the transfer is debited because the donor's net worth is reduced, whereas another account must be credited: exports, if goods are donated; services, if services are donated; or capital, if the recipient receives cash or a check. Suppose the American Red Cross donates $100,000 in goods for earthquake relief to Nicaragua. The balance-of-payments entries for this transaction would appear as follows:

	Debit	Credit
U.S. exports		$100,000
Unilateral transfer	$100,000	

Because double-entry bookkeeping ensures that debits equal credits, the sum of all transactions is zero. That is, the sum of the balance on the current account, the capital account, and the official reserves account must equal zero:

Current-account balance + Capital-account balance + Official reserves account = Balance of payments = 0

These features of balance-of-payments accounting are illustrated in Exhibit 5.1, which shows the U.S. balance of payments for 2002, and in Exhibit 5.2, which gives examples of entries in the U.S. balance-of-payments accounts.

Current Account

The balance on current account reflects the net flow of goods, services, income, and unilateral transfers. It includes exports and imports of merchandise (trade balance), service transactions (invisibles), and income transfers. The service account includes sales under military contracts, tourism, financial charges (banking and insurance), and transportation expenses (shipping and air travel). The income account was once part of the services account, but it has become so large in recent years that it is now shown separately. It

EXHIBIT 5.1 • THE U.S. BALANCE OF PAYMENTS FOR 2002[1] (U.S. $ BILLIONS)	
Credits: Sources of Foreign Exchange (+)	*Debits: Uses of Foreign Exchange (−)*

a: Exports of goods $681.9	*b:* Imports of civilian goods $1,164.7
Trade balance	= Deficit of $482.8
c: Exports of services (Fees earned, transportation receipts, foreign tourism in United States, etc.) 292.2	*d:* Imports of services (Fees paid out, transportation charges, U.S. tourism abroad, etc.) 227.4
Services balance	= Surplus of $64.8
e: Income receipts 255.5	*f:* Income payments 259.5
Income balance	= Deficit of $4.0
	g: Net unilateral transfers (gifts) 58.9
Current-account balance	= a + c + e − (b + d + f + g)
	= Deficit of $480.9
h: Capital account transactions, net (1.3)	
i: Foreign private investment in the United States 612.1	*j:* U.S. private investment overseas 175.3
k: Foreign official lending in the United States 94.9	*l:* U.S. government lending overseas 0.0
Capital-account balance	= h + i + k − (j + l)
	= Surplus of $530.4
	m: Net increase in U.S. official reserves 3.7
Official reserves balance	= Increase of $3.7
n: Statistical discrepancy (45.9)	

[1] Numbers may not sum exactly owing to rounding.

Source: Data from the Bureau of Economic Analysis, U.S. Department of Commerce, as published on their Web page, January 28, 2004.

includes investment income (interest and dividends) and employee compensation. Unilateral transfers include pensions, remittances, and other transfers overseas for which no specific services are rendered. In 2002, for example, the U.S. balance of trade registered a deficit of $482.8 billion, whereas the overall current-account deficit was $480.9 billion. The difference was accounted for by a $64.8 billion *surplus* on the services account and deficits of $4.0 billion and $58.9 billion, respectively, on the income account and in unilateral transactions. The United States ordinarily runs a deficit in the unilateral transfers account, but in 1991 it ran a surplus, largely accounted for by the $42.0 billion in contributions that the United States received from other countries to help pay for the Gulf War.

The U.S. current-account deficit at $480.9 billion in 2002 was the world's largest. In addition, as a percent of GDP, the deficit was 4.6 percent, higher even than its previous peak value of 4.5 percent in 2000. As shown in Exhibit 5.3, the forecast U.S. deficit for 2004 is one of the highest in the industrialized world.

EXHIBIT 5.2 • EXAMPLES OF ENTRIES IN THE U.S. BALANCE-OF-PAYMENTS ACCOUNTS

Credits	*Debits*
Current Account	
a: Sales of wheat to Great Britain; sales of computers to Germany	b: Purchases of oil from Saudi Arabia; purchases of Japanese automobiles
c: Sales of Phantom jets to Canada	d: Payments to German workers at U.S. bases in Germany
e: Licensing fees earned by Microsoft; spending by Japanese tourists at Disneyland	f: Hotel bills of U.S. tourists in Paris
	h: Profits on sales by Nestlé's U.S. affiliate
g: Interest earnings on loans to Argentina; profits on U.S.-owned auto plants abroad	i: Remittances by Mexican Americans to relatives in Mexico; Social Security payments to Americans living in Italy; economic aid to Pakistan
Capital Account	
j: Purchases by the Japanese of U.S. real estate; increases in Arab bank deposits in New York banks; purchases by the French of IBM stock; investment in plant expansion in Ohio by Honda	k: New investment in a German chemical plant by Du Pont; increases in U.S. bank loans to Mexico; deposits in Swiss banks by Americans; purchases of Japanese stocks and bonds by Americans
l: Purchases of U.S. Treasury bonds by Bank of Japan; increases in holdings of New York bank deposits by Saudi Arabian government	m: Deposits of funds by the U.S. Treasury in British banks; purchases of Swiss-franc bonds by the Federal Reserve
Official Reserve Account	
	n: Purchases of gold by the U.S. Treasury; increases in holdings of Japanese yen by the Federal Reserve

Capital Account

The capital account shows public and private lending and investment activities.

Capital-account transactions affect a nation's wealth and net creditor position. These transactions are classified as either portfolio, short-term, or direct investments. **Portfolio investments** are purchases of financial assets with a maturity greater than one year; *short-term investments* involve securities with a maturity of less than one year. **Direct investments** are those where management control is exerted, defined under U.S. rules as ownership of at least 10 percent of the equity. Government borrowing and lending are included in the balance on capital account. As shown in Exhibit 5.1, the U.S. balance on capital account in 2002 was a surplus of $530.4 billion.

Official Reserves Account

The official reserves account shows the net deficit or surplus on a nation's combined current and capital accounts.

The change in official reserves measures a nation's surplus or deficit on its current- and capital-account transactions by netting reserve liabilities from reserve assets. For example, a surplus will lead to an increase in official holdings of foreign currencies or gold or both; a deficit will normally cause a reduction in these assets. However, U.S. balance-of-payments deficits have not been matched exactly by net changes in reserve assets because foreigners have been willing to hold many billions of dollars (estimated at more than $100 billion) for liquidity and other purposes. Instead of being converted into foreign currencies, many dollars have been placed on deposit in the Eurodollar market. For most countries, however, there is a close correlation between balance-of-payments deficits and reserve declines. A drop in reserves will occur, for instance, when a nation sells gold to acquire foreign currencies that it can then use to meet a deficit in its balance of payments. In 2002, the United States ran a deficit of $3.7 billion in its official reserves.

EXHIBIT 5.3 • CURRENT-ACCOUNT BALANCES AS A PERCENTAGE OF GDP (2004 ESTIMATED)

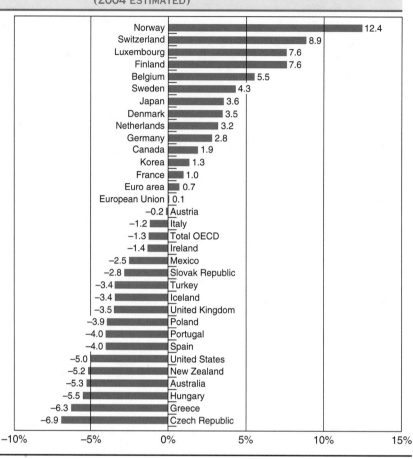

Source: Data from OECD Web site.

Balance-of-Payments Measures

There are several balance-of-payments definitions. The **basic balance** focuses on transactions considered to be fundamental to the economic health of a currency. Thus, it includes the balance on current account and long-term capital, but it excludes such ephemeral items as short-term capital flows, mainly bank deposits, that are heavily influenced by temporary factors—short-run monetary policy, changes in interest differentials, and anticipations of currency fluctuations.

Each of the different balance-of-payments measures has short-comings.

The **net liquidity balance** measures the change in private domestic borrowing or lending that is required to keep payments in balance without adjusting official reserves. Illiquid, private, short-term capital flows and errors and omissions are included in the balance; liquid assets and liabilities are excluded.

The **official reserve transactions balance** measures the adjustment required in official reserves to achieve balance-of-payments equilibrium. The assumption here is that official transactions are different from private transactions.

Each of these measures has shortcomings, primarily because of the increasing complexity of international financial transactions. For example, changes in the official reserve balance may now reflect investment flows as well as central bank intervention. Similarly, critics of the basic balance argue that the distinction between short- and long-term capital flows has become blurred. Direct investment is still determined by longer-term factors, but investment in stocks and bonds can be just as speculative as bank deposits and sold just as quickly. The astute international financial manager, therefore, must analyze the payments figures rather than rely on a single summarizing number.

The Missing Numbers

In going over the numbers in Exhibit 5.1, you will note an item referred to as a **statistical discrepancy**. This number reflects errors and omissions in collecting data on international transactions. In 2002, that item was –$45.9 billion. (A positive figure reflects a mysterious inflow of funds; a negative amount reflects an outflow.)

Typically, the statistical discrepancy entry for the United States is positive. For example, in 1990 it was +$66.8 billion. This discrepancy coincided with such worrisome foreign events as the Iraqi invasion of Kuwait, turmoil in Iran, unrest in Central and Latin America, and the upheaval in the Soviet Union. Many experts believe that the statistical discrepancy in that year was primarily the result of foreigners' surreptitiously moving money into what they deemed to be a safe political haven—the United States.

5.2 THE INTERNATIONAL FLOW OF GOODS, SERVICES, AND CAPITAL

Basic macroeconomic accounting identities link domestic spending and production to the current-account and capital-account balances.

This section provides an analytical framework that links the international flows of goods and capital to domestic economic behavior. The framework consists of a set of basic **macroeconomic accounting identities** that link domestic spending and production to savings, consumption, and investment behavior, and thence to the capital-account and current-account balances. By manipulating these equations, we can identify the nature of the links between the U.S. and world economies and assess the effects on the domestic economy of international economic policies, and vice versa. As we see in the next section, ignoring these links leads to political solutions to international economic problems—such as the trade deficit—that create greater problems. At the same time, authors of domestic policy changes are often unaware of the effect these changes can have on the country's international economic affairs.

Domestic Savings and Investment and the Capital Account

The national income and product accounts provide an accounting framework for recording the national product and showing how its components are affected by international transactions. This framework begins with the observation that **national income**, which is the same as **national product**, is either spent on consumption or saved:

$$National\ income = Consumption + Savings \tag{5.1}$$

Similarly, **national expenditure**, the total amount that the nation spends on goods and services, can be divided into spending on consumption and spending on domestic real investment. **Real investment** refers to plant and equipment, research and development, and other expenditures designed to increase the nation's productive capacity. This equation provides the second national accounting identity:

$$National\ spending = Consumption + Investment \tag{5.2}$$

Subtracting Equation 5.2 from Equation 5.1 yields a new identity:

$$National\ income - National\ spending = Savings - Investment \tag{5.3}$$

A nation whose income exceeds its spending will have a domestic savings surplus that must be invested abroad.

This identity says that if a nation's income exceeds its spending, savings will exceed domestic investment, yielding surplus capital. The surplus capital must be invested overseas (if it were invested domestically there would not be a capital surplus). In other words, savings equals domestic investment plus net foreign investment. Net foreign investment equals the nation's net public and private capital outflows plus the increase in official reserves. The net private and public capital outflows equal the capital-account deficit if the outflow is positive (a capital-account surplus if negative); the net increase in official reserves equals the balance on the official reserves account. In a freely floating exchange-rate system—that is, no government intervention and no official reserve transactions—excess savings will equal the capital-account deficit. Alternatively, a national savings deficit will equal the capital-account surplus (net borrowing from abroad); this borrowing finances the excess of national spending over national income.

A nation that produces more (less) than it spends will have a net capital outflow (inflow).

Here is the bottom line: A nation that produces more than it spends will save more than it invests domestically and will have a net capital outflow. This capital outflow will appear as some combination of a capital-account deficit and an increase in official reserves. Conversely, a nation that spends more than it produces will invest domestically more than it saves and have a net capital inflow. This capital inflow will appear as some combination of a capital-account surplus and a reduction in official reserves.

The Link Between the Current and Capital Accounts

Beginning again with national product, we can subtract from it spending on domestic goods and services. The remaining goods and services must equal exports. Similarly, if we subtract spending on domestic goods and services from total expenditures, the remaining spending must be on imports. Combining these two identities leads to another national income identity:

$$\textit{National income} - \textit{National spending} = \textit{Exports} - \textit{Imports} \qquad (5.4)$$

Equation 5.4 says that a current-account surplus arises when national output exceeds domestic expenditures; similarly, a current-account deficit is due to domestic expenditures' exceeding domestic output. Exhibit 5.4 illustrates this latter point for the United States. Moreover, when Equation 5.4 is combined with Equation 5.3, we have a new identity:

$$\textit{Savings} - \textit{Investment} = \textit{Exports} - \textit{Imports} \qquad (5.5)$$

The current-account balance must equal the net capital outflow.

According to Equation 5.5, if a nation's savings exceed its domestic investment, that nation will run a current-account surplus. This equation explains the Japanese current-account surplus: The Japanese have a very high savings rate, both in absolute terms and relative to their investment rate. Conversely, a nation such as the United States, which saves less than it invests, must run a current-account deficit. Noting that savings minus domestic investment equals net foreign investment, we have the following identity:

$$\textit{Net foreign investment} = \textit{Exports} - \textit{Imports} \qquad (5.6)$$

Japan is using its large current-account surplus to invest in the United States.

Equation 5.6 says that the balance on the current account must equal the net capital outflow; that is, any foreign exchange earned by selling abroad must be either spent on imports or exchanged for claims against foreigners. The net amount of these IOUs equals the nation's capital outflow. If the current account is in surplus, the country must be a net exporter of capital; a current-account deficit indicates that the nation is a net capital importer. This equation explains why Japan, with its large current-account surpluses, is a major capital exporter, whereas the United States, with its large current-account deficits, is a major capital importer. Bearing in mind that trade is goods plus services, to say that the United States has a **trade deficit** with Japan is simply to say that the United States is buying more goods and services from Japan than Japan is buying from the United States, and that Japan is investing more in the United States than the United States is investing in Japan. Between the United States and Japan, any deficit in the current account is exactly equal to the surplus in the capital account. Otherwise, there would be an imbalance in the foreign exchange market, and the exchange rate would change.

EXHIBIT 5.4 • THE TRADE BALANCE FALLS AS SPENDING RISES RELATIVE TO GDP

Another interpretation of Equation 5.6 is that the excess of goods and services bought over goods and services produced domestically must be acquired through foreign trade and must be financed by an equal amount of borrowing from abroad (the capital-account surplus and/or official reserves deficit). Thus, in a freely floating exchange-rate system, the current-account balance and the capital-account balance must exactly offset each other. With government intervention in the foreign exchange market, the sum of the current-account balance plus the capital-account balance plus the balance on the official reserves account must be zero. These relations are shown in Exhibit 5.5.

These identities are useful because they allow us to assess the efficacy of proposed "solutions" for improving the current-account balance. It is clear that a nation can neither reduce its current-account deficit, nor increase its current-account surplus unless it meets two conditions: (1) Raise national product relative to national spending, and (2) increase savings relative to domestic investment. A proposal to improve the current-account balance by reducing imports (say, via higher tariffs) that does not affect national output/spending and national savings/investment leaves the trade deficit the same; and the proposal cannot achieve its objective without violating fundamental accounting identities. With regard to Japan, a clear implication is that chronic Japanese trade surpluses are not reflective of unfair trade practices and restrictive import policies, but rather are the natural effect of differing cultures and philosophies regarding saving and consumption. As long as the Japanese prefer to save and invest rather than consume, the imbalance will persist.

These accounting identities also suggest that a current-account surplus is not necessarily a sign of economic vigor, nor is a current-account deficit necessarily a sign of weakness or of a lack of competitiveness. Indeed, economically healthy nations that provide good investment opportunities tend to run trade deficits because this is the only way to run a capital-account surplus. The United States ran trade deficits from early Colonial times to just before World War I, as Europeans sent investment capital to develop the continent. During its 300 years as a debtor nation—a net importer of capital—the United

To improve the current-account balance, domestic savings must be increased relative to domestic investment.

Current-account deficits (surpluses) are not necessarily signs of economic weakness (strength).

EXHIBIT 5.5 • LINKING NATIONAL ECONOMIC ACTIVITY WITH BALANCE-OF-PAYMENTS ACCOUNTS: BASIC IDENTITIES

	Our national product (Y)	–	Our total spending (E)
minus	Our spending for consumption	minus	Our spending for consumption

= | Our national savings (S) | – | Our investment in new real assets (I_d) |

= Net foreign investment, or the net increase in claims on foreigners and official reserve assets, e.g., gold (I_f)

	Our national product (Y)	–	Our total spending (E)
minus	Our spending on our own goods and services	minus	Our spending on our own goods and services

= | Our exports of goods and services (X) | – | Our imports of goods and services (M) |

= Balance on current account

= – (Balance on capital and official reserves accounts)

$$Y - E = S - I_d = X - M = I_f$$

Conclusions: A nation that produces more than it spends will save more than it invests, export more than it imports, and wind up with a capital outflow. A nation that spends more than it produces will invest more than it saves, import more than it exports, and wind up with a capital inflow.

States progressed from the status of a minor colony to the world's strongest power. Conversely, it ran surpluses while the infamous Smoot-Hawley tariff helped sink the world into depression. Similarly, during the 1980s, Latin America ran current-account surpluses because its dismal economic prospects made it unable to attract foreign capital. As Latin America's prospects improved in the early 1990s, money flowed in and it began running capital-account surpluses again—matched by offsetting current-account deficits.

> *Rapidly growing nations will import more.*

Note, too, that nations that grow rapidly will import more goods and services at the same time that weak economies will slow down or reduce their imports, because imports are positively related to income. As a result, the faster a nation grows relative to other economies, the larger its current-account deficit (or smaller its surplus). Conversely, slower-growing nations will have smaller current-account deficits (or larger surpluses). Hence, current-account deficits may reflect strong economic growth or a low level of savings, and current-account surpluses can signify a high level of savings or a slow rate of growth.

Because current-account deficits are financed by capital inflows, the cumulative effect of these deficits is to increase net foreign claims against the deficit nation and reduce that nation's net international wealth. Similarly, nations that consistently run current-account surpluses increase their net international wealth, where **net international wealth** is just the difference between a nation's investment abroad and foreign investment domestically.

> *The United States is now a huge international debtor.*

Sooner or later, deficit countries like the United States become net international debtors, and surplus countries like Japan become net creditors. For example, Exhibit 5.6 shows that the inevitable consequence of continued U.S. current-account deficits was to turn U.S. net international wealth (computed on a current cost basis) negative. In 1986, the United States became a net international debtor, reverting to the position it was in at the start of the 20th century. By the end of 2002, U.S. net international wealth was –$2.4 *trillion*.

Current-Account Deficits and Unemployment

One rationale for attempting to eliminate a current-account deficit is that such a deficit leads to unemployment. Underlying this rationale is the notion that imported goods and services are substituting for domestic goods and services and costing domestic jobs. For example, some have argued that every million-dollar increase in the U.S. trade deficit costs about 33 American jobs, assuming that the average worker earns about $30,000 a year ($1,000,000/$30,000 = 33). Hence, it is claimed, reducing imports would raise

EXHIBIT 5.6 • INTERNATIONAL INVESTMENT POSITION OF THE UNITED STATES: 1976–2002

Source: Data are investment positions calculated on a current cost basis by the U.S. Bureau of Economic Analysis at www.bea.doc.gov/bea/di1.htm.

domestic production and employment. However, the view that reducing a current-account deficit promotes jobs is based on single-entry bookkeeping.

If a country buys fewer foreign goods and services, it will demand less foreign exchange. As discussed earlier, this result will raise the value of the domestic currency, thereby reducing exports and encouraging the purchase of other imports. Jobs are saved in some industries, but other jobs are lost by the decline in exports and rise in other imports. Following this line of reasoning, the net impact of a trade deficit or surplus on jobs should be nil.

According to the apocalyptic claims of some politicians, however, the recent economic performance of the United States should have been dismal because of its huge current-account deficits. However, if the alternative story is correct—that a current-account deficit reflects excess spending and has little to do with the health of an economy—then there should be no necessary relation between economic performance and the current-account balance.

The appropriate way to settle this dispute is to examine the evidence. Recent research that examined the economic performance of the twenty-three OECD (Organization for Economic Cooperation and Development) countries during a thirty-eight-year period found no systematic relationship between trade deficits and unemployment rates.[1] This result is not surprising for those who have looked at U.S. economic performance over the past twenty years or so. During this period, the trade deficit soared, but the United States created jobs three times as fast as Japan and twenty times as fast as Germany. Also, in the same time period, America's GDP grew 43 percent faster than that of Japan or Germany, even though both nations had huge trade surpluses with the United States.

In general, no systematic relationship between net exports and economic growth should be expected—and none is to be found.[2] The evidence shows that current-account surpluses—in and of themselves—are neither good nor bad. They are not correlated with jobs, growth, decline, competitiveness, or weakness. What matters is why they occur.

Studies have found no systematic relationship between economic performance and the current-account balance.

Trade deficits, by themselves, are neither good nor bad.

[1] See David M. Gould, Roy J. Ruffin, and Graeme L. Woodbridge, "The Theory and Practice of Free Trade," *Federal Reserve Bank of Dallas Economic Review,* Fourth Quarter, 1993, pp. 1–16.

[2] See, for example, David M. Gould and Roy J. Ruffin, "Trade Deficits: Causes and Consequences," *Federal Reserve Bank of Dallas Economic Review,* Fourth Quarter, 1996, pp. 10–20. After analyzing a group of 101 countries over a thirty-year period, they conclude (p. 17) that "trade imbalances have little effect on rates of economic growth once we account for the fundamental determinants of economic growth."

The process of international payments equilibrium and its tie to both macroeconomic factors and exchange rates is shown in the case of Germany. With its mature industrial economy and aging population, western Germany has long run a current-account surplus. Modernization of the eastern German economy changed that. To finance reunification, Germany had to shift from being a large capital exporter to being a capital importer. Consequently, Germany had to increase its imports of goods and services relative to exports. This it did, as shown in Exhibit 5.7. For example, Germany's current account moved from a surplus of DM 70 billion (about 3 percent of GDP) in 1990 to a deficit of DM 30 billion (about 1.5 percent of GDP) in 1991. Such a drastic change could be brought about in one of two ways.

One possibility would have been to reduce domestic demand in Germany by private and government consumption or investment. However, cuts in capital spending would be unwise because they would mean less productive capacity in the future. Private consumption would have to be curbed through tax increases, which—even if temporary—would be unpopular, to say the least. Cutting non–unification-related government expenditures would have been politically difficult as well, given the strong constituencies behind that spending.

EXHIBIT 5.7 • REUNIFICATION TURNS GERMANY'S CURRENT-ACCOUNT SURPLUS INTO A DEFICIT THAT EXCEEDS THE U.S. DEFICIT (% OF GDP)

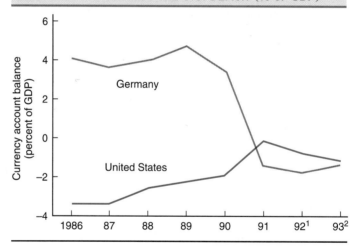

[1] Estimated.

[2] Projected.

Source: Adapted from *The Economist,* January 30, 1993, p. 59, © 1993.
The Economist Newspaper Group, Inc. Reprinted with permission. Further reproduction is prohibited.

The other alternative was to reduce demand for German exports and, at the same time, rely to a greater extent on imports to meet domestic demand. This path—which Germany chose—required its goods to become relatively more expensive to its trading partners (mostly fellow members of the European Monetary System) and foreign goods relatively less expensive to Germans. This shift in relative prices could be accomplished through some combination of higher inflation in Germany, appreciation of the DM, depreciation of foreign currencies relative to the DM, and deflation in fellow EMS members.

As we saw in Chapter 3, Germany was unwilling to accept inflation, and the ERM prevented exchange rate changes. That left only deflation in other EMS countries, until it too proved unacceptable and the system broke down in September 1992.

5.3 SUMMARY AND CONCLUSIONS

The balance of payments is an accounting statement of the international transactions of one nation over a specific period. The statement shows the sum of economic transactions of individuals, businesses, and government agencies located in one nation with those located in the rest of the world during the period. Thus, the U.S. balance of payments for a given year is an accounting of all transactions between U.S. residents and residents of all other countries during that year.

The statement is based on double-entry bookkeeping; every economic transaction recorded as a credit brings about an equal and offsetting debit entry, and vice versa. A debit entry shows a purchase of foreign goods, services, or assets, or a decline in liabilities to foreigners. A credit entry shows a sale of domestic goods, services, or assets, or an increase in liabilities to foreigners. For example, if a foreign company sells a car to a U.S. resident, a debit is recorded to indicate an increase in purchases made by the United States (the car); a credit is recorded to reflect an increase in liabilities to the foreigner (payment for the car).

The balance of payments is often divided into several components. Each shows a particular kind of transaction, such as merchandise exports or foreign purchases of U.S. government securities. Transactions that represent purchases and sales of goods and services in the current period are called the current account; those that represent capital transactions are called the capital account. Changes in official reserves appear on the official reserves account.

Double-entry bookkeeping ensures that debits equal credits; therefore, the sum of all transactions is zero. In the absence of official reserve transactions, a capital-account surplus must offset the current-account deficit, and a capital-account deficit must offset a current-account surplus.

The United States is currently running a large current-account deficit. Much public discussion about why the United States imports more than it exports has focused on claims of unfair trading practices or on the high value of the dollar. However, economic theory indicates that the total size of the current-account deficit is a macroeconomic phenomenon; there is a basic accounting identity that a nation's current-account deficit reflects excess domestic spending. Equivalently, a current-account deficit equals the excess of domestic investment over domestic savings.

QUESTIONS

1. In a freely floating exchange-rate system, if the current account is running a deficit, what are the consequences for the nation's balance on capital account and its overall balance of payments?

2. A current-account surplus is not always a sign of health; a current-account deficit is not always a sign of weakness. Comment.

3. Suppose Lufthansa buys $400 million worth of Boeing jets in 2005 and is financed by the U.S. Eximbank with a five-year loan that has no principal or interest payments due until 2006. What is the net impact of this sale on the U.S. current account, capital account, and overall balance of payments for 2005?

4. During the 1990s, Mexico and Argentina went from economic pariahs with huge foreign debts to countries posting strong economic growth and welcoming foreign investment. What would you expect these changes to do to their current-account balances?

5. Suppose the trade imbalances of the 1990s largely disappear during the next decade. What is likely to happen to the huge global capital flows of the 1990s? What is the link between the trade imbalances and the global movement of capital?

6. In the early 1990s, Japan underwent a recession that brought about a prolonged slump in consumer spending and capital investment. (Some estimates were that in 1994 only 65 percent of Japan's manufacturing capacity was being used.) At the same time, the U.S. economy emerged from its recession and began expanding rapidly. Under these circumstances, what would you predict would happen to the U.S. trade deficit with Japan?

7. According to the *World Competitiveness Report 1994*, with freer markets, Third World nations now are able to attract capital and technology from the advanced nations. As a result, they can achieve productivity close to Western levels while paying low wages. Hence, the low-wage Third World nations will run huge trade surpluses, creating either large-scale unemployment or sharply falling wages in the advanced nations. Comment on this apocalyptic scenario.

PROBLEMS

1. How would each of the following transactions show up on the U.S. balance-of-payments accounts?

   a. Payment of $50 million in Social Security to U.S. citizens living in Costa Rica

b. Sale overseas of 125,000 Elvis Presley CDs

c. Tuition receipts of $3 billion received by American universities from foreign students

d. Payment of $1 million to U.S. consultants A.D. Little by a Mexican company

e. Sale of a $100 million Eurobond issue in London by IBM

f. Investment of $25 million by Ford to build a parts plant in Argentina

g. Payment of $45 million in dividends to U.S. citizens from foreign companies

2. Set up the double-entry accounts showing the appropriate debits and credits associated with the following transactions:

a. ConAgra, a U.S. agribusiness, exports $80 million of soybeans to China and receives payment in the form of a check drawn on a U.S. bank.

b. The U.S. government provides refugee assistance to Somalia in the form of corn valued at $1 million.

c. Dow Chemical invests $500 million in a chemical plant in Germany financed by issuing bonds in London.

d. General Motors pays $5 million in dividends to foreign residents, who choose to hold the dividends in the form of bank deposits in New York.

e. The Bank of Japan buys up $1 billion in the foreign exchange market to hold down the value of the yen and uses these dollars to buy U.S. Treasury bonds.

f. Cemex, a Mexican company, sells $2 million worth of cement to a Texas company and deposits the check in a bank in Dallas.

g. Colombian drug dealers receive $10 million in cash for the cocaine they ship to the U.S. market. The money is smuggled out of the United States and then invested in U.S. corporate bonds on behalf of a Cayman Islands bank.

3. The following transactions (expressed in U.S. $ billions) take place during a year. Calculate the U.S. merchandise-trade, current-account, capital-account, and official reserves balances.

a. The United States exports $300 of goods and receives payment in the form of foreign demand deposits abroad.

b. The United States imports $225 of goods and pays for them by drawing down its foreign demand deposits.

c. The United States pays $15 to foreigners in dividends drawn on U.S. demand deposits here.

d. American tourists spend $30 overseas using traveler's checks drawn on U.S. banks here.

e. Americans buy foreign stocks with $60, using foreign demand deposits held abroad.

f. The U.S. government sells $45 in gold for foreign demand deposits abroad.

g. In a currency support operation, the U.S. government uses its foreign demand deposits to purchase $8 from private foreigners in the United States.

INTERNET RESOURCES

research.stlouisfed.org/fred2/ Web site of the Federal Reserve Bank of St. Louis that takes you directly to U.S. trade and balance of payments data that you can download into spreadsheets.

www.bea.doc.gov Web site of the Bureau of Economic Analysis (BEA). Contains data and articles on U.S. international trade and capital flows.

INTERNET EXERCISES

1. Which countries are the major customers for U.S. exports of goods and services? Which countries are the major exporters of goods and services to the United States?

2. Examine the U.S. balance of payments over the past year.

a. What is the current-account balance, the capital account balance, and the official reserves balance?

b. How have these balances changed from the previous year? What economic factors might account for these changes?

3. Based on historical data from the BEA, what is the relationship between U.S. trade balances and U.S. economic growth?

4. Select a country and analyze that country's balance of payments for eight to 12 years, subject to availability of data. You can find such data by using the Google search engine (at www.google.com) and typing in the country name and "Balance of Payments data" (include quote marks around the phrase). For example, the site for Japanese balance of payments data is www.mof.go.jp/e1c004.htm, and Canadian data can be found at www.statcan.ca/english/Pgdb/econ01a.htm. The analysis must

include examinations (presentation of statistical data with discussion) of the trade balance, current-account balance, capital-account balance, basic balance, and overall balance. Your report should also address the following issues:

a. What accounts for swings in these various balances over time?

b. What is the relationship between shifts in the current-account balance and changes in savings and investment? Include an examination of government budget deficits and surpluses, explaining how they are related to the savings and investment and current-account balances.[3]

---

[3] Project suggested by Donald T. Buck.

COUNTRY RISK ANALYSIS

People say they want clarification of the rules of the game, but I think it isn't very clear what isn't clear to them.

Adolfo Hegewisch Fernandez
Mexico's Subsecretary for Foreign Investment

Potential investors don't want flexibility, they want fixed rules of the game.

John Gavin
U.S. Ambassador to Mexico

CHAPTER LEARNING OBJECTIVES

- To define what country risk means from the standpoint of an MNC
- To describe the social, cultural, political, and economic factors that affect the general level of risk in a country and identify key indicators of country risk and economic health
- To describe what we can learn about economic development from the contrasting experiences of a variety of countries
- To describe the economic and political factors that determine a country's ability and willingness to repay its foreign debts

KEY TERMS

capital flight	international banking crisis of 1982
command economy (socialism)	market economy (capitalism)
controlled exchange rate system	monetizing the deficit
country risk	political economy
country risk analysis	political risk
debt relief	privatizing
expropriation	property rights
import-substitution development	statism
policy	terms-of-trade risk

Country risk analysis
involves assessing the
potential risks and
rewards of investing
and doing business
in a country.

Multinational firms must constantly assess the business environments of the countries they are already operating in as well as the ones they are considering investing in. Similarly, private and public investors alike are interested in determining which countries offer the best prospects for sound investments. This is the realm of **country risk analysis,** the assessment of the potential risks and rewards associated with making investments and doing business in a country. Ultimately, we are interested in whether sensible economic policies are likely to be pursued because countries adopting such policies will generally have good business environments in which enterprise can flourish. However, because political considerations often lead countries to pursue economic policies that are detrimental to business and to their own economic health, the focus of country risk analysis cannot be exclusively economic in nature. By necessity, it must also study the political factors that give rise to particular economic policies. This is the subject matter of **political economy**—the interaction of politics and economics. Such interactions occur on a continuous basis and affect not just monetary and fiscal (tax and spending) policies but also a host of other policies that affect the business environment, such as currency or trade controls, changes in labor laws, regulatory restrictions, and requirements for additional local production.

Country risk
depends on a
nation's economic
and political
policies.

By extension, the international economic environment is heavily dependent on the policies that individual nations pursue. Given the close linkage between a country's economic policies and the degree of exchange risk, inflation risk, and interest rate risk that multinational companies and investors face, it is vital in studying and attempting to forecast those risks to understand their causes. Simply put, no one can intelligently assess a country's risk profile without comprehending its economic and political policies and how those policies are likely to affect the country's prospects for economic growth. Similarly, attempts to forecast exchange rates, inflation rates, or interest rates are helped immensely by a deeper understanding of how those economic parameters are affected by national policies.

The purpose of this chapter is to provide a framework that can facilitate a formal assessment of country risk and its implications for corporate decision making. Both international banks and nonbank multinationals analyze country risk, but from different perspectives. Nonbank MNCs analyze country risk in order to determine the investment climate in various countries, whereas banks are interested in the country's ability to service its foreign debts. Country risk assessments may be used in investment analyses to screen out countries that are excessively risky or to monitor countries in which the firm is currently doing business to determine whether new policies are called for. Banks analyze country risk to determine which countries to lend to, the currencies in which to denominate their loans, and the interest rates to demand on these loans.

The chapter begins with a discussion of political risk and then moves to an analysis of the economic and political factors underlying country risk. The third section focuses on country risk from the perspective of an international bank.

6.1 MEASURING POLITICAL RISK

Although **expropriation**[1] is the most obvious and extreme form of **political risk**, there are other significant political risks, including currency or trade controls, changes in tax or labor laws, regulatory restrictions, and requirements for additional local production. The common denominator of such risks is not hard to identify: government intervention into the workings of the economy that affects, for good or ill, the value of the firm. Although the consequences usually are adverse, changes in the political environment can provide opportunities as well. The imposition of quotas on autos from Japan, for example, was undoubtedly beneficial to U.S. automobile manufacturers.

---

[1] The terms *expropriation* and *nationalization* are used interchangeably in this book and refer specifically to the taking of foreign property, with or without compensation.

The following discussion of the types of risks that multinational corporations are subject to is contained in the 1998 annual report of Lyondell Chemical Company.

ILLUSTRATION   *Lyondell Chemical Co. Faces Political Risks Overseas*

International operations and exports to foreign markets are subject to a number of risks, including currency exchange rate fluctuations, trade barriers, exchange controls, national and regional labor strikes, political risks and risks of increases in duties and taxes, as well as changes in laws and policies governing operations of foreign-based companies. In addition, earnings of foreign subsidiaries and intercompany payments may be subject to foreign income tax rules that may reduce cash flow available to meet required debt service and other obligations of the Company.

Political risk can be viewed from both a country-specific and a firm-specific perspective.

Despite the near-universal recognition among multinational corporations, political scientists, and economists of the existence of political risk, no unanimity has yet been reached about what constitutes that risk and how to measure it. The two basic approaches to viewing political risk are from a country-specific and a firm-specific perspective. The first perspective depends on country risk analysis, whereas the second depends on a more micro approach. This chapter focuses on macro indicators. Chapter 17 examines political risk from the perspective of an individual firm.

A number of commercial and academic political risk forecasting models are available today. These models normally supply country risk indices that attempt to quantify the level of political risk in each nation. Most of these indices rely on some measure(s) of the stability of the local political regime.

Political Stability

Measures of political stability may include the frequency of changes of government, the level of violence in the country (for example, violent deaths per 100,000 population), the number of armed insurrections, the extent of conflicts with other states, and so on. The basic function of these stability indicators is to determine how long the current regime will be in power and whether that regime also will be willing and able to enforce its foreign investment guarantees. Most companies believe that greater political stability means a safer investment environment.

Political risk models include both objective economic factors and subjective indicators of attitude toward property rights.

A basic problem in many Third World countries is that the local actors have all the external trappings of genuine nation-states—United Nations–endorsed borders, armies, foreign ministries, flags, currencies, national airlines—but they are nothing of the kind. They lack social cohesion, political legitimacy, and the institutional infrastructures necessary for economic growth. The latter include political institutions (such as a constitution and functioning legal system) that limit the powers of politicians and business leaders.

Economic Factors

Other frequently used indicators of political risk include economic factors such as inflation, balance-of-payments deficits or surpluses, and the growth rate of per capita GDP. The intention behind these measures is to determine whether the economy is in good shape or requires a quick fix, such as expropriation to increase government revenues or currency inconvertibility to improve the balance of payments. In general, the better a country's economic outlook, the less likely it is to face political and social turmoil that will inevitably harm foreign companies.

Subjective Factors

More subjective measures of political risk are based on a general perception of the country's attitude toward private enterprise: whether private enterprise is considered a necessary evil to be eliminated as soon as possible or whether it is actively welcomed. The attitude toward multinationals is particularly relevant and may differ from the feeling regarding local private ownership. Consider, for example, the former Soviet Union and other Eastern European countries that actively sought products, technology, and even joint ventures with Western firms while refusing to tolerate (until recently) domestic free enterprise. In general, most countries probably view foreign direct investment in terms of a cost/benefit trade-off and are neither for nor against it in principle.

An index that tries to incorporate all these economic, social, and political factors into an overall measure of the business climate, including the political environment, is the Profit Opportunity Recommendation (POR) rating, shown in Exhibit 6.1 for 2002. The scores of countries listed on the POR scale are based on an aggregation of the subjective assessments of a panel of experts. Note that the United States is ranked tenth overall on this scale in terms of political risk, behind countries such as Switzerland, Singapore, Taiwan, Japan, and Germany.

Political Risk and Uncertain Property Rights   Models such as POR are useful insofar as they provide an indication of the general level of political risk in a country. From an

EXHIBIT 6.1 • PROFIT OPPORTUNITY RECOMMENDATION RANKINGS, 1997

Low Risk (70–100)	POR Combined Score	High Risk (40–54)	POR Combined Score
Switzerland	82	Saudi Arabia	54
Singapore	77	Chile	52
Netherlands	73	South Africa	51
Taiwan (R.O.C.)	72	Czech Republic	50
Japan	72	Italy	50
Norway	71	Thailand	48
Germany	70	Hungary	46
		Kazakstan	46
Moderate Risk (55–69)		Poland	45
Austria	69	India	45
Belgium	67	Egypt	44
United States	66	Greece	43
Sweden	65	Russia	43
Finland	64	Iran	43
France	64	Philippines	43
Ireland	64	Vietnam	42
Canada	63	Colombia	41
Spain	62	Mexico	41
United Kingdom	62	Ukraine	41
Denmark	61	Peru	40
Korea (South)	58	Turkey	40
Malaysia	58	Brazil	40
China (P.R.C.)	58	Pakistan	40
Australia	57		
Portugal	57	**Prohibitive Risk (0–39)**	
		Indonesia	39
		Venezuela	36
		Ecuador	35
		Argentina	34

Source: Business Environment Risk Intelligence, by permission.

Political risk refers to uncertainty over property rights.

economic standpoint, political risk refers to uncertainty over **property rights.** If the government can expropriate either legal title to property or the stream of income it generates, then political risk exists. Political risk also exists if property owners may be constrained in the way they use their property. This definition of political risk encompasses government actions ranging from outright expropriation to a change in the tax law that alters the government's share of corporate income to laws that change the rights of private companies to compete against state-owned companies. Each action affects corporate cash flows and hence the value of the firm.

ILLUSTRATION　*Komineft Rhymes with Theft*

In early 1995, Komineft, a Russian oil company, instituted a 3-for-2 stock split but did not tell shareholders. It also decided that only those investors on the registry in May 1984 would get the new shares, thereby diluting by a third the stakes of those who had bought shares afterward, which included most foreign buyers. Komineft, though conceding there was a problem, insisted it had done nothing wrong. It was probably right. The few Russian laws there are to protect shareholders' interests are often contradictory, allowing Russian companies to ignore shareholder rights and get away with it. Although Komineft later reversed its position on the stock split, episodes such as this one have taken most of the luster off of investing in Russian companies.

Other investors in Russia have had similar experiences with vague and shifting property rights. For example, in February 1995, Texaco's $45 billion deal to drill in the Russian Arctic hit a last-minute snag when a regional production association suddenly demanded a 50 percent share of the profits. In addition, oil companies have suffered from arbitrary changes in tax and export laws despite the fact that when Western oil companies registered their joint ventures in 1991, the Soviet government assured them they would be able to export 100 percent of production tax-free. However, as the government struggled over cash shortages, the oil companies' "rights" disappeared. As a result, every foreign oil company operating in the former Soviet Union scaled back its operations there or pulled out altogether.

ILLUSTRATION　*Mr. Yampel Gets Trampled in Ukraine*

In August 2000, Jacob Yampel had just won a Ukrainian court decision in his battle to regain a 50 percent stake in a pharmaceutical factory. This stake had been taken from him by the plant's managers through a complicated series of transactions involving share dilution, transfer of plant assets to a new private company, doctored documents, and a bankruptcy declaration of the original joint venture. Unfortunately for Mr. Yampel, the losing side then enlisted the aid of the Ukrainian president. In a televised broadcast, President Leonid Kuchma said, "I often say … we must obey laws. But there is something higher than the law: the country's national interest. And this means the interests of our people, not of someone else." Twelve days later, Ukraine's High Arbitration Court overturned Mr. Yampel's victory on a technicality.

An official at the U.S. Embassy called the timing of the unfavorable court decision "suspicious" and said it was "likely to raise questions in the minds of investors about their ability to obtain a fair hearing … particularly if they have disputes with prominent domestic producers."[2]

---

[2] Tom Warner, "Lessons for Foreign Investors in Ukraine," *Wall Street Journal,* August 16, 2000, A18.

Mr. Yampel's plight is not that uncommon in Ukraine, a large, underdeveloped market that holds lucrative opportunities along with big risks. Although the government hopes to attract foreign investors by combining economic reforms with privatization, Ukrainian leaders are sending potential investors mixed messages about their attitude towards foreign business. In addition to Mr. Yampel's company, a number of U.S. firms have complained to the U.S. Congress about their treatment in Ukraine. Their grievances range from commercial disputes with government agencies or companies to bureaucratic interference to improper handling by the judicial system of their disputes with Ukrainian firms.

The key questions that companies should ask in assessing the degree of political risk they face in a country, particularly one undergoing a political and economic transition, are as follows:

Country risk is reduced by predictable and fair legal and regulatory systems.

- Has economic reform become institutionalized, thereby minimizing the chance of abrupt policy changes that would adversely affect an investment's value?

- Are the regulatory and legal systems predictable and fair? Constant rule changes involving foreign ownership, taxes, currency controls, trade, or contract law raise investment risk.

- Is the government reasonably competent, maintaining the value of its currency and preserving political stability?

ILLUSTRATION   *Hong Kong Loses Its Number One Ranking*

In May 2000, the Economist Intelligence Unit (a unit of *The Economist*) downgraded Hong Kong to sixth place from first in its annual ranking of the world's best places to do business in the next five years. According to the EIU, since the city's handover to China in 1997, China's political tampering and the gradual erosion of the rule of law had diminished Hong Kong's reputation for free-market policies. One worrisome factor, said the EIU, was the likelihood that the government would give preferential treatment to Chinese interests at the expense of foreign business.

ILLUSTRATION   *Unpredictable Philippine Courts Scare off Foreign Investors*

On August 13, 2003, the Philippines' Court of Appeals suspended central bank Governor Rafael Buenaventura and four senior deputies for a year without pay because they had shut down a failing Philippine bank three years earlier. This decision sent the Philippine peso plunging to a record low against the U.S. dollar and shook already precarious investor confidence. The reason was simple: In the Philippines' volatile political climate, with an unpredictable court system, the highly respected Mr. Buenaventura is a career banker and was one of the few stalwarts on whom investors and economists could base their forecasts of the Philippine economy. However, he was also a friend and appointee of President Gloria Arroyo's predecessor and political foe. Despite her denials, there is widespread speculation that President Arroyo engineered the court decision to remove Mr. Buenaventura. One consequence of legal decisions such as this one that are tainted by politics and corruption has been a 63 percent decline in foreign direct investment in the Philippines in the first half of 2003 compared to the same six months in 2002. Economists and foreign investors attribute this sharp drop in foreign investment, in part, to the tendency of Philippine courts to frequently involve themselves in business decisions in an arbitrary and capricious manner.

For example, in 2001, the Philippine Supreme Court ordered Singapore's Keppel Group to return a Philippine shipyard it had renovated and had been operating for seven years, saying that the 1994 legal provision that allowed Keppel to buy it was itself illegal. Similarly, in 1990, the Supreme Court stopped USI Far East Corp. of Taiwan from building a $370 million petrochemical plant in Batangas province because a congressman from Bataan sued to have the plant built in his province instead. When the Supreme Court agreed with him, USI promptly pulled out of the Philippines rather than become an easy target in an area plagued by communist guerillas and bandits.

Capital Flight   A useful indicator of the degree of political risk is the seriousness of capital flight. **Capital flight** refers to the export of savings by a nation's citizens because of fears about the safety of their capital. By its nature, capital flight is difficult to measure accurately because it is not directly observed in most cases. Nevertheless, one can usually infer the capital outflows, using balance-of-payments figures—particularly the entry labeled "errors and omissions." These estimates indicate that capital flight represents an enormous outflow of funds from developing countries.

> One good indicator of political risk is capital flight.

Between 1974 and 1982, Argentina borrowed $32.6 billion. Estimates of the level of capital flight from Argentina over the same period range from $15 billion to more than $27 billion.[3] These estimates would mean that capital flight amounted to between half and four-fifths of the entire inflow of foreign capital to Argentina. For Venezuela, the inflow was $27 billion over the same period, with capital flight estimated at between $12 billion and $22 billion. The inflow for Mexico was $79 billion between 1979 and 1984; the outflow has been estimated at between $26 billion and $54 billion for the same period. Other debtor countries, such as Nigeria and the Philippines, have also had large capital outflows. As conditions in many of these countries worsened, capital flight continued. As of the end of 1988, just prior to the end of the Latin American debt crisis, Morgan Guaranty estimated that Latin Americans held $243 billion in assets abroad, far exceeding the amount of loans to the region held by U.S. banks. And this excludes assets taken abroad before 1977. Exhibit 6.2 shows the breakdown of the $243 billion figure by country.

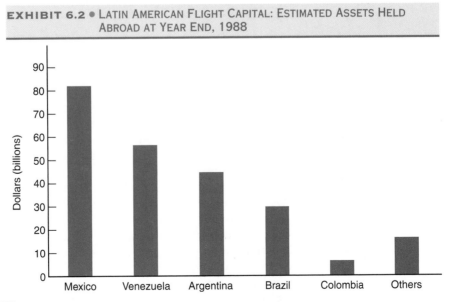

EXHIBIT 6.2 • LATIN AMERICAN FLIGHT CAPITAL: ESTIMATED ASSETS HELD ABROAD AT YEAR END, 1988

[3] These figures come from Steven Plaut, "Capital Flight and LDC Debt," *FRBSF Weekly Letter,* Federal Reserve Bank of San Francisco, January 8, 1988.

Capital flight occurs for several reasons, most of which have to do with inappropriate economic policies. These reasons include government regulations, controls, and taxes that lower the return on domestic investments. In countries where inflation is high and domestic inflation hedging is difficult or impossible, investors may hedge by shifting their savings to foreign currencies deemed less likely to depreciate. They may also make the shift when domestic interest rates are artificially held down by their governments or when they expect a devaluation of an overvalued currency.

Perhaps the most powerful motive for capital flight is political risk. In unstable political regimes (and in some stable ones), wealth is not secure from government seizure, especially when changes in regime occur. Savings may be shifted overseas to protect them. For example, the citizens of Hong Kong, which was turned over to communist China on July 1, 1997, responded to the anticipated change in regime by sending large sums of money abroad in advance.

Common sense dictates that if a nation's own citizens do not trust the government, then investment there is unsafe. After all, residents presumably have a better feel for conditions and government intentions than do outsiders. Thus, when analyzing investment or lending opportunities, multinational firms and international banks must note any apparent unwillingness of the nation's citizens to invest and lend in their own country.

Sound economic policies will reverse capital flight.

What is needed to halt capital flight are tough-minded economic policies—the kind of policies that make investors want to put their money to work instead of taking it out. As we shall see in the next section, these policies include cutting budget deficits and taxes, removing barriers to investment by foreigners, selling off state-owned enterprises, allowing for freer trade, and avoiding currency overvaluations that virtually invite people to ship their money elsewhere before the official exchange rate falls.

Such policies were employed in much of Latin America, with predictable results. As seen in Exhibit 6.3, beginning in 1990, capital flight was reversed, with private capital flooding back into Latin America. These capital inflows helped fuel the extraordinary performance of the Latin American stock markets that is discussed in Chapter 15. Unfortunately, after a few years of optimism, Latin America is again facing its old demons: low savings rates that make its countries dependent on foreign capital, overly centralized and costly governments, and an ineffectual political class. Tackling the entrenched interests that benefit from bloated public sectors requires a political leadership that has not materialized in Latin America. In response, private capital flows to Latin America have slowed markedly.

6.2 ECONOMIC AND POLITICAL FACTORS UNDERLYING COUNTRY RISK

We now examine in more detail some of the economic and political factors that contribute to the general level of risk in the country as a whole—termed **country risk**. The primary focus here is on how well the country is doing economically. As noted earlier, the better a nation's economic performance, the lower the likelihood that its government will take actions that adversely affect the value of companies operating there.

All countries entail some degree of political risk.

Although many of the examples used in this section involve less-developed countries (LDCs), high country risk is not confined to them. The same considerations affect developed countries as well. As we have already seen in Chapters 2 and 3, for example, Western European nations are currently confronting economic stagnation and business risk stemming from over-regulated economies, inflexible labor markets, and overly expansive and expensive social welfare states. Similarly, companies operating in the United States face systemic litigation risks and arbitrary changes in employment and environmental laws. Meanwhile, Japan is stuck with a rigid and highly regulated business system that puts too much power in the hands of the state and makes it difficult to adapt to a changed environment. Moreover, Japan has a banking system that refuses to face up to a problem of almost biblical proportions—an estimated $1.23

EXHIBIT 6.3 • PRIVATE CAPITAL RETURNS TO LATIN AMERICA

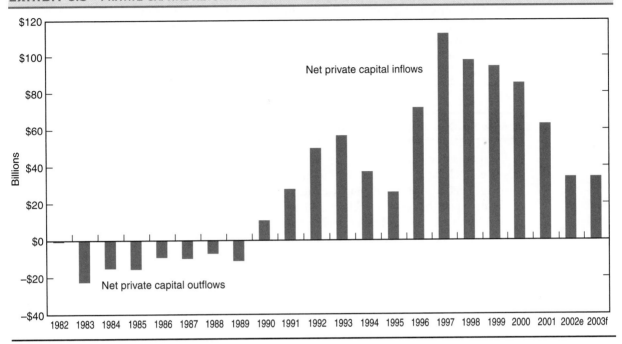

*e = estimated, f = forecast.

Sources: Bank for International Settlements, Inter-American Development Bank, and World Bank Group.

trillion in bad bank loans (in contrast, the U.S. savings and loan fiasco cost about $150 billion to resolve)—and a government that—fearing painful job losses, shuttered plants, and numerous bankruptcies if the problem is forcefully addressed—has gone along with this game of let's pretend that all is well. The failure to put insolvent borrowers out of their misery has left the Japanese economy loaded down with tens of thousands of sickly companies that are too weak to do anything except pile up more bad debts. Keeping these zombies alive also means that healthier rivals are unable to get the resources, customers, and funding they need to grow. The excess capacity also puts deflationary pressure on the Japanese economy. The result has been over a decade of economic stagnation, with politicians unwilling to induce the Japanese to take the bitter medicine needed to get their economy going again.

The bottom line is that no country offers a perfect business environment. Rather, countries are better or worse than average for doing business. We now examine key factors that determine the economic performance of a country and its degree of risk.

Fiscal Irresponsibility

Fiscal irresponsibility and monetary instability tend to go hand-in-hand.

To begin, fiscal irresponsibility—excessive government spending—is one sign of a country likely to be risky because it will probably have an insatiable appetite for money. Thus, one country risk indicator is the government deficit as a percentage of gross domestic product. The higher this figure, the more the government is promising to its citizens relative to the resources it is extracting in payment.[4] This gap lowers the possibility that the

---

[4] An increasingly important driver of government deficits and high taxes worldwide is state-run pension and retiree health care plans, such as Social Security and Medicare in the United States. Most of these plans are funded on a pay-as-you-go basis in which the payroll taxes of current workers are paid directly in benefits to current retirees; there are no savings to draw on for future beneficiaries. That leaves them vulnerable to a declining workforce and an increasing number of dependents, which is the situation in most developed nations today. And it will only get worse. As populations age and there are fewer workers to pay taxes for each person drawing pension and medical benefits, these plans will run ever-larger deficits. The political will to deal with these deficits by cutting benefits or raising taxes sharply is often lacking owing to the voting power of the elderly and the resistance of the young.

government can meet its promises without resorting to expropriations of property, raising taxes, or printing money. These actions, in turn, will adversely affect the nation's economic health. Expropriation will cause capital flight and dry up new investment; raising taxes will adversely affect incentives to work, save, and take risks; and printing money to finance a government deficit—known as **monetizing the deficit**—will result in monetary instability, high inflation, high interest rates, and currency depreciation.

ILLUSTRATION   *Japan as Number One in Fiscal Irresponsibility*

Even apparently stable countries are not immune to fiscal irresponsibility. For example, since 1992, Japan has attempted to kick-start its long-suffering economy by running huge budget deficits, the traditional Keynesian remedy for an economic downturn. Aside from giving Japan the highest debt-to-GDP ratio in the developed world (see Exhibit 6.4A), the end result has been a Japanese economy mired in a seemingly endless recession—and a clear repudiation of Keynesian economics (Exhibit 6.4B shows that after deficit spending totaling some $1.03 trillion over the ten-year period 1992–2001, Japan's GDP grew an average of 0.9 percent annually during this period—with four recessions thrown in for good measure—in contrast to average annual growth of 4.1 percent during the preceding ten-year period).[5] Only when Japan refocuses its anti-recessionary efforts away from fiscal stimulus and toward structural reforms—privatization and deregulation of its economy along with cleaning up its bad bank loan problem so that credit can start flowing again to healthy companies and allowing insolvent companies to go bankrupt—will it end its decade-long economic stagnation.[6]

EXHIBIT 6.4A • GROSS GOVERNMENT DEBT AS A PERCENTAGE OF GDP: 1992 AND 2001

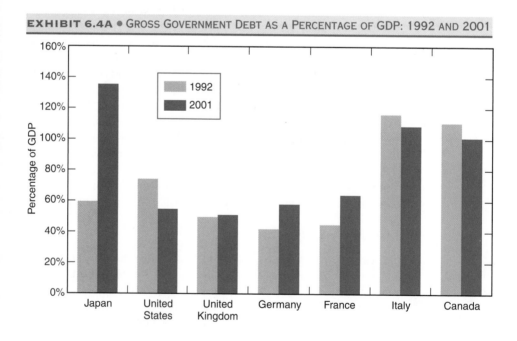

---

[5] Another apparent side effect of Japan's recent experience is to have silenced the numerous Japanologists who were exhorting the United States to emulate Japanese economic policies.

[6] Many observers have pointed to Japan's hostility towards competition in many aspects of its economic life as being a key roadblock to its recovery. In inefficient sectors such as construction and distribution, for example, losers continue to be propped up by government policy instead of being allowed to fail. Similarly, farming, health care, and education largely exclude private companies, thereby depriving Japan of the innovation that has driven its export-oriented industries and hobbling its economic growth. Not surprisingly, the lack of competition in its domestic economy makes Japan one of the highest-cost nations in the world.

EXHIBIT 6.4B • JAPANESE ECONOMIC PERFORMANCE OVER THE PAST DECADE: 1992–2001

Monetary Instability

Large government deficits are often monetized and result in high inflation.

As we saw in Chapter 4, according to modern monetary theory, inflation is the logical outcome of an expansion of the money supply in excess of real output growth. Large and unpredictable changes in the money supply lead to high and volatile inflation. Rapid expansion in the money supply is typically traceable to large government deficits that the central bank monetizes.

ILLUSTRATION   *Zimbabwe Descends into Chaos*

Zimbabwe, formerly known as Rhodesia, used to be an industrial powerhouse in Africa, second only to South Africa in the region. It has roads, factories, telephones, fertile farmland, and some of the most educated people in Africa. But the country is now undergoing an industrial revolution in reverse. Its factories are grinding to a halt for want of power and spare parts; its great mineral wealth is staying underground; tourism has plummeted; and the shelves in its shops are largely bare. These tribulations can be laid at the door of President Robert Mugabe, leader of the party that liberated Zimbabwe from white rule, and his policies. To soothe disgruntled veterans of the war against white rule, he gave 50,000 of them huge bales of cash that he borrowed or printed (Zimbabwe already had a large budget deficit). To win over rural black voters, he offered them free land—not idle state-owned land, but land belonging to white commercial farmers (who tend to back the opposition party). The peasants who settled on this land did not have the training or capital to properly farm it, so agricultural production has plummeted.

His policies had their predictable results. By voiding property rights, Mr. Mugabe killed investment. By monetizing the large budget deficit (in 2000 Zimbabwe spent more than twice what it received in tax revenues), he sparked inflation (running at an annual rate of 400 percent in July 2003). In a vain attempt to curb this inflation, Mr. Mugabe imposed price controls on fuel and food, leading to shortages. The government also started issuing treasury bills yielding far less than the rate of inflation. Since no one would buy them voluntarily, the regime forced institutional investors to put 45 percent of their portfolios into government paper.

The high inflation forced the Zim dollar to devalue in February 2003 from its previous official exchange rate of Z$55/U.S.$ to Z$824/U.S.$. Nonetheless, with a black market rate of Z$5,500/U.S.$, the Zim dollar is still greatly overvalued at its new official exchange rate. Only the government can get U.S. dollars at the official rate, and only by forcing exporters to surrender 40 percent of their hard-currency earnings. Many previously honest businessmen have turned to smuggling; others have gone bankrupt.

In response to these policies, the economy has nosedived. Although it is difficult to determine with precision just how bad things have gotten because of poor quality data, economists estimate that between 1997 and 2002, income per capita has fallen by at least 25 percent and possibly more than 50 percent.

Controlled Exchange Rate System

A key country risk indicator is an overvalued currency.

The economic problems presented by a fiscally and monetarily irresponsible government are compounded by having a **controlled exchange rate system,** where currency controls are used to fix the exchange rate. A controlled rate system goes hand in hand with an overvalued local currency, which is the equivalent of taxing exports and subsidizing imports. The risk of tighter currency controls and the ever-present threat of a devaluation encourage capital flight. Similarly, multinational firms will try to repatriate their local affiliates' profits rather than reinvest them. A controlled rate system also leaves the economy with little flexibility to respond to changing relative prices and wealth positions, exacerbating any unfavorable trend in the nation's *terms of trade,* the weighted average of the nation's export prices relative to its import prices—that is, the exchange rate between exports and imports.

Wasteful Government Spending

Another indicator of potential increased country risk is the amount of unproductive spending in the economy. To the extent that capital from abroad is used to subsidize consumption or is wasted on showcase projects, the government will have less wealth to draw on to repay the nation's foreign debts and is more likely to resort to exchange controls, higher taxes, and the like. In addition, funds diverted to the purchase of assets abroad (capital flight) will not add to the economy's dollar-generating capacity unless investors feel safe in repatriating their overseas earnings.

Resource Base

The resource base of a country consists of its natural, human, and financial resources. Other things being equal, a nation with substantial natural resources, such as oil or copper, is a better economic risk than is one without those resources. However, typically, all is not equal. Hence, nations such as South Korea and Taiwan turn out to be better risks than resource-rich Argentina and Brazil. The reason has to do with the quality of human resources and the degree to which these resources are allowed to be put to their most efficient use.

Political stability and free markets promote economic growth.

A nation with highly skilled and productive workers, a large pool of scientists and engineers, and ample management talent will have many of the essential ingredients needed to pursue a course of steady growth and development. Three additional factors are necessary: (1) a stable political system that encourages hard work and risk taking by allowing entrepreneurs to reap the rewards (and bear the losses) from their activities, (2) a flexible labor market that permits workers to be allocated to those jobs in which they will be the most productive, and (3) a free-market system that ensures that the prices people respond to correctly signal the relative desirability of engaging in different activities. In this way, the nation's human and natural resources will be put to their most efficient uses. The evidence by now is overwhelming that free markets bring wealth and that endless state meddling brings waste. The reason is simple: Unlike a government-controlled economy, free markets do not tolerate and perpetuate mistakes.

Country Risk and Adjustment to External Shocks

Countries that fail to adjust quickly to external economic shocks face future problems.

Recent history shows that the impact of external shocks is likely to vary from nation to nation; some countries deal successfully with these shocks, and others succumb to them. The evidence suggests that domestic policies play a critical role in determining how effectively a particular nation will deal with external shocks. Asian nations, for example, successfully coped with falling commodity prices, rising interest rates, and rising exchange rates during the 1980s because their policies promoted timely internal and external adjustment, as is manifest in relatively low inflation rates and small current-account deficits.

The opposite happened in Latin America, where most countries accepted the then-prevalent ideology that growth is best promoted by an **import-substitution development strategy** characterized by extensive state ownership, controls, and policies to encourage import substitution. Many of these countries took over failing private businesses, nationalized the banks, protected domestic companies against imports, ran up large foreign debts, and heavily regulated the private sector. Whereas the "East Asian Tigers"—Hong Kong, South Korea, Taiwan, and Singapore—tested their ability to imitate and innovate in the international marketplace, Latin American producers were content with the exploitation of the internal market, charging prices that were typically several times the international price for their goods. The lack of foreign competition has contributed to long-term inefficiency among Latin American manufacturers.

Statist policies that downgraded the role of market forces underlie Latin America's economic problems.

In addition, by raising the cost of imported materials and products used by the export sector, the Latin American import-substitution development strategies worsened their international competitive position, leaving the share of exports in GDP far below that of other LDCs. Moreover, state expenditures on massive capital projects diverted resources from the private sector and exports. Much of the investment went to inefficient state enterprises, leading to wasted resources and large debts.

The decline in commodity prices and the simultaneous rise in real interest rates in the early 1980s should have led to reduced domestic consumption. However, fearing that spending cuts would threaten social stability, Latin American governments delayed cutting back on projects and social expenditures. The difference between consumption and production was made up by borrowing overseas, thereby enabling their societies to temporarily enjoy artificially high standards of living.

Latin American governments also tried to stimulate their economies by increasing state spending, fueled by high rates of monetary expansion. This response exacerbated their difficulties because the resulting high rates of inflation combined with their fixed exchange rates to boost real exchange rates substantially and resulted in higher imports and lower exports. Moreover, the overvalued exchange rates, interest rate controls, and political uncertainties triggered massive capital flight from the region—estimated at up to $100 billion during the two-year period of 1981–1982. The result was larger balance-of-payments deficits that necessitated more foreign borrowing and higher debt-service requirements. Moreover, in an attempt to control inflation, the Latin American governments imposed price controls and interest rate controls. These controls led to further capital flight and price rigidity. Distorted prices gave the wrong signals to the residents, sending consumption soaring and production plummeting.

Market-Oriented versus Statist Policies

The great economic lesson of the ill-fated, post–World War II experiment in Communism is that markets work and command economies do not. The truly extraordinary difference in the economic results of these two systems—contrast the disparate experiences of East Germany and West Germany; North Korea and South Korea; and Hong Kong, Taiwan, and China under Mao—stems directly from their diametrically opposite means of organizing economic activity. In a **market economy**—also known as **capitalism**—economic decisions are made by individual decision makers based on prices—of goods, services, capital, labor, land, and other resources. In a **command economy**—often termed **socialism**—people at the top decide what is to be produced, how it is to be produced, and where it is to be produced, and then command others to follow the central plan.

Economic activity can be organized through markets or by command.

Why Capitalism Works

The core distinction between a market economy and a command economy, and the one that accounts for the huge disparity in their performances, is the different ways in which they harness information and incentives. Given that resources are scarce, economic decisions involve a series of tradeoffs. In order to make these trade-offs successfully, command economies demand that all the fragments of knowledge existing in different minds be brought together in the mind of the central planner, an impossible informational requirement. Markets work because economic decisions are made by those who have the information necessary to determine the trade-offs that must be made and the suitability of those trade-offs, given their own unique skills, circumstances, and preferences combined with market prices that signal the relative values and costs placed on those activities by society. Of equal importance, in a market economy, people have the incentives to efficiently act on that information.

Statist Policies Constrain Growth

Most countries today have a mixture of market and command economies. Pure command economies are rare nowadays—only Cuba and North Korea remain—and markets tend to predominate in the production and distribution of goods and services around the world. However, many nations follow *statist* policies in which markets are combined with heavy government intervention in their economies through various regulations and tax and spending policies. In addition, so-called critical industries, such as air transportation, mining, telecommunications, aerospace, oil, and power generation, are typically owned or controlled by the state. As a result, economic power is often heavily centralized in the state, usually with harmful consequences for wealth creation.

The centralization of economic power in much of the Third World turned the state into a huge patronage machine and spawned a swollen and corrupt bureaucracy to administer the all-encompassing rules and regulations. Avaricious elites, accountable to no one, used the labyrinthine controls and regulations to enrich themselves and further the interests of their own ethnic groups or professional class at the expense of national economic health and well-being.

Third World nations are promoting the private sector and individual initiative in an attempt to stimulate economic growth.

Why Statist Policies Persist

Many of these countries are finally rejecting their earlier statist policies and trying to stimulate the private sector and individual initiative. The experience in countries that are reforming their economies—including the former Soviet Union, China, and India, as well as much of Latin America—illustrates that it is far easier to regulate and extend the state's reach than to deregulate and retrench. When the state becomes heavily involved in the economy, many special interests from the state bureaucracy, business, labor, and consumer groups come to rely on state benefits. Of course, they actively oppose reforms that curtail their subsidies.

The process of reform is greatly complicated by egalitarian ideologies that deprecate private success while justifying public privilege and by the pervasiveness of the state, which distorts the reward pattern and makes it easier to get rich by politics rather than by industry, by connections rather than by performance. These ideologies tend to take investment and the provision of productive capacity for granted (they like capital but dislike capitalists), while being generally more concerned with redistributing the benefits and mitigating the costs of economic progress than with protecting its foundations.

The message is clear. In evaluating a nation's riskiness, it is not sufficient to identify factors—such as real interest shocks or world recession—that would systematically affect the economies of all foreign countries to one extent or another. It is necessary also to determine the susceptibility of the various nations to these shocks. This determination requires a focus on the financial policies and development strategies pursued by the different nations.

Key Indicators of Country Risk and Economic Health

Based on the preceding discussion, some of the common characteristics of high country risk are:

Pervasive government intervention in the economy, along with high tax and spending policies, reduces growth and increases country risk.

- A large government deficit relative to GDP
- A high rate of money expansion, especially if it is combined with a relatively fixed exchange rate
- Substantial government expenditures yielding low rates of return
- Price controls, interest rate ceilings, trade restrictions, rigid labor laws, and other government-imposed barriers to the smooth adjustment of the economy to changing relative prices
- High tax rates that destroy incentives to work, save, and invest
- Vast state-owned firms run for the benefit of their managers and workers
- A citizenry that demands, and a political system that accepts, government responsibility for maintaining and expanding the nation's standard of living through public-sector spending and regulations (the less stable the political system, the more important this factor will likely be)
- Pervasive corruption that acts as a large tax on legitimate business activity, holds back development, discourages foreign investment, breeds distrust of capitalism, and weakens the basic fabric of society
- The absence of basic institutions of government—a well-functioning legal system, reliable regulation of financial markets and institutions, and an honest civil service

Alternatively, positive indicators of a nation's long-run economic health include the following:

Market-oriented policies improve a nation's economic health and its credit-worthiness.

- *A structure of incentives that rewards risk taking in productive ventures.* People have clearly demonstrated that they respond rationally to the incentives they face, given the information and resources available to them. This statement is true whether we are talking about shopkeepers in Nairobi or bankers in New York. A necessary precondition for productive investment to take place is secure legal rights to own and sell at least some forms of property. If property is not secure, people have an incentive to consume their resources immediately or transfer them overseas, lest they be taken away. Low taxes are also important because they encourage productive efforts and promote savings and investment.
- *A legal structure that stimulates the development of free markets.* Wealth creation is made easier by stable rules governing society and fair and predictable application of laws administered by a judicial system free of corruption. Such a legal structure, which replaces official whim with the rule of law, combined with a system of property rights and properly enforceable contracts, facilitates the development of free markets. The resulting market price signals are most likely to contain the data and provide the incentives that are essential to making

efficient use of the nation's resources. Free markets, however, do more than increase economic efficiency. By quickly rewarding success and penalizing failure, they also encourage successful innovation and economic growth. Conversely, the lack of a rule of law and a well-defined commercial code, as in Russia, and the persistence of corruption, as in much of Africa and Latin America, hampers the development of a market economy by making it difficult to enforce contracts and forcing businesses to pay protection money to thugs, bureaucrats, or politicians.

- *Minimal regulations and economic distortions.* Complex regulations are costly to implement and waste management time and other resources. Moreover, reduced government intervention in the economy lowers the incidence of corruption. After all, why bribe civil servants if their ability to grant economic favors is minimal? Instead, the way to succeed in an unregulated economy is to provide superior goods and services to the market.

- *Clear incentives to save and invest.* In general, when there are such incentives—that is, the economic rules of the game are straightforward and stable, property rights are secure, taxes on investment returns are low, and there is political stability—a nation's chances of developing are maximized.

- *An open economy.* Free trade not only increases competition and permits the realization of comparative advantage, it also constrains government policies and makes them conform more closely to those policies conducive to increases in living standards and rapid economic growth. An open economy strengthens the rule of law as well because it must compete for investment capital by demonstrating that it protects property rights.

- *Stable macroeconomic policies.* Macroeconomic stability, largely promoted by a stable monetary policy, reduces economic risk and leads to lower inflation and lower real interest rates. The resulting increase in the willingness of people to save and entrepreneurs to invest in the domestic economy stimulates economic growth.

The sorry economic state of Eastern Europe under communism dramatically illustrates the consequences of pursuing policies that are the exact opposite of those recommended. Thus, the ability of the Eastern European countries to share in the prosperity of the Western world depends critically on reversing the policies they followed under communist rule.

Similarly, investors assessing the prospects for Western nations would also do well to recognize the benefits of markets and incentives. Government economic intervention in the form of subsidies and regulations is appealing to many, but governments make poor venture capitalists and for a simple reason: Industries not yet born do not have lobbyists, whereas old and established ones have lots of them. The net result is that the bulk of subsidies go to those industries resisting change. For example, Germany spends more on subsidies for powerful smokestack industries such as shipbuilding and coal mining than to support basic research. Until recently, it also sheltered the state-owned telecommunications monopoly, Deutsche Telekom, and its suppliers, such as Siemens, from most foreign competition;[7] government sheltering in turn dampens innovation across a range of industries. When government does invest in high-tech industries, it usually botches the job. Examples are legion, including the tens of billions of wasted tax dollars spent to develop European software, semiconductor, computer, and aerospace industries.

Low taxes and minimal regulation improve a nation's growth prospects.

Governments make poor venture capitalists.

---

[7] The German telecommunications industry was deregulated in 1998. However, Deutsche Telekom is still majority-owned by the German government.

ILLUSTRATION   *The 1948 West German Erhard Reforms*

At the end of World War II, the German economy lay in ruins. Industrial output in 1948 was one-third its 1936 level because of a massive disruption in production and trade patterns. Aside from the devastation caused by the war, economic disruption was aggravated by wartime money creation, price controls, and uncertainty about economic policy. Each day vast, hungry crowds traveled to the countryside to barter food from farmers; an extensive black market developed; and cigarettes replaced currency in many transactions.

In June 1948, Ludwig Erhard, West Germany's economic czar, announced an extensive reform package. This package created a new currency, the Deutsche mark (DM), and dismantled most price controls and rationing ordinances. It also implemented a restrictive monetary policy, lowered tax rates, and provided incentives for investment.

Erhard's reforms almost immediately established sound and stable macroeconomic conditions and led to the German "economic miracle." Consumer prices initially rose by 20 percent, but inflation then subsided to an average annual rate of about 1 percent between 1949 and 1959. Goods that had been hoarded or sold only in the black market flooded the market. Industrial production increased 40 percent in the second half of 1948 and then tripled over the next ten years. Real GDP and productivity also grew rapidly. Although unemployment rose from 3 percent in the first half of 1948 to more than 10 percent in the first half of 1950, it then disappeared over the next eight years. In 1958, the DM became convertible.

Economic reform could not have produced such dramatic results if West Germany had not had key structural elements already in place. It had the legal framework necessary for a market economy, many intact businesses, and skilled workers and managers. Marshall Plan money helped, but without the reforms, any aid would have been wasted.

The hard fact is that the LDCs must rely on self-help to cope with their problems.

Market-Oriented Policies Work   As the West German example illustrates, realism demands that nations—especially those in the Third World and Eastern Europe—come to terms with their need to rely more on self-help. The most successful economies, such as Hong Kong, South Korea, and Taiwan, demonstrate the importance of aligning domestic incentives with world market conditions. As a result of their market-oriented policies, Asian nations have had remarkable economic success over the past three decades as reflected in their strong economic growth and rising standards of living. Their recent problems just reinforce the importance of such policies: When Asian nations substituted the visible hand of state intervention for the invisible hand of the market in allocating capital, they helped create the financial crisis that rocked Asia in 1997. The evidence indicates that the more distorted the prior economic policies, the more severe the crisis, with Indonesia, South Korea, Thailand, and Malaysia being hit much harder than Hong Kong, Taiwan, and Singapore.

Like it or not, nations must make their way in an increasingly competitive world economy that puts a premium on self-help and has little time for the inefficiency and pretension of **statism**—that is, the substitution of state-owned or state-guided enterprises for the private sector—as the road to economic success. Statism destroys initiative and leads to economic stagnation. Free enterprise is the road to prosperity.

Market-oriented reform, including cutting government spending, is key to economic health.

This recognition—that countries cannot realize the benefits of capitalism without the institutions of capitalism—is dawning in even the most socialist countries of Europe, Asia, and Latin America. For example, in 1989, Vietnamese families were given the right to work their own land and sell their output at market prices. Within a year, rice production rose so dramatically that Vietnam went from the edge of famine to the world's third-largest rice exporter. Market-oriented reform of Eastern European and LDC economic policies lies at the heart of any credible undertaking to secure these nations' economic and financial rehabilitation. The first and most critical step is to cut government spending. In practical terms, cutting government spending means reducing the bloated public sectors that permeate most Latin American, African, and ex-communist countries.

Latin American countries have made great strides in reforming the public sector.

Market-Oriented Reform in Latin America Reform of the public sector has probably gone the furthest in Latin America, where, shocked by the severe miseries of the 1980s (known in Latin America as the *Lost Decade*), many of these countries abandoned the statism, populism, and protectionism that have crippled their economies since colonial times. Chile and Colombia have embarked on fairly comprehensive reform programs, emphasizing free markets and sound money, and, despite some backsliding and significant problems with corruption, Mexico has made surprisingly good headway (see Exhibit 6.5 for a summary of the changes in Mexico's economic policies). We saw in Chapter 2 that Argentina also undertook radical reform of its economy, highlighted by **privatizing**—returning to the private sector from the public sector—major activities and galvanizing the private sector by deregulation and the elimination of protectionism, although it has since engaged in backsliding. Poland has instituted a radical set of market reforms as well. The next big challenge for all these countries is to revamp the entire civil service, including police, regulatory agencies, judiciaries, and all the other institutions necessary for the smooth functioning of a market economy. The United States offers a persuasive example of how well-constructed institutions permit enterprising people of diverse cultures to flourish together.

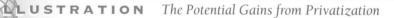

ILLUSTRATION *The Potential Gains from Privatization*

A recent study points to the potential gains from privatization.[8] Government-owned entities in India own about 43 percent of the country's capital stock and account for about 15 percent of nonagricultural employment. However, according to Exhibit 6.6, the labor (capital) productivity of public sector entities relative to that of their private sector competitors varies from 11 percent for labor (20 percent for capital) to 50 percent (88 percent) and averages just 26 percent (63 percent). Two factors largely account for these stark differences: (1) Public sector companies experience little pressure to perform better and (2) the government subsidies they receive means they can survive despite their extraordinary inefficiency. Privatizing these government entities would

EXHIBIT 6.5 • MEXICO'S ECONOMIC POLICIES: THEN AND NOW

Old Mexican Model	New Mexican Model
Large budget deficits	Fiscal restraint
Rapid expansion of money supply	Monetary discipline
Nationalization	Privatizations
Restricted foreign direct investment	Attract foreign direct investment
High tax rates	Tax reform
Import substitution	Trade liberalization
Controlled currency	End currency controls
Price and interest rate controls	Prices and interest rates set by market
Government-dominated economy	Reduced size and scope of government

---

[8] Amadeo M. Di Lodovico, William W. Lewis, Vincent Palmade, and Shirish Sankhe, "India—From Emerging to Surging," *The McKinsey Quarterly* 4 (2001): 1–5.

boost productivity, save on subsidies, and give their customers better products and services at lower prices. Despite these benefits, intense opposition from politicians, unions, and the media has largely frozen India's privatization program and held progress in broader economic reform to a glacial pace.

EXHIBIT 6.6 • INDIAN GOVERNMENT OWNERSHIP HURTS PRODUCTIVITY

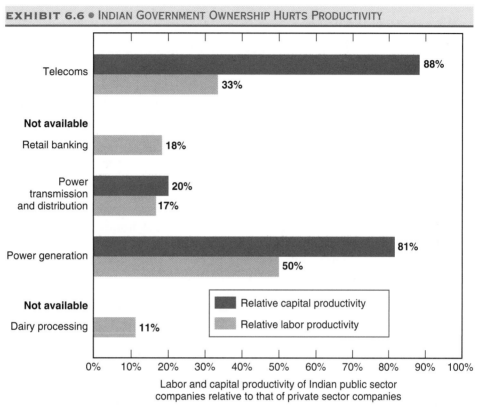

Labor and capital productivity of Indian public sector companies relative to that of private sector companies

Obstacles to Economic Reform   Yet in the best of circumstances, structural reform meets formidable political obstacles: labor unions facing job and benefit losses, bureaucrats fearful of diminished power and influence (not to mention their jobs), and local industrialists concerned about increased competition and reduced profitability. All are well aware that the benefits of restructuring are diffuse and materialize only gradually, while they must bear the costs immediately. Many are also trapped by a culture that sanctifies the state and distrusts the market's ability to bring about fair or wise results. This distrust reflects an ideology that equates inequality with inequity and is unwilling to accept the fact that the prospect of large rewards for some is the fuel that drives the economic engine of growth.

> Structural reform is necessary, but politically unpopular.

Despite these obstacles, reducing state subsidies on consumer goods and to inefficient industries, privatizing bloated state enterprises to boost productivity and force customer responsiveness, removing trade barriers and price controls, and freeing interest rates and the exchange rate to move to market levels are probably the most straightforward and workable solutions to economic stagnation. These actions, if implemented, can increase output (by making the economy more efficient), reduce consumption and therefore increase the quantity of goods available for export. They will also discourage capital flight and stimulate domestic savings and investment.

The simple truth is that a nation's success is not a function of the way its government harnesses resources, manages workers, or distributes wealth. Rather, economic success depends on the ability and willingness of a nation's people to work hard and take risks in the hopes of a better life. From this perspective, the state's best strategy is to provide basic stability—and little else—thereby permitting the humble to rise and the great to fall.

6.3 COUNTRY RISK ANALYSIS IN INTERNATIONAL BANKING

This section explores country risk from a bank's standpoint, the possibility that borrowers in a country will be unable or unwilling to service or repay their debts to foreign lenders in a timely manner. Countries that default will lose access, at least temporarily, to the international financial markets. For many borrowers, this penalty is severe enough that they do not voluntarily default on their bank loans. Thus, countries will sometimes go to extraordinary lengths to continue servicing their debts. Bank country risk analysis can, therefore, focus largely on ability to repay rather than willingness to repay. Consequently, the essence of country risk analysis at commercial banks is an assessment of factors that affect the likelihood that a country, such as Mexico, will be able to generate sufficient dollars to repay foreign debts as these debts come due.

> Banks face country risk on their international loans—the risk that foreign borrowers will be unable to repay their loans on time.

These factors are both economic and political and are very similar to those we already examined in analyzing country risk from an MNC's perspective. Among economic factors often pointed to are the country's resource base and its external financial position. Most important, however, are the quality and effectiveness of a country's economic and financial management policies. The evidence from those countries that have defaulted on their international debts is that all too often the underlying causes of country risk are homegrown, with massive corruption, bloated bureaucracies, and government intervention in the economy leading to inefficient and uncompetitive industries and huge amounts of capital squandered on money-losing ventures. In addition, poor macroeconomic policies have made their own contribution to economic instability. Many of these countries have large budget deficits that they monetized, leading to high rates of inflation, overvalued currencies, and periodic devaluations. The deficits stem from too many promises that cannot be met from available resources and high tax rates that result in tax evasion, low revenue collections, and further corruption.

Political factors that underlie country risk include the degree of political stability of a country and the extent to which a foreign entity, such as the United States, is willing to implicitly stand behind the country's external obligations. Lending to a private-sector borrower also exposes a bank to commercial risks, in addition to country risk. Because these commercial risks are generally similar to those encountered in domestic lending, they are not treated separately.

Country Risk and the Terms of Trade

> Default risk on a country's debts partly depends on how the government responds to a change in its terms of trade.

What ultimately determines a nation's ability to repay foreign loans is that nation's ability to generate U.S. dollars and other hard currencies. This ability, in turn, is based on the nation's terms of trade. Most economists would agree that these terms of trade are largely independent of the nominal exchange rate, unless the observed exchange rate has been affected by government intervention in the foreign exchange market.

In general, if its terms of trade increase, a nation will be a better credit risk. Alternatively, if its terms of trade decrease, a nation will be a poorer credit risk. This **terms-of-trade risk**, however, can be exacerbated by political decisions. When a nation's terms of trade improve, foreign goods become relatively less expensive, the nation's standard of living rises, and consumers and businesses become more dependent on imports. However, because there is a large element of unpredictability to relative price changes, shifts in the terms of trade also will be unpredictable. When the nation's terms of trade decline, as must inevitably happen when prices fluctuate randomly, the government will face political pressure to maintain the nation's standard of living.

Capital flight exacer-
bated the debt crisis.

As we saw in Section 6.2, a typical response is for the government to fix the exchange rate at its former (and now overvalued) level—that is, to subsidize the price of dollars. Loans made when the terms of trade improved are now doubly risky: first, because the terms of trade have declined and, second, because the government is maintaining an *overvalued currency,* further reducing the nation's net inflow of dollars. The deterioration in the trade balance usually results in added government borrowing. Capital flight exacerbates this problem, as residents recognize the country's deteriorating economic situation.

To summarize, a terms-of-trade risk can be exacerbated if the government tries to avoid the necessary drop in the standard of living when the terms of trade decline by maintaining the old and now-overvalued exchange rate. In reality, of course, this element of country risk is a political risk. The government is attempting by political means to hold off the necessary economic adjustments to the country's changed wealth position.

A key issue, therefore, in assessing country risk is the speed with which a country adjusts to its new wealth position. In other words, how fast will the necessary austerity policy be implemented? The speed of adjustment will be determined in part by the government's perception of the costs and benefits associated with austerity versus default.

The Government's Cost/Benefit Calculus

The cost of austerity is determined primarily by the nation's external debts relative to its wealth, as measured by its gross domestic product. The lower this ratio, the lower the relative amount of consumption that must be sacrificed to meet a nation's foreign debts.

The cost of default is the likelihood of being cut off from international credit. This possibility brings with it its own form of austerity. Most nations will follow this path only as a last resort, preferring to stall for time in the hope that something will happen in the interim. That something could be a bailout by the IMF, the Bank for International Settlements, the Federal Reserve, or some other major central bank. The bailout decision is largely a political decision. It depends on the willingness of citizens of another nation, usually the United States, to tax themselves on behalf of the country involved.[9] This willingness is a function of two factors: (1) the nation's geopolitical importance to the United States and (2) the probability that the economic adjustments that would be necessary if the country were not bailed out will result in unacceptable political turmoil.

Highly variable
terms of trade and
an unstable political
system magnify
country risk.

The more a nation's terms of trade fluctuate and the less stable its political system, the greater the odds the government will face a situation that will tempt it to hold off on the necessary adjustments. Terms-of-trade variability probably will be inversely correlated with the degree of product diversification in the nation's trade flows. With limited diversification—for example, dependence on the export of one or two primary products or on imports heavily weighted toward a few commodities—the nation's terms of trade are likely to be highly variable. This characterizes the situation facing many Third World countries. It also describes, in part, the situation of those OECD (Organization for Economic Cooperation and Development) nations heavily dependent on oil imports.

Lessons from the International Debt Crisis

During the 1970s and early 1980s, international banks lent hundreds of billions of dollars to less-developed countries and communist countries. Most of the money was squandered on all sorts of extravagant and profitless projects, from Amazon highways to highly automated steel mills in Africa. These loans made sense, however, only as long as banks and their depositors

---

[9] See Tamir Agmon and J. K. Dietrich, "International Lending and Income Redistribution: An Alternative View of Country Risk," *Journal of Banking and Finance,* December 1983, pp. 483–495, for a discussion of this point.

were willing to suspend their disbelief about the risks of international lending. By now, the risks are big and obvious, particularly in light of the **international banking crisis of 1982**.

Onset of the Crisis   This crisis began in August 1982, when Mexico announced that it was unable to meet its regularly scheduled payments to international creditors. Shortly thereafter, Brazil and Argentina (the second- and third-largest debtor nations) found themselves in a similar situation. By the spring of 1983, about twenty-five less-developed countries—accounting for two-thirds of the international banks' claims on this group of countries—were unable to meet their debt payments as scheduled and had entered into loan-rescheduling negotiations with the creditor banks. Altogether, the LDCs defaulted on several hundred billion dollars worth of debt. Lending to LDCs dried up, but this was the equivalent of locking the barn door after the horses had escaped.

Reform Takes Hold   By late 1983, the intensity of the international debt crisis began to ease as the world's economic activities picked up—boosting the LDCs' export earnings—and as the orderly rescheduling of many overdue international loans was completed. However, it was not until 1991 that net international bank lending (new loans net of loans repaid) turned positive again, following on the heels of the dramatic economic reforms under way in many LDCs. The major reason for the drop in international lending activity through the 1980s was the difficulty the LDC debtor nations had in achieving sustained economic growth. The LDCs required capital formation to grow but the banks first wanted to see economic reforms that would improve the odds that the LDCs would be able to service their debts.

Debt Relief   Many of the LDCs pushed for **debt relief**—that is, reducing the principal or interest payments, or both, on loans. However, the middle-income debtor nations were neither very poor nor insolvent. They possess considerable human and natural resources, reasonably well-developed infrastructures and productive capacities, and the potential for substantial growth in output and exports given sound economic policies. In addition, many of these countries possess considerable wealth—much of it invested abroad.

Although debt burdens exacerbated the economic problems faced by these countries, all too often the underlying causes were to be found in patronage-bloated bureaucracies, overvalued currencies, massive corruption, and politically motivated government investments in money-losing ventures. These countries also suffered from markets that were distorted by import protection for inefficient domestic producers and government favors for politically influential groups. For these countries, debt relief was at best an ineffectual substitute for sound macroeconomic policy and major structural reform; relief would only have weakened discipline over economic policy and undermined support for structural reform.

The Crisis Ends   Ten years after it began, the decade-long Latin American debt crisis ended in July 1992 with the signing of an agreement with Brazil to restructure the $44 billion it owed foreign banks. In the end, however, it was not negotiation that cut the Gordian knot of Latin American debt—no new money until Latin America showed economic growth, yet growth required new money—but genuine economic reforms, forced on unwilling governments by the unrelenting pressures of the debt crisis. Mexico and Chile, hopelessly mired in debt, so thoroughly reformed their economies, spurring economic growth in the process, that they were able to raise new money from the international capital markets. These economic reforms included opening their markets to imports, tearing down barriers to foreign investment, selling off state-owned companies, instituting tight money policies, and cutting government deficits. The examples of Mexico and Chile led others, such as Argentina and Venezuela, to change their policies as well—at least for a while (Argentina and Venezuela have subsequently elected populist presidents who reversed many of these policies).

> With the onset of the international debt crisis in 1982, banks pulled back sharply on their international lending.

> The key to solving the international debt crisis was economic reform that improved the prospects for economic growth.

Lessons from Successful Economic Reform   The experiences of Mexico, Chile, and Argentina—countries that successfully implemented economic reform programs (despite Argentina's later backsliding)—show that they all met the following criteria:[10]

LDC debtors had to rely on self-help rather than debt relief to cope with their problems.

- A head of state who demonstrates strong will and political leadership
- A viable and comprehensive economic plan that is implemented in a proper sequence
- A motivated and competent economic team working in harmony
- Belief in the plan from the head of state, the cabinet, and other senior officials
- An integrated program to sell the plan to all levels of society through the media

These criteria are applicable not only to Latin America but to all LDCs anywhere in the world. Even with the best of intentions, however, economic reform is painful and difficult to make stick unless all levels of society are convinced that instituting free-market policies will bring the long-term benefits of sustained growth.

Recent experience has also shown that crises are less severe and more avoidable if countries follow sensible (and credible) monetary and fiscal policies, limit their short-term foreign borrowing, and strengthen their financial systems. The need to pursue sound economic policies is particularly important for countries, like China, that have liberalized their economies and become more subject to market forces.

6.4 SUMMARY AND CONCLUSIONS

From the standpoint of a multinational corporation, country risk analysis is the assessment of factors that influence the likelihood that a country will have a healthy investment climate. A favorable business environment depends on the existence of a stable political and economic system in which entrepreneurship is encouraged and free markets predominate. Under such a system, resources are most likely to be allocated to their highest-valued uses, and people will have the greatest incentive to take risks in productive ventures.

Several costly lessons have led to a new emphasis on country risk analysis in international banking as well. From the bank's standpoint, country risk—the credit risk on loans to a nation—is largely determined by the real cost of repaying the loan versus the real wealth that the country has to draw on. These parameters, in turn, depend on the variability of the nation's terms of trade and the government's willingness to allow the nation's standard of living to adjust rapidly to changing economic fortunes.

The experience of those countries that have made it through the international debt crisis suggests that others in a similar situation can get out only if they institute broad systemic reforms. Their problems are caused by governments spending too much money they do not have to meet promises they should not make. They create public-sector jobs for people to do things they should not do and subsidize companies to produce high-priced goods and services. These countries need less government and fewer bureaucratic rules. Debt forgiveness or further capital inflows would only tempt these nations to postpone economic adjustment further.

QUESTIONS

1. What are some indicators of country risk? Of country health?
2. What can we learn about economic development and political risk from the contrasting experiences of East and West Germany, North and South Korea, and China and Taiwan, Hong Kong, and Singapore?
3. What role do property rights and the price system play in national development and economic efficiency?
4. What indicators would you look for in assessing the political riskiness of an investment in Eastern Europe?
5. Exhibit 6.5 describes some economic changes that have been instituted by Mexico in recent years.
   a. What are the likely consequences of those changes?
   b. Who are the winners and the losers from these economic changes?

---

[10] These criteria appear in William R. Rhodes, "Third World Debt: The Disaster That Didn't Happen," *The Economist*, September 12, 1992, pp. 21–23.

PROBLEMS

1. Comment on the following statement discussing Mexico's recent privatization: "Mexican state companies are owned in the name of the people but are run and now privatized to benefit Mexico's ruling class."

2. In the early 1990s, China decided that by 2000 it would boost its electricity-generating capacity by more than half. To do that, it is planning on foreigners investing at least $20 billion of the roughly $100 billion tab. However, Beijing has informed investors that, contrary to their expectations, they will not be permitted to hold majority stakes in large power-plant or equipment-manufacturing ventures. In addition, Beijing has insisted on limiting the rate of return that foreign investors can earn on power projects. Moreover, this rate of return will be in local currency without official guarantees that the local currency can be converted into dollars, and it will not be permitted to rise with the rate of inflation. Beijing says that if foreign investors fail to invest in these projects, it will raise the necessary capital by issuing bonds overseas. However, these bonds will not carry the "full faith and credit of the Chinese government."

   a. What problems do you foresee for foreign investors in China's power industry?

   b. What options do potential foreign investors have to cope with these problems?

   c. How credible is the Chinese government's fallback position of issuing bonds overseas to raise capital in lieu of foreign direct investment?

3. The president of Mexico has asked you to advise him on the likely economic consequences of the following five policies designed to improve Mexico's economic environment. Describe the consequences of each policy, and evaluate the extent to which these proposed policies will achieve their intended objective.

   a. Expand the money supply to drive down interest rates and stimulate economic activity.

   b. Increase the minimum wage to raise the incomes of poor workers.

   c. Impose import restrictions on most products to preserve the domestic market for local manufacturers and thereby increase national income.

   d. Raise corporate and personal tax rates from 50 percent to 70 percent to boost tax revenues and reduce the Mexican government deficit.

   e. Fix the nominal exchange rate at its current level in order to hold down the cost to Mexican consumers of imported necessities (assume that inflation is currently 100 percent annually in Mexico).

BIBLIOGRAPHY

Agmon, Tamir, and J. K. Dietrich. "International Lending and Income Redistribution: An Alternative View of Country Risk," *Journal of Banking and Finance,* December 1983, pp. 483–495.

Kobrin, Stephen J. "Political Risk: A Review and Reconsideration." *Journal of International Business Studies,* Spring–Summer 1979, pp. 67–80.

Krueger, Anne O. "Asian Trade and Growth Lessons." *American Economic Review,* May 1990, pp. 108–112.

Landes, David S. "Why Are We So Rich and They So Poor?" *American Economic Review,* May 1990, pp. 1–13.

Lessard, Donald R., and John Williamson, eds. *Capital Flight and Third World Debt.* Washington, D.C.: Institute for International Economics, 1987.

Plaut, Steven. "Capital Flight and LDC Debt," *FRBSF Weekly Letter,* Federal Reserve Bank of San Francisco, January 8, 1988.

Rhodes, William R. "Third World Debt: The Disaster That Didn't Happen," *The Economist,* September 12, 1992, pp. 21–23.

Shapiro, Alan C. "The Management of Political Risk." *Columbia Journal of World Business,* Fall 1981, pp. 45–56.

————. "Risk in International Banking." *Journal of Financial and Quantitative Analysis,* December 1982, pp. 727–739.

————. "Currency Risk and Country Risk in International Banking." *Journal of Finance,* July 1985, pp. 881–891.

INTERNET RESOURCES

www.moodys.com Web site of Moody's. Contains country risk ratings and analyses.

www.standardandpoors.com Web site of Standard & Poor's. Contains country risk ratings and analyses.

INTERNET EXERCISES

1. What country risk factors do Moody's and Standard & Poor's emphasize?

2. Pick out a country (e.g., Argentina, China). What is the general assessment of your pick's country risk? Has it increased or decreased over the past year? What factors caused this change?

CASE I.1
WILL ARGENTINA DEVALUE ITS PESO?

In November 2000, Mike Lanning was reacting to reports that Argentina might devalue its peso. Such a decision would have important ramifications for his company, Wessen Development Inc., (WDI). WDI is contemplating entering a joint venture with IRSA, the largest developer of shopping malls in Argentina, to construct a new shopping mall on the outskirts of Buenos Aires. The new shopping center, codenamed Mega, would include a Jumbo supermarket, 150 retail outlets, a movie theater with sixteen screens, a video game center, and a bowling alley. Mr. Lanning believes there is still much room for growth in shopping centers, especially outside of Buenos Aires. He notes that Argentina has 0.04 square meters of shopping center space per habitant. By comparison, in the United States there are 0.7 square meters of shopping center space per habitant, or nearly twenty times the space found in Argentina. Moreover, in Argentina's interior, where entertainment opportunities are limited, shopping centers—with their movie theaters, entertainment centers, restaurants, and stores—make a good place for a family outing.

Despite these promising prospects for Mega and other shopping projects, he is greatly concerned that the slowdown in Argentine economic activity and high unemployment rate could lead to renewed pressure to rescind the Convertibility Act and devalue the peso. Exhibit I 1.1 contains key Argentine economic indicators. One of the problems pointed to by opponents of convertibility is that Argentina is especially vulnerable to external shocks because of its currency board, which fixes the peso at par with the dollar and requires that the monetary base be fully backed by international reserves. Any turmoil in global capital markets, such as occurred during the Mexican, Asian, Russian, and Brazilian crises, leads to capital outflows, which push interest rates up and restrict the government's access to international debt markets. The currency board also makes Argentina exposed to devaluations by its Brazilian neighbor, such as occurred in January 1999. Argentina sends more than 30 percent of its exports to Brazil, so a devaluation of the Brazilian *real* makes Argentine business less competitive in its most important market. A *real* devaluation also gives Brazilian producers a competitive edge over their Argentinian counterparts in the Argentine market as well.

EXHIBIT I 1.1 • KEY ARGENTINE ECONOMIC INDICATORS

Key indicators	*1997*	*1998*	*1999*	
GDP ($ billions)	293.0	298.3	282.9	
Real GDP growth (%)	8.1	3.9	−3.1	
Consumer price inflation (%)	0.5	0.9	−1.2	
Population (millions)	35.7	36.1	36.6	
Exports of goods ($ millions)	26,431	26,441	23,316	
Imports of goods ($ millions)	28,554	29,558	24,145	
Current-account balance ($ millions)	−11,954	−14,274	−12,152	
Foreign-exchange reserves excluding gold ($ billions)	22,320	24,752	26,252	
Total external debt ($ billions)	130.8	144.1	148.6	
Debt-service ratio (%)	50.2	57.6	63.1	
Exchange rate (Ps:US$)	1	1	1	
Key indicators (forecast)	*2000*	*2001*	*2002*	*2003*
Real GDP growth (%)	0.8	3.7	3.4	3.7
Consumer price inflation (%)	−0.9	−0.7	0.4	1.3
Budget balance (% of GDP)	−2.1	−1.5	−0.8	−0.1
Current-account balance (% of GDP)	−4.2	−4.4	−3.6	−3.9
Money-market rate (%)	6.9	6.7	6.4	7
Exchange rate (Ps:US$)	1	1	1	1

A rise in interest rates and reduced access to capital or a devaluation of the *real* will slow down economic growth or even push the country deeper into recession, something Argentina does not need with its double-digit unemployment rate.[1] Under the currency board system, Argentine prices will drop in response to a recession, thereby bringing the economy back to equilibrium, but the adjustment mechanism is costly and protracted.

A peso devaluation, on the other hand, could improve the competitiveness of Argentine exports and import-competing products as well as reduce real interest rates (once the threat of devaluation was gone). A decline in real interest rates along with improved trade prospects, in turn, would stimulate Argentine economic activity and reduce unemployment. The latter effects would help boost government tax revenues as well and could reduce its unemployment compensation and other social spending.

However, devaluation has its own problems. For one thing, most of Argentina's liabilities are denominated in dollars (see Exhibit I 1.2 for an accounting of these dollar-denominated liabilities). A devaluation of the peso would lead to a redistribution of wealth to creditors from debtors, with much of this redistribution occurring between foreign creditors and Argentine debtors. However, the inflation that would follow a devaluation of the peso would mitigate this wealth redistribution somewhat although it would bring its own set of problems.

Peso devaluation would also reduce the equity of Argentine banks and private companies. Even if all domestic private and public dollar-denominated debt were to be honored in pesos, a devaluation of the peso would put substantial pressure on bank capital. As shown in Exhibit I 1.3, at a new peso:dollar exchange rate of 1.7:1, bank capital would go to zero. It would take a much larger peso devaluation (1 to 3.5) to wipe out non-bank capital. The higher peso costs of servicing the Argentine government's foreign debts following a peso devaluation would increase the budget deficit as well. According to Exhibit I 1.4, a devaluation of the peso to 1.7 would increase the Argentine deficit by over 50 percent, to 2.9 percent of GDP from 1.9 percent.

In talking to some investment bankers, Mike Lanning was made aware that pressure for a peso devaluation would likely decline if the promised monetary easing by the Federal Reserve takes place. Lower U.S. interest rates would lead to lower Argentine rates and stronger economic growth.

Another option being considered is unilateral dollarization, whereby Argentina would replace the peso with the dollar. Dollarization, it is argued, would enhance the credibility of Argentina's commitment to monetary and exchange rate stability. Despite the currency board, the Argentine peso is not fully credible. Hence, any shocks from global financial crises result in widening spreads between peso- and dollar-denominated bonds, leaving the Argentine economy with high credit costs, less investment, and slower economic growth. Proponents claim that dollarization, by reducing the risk of devaluation, would result in lower Argentine interest rates and faster economic growth. The tradeoff is the loss of monetary policy options that would ensue once the Argentine peso is completely abolished. Most important of these is that dollarization appears to preclude a "lender of last resort." However, Argentina has a limited lender-of-last-resort capacity through its Contingent Repurchase Facility, which offers a temporary source of funds to illiquid banks. This facility, which was arranged in 1996, gives Argentina the option to sell government bonds to a group of international banks under a repurchase agreement. Another cost of dollarization would be the Argentine government's loss of seigniorage. Currently, the currency board stands ready to convert pesos into dollars but it invests its

---

[1] It should be noted that many analysts attribute the high unemployment rate to Argentina's rigid labor laws rather than to peso overvaluation. Other analysts have pointed to the deteriorating education system as causing wage stagnation and increased demands by the Peronist labor unions for job security.

EXHIBIT I 1.2 • DOLLAR-DENOMINATED ARGENTINE LIABILITIES

	Local creditors	*Foreign creditors*	*Total*
Non-financial public sector and central bank	$32,200	$ 81,000	$113,200
Non-financial private sector	46,700	35,100	81,800
Financial sector	2,100	23,600	25,700
U.S. dollar liabilities (total)	$81,000	$139,700	$220,700

EXHIBIT I 1.3 • PRIVATE-SECTOR IMPACT OF PESO DEVALUATION

| | | Post-Devaluation Scenarios | | |
	Current	1	2	3
Exchange rate	1.00	1.40	1.70	3.47
Non-financial sector (millions of pesos)				
Assets	80,890	80,890	80,890	80,890
Liabilities	38,046	44,988	50,211	80,890
Equity	42,843	35,892	30,678	0
Change in equity		−16.2%	−28.4%	−100.0%
Banks (millions of pesos)				
Assets	155,023	155,023	155,023	
Liabilities	138,229	147,962	155,023	
Equity	16,794	7,061	0	
Change in equity		−58.0%	−100.0%	

EXHIBIT I 1.4 • PUBLIC-SECTOR IMPACT OF PESO DEVALUATION
(IN PESOS UNLESS OTHERWISE INDICATED)

| | | Post-Devaluation Scenarios | |
	Current	1	2
Exchange rate	1.00	1.40	1.70
Total revenues	54,900	54,900	54,900
Primary spending	52,800	52,800	52,800
Primary balance*	2,100	2,100	2,100
Interest payments	8,000	10,063	11,560
Pesos	640	640	640
U.S. dollars	7,360	9,423	10,920
– To local creditors	2,355	2,355	2,355
– To foreign creditors	5,005	7,068	8,565
Central bank revenue	400	1,128	1,368
Fiscal balance	(5,500)	(6,835)	(8,092)
Fiscal balance (% of GDP)	−1.9%	−2.4%	−2.9%

*Primary balance refers to the government's pre-interest balance.

dollars in interest-bearing assets. These assets would have to be sold off to get the cash to replace the pesos currently in circulation.

Mike Lanning also realized that he had to consider the consequences of these alternative currency scenarios for his own projects as well as the likelihood of their materializing.

QUESTIONS

1. What are the pros and cons of Argentine peso devaluation?

2. Given these pros and cons, what is the likelihood that Argentina will devalue its peso?

3. What are the pros and cons of dollarization?

4. What are the likely consequences of peso devaluation for the Mega project?

5. What effects would dollarization likely have on the Mega project?

6. What alternatives are available to stimulate Argentina's economic growth independent of exchange rate policy?

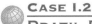

CASE I.2
BRAZIL FIGHTS A *REAL* BATTLE

In 1994, with inflation running at close to 50 percent *monthly* and Brazil's economy near collapse, Fernando Cardoso was elected president. A former socialist mugged by reality, Cardoso opened the economy, adopted a number of free-market policies, stabilized the currency, and brought inflation down to just 7 percent annually by 1997. Now the Asian financial turmoil is threatening President Cardoso's proudest achievement and the cornerstone of his popularity: a stable Brazilian *real*. Fallout from the Asian crisis has been more acute in Brazil than elsewhere in Latin America, partly because speculators believe that the *real* is overvalued. They also see parallels to Asia in Brazil's large trade deficit financed by foreign capital inflows. The pressure on the *real* has been ratcheted up because Brazilian financial players are unusually aggressive and sophisticated, traits that are a legacy of the past three decades when rampant inflation and abrupt policy shifts forced traders to be brutally pragmatic and move quickly to survive.

The speculators may have met their match in President Cardoso, however. Cardoso is unlikely to give up easily because he has staked Brazil's fortunes, and his own, on the *Real Plan,* which he had introduced in 1993 while he was finance minister. Its linchpin is a crawling peg designed to end the cycle of runaway inflation followed by massive devaluations that has given Brazil thirty years of economic chaos and eroded living standards for much of the population. By permitting only a tightly controlled and limited 0.6 percent depreciation of the *real* against the dollar each month (see Exhibit I 2.1), Cardoso has managed to halt Brazil's hyperinflation and bring a new confidence that is spurring foreign investment (see Exhibit I 2.2 for statistics on the Brazilian economy). However, Brazil's current account deficit is mounting, its foreign exchange reserves are falling, and financial markets are getting nervous that the *real* will suffer the same fate as that of the Asian currencies. The loss of confidence in the *real* is showing up in the form of capital flight, with $10 billion fleeing Brazil in the last two weeks of October 1997 alone.

In addition, a fractious Congress has kept President Cardoso from carrying out the budgetary reforms that would allow him to control the fiscal deficits that have been the engine of hyperinflation and thereby institutionalize Brazil's newfound macroeconomic stability. These reforms, which include revamping the tax, civil service, and social

EXHIBIT I 2.1 • BRAZIL'S CRAWLING PEG LEADS TO A GRADUAL DEVALUATION OF THE *REAL* AGAINST THE U.S. DOLLAR

Source: *International Financial Statistics*, various editions.

EXHIBIT I 2.2 • KEY BRAZILIAN ECONOMIC STATISTICS (IN U.S. $ BILLIONS UNLESS OTHERWISE INDICATED)

	1990	*1991*	*1992*	*1993*	*1994*	*1995*	*1996*	*1997*
Gross domestic product	$445.9	$386.2	387.3	$429.7	$543.1	$705.4	$775.4	$803.0
Current-account balance	−$3.8	−$1.5	$6.1	$0.0	−$1.2	−$18.1	−$24.3	−$33.8
Current-account balance (% of GDP)	−0.9%	−0.4%	1.6%	0.0%	−0.2%	−2.6%	−3.1%	−4.2%
Budget deficit (% of GDP)[1]	−1.4%	−1.4%	2.2%	−0.2%	−1.3%	4.8%	3.9%	5.9%
Foreign investment[2]	$0.8	$3.9	$16.4	$15.8	$23.8	$25.8	$34.3	$55.1
Portolio	$0.5	$3.8	$14.5	$15.0	$21.6	$22.6	$24.7	$37.2
Direct	$0.3	$0.1	$1.9	$0.9	$2.2	$3.3	$9.6	$17.9
Reserves excluding gold	$7.4	$8.0	$22.5	$30.6	$37.1	$49.7	$58.3	$51.4
Exchange rate (end of period, reais/$)[3]	0.000064	0.0004	0.005	0.119	0.846	0.973	1.039	1.116
Inflation (consumer price index)	1657.7%	493.8%	1156.0%	2828.7%	992.0%	25.9%	11.3%	7.2%
U.S. inflation rate (CPI)	5.4%	4.2%	3.2%	3.0%	2.6%	2.8%	3.0%	2.3%

[1] A negative sign indicates a budget surplus.

[2] Other components of foreign investment are relatively minor.

[3] Exchange rate for the *real* prior to 1994 reflects the effects of two earlier currency replacements.

Source: Current Bank of Brazil Bulletin, April 1998 and *Economic Report of the President,* February 1998.

security systems, and privatizing key industries from telecom to mining, would allow Brazil to consolidate the economic gains it has already made, give investors greater confidence in the economy's future, and speed up Brazil's growth rate. As of now, Brazil has a bloated public sector (government workers cannot be dismissed, regardless of performance), large budget deficits (5.9 percent of GDP in 1997), protected industries, high tax rates with low tax collections, and one of the most unequal distributions of income and wealth in the world. One legacy of Brazil's large budget deficits is that the country must now roll over about $20 billion a month in government debt.

Nonetheless, until the Asian crisis hit, investors had responded to currency stabilization and the free-market reforms already begun by pushing up the Brazilian bolsa (stock market) by about 158 percent from January 1994, when the *Real Plan* took hold, to October 1997 (see Exhibit I 2.3). However, contagion from the Asian crisis has recently pummeled the bolsa, sending it down 29 percent from August through October.

Although it now appears that Cardoso will have to wait until his second term in office to carry out most of the proposed reforms, he is nonetheless reputed to be preparing a new push on his long-stalled reform program. One of the stalled reforms is a bill to privatize the Brazilian social security system. This system, which pays out benefits to some workers in their 40s, is widely viewed as contributing to a Brazilian savings rate of just 16 percent of GDP (to put this number into perspective, Asian countries average closer to 30 percent). Until the presidential election in October 1998, Cardoso expects to maintain a tight-money policy that will support the *real* and, it is hoped, prevent the trade deficit from spiraling out of control. In addition to raising interest rates, the government's main weapon to stanch Brazil's fiscal and trade deficits is a newly invigorated privatization program. In the first half of 1997, a large share of the $7.4 billion in foreign direct investment came in the form of purchases of state-owned businesses. Altogether, Brazil expects to take in an estimated $17 billion from privatizations in 1997 and at least $22 billion in 1998.

Fortunately, the government is making enough progress toward economic reform to continue to entice foreign investors, who appear mesmerized by Brazil's enormous potential. With a population of 160

EXHIBIT I 2.3 • BRAZILIAN BOLSA IN U.S. DOLLARS: JANUARY 1995–NOVEMBER 1997

Source: Morgan Stanley Capital International.

million and an estimated GDP of about $800 billion that has grown at an average rate of more than 4 percent annually since 1993 (see Exhibit I 2.4), Brazil is by far the largest market in Latin America (representing about 45 percent of total Latin American GDP) and provides a launching pad for investments throughout the region. Moreover, it is rapidly industrializing, as evidenced by the fact that industrial products now account for 75 percent of Brazil's exports. Historically, coffee made up 80 percent of exports; now it accounts for only about 5 percent.

Rather than devaluing the currency, the traditional response by Brazilian governments faced with speculative attacks, Brazil's central bank—the Banco Central do Brazil—has defended the *Real Plan* by doubling the basic interest rate to 43 percent (see Exhibit I 2.5) and spending the nation's dollar reserves to buy up excess reais (plural of *real*). In early November 1997, Cardoso also managed to push through Congress some budgetary reforms along with $18 billion in spending cuts and tax increases, equivalent to more than 2 percent of GDP. The *real's* defense is not cost-free, however. The high real interest rates are expected to slow GDP growth in 1998 to 1.5 percent, from 3 percent in 1997. They are also pushing up the unemployment rate and worsening the credit quality of Brazil's banks. Cardoso's economic reforms have been attacked as benefiting the

wealthy and coming at the expense of the poor, who are the first to lose their jobs. These charges are worrisome in a presidential-election year. Some observers have argued that by increasing the pace of the devaluations, Brazil could afford to lower interest rates and boost growth and jobs—and at the same time improve Cardoso's prospects in next October's presidential elections. However, many analysts believe that any significant deviation from the *Real Plan,* especially before an election, would look like politics as usual and cast doubt on the sustainability of all economic reforms. Backsliding on currency stability is also likely to be unpopular. The *Real Plan* has made politicians and the populace aware of the strong link between devaluation and inflation. Thus, any policy changes that threaten the low inflation wrought by currency stability is likely to be politically risky. However, the recent austerity measures are also unpopular and are eroding Cardoso's approval ratings. With a recession looming as Brazil enters into an election year, Cardoso's supporters fear that rising joblessness will cut deeply into his electoral chances.

Banks and other financial institutions have found that speculating against the *real* is an expensive and difficult proposition because the Banco do Brazil maintains a wide range of controls on the foreign exchange market. One of the most onerous and costly requires that buyers of dollars deposit a large

EXHIBIT I 2.4 • BRAZIL'S ECONOMIC GROWTH RATE: 1990–1997

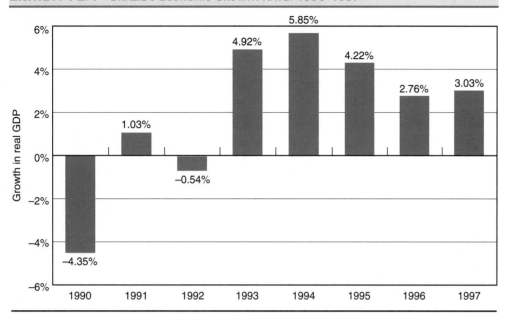

Source: Central Bank of Brazil Bulletin, April 1998.

EXHIBIT I 2.5 • BRAZILIAN INTEREST RATES

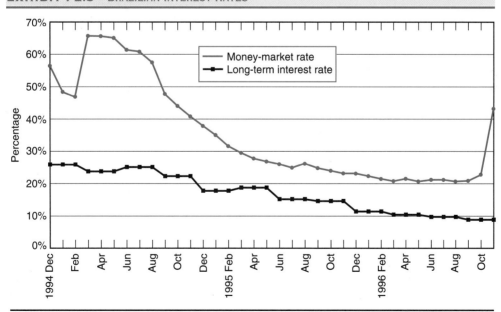

Source: Central Bank of Brazil Bulletin, April 1998.

portion of them in special, low-interest accounts with the central bank. In times of intense speculative pressure, the central bank has cut the interest rate paid on these accounts to zero. Thus investors who borrowed reais and converted them to dollars would start losing money the moment they deposited them with the central bank, unless the *real* fell enough to offset the loss of interest.

QUESTIONS

1. How does Brazil hope to control its current-account deficit through a tight monetary policy? What alternatives are available to control Brazil's current-account deficit?

2. How will Brazil's tight money policy affect its fiscal deficit? How will it affect Brazil's real (inflation-adjusted) interest rates, both short-term and long-term rates?

3. Why have Brazil's interest rates generally fallen in recent years?

4. How would reform and privatization of the social security system improve Brazil's savings rate? What would be the likely consequences of this improvement for Brazil's current-account balance and the *real*'s value? Explain.

5. What are the costs and benefits of using currency controls to defend the *real*?

6. Why might speculators view the *real* as being overvalued? Based on the data in the case, what is your best estimate as to the *real*'s degree of overvaluation?

7. What are the tradeoffs that President Cardoso must consider in deciding whether to accelerate the *real*'s depreciation?

8. Could Brazil have avoided the recessionary impacts of its monetary policy if it had devalued the *real* instead?

9. What would a Brazilian devaluation do to the currencies and economies of Argentina and Chile, its neighbors and largest trading partners?

10. What is the link between Brazil's budget deficits and its historical hyperinflation?

11. What mix of fiscal and monetary policy would you recommend to President Cardoso? Should he devalue or defend the *real*?

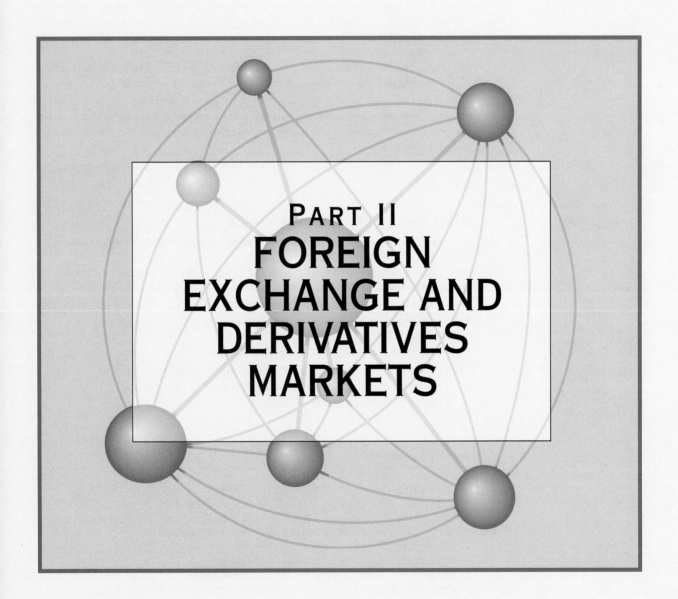

PART II
FOREIGN EXCHANGE AND DERIVATIVES MARKETS

THE FOREIGN EXCHANGE MARKET

The Spaniards coming into the West Indies had many commodities of the country which they needed, brought unto them by the inhabitants, to who when they offered them money, goodly pieces of gold coin, the Indians, taking the money, would put it into their mouths, and spit it out to the Spaniards again, signifying that they could not eat it, or make use of it, and therefore would not part with their commodities for money, unless they had such other commodities as would serve their use.

Edward Leigh (1671)

CHAPTER LEARNING OBJECTIVES

- To describe the organization of the foreign exchange market and distinguish between the spot and forward markets
- To distinguish between different methods of foreign exchange quotation and convert from one method of quotation to another
- To read and explain foreign currency quotations as they appear in *The Wall Street Journal*
- To identify profitable currency arbitrage opportunities and calculate the profits associated with these arbitrage opportunities
- To describe the mechanics of spot currency transactions
- To explain how forward contracts can be used to reduce currency risk
- To list the major users of forward contracts and describe their motives
- To calculate forward premiums and discounts

KEY TERMS

American terms
arbitrageurs
bid–ask spread
Clearing House Interbank Payments
   System (CHIPS)
contract note
cross rate
currency arbitrage
direct quotation
electronic trading
European terms
exchange risk
fed funds
FedWire
foreign exchange brokers
foreign exchange market
foreign exchange quotes

forward contract
forward discount
forward market
forward premium
forward price
hedgers
Herstatt risk
indirect quotation
interbank market
liquidity
long
no-arbitrage condition
nostro account
outright rate
position sheet
settlement risk
short

Society for Worldwide Interbank Financial
   Telecommunications (SWIFT)
speculators
spot market
spot price

swap
swap rate
traders
triangular currency arbitrage
value date

The volume of international transactions has grown enormously over the past fifty years. Exports of goods and services by the United States now total more than 10 percent of gross domestic product. For both Canada and Great Britain, this figure exceeds 25 percent. Imports are about the same size. Similarly, annual capital flows involving hundreds of billions of dollars occur between the United States and other nations. International trade and investment of this magnitude would not be possible without the ability to buy and sell foreign currencies. Currencies must be bought and sold because the U.S. dollar is not the acceptable means of payment in most other countries. Investors, tourists, exporters, and importers must exchange dollars for foreign currencies, and vice versa.

The trading of currencies takes place in foreign exchange markets whose primary function is to facilitate international trade and investment. Knowledge of the operation and mechanics of these markets, therefore, is important for any fundamental understanding of international financial management. This chapter provides this information. It discusses the organization of the most important foreign exchange market—the interbank market—including the spot market, the market in which currencies are traded for immediate delivery, and the forward market, in which currencies are traded for future delivery. Chapter 8 examines the currency futures and options markets.

7.1 ORGANIZATION OF THE FOREIGN EXCHANGE MARKET

The foreign exchange market permits people to exchange purchasing power denominated in different currencies.

If there were a single international currency, there would be no need for a foreign exchange market. As it is, in any international transaction, at least one party is dealing in a foreign currency. The purpose of the **foreign exchange market** is to permit transfers of purchasing power denominated in one currency to another—that is, to trade one currency for another currency. For example, a Japanese exporter sells automobiles to a U.S. dealer for dollars, and a U.S. manufacturer sells machine tools to a Japanese company for yen. Ultimately, however, the U.S. company will likely be interested in receiving dollars, whereas the Japanese exporter will want yen. Similarly, an American investor in Swiss-franc-denominated bonds must convert dollars into francs, and Swiss purchasers of U.S. Treasury bills require dollars to complete these transactions. It would be inconvenient, to say the least, for individual buyers and sellers of foreign exchange to seek out one another, so a foreign exchange market has developed to act as an intermediary.

Major banks trade with one other in the interbank market.

Most currency transactions are channeled through the worldwide **interbank market**, the wholesale market in which major banks trade with one another. This market, which accounts for about 59 percent of foreign exchange transactions, is normally referred to as *the* foreign exchange market. It is dominated by about twenty major banks. In the **spot market**, currencies are traded for immediate delivery, which is actually within two business days after the transaction has been concluded. In the **forward market**, contracts are made to buy or sell currencies for future delivery. Spot transactions account for about 33 percent of the market, with forward transactions accounting for another 11 percent. The remaining 56 percent of the market consists of **swap** transactions, which involve a package of a spot and a forward contract.[1]

---

[1] These volume estimates appear in "Triennial Central Bank Survey: Foreign Exchange and Derivatives Market Activity in 2001," Bank for International Settlements (BIS), Basle, March 2002.

The foreign exchange market is not a physical place; rather, it is an electronically linked network of banks, foreign exchange brokers, and dealers whose function is to bring together buyers and sellers of foreign exchange. The foreign exchange market is not confined to any one country but is dispersed throughout the leading financial centers of the world: London, New York, Paris, Zurich, Amsterdam, Tokyo, Hong Kong, Toronto, Frankfurt, Milan, and other cities.

Trading has historically been done by telephone, telex, or the SWIFT system. **SWIFT (Society for Worldwide Interbank Financial Telecommunications)**, an international bank-communications network, electronically links all brokers and traders. The SWIFT network connects more than 7,000 banks and broker-dealers in 192 countries and processes more than five million transactions a day, representing about $5 trillion in payments. Its mission is to quickly transmit standard forms to allow its member banks to automatically process data by computer. All types of customer and bank transfers are transmitted, as well as foreign exchange deals, bank account statements, and administrative messages. To use SWIFT, the corporate client must deal with domestic banks that are subscribers and with foreign banks that are highly automated. Like many other proprietary data networks, SWIFT is facing growing competition from Internet-based systems that allow both banks and nonfinancial companies to connect to a secure payments network.

> The SWIFT network is an integral part of the foreign exchange market.

Foreign exchange traders in each bank usually operate out of a separate foreign exchange trading room. Each trader has several telephones and is surrounded by terminals displaying up-to-the-minute information. It is a hectic existence, and many traders burn out by age 35. Most transactions are based on verbal communications; written confirmation occurs later. Hence, an informal code of moral conduct has evolved over time in which the foreign exchange dealers' word is their bond. Today, however, much of the telephone-based trading has been replaced by electronic brokering.

Although one might think that most foreign exchange trading is derived from export and import activities, this turns out not to be the case. In fact, trade in goods and services accounts for less than 5 percent of foreign exchange trading. More than 95 percent of foreign exchange trading relates to cross-border purchases and sales of assets, that is, to international capital flows.

Currency trading takes place 24 hours a day, but the volume varies depending on the number of potential counterparties available. Exhibit 7.1 indicates how participation levels in the global foreign exchange market vary by tracking electronic trading conversations per hour.

The Participants

> Major users of forward contracts include arbitragers, traders, hedgers, and speculators.

The major participants in the foreign exchange market are the large commercial and investment banks; foreign exchange brokers in the interbank market; commercial customers, primarily multinational corporations; and central banks, which intervene in the market from time to time to smooth exchange rate fluctuations or to maintain target exchange rates. Central bank intervention involving buying or selling in the market is often indistinguishable from the foreign exchange dealings of commercial banks or of other private participants.

Only the head offices or regional offices of the major commercial and investment banks are actually market makers—that is, they actively deal in foreign exchange for their own accounts. These banks stand ready to buy or sell any of the major currencies on a more or less continuous basis. Exhibit 7.2 lists some of the major financial institutions that are market makers and their estimated market shares.

A large fraction of the interbank transactions in the United States is conducted through **foreign exchange brokers**, specialists in matching net supplier and demander banks. These brokers receive a small commission on all trades (traditionally, 1/32 of 1 percent in the U.S.

EXHIBIT 7.1 • THE CIRCADIAN RHYTHMS OF THE FX MARKET

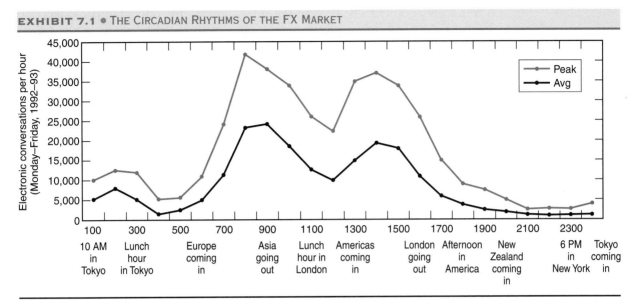

Note: Time (0100–2400) hours, Greenwich Mean Time.

Source: Reuters. Chart appears in Sam Y. Cross. *All About...the Foreign Exchange Market in the United States,* Federal Reserve Bank of New York, www.ny.frb.org/pihome/addpub.

EXHIBIT 7.2 • LEADING FOREIGN EXCHANGE TRADERS IN 2003

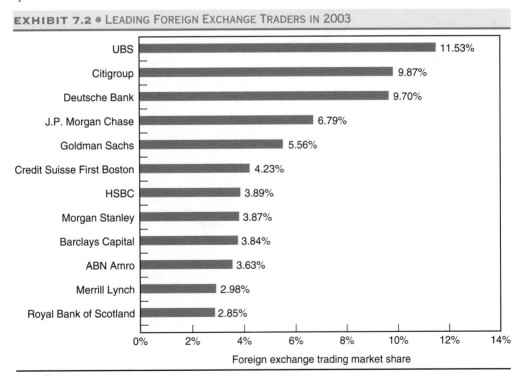

Source: Euromoney.

Foreign exchange brokers provide information and anonymity to banks trading in the inter-bank market.

market, which translates into $312.50 on a $1 million trade). Some brokers tend to special-ize in certain currencies, but they all handle major currencies such as the pound sterling, Canadian dollar, euro, and Swiss franc. Brokers supply information (at which rates various banks will buy or sell a currency); they provide anonymity to the participants until a rate is agreed to (because knowing the identity of the other party may give dealers an insight into whether that party needs or has a surplus of a particular currency); and they help banks min-imize their contacts with other traders (one call to a broker may substitute for half a dozen calls to traders at other banks). As in the stock market, the role of human brokers has declined as electronic brokers have significantly increased their share of the foreign exchange business.

Commercial and central bank customers buy and sell foreign exchange through their banks. However, most small banks and local offices of major banks do not deal directly in the interbank market. Rather, they typically will have a credit line with a large bank or with their home office. Thus, transactions with local banks will involve an extra step. The customer deals with a local bank that in turn deals with its head office or a major bank. The various linkages between banks and their customers are depicted in Exhibit 7.3. Note that the diagram includes linkages with currency futures and options markets, which we will examine in the next chapter.

The major participants in the forward market can be categorized as arbitrageurs, traders, hedgers, and speculators. **Arbitrageurs** seek to earn risk-free profits by taking advantage of differences in interest rates among countries. They use forward contracts to eliminate the exchange risk involved in transferring their funds from one nation to another.

Traders use forward contracts to eliminate or cover the risk of loss on export or import orders that are denominated in foreign currencies. More generally, a forward-covering transaction is related to a specific payment or receipt expected at a specified point in time.

Hedgers, mostly multinational firms, engage in forward contracts to protect the home currency value of various foreign currency-denominated assets and liabilities on their balance sheets that are not to be realized over the life of the contracts.

> The major partici-
> pants in the foreign
> exchange market
> include hedgers,
> traders, arbitrageurs,
> and speculators.

EXHIBIT 7.3 • STRUCTURE OF FOREIGN EXCHANGE MARKETS

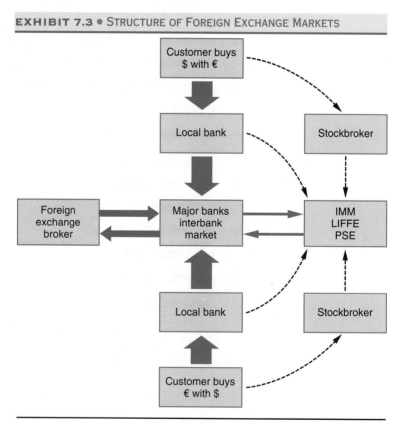

Note: The International Money Market (IMM) Chicago trades foreign exchange futures and euro futures options. The London International Financial Futures Exchange (LIFFE) trades foreign exchange futures. The Philadelphia Stock Exchange (PSE) trades foreign currency options.

Source: Federal Reserve Bank of St. Louis, *Review,* March 1984, p. 9, revised.

Arbitrageurs, traders, and hedgers seek to reduce (or eliminate, if possible) their exchange risks by "locking in" the exchange rate on future trade or financial operations.

In contrast to these three types of forward market participants, **speculators** actively expose themselves to currency risk by buying or selling currencies forward in order to profit from exchange rate fluctuations. Their degree of participation does not depend on their business transactions in other currencies; instead, it is based on prevailing forward rates and their expectations for spot exchange rates in the future.

The Clearing System   Technology has standardized and sped up the international transfers of funds, which is at the heart of clearing, or settling, foreign exchange transactions. In the United States, where all foreign exchange transactions involving dollars are cleared, electronic funds transfers take place through the **Clearing House Interbank Payments System,** or **CHIPS.** CHIPS is a computerized network developed by the New York Clearing House Association for transfer of international dollar payments, linking about 150 depository institutions that have offices or affiliates in New York City. Currently, CHIPS handles about 105,000 interbank transfers daily valued at $350 billion. The transfers represent about 90 percent of all interbank transfers relating to international dollar payments.

> *Most dollar trades in the foreign exchange market are cleared through CHIPS.*

The New York Fed (Federal Reserve Bank) has established a settlement account for member banks into which debit settlement payments are sent and from which credit settlement payments are disbursed. Transfers between member banks are netted out and settled at the close of each business day by sending or receiving **FedWire** transfers of **fed funds** through the settlement account. Fed funds are deposits held by member banks at Federal Reserve branches.

The FedWire system is operated by the Federal Reserve and is used for domestic money transfers. FedWire allows almost instant movement of balances between institutions that have accounts at the Federal Reserve Banks. A transfer takes place when an order to pay is transmitted from an originating office to a Federal Reserve Bank. The account of the paying bank is charged, and the receiving bank's account is credited with fed funds.

To illustrate the workings of CHIPS, suppose Fuji Bank has sold U.S.$15 million to Citigroup in return for ¥1.5 billion to be paid in Tokyo. In order for Fuji Bank to complete its end of the transaction, it must transfer $15 million to Citigroup. To do this, Fuji Bank enters the transaction into its CHIPS terminal, providing the identifying codes for the sending and receiving banks. The message—the equivalent of an electronic check—is then stored in the CHIPS central computer.

As soon as Fuji Bank approves and releases the "stored" transaction, the message is transmitted from the CHIPS computer to Citigroup. The CHIPS computer also makes a permanent record of the transaction and makes appropriate debits and credits in the CHIPS accounts of Fuji Bank and Citigroup, as both banks are members of CHIPS. Immediately after the closing of the CHIPS network at 4:30 P.M. (eastern time), the CHIPS computer produces a settlement report showing the net debit or credit position of each member bank.

Member banks with debit positions have until 5:45 P.M. (eastern time) to transfer their debit amounts through FedWire to the CHIPS settlement account on the books of the New York Fed. The Clearing House then transfers those fed funds via FedWire out of the settlement account to those member banks with net creditor positions. The process usually is completed by 6:00 P.M. (eastern time).

Electronic Trading   A major structural change in the foreign exchange market occurred in April 1992 when Reuters, the news company that supplies the foreign exchange market with the screen quotations used in telephone trading, introduced a new service that added automatic execution to the process, thereby creating a genuine screen-based market. Other quote vendors, such as EBS, Telerate, and Quotron, introduced their own automatic systems. These **electronic trading** systems offer automated matching.

> *Electronic trading systems offer automated matching of buy and sell orders.*

Traders enter buy and sell orders directly into their terminals on an anonymous basis, and these prices are visible to all market participants. Another trader, anywhere in the world, can execute a trade by simply hitting two buttons.

The introduction of automated trading has reduced the cost of trading, partly by eliminating foreign exchange brokers and partly by reducing the number of transactions traders had to engage in to obtain information on market prices. The new systems replicate the order matching and the anonymity that brokers offer, and they do it more cheaply. For example, small banks can now deal directly with each other instead of having to channel trades through larger ones. At the same time, automated systems threaten the oligopoly of information that has underpinned the profits of those who now do most foreign exchange business. These new systems gather and publish information on the prices and quantities of currencies as they are actually traded, thereby revealing details of currency trades that until now the traders have profitably kept to themselves. Such comparisons are facilitated by new Internet-based foreign exchange systems designed to help users reduce costs by allowing them to compare rates offered by a range of banks. The largest such system, FXall, teams some of the biggest participants in the foreign exchange market—including J.P. Morgan Chase, Citigroup, Goldman Sachs, CSFB, UBS Warburg, Morgan Stanley, and Bank of America—to offer a range of foreign exchange services over the Internet.

Automated trading threatens the information oligopoly held by currency traders today.

The key to the widespread use of computerized foreign-currency trading systems is **liquidity**, as measured by the difference between the rates at which dealers can buy and sell currencies. Liquidity, in turn, requires reaching a critical mass of users. If enough dealers are putting their prices into the system, then users have greater assurance that the system will provide them with the best prices available. That critical mass has been achieved. According to the Bank for International Settlements, in 2000, 85 percent to 95 percent of interbank trading in the major currencies was conducted using electronic brokers.[2]

Size

The foreign exchange market is the largest financial market in the world.

The foreign exchange market is by far the largest financial market in the world. A survey of the world's central banks by the Bank for International Settlements placed the average foreign exchange trading volume in 1998 at $1.5 trillion daily, or $375 trillion a year.[3] This figure compares with an average daily trading volume of about $25 billion on the New York Stock Exchange. As another benchmark, the U.S. gross domestic product was approximately $11 trillion in 2003. However, after peaking in 1998, foreign currency trading volumes fell, largely because the replacement of twelve European currencies with the euro, combined with the rise of electronic trading, greatly reduced the number of currency transactions. By 2001, the daily foreign exchange volume had fallen to $1.2 trillion[4] and remained at that level as of 2003.[5]

According to data from the 2001 triennial survey by the Bank for International Settlements, London is by far the world's largest currency trading market, with daily turnover in 2001 estimated at $504 billion, more than that of the next two markets—New York, at $254 billion, and Tokyo, at $147 billion—combined.[6] Exhibit 7.4A shows that the eight biggest financial centers have seen trading volume fall by an average of 20 percent since the last BIS survey was conducted, a sharp turnaround from the average increase of 25 percent between 1995 and 1998. Despite its recent decline, foreign exchange trading has historically outpaced the growth of international trade and the world's output of goods and services. The explosive growth in currency trading since

---

[2] See *BIS 71st Annual Report*, p. 99.

[3] Survey results appear in "Central Bank Survey of Foreign Exchange and Derivatives Market Activity 1998," *op. cit.*, p. 1.

[4] Reported in the *BIS 71st Annual Report*, p. 98.

[5] Gregory Zuckerman, "UBS Cleans Up in Currency-Trading Corner," *Wall Street Journal*, May 27, 2003, C1, C5.

[6] "Triennial Central Bank Survey: Foreign Exchange and Derivatives Market Activity in 2001," *op cit.*

EXHIBIT 7.4A • DAILY FOREIGN EXCHANGE TRADING VOLUME BY FINANCIAL CENTER

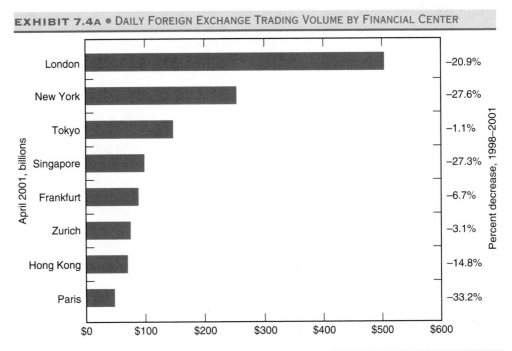

EXHIBIT 7.4B • DAILY GLOBAL FOREIGN EXCHANGE TRADING VOLUME

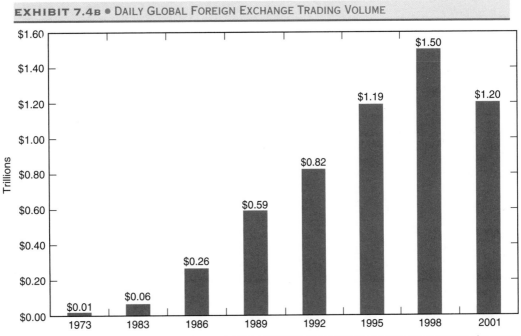

Source: Bank for International Settlements surveys.

Foreign exchange trading has grown dramatically in the past twenty years.

1973—daily volume was estimated at $10 billion in 1973 (see Exhibit 7.4B)—has been attributed to the growing integration of the world's economies and financial markets, as well as a growing desire among companies and financial institutions to manage their currency risk exposure more actively. Dollar/DM trades used to be the most common, but with the replacement of the DM and 11 other currencies with the euro, dollar/euro trades have the biggest market share (30 percent) with dollar/yen trades at 20 percent and dollar/sterling trades at 11 percent.

7.2 THE SPOT MARKET

This section examines the spot market in foreign exchange. It covers spot quotations, transaction costs, and the mechanics of spot transactions.

Spot Quotations

Most banks quote all currencies against the U.S. dollar when trading among themselves.

Almost all major newspapers print a daily list of exchange rates. For major currencies, up to four different **foreign exchange quotes** (prices) are displayed. One is the **spot price.** The others might include the 30-day, 90-day, and 180-day **forward prices.** These quotes are for trades among dealers in the interbank market. When interbank trades involve dollars (about 60 percent of such trades do), these rates will be expressed in either **American terms** (numbers of U.S. dollars per unit of foreign currency) or **European terms** (number of foreign currency units per U.S. dollar). Exhibit 7.5 lists quotes in American and

EXHIBIT 7.5 • FOREIGN EXCHANGE RATES[1] (WEDNESDAY, JANUARY 28, 2004)

Country	Currency Symbol	U.S. $ Equiv.	Currency per U.S. $	Country	Currency Symbol	U.S. $ Equiv.	Currency per U.S. $
Argentina (Peso)	ARS	0.3436	2.9104	New Zealand (Dollar)	NZD	0.6772	1.4767
Australia (Dollar)	AUD	0.7737	1.2925	Norway (Krone)	NOK	0.1434	6.9735
Bahrain (Dinar)	BHD	2.6526	0.377	Pakistan (Rupee)	PKR	0.01746	57.274
Brazil (Real)	BRL	0.3439	2.9078	Peru (New Sol)	PEN	0.2866	3.4892
Canada (Dollar)	CAD	0.7545	1.3254	Philippines (Peso)	PHP	0.0179	55.866
1 Month Forward		0.7536	1.327	Poland (Zloty)	PLN	0.2661	3.758
3 Months Forward		0.752	1.3298	Russia (Ruble)-a	RUR	0.03509	28.498
6 Months Forward		0.7501	1.3332	Saudi Arabia (Riyal)	SAR	0.2667	3.7495
Chile (Peso)	CLP	0.001701	587.89	Singapore (Dollar)	SGD	0.5902	1.6943
China (Renminbi)	CNY	0.1208	8.2781	Slovak Republic (Koruna)	SKK	0.03074	32.531
Colombia (Peso)	COP	0.000364	2,745.70	South Africa (Rand)	ZAR	0.1434	6.9735
Czech Republic (Koruna)							
Commercial Rate	CZK	0.038	26.316	South Korea (Won)	KRW	0.000854	1,171.50
Denmark (Krone)	DKK	0.1676	5.9666	Sweden (Krona)	SEK	0.1368	7.3099
Ecuador (U.S. Dollar)-e	USD	1.0	1.0	Switzerland (Franc)	CHF	0.7967	1.2552
Egypt Pound	EGP	0.1625	6.155	1 Month Forward		0.7972	1.2544
Hong Kong (Dollar)	HKD	0.1287	7.77	3 Months Forward		0.7984	1.2525
Hungary (Forint)	HUF	0.004759	210.13	6 Months Forward		0.8002	1.2497
India (Rupee)	INR	0.02203	45.393	Taiwan (Dollar)	TWD	0.03	33.333
Indonesia (Rupiah)	IDR	0.000119	8,417.50	Thailand (Baht)	THB	0.02555	39.139
Israel (Shekel)	ILS	0.2231	4.4823	Turkish (Lira)	TRL	7.5E-07	1,333,333
Japan (Yen)	JPY	0.009432	106.02	U.K. (Pound)	GBP	1.8220	0.5488
1 Month Forward		0.00944	105.93	1 Month Forward		1.8180	0.5501
3 Months Forward		0.009459	105.72	3 Months Forward		1.8086	0.5529
6 Months Forward		0.009488	105.4	6 Months Forward		1.7949	0.5571
Jordan (Dinar)	JOD	1.4104	0.709	United Arab (Dirham)	AED	0.2722	3.6738
Kuwait (Dinar)	KWD	3.3927	0.2948	Uruguay (Peso) Financial	UYU	0.034	29.412
Lebanon (Pound)	LBP	0.00066	1,514.50	Venezuela (Bolivar)	VEB	0.000626	1,597.40
Malaysia (Ringitt)-b	MYR	0.2632	3.7994				
Malta (Lira)	MTL	2.9115	0.3435	Special Drawing Rights	SDR	1.4931	0.6697
Mexico (Peso)	MXN	0.09112	10.975	Euro	EUR	1.2488	0.8008

Special Drawing Rights (SDR) are based on exchange rates for the U.S., British, and Japanese currencies. *Source:* International Monetary Fund.

[1] These foreign exchange rates are mid-range rates that apply to trading among banks in amounts of $1 million and more, as quoted at 4 P.M. Eastern time.

Source: Reuters.

The financial press contains daily spot and forward quotations for most major currencies.

European terms side by side along with the currency's abbreviation. For example, on January 28, 2004, the American quote for the Swiss franc was SFr 1 = $0.7967 (also expressed as $0.7967/SFr), and the European quote was $1 = SFr 1.2552 (or SFr 1.2552/$). Nowadays, in trades involving dollars, all except U.K. and Irish exchange rates are expressed in European terms.

In their dealings with nonbank customers, banks in most countries use a system of **direct quotation.** A direct exchange rate quote gives the home currency price of a certain quantity of the foreign currency quoted (usually 100 units, but only one unit in the case of the U.S. dollar or the pound sterling). For example, the price of foreign currency is expressed in Swiss francs (SFr) in Switzerland and in euros in Germany. Thus, in Switzerland the euro might be quoted at SFr 1.5, whereas in Germany the franc would be quoted at €0.67.

There are exceptions to this rule, though. Banks in Great Britain quote the value of the pound sterling (£) in terms of the foreign currency—for example, £1 = $1.4420. This method of **indirect quotation** is also used in the United States for domestic purposes and for the Canadian dollar. In their foreign exchange activities abroad, however, U.S. banks adhere to the European method of direct quotation.

American and European terms and direct and indirect quotes are related as follows:

American terms	*European terms*
U.S. dollar price per unit of foreign currency	Foreign currency units per dollar
(for example, $0.009251/¥)	(for example, ¥108.10/$)
A direct quote in the United States	A direct quote outside the United States
An indirect quote outside the United States	An indirect quote in the United States

Currency quotations are given in pairs, the first being the bid or buy rate and the second being the ask or sell rate.

Banks do not normally charge a commission on their currency transactions, but they profit from the spread between the buying and selling rates on both spot and forward transactions. Quotes are always given in pairs because a dealer usually does not know whether a prospective customer is in the market to buy or to sell a foreign currency. The first rate is the buy, or bid, price; the second is the sell, or ask, or offer, rate. Suppose the pound sterling is quoted at $1.7442–53. This quote means that banks are willing to buy pounds at $1.7442 and sell them at $1.7453. If you are a customer of the bank, you can expect to sell pounds to the bank at the bid rate of $1.7442 and buy pounds from the bank at the ask rate of $1.7453. The dealer will profit from the spread of $0.0011 ($1.7442 – $1.7453) between the bid and ask rates.

In practice, because time is money, dealers do not quote the full rate to each other; instead, they quote only the last two digits of the decimal. Thus, sterling would be quoted at 42–53 in the above example. Any dealer who is not sufficiently up-to-date to know the preceding numbers will not remain in business for long.

Note that when American terms are converted to European terms or direct quotations are converted to indirect quotations, bid and ask quotes are reversed; that is, the reciprocal of the American (direct) bid becomes the European (indirect) ask, and the reciprocal of the American (direct) ask becomes the European (indirect) bid. So, in the previous example, the reciprocal of the American bid of $1.7442/£ becomes the European ask of £0.5733/$, and the reciprocal of the American ask of $1.7453/£ equals the European bid of £0.5730/$, resulting in a direct quote for the dollar in London of £0.5730–33. Note, too, that the banks will always buy low and sell high.

Transaction Costs The **bid–ask spread**—that is, the spread between bid and ask rates for a currency—is based on the breadth and depth of the market for that currency as well as on the currency's volatility. The spread repays traders for the costs they incur in currency dealing—including earning a profit on the capital tied up in their business—and compensates them for the risks they bear. It is usually stated as a percentage cost of transacting in the foreign exchange market, which is computed as follows:

$$\text{Percent spread} = \frac{\text{Ask price} - \text{Bid price}}{\text{Ask price}} \times 100$$

For example, with pound sterling quoted at \$1.7442–53, the percentage spread equals 0.063 percent:

$$\text{Percent spread} = \frac{1.7453 - 1.7442}{1.7453} \times 100 = 0.063\%$$

The bid-ask spread is narrower for widely traded currencies and for less volatile currencies.

For widely traded currencies, such as the pound, euro, Swiss franc, and yen, the spread used to be on the order of 0.05 percent to 0.08 percent.[7] However, the advent of sophisticated electronic trading systems has pushed the spreads on trades of \$1 million or more to a tiny 0.02 percent.[8] Less heavily traded currencies, and currencies having greater volatility, have higher spreads. In response to their higher spreads and volatility (which increases the opportunity for profit when trading for the bank's own account), the large banks have expanded their trading in emerging market currencies, such as the Czech koruna, Russian ruble, Turkish lira, and Zambian kwacha. Although these currencies currently account for less than 5 percent of the global foreign exchange market, the forecast is for rapid growth, in line with growing investment in emerging markets.

Mean forward currency bid–ask spreads are larger than spot spreads, but they are still small in absolute terms, ranging from 0.09 percent to 0.15 percent for actively traded currencies. There is a growing forward market for emerging currencies, but because of the thinness of this market and its lack of liquidity, the bid–ask spreads are much higher.

Foreign exchange quotes for individuals and firms differ from those given in the financial press.

The quotes found in the financial press are not those that individuals or firms would get at a local bank. Unless otherwise specified, these quotes are for transactions in the interbank market exceeding \$1 million. (The standard transaction amount in the interbank market is now about \$10 million.) But competition ensures that individual customers receive rates that reflect, even if they do not necessarily equal, interbank quotations. For example, a trader may believe that he or she can trade a little more favorably than the market rates indicate—that is, buy from a customer at a slightly lower rate or sell at a somewhat higher rate than the market rate. Thus, if the current spot rate for the Swiss franc is \$0.6967–72, the bank may quote a customer a rate of \$0.6964–75. On the other hand, a bank that is temporarily short in a currency may be willing to pay a slightly more favorable rate; or if the bank has overbought a currency, it may be willing to sell that currency at a somewhat lower rate.

For these reasons, many corporations will shop around at several banks for quotes before committing themselves to a transaction. On large transactions, customers also may get a rate break inasmuch as it ordinarily does not take much more effort to process a large order than a small order.

The market for traveler's checks and smaller currency exchanges, such as might be made by a traveler going abroad, is quite separate from the interbank market. The spread on these smaller exchanges is much wider than that in the interbank market, reflecting the higher average costs banks incur on such transactions. As a result, individuals and

---

[7] Data on mean spot and forward bid–ask spreads appear in Hendrik Bessembinder, "Bid–Ask Spreads in the Interbank Foreign Exchange Markets," *Journal of Financial Economics,* June 1994, pp. 317–348.

[8] Zuckerman, "UBS Cleans Up in Currency-Trading Corner," *op cit.*

firms involved in smaller retail transactions generally pay a higher price when buying and receive a lower price when selling foreign currency than those quoted in newspapers.

Cross Rates Because most currencies are quoted against the dollar, it may be necessary to work out the **cross rates** for currencies other than the dollar. For example, if the euro is selling for $1.20 and the buying rate for the Swiss franc is $0.80, then the €/SFr cross rate is €1 = SFr 1.5. A somewhat more complicated cross-rate calculation would be the following. Suppose that the European quotes for the Japanese yen and the South Korean won are as follows:

Japanese yen: ¥135.62/U.S.$

South Korean won: W763.89/U.S.$

In this case, the cross rate of yen per won can be calculated by dividing the rate for the yen by the rate for the won, as follows:

$$\frac{\text{Japanese yen/U.S. dollar}}{\text{Korean won/U.S. dollar}} = \frac{¥135.62/\text{U.S.\$}}{W763.89/\text{U.S.\$}} = ¥0.17754 / W$$

Exhibit 7.6 contains cross rates for major currencies on January 28, 2004.

Cross exchange rates can be computed for currency pairs that do not involve the dollar.

ILLUSTRATION *Calculating the Direct Quote for the British Pound in Zurich*

Suppose sterling is quoted at $1.4419–36, and the Swiss franc is quoted at $0.6250–67. What is the direct quote for the pound in Zurich?

Solution. The bid rate for the pound in Zurich can be found by realizing that selling pounds for SFr is equivalent to combining two transactions: (1) selling pounds for dollars at the bid rate of $1.4419 and (2) converting those dollars into SFr 1.4419/0.6267 = SFr 2.3008 per pound at the ask rate of $0.6267. Similarly, the franc cost of buying one pound (the ask rate) can be found by first buying $1.4436 (the ask rate for £1) with SFr and then using those dollars to buy one pound. Because buying dollars for francs is equivalent to selling francs for dollars (at the bid rate of $0.6250), it will take SFr 1.4436/0.6250 = SFr 2.3098 to acquire the $1.4436 needed to buy one pound. Thus, the direct quotes for the pound in Zurich are SFr 2.3008–98.

Note that in calculating the cross rates you should always assume that you have to sell a currency at the lower (or bid) rate and buy it at the higher (or ask) rate, giving you the worst possible rate. This method of quotation is how banks make money in foreign exchange.

EXHIBIT 7.6 ● KEY CURRENCY CROSS RATES[1] (FOR LATE NEW YORK TRADING WEDNESDAY, JANUARY 28, 2004)

Dollar	Euro	Pound	SFranc	Peso	Yen	CdnDlr
1.3254	1.6551	2.4148	1.0559	0.1208	0.0125	...
106.02	132.4	193.17	84.468	9.6607	...	79.994
10.975	13.705	19.996	8.7434	...	0.1035	8.2803
1.2552	1.5675	2.2869	...	0.1144	0.0118	0.947
0.5488	0.6854	...	0.4373	0.05	0.0052	0.4141
0.8008	...	1.459	0.638	0.073	0.0076	0.6042
...	1.2488	1.822	0.7967	0.0911	0.0094	0.7545

[1] These foreign exchange rates are mid-range rates that apply to trading among banks in amounts of $1 million and more, as quoted at 4 P.M. Eastern time.

Source: Reuters.

I L L U S T R A T I O N   *Calculating the Direct Quote for the Brazilian* **Real** *in Bangkok*

Suppose that the Brazilian *real* is quoted at R 0.9955–1.0076/U.S.$ and the Thai baht is quoted at B 25.2513–3986. What is the direct quote for the *real* in Bangkok?

Solution. Analogous to the prior example, the direct bid rate for the *real* in Bangkok can be found by recognizing that selling reais (plural of *real*) in exchange for baht is equivalent to combining two transactions: (1) selling the *real* for dollars (which is the same as buying dollars with reais) at the ask rate of R 1.0076/U.S.$ and (2) selling those dollars for baht at the bid rate of B 25.2513/U.S.$. These transactions result in the bid cross rate for the *real* being the bid rate for the baht divided by the ask rate for the *real*:

$$\text{Bid cross rate for the real} = \frac{\text{Bid rate for Thai baht/U.S.\$}}{\text{Ask rate for Brazilian real/U.S.\$}} = \frac{25.2513}{1.0076} = B\ 25.0608/R$$

Similarly, the baht cost of buying the *real* (the ask cross rate) can be found by first buying dollars for Thai baht at the ask rate of B 25.3986/U.S.$ and then selling those dollars to buy Brazilian reais at the bid rate of R 0.9955/U.S.$. Combining these transactions yields the ask cross rate for the *real* being the ask rate for the baht divided by the bid rate for the *real*:

$$\text{Ask cross rate for the real} = \frac{\text{Ask rate for Thai baht/U.S.\$}}{\text{Bid rate for Brazilian real/U.S.\$}} = \frac{25.3986}{0.9955} = B\ 25.5134/R$$

Thus, the direct quotes for the *real* in Bangkok are B 25.0608–5134.

A growing percentage of foreign exchange trades don't involve the dollar.

Currency Arbitrage   Until recently, the pervasive practice among bank dealers was to quote all currencies against the U.S. dollar when trading among themselves. Now, however, a growing percentage of currency trades does not involve the dollar. For example, Swiss banks may quote the euro against the Swiss franc, and German banks may quote pounds sterling in terms of euros. Exchange traders are continually alert to the possibility of taking advantage, through **currency arbitrage** transactions, of exchange rate inconsistencies in different money centers. These transactions involve buying a currency in one market and selling it in another. Such activities tend to keep exchange rates uniform in the various markets.

Currency arbitrage transactions also explain why such profitable opportunities are fleeting. In the process of taking advantage of an arbitrage opportunity, the buying and selling of currencies tends to move rates in a manner that eliminates the profit opportunity in the future. When profitable arbitrage opportunities disappear, we say that the **no-arbitrage condition** holds. If this condition is violated on an ongoing basis, we would wind up with a money machine, as shown in the following example.

Traders take advantages of differences in exchange rate quotations among markets through currency arbitrage.

Suppose the pound sterling is bid at $1.5422 in New York and the euro is offered at $0.9251 in Frankfurt. At the same time, London banks are offering pounds sterling at €1.6650. An astute trader would sell dollars for euros in Frankfurt, use the euros to acquire pounds sterling in London, and sell the pounds in New York.

Specifically, if the trader begins in New York with $1 million, he could acquire €1,080,964.22 for $1 million in Frankfurt (1 million/0.9251), sell these euros for £649,227.76 in London (1,080,964.22/1.6650), and resell the pounds in New York for $1,001,239.05 (649,227.76 × 1.5422). Thus, a few minutes' work would yield a profit of $1,239.05. In effect, by arbitraging through the euro, the trader would be able to acquire sterling at $1.5403 in London ($0.9251 × 1.6650) and sell it at $1.5422 in New York. This sequence of transactions, known as **triangular currency arbitrage**, is depicted in Exhibit 7.7.

EXHIBIT 7.7 • TRIANGULAR CURRENCY ARBITRAGE

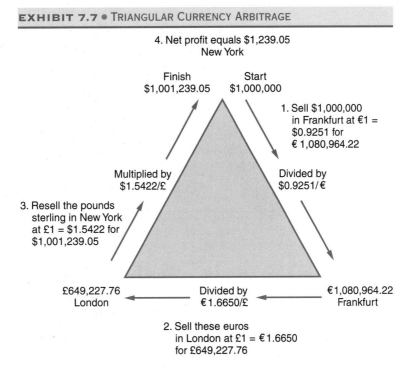

In the preceding example, the arbitrage transactions would tend to cause the euro to appreciate vis-à-vis the dollar in Frankfurt and to depreciate against the pound sterling in London; at the same time, sterling would tend to fall in New York against the dollar. Acting simultaneously, these currency changes will quickly eliminate profits from this set of transactions, thereby enforcing the no-arbitrage condition. Otherwise, a money machine would exist, opening up the prospect of unlimited risk-free profits. Such profits would quickly attract other traders, whose combined buying and selling activities would bring exchange rates back into equilibrium almost instantaneously.

Opportunities for profitable currency arbitrage have been greatly reduced in recent years, given the extensive network of people—aided by high-speed, computerized information systems—who are continually collecting, comparing, and acting on currency quotes in all financial markets. The practice of quoting rates against the dollar makes currency arbitrage even simpler. The result of this activity is that rates for a specific currency tend to be the same everywhere, with only minimal deviations due to transaction costs.

> Ready access to information has reduced opportunities for profitable currency arbitrage.

![globe icon] **ILLUSTRATION**   *Calculating the Direct Quote for the Euro in New York*

If the direct quote for the dollar is €0.95 in Frankfurt, and transaction costs are 0.4 percent, what are the minimum and maximum possible direct quotes for the euro in New York?

Solution. The object here is to find the *no-arbitrage* range of euro quotes—that is, the widest bid–ask spread within which any potential arbitrage profits are eaten up by transaction costs. It can be found as follows. Begin with an arbitrageur who converts $1 into euros in Frankfurt. The arbitrageur would receive €0.95 × 0.996, after paying transaction costs of 0.4 percent. Converting these euros into dollars in New York at a direct quote of e, the arbitrageur would keep $0.95 \times 0.996 \times e \times 0.996$. The no-arbitrage condition requires that this quantity must be less than or equal to $1 (otherwise there would be a money machine), or $e \leq 1/[0.95(0.996)^2] = \$1.0611$. Alternatively, an arbitrageur who converted $1 into euros in New York at a rate of e, took those euros to Frankfurt and exchanged them for dollars, would wind up—after paying transaction costs in both New

York and Frankfurt—with $(1/e) \times 0.996 \times 1/0.95 \times 0.996$. Because the no-arbitrage condition requires that this quantity must not exceed $1, $(0.996)^2 \times (1/0.95e) \leq 1$, or $e \geq$ 1.0442. Combining these two inequalities yields $1.0442 \leq e \leq \$1.0611$.

Settlement Date The **value date** for spot transactions, the date on which the monies must be paid to the parties involved, is set as the second working day after the date on which the transaction is concluded. Thus, a spot deal entered into on Thursday in Paris will not be settled until the following Monday (French banks are closed on Saturdays and Sundays). It is possible, although unusual, to get one-day or even same-day value, but the rates will be adjusted to reflect interest differentials on the currencies involved.

Exchange Risk Bankers also act as market makers, as well as agents, by taking positions in foreign currencies, thereby exposing themselves to **exchange risk.** The immediate adjustment of quotes as traders receive and interpret new political and economic information is the source of both exchange losses and gains by banks active in the foreign exchange market. For instance, suppose a trader quotes a rate of £1:$1.3012 for £500,000, and it is accepted. The bank will receive $650,600 in return for the £500,000. If the bank does not have an offsetting transaction, it may decide within a few minutes to cover its exposed position in the interbank market. If during this brief delay, news of a lower-than-expected British trade deficit reaches the market, the trader may be unable to purchase pounds at a rate lower than $1.3101. Because the bank would have to pay $655,050 to acquire £500,000 at this new rate, the result is a $4,450 ($655,050 − $650,600) exchange loss on a relatively small transaction within just a few minutes. Equally possible, of course, is a gain if the dollar strengthens against the pound.

Clearly, as a trader becomes more and more uncertain about the rate at which she can offset a given currency contract with other dealers or customers, she will demand a greater profit to bear this added risk. This expectation translates into a wider bid–ask spread. For example, during a period of volatility in the exchange rate between the Swiss franc and U.S. dollar, a trader will probably quote a customer a bid for francs that is distinctly lower than the last observed bid in the interbank market; the trader will attempt to reduce the risk of buying francs at a price higher than that at which she can eventually resell them. Similarly, the trader may quote a price for the sale of francs that is above the current asking price.

Bankers acting as marketmakers, by taking positions in foreign currencies, expose themselves to exchange risk.

The Mechanics of Spot Transactions

Foreign exchange transactions are based on verbal agreements, later supplemented by a contract note.

The simplest way to explain the process of actually settling transactions in the spot market is to work through an example. Suppose a U.S. importer requires HK$1 million to pay his Hong Kong supplier. After receiving and accepting a verbal quote from the trader of a U.S. bank, the importer will be asked to specify two accounts: (1) the account in a U.S. bank that he wants debited for the equivalent dollar amount at the agreed exchange rate—say, U.S.$0.1293 per Hong Kong dollar, and (2) the Hong Kong supplier's account that is to be credited by HK$1 million.

On completion of the verbal agreement, the trader will forward to the settlement section of her bank a dealing slip containing the relevant information. That same day, a **contract note**—which includes the amount of the foreign currency (HK$1 million), the dollar equivalent at the agreed rate ($129,300 = 0.1293 × 1 million), and confirmation of the payment instructions—will be sent to the importer. The settlement section will then cable the bank's correspondent (or branch) in Hong Kong, requesting transfer of HK$1 million from its **nostro account**—working balances maintained with the correspondent to facilitate delivery and receipt of currencies—to the account specified by the importer.

On the value date, the U.S. bank will debit the importer's account, and the exporter will have his account credited by the Hong Kong correspondent.

At the time of the initial agreement, the trader provides a clerk with the pertinent details of the transaction. The clerk, in turn, constantly updates a **position sheet** that shows the bank's position by currency, as well as by maturities of forward contracts. A number of the major international banks have fully computerized this process to ensure accurate and instantaneous information on individual transactions and on the bank's cumulative currency exposure at any time. The head trader will monitor this information for evidence of possible fraud or excessive exposure in a given currency.

As spot transactions are normally settled two working days later, a bank is never certain until one or two days after the deal is concluded whether the payment due the bank has actually been made. To keep this credit risk in bounds, most banks will transact large amounts only with prime names (other banks or corporate customers).

A different type of credit risk is **settlement risk**, also known as **Herstatt risk**. Herstatt risk, named after a German bank that went bankrupt after losing a fortune speculating on foreign currencies, is the risk that a bank will deliver currency on one side of a foreign exchange deal only to find that its counterparty has not sent any money in return. This risk arises because of the way foreign currency transactions are settled. Settlement requires a cash transfer from one bank's account to another at the central banks of the currencies involved. However, if those banks are in different time zones, there may be a delay. In the case of Herstatt, German regulators closed the bank after it had received Deutsche marks in Frankfurt but before it had delivered dollars to its counterparty banks (because the New York market had not yet opened).

Because central banks have been slow to deal with this problem, some banks have begun to pool their trades in a particular currency, canceling out offsetting ones and settling the balance at the end of the day. In 2002, about sixty of the world's biggest banks went further and established CLS Bank, a global clearing bank that takes details of all trades in seven main currencies (U.S., Canadian, and Australian dollars, euro, yen, pound, and Swiss franc), with more to come, and gives member banks an orderly schedule of when each bank must make payments during the following day to honor them. A single payment of a few million dollars, yen, or euros is then enough to settle a bank's multiple trades scheduled in that currency for that day. For example, on October 29, 2002, CLS Bank settled 15,200 transactions, totaling $395 billion, which required only $17 billion of payments between member banks, a 96 percent reduction.

> Settlement risk is a risk associated with foreign exchange contracts.

7.3 THE FORWARD MARKET

Forward exchange operations carry the same credit risk as spot transactions but for longer periods of time; however, there are significant exchange risks involved.

A **forward contract** between a bank and a customer (which could be another bank) calls for delivery, at a fixed future date, of a specified amount of one currency against dollar payment; the exchange rate is fixed at the time the contract is entered into. Although the euro is the most widely traded currency at present, active forward markets exist for the pound sterling, the Canadian dollar, the Japanese yen, and the Swiss franc. In general, forward markets for the currencies of less-developed countries (LDCs) are either limited or nonexistent.

In a typical forward transaction, for example, a U.S. company buys textiles from England with payment of £1 million due in 90 days. Thus, the importer is **short** pounds—that is, it owes pounds for future delivery. Suppose the spot price of the pound is $1.71. During the next 90 days, however, the pound might rise against the dollar, raising the dollar

> Companies can reduce their exchange risk by using forward contracts to lock in the exchange rate on future currency transactions.

cost of the textiles. The importer can guard against this exchange risk by immediately negotiating a 90-day forward contract with a bank at a price of, say, £1 = $1.72. According to the
forward contract, in 90 days the bank will give the importer £1 million (which it will use to
pay for its textile order), and the importer will give the bank $1.72 million, which is the dol-
lar equivalent of £1 million at the forward rate of $1.72.

In technical terms, the importer is offsetting a short position in pounds by going
long in the forward market—that is, by buying pounds for future delivery. In effect, use
of the forward contract enables the importer to convert a short underlying position in
pounds to a zero net exposed position, with the forward contract receipt of £1 million
canceling out the account payable of £1 million and leaving the importer with a net liability of $1,720,000:

Importer's T-Account

Forward contract receipt	£1,000,000	Account payable	£1,000,000
		Forward contract payment	$1,720,000

According to this T-account, the forward contract allows the importer to convert an
unknown dollar cost (1 million $\times e_1$, where e_1 is the unknown spot exchange rate—$/£—
in 90 days) into a known dollar cost ($1,720,000), thereby eliminating all exchange risk
on this transaction.

Exhibit 7.8 plots the importer's dollar cost of the textile shipment with and without
the use of a forward contract. It also shows the gain or loss on the forward contract as a
function of the contracted forward price and the spot price of the pound when the contract matures.

The gains and losses from long and short forward positions are related to the difference between the contracted forward price and the spot price of the underlying currency
at the time the contract matures. In the case of the textile order, the importer is committed to buy pounds at $1.72 apiece. If the spot rate in 90 days is less than $1.72, the
importer will suffer an implicit loss on the forward contract because it is buying pounds

*Forward contract
gains or losses stem
from the difference
between the forward
rate and the spot
rate at maturity of
the forward contract.*

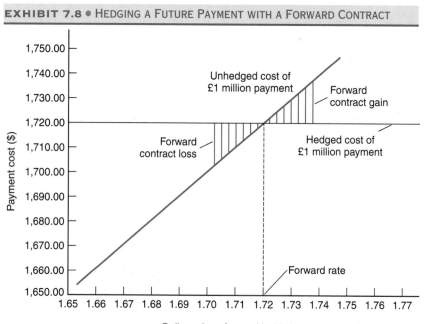

EXHIBIT 7.8 • HEDGING A FUTURE PAYMENT WITH A FORWARD CONTRACT

for more than the prevailing value. However, if the spot rate in 90 days exceeds $1.72, the importer will enjoy an implicit profit because the contract obliges the bank to sell the pounds at a price less than current value.

Three points are worth noting. First, the gain or loss on the forward contract is unrelated to the current spot rate of $1.71. Second, the forward contract gain or loss exactly offsets the change in the dollar cost of the textile order that is associated with movements in the pound's value. For example, if the spot price of the pound in 90 days is $1.75, the importer's cost of delivery is $1.75 million. However, the forward contract has a gain of $30,000, or 1 million × (1.75 − 1.72). The net cost of the textile order when covered with a forward contract is $1.72 million, no matter what happens to the spot exchange rate in 90 days. (Chapter 10 elaborates on the use of forward contracts to manage exchange risk.) Third, the forward contract is not an option contract. Both parties must perform the agreed-on behavior, unlike the situation with an option in which the buyer can choose whether to exercise the contract or allow it to expire. The bank must deliver the pounds, and the importer must buy them at the prearranged price. Options are discussed in Chapter 8.

Forward Quotations

A foreign currency is at a forward discount (premium) if the forward rate expressed in dollars is below (above) the spot rate.

Forward rates can be expressed in two ways. Commercial customers are usually quoted the actual price, otherwise known as the **outright rate**. In the interbank market, however, dealers quote the forward rate only as a discount from, or a premium on, the spot rate. This forward differential is known as the **swap rate**. As explained in Chapter 4, a foreign currency is at a **forward discount** if the forward rate expressed in dollars is below the spot rate, whereas a **forward premium** exists if the forward rate is above the spot rate. As we see in the next section, the forward premium or discount is closely related to the difference in interest rates on the two currencies.

According to Exhibit 7.5, spot Japanese yen on January 28, 2004, sold at $0.009432, whereas 180-day forward yen were priced at $0.009488. Based on these rates, the swap rate for the 180-day forward yen was quoted as a 56-point premium (0.009488 − 0.009432), where a point, or "pip," refers to the last digit quoted. Similarly, because the 90-day British pound was quoted at $1.8086 while the spot pound was $1.8220, the 90-day forward British pound sold at a 134-point discount.

Based on Equation 4.1 from Chapter 4, which is repeated here as Equation 7.1, the forward premium or discount on a foreign currency may also be expressed as an annualized percentage deviation from the spot rate using the following formula:

$$\text{Forward premium or discount on foreign currency} = \frac{\text{Forward rate} - \text{Spot rate}}{\text{Spot rate}} \times \frac{360}{\text{Forward contract number of days}} \qquad (7.1)$$

where the exchange rate is stated in domestic currency units per unit of foreign currency.

Thus, on January 28, 2004, the 180-day forward Japanese yen was selling at a 1.19 percent annualized premium:

$$\text{Forward premium annualized} = \frac{0.009488 - 0.009432}{0.009432} \times \frac{360}{180} = 0.0119$$

The 90-day British pound was selling at a 2.94 percent annualized discount:

$$\text{Forward discount annualized} = \frac{1.8086 - 1.8220}{1.8220} \times \frac{360}{90} = -0.0294$$

A swap rate can be converted into an outright rate by adding the premium (in points) to, or subtracting the discount (in points) from, the spot rate. Although the swap rates do not carry plus or minus signs, you can determine whether the forward rate is at a discount or a premium using the following rule: When the forward bid in points is smaller than the ask rate in points, the forward rate is at a premium and the points should be added to the spot price to compute the outright quote. Conversely, if the bid in points exceeds the ask in points, the forward rate is at a discount and the points must be subtracted from the spot price to get the outright quotes.[9]

Suppose the following quotes are received for spot, 30-day, 90-day, and 180-day Swiss francs (SFr) and pounds sterling:

Spot	30-day	90-day	180-day
£: $2.0015–30	19–17	26–22	42–35
SFr: $0.6963–68	4–6	9–14	25–38

Bearing in mind the practice of quoting only the last two digits, a dealer would quote sterling at 15–30, 19–17, 26–22, 42–35 and Swiss francs at 63–68, 4–6, 9–14, 25–38.
The outright rates are shown in the following chart.

	£			SFr		
Maturity	*Bid*	*Ask*	*Spread (%)*	*Bid*	*Ask*	*Spread (%)*
Spot	$2.0015	$2.0030	0.075	$0.6963	$0.6968	0.072
30-day	1.9996	2.0013	0.085	0.6967	0.6974	0.100
90-day	1.9989	2.0008	0.095	0.6972	0.6982	0.143
180-day	1.9973	1.9995	0.110	0.6988	0.7006	0.257

The bid-ask spread on forward contracts rises with currency volatility and contract maturity.

Thus, the Swiss franc is selling at a premium against the dollar, and the pound is selling at a discount. Note the slightly wider percentage spread between outright bid and ask on the Swiss franc compared with the spread on the pound. This difference is due to the broader market in pounds. Note, too, the widening of spreads by maturity for both currencies. This widening is caused by the greater uncertainty surrounding future exchange rates.

Exchange Risk   Spreads in the forward market are a function of both the breadth of the market (volume of transactions) in a given currency and the risks associated with forward contracts. The risks, in turn, are based on the variability of future spot rates. Even if the spot market is stable, there is no guarantee that future rates will remain invariant. This uncertainty will be reflected in the forward market. Furthermore, because beliefs about distant exchange rates are typically less secure than those about nearer-term rates, uncertainty will increase with lengthening maturities of forward contracts. Dealers will quote wider spreads on longer-term forward contracts to compensate themselves for the risk of being unable to reverse their positions profitably. Moreover, the greater unpredictability of future spot rates may reduce the number of market participants. This increased thinness

---

[9] This rule is based on two factors: (1) The buying rate, be it for spot or forward delivery, is always less than the selling price; and (2) the forward bid–ask spread always exceeds the spot bid–ask spread. In other words, you can always assume that the bank will be buying low and selling high and that bid–ask spreads widen with the maturity of the contract.

will further widen the bid–ask spread because it magnifies the dealer's risk in taking even a temporary position in the forward market.

Cross Rates   Forward cross rates are figured in much the same way as spot cross rates. For instance, suppose a customer wants to sell 30-day forward euros against yen delivery. The market rates (expressed in European terms of foreign currency units per dollar) are as follows:

€: $ spot	0.81070–0.81103
30-day forward	0.81170–0.81243
¥: $ spot	107.490–107.540
30-day forward	107.347–107.442

Based on these rates, the forward cross rate for yen in terms of euros is found as follows: Forward euros are sold for dollars—that is, dollars are bought at the euro forward selling price of €0.81243 = $1—and the dollars to be received are simultaneously sold for 30-day forward yen at a rate of ¥107.347. Thus, €0.81243 = ¥107.347, or the forward buying rate for yen is €0.81243/107.347 = €0.0075683. Similarly, the forward selling rate for yen against euros (euros received per yen sold forward) is €0.81170/107.442 = €0.0075548. The spot buying rate for yen is €0.81103/107.490 = €0.0075452. Hence, based on its ask price, the yen is trading at an annualized 3.67 percent premium against the euro in the 30-day forward market:

$$\begin{matrix} \text{Forward premium} \\ \text{annualized} \end{matrix} = \frac{0.0075683 - 0.0075452}{0.0075452} \times \frac{360}{30} = 3.67\%$$

Forward Contract Maturities

Forward contracts are normally available for 30-day, 60-day, 90-day, 180-day, or 360-day delivery. Banks will also tailor forward contracts for odd maturities (e.g., 77 days) to meet their customers' needs. Longer-term forward contracts can usually be arranged for widely traded currencies, such as the pound sterling, euro, or Japanese yen; however, the bid–ask spread tends to widen for longer maturities. As with spot rates, these spreads have widened for almost all currencies since the early 1970s, probably because of the greater turbulence in foreign exchange markets. For widely traded currencies, the 90-day bid–ask spread can vary from 0.1 percent to 1 percent.

Forward contracts going out past one year are available for widely-traded currencies.

7.4 SUMMARY AND CONCLUSIONS

In this chapter, we saw that the primary function of the foreign exchange market is to transfer purchasing power denominated in one currency to another and thereby facilitate international trade and investment. The foreign exchange market consists of two tiers: the interbank market, in which major banks trade with each other, and the retail market, in which banks deal with their commercial customers.

In the spot market, currencies are traded for settlement within two business days after the transaction has been concluded. In the forward market, contracts are made to buy or sell currencies for future delivery. Spot and forward quotations are given either in American terms—the dollar price of a foreign currency—or in European terms—the foreign currency price of a dollar. Quotations can also be expressed on a direct basis—the home currency price of another currency—or an indirect basis—the foreign currency price of the home currency.

The major participants in the forward market are categorized as arbitrageurs, traders, hedgers, and speculators. Forward rates can be stated on an outright basis or as a discount from, or a premium on, the spot rate. This forward differential is known as the swap rate. Because most currencies are quoted against the dollar, the exchange rate between two nondollar currencies—known as a cross rate—must be calculated on the basis of their direct quotes against the dollar.

QUESTIONS

1. Answer the following questions using the data in Exhibit 7.5.
   a. How many Swiss francs can you get for one dollar?
   b. How many dollars can you get for one Swiss franc?
   c. What is the three-month forward rate for the Swiss franc?
   d. Is the Swiss franc selling at a forward premium or discount?
   e. What is the 90-day forward discount or premium on the Swiss franc?

2. What risks confront dealers in the foreign exchange market? How can they cope with those risks?
3. Suppose a currency increases in volatility. What is likely to happen to its bid–ask spread? Why?
4. Who are the principal users of the forward market? What are their motives?
5. How does a company pay for the foreign exchange services of a commercial bank?

PROBLEMS

1. The $/€ exchange rate is €1 = $0.95, and the €/SFr exchange rate is SFr 1 = €0.71. What is the SFr/$ exchange rate?
2. Suppose the direct quote for sterling in New York is 1.1110–5.
   a. How much would £500,000 cost in New York?
   b. What is the direct quote for dollars in London?
3. Using the data in Exhibit 7.5, calculate the 30-day, 90-day, and 180-day forward premiums for the Canadian dollar.
4. An investor wishes to buy euros spot (at $0.9080) and sell euros forward for 180 days (at $0.9146).
   a. What is the swap rate on euros?
   b. What is the forward premium or discount on 180-day euros?
5. Suppose Credit Suisse quotes spot and 90-day forward rates on the Swiss franc of $0.7957–60, 8–13.
   a. What are the outright 90-day forward rates that Credit Suisse is quoting?
   b. What is the forward discount or premium associated with buying 90-day Swiss francs?
   c. Compute the percentage bid–ask spreads on spot and forward Swiss francs.
6. Suppose Dow Chemical receives quotes of $0.009369–71 for the yen and $0.03675–6 for the Taiwan dollar (NT$).
   a. How many U.S. dollars will Dow Chemical receive from the sale of ¥50 million?
   b. What is the U.S. dollar cost to Dow Chemical of buying ¥1 billion?
   c. How many NT$ will Dow Chemical receive for U.S.$500,000?
   d. How many yen will Dow Chemical receive for NT$200 million?
   e. What is the yen cost to Dow Chemical of buying NT$80 million?

7. Suppose the euro is quoted at 0.7064–80 in London and the pound sterling is quoted at 1.6244–59 in Frankfurt.
   a. Is there a profitable arbitrage situation? Describe it.
   b. Compute the percentage bid–ask spreads on the pound and euro.
8. As a foreign exchange trader at Sumitomo Bank, you have a customer who would like spot and 30-day forward yen quotes on Australian dollars. Current market rates are

	Spot	30-day
	¥101.37–85/U.S.$1	15–13
	A$1.2924–44/U.S.$1	20–26

   a. What bid and ask yen cross rates would you quote on spot Australian dollars?
   b. What outright yen cross rates would you quote on 30-day forward Australian dollars?
   c. What is the forward premium or discount on buying 30-day Australian dollars against yen delivery?
9. Suppose Air France receives the following indirect quotes in New York: €0.92–3 and £ 0.63–4. Given these quotes, what range of £/€ bid and ask quotes in Paris will permit arbitrage?
10. On checking the Telerate screen, you see the following exchange rate and interest rate quotes:

Currency	90-Day Interest Rates (annualized)	Spot Rates	90-Day Forward Rates
Dollar	4.99%–5.03%		
Swiss franc	3.14%–3.19%	$0.711–22	$0.726–32

   a. Can you find an arbitrage opportunity?
   b. What steps must you take to capitalize on it?
   c. What is the profit per $1 million arbitraged?

BIBLIOGRAPHY

Bessembinder, Hendrik. "Bid-Ask Spreads in the Interbank Foreign Exchange Markets." *Journal of Financial Economics,* June 1994, pp. 317–348.

Fama, Eugene. "Forward and Spot Exchange Rates." *Journal of Monetary Economics* 14, 1984, pp. 319–338.

Glassman, Debra. "Exchange Rate Risk and Transactions Costs: Evidence from Bid-Ask Spreads." *Journal of International Money and Finance,* December 1987, pp. 479–491.

Kubarych, Roger M. *Foreign Exchange Markets in the United States.* New York: Federal Reserve Bank of New York, 1983.

Strongin, Steve. "International Credit Market Connections." *Economic Perspectives,* July/August 1990, pp. 2–10.

INTERNET RESOURCES

www.imf.org/external/fin.htm IMF Web site that contains exchange rate quotes for selected currencies.

www.ny.frb.org/markets/fxrates/noon.cfm Web site of the Federal Reserve Bank of New York that lists daily noon foreign exchange rates.

www.oanda.com Contains a wide variety of current and historical exchange rate data along with stories relating to foreign exchange and links to the world's central banks.

www.ny.frb.org/education/addpub/usfxm/ List of online publications by the Federal Reserve Bank of New York that offer detailed information about the foreign exchange market in the United States.

www.bis.org/publ/index.htm Contains the BIS Annual Report, statistics on derivatives, external debt, foreign exchange market activity, and so on.

emgmkts.com/pricing/fxclose.htm Contains a wide variety of data on financial markets worldwide, including foreign exchange and interest rate data.

www.bloomberg.com Web site for Bloomberg. Contains a wide variety of data on financial markets worldwide, including foreign exchange and interest rate data.

INTERNET EXERCISES

1. Find the latest quotes for the euro, pound, and yen. By how much did these currencies rise or fall against the dollar in the last day?

2. Have emerging market currencies generally risen or fall in the past day? You can use the Emerging Markets Companion for these data or the IMF Web site.

3. What was the volume of forward contracts traded in the past year? You can use data from the BIS Annual Report to answer this question.

4. Find the currency cross rates provided by Bloomberg for the euro/pound and euro/yen. Using these rates, calculate what the pound/yen cross rate should be. Compare your calculated pound/yen cross rate to the one reported by Bloomberg. Are the two cross rates the same?

CURRENCY FUTURES AND OPTIONS MARKETS

I dipt into the future far as human eye could see, Saw the vision of the world and all the wonder that would be.

Alfred, Lord Tennyson (1842)

CHAPTER LEARNING OBJECTIVES

- To explain what currency futures and options contracts are and to describe the organization of the markets in which these contracts are traded
- To distinguish between currency forward and futures contracts
- To distinguish between currency futures and options contracts
- To describe the advantages and disadvantages of futures contracts relative to forward contracts
- To explain how currency futures and options contracts can be used to manage currency risk and to speculate on future currency movements
- To identify the basic factors that determine the value of a currency option
- To read and interpret the prices of currency futures and options contracts as they appear in the *Wall Street Journal*

KEY TERMS

American option
at-the-money
bear spread
break-even price
bull spread
call option
Chicago Mercantile Exchange
currency futures
currency option
currency spread
derivatives
European option
exchanged-traded option
exercise price
expiration date
futures contract
futures option
initial margin
International Monetary Market
in-the-money
intrinsic value
knockout option
listed option

maintenance margin
maintenance performance bond
margin call
marking to market
offsetting trade
open interest
out-of-the-money
OTC currency option
outstrike
over-the-counter (OTC) market
performance bond
performance bond call
Philadelphia Stock Exchange (PHLX)
put option
retail market
round trip
strike price
time value
United Currency Options Market
  (UCOM)
Virtual Currency Option
wholesale market

Foreign currency futures and options contracts are examples of the new breed of financial instrument known as derivatives. Financial **derivatives** are contracts that derive their value from some underlying asset (such as a stock, bond, or currency), reference rate (such as a 90-day Treasury bill rate), or index (such as the S&P 500 stock index). Popular derivatives include swaps, forwards, futures, and options. Chapter 7 discussed forward contracts, and Chapter 9 discusses swaps. This chapter describes the nature and valuation of currency futures and options contracts and shows how they can be used to manage foreign exchange risk or take speculative positions on currency movements. It also shows how to read the prices of these contracts as they appear in the financial press.

8.1 FUTURES CONTRACTS

Currency futures contracts are patterned after grain and commodity futures contracts.

The **Chicago Mercantile Exchange** (CME) provides an outlet for currency speculators and for those looking to reduce their currency risks. Trade takes place in **currency futures,** which are contracts for specific quantities of given currencies; the exchange rate is fixed at the time the contract is entered into, and the delivery date is set by the board of directors of the CME. These contracts are patterned after those for grain and commodity futures contracts, which have been traded on Chicago's exchanges for over 100 years.

Currency futures contracts are currently available for the Australian dollar, Brazilian real, British pound, Canadian dollar, euro, Japanese yen, Mexican peso, New Zealand dollar, Norwegian krone, Russian ruble, South African rand, Swedish krona, and Swiss franc. The CME is continually experimenting with new contracts. Those that meet the minimum volume requirements are added, and those that do not are dropped. For example, the CME recently added a number of cross-rate contracts, such as EC/JY and AD/SF cross-rate contracts, while dropping contracts in the Dutch guilder (before it was replaced by the euro). By taking the U.S. dollar out of the equation, cross-rate futures allow one to hedge directly the currency risk that arises in dealing with nondollar currencies. The number of contracts outstanding at any one time is called the **open interest.**

Private individuals are encouraged, rather than discouraged, to participate in the market. Contract sizes are standardized by amount of foreign currency—for example, £62,500, C$100,000, and SFr 125,000. Exhibit 8.1 shows contract specifications for some of the currencies traded. Leverage is high; margin requirements average less than 2 percent of the value of the futures contract. The leverage assures that investors' fortunes will be decided by tiny swings in exchange rates.

The contracts have minimum price moves, which generally translate into about $10–$12 per contract. At the same time, most exchanges set daily price limits on their contracts that restrict the maximum daily price move. When these limits are reached, additional margin requirements are imposed and trading may be halted for a short time.

Traders charge commissions on futures contracts rather than using the bid–ask spreads found in the forward market.

Instead of using the bid–ask spreads found in the interbank market, traders charge commissions. Though commissions will vary, a **round trip**—that is, one buy and one sell—costs as little as $15. This cost works out to less than 0.02 percent of the value of a sterling contract. The low cost, along with the high degree of leverage, has provided a major inducement for speculators to participate in the market. Other market participants include importers and exporters, companies with foreign currency assets and liabilities, and bankers.

Although volume in the futures market is still small compared with that in the forward market, it can be viewed as an expanding part of a growing foreign exchange market. As we will see shortly, the different segments of this market are linked by arbitrage.

The CME is still the dominant trader, but other exchanges also trade futures contracts. The most important of these competitors include the London International Financial Futures Exchange (LIFFE), the Chicago Board of Trade (CBOT), the New York Mercantile

EXHIBIT 8.1 • CONTRACT SPECIFICATIONS FOR FOREIGN CURRENCY FUTURES*

	Australian Dollar	*British Pound*	*Canadian Dollar*	*Euro FX*	*Japanese Yen*	*Mexican Peso*	*Swiss Franc*
Contract size	A$100,000	£62,500	C$100,000	€125,000	¥12,500,000	P500,000	SFr 125,000
Symbol	AD	BP	CD	EC	JY	MP	SF
Performance bond requirements							
Initial	$1,485	$1,350	$608	$2,025	$2,025	$3,125	$1,452
Maintenance	$1,100	$1,000	$450	$1,500	$1,500	$2,500	$1,075
Minimum price change	$0.0001 (1 pt.)	$0.0002 (2 pts.)	$0.0001 (1 pt.)	$0.0001 (1 pt.)	$0.000001 (1 pt.)	$0.000025	$0.0001 (1 pt.)
Value of 1 point	$10.00	$6.25	$10.00	$12.50	$12.50	$12.50	$12.50
Months traded	March, June, September, December						
Trading hours	7:20 A.M.–2:00 P.M. (Central Time)						
Last day of trading	The second business day immediately preceding the third Wednesday of the delivery month						

* Effective as of January 22, 2002. The CME still calls the margin requirements initial and maintenance on its Web site.
Source: Data collected from Chicago Mercantile Exchange's Web site at www.cme.com.

Exchange, the Philadelphia Stock Exchange (PHLX), the Singapore International Monetary Exchange (SIMEX), Deutsche Termin Borse (DTB) in Frankfurt, the Hong Kong Futures Exchange (HKFE), the Marché à Termes des Instruments Financiers (MATIF) in Paris, and the Tokyo International Financial Futures Exchange (TIFFE).

A notable feature of the CME and other futures markets is that deals are struck by brokers face to face on a trading floor rather than over the telephone. There are other, more important distinctions between the futures and forward markets.

Forward Contract versus Futures Contract

One way to understand futures contracts is to compare them with forward contracts. **Futures contracts** are standardized contracts that trade on organized futures markets for specific delivery dates only. In the case of the CME, the most actively traded currency futures contracts are for March, June, September, and December delivery. Contracts expire two business days before the third Wednesday of the delivery month. Contract sizes and maturities are standardized, so all participants in the market are familiar with the types of contracts available, a situation that facilitates trading. Forward contracts, on the other hand, are private deals between two individuals who can sign any type of contract they agree on. For example, two individuals may sign a forward contract for €70,000 in twenty months to be paid in Swiss francs. However, CME contracts trade only in round lots of €125,000 priced in U.S. dollars and with a limited range of maturities available. With only a few standardized contracts traded, the trading volume in available contracts is higher, leading to superior liquidity, smaller price fluctuations, and lower transaction costs.

Once a trade is confirmed, the exchange's clearing house—backed by its members' capital—becomes the legal counterparty to both the buyer and seller of the futures contract. The exchange members, in effect, guarantee both sides of a contract, largely eliminating the default risks of trading. Members of the futures exchange support their guarantee through margin requirements, marking contracts to market daily (explained later), and maintaining a guarantee fund in the event a member defaults. In contrast, a forward contract is a private deal between two parties and is subject to the risk that either side may default on the terms of the agreement.

Futures contracts are standardized contracts traded on an organized exchange, whereas forward contracts are non-standardized private deals.

The contract specifications in Exhibit 8.1 show the margin requirements (now called performance bonds by the CME). The **performance bond** (previously referred to as the **initial margin**) shows how much money must be in the account balance when the contract is entered into. This amount is $1,350 in the case of the pound. A **performance bond call** (formerly referred to as a **margin call**) is issued if—because of losses on the futures contract—the balance in the account falls below the **maintenance performance bond** (formerly referred to as the **maintenance margin**), which is $1,000 for the pound. At that time, enough new money must be added to the account balance to bring it up to the performance bond. For example, suppose you start with an initial balance of $1,500 ($150 in excess of the performance bond of $1,350) in your account on a pound futures contract and your contract loses, say, $600 in value. It is now $900, which is $100 below the maintenance performance bond of $1,000. Hence, you must add $450 to your account to meet the performance bond requirement ($1,500 − $600 + $450 = $1,350).

The CME periodically revises its performance bond requirements in line with changing currency volatilities using a computerized risk management program call *SPAN,* which stands for Standard Portfolio Analysis of Risk. Note also that the performance bond requirements set by the CME are minimums; brokers often require higher performance bonds on more volatile currency contracts.

Profits and losses of futures contracts are paid over every day at the end of trading, a practice called **marking to market**. This daily-settlement feature can best be illustrated with an example. On Tuesday morning, an investor takes a long position in a Swiss franc futures contract that matures on Thursday afternoon. The agreed-on price is $0.75 for SFr 125,000. To begin, the investor must deposit into his account a performance bond of $1,452. At the close of trading on Tuesday, the futures price has risen to $0.755. Because of daily settlement, three things occur. First, the investor receives his cash profit of $625 (125,000 × 0.005). Second, the existing futures contract with a price of $0.75 is canceled. Third, the investor receives a new futures contract with the prevailing price of $0.755. Thus, the value of the futures contracts is set to zero at the end of each trading day.

At Wednesday close, the price has declined to $0.743. The investor must pay the $1,500 loss (125,000 × 0.012) to the other side of the contract and trade in the old contract for a new one with a price of $0.743. At Thursday close, the price drops to $0.74, and the contract matures. The investor pays his $375 loss to the other side and takes delivery of the Swiss francs, paying the prevailing price of $0.74. The investor has had a

Futures contracts are marked to market, meaning that contract profits and losses are paid over each day at the end of trading.

EXHIBIT 8.2 • AN EXAMPLE OF DAILY SETTLEMENT WITH A FUTURES CONTRACT

Time	*Action*	*Cash Flow*
Tuesday morning	Investor buys SFr futures contract that matures in two days. Price is $0.75.	None
Tuesday close	Futures price rises to $0.755. Position is marked to market.	Investor receives 125,000 × (0.755 − 0.75) = $625
Wednesday close	Futures price drops to $0.743. Position is marked to market.	Investor pays 125,000 × (0.755 − 0.743) = $1,500
Thursday close	Futures price drops to $0.74. (1) Contract is marked to market. (2) Investor takes delivery of SFr 125,000.	(1) Investor pays 125,000 × (0.743 − 0.74) = $375 (2) Investor pays 125,000 × 0.74 = $92,500 Net loss on the futures contract = $1,250

net loss on the contract of $1,250 ($625 – $1,500 – $375) before paying his commission. Exhibit 8.2 details the daily settlement process.

Daily settlement reduces default risk.

Daily settlement reduces the default risk of futures contracts relative to forward contracts. Every day, futures investors must pay over any losses or receive any gains from the day's price movements. These gains or losses are generally added to or subtracted from the investor's account. An insolvent investor with an unprofitable position would be forced into default after only one day's trading rather than being allowed to build up huge losses that lead to one large default at the time the contract matures (as could occur with a forward contract). For example, if the investor decided to keep his contract in force, rather than closing it out on Wednesday, he would have had a performance bond call because his account would have fallen below the maintenance performance bond of $1,075. His performance bond call would be for $875 ($1,452 + $625 – $1,500 + $875 = $1,452) at the close of Wednesday trading in order to meet his $1,452 performance bond; that is, the investor would have had to add $875 to his account to maintain his futures contract.

Futures contracts can also be closed out with an **offsetting trade**. For example, if a company's long position in euro futures has proved to be profitable, it need not literally take delivery of the euros when the contract matures. Rather, the company can sell futures contracts on a like amount of euros just prior to the maturity of the long position. The two positions cancel on the books of the futures exchange, and the company receives its profit in dollars. Exhibit 8.3 summarizes these and other differences between forward and futures contracts.

 ILLUSTRATION   *Computing Gains, Losses, and Performance Bond Calls on a Futures Contract*

On Monday morning, you short one CME yen futures contract containing ¥12,500,000 at a price of $0.009433. Suppose the broker requires a performance bond of $4,590 and a maintenance performance bond of $3,400. The settlement prices for Monday through Thursday are $0.009542, $0.009581, $0.009375, and $0.009369, respectively. On Friday, you close out the contract at a price of $0.009394. Calculate the daily cash flows on your account. Describe any performance bond calls on your account. What is your cash balance with your broker as of the close of business on Friday? Assume that you begin with an initial balance of $4,590 and that your round-trip commission was $27.
Solution:

Time	*Action*	*Cash Flow on Contract*
Monday morning	Sell one CME yen futures contract. Price is $0.009433.	None.
Monday close	Futures price rises to $0.009542. Contract is marked-to-market.	You pay out 12,500,000 × (0.009433 – 0.009542) = –$1,362.50
Tuesday close	Futures price rises to $0.009581. Contract is marked-to-market.	You pay out an additional 12,500,000 × (0.009542 – 0.009581) = –$487.50
Wednesday close	Futures price falls to $0.009375. Contract is marked-to-market.	You receive 12,500,000 × (0.009581 – 0.009375) = +$2,575.00
Thursday close	Futures price falls to $0.009369. Contract is marked-to-market.	You receive an additional 12,500,000 × (0.009375 – 0.009369) = +$75.00
Friday	You close out your contract at a futures price of $0.009394.	You pay out 12,500,000 × (0.009369 – 0.009394) = –$312.50
		You pay out a round-trip commission = –$27.00
		Net gain on the futures contract $460.50

Your performance bond calls and cash balances as of the close of each day were as follows:

Monday   With a loss of $1,362.50, your account balance falls to $3,227.50 ($4,590 – $1,362.50). You must add $1,362.50 ($4,590 – $3,227.50) to your account to meet the performance bond of $4,590.

Tuesday   With an additional loss of $487.50, your balance falls to $4,102.50 ($4,590 – $487.50). You must add $487.50 to your account to meet the performance bond of $4,590.

Wednesday With a gain of $2,575, your balance rises to $7,165.

Thursday   With a gain of $75, your account balance rises further to $7,240.

Friday   With a loss of $312.50, your account balance falls to $6,927.50. After subtracting the round-trip commission of $27, your account balance ends at $6,900.50.

EXHIBIT 8.3 ● BASIC DIFFERENCES BETWEEN FORWARD AND FUTURES CONTRACTS

1. **Trading:**
   Forward contracts are traded by telephone or telex.
   Futures contracts are traded in a competitive arena.

2. **Regulation:**
   The forward market is self-regulating.
   The IMM is regulated by the Commodity Futures Trading Commission.

3. **Frequency of Delivery:**
   More than 90 percent of all forward contracts are settled by actual delivery.
   By contrast, less than 1 percent of the IMM futures contracts are settled by delivery.

4. **Size of Contract:**
   Forward contracts are individually tailored and tend to be much larger than the standardized contracts on the futures market.
   Futures contracts are standardized in terms of currency amount.

5. **Delivery Date:**
   Banks offer forward contracts for delivery on any date.
   IMM futures contracts are available for delivery on only a few specified dates a year.

6. **Settlement:**
   Forward contract settlement occurs on the date agreed on between the bank and the customer.
   Futures contract settlements are made daily via the Exchange's Clearing House; gains on position values may be withdrawn and losses are collected daily. This practice is known as marking to market.

7. **Quotes:**
   Forward prices generally are quoted in European terms (units of local currency per U.S. dollar).
   Futures contracts are quoted in American terms (dollars per one foreign currency unit).

8. **Transaction Costs:**
   Costs of forward contracts are based on bid–ask spread.
   Futures contracts entail brokerage fees for buy and sell orders.

9. **Margins:**
   Margins are not required in the forward market.
   Margins are required of all participants in the futures market.

10. **Credit Risk:**
    The credit risk is borne by each party to a forward contract. Credit limits must therefore be set for each customer.
    The Exchange's Clearing House becomes the opposite side to each futures contract, thereby reducing credit risk substantially.

Advantages and Disadvantages of Futures Contracts   The smaller size of a futures contract and the freedom to liquidate the contract at any time before its matu-rity in a well-organized futures market differentiate the futures contract from the for-ward contract. These features of the futures contract attract many users. On the other hand, the limited number of currencies traded, the limited delivery dates, and the rigid contractual amounts of currencies to be delivered are disadvantages of the futures con-tract to many commercial users. Only by chance will contracts conform exactly to cor-porate requirements. The contracts are of value mainly to those commercial customers who have a fairly stable and continuous stream of payments or receipts in the traded foreign currencies.

Arbitrage between the Futures and Forward Markets   Arbitrageurs play an important role on the CME. They translate CME futures rates into interbank forward rates and, by realizing profit opportunities, keep CME futures rates in line with bank forward rates.

ILLUSTRATION   *Forward-Futures Arbitrage*

Suppose the interbank forward bid for June 18 on pounds sterling is $1.2927 at the same time that the price of CME sterling futures for delivery on June 18 is $1.2915. How could the dealer use arbitrage to profit from this situation?

Solution. The dealer would simultaneously buy the June sterling futures contract for $80,718.75 (62,500 × $1.2915) and sell an equivalent amount of sterling forward, worth $80,793.75 (62,500 × $1.2927), for June delivery. Upon settlement, the dealer would earn a profit of $75. Alternatively, if the markets come back together before June 18, the dealer can unwind his position (by simultaneously buying £62,500 forward and selling a futures contract, both for delivery on June 18) and earn the same $75 profit. Although the amount of profit on this transaction is tiny, it becomes $7,500 if 100 futures contracts are traded.

Such arbitrage transactions as described in the "Forward-Futures Arbitrage" illus-tration will bid up the futures price and bid down the forward price until approximate equality is restored. The word *approximate* is used because there is a difference between the two contracts. Unlike the forward contract, where gains or losses are not realized until maturity, marking to market means that day-to-day futures contract gains (or losses) will have to be invested (or borrowed) at uncertain future interest rates. However, a study of actual rates for the British pound, Canadian dollar, Deutsche mark, Swiss franc, and Japanese yen found that forward and futures prices do not differ significantly.[1]

8.2 CURRENCY OPTIONS

Whatever advantages the forward or the futures contract might hold for its purchaser, the two contracts have a common disadvantage: Although they protect the holder against the risk of adverse movements in exchange rates, they also eliminate the possibility of gaining a wind-fall profit from favorable movements. This disadvantage was apparently one of the consider-ations that led some commercial banks to offer **currency options** to their customers. Exchange-traded currency options were first offered in 1983 by the **Philadelphia Stock**

---

[1] Bradford Cornell and Marc Reinganum, "Forward and Futures Prices: Evidence from the Foreign Exchange Markets," *Journal of Finance,* December 1981, pp. 1035–1045.

Exchange (PHLX), where they are now traded on the **United Currency Options Market (UCOM)**. Currency options are one of the fastest growing segments of the global foreign exchange market, currently accounting for as much as 7 percent of daily trading volume.

In principle, an *option* is a financial instrument that gives the holder the right—but not the obligation—to sell (put) or buy (call) another financial instrument at a set price and expiration date. The seller of the put option or call option must fulfill the contract if the buyer so desires it. Because the option not to buy or sell has value, the buyer must pay the seller of the option some premium for this privilege. As applied to foreign currencies, **call options** give the customer the right to purchase—and **put options** give the right to sell—the contracted currencies at the **expiration date**. Note that because a foreign exchange transaction has two sides, a call (put) option on a foreign currency can be considered a foreign currency put (call) option on the domestic currency. For example, the right to buy euros against dollar payment is equivalent to the right to sell dollars for euro payment. An **American option** can be exercised at any time up to the expiration date; a **European option** can be exercised only at maturity.

An option that would be profitable to exercise at the current exchange rate is said to be **in-the-money**. Conversely, an **out-of-the-money** option is one that would not be profitable to exercise at the current exchange rate. The price at which the option is exercised is called the **exercise price** or **strike price**. An option whose exercise price is the same as the spot exchange rate is termed **at-the-money**. That is,

> *Currency options give holders the right, but not the obligation, to sell (put) or buy (call) the contracted currency at a set price and expiration date.*

Option Description	*Strike Price Relative to Spot Rate*	*Effect of Immediate Exercise*
In-the-money	Strike price < spot rate	Profit
At-the-money	Strike price = spot rate	Indifference
Out-of-the-money	Strike price > spot rate	Loss

> *An out-of-the-money option is worthless on its expiration date.*

Using Currency Options

To see how currency options might be used, consider a U.S. importer with a €62,500 payment to make to a German exporter in sixty days. The importer could purchase a European call option to have the euros delivered to him at a specified exchange rate (the strike price) on the due date. Suppose the option premium is $0.02 per euro and the exercise price is $1.14. The importer has paid $1,250 for a €114 call option, which gives him the right to buy €62,500 at a price of $1.14 per euro at the end of sixty days. If at the time the importer's payment falls due, the value of the euro has risen to, say, $1.20, the option would be in-the-money. In this case, the importer exercises his call option and purchases euros for $1.14. The importer would earn a profit of $3,750 (62,500 × 0.06), which would more than cover the $1,250 cost of the option. If the rate has declined below the contracted rate to, say, $1.11, the €114 option would be out-of-the-money. Consequently, the importer would let the option expire and purchase the euros in the spot market. Despite losing the $1,250 option premium, the importer would still be $625 better off than if he had locked in a rate of $1.14 with a forward or futures contract.

Exhibit 8.4 illustrates the importer's gains or losses on the call option. At a spot rate on expiration of $1.14 or lower, the option will not be exercised, resulting in a loss of the $1,250 option premium. Between $1.14 and $1.16, the option will be exercised, but the gain is insufficient to cover the premium. The **break-even price**—at which the gain on the option just equals the option premium—is $1.16. Above $1.16 per euro, the option is sufficiently deep in-the-money to cover the option premium and yield a—potentially unlimited—net profit.

Because this is a zero-sum game, the profit from selling a call, shown in Exhibit 8.5, is the mirror image of the profit from buying the call. For example, if the spot rate at expiration is above $1.16/€, the call option writer is exposed to potentially unlimited losses.

Buy an option (handwritten)

EXHIBIT 8.4 • PROFIT FROM BUYING A CALL OPTION FOR VARIOUS SPOT PRICES AT EXPIRATION

let expire buy in market out-lose premium (handwritten)

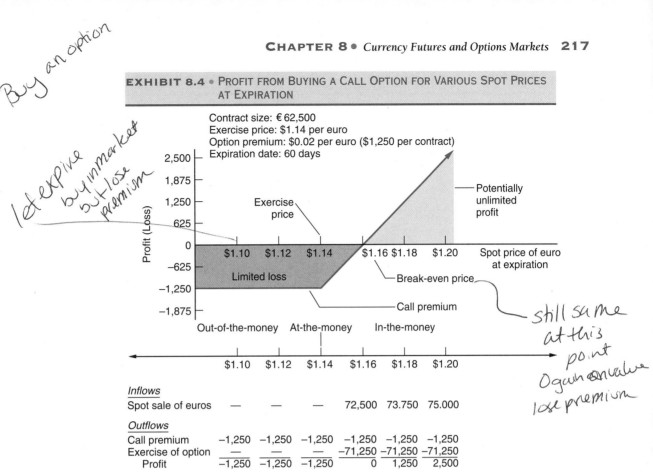

Contract size: € 62,500
Exercise price: $1.14 per euro
Option premium: $0.02 per euro ($1,250 per contract)
Expiration date: 60 days

still same at this point. 0 gain on value lose premium (handwritten)

	$1.10	$1.12	$1.14	$1.16	$1.18	$1.20
Inflows						
Spot sale of euros	—	—	—	72,500	73.750	75.000
Outflows						
Call premium	−1,250	−1,250	−1,250	−1,250	−1,250	−1,250
Exercise of option	—	—	—	−71,250	−71,250	−71,250
Profit	−1,250	−1,250	−1,250	0	1,250	2,500

The profit from buying a call (put) option is the mirror image of the profit from selling a call (put) option.

An in-the-money option will show a loss if the gain is less than the option premium.

Why would an option writer accept such risks? For one thing, the option writer may already be long euros, effectively hedging much of the risk. Alternatively, the writer might be willing to take a risk in the hope of profiting from the option premium because of a belief that the euro will depreciate over the life of the contract. If the spot rate at expiration is $1.14 or less, the option ends out-of-the-money and the call option writer gets to keep the full $1,250 premium. For spot rates between $1.14 and $1.16, the option writer still earns a profit, albeit a diminishing one.

In contrast to the call option, a put option at the same terms (exercise price of $1.14 and put premium of $0.02 per euro) would be in-the-money at a spot price of $1.11 and out-of-the-money at $1.20. Exhibit 8.6 illustrates the profits available on this euro put option. If the spot price falls to, say, $1.08, the holder of a put option will deliver €62,500 worth $67,500 (1.08 × 62,500) and receive $71,250 (1.14 × 62,500). The option holder's profit, net of the $1,250 option premium, is $2,500. As the spot price falls further, the value of the put option rises. At the extreme, if the spot rate falls to zero, the buyer's profit on the contract will reach $70,000 (1.14 × 62,500 − 1,250). Below a spot rate of $1.12, the gain on the put option will more than cover the $1,250 option premium. Between $1.12—the breakeven price for the put option—and $1.14, the holder would exercise the option, but the gain would be less than the option premium. At spot prices above $1.14, the holder would not exercise the option and so would lose the $1,250 premium. Both the put and the call options will be at-the-money if the spot rate in 60 days is $1.14, and the call or put option buyer will lose the $1,250 option premium.

As in the case of the call option, the writer of the put option will have a payoff profile that is the mirror image of the buyer's. We see in Exhibit 8.7 that if the spot rate at expiration is $1.14 or higher, the option writer gets to keep the full $1,250 premium. As the spot rate falls below $1.14, the option writer earns a decreasing profit down to $1.12.

EXHIBIT 8.5 • PROFIT FROM SELLING A CALL OPTION FOR VARIOUS SPOT PRICES AT EXPIRATION

	$1.10	$1.12	$1.14	$1.16	$1.18	$1.20
Inflows						
Call premium	1,250	1,250	1,250	1,250	1,250	1,250
Exercise of option	–	–	–	71,250	71,250	71,250
Outflows						
Spot purchase of euros	–	–	–	–72,500	–73,750	–75,000
Profit	1,250	1,250	1,250	0	–1,250	–2,500

For spot rates below $1.12, the option writer is exposed to increasing losses, up to a maximum potential loss of $70,000 ($1.12 × 62,500). The writer of the put option will accept these risks in the hope of profiting from the put premium. These risks may be minimal if the put option writer is already short euros.

ILLUSTRATION   *Speculating with a Japanese Yen Call Option*

In March, a speculator who is gambling that the yen will appreciate against the dollar pays $680 to buy a yen June 81 call option. This option gives the speculator the right to buy ¥6,250,000 in June at an exchange rate of ¥1 = $0.0081 (the 81 in the contract description is expressed in hundredths of a cent). By the expiration date in June, the yen spot price has risen to $0.0083. What is the investor's net return on the contract?

Solution. Because the call option is in-the-money by 0.02 cents, the investor will realize a gain of $1,250 ($0.0002 × 6,250,000) on the option contract. This amount less the $680 paid for the option produces a gain on the contract of $570.

Currency options can be used to hedge contingent foreign currency cash flows.

Typical users of currency options might be financial firms holding large investments overseas where sizable unrealized gains have occurred because of exchange rate changes and where these gains are thought likely to be partially or fully reversed. Limited use of currency options has also been made by firms that have a foreign currency inflow or outflow that is possibly forthcoming but not definitely. In such cases, where future foreign currency cash flows are contingent on an event such as acceptance of a bid, long call or put positions can be safer hedges than either futures or forwards.

EXHIBIT 8.6 • PROFIT FROM BUYING A PUT OPTION FOR VARIOUS SPOT PRICES AT EXPIRATION

	$1.08	$1.10	$1.12	$1.14	$1.16	$1.18
Inflows						
Exercise of option	71,250	71,250	71,250	—	—	—
Outflows						
Put premium	−1,250	−1,250	−1,250	−1,250	−1,250	−1,250
Spot purchase of euros	−67,500	−68,750	−70,000	—	—	—
Profit	2,500	1,250	0	−1,250	−1,250	−1,250

For example, assume that a U.S. investor makes a firm bid in pounds sterling to buy a piece of real estate in London. If the firm wishes to hedge the dollar cost of the bid, it can buy pounds forward so that if the pound sterling appreciates, the gain on the forward contract will offset the increased dollar cost of the prospective investment. But if the bid is eventually rejected, and if the pound has fallen in the interim, losses from the forward position will have no offset. If no forward cover is taken and the pound appreciates, the real estate will cost more than expected.

Currency call options can provide a better hedge in such a case. Purchased-pound call options would provide protection against a rising pound; and yet, if the bid were rejected and the pound had fallen, the uncovered hedge loss would be limited to the premium paid for the calls. Note that a U.S. company in the opposite position, such as one bidding to supply goods or services priced in pounds to a British project, whose receipt of future pound cash inflows is contingent on acceptance of its bid, would use a long pound put position to provide the safest hedge.

Currency options can also be used by speculators.

Currency options also can be used by pure speculators, those without an underlying foreign currency transaction to protect against. The presence of speculators in the options markets adds to the breadth and depth of these markets, thereby making them more liquid and lowering transactions costs and risk.

Currency Spread   A **currency spread** allows speculators to bet on the direction of a currency but at a lower cost than buying a put or a call option alone. It involves buying an option at one strike price and selling a similar option at a different strike price. The currency spread limits the holder's downside risk on the currency bet but at the cost of limiting the position's upside potential. As shown in Exhibit 8.8a, a spread designed to bet on a currency's appreciation—also called a **bull spread**—would involve buying a call at one strike price and selling another call at a higher strike price. The net premium paid for

EXHIBIT 8.7 • PROFIT FROM SELLING A PUT OPTION FOR VARIOUS SPOT PRICES AT EXPIRATION

	$1.08	$1.10	$1.12	$1.14	$1.16	$1.18
Inflows						
Put premium	1,250	1,250	1,250	1,250	1,250	1,250
Spot sale of euros	67,500	68,750	70,000	–	–	–
Outflows						
Exercise of option	–71,250	–71,250	–71,250	–	–	–
Profit	–2,500	–1,250	0	1,250	1,250	1,250

this position is positive because the former call will be higher priced than the latter (with a lower strike, the option is less out-of-the-money) but it will be less than the cost of buying the former option alone. At the same time, the upside is limited by the strike price of the latter option. Exhibit 8.8b shows the payoff profile of a currency spread designed to bet on a currency's decline. This spread—also called a **bear spread**—involves buying a put at one strike price and selling another put at a lower strike price.

Currency spreads allow speculators to place a low-cost bet on the direction of a currency.

Knockout Options Another way to bet on currency movements at a lower cost than buying a call or a put alone is to use knockout options. A **knockout option** is similar to a standard option except that it is canceled—that is, knocked out—if the exchange rate crosses, even briefly, a pre-defined level called the **outstrike**. If the exchange rate breaches this barrier, the holder cannot exercise this option, even if it ends up in-the-money. Knockout options, also known as *barrier options,* are less expensive than standard currency options precisely because of this risk of early cancellation.

A knockout option is canceled prior to maturity if the exchange rate crosses a predefined level called the outstrike.

There are different types of knockout options. For example, a *down-and-out call* will have a positive payoff to the option holder if the underlying currency strengthens but is canceled if it weakens sufficiently to hit the outstrike. Conversely, a *down-and-out put* has a positive payoff if the currency weakens but will be canceled if it weakens beyond the outstrike. In addition to lowering cost (albeit at the expense of less protection), down-and-out options are useful when a company believes that if the foreign currency declines below a certain level, it is unlikely to rebound to the point that it will cause the company losses. *Up-and-out options* are canceled if the underlying currency strengthens beyond the outstrike. In contrast to the previous knockout options, *down-and-in* and *up-and-in options* come into existence if and only if the currency crosses a preset barrier. The pricing of these options is extremely complex.

EXHIBIT 8.8 • CURRENCY SPREADS

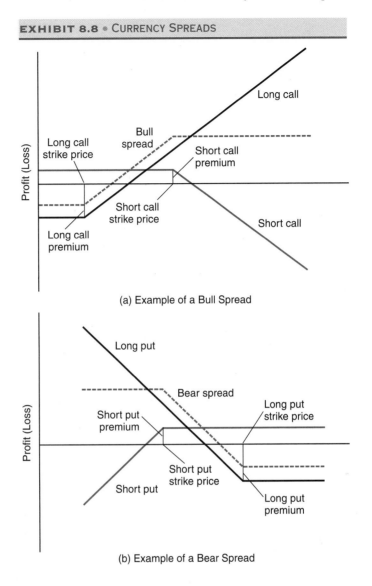

(a) Example of a Bull Spread

(b) Example of a Bear Spread

Option Pricing and Valuation

Options have both intrinsic value and time value.

From a theoretical standpoint, the value of an option comprises two components: intrinsic value and time value. The **intrinsic value** of the option is the amount by which the option is in-the-money, or $S - X$, where S is the current spot price and X the exercise price. In other words, the intrinsic value equals the immediate exercise value of the option. Thus, the further into the money an option is, the more valuable it is. An out-of-the-money option has no intrinsic value. For example, the intrinsic value of a call option on Swiss francs with an exercise price of $0.74 and a spot rate of $0.77 would be $0.03 per franc. The intrinsic value of the option for spot rates that are less than the exercise price is zero. Any excess of the option value over its intrinsic value is called the **time value** of the contract. An option will generally sell for at least its intrinsic value. The more out-of-the-money an option is, the lower the option price. These features are shown in Exhibit 8.9.

During the time remaining before an option expires, the exchange rate can move so as to make exercising the option profitable or more profitable. That is, an out-of-the-money option can move into the money, or one already in-the-money can become more so. The chance that an option will become profitable or more profitable is always greater

EXHIBIT 8.9 • THE VALUE OF A CALL OPTION BEFORE MATURITY

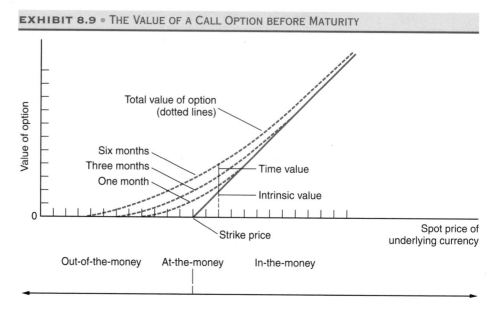

The value of a currency option rises with both contract maturity and increases in exchange rate volatility.

than zero. Consequently, the time value of an option is always positive for an out-of-the-money option and is usually positive for an in-the-money option. Moreover, the more time that remains until an option expires, the higher the time value tends to be. For example, an option with six months remaining until expiration will tend to have a higher price than an option with the same strike price but with only three months until expiration. As the option approaches its maturity, the time value declines to zero.

The value of an American option always exceeds its intrinsic value because the time value is always positive up to the expiration date. For example, if $S > X$, then $C(X) > S - X$, where $C(X)$ is the dollar price of an American call option on one unit of foreign currency. However, the case is more ambiguous for a European option because increasing the time to maturity may not increase its value, given that it can be exercised only on the maturity date.[2] That is, a European currency option may be in-the-money before expiration, yet it may be out-of-the-money by the maturity date.

Before expiration, an out-of-the-money option has only time value, but an in-the-money option has both time value and intrinsic value. At expiration, an option can have only intrinsic value. The time value of a currency option reflects the probability that its intrinsic value will increase before expiration; this probability depends, among other things, on the volatility of the exchange rate. An increase in currency volatility increases the chance of an extremely high or low exchange rate at the time the option expires. The chance of a very high exchange rate benefits the call owner. The chance of a very low exchange rate, however, is irrelevant; the option will be worthless for any exchange rate less than the striking price, whether the exchange rate is "low" or "very low." Inasmuch as the effect of increased volatility is beneficial, the value of the call option is higher. Put options similarly benefit from increased volatility in the exchange rate.

Another aspect of time value involves interest rates. In general, options have a present intrinsic value, determined by the exercise price and price of the underlying asset. Because the option is a claim on a specified amount of an asset over a period of time into the future, that claim must have a return in line with market interest rates on comparable instruments. Therefore, a rise in the interest rate will cause call values to rise and put values to fall.

---

[2] For a technical discussion of foreign currency option pricing, see Mark B. Garman and Steven W. Kohlhagen, "Foreign Currency Option Values," *Journal of International Money and Finance*, December 1983, pp. 231–237.

The price of a currency option is affected by both domestic and foreign interest rates.

Pricing foreign currency options is more complex because it requires consideration of both domestic and foreign interest rates. A foreign currency is normally at a forward premium or discount vis-à-vis the domestic currency. As we saw in Chapter 4, this forward premium or discount is determined by relative interest rates. Consequently, for foreign currency options, call values rise and put values fall when the domestic interest rate increases or the foreign interest rate decreases.

The flip side of a more valuable put or call option is a higher option premium. Hence, options become more expensive when exchange rate volatility rises. Similarly, when the domestic-foreign interest rate differential increases, call options become more expensive and put options less expensive. These elements of option valuation are summarized in Exhibit 8.10.

Using Forward or Futures Contracts versus Options Contracts

Suppose that on July 1, an American company makes a sale for which it will receive €125,000 on September 1. The firm will want to convert those euros into dollars, so it is exposed to the risk that the euro will fall below its current spot rate of $0.9922 in the meantime. The firm can protect itself against a declining euro by selling its expected euro receipts forward (using a futures contract at a futures rate of $0.9956) or by buying a euro put option.

Exhibit 8.11 shows possible results for each choice, using options with strike prices just above and just below the spot exchange of July 1 ($0.98 and $1.00). The example assumes a euro decline to $0.9542 and the consequent price adjustments of associated futures and options contracts. The put quotes are the option premiums per euro. Thus, the dollar premium associated with a particular quote equals the quote multiplied by the number of euros covered by the put options. For example, the quote of $0.0059 for a September put option with a strike price of 98 (in cents) represents a premium for covering the exporter's €125,000 transaction equal to $0.0059 × 125,000 = $737.50.

In the example just described, a decision to remain unhedged would yield a loss of 125,000 × (0.9922 − 0.9542), or $4,750. The outcomes of the various hedge possibilities are shown in Exhibit 8.12.

EXHIBIT 8.10 • CURRENCY OPTION PRICING AND VALUATION

Price Equals the Sum of	*Intrinsic Value*	*Time Value*
	The amount by which the option is in-the-money	The amount by which the price of the contract exceeds its intrinsic value
Call option	$= S - X$, where S is the current spot price and X the exercise price Intrinsic value is zero if $S - X < 0$	Positively affected by an increase in: • time to expiration (usually) • volatility • domestic – foreign interest rate differential
Put option	$= X - S$ Intrinsic value is zero if $X - S < 0$	Positively affected by an increase in: • time to expiration (usually) • volatility • foreign – domestic interest rate differential

EXHIBIT 8.11 • DECLINING EXCHANGE RATE SCENARIO

	July 1	September 1
Spot	$0.9922	$0.9542
September futures	0.9956	0.9558
September 98 put	0.0059	0.0261
September 100 put	0.0144	0.0460

EXHIBIT 8.12 • HEDGING ALTERNATIVES: OFFSETTING A $4,750 LOSS DUE TO A DECLINING EURO

Result of Selling Futures

$(0.9956 - 0.9558) \times 125,000 = \$4,975$ profit

Results of Buying Put Options

98 put: $(0.0261 - 0.0059) \times 125,000 = \$2,525$ profit

100 put: $(0.0460 - 0.0144) \times 125,000 = \$3,950$ profit

Exhibit 8.12 demonstrates the following differences between the futures and options hedging strategies:

1. The futures hedge offers the closest offset to the loss due to the decline of the euro.
2. The purchase of the in-the-money put option (the 100 strike price) offers greater protection (but at a higher premium) than the out-of-the-money put (the 98 strike price).

Note that the September futures price is unequal to the spot rate on September 1 because settlement is not until later in the month. As the euro declines in value, the company will suffer a larger loss on its euro receivables, to be offset by a further increase in the value of the put and futures contracts.

Although the company wants to protect against the possibility of a euro depreciation, what would happen if the euro appreciated? To answer this question—so as to assess fully the options and futures hedge strategies—assume the hypothetical conditions in Exhibit 8.13.

In this scenario, the rise in the euro would increase the value of the unhedged position by $125,000 \times (1.0338 - 0.9922)$, or $5,200. This gain would be offset by losses on the futures or options contracts, as shown in Exhibit 8.14.

We can see that the futures hedge again provides the closest offset. Because these hedges generate losses, however, the company would be better served under this scenario by the smallest offset. With rapidly rising exchange rates, the company would benefit most from hedging with a long put position as opposed to a futures contract; conversely, with rapidly falling exchange rates, the company would benefit most from hedging with a futures contract.

> Futures or forward contracts are better suited than options to hedge known future foreign currency cash flows.

EXHIBIT 8.13 • RISING EXCHANGE RATE SCENARIO

	July 1	September 1
Spot	$0.9922	$1.0338
September futures	0.9956	1.0374
September 98 put	0.0059	0.0001
September 100 put	0.0144	0.0001

EXHIBIT 8.14 • HEDGING ALTERNATIVES: OFFSETTING
A $5,200 GAIN DUE TO A RISING EURO

Result of Selling Futures

$(1.0374 - 0.9956) \times 125,000 = \$5,225$ loss

Results of Buying Put Options

98 put: $(0.0059 - 0.0001) \times 125,000 = \$725$ loss

100 put: $(0.0144 - 0.0001) \times 125,000 = \$1,787.50$ profit

---

Market Structure

Options are purchased and traded either on an organized exchange (such as the United Currency Options Market of the PHLX) or in the **over-the-counter (OTC) market**. **Exchange-traded options** or **listed options** are standardized contracts with predetermined exercise prices, and standard expiration months (March, June, September, and December plus two near-term months). United Currency Options Market (UCOM) options are available in six currencies—the Australian dollar, British pound, Canadian dollar, euro, Japanese yen, and Swiss franc—and are traded in standard contracts half the size of the CME futures contracts. The euro contracts have replaced contracts in the Deutsche mark and French franc. Cross-rate options are also available for the €/¥ and £/€. The cross-rate options serve the same hedging function as cross-rate futures. Contract specifications are shown in Exhibit 8.15. The PHLX trades both American-style and European-style currency options. It also trades month-end options (listed as EOM, or end of month), which ensure the availability of a short-term (at most, a two- or sometimes three-week) currency option at all times, and long-term options, which extend the available expiration months on PHLX dollar-based and cross-rate contracts—providing for 18- and 24-month European-style options.

In 1994, the PHLX introduced a new option contract, called the **Virtual Currency Option**, which is settled in U.S. dollars rather than in the underlying currency. Virtual Currency Options, also called 3-Ds (dollar-denominated delivery), just formalize the reality that practically no exchange-traded options involve the payment or delivery of the underlying currency. Currently, 3-D options on all six traded currencies are available. They are European-style options that have maturities ranging from one week to nine months, and they settle weekly (meaning that each week a new contract is listed). They expire on Monday mornings, so hedging currency risk over a weekend is easy.

The PHLX also offers customized currency options, which allow users to customize various aspects of a currency option, including choice of exercise price, expiration date (up to two years out), and premium quotation as either units of currency or percent of underlying value. Customized currency options can be traded on any combination of the six currencies for which standardized options are available, along with the Mexican peso and the U.S. dollar.[3] The contract size is the same as that for standardized contracts in the underlying currency. Other organized options exchanges are located in Amsterdam (European Options Exchange), Chicago (Chicago Mercantile Exchange), and Montreal (Montreal Stock Exchange).

Over-the-counter (OTC) *options* are contracts whose specifications are generally negotiated as to the amount, exercise price and rights, underlying instrument, and expiration. **OTC currency options** are traded by commercial and investment banks in virtually all financial centers. OTC activity is concentrated in London and New York, and it centers on the major currencies, most often involving U.S. dollars against pounds

Currency options are traded both on organized exchanges and in the over-the-counter markets.

Virtual currency options are settled in dollars rather than in the underlying currency.

The terms on OTC options are generally negotiated as opposed to being standardized like exchange-listed options.

---

[3] The Australian dollar may be matched only against the U.S. dollar.

EXHIBIT 8.15 • PHILADELPHIA STOCK EXCHANGE CURRENCY OPTIONS SPECIFICATIONS

	Australian Dollar	British Pound	Canadian Dollar	Euro	Swiss Franc	Japanese Yen
Symbol						
American style	XAD	XBP	XCD	XEU	XSF	XJY
European style	CAD	CBP	CCD	ECU	CSF	CJY
Contract size	A$50,000	£31,250	C$50,000	€ 62,500	SFr 62,500	¥6,250,000
Exercise Price Intervals	1¢	2¢[1]	0.5¢	1¢	1¢[1]	0.01¢[1]
Premium Quotations	Cents per unit	Cents per unit	Cents per unit	Cents per unit	Cents per unit	Hundredths of a cent per unit
Minimum Price Change	$0.(00)01	$0.(00)01	$0.(00)01	$0.(00)01	$0.(00)01	$0.(0000)01
Minimum Contract Price Change	$5.00	$3.125	$5.00	$6.25	$6.25	$6.25

Expiration Months ———————————— March, June, September, and December + two near-term months ———

Exercise Notice ———————————— No automatic exercise of in-the-money options —————————

Expiration Date — Friday before third Wednesday of the expiring month (Friday is also the last trading day)

Expiration Settlement Date ———————————— Third Wednesday of month ————————————

Daily Price Limits ———————————————— None ————————————————

Issuer & Guarantor ———————————— Options Clearing Corporation (OCC) ————————————

Margin for Uncovered Writer ——— Option premium plus 4% of the underlying contract value less out-of-the-money amount, if any, to a minimum of the option premium plus 3/4% of the underlying contract value.
Contract value equal spot price times unit of currency per contract.

Position & Exercise Limits ———————————— 100,000 contracts ————————————

Trading Hours ———————————— 2:30 A.M.–2:30 P.M. Philadelphia time, Monday through Friday[2] ———

[1] Exercise price intervals for £ (1¢), SFr (0.5¢), and ¥ (0.005¢) in the three near-term months only.
[2] Trading hours for the Canadian dollar are 7:00 A.M–2:30 P.M. Philadelphia time, Monday through Friday.
Source: Philadelphia Stock Exchange, Web site, www.phlx.com.

sterling, euros, Swiss francs, Japanese yen, and Canadian dollars. Branches of foreign banks in the major financial centers are generally willing to write options against the currency of their home country. For example, Australian banks in London write options on the Australian dollar. Generally, OTC options are traded in round lots, commonly $5 million–$10 million in New York and $2 million–$3 million in London. The average maturity of OTC options ranges from two to six months, and very few options are written for more than one year. American options are most common, but European options are popular in Switzerland and Germany because of familiarity.

The OTC options market consists of two sectors: (1) a **retail market** composed of nonbank customers who purchase from banks what amounts to customized insurance against adverse exchange rate movements, and (2) a **wholesale market** among commercial banks, investment banks, and specialized trading firms; this market may include interbank OTC trading or trading on the organized exchanges. The interbank market in

The OTC options market consists of a retail market and a wholesale market.

currency options is analogous to the interbank markets in spot and forward exchange. Banks use the wholesale market to hedge, or "reinsure," the risks undertaken in trading with customers and to take speculative positions in options.

Most retail customers for OTC options are either corporations active in international trade or financial institutions with multicurrency asset portfolios. These customers could purchase foreign exchange puts or calls on organized exchanges, but they generally turn to the banks for options in order to find precisely the terms that match their needs. Contracts are generally tailored with regard to amount, strike price, expiration date, and currency.

The existence of OTC currency options predates exchange-traded options by many years, but trading in OTC options grew rapidly at the same time that PHLX trading began. The acceleration in the growth of options trading in both markets appears to spring from the desire by companies to manage foreign currency risks more effectively and, in particular, from an increased willingness to pay a fee to transfer such risks to another party. Most commentators suggest that corporate demand has increased because the greater volatility of exchange rates has increasingly exposed firms to risks from developments that are difficult to predict and beyond their control.

The growth of listed options, especially for "wholesale" purposes, apparently is putting pressure on the OTC markets for greater standardization in interbank trading. In some instances, OTC foreign currency options are traded for expiration on the third Wednesday of March, June, September, and December, to coincide with expiration dates on the U.S. exchanges.

> The buyer of an option can lose only the premium, whereas the seller's potential loss is unlimited.

Although the buyer of an option can lose only the premium paid for the option, the seller's risk of loss is potentially unlimited. Because of this asymmetry between income and risk, few retail customers are willing to write options. For this reason, the market structure is distinctly asymmetrical when compared with the ordinary market for spot and forward foreign exchange, where there is a balance between customers who are purchasing or selling currency and where the interbank market likewise has a reasonable balance.

Futures Options

In January 1984, the CME introduced a market in options on DM (now replaced by euro) futures contracts. Since then, the **futures option** market has grown to include options on futures in the Australian dollar, Brazilian real, British pound, Canadian dollar, euro, Japanese yen, Mexican peso, New Zealand dollar, Russian ruble, South African rand, and Swiss franc as well. Trading involves purchases and sales of puts and calls on a contract calling for delivery of a standard CME futures contract in the currency rather than the currency itself. When such a contract is exercised, the holder receives a short or long position in the underlying currency futures contract that is marked-to-market, providing the holder with a cash gain. (If there were a loss on the futures contract, the option would not be exercised.) Specifically,

1. If a call futures option contract is exercised, the holder receives a long position in the underlying futures contract plus an amount of cash equal to the current futures price minus the strike price.

2. If a put futures option is exercised, the holder receives a short position in the futures contract plus an amount of cash equal to the strike price minus the current futures price.

The seller of these options has the opposite position to the holder after exercise: a cash outflow plus a short futures position on a call and a long futures position on a put option.

ILLUSTRATION   *Exercising a Pound Call Futures Option Contract*

An investor is holding a pound call futures option contract for June delivery (representing £62,500) at a strike price of $1.5050. The current price of a pound futures contract due in June is $1.5148. What will the investor receive if she exercises her futures option?

Solution. The investor will receive a long position in the June futures contract established at a price of $1.5050 and the option writer has a short position in the same futures contract. These positions are immediately marked to market, triggering a cash payment to the investor from the option writer of 62,500 × ($1.5148 – $1.5050) = $612.50. If the investor desires, she can immediately close out her long futures position at no cost, leaving her with the $612.50 payoff.

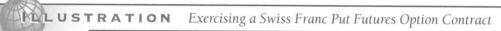

ILLUSTRATION   *Exercising a Swiss Franc Put Futures Option Contract*

An investor is holding one Swiss franc March put futures option contract (representing SFr 125,000) at a strike price of $0.8132. The current price of a Swiss franc futures contract for March delivery is $0.7950. What will the investor receive if she exercises her futures option?

Solution. The investor will receive a short position in the March futures contract established at a price of $0.8132, and the option writer has a long position in the same futures contract. These positions are immediately marked to market and the investor will receive a cash payment from the option writer of 125,000 × ($0.8132 – 0.7950) = $2,275. If the investor desires, she can immediately close out her short futures position at no cost, leaving her with the $2,275 payoff.

A futures option contract has this advantage over a futures contract: With a futures contract, the holder must deliver one currency against the other or reverse the contract, regardless of whether this move is profitable. In contrast, with the futures option contract, the holder is protected against an adverse move in the exchange rate but may allow the option to expire unexercised if using the spot market would be more profitable.

8.3 READING CURRENCY FUTURES AND OPTIONS PRICES

Futures and options prices appear daily in the financial press and are straightforward to read.

Futures and exchange-listed options prices appear daily in the financial press. Exhibit 8.16 shows prices for January 27, 2004, as displayed in the *Wall Street Journal* on the following day. Futures prices on the CME are listed for seven currencies, with two to three contracts quoted for each currency: March and June 2004 for all currencies, and September and December 2004 for two currencies. Included are the opening and last settlement (settle) prices, the change from the previous trading day, the range for the day, and the number of contracts outstanding (open interest). For example, the March euro futures contract opened at $1.2445 per euro and closed at $1.2613, up $0.016 per euro relative to its previous closing price of $1.2453. Futures prices are shown in Exhibit 8.16a.

Exhibit 8.16b shows the Chicago Mercantile Exchange (CME) options on these futures contracts. To interpret the numbers in this column, consider the March call options. These are rights to buy the March euro futures contract at specified prices—the strike prices. For example, the call option with a strike price of 12500 means that you can

EXHIBIT 8.16 • FOREIGN CURRENCY FUTURES AND OPTIONS CONTRACTS

Currency Futures

	OPEN	HIGH	LOW	SETTLE	CHG	LIFETIME HIGH	LIFETIME LOW	OPEN INT

Japanese Yen (CME)-¥12,500,000; $ per ¥
| Mar | .9418 | .9497 | .9413 | .9486 | .0067 | .9497 | .8240 | 149,231 |
| June | .9491 | .9519 | .9456 | .9514 | .0067 | .9519 | .8496 | 7,745 |

Est vol 21,821; vol Mon 17,853; open int 157,046, +616.

Canadian Dollar (CME)-CAD 100,000; $ per CAD
Mar	.7650	.7655	.7583	.7648	.0048	.7863	.6150	58,647
June	.7580	.7635	.7575	.7626	.0048	.7850	.6201	3,398
Sept	.7590	.7620	.7590	.7610	.0048	.7815	.6505	1,556

Est vol 17,582; vol Mon 12,122; open int 64,537, -1,121.

British Pound (CME)-£62,500; $ per £
| Mar | 1.8069 | 1.8222 | 1.7950 | 1.8194 | .0151 | 1.8488 | 1.5654 | 61,708 |
| June | 1.7938 | 1.8100 | 1.7844 | 1.8054 | .0151 | 1.8373 | 1.6080 | 117 |

Est vol 13,322; vol Mon 12,907; open int 62,190, +1,167.

Swiss Franc (CME)-CHF 125,000; $ per CHF
| Mar | .7962 | .8087 | .7950 | .8066 | .0104 | .8249 | .7060 | 40,352 |
| June | .8100 | .8100 | .8082 | .8082 | .0104 | .8248 | .7117 | 188 |

Est vol 13,420; vol Mon 10,863; open int 40,644, -671.

Australian Dollar (CME)-AUD 100,000; $ per AUD
| Mar | .7635 | .7769 | .7635 | .7750 | .0095 | .7769 | .5193 | 57,799 |
| June | .7566 | .7680 | .7566 | .7666 | .0094 | .7680 | .5645 | 803 |

Est vol 8,594; vol Mon 5,880; open int 58,897, -434.

Mexican Peso (CME)-MXN 500,000; $ per MXN
| Mar | .09122 | .09160 | .09087 | .09110 | -0010 | .09330 | .08600 | 40,564 |
| June | .09040 | .09045 | .09010 | .09005 | -0010 | .09125 | .08495 | 543 |

Est vol 4,718; vol Mon 8,026; open int 41,626, -2,549.

Euro/US Dollar (CME)-€125,000; $ per €
Mar	1.2445	1.2639	1.2422	1.2613	.0160	1.2875	1.0425	124,167
June	1.2401	1.2606	1.2401	1.2584	.0160	1.2837	1.0570	1,052
Dec	1.2518	1.2542	1.2518	1.2537	.0160	1.2755	1.0735	212

Est vol 75,779; vol Mon 75,946; open int 125,760, +489.

(a)

Currency Futures Options

Japanese Yen (CME)
12,500,000 yen; cents per 100 yen
STRIKE Price	CALLS-SETTLE Feb	Mar	Apr	PUTS-SETTLE Feb	Mar	Apr
9400	1.11	1.67	...	0.25	0.81	...
9450	0.79	1.40	...	0.43	1.04	...
9500	0.53	1.16	...	0.67	1.30	...
9550	0.34	0.96	...	0.98	...	...
9600	0.22	0.80	...	...	1.94	...
9650	0.15	0.66	...	...	...	...

Est vol 1,039 Mn 337 calls 699 puts
Op int Mon 20,069 calls 18,654 puts

Canadian Dollar (CME)
100,000 Can.$, cents per Can.$
Price	Feb	Mar	Apr	Feb	Mar	Apr
7550	...	1.51	...	0.20	0.55	...
7600	0.78	1.20	...	0.32	0.74	...
7650	0.48	0.93	...	0.52	0.97	...
7700	0.30	0.72	...	0.84	1.26	...
7750	0.18	0.55	...	1.22	1.59	...
7800	0.11	0.42	...	1.65	1.96	...

Est vol 299 Mn 81 calls 323 puts
Op int Mon 12,537 calls 9,488 puts

British Pound (CME)
62,500 pounds; cents per pound
Price	Feb	Mar	Apr	Feb	Mar	Apr
1800	2.54	3.52	...	0.60	1.58	...
1810	1.78	2.92	...	0.84	1.98	...
1820	1.16	2.38	...	1.22	2.44	...
1830	0.84	1.92	...	1.90	2.98	...
1840	0.56	1.54	...	2.62	3.60	...
1850	0.40	1.22	1.49	...	...	...

Est vol 193 Mn 114 calls 49 puts
Op int Mon 5,561 calls 4,437 puts

Swiss Franc (CME)
125,000 francs; cents per franc
Price	Feb	Mar	Apr	Feb	Mar	Apr
7950	...	1.90	...	0.26	0.74	...
8000	1.06	1.60	...	0.40	0.94	...
8050	0.76	1.33	...	0.60	1.17	...
8100	0.51	1.08	...	0.85	1.42	...
8150	0.35	0.89	...	1.19	1.73	...
8200	0.24	0.72	...	1.58	2.06	...

Est vol 90 Mn 238 calls 137 puts
Op int Mon 1,625 calls 1,581 puts

Euro Fx (CME)
125,000 euros; cents per euro
Price	Feb	Mar	Apr	Feb	Mar	Apr
12500	1.64	2.45	2.87	0.51	1.32	2.03
12550	1.31	2.16	...	0.68	1.53	...
12600	1.03	1.89	2.37	0.90	1.76	2.53
12650	0.81	1.66	2.14	1.18	2.03	2.80
12700	...	1.45	1.93	1.49	2.32	...
12750	0.46	1.25	...	1.83	2.62	...

Est vol 4,111 Mn 2,914 calls 4,025 puts
Op int Mon 34,750 calls 40,523 puts

(b)

purchase an option to buy a March euro futures contract, up to the March settlement date, for $1.2500 per euro. This option will cost $0.0245 per euro, or $3,062.50, plus brokerage commission, for a €125,000 contract. The price is high because the option is in-the-money. In contrast, the March futures option with a strike price of 12750, which is out-of-the-money, costs only $0.0125 per euro, or $1,562.50 for one contract. These option prices indicate that the market expects the dollar price of the euro to exceed $1.2500 but not to rise much above $1.2750 by March.

As we have just seen, a futures call option allows you to buy the relevant futures contract, which is settled at maturity. On the other hand, the Philadelphia call options contract is an option to buy foreign exchange spot, which is settled when the call option is exercised; the buyer receives foreign currency immediately.

Price quotes usually reflect this difference. For example, PHLX call options for the March euro with a strike price of $1.2500, are $0.0356 per euro (versus $0.0245 for the March futures call option), or $2,225, plus brokerage fees, for one contract of €62,500. Brokerage fees here would be about the same as on the CME: about $16 per transaction round trip per contract.[4] Exhibit 8.17 summarizes how to read price quotations for futures using a euro illustration.

---

[4] The *Wall Street Journal* no longer publishes PHLX currency option prices so the January option price was taken from the PHLX's Web site.

EXHIBIT 8.17 • How to Read Futures Quotations

Trading activity can be monitored daily in the business pages of most major newspapers. The following displays are illustrations of the way these prices are shown.

Futures

EURO (CME)—125,000 euros; $ per euro

	Open	High	Low	Settle	Chg	Lifetime High	Low	Open Interest
Mar	0.8711	0.8782	0.8703	0.8764	+0.0053	0.9205	0.8646	143,059
June	0.8680	0.8750	0.8673	0.8732	+0.0053	0.9162	0.8607	8,202
Sept	0.8690	0.8654	0.8690	0.8708	+0.0053	0.9130	0.8610	296

Est. vol. 45,259; vol. Wed. 32,307 ; open int. 151,594 – 2,049

1. Prices represent the open, high, low, and settlement (or closing) price for the previous day.
2. Contract delivery months that are currently traded.
3. Number of contracts traded in the previous two trading sessions.
4. One day's change in the settlement price.
5. The total of the right column, and the change from the prior trading day.
6. The extreme prices recorded for the contract over its trading life.
7. The number of contracts still in effect at the end of the previous day's trading session. Each unit represents a buyer *and* a seller who still have a contract position.

8.4 SUMMARY AND CONCLUSIONS

In this chapter, we examined the currency futures and options markets and looked at some of the institutional characteristics and mechanics of these markets. We saw that currency futures and options offer alternative hedging (and speculative) mechanisms for companies and individuals. Like forward contracts, futures contracts must be settled at maturity. By contrast, currency options give the owner the right but not the obligation to buy (call option) or sell (put option) the contracted currency. An American option can be exercised at any time up to the expiration date; a European option can be exercised only at maturity.

Futures contracts are standardized contracts that trade on organized exchanges. Forward contracts, on the other hand, are custom-tailored contracts, typically entered into between a bank and its customers. Options contracts are sold on both organized exchanges and in the over-the-counter (OTC) market. Like forward contracts, OTC options are contracts whose specifications are generally negotiated as to the terms and conditions between a bank and its customers.

QUESTIONS

1. On April 1, the spot price of the British pound was $1.86 and the price of the June futures contract was $1.85. During April the pound appreciated, so that by May 1 it was selling for $1.91. What do you think happened to the price of the June pound futures contract during April? Explain.

2. What are the basic differences between forward and futures contracts? Between futures and options contracts?

3. A forward market already existed, so why was it necessary to establish currency futures and currency options contracts?

4. Suppose that Texas Instruments (TI) must pay a French supplier €10 million in 90 days.
   a. Explain how TI can use currency futures to hedge its exchange risk. How many futures contracts will TI need to fully protect itself?

   b. Explain how TI can use currency options to hedge its exchange risk. How many options contracts will TI need to fully protect itself?
   c. Discuss the advantages and disadvantages of using currency futures versus currency options to hedge TI's exchange risk.

5. Suppose that Bechtel Group wants to hedge a bid on a Japanese construction project. But because the yen exposure is contingent on acceptance of its bid, Bechtel decides to buy a put option for the ¥15 billion bid amount rather than sell it forward. In order to reduce its hedging cost, however, Bechtel simultaneously sells a call option for ¥15 billion with the same strike price. Bechtel reasons that it wants to protect its downside risk on the contract and is willing to sacrifice the upside potential in order to collect the call premium. Comment on Bechtel's hedging strategy.

PROBLEMS

1. On Monday morning, an investor takes a long position in a pound futures contract that matures on Wednesday afternoon. The agreed-upon price is $1.78 for £62,500. At the close of trading on Monday, the futures price has risen to $1.79. At Tuesday close, the price rises further to $1.80. At Wednesday close, the price falls to $1.785, and the contract matures. The investor takes delivery of the pounds at the prevailing price of $1.785. Detail the daily settlement process (see Exhibit 8.3). What will be the investor's profit (loss)?

2. Suppose that the forward ask price for March 20 on euros is $0.9127 at the same time that the price of CME euro futures for delivery on March 20 is $0.9145. How could an arbitrageur profit from this situation? What will be the arbitrageur's profit per futures contract (contract size is €125,000)?

3. Suppose that DEC buys a Swiss franc futures contract (contract size is SFr 125,000) at a price of $0.83. If the spot rate for the Swiss franc at the date of settlement is SFr 1 = $0.8250, what is DEC's gain or loss on this contract?

4. On January 10, Volkswagen agrees to import auto parts worth $7 million from the United States. The parts will be delivered on March 4 and are payable immediately in dollars. VW decides to hedge its dollar position by entering into CME futures contracts. The spot rate is $0.8947/€, and the March futures price is $0.9002/€.

   a.. Calculate the number of futures contracts that VW must buy to offset its dollar exchange risk on the parts contract.

   b. On March 4, the spot rate turns out to be $0.8952/€, while the March futures price is $0.8968/€. Calculate VW's net euro gain or loss on its futures position. Compare this figure with VW's gain or loss on its unhedged position.

5. Citigroup sells a call option on euros (contract size is €500,000) at a premium of $0.04 per euro. If the exercise price is $0.91 and the spot price of the euro at date of expiration is $0.93, what is Citigroup's profit (loss) on the call option?

6. Suppose you buy three June PHLX euro call options with a 90 strike price at a price of 2.3 (¢/€).

   a. What would be your total dollar cost for these calls, ignoring broker fees?

   b. After holding these calls for 60 days, you sell them for 3.8 (¢/€). What is your net profit on the contracts, assuming that brokerage fees on both entry and exit were $5 per contract and that your opportunity cost was 8 percent per annum on the money tied up in the premium?

7. Apex Corporation must pay its Japanese supplier ¥125 million in three months. It is thinking of buying 20 yen call options (contract size is ¥6.25 million) at a strike price of $0.00800 in order to protect against the risk of a rising yen. The premium is 0.015 cents per yen. Alternatively, Apex could buy ten three-month yen futures contracts (contract size is ¥12.5 million) at a price of $0.007940/¥. The current spot rate is ¥1 = $0.007823. Apex's treasurer believes that the most likely value for the yen in 90 days is $0.007900, but the yen could go as high as $0.008400 or as low as $0.007500.

   a. Diagram Apex's gains and losses on the call option position and the futures position within its range of expected prices (see Exhibit 8.4). Ignore transaction costs and margins.

   b. Calculate what Apex would gain or lose on the option and futures positions if the yen settled at its most likely value.

   c. What is Apex's break-even future spot price on the option contract? On the futures contract?

   d. Calculate and diagram the corresponding profit and loss and break-even positions on the futures and options contracts for the sellers of these contracts.

BIBLIOGRAPHY

Bates, David S. "Jumps and Stochastic Volatility: Exchange Rate Processes Implicit in PHLX Deutschemark Options." Wharton School Working Paper, 1993.

Black, Fischer, and Myron Scholes, "The Pricing of Options and Corporate Liabilities," *Journal of Political Economy,* May–June 1973, pp. 637–659.

Bodurtha, James, N., Jr., and Georges R. Courtadon. "Tests of an American Option Pricing Model on the Foreign Currency Options Market." *Journal of Financial and Quantitative Analysis,* June 1987, pp. 153–167.

Chicago Mercantile Exchange. *Using Currency Futures and Options.* Chicago: CME, 1987.

Cornell, Bradford, and Marc Reinganum. "Forward and Futures Prices: Evidence from the Foreign Exchange Markets." *Journal of Finance,* December 1981, pp. 1035–1045.

Garman, Mark B., and Steven W. Kohlhagen. "Foreign Currency Option Values." *Journal of International Money and Finance,* December 1983, pp. 231–237.

Jorion, Phillipe. "On Jump Processes in the Foreign Exchange and Stock Markets." *Review of Financial Studies* 1, no. 4 (1988): 427–445.

Shastri, Kuleep, and Kulpatra Wethyavivorn. "The Valuation of Currency Options for Alternate Stochastic Processes." *Journal of Financial Research,* Winter 1987, pp. 283–293.

INTERNET RESOURCES

www.ny.frb.org/markets/impliedvolatility.html Web site of the Federal Reserve Bank of New York that lists implied volatilities for foreign currency options.

www.bis.org/publ/index.htm Web site of the Bank for International Settlements that lists downloadable publications such as BIS Annual Report, statistics on derivatives, external debt, foreign exchange market activity, and so on.

www.cme.com Web site of the Chicago Mercantile Exchange (CME). Contains information and quotes on currency futures and options contracts.

www.phlx.com Web site of the Philadelphia Stock Exchange (PHLX). Contains information and quotes on currency options contracts.

INTERNET EXERCISES

1. What currency futures contracts are currently being traded on the CME?
2. Have currency futures prices generally risen or fallen in the past day?
3. What currency options contracts are currently traded on the PHLX?

SWAPS AND INTEREST RATE DERIVATIVES

Man is not the creature of circumstances, circumstances are the creatures of men.

Benjamin Disraeli (1826)

CHAPTER LEARNING OBJECTIVES

- To describe interest rate and currency swaps and explain how they can be used to reduce financing costs and risk
- To calculate the appropriate payments and receipts associated with a given interest rate or currency swap
- To identify the factors that underlie the economic benefits of swaps
- To describe the use of forward forwards, forward rate agreements, and Eurodollar futures to lock in interest rates on future loans and deposits and hedge interest rate risk

KEY TERMS

all-in cost	floating rate
basis swap	forward forward
coupon swap	forward rate agreement
currency swap	interest rate/currency swap
dual currency bond	interest rate swap
Eurobond	London Interbank Offered Rate
Eurocurrency	(LIBOR)
Eurodollar futures	notional principal
exchange of principals	right of offset
fixed rate	swap

This chapter examines several currency and interest rate derivatives that multinational corporations can use to fund their foreign investments and manage their interest rate risk. These derivatives include interest rate, currency, and interest rate/currency swaps and interest rate forward and futures contracts. Each of them presents opportunities to the multinational firm to reduce financing costs and/or risk.

9.1 INTEREST RATE AND CURRENCY SWAPS

Swaps can facilitate innovative, complex financings that reduce costs and risk.

Corporate financial managers can use **swaps** to arrange complex, innovative financings that reduce borrowing costs and increase control over interest rate risk and foreign currency exposure. For example, General Electric points out in its 1999 Annual Report that it and its subsidiary General Electric Capital Services (GECS) use swaps both to reduce funding costs and to hedge risk:

> *Swaps of interest rates and currencies are used by GE and GECS to optimize funding costs for a particular funding strategy. A cancelable interest rate swap was used by GE to hedge an investment position. Interest rate and currency swaps, along with purchased options and futures, are used by GECS to establish specific hedges of mortgage-related assets and to manage net investment exposures.*

As a result of the deregulation and integration of national capital markets and extreme interest rate and currency volatility, the relatively new swaps market has experienced explosive growth, with the Bank for International Settlements (BIS) estimating outstanding interest rate and currency swaps as of June 30, 2001, of $61.5 trillion.[1] Few Eurobonds are issued without at least one swap behind them to give the borrower cheaper or in some way more desirable funds.

This section discusses the structure and mechanics of the two basic types of swaps—interest rate swaps and currency swaps—and shows how swaps can be used to achieve diverse goals. Swaps have had a major impact on the treasury function, permitting firms to tap new capital markets and to take further advantage of innovative products without an increase in risk. Through the swap, they can trade a perceived risk in one market or currency for a liability in another. The swap has led to a refinement of risk management techniques, which in turn has facilitated corporate involvement in international capital markets.

Interest Rate Swaps

Parties to an interest rate swap exchange interest rate payments for a specific maturity on an agreed-upon notional amount.

An **interest rate swap** is an agreement between two parties to exchange U.S. dollar interest payments for a specific maturity on an agreed-upon notional amount. The term *notional* refers to the theoretical principal underlying the swap. Thus, the **notional principal** is simply a reference amount against which the interest is calculated. No principal ever changes hands. Maturities range from less than a year to more than fifteen years; however, most transactions fall within a two-year to ten-year period. The two main types are coupon swaps and basis swaps. In a **coupon swap**, one party pays a *fixed rate* calculated at the time of trade as a spread to a particular Treasury bond, and the other side pays a *floating rate* that resets periodically throughout the life of the deal against a designated index. In a **basis swap**, two parties exchange floating interest payments based on different reference rates. Using this relatively straightforward mechanism, interest rate swaps transform debt issues, assets, liabilities, or any cash flow from type to type and—with some variation in the transaction structure—from currency to currency.

---

[1] "Triennial Central Bank Survey: Foreign Exchange and Derivatives Market Activity in 2001," Bank for International Settlements, Basle, March 2002, Table C.6, p. 26.

The most important reference rate in swap and other financial transactions is the **London Interbank Offered Rate (LIBOR)**. LIBOR is the average interest rate offered by a specific group of multinational banks in London (selected by the British Bankers Association for their degree of expertise and scale of activities) for U.S. dollar deposits of a stated maturity and is used as a base index for setting rates of many floating rate financial instruments, especially in the Eurocurrency and Eurobond markets. A **Eurocurrency** is a dollar or other freely convertible currency deposited in a bank outside its country of origin. For example, a dollar on deposit in London is a Eurodollar. A **Eurobond** is a bond sold outside the country in whose currency it is denominated. So, for example, a dollar bond sold in Paris by IBM would be a Eurobond. Eurobonds can carry either fixed rates or floating rates. **Fixed-rate** bonds have a fixed coupon, whereas **floating-rate** issues have variable coupons that are reset at fixed intervals, usually every three to six months. The new coupon is set at a fixed margin above a mutually agreed-upon reference rate such as LIBOR.

The Classic Swap Transaction   Counterparties A and B both require $100 million for a five-year period. To reduce their financing risks, counterparty A would like to borrow at a fixed rate, whereas counterparty B would prefer to borrow at a floating rate. Suppose that A is a company with a BBB rating and B is a AAA-rated bank. Although A has good access to banks or other sources of floating-rate funds for its operations, it has difficulty raising fixed-rate funds from bond issues in the capital markets at a price it finds attractive. By contrast, B can borrow at the finest rates in either market. The cost to each party of accessing either the fixed-rate or the floating-rate market for a new five-year debt issue is as follows:

Borrower	Fixed-Rate Available	Floating-Rate Available
Counterparty A: BBB-rated	8.5%	6-month LIBOR + 0.5%
Counterparty B: AAA-rated	7.0%	6-month LIBOR
Difference	1.5%	0.5%

It is obvious that there is an anomaly between the two markets: One judges that the difference in credit quality between a AAA-rated firm and a BBB-rated firm is worth 150 basis points; the other determines that this difference is worth only 50 basis points (a basis point equals 0.01 percent). Through an interest rate swap, both parties can take advantage of the 100 basis-point spread differential.

To begin, A will take out a $100 million, five-year floating-rate Eurodollar loan from a syndicate of banks at an interest rate of LIBOR plus 50 basis points. At the same time, B will issue a $100 million, five-year Eurobond carrying a fixed rate of 7 percent. A and B then will enter into the following interest rate swaps with BigBank. Counterparty A agrees that it will pay BigBank 7.35 percent for five years, with payments calculated by multiplying that rate by the $100 million notional principal amount. In return for this payment, BigBank agrees to pay A six-month LIBOR (LIBOR6) over five years, with reset dates matching the reset dates on its floating-rate loan. Through the swap, A has managed to turn a floating-rate loan into a fixed-rate loan costing 7.85 percent.

In a similar fashion, B enters into a swap with BigBank whereby it agrees to pay six-month LIBOR to BigBank on a notional principal amount of $100 million for five years in exchange for receiving payments of 7.25 percent. Thus, B has swapped a fixed-rate loan for a floating-rate loan carrying an effective cost of LIBOR6 minus 25 basis points.

Why would BigBank or any financial intermediary enter into such transactions? The reason BigBank is willing to enter into such contracts is more evident when looking at the transaction in its entirety. This classic swap structure is shown in Exhibit 9.1.

A swap can convert a floating-rate loan into a fixed-rate loan and vice versa.

EXHIBIT 9.1 • CLASSIC SWAP STRUCTURE

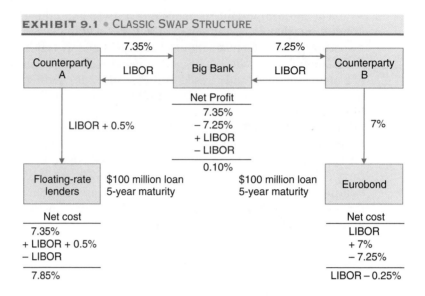

As a financial intermediary, BigBank puts together both transactions. The risks net out, and BigBank is left with a spread of 10 basis points:

Receive (from A)	7.35%
Pay (to B)	(7.25%)
Receive (from B)	LIBOR
Pay (to A)	(LIBOR)
Net	10 basis points

BigBank thus receives compensation equal to $100,000 annually for the next five years on the $100 million swap transaction.

Cost Savings Associated with Swaps   The example just discussed shows the risk-reducing potential of interest rate swaps. Swaps also may be used to reduce costs. Their ability to do so depends on a difference in perceived credit quality across financial markets. In essence, interest rate swaps exploit the comparative advantages—if they exist—enjoyed by different borrowers in different markets, thereby increasing the options available to both borrower and investor.

Returning to the previous example, we can see that there is a spread differential of 100 basis points between the cost of fixed- and floating-rate borrowing for A and B which the interest rate swap has permitted the parties to share among themselves as follows:

Party	Normal Funding Cost (%)	Cost After Swap (%)	Difference (%)
Counterparty A	8.50	7.85	0.65
Counterparty B	LIBOR	LIBOR − 0.25	0.25
BigBank	—	—	0.10
		Total	1.00

In this example, A lowers its fixed-rate costs by 65 basis points, B lowers its floating-rate costs by 25 basis points, and BigBank receives 10 basis points for arranging the transaction and bearing the credit risk of the counterparties.

Swaps can reduce costs for both parties if there is a difference in perceived credit quality across financial markets.

You might expect that the process of financial arbitrage would soon eliminate any such cost savings opportunities associated with a mispricing of credit quality. Despite this efficient markets view, many players in the swaps market believe that such anomalies in perceived credit risk continue to exist. The explosive growth in the swaps market supports this belief. It may also indicate the presence of other factors, such as differences in information and risk aversion of lenders across markets, that are more likely to persist.

 ILLUSTRATION   *Payments on a Two-Year Fixed-for-Floating Interest Rate Swap*

Suppose that on December 31, 2004, IBM issues a two-year, floating-rate bond in the amount of $100 million on which it pays LIBOR6 − 0.5 percent semiannually, with the first payment due at the end of June 2005. Because IBM would prefer fixed-rate payments, it enters into a swap with Citibank as the intermediary on December 31, 2004. Under the swap contract, IBM agrees to pay Citibank an annual rate of 8 percent and will receive LIBOR6. All payments are made on a semiannual basis. In effect, IBM has used a swap to convert its floating-rate debt into a fixed-rate bond yielding 7.5 percent.

To see how the payments on the swap are computed, suppose that LIBOR6 on December 31, 2004, is 7 percent. On June 30, 2005, IBM will owe Citibank $4 million ($0.5 \times 0.08 \times \$100$ million) and will receive in return $3.5 million ($0.5 \times 0.07 \times \$100$ million). Net, IBM will pay Citibank $0.5 million. IBM will also pay its bondholders $3.25 million [$0.5 \times (0.07 - 0.005) \times \$100$ million]. Combining the swap and the bond payments, IBM will pay out $3.75 million, which converts into a coupon rate of 7.5 percent paid semiannually. On subsequent reset periods, payments will vary with LIBOR6 (see Exhibit 9.2 for possible payments).

Currency Swaps

Interest rate swaps can be arranged across currencies.

Swap contracts also can be arranged across currencies. Such contracts are known as currency swaps and can help manage both interest rate and exchange rate risk. Many financial institutions count the arranging of swaps, both domestic and foreign currency, as an important line of business.

Technically, a **currency swap** is an exchange of debt-service obligations denominated in one currency for the service on an agreed upon principal amount of debt denominated in another currency. By swapping their future cash-flow obligations, the counterparties are able to replace cash flows denominated in one currency with cash flows in a more desired currency. In this way, company A, which has borrowed, say, Japanese yen at a fixed interest rate, can transform its yen debt into a fully hedged dollar liability

EXHIBIT 9.2 ● SWAP PAYMENTS OVER THE TWO-YEAR LIFE OF IBM'S SWAP

Period Ending	LIBOR6	Fixed-Rate Payment to Citibank	Floating-Rate Payment from Citibank	Net Payment to Citibank	Payment to Bondholders	Net Payment by IBM
June 2005	7%	$4,000,000	$3,500,000	$500,000	$3,250,000	$3,750,000
December 2005	6%	$4,000,000	$3,000,000	$1,000,000	$2,750,000	$3750,000
June 2006	8%	$4,000,000	$4,000,000	$0	$3,750,000	$3,750,000
December 2006	9%	$4,000,000	$4,500,000	-$500,000	$4,250,000	$3,750,000

by exchanging cash flows with counterparty B. As illustrated in Exhibit 9.3, the two loans that comprise the currency swap have parallel interest and principal repayment schedules. At each payment date, company A will pay a fixed interest rate in dollars and receive a fixed rate in yen. The counterparties also exchange principal amounts at the start and the end of the swap arrangement (denoted as time T in the diagram).

In effect, a U.S. firm engaged in a currency swap has borrowed foreign currency and converted its proceeds into dollars, while simultaneously arranging for a counterparty to make the requisite foreign currency payment in each period. In return for this foreign currency payment, the firm pays an agreed-upon amount of dollars to the counterparty. Given the fixed nature of the periodic exchanges of currencies, the currency swap is equivalent to a package of forward contracts. For example, in the dollar:yen swap just discussed, firm A has contracted to sell fixed amounts of dollars forward for fixed amounts of yen on a series of future dates.

The counterparties to a currency swap will be concerned about their **all-in cost**—that is, the effective interest rate on the money they have raised. This interest rate is calculated as the discount rate that equates the present value of the future interest and principal payments to the net proceeds received by the issuer.

Currency swaps contain the **right of offset**, which gives each party the right to offset any nonpayment of principal or interest with a comparable nonpayment. Absent a right of offset, default by one party would not release the other from making its contractually obligated payments. Moreover, because a currency swap is not a loan, it does not appear as a liability on the parties' balance sheets.

Although the structure of currency swaps differs from interest rate swaps in a variety of ways, the major difference is that with a currency swap, there is always an exchange of principal amounts at maturity at a predetermined exchange rate. Thus, the swap contract behaves like a long-dated forward foreign exchange contract, where the forward rate is the current spot rate.

> The exchange of principals at maturity in a currency swap offsets the interest differential between the currencies.

That there is always an exchange of principal amounts at maturity can be explained as follows. Assume that the prevailing coupon rate is 8 percent in one currency and 5 percent in the other currency. What would persuade an investor to pay 8 percent and receive 300 basis points less? The answer lies in the spot and long-term forward exchange rates and how

EXHIBIT 9.3 ● DIAGRAM OF A FIXED FOR FIXED CURRENCY SWAP

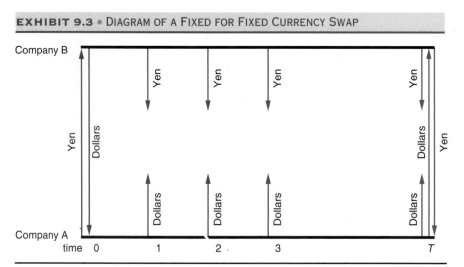

Company A issues yen debt and exchanges the yen principal amount for dollars with company B, which has issued dollar debt. At each subsequent interest date, A pays dollar interest to B and receives yen interest from B. A uses the yen it receives from B to service its yen debt. At maturity, there is a final interest exchange and an exchange of principal amounts.

currency swaps adjust to compensate for the differentials. According to interest rate parity theory, forward rates are a direct function of the interest rate differential for the two currencies involved. As a result, a currency with a lower interest rate has a correspondingly higher forward exchange value. It follows that future exchange of currencies at the present spot exchange rate would offset the current difference in interest rates. This **exchange of principals** is what occurs in every currency swap at maturity based on the original amounts of each currency and, by implication, is done at the original spot exchange rate.

In the classic currency swap, the counterparties exchange fixed-rate payments in one currency for fixed-rate payments in another currency. The hypothetical example of a swap between Dow and Michelin illustrates the structure of a fixed-for-fixed currency swap.

ILLUSTRATION   *Dow Chemical Swaps Fixed-for-Fixed with Michelin*

EXHIBIT 9.4 • EXAMPLE OF A FIXED-FOR-FIXED EURO U.S. DOLLAR CURRENCY SWAP

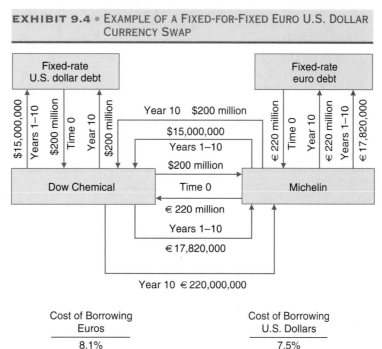

Cost of Borrowing Euros	Cost of Borrowing U.S. Dollars
8.1%	7.5%

Suppose that Dow Chemical is looking to hedge some of its euro exposure by borrowing in euros. At the same time, French tire manufacturer Michelin is seeking dollars to finance additional investment in the U.S. market. Both want the equivalent of $200 million in fixed-rate financing for ten years. Dow can issue dollar-denominated debt at a coupon rate of 7.5 percent or euro-denominated debt at a coupon rate of 8.25 percent. Equivalent rates for Michelin are 7.7 percent in dollars and 8.1 percent in euros. Given that both companies have similar credit ratings, it is clear that the best way for them to borrow in the other's currency is to issue debt in their own currencies and then swap the proceeds and future debt-service payments.

Assuming a current spot rate of €1.1/$, Michelin would issue €220 million in 8.1 percent debt and Dow Chemical would float a bond issue of $200 million at 7.5 percent. The coupon payments on these bond issues are €17,820,000 (0.081 × €220 million) and $15 million (0.075 × $200 million), respectively, giving rise to the following debt-service payments:

Year	Michelin	Dow Chemical
1–10	€17,820,000	$15,000,000
10	€220,000,000	$200,000,000

After swapping the proceeds at time 0 (now), Dow Chemical winds up with €220 million in euro debt and Michelin has $200 million in debt to service. In subsequent years, they would exchange coupon payments and the principal amounts at repayment. The cash inflows and outflows for both parties are summarized in Exhibit 9.4. The net result is that the swap enables Dow to borrow fixed-rate euros indirectly at 8.1 percent, saving 15 basis points relative to its 8.25 percent cost of borrowing euros directly, and Michelin can borrow dollars at 7.5 percent, saving 20 basis points relative to its direct cost of 7.7 percent.

Interest Rate/Currency Swaps   Although the currency swap market began with fixed-for-fixed swaps, most such swaps today are interest rate/currency swaps. As its name implies, an **interest rate/currency swap** combines the features of both a currency swap and an interest rate swap. This swap is designed to convert a liability in one currency with a stipulated type of interest payment into one denominated in another currency with a different type of interest payment. The most common form of interest rate/currency swap converts a fixed-rate liability in one currency into a floating-rate liability in a second currency. We can use the previous example of Dow Chemical and Michelin to illustrate the mechanics of a fixed-for-floating currency swap.

Most currency swaps also involve fixed-for-floating interest rate swaps.

ILLUSTRATION   *Dow Chemical Swaps Fixed-for-Floating with Michelin*

Suppose that Dow Chemical decides it prefers to borrow floating-rate euros instead of fixed-rate euros, whereas Michelin maintains its preference for fixed-rate dollars. Assume that Dow Chemical can borrow floating-rate euros directly at LIBOR + 0.35 percent, versus a cost to Michelin of borrowing floating-rate euros of LIBOR + 0.125 percent. As before, given Dow's cost of borrowing dollars of 7.5 percent, versus Michelin's cost of 7.7 percent,

EXHIBIT 9.5 ● EXAMPLE OF A FIXED-FOR-FLOATING CURRENCY SWAP

Fixed-rate U.S. dollar debt	Floating-rate Euro debt

$200 million — Time 0
Interest at 7.5% — Years 1–10
$200 million — Year 10

€ 220 million — Time 0
Interest at LIBOR + 0.125% — Years 1–10
€ 220 million — Year 10

$200 million — Year 10
Interest at 7.5% — Years 1–10
$200 million — Time 0

Dow Chemical   **Michelin**

€ 220 million — Time 0
Interest at LIBOR + 0.125% — Years 1–10
€ 220 million — Year 10

Cost of Borrowing
Euros
─────────
LIBOR + 0.125%

Cost of Borrowing
U.S. Dollars
─────────
7.5%

the best way for them to achieve their currency and interest rate objectives is to issue debt in their own currencies and then swap the proceeds and future debt-service payments.

Exhibit 9.5 summarizes the cash inflows and outflows for both parties. The net result of the swap is that Dow Chemical can borrow euros indirectly at a floating rate of LIBOR + 0.125 percent, saving 22.5 basis points relative to its cost of borrowing floating-rate euros directly. Michelin's cost of borrowing fixed-rate dollars remains at 7.5 percent, a savings of 20 basis points.

Swaps are arranged by financial intermediaries who charge fees for their services.

The two examples of Dow Chemical and Michelin have them dealing directly with one another. In practice, they would use a financial intermediary, such as a commercial bank or an investment bank, as either a broker or a dealer to arrange the swap. As a broker, the intermediary simply brings the counterparties together for a fee. In contrast, if the intermediary acts as a dealer, it not only arranges the swap, but it also guarantees the swap payments that each party is supposed to receive. Because the dealer guarantees the parties to the swap arrangement against default risk, both parties will be concerned with the dealer's credit rating. Financial intermediaries in the swap market must have high credit ratings because most intermediaries these days act as dealers.

Dual Currency Bonds have the interest payments stated in one currency and the principal repayment in a second currency.

Dual Currency Bond Swaps   Another variant on the currency swap theme is a currency swap involving a **dual currency bond**—one that has the issue's proceeds and interest payments stated in foreign currency and the principal repayment stated in dollars. An example of a dual currency bond swap is the one involving the Federal National Mortgage Association (FNMA or Fannie Mae). On October 1, 1985, FNMA agreed to issue ten-year, 8 percent coupon debentures in the amount of ¥50 billion (with net proceeds of ¥49,687,500,000) and to swap these yen for just over $209 million (an implied swap rate of ¥237.5479/$1). In return, Fannie Mae agreed to pay interest averaging about $21 million annually and to redeem these bonds at the end of ten years at a cost of $240,400,000. Exhibit 9.6 shows the detailed yen and dollar cash flows associated with this currency swap. The net effect of this swap was to give Fannie Mae an all-in dollar cost of 10.67 percent annually. In other words, regardless of what happened to the yen:dollar exchange rate in the future, Fannie Mae's dollar cost on its yen bond issue would remain at 10.67 percent. The 10.67 percent figure is the interest rate that just equates the dollar figures in column 2 to zero.

Let us illustrate the mechanics of this swap. Note that at the end of the first year, FNMA is obligated to pay its bondholders ¥4 billion in interest (an 8 percent coupon payment on a ¥50 billion face value debenture). To satisfy this obligation, FNMA pays $18,811,795 to Nomura, which in turn makes the ¥4 billion interest payment. As column 3 of Exhibit 9.6 shows, FNMA has effectively contracted with Nomura to buy ¥4 billion forward for delivery in one year at a forward rate of ¥212.6325.

Similarly, FNMA satisfies its remaining yen obligations (shown in column 1) by paying a series of dollar amounts (shown in column 2) to Nomura, which in turn makes the required yen payments. The exchange of fixed dollar payments in the future for fixed yen payments in the future is equivalent to a sequence of forward contracts entered into at the forward exchange rates shown in column 3. Since the actual spot rate at the time the swap was entered into (August 29, 1985) was about ¥240/$1, the implicit forward rates on these forward contracts reveal that the yen was selling at a forward premium relative to the dollar; that is, it cost fewer yen to buy a dollar in the forward market than in the spot market. The reason the yen was selling at a forward premium was the same reason that Fannie Mae was borrowing yen: At this time, the interest rate on yen was below the interest rate on dollars.

Since this particular issue was a dual currency bond, with the issue's proceeds and interest payments stated in yen and the principal repayment stated in dollars, the final payment is stated in dollars only. However, it should be noted that by agreeing to

EXHIBIT 9.6 • CASH FLOWS ASSOCIATED WITH YEN DEBENTURE CURRENCY SWAP

Payment Date	Payment on Dual Currency Debenture	Dollar Payment Under Swap	Yen:Dollar Exchange Rate
October 1, 1985	−¥49,687,500,000*	−$209,168,297**	¥237.3777/$1
October 1, 1986	¥4,000,000,000	$18,811,795	¥212.6325/$1
October 1, 1987	¥4,000,000,000	$19,124,383	¥209.1571/$1
October 1, 1988	¥4,000,000,000	$19,464,369	¥205.5037/$1
October 1, 1989	¥4,000,000,000	$19,854,510	¥201.4656/$1
October 1, 1990	¥4,000,000,000	$20,304,260	¥197.0030/$1
October 1, 1991	¥4,000,000,000	$20,942,380	¥191.0003/$1
October 1, 1992	¥4,000,000,000	$21,499,717	¥186.0490/$1
October 1, 1993	¥4,000,000,000	$22,116,875	¥180.8574/$1
October 1, 1994	¥4,000,000,000	$22,723,857	¥176.0265/$1
October 1, 1995	¥4,000,000,000	$23,665,098	¥169.0253/$1
October 1, 1995	$240,400,000	$240,400,000	¥207.9867/$1

*This figure is the ¥50 billion face amount net of issue expenses.
**Net proceeds received after reimbursing underwriters for expenses of $150,000.

a principal repayment of $240,400,000, instead of ¥50 billion, Fannie Mae actually was entering into the equivalent of a long-dated forward contract at an implicit forward rate of ¥207.9867/$1 (¥50 billion/$240,400,000).

Economic Advantages of Swaps

Swaps provide economic benefits to both parties when barriers to arbitrage exist.

Swaps provide a real economic benefit to both parties only if a barrier exists to prevent arbitrage from functioning fully. Such impediments may include legal restrictions on spot and forward foreign exchange transactions, different perceptions by investors of risk and creditworthiness of the two parties, appeal or acceptability of one borrower to a certain class of investor, tax differentials, and so forth.[2]

Swaps also allow firms who are parties to the contracts to lower their cost of foreign exchange risk management by arbitraging their relative access to different currency markets. A borrower whose paper is much in demand in one currency can obtain a cost saving in another currency sector by raising money in the former and swapping the funds into the latter currency. A U.S. corporation, for example, may want to secure fixed-rate funds in euros in order to reduce its euro exposure, but it may be hampered in doing so because it is a relatively unknown credit in the German financial market. In contrast, a German company that is well established in its own country may desire floating-rate dollar financing but is relatively unknown in the U.S. financial market.

In such a case, a bank intermediary familiar with the funding needs and "comparative advantages" in borrowing of both parties may arrange a currency swap. The U.S. company borrows floating-rate dollars, and the German company borrows fixed-rate euros. The two companies then swap both principal and interest payments. When the term of the swap matures, say, in five years, the principal amounts revert to the original holder. Both parties receive a cost savings because they initially borrow in the market where they have a comparative advantage and then swap for their preferred liability. In general currency,

[2] This explanation is provided in Clifford W. Smith, Jr., Charles W. Smithson, and Lee M. Wakeman, "The Evolving Market for Swaps," *Midland Corporate Finance Journal,* Winter 1986, pp. 20–32.

swaps allow the parties to the contract to arbitrage their relative access to different currency markets. A borrower whose paper is much in demand in one currency can obtain a cost saving in another currency sector by raising money in the former and swapping the funds into the latter currency.

Currency swaps are, therefore, often used to provide long-term financing in foreign currencies. This function is important because in many foreign countries long-term capital and forward foreign exchange markets are notably absent or not well developed. Swaps are one vehicle that provides liquidity to these markets.

In effect, swaps allow the transacting parties to engage in some form of tax, regulatory-system, or financial-market arbitrage. If the world capital market were fully integrated, the incentive to swap would be reduced because fewer arbitrage opportunities would exist. However, even in the United States, where financial markets function freely, interest rate swaps are very popular and are credited with cost savings.

9.2 INTEREST RATE FORWARDS AND FUTURES

Companies can also use forward and futures contracts to manage their interest rate risk.

In addition to swaps, companies can use a variety of forward and futures contracts to manage their interest rate expense and risk. These contracts include forward forwards, forward rate agreements, and Eurodollar futures. All of them allow companies to lock in interest rates on future loans and deposits.

Forward Forwards

A **forward forward** is a contract that fixes an interest rate today on a future loan or deposit. The contract specifies the interest rate, the principal amount of the future deposit or loan, and the start and ending dates of the future interest rate period.

 ILLUSTRATION   *Telecom Argentina Fixes a Future Loan Rate*

Suppose that Telecom Argentina needs to borrow $10 million in six months for a three-month period. It could wait six months and borrow the money at the then-current interest rate. Rather than risk a significant rise in interest rates over the next six months, however, Telecom Argentina decides to enter into a forward forward with Daiwa Bank that fixes this rate at 8.4 percent per annum. This contract guarantees that six months from today, Daiwa Bank will lend Telecom Argentina $10 million for a three-month period at a rate of 2.1 percent (8.4 percent/4). In return, nine months from today, Telecom Argentina will repay Daiwa the principal plus interest on the loan, or $10,210,000 ($10 million × 1.021).

The forward forward rate on a loan can be found through arbitrage. For example, suppose that a company wishes to lock in a six-month rate on a $1 million Eurodollar deposit to be placed in three months. It can buy a forward forward or it can create its own. To illustrate this process, suppose that the company can borrow or lend at LIBOR. Then the company can derive a three-month forward rate on LIBOR6 by simultaneously borrowing the present value of $1 million for three months and lending that same amount of money for nine months. If three-month LIBOR (LIBOR3) is 6.7 percent, the company will borrow $1 million/(1 + 0.067/4) = $983,526 today and lend that same amount for nine months. If nine-month LIBOR (LIBOR9) is 6.95 percent, at the end of nine months the company will receive $983,526 × (1 + 0.0695 × 3/4) = $1,034,792. The cash flows on these transactions are

+$983,526   +$1,034,792

	3 months		9 months
−$983,526		−$1,000,000	

Notice that the borrowing and lending transactions are structured so that the only net cash flows are the cash outlay of $1 million in three months and the receipt of $1,034,792 in nine months. These transactions are equivalent to investing $1 million in three months and receiving back $1,034,792 in nine months. The interest receipt of $34,792, or 3.479 percent for six months, is equivalent to a rate of 6.958 percent per annum.

The process of arbitrage will ensure that the actual forward rate for LIBOR6 in three months will almost exactly equal the "homemade" forward forward rate.

Forward Rate Agreement

Forward forwards and forward rate agreements fix interest rates today on future loans or deposits.

In recent years, forward forwards have been largely displaced by the forward rate agreement. A **forward rate agreement** (FRA) is a cash-settled, over-the-counter forward contract that allows a company to fix an interest rate to be applied to a specified future interest period on a notional principal amount. It is analogous to a forward foreign currency contract, but instead of exchanging currencies, the parties to an FRA agree to exchange interest payments. As of year end 2000, the estimated notional amount of FRAs outstanding was $6.4 trillion.[3]

The formula used to calculate the interest payment on a LIBOR-based FRA is

$$\text{Interest payment} = \text{notional principal} \times \frac{(\text{LIBOR} - \text{forward rate})(\text{days}/360)}{1 + \text{LIBOR} \times (\text{days}/360)} \quad (9.1)$$

where *days* refers to the number of days in the future interest period. The discount reflects the fact that the FRA payment occurs at the start of the loan period, whereas the interest expense on a loan is not paid until the loan's maturity. To equate the two, the differential interest expense must be discounted back to its present value using the actual interest rate. The example of Unilever shows how a borrower can use an FRA to lock in the interest rate applicable for a future loan.

 ILLUSTRATION   *Unilever Uses an FRA to Fix the Interest Rate on a Future Loan*

Suppose that Unilever needs to borrow $50 million in two months for a six-month period. To lock in the rate on this loan, Unilever buys a "2 × 6" FRA on LIBOR at 6.5 percent from Bankers Trust for a notional principal of $50 million. This means that Bankers Trust has entered into a two-month forward contract on six-month LIBOR. Two months from now, if LIBOR6 exceeds 6.5 percent, Bankers Trust will pay Unilever the difference in interest expense. If LIBOR6 is less than 6.5 percent, Unilever will pay Bankers Trust the difference.

Assume that in two months LIBOR6 is 7.2 percent. Because this rate exceeds 6.5 percent, and assuming 182 days in the six-month period, Unilever will receive from Bankers Trust a payment determined by Equation 9.1 of

$$\text{Interest payment} = \$50,000,000 \times \frac{(0.072 - 0.065)(182/360)}{1 + 0.072 \times (182/360)} = \$170,730$$

In addition to fixing future borrowing rates, FRAs can also be used to fix future deposit rates. Specifically, by selling an FRA, a company can lock in the interest rate applicable for a future deposit.

---

[3] *BIS Quarterly Review*, September 2001, p. 89.

Eurodollar Futures

Eurodollar futures
lock in future inter-
est rates and are
marked to market
daily.

A **Eurodollar future** is a cash-settled futures contract on a three-month, $1 million Eurodollar deposit that pays LIBOR. These contracts are traded on the Chicago Mercantile Exchange (CME), the London International Financial Futures Exchange (LIFFE), and the Singapore International Monetary Exchange (SIMEX). Eurodollar futures contracts are traded for March, June, September, and December delivery. Contracts are traded out to three years, with a high degree of liquidity out to two years.

Eurodollar futures act like FRAs in that they help lock in a future interest rate and are settled in cash. However, unlike FRAs, they are marked to market daily. (As in currency futures, this means that gains and losses are settled in cash each day.) The price of a Eurodollar futures contract is quoted as an index number equal to 100 minus the annualized forward interest rate. For example, suppose the current futures price is 91.68. This price implies that the contracted-for LIBOR3 rate is 8.32 percent, that is, 100 minus 91.68. The value of this contract at inception is found by use of the following formula:

$$\text{Initial value of Eurodollar futures contract} = \$1,000,000\,[1 - 0.0832(90/360)] = \$979,200$$

The interest rate is divided by four to convert it into a quarterly rate. At maturity, the cash settlement price is determined by subtracting LIBOR3 on that date from 100. Whether the contract gained or lost money depends on whether cash LIBOR3 at settlement is greater or less than 8.32 percent. If LIBOR3 at settlement is 7.54 percent, the Eurodollar future on that date is valued at $981,150:

$$\text{Settlement value of Eurodollar futures contract} =$$
$$\$1,000,000[1 - 0.0754(90/360)] = \$981,150$$

Borrowers will sell
and investors will
buy Eurodollar
futures contracts to
lock in a future
interest rate.

At this price, the buyer has earned $1,950 ($981,150 − $979,200) on the contract. As can be seen from the formula for valuing the futures contract, each basis point change in the forward rate translates into $25 for each contract ($1 million × 0.0001/4), with increases in the forward rate reducing the contract's value and decreases raising its value. For example, if the forward rate rose three basis points, a long position in the contract would lose $75. This arithmetic suggests that borrowers looking to lock in a future cost of funds would sell futures contracts because increases in future interest rates would be offset by gains on the short position in the futures contracts. Conversely, investors seeking to lock in a forward interest rate would buy futures contracts because declines in future rates would be offset by gains on the long position in the futures contracts.

Before the settlement date, the forward interest rate embedded in the futures contract is unlikely to equal the prevailing LIBOR3. For example, on January 6, 1995, the June 1995 Eurodollar futures contract closed at an index price of 92.22, implying a forward rate of 7.78 percent (100 − 92.22). Actual LIBOR3 on January 6 was 6.4375 percent. The discrepancy between the two rates reflects the fact that the 7.78 percent rate represented a three-month implied forward rate as of June 19, 1995, which was 164 days in the future. The forward rate is based on the difference between 164-day LIBOR and LIBOR on a 254-day deposit (which matures on September 17, 1995, 90 days after the 164-day deposit).

The actual LIBOR3 used is determined by the respective exchanges. Both the CME and LIFFE conduct a survey of banks to establish the closing value for LIBOR3. Accordingly, contracts traded on the two exchanges can settle at slightly different values. SIMEX uses the CME's settlement price for its contracts.

Contracts traded on the CME and SIMEX have identical contractual provisions. Those two exchanges have an offset arrangement whereby contracts traded on one exchange can be converted into equivalent contracts on the other exchange. Accordingly, the two contracts are completely fungible. LIFFE does not participate in this arrangement.

ILLUSTRATION *Using a Futures Contract to Hedge a Forward Borrowing Rate*

In late June, a corporate treasurer projects that a shortfall in cash flow will require a $10 million bank loan on September 16. The contractual loan rate will be LIBOR3 + 1 percent. LIBOR3 is currently at 5.63 percent. The treasurer can use the September Eurodollar futures, which are currently trading at 94.18, to lock in the forward borrowing rate. This price implies a forward Eurodollar rate of 5.82 percent (100 − 94.18). By selling ten September Eurodollar futures contract, the corporate treasurer ensures a borrowing rate of 6.82 percent for the three-month period beginning September 16. This rate reflects the bank's 1 percent spread above the rate locked in through the futures contract.

9.3 SUMMARY AND CONCLUSIONS

Multinational corporations can use creative financing to achieve various objectives, such as lowering their cost of funds, cutting taxes, and reducing political risk. This chapter focused on two such techniques—interest rate and currency swaps and interest rate forward and futures contracts.

Interest and currency swaps involve a financial transaction in which two counterparties agree to exchange streams of payments over time. In an interest rate swap, no actual principal is exchanged either initially or at maturity, but interest payment streams are exchanged according to predetermined rules and are based on an underlying notional amount. The two main types are coupon swaps (or fixed rate to floating rate) and basis swaps (from floating rate against one reference rate to floating rate with another reference rate).

Currency swap refers to a transaction in which two counterparties exchange specific amounts of two currencies at the outset and repay over time according to a predetermined rule that reflects both interest payments and amortization of principal. A cross-currency interest rate swap involves swapping fixed-rate flows in one currency to floating-rate flows in another.

Interest forward and futures contracts enable companies to manage their interest rate expense and risk. These contracts include forward forwards, forward rate agreements, and Eurodollar futures. All of them allow companies to lock in interest rates on future loans and deposits. A forward forward is a contract that fixes an interest rate today on a future loan or deposit. The contract specifies the interest rate, the principal amount of the future deposit or loan, and the start and ending dates of the future interest rate period.

A forward rate agreement is a cash-settled, over-the-counter forward contract that allows a company to fix an interest rate to be applied to a specified future interest period on a notional principal amount. Eurodollar futures, which are based on a three-month, $1 million Eurodollar deposit that pays LIBOR, act like FRAs in that they help lock in a future interest rate and are settled in cash. However, unlike FRAs they are marked to market daily. Eurodollar futures contracts are traded on several U.S. and overseas exchanges.

QUESTIONS

1. What is an interest rate swap? What is the difference between a basis swap and a coupon swap?

2. What is a currency swap?

3. Comment on the following statement. "In order for one party to a swap to benefit, the other party must lose."

4. The Swiss Central Bank bans the use of Swiss francs for Eurobond issues. Explain how currency swaps can be used to enable foreign borrowers who want to raise Swiss francs through a bond issue outside of Switzerland to get around this ban.

5. Explain how IBM can use a forward rate agreement to lock in the cost of a one-year $25 million loan to be taken out in six months. Alternatively, explain how IBM can lock in the interest rate on this loan by using Eurodollar futures contracts. What is the major difference between using the FRA and the futures contract to hedge IBM's interest rate risk?

PROBLEMS

1. Dell Computers would like to borrow pounds, and Virgin Airlines wants to borrow dollars. Because Dell is better known in the United States, it can borrow on its own dollars at 7 percent and pounds at 9 percent, whereas Virgin can on its own borrow dollars at 8 percent and pounds at 8.5 percent.

   a. Suppose Dell wants to borrow £10 million for two years, Virgin wants to borrow $16 million for two years, and the current ($/£) exchange rate is $1.60. What swap transaction would accomplish this objective? Assume the counterparties would exchange principal and interest payments with no rate adjustments.

   b. What savings are realized by Dell and Virgin?

   c. Suppose, in fact, that Dell can borrow dollars at 7 percent and pounds at 9 percent, whereas Virgin can borrow dollars at 8.75 percent and pounds at 9.5 percent. What range of interest rates would make this swap attractive to both parties?

   d. Based on the scenario in part (c), suppose Dell borrows dollars at 7 percent and Virgin borrows pounds at 9.5 percent. If the parties swap their currency proceeds, with Dell paying 8.75 percent to Virgin for pounds and Virgin paying 7.75 percent to Dell for dollars, what are the cost savings to each party?

2. In May 1988, Walt Disney Productions sold to Japanese investors a 20-year stream of projected yen royalties from Tokyo Disneyland. The present value of that stream of royalties, discounted at 6 percent (the return required by the Japanese investors), was ¥93 billion. Disney took the yen proceeds from the sale, converted them to dollars, and invested the dollars in bonds yielding 10 percent. According to Disney's chief financial officer, Gary Wilson, "In effect, we got money at a 6 percent discount rate, reinvested it at 10 percent, and hedged our royalty stream against yen fluctuations—all in one transaction."

   a. At the time of the sale, the exchange rate was ¥124 = $1. What dollar amount did Disney realize from the sale of its yen proceeds?

   b. Demonstrate the equivalence between Walt Disney's transaction and a currency swap. (*Hint:* A diagram would help.)

   c. Comment on Gary Wilson's statement. Did Disney achieve the equivalent of a free lunch through its transaction?

3. Suppose that IBM would like to borrow fixed-rate yen, whereas Korea Development Bank (KDB) would like to borrow floating-rate dollars. IBM can borrow fixed-rate yen at 4.5 percent or floating-rate dollars at LIBOR + 0.25 percent. KDB can borrow fixed-rate yen at 4.9 percent or floating-rate dollars at LIBOR + 0.8 percent.

   a. What is the range of possible cost savings that IBM can realize through an interest rate/currency swap with KDB?

   b. Assuming a notional principal equivalent to $125 million and a current exchange rate of ¥105/$, what do these possible cost savings translate into in yen terms?

   c. Redo Parts a and b assuming that the parties use Bank of America, which charges a fee of 8 basis points to arrange the swap.

4. At time *t*, 3M borrows ¥12.8 billion at an interest rate of 1.2 percent, paid semiannually, for a period of two years. It then enters into a two-year yen/dollar swap with Bankers Trust (BT) on a notional principal amount of $100 million (¥12.8 billion at the current spot rate). Every six months, 3M pays BT U.S. dollar LIBOR6, while BT makes payments to 3M of 1.3 percent annually in yen. At maturity, BT and 3M reverse the notional principals. Assume that LIBOR6 (annualized) and the ¥/$ exchange rate evolve as follows.

Time (months)	LIBOR6	¥/$ (spot)	Net $ receipt (+)/ payment (−)
t	5.7%	128	
t + 6	5.4%	132	
t + 12	5.3%	137	
t + 18	5.9%	131	
t + 24	5.8%	123	

   a. Calculate the *net* dollar amount that 3M pays to BT ("−") or receives from BT ("+") in each six-month period.

   b. What is the all-in dollar cost of 3M's loan?

   c. Suppose 3M decides at *t* + 18 to use a six-month forward contract to hedge the *t* + 24 receipt of yen from BT. Six-month interest rates (annualized) at *t* + 18 are 5.9 percent in dollars and 2.1 percent in yen. With this hedge in place, what fixed dollar amount would 3M have paid (received) at time *t* + 24? How does this amount compare to the *t* + 24 net payment computed in Part a?

   d. Does it make sense for 3M to hedge its receipt of yen from BT? Explain.

5. Suppose LIBOR3 is 7.93 percent and LIBOR6 is 8.11 percent. What is the forward forward rate for a LIBOR3 deposit to be placed in three months?

6. Suppose that Skandinaviska Ensilden Banken (SEB), the Swedish bank, funds itself with three-month Eurodollar time deposits at LIBOR. Assume that Alfa Laval comes to SEB seeking a one-year, fixed-rate loan of $10 million, with interest to be paid quarterly. At the time of the loan disbursement, SEB raises three-month

funds at 5.75 percent but has to roll over this funding in three successive quarters. If it does not lock in a funding rate and interest rates rise, the loan could prove to be unprofitable. The three quarterly refunding dates fall shortly before the next three Eurodollar futures-contract expirations in March, June, and September.

a. At the time the loan is made, the price of each contract is 94.12, 93.95, and 93.80. Show how SEB can use Eurodollar futures contracts to lock in its cost of funds for the year. What is SEB's hedged cost of funds for the year?

d. Suppose that the settlement prices of the March, June, and September contracts are, respectively, 92.98, 92.80, and 92.66. What would have been SEB's unhedged cost of funding the loan to Alfa Laval?

BIBLIOGRAPHY

Smith, Clifford W., Jr., Charles W. Smithson, and Lee M. Wakeman. "The Evolving Market for Swaps." *Midland* *Corporate Finance Journal,* Winter 1986, pp. 20–32.

INTERNET RESOURCES

www.bis.org/publ/index.htm Web site of the Bank for International Settlements that lists downloadable publications such as the BIS Annual Report, statistics on derivatives, external debt, foreign exchange market activity, and so on.

www.isda.org Web site of the International Swaps and Derivatives Association (ISDA). Provides information and data on swaps and other derivatives.

INTERNET EXERCISES

1. What were the volumes of interest and currency swaps during the past year? How do these figures compare to those from the previous year?

2. What risk factors associated with swaps does the ISDA discuss on its Web site?

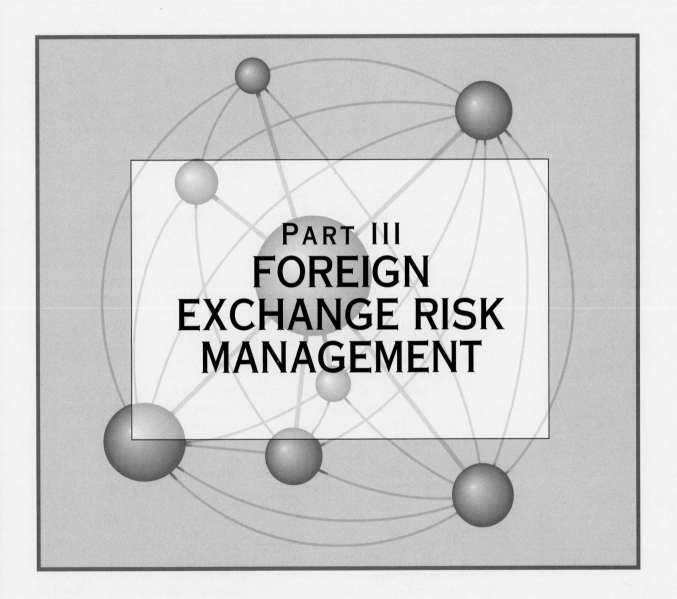

PART III
FOREIGN EXCHANGE RISK MANAGEMENT

MEASURING AND MANAGING TRANSLATION AND TRANSACTION EXPOSURE

The stream of time sweeps away errors, and leaves the truth for the inheritance of humanity.

George Brandes

CHAPTER LEARNING OBJECTIVES

- To define translation and transaction exposure and distinguish between the two
- To describe the four principal currency translation methods available and to calculate translation exposure using these different methods
- To describe and apply the current (FASB-52) currency translation method prescribed by the Financial Accounting Standards Board
- To identify the basic hedging strategy and techniques used by firms to manage their currency transaction and translation risks
- To explain how a forward market hedge works
- To explain how a money-market hedge works
- To describe how foreign currency contract prices should be set to factor in exchange rate change expectations
- To describe how currency risk-sharing arrangements work
- To explain when foreign currency options are the preferred hedging technique
- To describe the costs associated with using the different hedging techniques
- To describe and assess the economic soundness of the various corporate hedging objectives
- To explain the advantages and disadvantages of centralizing foreign exchange risk management

KEY TERMS

accounting exposure
balance-sheet exposure
cross-hedge
currency call option
currency collar
currency options
currency put option
currency risk sharing
current exchange rate
current/noncurrent method
current rate method
cylinder

economic exposure
exposure netting
Financial Accounting Standards Board
foreign exchange risk
forward market hedge
functional currency
funds adjustment
hard currency
hedging
historical exchange rate
hyperinflationary country
monetary/nonmonetary method

money-market hedge
neutral zone
operating exposure
opportunity cost
price adjustment clause
range forward
reporting currency

risk shifting
soft currency
*Statement of Financial Accounting Standards
    No. 52*
temporal method
transaction exposure
translation exposure

The pressure to monitor and manage foreign currency risks has led many companies to develop sophisticated computer-based systems to keep track of their foreign exchange exposure and aid in managing that exposure. The general concept of *exposure* refers to the degree to which a company is affected by exchange rate changes. This impact can be measured in several ways. As so often happens, economists tend to favor one approach to measuring foreign exchange exposure, while accountants favor an alternative approach. This chapter deals with the measurement and management of accounting exposure, including both translation and transaction exposure. Management of accounting exposure centers around the concept of hedging. **Hedging** a particular currency exposure means establishing an offsetting currency position so that whatever is lost or gained on the original currency exposure is exactly offset by a corresponding foreign exchange gain or loss on the currency hedge. Regardless of what happens to the future exchange rate, therefore, hedging locks in a dollar (home currency) value for the currency exposure. In this way, hedging can protect a firm from unforeseen currency movements.

10.1 ALTERNATIVE MEASURES OF FOREIGN EXCHANGE EXPOSURE

The three basic types of exposure are accounting exposure, transaction exposure, and operating exposure.

The three basic types of exposure are translation exposure, transaction exposure, and operating exposure. Transaction exposure and operating exposure combine to form economic exposure. Exhibit 10.1 illustrates and contrasts translation, transaction, and operating exposure. As can be seen, these exposures cannot always be neatly separated but instead overlap to some extent.

Translation Exposure

Translation exposure arises from the need to convert foreign currency accounts, revenues, and expenses into the home currency.

Translation exposure, also known as **accounting exposure**, arises from the need, for purposes of reporting and consolidation, to convert the financial statements of foreign operations from the local currencies (LC) involved to the home currency (HC). If exchange rates have changed since the previous reporting period, this *translation*, or restatement, of those assets, liabilities, revenues, expenses, gains, and losses that are denominated in foreign currencies will result in foreign exchange gains or losses. The possible extent of these gains or losses is measured by the translation exposure figures. The rules that govern translation are devised by an accounting association such as the **Financial Accounting Standards Board** in the United States, the parent firm's government, or the firm itself. This chapter focuses on **Statement of Financial Accounting Standards No. 52**—the present currency translation method prescribed by the Financial Accounting Standards Board (FASB).

Transaction Exposure

Transaction exposure results from transactions that give rise to known, contractually binding future foreign-currency–denominated cash inflows or outflows. As exchange rates change between now and when these transactions settle, so does the value of their

EXHIBIT 10.1 • COMPARISON OF TRANSLATION, TRANSACTION, AND OPERATING EXPOSURE

Translation Exposure	*Operating Exposure*
Changes in income statement items and the book value of balance sheet assets and liabilities that are caused by an exchange rate change. The resulting exchange gains and losses are determined by accounting rules and are paper only. The measurement of accounting exposure is retrospective in nature as it is based on activities that occurred in the past.	Changes in the amount of future operating cash flows caused by an exchange rate change. The resulting exchange gains or losses are determined by changes in the firm's future competitive position and are real. The measurement of operating exposure is prospective in nature as it is based on future activities.
Impacts: Balance sheet assets and liabilities and income statement items that already exist.	*Impacts:* Revenues and costs associated with future sales.

Exchange rate
change occurs

Impacts: Contracts already entered into, but . . . to be settled at a later date.

Transaction Exposure

Changes in the value of outstanding foreign-currency–denominated contracts (i.e., contracts that give rise to future foreign currency cash flows) that are brought about by an exchange rate change. The resulting exchange gains and losses are determined by the nature of the contracts already entered into and are real. The measurement of transaction exposure mixes the retrospective and prospective because it is based on activities that occurred in the past but will be settled in the future. Contracts already on the balance sheet are part of accounting exposure, whereas contracts not yet on the balance sheet are part of operating exposure.

Transaction and operating exposure are cash flow exposures.

associated foreign currency cash flows, leading to currency gains and losses. Examples of transaction exposure for a U.S. company would be the account receivable associated with a sale denominated in euros or the obligation to repay a Japanese yen debt. Although transaction exposure is rightly part of economic exposure, it is usually lumped under accounting exposure. In reality, transaction exposure overlaps with both accounting and operating exposure. Some elements of transaction exposure, such as foreign-currency-denominated accounts receivable and debts, are included in a firm's accounting exposure because they already appear on the firm's balance sheet. Other elements of transaction exposure, such as foreign currency sales contracts that have been entered into but where the goods have not yet been delivered (and so receivables have not yet been created), do not appear on the firm's current financial statements and instead are part of the firm's operating exposure.

Operating Exposure

Operating exposure measures the extent to which currency fluctuations can alter a company's future operating cash flows; that is, its future revenues and costs. Any company whose revenues or costs are affected by currency changes has operating exposure, even if it is a purely domestic corporation and has all its cash flows denominated in home currency.

The two cash-flow exposures—operating exposure and transaction exposure—combine to equal a company's economic exposure. In technical terms, **economic exposure** is the extent to which the value of the firm—as measured by the present value of its expected cash flows—will change when exchange rates change.

10.2 ALTERNATIVE CURRENCY TRANSLATION METHODS

Companies with international operations will have foreign-currency-denominated assets and liabilities, revenues, and expenses. However, because home-country investors and the entire financial community are interested in home currency values, the foreign currency balance sheet accounts and income statement must be assigned HC values. In particular, the financial statements of an MNC's overseas subsidiaries must be translated from local currency to home currency before consolidation with the parent's financial statements.

If currency values change, foreign exchange translation gains or losses may result. Assets and liabilities that are translated at the current (postchange) exchange rate are considered to be exposed; those translated at a historical (prechange) exchange rate will maintain their historic HC values and, hence, are regarded as not exposed. Translation exposure is simply the difference between exposed assets and exposed liabilities. The controversies among accountants center on which assets and liabilities are exposed and on when accounting-derived foreign exchange gains and losses should be recognized (reported on the income statement). A crucial point to realize in putting these controversies in perspective is that such gains or losses are of an accounting nature—that is, no cash flows are necessarily involved.

Four principal translation methods are available: the current/noncurrent method, the monetary/nonmonetary method, the temporal method, and the current rate method. In practice, there are also variations of each method.

The four principal translation methods are the current/noncurrent, monetary/nonmonetary, temporal, and current rate methods.

Current/Noncurrent Method

At one time, the **current/noncurrent method,** whose underlying theoretical basis is maturity, was used by almost all U.S. multinationals. With this method, all the foreign subsidiary's current assets and liabilities are translated into home currency at the **current exchange rate.** Each noncurrent asset or liability is translated at its **historical exchange rate**—that is, at the rate in effect at the time the asset was acquired or the liability was incurred. Hence, a foreign subsidiary with positive local currency working capital will give rise to a translation loss (gain) from a devaluation (revaluation) with the current/noncurrent method, and vice versa if working capital is negative.

The income statement is translated at the average exchange rate of the period, except for those revenues and expense items associated with noncurrent assets or liabilities. The latter items, such as depreciation expense, are translated at the same rates as the corresponding balance sheet items. Thus, it is possible to see different revenue and expense items with similar maturities being translated at different rates.

Monetary/Nonmonetary Method

The **monetary/nonmonetary method** differentiates between *monetary* assets and liabilities—that is, those items that represent a claim to receive, or an obligation to pay, a fixed amount of foreign currency units—and *nonmonetary,* or physical, assets and liabilities. Monetary items (for example, cash, accounts payable and receivable, and long-term debt) are translated at the current rate; nonmonetary items (for example, inventory, fixed assets, and long-term investments) are translated at historical rates.

Income statement items are translated at the average exchange rate during the period, except for revenue and expense items related to nonmonetary assets and liabilities. The latter items, primarily depreciation expense and cost of goods sold, are translated at the same rate as the corresponding balance sheet items. As a result, the cost of goods sold may be translated at a rate different from that used to translate sales.

Temporal Method

The **temporal method** appears to be a modified version of the monetary/nonmonetary method. The only difference is that under the monetary/nonmonetary method, inventory is always translated at the historical rate. Under the temporal method, inventory is normally translated at the historical rate, but it can be translated at the current rate if the inventory is shown on the balance sheet at market values. Despite the similarities, the theoretical bases of the two methods are different. The choice of exchange rate for translation is based on the type of asset or liability in the monetary/nonmonetary method; in the temporal method, it is based on the underlying approach to evaluating cost (historical versus market). Under a historical cost accounting system, as the United States now has, most accounting theoreticians probably would argue that the temporal method is the appropriate method for translation.

Income statement items normally are translated at an average rate for the reporting period. However, cost of goods sold and depreciation and amortization charges related to balance sheet items carried at past prices are translated at historical rates.

Current Rate Method

The **current rate method** is the simplest: All balance sheet and income items are translated at the current rate. This method is widely employed by British companies. Under this method, if a firm's foreign-currency-denominated assets exceed its foreign-currency–denominated liabilities, a devaluation must result in a loss and a revaluation must result in a gain. One variation is to translate all assets and liabilities except net fixed assets at the current rate.

> The current rate method requires all foreign currency balance sheet and income items to be translated at the current exchange rate.

Exhibit 10.2 applies the four methods to a hypothetical balance sheet that is affected by both a 25 percent devaluation and a 37.5 percent revaluation. Depending on the method chosen, the translation results for the LC devaluation can range from a loss of $205,000 to a gain of $215,000; LC revaluation results can vary from a gain of $615,000 to a loss of $645,000. The assets and liabilities that are considered exposed under each method are the ones that change in dollar value. Note that the translation gains or losses for each method show up as the change in the equity account. For example, the LC devaluation combined with the current rate method results in a $205,000 reduction in the equity account ($1,025,000 – $820,000), which equals the translation loss for this method. Another way to calculate this loss is to take the net LC translation exposure, which equals exposed assets minus exposed liabilities (for the current rate method this figure is LC 4,100,000, which, not coincidentally, equals its equity value) and multiply it by the $0.05 ($0.25 – $0.20) change in the exchange rate. This calculation yields a translation loss of $205,000 ($0.05 × 4,100,000), the same as calculated in Exhibit 10.2.

EXHIBIT 10.2 FINANCIAL STATEMENT IMPACT OF TRANSLATION ALTERNATIVES (U.S. $ THOUSANDS)

	Local Currency	U.S. Dollars Prior to Exchange Rate Change (LC 4 = $1)	After Devaluation of Local Currency (LC 5 = $1)				After Revaluation of Local Currency			
			Monetary/ Non-monetary	Temporal	Current/ Non-current	Current Rates for All Assets and Liabilities	Monetary/ Non-monetary	Temporal	Current/ Non-current	Current Rates for All Assets and Liabilities
Assets										
Current assets										
Cash, marketable securities, and receivables	LC 2,600	$ 650	$ 520	$ 520	$ 520	$ 520	$ 1,040	$ 1,040	$ 1,040	$ 1,040
Inventory (at market)	3,600	900	900	720	720	720	900	1,440	1,440	1,440
Prepaid expenses	200	50	50	50	40	40	50	50	80	80
Total current assets	6,400	1,600	1,470	1,290	1,280	1,280	1,990	2,530	2,560	2,560
Fixed assets less accumulated depreciation	3,600	900	900	900	900	720	900	900	900	1,440
Goodwill	1,000	250	250	250	250	200	250	250	250	400
Total assets	LC 11,000	$ 2,750	$ 2,620	$ 2,440	$ 2,430	$ 2,200	$ 3,140	$ 3,680	$ 3,710	$ 4,400
Liabilities										
Current liabilities	3,400	850	680	680	680	680	1,360	1,360	1,360	1,360
Long-term debt	3,000	750	600	600	750	600	1,200	1,200	750	1,200
Deferred income taxes	500	125	100	100	125	100	200	200	125	200
Total liabilities	6,900	1,725	1,380	1,380	1,555	1,380	2,760	2,760	2,235	2,760
Capital stock	1,500	375	375	375	375	375	375	375	375	375
Retained earnings	2,600	650	865	685	500	445	5	545	1,100	1,265
Total equity	4,100	1,025	1,240	1,060	875	820	380	920	1,475	1,640
Total liabilities plus equity	LC 11,000	$ 2,750	$ 2,620	$ 2,440	$ 2,430	$ 2,200	$ 3,140	$ 3,680	$ 3,710	$ 4,400
Translation gain (loss)	—	—	$ 215	$ 35	$ (150)	$ (205)	$ (645)	$ (105)	$ 450	$ 615

Another way to calculate this loss is to multiply the net dollar translation exposure by the fractional change in the exchange rate, or $1,025,000 × 0.05/0.25 = $205,000. Either approach gives the correct answer.

10.3 STATEMENT OF FINANCIAL ACCOUNTING STANDARDS No. 52

FASB-52, the current translation standard, mandates use of the current rate method.

The current translation standard—*Statement of Financial Accounting Standards No. 52* (FASB-52)—was adopted in 1981.[1] According to FASB-52, firms must use the current rate method to translate foreign-currency–denominated assets and liabilities into dollars. All foreign currency revenue and expense items on the income statement must be translated at either the exchange rate in effect on the date these items are recognized or at an appropriately weighted average exchange rate for the period. The most important aspect of this standard is that most FASB-52 translation gains and losses bypass the income statement and are accumulated in a separate equity account on the parent's balance sheet. This account is usually called something like "cumulative translation adjustment."

FASB-52 distinguishes between the functional currency and the reporting currency.

FASB-52 differentiates between the functional currency and the reporting currency. An affiliate's **functional currency** is the currency of the primary economic environment in which the affiliate generates and expends cash. If the enterprise's operations are relatively self-contained and integrated within a particular country, the functional currency will generally be the currency of that country. An example of this case would be an English affiliate that both manufactures and sells most of its output in England. Alternatively, if the foreign affiliate's operations are a direct and integral component or extension of the parent company's operations, the functional currency will be the U.S. dollar. An example of this would be a Hong Kong assembly plant for radios that sources the components in the United States and sells the assembled radios in the United States. It is also possible that the functional currency is neither the local currency nor the dollar but, rather, a third currency. However, in the remainder of this chapter, we will assume that if the functional currency is not the local currency, then it is the U.S. dollar.

The functional currency is the currency of the primary economic environment in which the affiliate generates and expends cash.

Guidelines for selecting the appropriate functional currency are presented in Exhibit 10.3. There is sufficient ambiguity to give companies some leeway in selecting the functional currency. However, in the case of a **hyperinflationary country**—defined as one that has cumulative inflation of approximately 100 percent or more over a three-year period—the functional currency must be the dollar.

Companies will usually explain in the notes to their annual report how they accounted for foreign currency translation. A typical statement is that found in Dow Chemical's 1999 Annual Report:

> *The local currency has been primarily used as the functional currency throughout the world. Translation gains and losses of those operations that use local currency as the functional currency, and the effects of exchange rate changes on transactions designated as hedges of net foreign investments, are included in "Accumulated other*

[1] The previous translation standard, *Statement of Financial Accounting Standards No. 8* (or FASB-8), was based on the temporal method. Its principal virtue was its consistency with generally accepted accounting practice that requires balance sheet items to be valued (translated) according to their underlying measurement basis (that is, current or historical). Almost immediately upon its adoption, however, controversy ensued over FASB-8. A major source of corporate dissatisfaction with FASB-8 was the ruling that all reserves for currency losses be disallowed. Before FASB-8, many companies established a reserve and were able to defer unrealized translation gains and losses by adding them to, or charging them against, the reserve. In that way, corporations generally were able to cushion the impact of sharp changes in currency values on reported earnings. With FASB-8, however, fluctuating values of pesos, pounds, yen, Canadian dollars, and other foreign currencies often had far more impact on profit-and-loss statements than did the sales and profit margins of multinational manufacturers' product lines.

EXHIBIT 10.3 • FACTORS INDICATING THE APPROPRIATE FUNCTIONAL CURRENCY

Foreign Unit's	Local Currency Indicators	Dollar Indicator
Cash flows	Primarily in the local currency; do not directly affect parent company cash flows	Direct impact on parent company; cash flow available for remittance
Sales prices	Not responsive to exchange rate changes in the short run; determined more by local conditions	Determined more by worldwide competition; affected in the short run by exchange rate changes
Sales market	Active local market for entity's products	Products sold primarily in the United States; sales contracts denominated in dollars
Expenses	Labor, materials, and other costs denominated primarily in local currency	Inputs primarily from sources in the United States or otherwise denominated in dollars
Financing	Primarily in local currency; operations generate sufficient funds to service these debts	Primarily from the parent company or otherwise denominated in dollars; operations don't generate sufficient dollars to service its dollar debts
Intercompany transactions	Few intracorporate transactions; little connection between local and parent operations	High volume of intracorporate transactions; extensive interrelationship between local and parent operations

comprehensive income." Where the U.S. dollar is used as the functional currency, foreign currency gains and losses are reflected in income.

The **reporting currency** is the currency in which the parent firm prepares its own financial statements—that is, U.S. dollars for a U.S. firm. FASB-52 requires that the financial statements of a foreign unit first be stated in the functional currency, using generally accepted accounting principles of the United States. At each balance sheet date, any assets and liabilities denominated in a currency other than the functional currency of the recording entity must be adjusted to reflect the current exchange rate on that date. Transaction gains and losses that result from adjusting assets and liabilities denominated in a currency other than the functional currency, or from settling such items, generally must appear on the foreign unit's income statement. The only exceptions to the general requirement to include transaction gains and losses in income as they arise are listed as follows:

> The reporting currency is the currency in which the parent company prepares its own financial statements.

1. Gains and losses attributable to a foreign currency transaction that is designated as an economic hedge of a net investment in a foreign entity must be included in the separate component of shareholders' equity in which adjustments arising from translating foreign currency financial statements are accumulated. An example of such a transaction would be a euro borrowing by a U.S. parent. The transaction would be designated as a hedge of the parent's net investment in its German subsidiary.

> Under FASB-52, transaction gains or losses are generally included in the income statement, whereas translation gains or losses are not.

2. Gains and losses attributable to intercompany foreign currency transactions that are of a long-term investment nature must be included in the separate

component of shareholders' equity. The parties to the transaction in this case are accounted for by the equity method in the reporting entity's financial statements.

3. Gains and losses attributable to foreign currency transactions that hedge identifiable foreign currency commitments are to be deferred and included in the measurement of the basis of the related foreign transactions.

The requirements regarding translation of transactions apply both to transactions entered into by a U.S. company and denominated in a currency other than the U.S. dollar and to transactions entered into by a foreign affiliate of a U.S. company and denominated in a currency other than its functional currency. Thus, for example, if a German subsidiary of a U.S. company owed $180,000 and the euro declined from $1.20 to $1.00, the euro amount of the liability would increase from €150,000 (180,000/1.20) to €180,000 (180,000/1.00), for a loss of €30,000. If the subsidiary's functional currency is the euro, the €30,000 loss must be translated into dollars at the average exchange rate for the period (say, $1.10), and the resulting amount ($33,000) must be included as a transaction loss in the U.S. company's consolidated statement of income. This loss results even though the liability is denominated in the parent company's reporting currency because the subsidiary's functional currency is the euro, and its financial statements must be measured in terms of that currency. Similarly, under FASB-52, if the subsidiary's functional currency is the U.S. dollar, no gain or loss will arise on the $180,000 liability.

After all financial statements have been converted into the functional currency, the functional currency statements are then translated into dollars, with translation gains and losses flowing directly into the parent's foreign exchange equity account.

If the functional currency is the dollar, the unit's local currency financial statements must be remeasured in dollars. The objective of the remeasurement process is to produce the same results that would have been reported if the accounting records had been kept in dollars rather than the local currency. Translation of the local currency accounts into dollars takes place according to the temporal method; thus, the resulting translation gains and losses *must* be included in the income statement.

A large majority of firms have opted for the local currency as the functional currency for most of their subsidiaries. The major exceptions are those subsidiaries operating in highly inflationary countries; they must use the dollar as their functional currency.

Most firms select the local currency as the functional currency.

Application of FASB No. 52

Sterling Ltd., the British subsidiary of a U.S. company, started business and acquired fixed assets at the beginning of a year when the exchange rate for the pound sterling was £1 = $1.50. The average exchange rate for the period was $1.40, the rate at the end of the period was $1.30, and the historical rate for inventory was $1.45. Refer to Exhibits 10.4 and 10.5 for the discussion that follows.

During the year, Sterling Ltd. has income after tax of £20 million, which goes into retained earnings—that is, no dividends are paid. Thus, retained earnings rise from 0 to £20 million. Exhibit 10.4 shows how the income statement would be translated into dollars under two alternatives: (1) The functional currency is the pound sterling, and (2) the functional currency is the U.S. dollar.

If the functional currency is the pound sterling, Sterling Ltd. will have a translation loss of $22 million, which bypasses the income statement (because the functional currency is identical to the local currency) and appears on the balance sheet as a separate

EXHIBIT 10.4 ● TRANSLATION OF STERLING LTD.'S INCOME STATEMENT UNDER FASB-52 (MILLIONS)

| | | Functional Currency | | | |
| | | Pound Sterling | | U.S. Dollar | |
	Pound Sterling	Rates Used	U.S. Dollars	Rates Used	U.S. Dollars
Revenue	£120	$1.40	$168	$1.40	$168
Cost of goods sold	(50)	1.40	(70)	1.45	(73)
Depreciation	(20)	1.40	(28)	1.50	(30)
Other expenses, net	(10)	1.40	(14)	1.40	(14)
Foreign exchange gain					108
Income before taxes	40		56		159
Income taxes	(20)	1.40	(28)		(28)
Net income	£ 20		$ 28		$131
Ratios					
Net income to revenue	0.17		0.17		0.78
Gross profit to revenue	0.58		0.58		0.57
Debt to equity	7.33		7.33		4.07

EXHIBIT 10.5 ● TRANSLATION OF STERLING LTD.'S BALANCE SHEET UNDER FASB-52 (MILLIONS)

| | | Functional Currency | | | |
| | | Pound Sterling | | U.S. Dollar | |
	Pound Sterling	Rates Used	U.S. Dollars	Rates Used	U.S. Dollars
Assets					
Cash	£ 100	$1.30	$ 130	$1.30	$ 130
Receivables	200	1.30	260	1.30	260
Inventory	300	1.30	390	1.45	435
Fixed assets, net	400	1.30	520	1.50	600
Total assets	£1,000		$1,300		$1,425
Liabilities					
Current liabilities	180	1.30	234	1.30	234
Long-term debt	700	1.30	910	1.30	910
Stockholders' equity					
Common stock	100	1.50	150	1.50	150
Retained earnings	20		28		131
Cumulative translation adjustment			(22)		
Total liabilities plus equity	£1,000		$1,300		$1,425

item called *cumulative translation adjustment* under the stockholders' equity account. The translation loss is calculated as the number that reconciles the equity account with the remaining translated accounts to balance assets with liabilities and equity. Exhibit 10.5 shows the balance sheet translations for Sterling Ltd. under the two alternative functional currencies.

Similarly, if the dollar is the functional currency, the foreign exchange translation gain of $108 million, which appears on Sterling Ltd.'s income statement (because the functional currency differs from the local currency), is calculated as the difference between translated income before currency gains ($23 million) and the retained earnings figure ($131 million). This amount just balances Sterling Ltd.'s books.

Two comments are appropriate here.

1. Fluctuations in reported earnings in the preceding example are reduced significantly under FASB-52 when the local currency is the functional currency, as compared with the case when the U.S. dollar is the functional currency.

2. Key financial ratios and relationships—such as net income-to-revenue, gross profit, and debt-to-equity—are the same when translated into dollars under FASB-52, using the local currency as the functional currency, as they are in the local currency financial statements. These ratios and relationships are significantly different if the dollar is used as the functional currency. The ratios appear at the bottom of Exhibit 10.4.

10.4 TRANSACTION EXPOSURE

Companies often include transaction exposure as part of their accounting exposure, although as a cash-flow exposure it is rightly part of a company's economic exposure. As we have seen, *transaction exposure* stems from the possibility of incurring future exchange gains or losses on transactions already entered into and denominated in a foreign currency. For example, when IBM sells a mainframe computer to Royal Dutch Shell in England, it typically will not be paid until a later date. If that sale is priced in pounds, IBM has a pound transaction exposure.

A company's transaction exposure is measured currency by currency and equals the difference between contractually fixed future cash inflows and outflows in each currency. Some of these unsettled transactions, including foreign-currency-denominated debt and accounts receivable, are already listed on the firm's balance sheet. However, other obligations, such as contracts for future sales or purchases, are not.

 ILLUSTRATION *Computing Transaction Exposure*

Suppose Boeing Airlines sells five 747s to Garuda, the Indonesian airline, in rupiahs. The rupiah price is Rp 140 billion. To help reduce the impact on Indonesia's balance of payments, Boeing agrees to buy parts from various Indonesian companies worth Rp 55 billion.

    a. If the spot rate is $0.004/Rp, what is Boeing's net rupiah transaction exposure?

Solution. Boeing's net rupiah exposure equals its projected rupiah inflows minus its projected rupiah outflows, or Rp 140 billion − Rp 55 billion = Rp 85 billion. Converted into dollars at the spot rate of $0.004/Rp, Boeing's transaction exposure equals $340 million.

b. If the rupiah depreciates to $0.0035/Rp, what is Boeing's transaction loss?

Solution. Boeing will lose an amount equal to its rupiah exposure multiplied by the change in the exchange rate, or 85 billion (0.004 – 0.0035) = $42.5 million. This loss can also be determined by multiplying Boeing's exposure in dollar terms, by the fractional change in the exchange rate, or 340 million (0.0005/0.004) = $42.5 million.

Although translation and transaction exposures overlap, they are not synonymous. Some items included in translation exposure, such as inventories and fixed assets, are excluded from transaction exposure, whereas other items included in transaction exposure, such as contracts for future sales or purchases, are not included in translation exposure. Thus, it is possible for transaction exposure in a currency to be positive and translation exposure in that same currency to be negative and vice versa. For example, Sterling Ltd. has translation exposure of £120,000 (£1 million – £880,000). At the same time, ignoring off-balance sheet items, it has transaction exposure of –£580,000 (by eliminating £700,000 in inventory and fixed assets from our calculations).

10.5 DESIGNING A HEDGING STRATEGY

Successful hedging requires an operational set of goals.

We now come to the problem of managing exposure by means of hedging. As mentioned earlier, hedging a particular currency exposure means establishing an offsetting currency position so as to lock in a dollar (home currency) value for the currency exposure and thereby eliminate the risk posed by currency fluctuations. A variety of hedging techniques are available for managing exposure, but before a firm uses them it must decide on which exposures to manage and how to manage them. Addressing these issues successfully requires an operational set of goals for those involved in exchange risk management. Failure to set out objectives can lead to possibly conflicting and costly actions on the part of employees. Although many firms do have objectives, their goals are often so vague and simplistic (for example, "eliminate all exposure" or "minimize reported foreign exchange losses") that they provide little realistic guidance to managers.[2] For example, should an employee told to eliminate all exposure do so by using forward contracts and currency options, or by borrowing in the local currency? And if hedging is not possible in a particular currency, should sales in that currency be forgone even if it means losing potential profits? The latter policy is likely to present a manager with the dilemma of choosing between the goals of increased profits and reduced exchange losses. Moreover, reducing translation exposure could increase transaction exposure and vice versa. What trade-offs, if any, should a manager be willing to make between these two types of exposure?

These and similar questions demonstrate the need for a coherent and effective strategy. The following elements are suggested for an effective exposure management strategy:[3]

1. Determine the types of exposure to be monitored.
2. Formulate corporate objectives and give guidance in resolving potential conflicts in objectives.
3. Ensure that these corporate objectives are consistent with maximizing shareholder value and can be implemented.
4. Clearly specify who is responsible for which exposures, and detail the criteria by which each manager is to be judged.

---

[2] Dow Chemical stated in its 1999 Annual Report that the primary objective of its hedging activity is "to optimize the U.S. dollar value of the Company's assets, liabilities and future cash flows with respect to exchange rate fluctuations." While a laudable objective, it is difficult to determine what specific actions a manager should take to accomplish it.

[3] Most of these elements are suggested in Thomas G. Evans and William R. Folks, Jr., "Defining Objectives for Exposure Management," *Business International Money Report*, February 2, 1979, pp. 37–39.

5. Make explicit any constraints on the use of exposure-management techniques, such as limitations on entering into forward contracts.

6. Identify the channels by which exchange rate considerations are incorporated into operating decisions that will affect the firm's exchange risk posture.

7. Develop a system for monitoring and evaluating exchange risk management activities.

Objectives

The usefulness of a hedging strategy depends on its quality and acceptability.

The usefulness of a particular hedging strategy depends on both *acceptability* and *quality.* Acceptability refers to approval by those in the organization who will implement the strategy, and quality refers to the ability to provide better decisions. To be acceptable, a hedging strategy must be consistent with top management's values and overall corporate objectives. In turn, these values and objectives are strongly motivated by management's beliefs about financial markets and how its performance will be evaluated. The quality, or value to the shareholders, of a particular hedging strategy is, therefore, related to the congruence between those perceptions and the realities of the business environment.

The most frequently occurring objectives, explicit and implicit, in management behavior include the following:[4]

Corporate hedging objectives should reflect management's beliefs about how financial markets work.

1. *Minimize translation exposure.* This common goal necessitates a complete focus on protecting foreign-currency-denominated assets and liabilities from changes in value due to exchange rate fluctuations. Given that translation and transaction exposures are not synonymous, reducing the former could cause an increase in the latter (and vice versa).

2. *Minimize quarter-to-quarter (or year-to-year) earnings fluctuations owing to exchange rate changes.* This goal requires a firm to consider both its translation exposure and its transaction exposure.

3. *Minimize transaction exposure.* This objective involves managing a subset of the firm's true cash-flow exposure.

4. *Minimize economic exposure.* To achieve this goal, a firm must ignore accounting earnings and concentrate on reducing cash-flow fluctuations stemming from currency fluctuations.

5. *Minimize foreign exchange risk management costs.* This goal requires a firm to balance off the benefits of hedging with its costs. It also assumes risk neutrality.

6. *Avoid surprises.* This objective involves preventing large foreign exchange losses.

The most appropriate way to rank these objectives is on their consistency with the overarching goal of maximizing shareholder value. To establish what hedging can do to further this goal, we return to our discussion of total risk in Chapter 1. In that discussion, we saw that total risk tends to adversely affect a firm's value by leading to lower sales and higher costs. Consequently, actions taken by a firm that decrease its total risk will improve its sales and cost outlooks, thereby increasing its expected cash flows.

Reducing total risk can also ensure that a firm will not run out of cash to fund its planned investment program. Otherwise, potentially profitable investment opportunities may be passed up because of corporate reluctance to tap the financial markets when internally generated cash is insufficient.[5]

---

[4] See, for example, David B. Zenoff, "Applying Management Principles to Foreign Exchange Exposure," *Euromoney,* September 1978, pp. 123–130.

[5] This explanation appears in Kenneth Froot, David Scharfstein, and Jeremy Stein, "A Framework for Risk Management," *Harvard Business Review,* November 1994, pp. 91–102. The reluctance to raise additional external capital may stem from the problem of *information asymmetry*—this problem arises when one party to a transaction knows something relevant to the transaction that the other party does not know—which could lead investors to impose higher costs on the company seeking capital.

This and other explanations for hedging all relate to the idea that there is likely to be an inverse relation between total risk and shareholder value.[6] Given these considerations, the view taken here is that the basic purpose of hedging is to reduce exchange risk, where exchange risk is defined as that element of cash-flow variability attributable to currency fluctuations. This is Objective 4.

To the extent that earnings fluctuations or large losses can adversely affect the company's perceptions in the minds of potential investors, customers, employees, and so on, there may be reason to also pay attention to Objectives 2 and 6.[7] However, despite these potential benefits, there are likely to be few, if any, advantages to devoting substantial resources to managing earnings fluctuations or accounting exposure more generally (Objectives 1 and 3). To begin, trying to manage accounting exposure is inconsistent with a large body of empirical evidence that investors have the uncanny ability to peer beyond the ephemeral and concentrate on the firm's true cash-flow-generating ability. In addition, whereas balance sheet gains and losses can be dampened by hedging, operating earnings will also fluctuate in line with the combined and offsetting effects of currency changes and inflation. Moreover, hedging costs themselves will vary unpredictably from one period to the next, leading to unpredictable earnings changes. Thus, it is impossible for firms to protect themselves from earnings fluctuations due to exchange rate changes except in the very short run.

Given the questionable benefits of managing accounting exposure, the emphasis in this text is on managing economic exposure. However, this chapter describes the techniques used to manage transaction and translation exposure because many of these techniques are equally applicable to hedging cash flows.

In operational terms, hedging to reduce the variance of cash flows translates into the following exposure management goal: *to arrange a firm's financial affairs in such a way that however the exchange rate may move in the future, the effects on dollar returns are minimized.* This objective is not universally subscribed to, however. Instead, many firms follow a selective hedging policy designed to protect against anticipated currency movements. A selective hedging policy is especially prevalent among those firms that organize their treasury departments as profit centers. In such firms, the desire to reduce the expected costs of hedging (Objective 5)—and thereby increase profits—often leads to taking higher risks by hedging only when a currency change is expected and going unhedged otherwise.

If financial markets are efficient, however, firms cannot hedge against *expected* exchange rate changes. Interest rates, forward rates, and sales-contract prices should already reflect currency changes that are anticipated, thereby offsetting the loss-reducing benefits of hedging with higher costs. In the case of Mexico, for instance, the one-year forward discount in the futures market was close to 100 percent just before the peso was floated in 1982. The unavoidable conclusion is that a firm can protect itself only against *unexpected* currency changes.

Moreover, there is always the possibility of bad timing. For example, big Japanese exporters such as Toyota and Honda have incurred billions of dollars in foreign exchange losses. One reason for these losses is that Japanese companies often try to predict where the dollar is going and hedge (or not hedge) accordingly. At the beginning of 1994, many thought that the dollar would continue to strengthen, and thus they failed to hedge their exposure. When the dollar plummeted instead, they lost billions. The lesson is that firms that try simultaneously to use hedging to both reduce risk and to beat the market may end up with more risk, not less.

---

[6] For a good summary of these other rationales for corporate hedging, see Matthew Bishop, "A Survey of Corporate Risk Management," *The Economist,* February 10, 1996, special section.

[7] Fluctuating earnings could also boost a company's taxes by causing it to alternate between high and low tax brackets (see Rene Stulz, "Rethinking Risk Management," Ohio State University working paper).

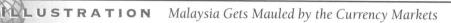

ILLUSTRATION *Malaysia Gets Mauled by the Currency Markets*

In January 1994, Bank Negara, Malaysia's central bank, declared war on "currency speculators" who were trying to profit from an anticipated rise in the Malaysian dollar. The timing of this declaration struck a nerve among currency traders because Bank Negara had itself long been a major speculator in the currency markets—a speculator whose boldness was matched only by its incompetence. During the two-year period 1992–1993, Bank Negara had foreign exchange losses of M$14.7 billion (U.S.$5.42 billion). It seems that even central banks are not immune to the consequences of market efficiency—and stupidity.

Costs and Benefits of Standard Hedging Techniques

Standard techniques for responding to anticipated currency changes are summarized in Exhibit 10.6. Such techniques, however, are vastly overrated in terms of their ability to minimize hedging costs.

Costs of Hedging   If a devaluation is unlikely, hedging may be a costly and inefficient way of doing business. If a devaluation is expected, the cost of using the techniques (like the cost of local borrowing) rises to reflect the anticipated devaluation. Just before the August 1982 peso devaluation, for example, every company in Mexico was trying to delay peso payments. Of course, this technique cannot produce a net gain because one company's payable is another company's receivable. As another example, if one company wants peso trade credit, another must offer it. Assuming that both the borrower and the lender are rational, a deal will not be struck until the interest cost rises to reflect the expected decline in the peso.

> Even shifting funds from one country to another is not a costless means of hedging. The net effect of speeding up remittances while delaying receipt of intercompany receivables is to force a subsidiary in a devaluation-prone country to increase its local currency

Hedging exchange risk costs money and should be evaluated like any other purchase of insurance.

EXHIBIT 10.6 • BASIC HEDGING TECHNIQUES

Depreciation	Appreciation
• Sell local currency forward	• Buy local currency forward
• Buy a local currency put option	• Buy a local currency call option
• Reduce levels of local currency cash and marketable securities	• Increase levels of local currency cash and marketable securities
• Tighten credit (reduce local currency receivables)	• Relax local currency credit terms
• Delay collection of hard currency receivables	• Speed up collection of soft currency receivables
• Increase imports of hard currency goods	• Reduce imports of soft currency goods
• Borrow locally	• Reduce local borrowing
• Delay payment of accounts payable	• Speed up payment of accounts payable
• Speed up dividend and fee remittances to parent and other subsidiaries	• Delay dividend and fee remittances to parent and other subsidiaries
• Speed up payment of intersubsidiary accounts payable	• Delay payment of intersubsidiary accounts payable
• Delay collection of intersubsidiary accounts receivable	• Speed up collection of intersubsidiary accounts receivable
• Invoice exports in foreign currency and imports in local currency	• Invoice exports in local currency and imports in foreign currency

(LC) borrowings to finance the additional working capital requirements. The net cost of shifting funds, therefore, is the cost of the LC loan minus the profit generated from use of the funds—for example, prepaying a hard currency loan—with both adjusted for expected exchange rate changes. As mentioned previously, loans in local currencies subject to devaluation fears carry higher interest rates that are likely to offset any gains from LC devaluation.

Reducing the level of cash holdings to lower exposure can adversely affect a subsidiary's operations, whereas selling LC-denominated marketable securities can entail an opportunity cost (the lower interest rate on hard currency securities). A firm with excess cash or marketable securities should reduce its holdings regardless of whether a devaluation is anticipated. After cash balances are at the minimum level, however, any further reductions will involve real costs that must be weighed against the expected benefits.

Invoicing exports in the foreign currency and imports in the local currency may cause the loss of valuable sales or may reduce a firm's ability to extract concessions on import prices. Similarly, tightening credit may reduce profits more than costs.

In summary, hedging exchange risk costs money and should be scrutinized like any other purchase of insurance. The costs of these hedging techniques are summarized in Exhibit 10.7.

Benefits of Hedging　A company can benefit from the preceding techniques only to the extent that it can forecast future exchange rates more accurately than the general market. For example, if the company has a foreign currency cash inflow, it would hedge only if the forward rate exceeds its estimate of the future spot rate. Conversely, with a foreign currency cash outflow, it would hedge only if the forward rate was below its estimated future spot rate. In this way, it would apparently be following the profit-guaranteeing dictum of buy low–sell high. The key word, however, is *apparently,* because attempting to

Attempting to profit from expected exchange rate changes is speculation, not hedging.

EXHIBIT 10.7 ● COST OF THE BASIC HEDGING TECHNIQUES

Depreciation	*Costs*
● Sell local currency forward	● Transaction costs; difference between forward and future spot rates
● Buy a local currency put option	● Put option premium
● Reduce levels of local currency cash and marketable securities	● Operational problems; opportunity cost (loss of higher interest rates on LC securities)
● Tighten credit (reduce local currency receivables)	● Lost sales and profits
● Delay collection of hard currency receivables	● Cost of financing additional receivables
● Increase imports of hard currency goods	● Financing and holding costs
● Borrow locally	● Higher interest rates
● Delay payment of accounts payable	● Harm to credit reputation
● Speed up dividend and fee remittances to parent and other subsidiaries	● Borrowing cost if funds not available or loss of higher interest rates if LC securities must be sold
● Speed up payment of intersubsidiary accounts payable	● Opportunity cost of money
● Delay collection of intersubsidiary accounts receivable	● Opportunity cost of money
● Invoice exports in foreign currency and imports in local currency	● Lost export sales or lower price; premium price for imports

profit from foreign exchange forecasting is speculating rather than hedging. The hedger is well advised to assume that the market knows as much as he or she does. Those who feel that they have superior information may choose to speculate, but this activity should not be confused with hedging.

ILLUSTRATION   *Selective Hedging*

In March, Multinational Industries, Inc. (MII), assessed the September spot rate for sterling at the following rates:

$1.30/£ with probability 0.15

$1.35/£ with probability 0.20

$1.40/£ with probability 0.25

$1.45/£ with probability 0.20

$1.50/£ with probability 0.20

a. What is the expected spot rate for September?

Solution. The expected future spot rate is 1.30(0.15) + 1.35(0.2) + 1.40(0.25) + 1.45(0.20) + 1.50(0.20) = $1.405.

b. If the six-month forward rate is $1.40, should the firm sell forward its £500,000 pound receivables due in September?

Solution. If MII sells its pound proceeds forward, it will lock in a value of $700,000 (1.40 × 500,000). Alternatively, if it decides to wait until September and sell its pound proceeds in the spot market, it expects to receive $702,500 (1.405 × 500,000). Based on these figures, if MII wants to maximize expected profits, it should retain its pound receivables and sell the proceeds in the spot market upon receipt.

c. What factors are likely to affect Multinational Industries' hedging decision?

Solution. Risk aversion could lead MII to sell its receivables forward to hedge their dollar value. However, if MII has pound liabilities, they could provide a natural hedge and reduce (or eliminate) the amount necessary to hedge. The existence of a cheaper hedging alternative, such as borrowing pounds and converting them to dollars for the duration of the receivables, would also make undesirable the use of a forward contract. This latter situation assumes that interest rate parity is violated. The tax treatment of foreign exchange gains and losses on forward contracts could also affect the hedging decision.

Companies can take advantage of tax asymmetries and market imperfections to lower their cost of hedging.

Under some circumstances, a company may benefit at the expense of the local government without speculating. Such a circumstance would involve the judicious use of market imperfections or existing tax asymmetries, or both. In the case of an overvalued currency, such as the Mexican peso in 1982, if exchange controls are not imposed to prevent capital outflows and if hard currency can be acquired at the official exchange rate, then money can be moved out of the country via intercompany payments. For instance, a subsidiary can speed payments of intercompany accounts payable, make immediate purchases from other subsidiaries, or speed remittances to the parent. Unfortunately, governments are not unaware of these tactics. During a currency crisis, when hard currency is scarce, the local government can be expected to block such transfers or at least make them more expensive.

Another often-cited reason for market imperfection is that individual investors may not have equal access to capital markets. For example, because forward exchange markets exist only for the major currencies, hedging often requires local borrowing in heavily regulated capital markets. As a legal citizen of many nations, the MNC normally has greater access to these markets.

Similarly, if forward contract losses are treated as a cost of doing business, whereas gains are taxed at a lower capital gains rate, the firm can engage in tax arbitrage. In the absence of financial market imperfections or tax asymmetries, however, the net expected value of hedging over time should be zero. Despite the questionable value to shareholders of hedging **balance-sheet exposure** or even transaction exposure, however, managers often try to reduce these exposures because they are evaluated, at least in part, on translation or transaction gains or losses.

In one area, however, companies can reduce their exchange risk at no cost. This costless hedging technique is known as exposure netting.

Exposure Netting   **Exposure netting** involves offsetting exposures in one currency with exposures in the same or another currency, where exchange rates are expected to move in a way such that losses (gains) on the first exposed position will be offset by gains (losses) on the second currency exposure. This portfolio approach to hedging recognizes that the total variability or risk of a currency exposure portfolio will be less than the sum of the individual variabilities of each currency exposure considered in isolation. The assumption underlying exposure netting is that the net gain or loss on the entire currency exposure portfolio is what matters, rather than the gain or loss on any individual monetary unit.

Centralization versus Decentralization

Centralization of exchange risk management reduces the amount of hedging needed to achieve a given level of safety.

In the area of **foreign exchange risk** management, there are good arguments both for and against centralization. Favoring centralization is the reasonable assumption that local treasurers want to optimize their own financial and exposure positions, regardless of the overall corporate situation. An example is a multibillion-dollar U.S. consumer-goods firm that gives its affiliates a free hand in deciding on their hedging policies. The firm's local treasurers ignore the possibilities available to the corporation to trade off positive and negative currency exposure positions by consolidating exposure worldwide. If subsidiary A sells to subsidiary B in sterling, then from the corporate perspective, these sterling exposures net out on a consolidated translation basis (but only before tax). If A or B or both hedge their sterling positions, however, unnecessary hedging takes place, or a zero sterling exposure turns into a positive or negative position. Furthermore, in their dealings with external customers, some affiliates may wind up with a positive exposure and others with a negative exposure in the same currency. Through lack of knowledge or incentive, individual subsidiaries may undertake hedging actions that increase rather than decrease overall corporate exposure in a given currency.

A further benefit of centralized exposure management is the ability to take advantage, through exposure netting, of the portfolio effect discussed previously. Thus, centralization of exchange risk management should reduce the amount of hedging required to achieve a given level of safety.

After the company has decided on the maximum currency exposure it is willing to tolerate, it can then select the cheapest option(s) worldwide to hedge its remaining exposure. Tax effects can be crucial at this stage, in computing both the amounts to hedge and the costs involved, but only headquarters will have the required global perspective. Centralized management also is needed to take advantage of the before-tax hedging cost variations that are likely to exist among subsidiaries because of market imperfections.

All these arguments for centralization of currency risk management are powerful. Against the benefits must be weighed the loss of local knowledge and the lack of incentive for local managers to take advantage of particular situations that only they may be familiar with. Companies that decentralize the hedging decision may allow local units to manage their own exposures by engaging in forward contracts with a central unit at negotiated rates. The central unit, in turn, may or may not lay off these contracts in the marketplace.

Managing Risk Management

Several spectacular risk management failures point to the need to monitor and supervise risk managers.

A number of highly publicized cases of derivatives-related losses have highlighted the potential dangers in the use of derivatives such as futures and options. Although these losses did not involve the use of currency derivatives, several lessons for risk management can be drawn from these cases, which include the bankruptcies of Orange County and Barings PLC and the huge losses taken at Metallgesellschaft, Kidder Peabody, Sumitomo, Union Bank of Switzerland, and Procter & Gamble. The most important lesson to be learned is that risk management failures have their origins in inadequate systems and controls rather than from any risk inherent in the use of derivatives themselves. In every case of large losses, senior management did not understand fully the activities of those taking positions in derivatives and failed to monitor and supervise their activities adequately. Some specific lessons include the following.

First, segregate the duties of those trading derivatives from those supposed to monitor them. For example, Nicholas Leeson, the trader who sank Barings, was in charge of trading and also kept his own books. When he took losses, he covered them up and doubled his bets. Similarly, the manager responsible for the profits generated by trading derivatives at UBS also oversaw the risks of his position. No one else at the bank was allowed to examine the risks his department was taking. And a rogue trader at Sumitomo, who lost $1.8 billion, oversaw the accounts that kept track of his dealings. These conflicts of interest are a recipe for disaster. Second, derivatives positions should be limited to prevent the possibility of catastrophic losses, and they should be marked to market every day to avoid the possibility of losses going unrecognized and being allowed to accumulate. As in the cases of Barings and Sumitomo, traders who can roll over their positions at non-market prices tend to make bigger and riskier bets to recoup their losses.

Third, compensation arrangements should be designed to shift more of the risk onto the shoulders of those taking the risks. For example, deferring part of traders' salaries until their derivatives positions actually pay off would make them more cognizant of the risks they are taking. Fourth, one should pay attention to warning signs. For example, Barings was slow to respond to an audit showing significant discrepancies in Leeson's accounts. Similarly, Kidder Peabody's executives ignored a government-bond trader who was generating record profits while supposedly engaged in risk-free arbitrage. A related lesson is that there's no free lunch. Traders and others delivering high profits deserve special scrutiny by independent auditors. The auditors must pay particular attention to the valuation of *exotic derivatives*—specialized contracts not actively traded. Given the lack of ready market prices for exotics, it is easy for traders to overvalue their positions in exotics without independent oversight. Finally, those who value reward above risk will likely wind up with risk at the expense of reward.

ILLUSTRATION   *The Luck of the Irish Eludes Allied Irish Banks*

In February 2002, Allied Irish Banks announced that a rogue trader at its U.S. unit lost $750 million through unauthorized foreign-exchange trades. Allied said John Rusnak, a foreign-exchange dealer at its U.S. unit Allfirst, tried to disguise huge losses through fictitious foreign-exchange trades over the past year. Traders in the foreign-exchange market believe that Mr. Rusnak bet on the wrong direction of the Japanese yen, which was the only currency that moved enough during that period to have enabled a trader to pile up such colossal losses. The foreign-exchange trades at issue were believed by the bank to have been hedged with currency options to reduce their risk. As it turned out, however, the options that Mr. Rusnak claimed to have bought were fictitious, leaving the bank with enormous "naked" (unhedged) foreign-exchange positions. As his losses piled up, he placed even larger foreign currency bets, which turned sour as well. Bank analysts said the episode raised serious issues about the risk-management controls in place at Allied and throughout the entire banking industry that are supposed to prevent the kinds of events that apparently hit Allied.

10.6 MANAGING TRANSLATION EXPOSURE

To hedge translation exposure, decrease soft currency assets (hard currency liabilities) and increase soft currency liabilities (hard currency assets).

Firms have three available methods for managing their translation exposure: (1) adjusting fund flows, (2) entering into forward contracts, and (3) exposure netting. The basic hedging strategy for reducing translation exposure shown in Exhibit 10.8 uses these methods. Essentially, the strategy involves increasing **hard currency** (likely to appreciate) assets and decreasing **soft currency** (likely to depreciate) assets, while simultaneously decreasing hard currency liabilities and increasing soft currency liabilities. For example, if a devaluation appears likely, the basic hedging strategy will be executed as follows: Reduce the level of cash, tighten credit terms to decrease accounts receivable, increase LC borrowing, delay accounts payable, and sell the weak currency forward. An expected currency appreciation would trigger the opposite tactics.

Despite their prevalence among firms, these hedging activities are not automatically valuable. As discussed in the previous section, if the market already recognizes the likelihood of currency appreciation or depreciation, this recognition will be reflected in the costs of the various hedging techniques. Only if the firm's anticipations differ from the market's and are also superior to the market's can hedging lead to reduced costs. Otherwise, the principal value of hedging would be to protect a firm from unforeseen currency fluctuations.

Funds Adjustment

Most techniques for hedging an impending local currency (LC) devaluation reduce LC assets or increase LC liabilities, thereby generating LC cash. If accounting exposure is to be reduced, these funds must be converted into hard currency assets. For example, a company will reduce its translation loss if, before an LC devaluation, it converts some of its LC cash holdings to the home currency. This conversion can be accomplished, either directly or indirectly, by means of funds adjustment techniques.

Companies can hedge their exposure by altering the amounts or currencies of their planned cash flows.

Funds adjustment involves altering either the amounts or the currencies (or both) of the planned cash flows of the parent or its subsidiaries to reduce the firm's local currency accounting exposure. If an LC devaluation is anticipated, direct funds-adjustment methods include pricing exports in hard currencies and imports in the local currency, investing in hard currency securities, and replacing hard currency borrowings with local currency loans. The indirect methods, which are elaborated upon in Chapter 20, include adjusting transfer prices on the sale of goods between affiliates; speeding up the payment of dividends, fees, and royalties; and adjusting the leads and lags of intersubsidiary accounts. The last method, which is the one most frequently used by multinationals, involves speeding up the payment of intersubsidiary accounts payable and delaying the collection of intersubsidiary accounts receivable. These hedging procedures for devaluations would be reversed for revaluations (see Exhibit 10.6).

EXHIBIT 10.8 ● BASIC STRATEGY FOR HEDGING TRANSLATION EXPOSURE

	Assets	*Liabilities*
Hard currencies (Likely to appreciate)	Increase	Decrease
Soft currencies (Likely to depreciate)	Decrease	Increase

Some of these techniques or tools may require considerable lead time and—as is the case with a transfer price—once they are introduced, they cannot easily be changed. In addition, techniques such as transfer price, fee and royalty, and dividend flow adjustments fall into the realm of corporate policy and are not usually under the treasurer's control, although this situation may be changing. It is, therefore, incumbent on the treasurer to educate other decision makers about the impact of these tools on the costs and management of corporate exposure.

Although entering forward contracts is the most popular coverage technique, the leading and lagging of payables and receivables is almost as important. For those countries in which a formal market in LC forward contracts does not exist, leading and lagging and LC borrowing are the most important techniques. The bulk of international business, however, is conducted in those few currencies for which forward markets do exist.

Forward contracts can reduce a firm's translation exposure by creating an offsetting asset or liability in the foreign currency. For example, suppose that IBM U.K. has translation exposure of £40 million (that is, sterling assets exceed sterling liabilities by that amount). IBM U.K. can eliminate its entire translation exposure by selling £40 million forward. Any loss (gain) on its translation exposure will then be offset by a corresponding gain (loss) on its forward contract. Note, however, that the gain (or loss) on the forward contract is of a cash-flow nature and is netted against an unrealized translation loss (or gain).

Selecting convenient (less risky) currencies for invoicing exports and imports and adjusting transfer prices are two techniques that are less frequently used, perhaps because of constraints on the use of those techniques. It is often difficult, for instance, to make a customer or supplier accept billing in a particular currency.

Exposure netting is an additional exchange-management technique that is available to multinational firms with positions in more than one foreign currency or with offsetting positions in the same currency. As defined earlier, this technique involves offsetting exposures in one currency with exposures in the same or another currency such that gains and losses on the two currency positions will offset each other.

Sidenote (left margin): Forward contracts are the most popular hedging tool.

Evaluating Alternative Hedging Mechanisms

Sidenote (left margin): Firms should adjust fund flows whenever it is profitable to do so on a covered basis, regardless of the impact on accounting exposure.

Ordinarily, the selection of a funds-adjustment strategy cannot proceed by evaluating each possible technique separately without risking suboptimization; for example, whether a firm chooses to borrow locally is not independent of its decision to use or not use those funds to import additional hard currency inventory. However, where the level of forward contracts that the financial manager can enter into is unrestricted, the following two-stage methodology allows the optimal level of forward transactions to be determined apart from the selection of what funds-adjustment techniques to use.[8] Moreover, this methodology is valid regardless of the manager's (or firm's) attitude toward risk.

Stage 1: Compute the profit associated with each funds-adjustment technique on a covered after-tax basis. Transactions that are profitable on a covered basis ought to be undertaken regardless of whether they increase or decrease the firm's accounting exposure. However, such activities should not be termed *hedging*; rather, they involve the use of *arbitrage* to exploit market distortions.

Stage 2: Any unwanted exposure resulting from the first stage can be corrected in the forward market. Stage 2 is the selection of an optimal level of forward transactions based on the firm's initial exposure, adjusted for the impact on exposure of decisions made in stage 1. Where the forward market is nonexistent, or where access to it is limited, the firm must determine both the techniques to use and their appropriate levels. In the latter case, a comparison of the net cost of a funds-adjustment technique with the

---

[8] This methodology is presented in William R. Folks, Jr., "Decision Analysis for Exchange Risk Management," *Financial Management*, Winter 1972, pp. 101–112.

anticipated currency depreciation will indicate whether the hedging transaction is profitable on an expected-value basis.

10.7 MANAGING TRANSACTION EXPOSURE

Transaction exposure can be managed by entering into offsetting foreign currency transactions.

As we saw in Section 10.1, transaction exposure arises whenever a company is committed to a foreign-currency-denominated transaction. Since the transaction will result in a future foreign currency cash inflow or outflow, any change in the exchange rate between the time the transaction is entered into and the time it is settled in cash will lead to a change in the dollar (HC) amount of the cash inflow or outflow. Protective measures to guard against transaction exposure involve entering into foreign currency transactions whose cash flows exactly offset the cash flows of the transaction exposure.

These protective measures include using forward contracts, price adjustment clauses, currency options, and borrowing or lending in the foreign currency. For example, General Electric explained its hedging activities in its 1999 Annual Report as follows:

> *Financial results of GE's international activities reported in U.S. dollars are affected by currency exchange. A number of techniques are used to manage the effects of currency exchange, including selective borrowings in local currencies and selective hedging of significant cross-currency transactions. Principal currencies are the major European currencies, including the euro, as well as the Japanese yen and the Canadian dollar.*
>
> *CURRENCY FORWARDS AND OPTIONS are employed by GE and GECS [GE Capital Services] to manage exposures to changes in currency exchange rates associated with commercial purchase and sale transactions.... These financial instruments generally are used to fix the local currency cost of purchased goods or services or selling prices denominated in currencies other than the functional currency. Currency exposures that result from net investments in affiliates are managed principally by funding assets denominated in local currency with debt denominated in those same currencies. In certain circumstances, net investment exposures are managed using currency forwards and currency swaps.*

Alternatively, the company could try to invoice all transactions in dollars and to avoid transaction exposure entirely. However, eliminating transaction exposure does not eliminate all foreign exchange risk. The firm still is subject to exchange risk on its future revenues and costs—its operating cash flows.

In a forward market hedge, any exchange gain or loss on the forward contract will be offset by a corresponding exchange loss or gain on the underlying transaction.

We will now look at the various techniques for managing transaction exposure by examining the case of General Electric's euro exposure. Suppose that on January 1, GE is awarded a contract to supply turbine blades to Lufthansa, the German airline. On December 31, GE will receive payment of €10 million for these blades. The most direct way for GE to hedge this receivable is to sell a €10 million forward contract for delivery in one year. Alternatively, it can use a money-market hedge, which would involve borrowing €10 million for one year, converting it into dollars, and investing the proceeds in a security that matures on December 31. As we will see, if interest rate parity holds, the two methods will yield the same results. GE can also manage its transaction exposure through risk shifting, risk sharing, exposure netting, and currency options.

Forward Market Hedge

In a **forward market hedge**, a company that is long a foreign currency will sell the foreign currency forward, whereas a company that is short a foreign currency will buy the currency forward. In this way, the company can fix the dollar value of future foreign currency cash flow. For example, by selling forward the proceeds from its sale of turbine blades, GE can effectively transform the currency denomination of its €10 million receivable from euros to dollars, thereby eliminating all currency risk on the sale. For example, suppose the current spot price for the euro is $1.00/€, and the one-year forward rate is $0.957/€. Then, a forward sale of €10 million for delivery in one year will yield GE $9.57 million on December 31. Exhibit 10.9 shows the cash-flow consequences of combining the forward sale with the euro receivable, given three possible exchange rate scenarios.

Regardless of what happens to the future spot rate, Exhibit 10.9 demonstrates that GE still gets to collect $9.57 million on its turbine sale. Any exchange gain or loss on the forward contract will be offset by a corresponding exchange loss or gain on the receivable. The effects of this transaction also can be seen with the following simple T-account describing GE's position as of December 31:

December 31: GE T-Account (millions)

Account receivable	€10.00	Forward contract payment	€10.00
Forward contract receipt	$9.57		

Without hedging, GE will have a €10 million asset whose value will fluctuate with the exchange rate. The forward contract creates an equal euro liability, offset by an asset worth $9.57 million dollars. The euro asset and liability cancel each other out, and GE is left with a $9.57 million asset.

This example illustrates another point as well: *Hedging with forward contracts eliminates the downside risk at the expense of forgoing the upside potential.*

The True Cost of Hedging   Exhibit 10.9 also shows that the true cost of hedging cannot be calculated in advance because it depends on the future spot rate, which is unknown at the time the forward contract is entered into. In the GE example, the actual cost of hedging can vary from +$430,000 to –$570,000; a plus (+) represents a cost, and a minus (–) represents a negative cost or a gain. In percentage terms, the cost varies from –5.7 percent to +4.3 percent.

This example points out the distinction between the traditional method of calculating the cost of a forward contract and the correct method, which measures its opportunity cost. Specifically, the cost of a forward contract is usually measured as its forward discount or premium:

The true cost of hedging is an opportunity cost that depends on the future spot rate on the date of settlement.

$$\frac{f_1 - e_0}{e_0}$$

where e_0 is the current spot rate (dollar price) of the foreign currency and f_1 is the forward rate. In GE's case, this cost would equal 4.3 percent.

EXHIBIT 10.9 • POSSIBLE OUTCOMES OF FORWARD MARKET HEDGE AS OF DECEMBER 31

Spot Exchange Rate	Value of Original Receivable (1)	+	Gain (Loss) on Foward Contract (2)	=	Total Cash Flow (3)
€1 = $1.00	$10,000,000		($430,000)		$9,570,000
€1 = $0.957	9,570,000		0		$9,570,000
€1 = $0.90	9,000,000		570,000		$9,570,000

However, this approach is wrong because the relevant comparison must be between the dollars per unit of foreign currency received with hedging, f_1, and the dollars received in the absence of hedging, e_1, where e_1 is the future (unknown) spot rate on the date of settlement. That is, the real cost of hedging is an **opportunity cost**. In particular, if the forward contract had not been entered into, the future value of each unit of foreign currency would have been e_1 dollars. Thus, the true dollar cost of the forward contract per dollar's worth of foreign currency sold forward equals

$$\frac{f_1 - e_1}{e_0}$$

The expected cost (value) of a forward contract depends on whether or not a risk premium or other source of bias exists. Absent such bias, the expected cost of hedging via a forward contract will be zero. Otherwise, there would be an arbitrage opportunity. Suppose, for example, that management at General Electric believes that despite a one-year forward rate of $0.9570, the euro will actually be worth about $0.9775 on December 31. Then GE could profit by buying (rather than selling) euros forward for one year at $0.9570 and, on December 31, completing the contract by selling euros in the spot market at $0.9775. If GE is correct, it will earn $0.0205 (0.9775 – 0.9570) per euro sold forward. On a €10 million forward contract, this profit would amount to $205,000—a substantial reward for a few minutes of work.

In an efficient market, the expected cost of a forward contract is zero.

The prospect of such rewards would not go unrecognized for long, which explains why, on average, the forward rate appears to be unbiased. Therefore, unless GE or any other company has some special information about the future spot rate that it has good reason to believe is not adequately reflected in the forward rate, it should accept the forward rate's predictive validity as a working hypothesis and avoid speculative activities. After the fact, of course, the actual cost of a forward contract will turn out to be positive or negative (unless the future spot rate equals the forward rate), but the sign cannot be predicted in advance.

On the other hand, the evidence presented in Chapter 4 points to the possibility of bias in the forward rate at any point in time. The nature of this apparent bias suggests that the selective use of forward contracts in hedging may reduce expected hedging costs; but beware of the peso problem—the possibility that historical returns may be unrepresentative of future returns. The specific cost-minimizing selective hedging policy to take advantage of this bias would depend on whether you are trying to hedge a long or a short position in a currency. The policy is as follows:

- If you are long a currency, hedge (by selling forward) if the currency is at a forward premium; if the currency is at a forward discount, do not hedge.

- If you are short a currency, hedge (by buying forward) if the currency is selling at a forward discount; if the currency is at a forward premium, do not hedge.

As discussed in Section 10.5 ("Designing a Hedging Strategy"), however, this selective hedging policy does not come free; it may reduce expected costs but at the expense of higher risk. Absent other considerations, therefore, the impact on shareholder wealth of selective hedging via forward contracts should be minimal, with any expected gains likely to be offset by higher risk.

Money-Market Hedge

An alternative to a forward market hedge is to use a money-market hedge. A **money-market hedge** involves simultaneous borrowing and lending activities in two different currencies to lock in the dollar value of a future foreign currency cash flow. For example, suppose Euro and U.S. dollar interest rates are 15 percent and 10 percent, respectively. Using a

A money market hedge uses simultaneous borrowing and lending activities in two different currencies to eliminate a transaction exposure.

money-market hedge, General Electric will borrow €(10/1.15) million = €8.70 million for one year, convert it into $8.7 million in the spot market, and invest the $8.7 million for one year. On December 31, GE will receive 1.10 × $8.7 million = $9.57 million from its dollar investment. GE will then use the proceeds of its euro receivable, collectible on that date, to repay the 1.15 × €8.70 million = €10 million it owes in principal and interest. As Exhibit 10.10 shows, the exchange gain or loss on the borrowing and lending transactions exactly offsets the dollar loss or gain on GE's euro receivable.

The gain or loss on the money-market hedge can be calculated simply by subtracting the cost of repaying the euro debt from the dollar value of the investment. For example, in the case of an end-of-year spot rate of $1.00, the €10 million in principal and interest will cost $10 million to repay. The return on the dollar investment is only $9.57 million, leaving a loss on the money-market hedge of $430,000.

We can also view the effects of this transaction with the simple T-account used earlier:

December 31: GE T-Account (millions)

| Account receivable | €10.00 | Loan repayment (including interest) | €10.00 |
| Investment return (including interest) | $9.57 | | |

As with the forward contract, the euro asset and liability (the loan repayment) cancel each other out, and GE is left with a $9.57 million asset (its investment).

A money market hedge is equivalent to a forward contract if interest rate parity holds.

The equality of the net cash flows from the forward market and money-market hedges is not coincidental. The interest rates and forward and spot rates were selected so that interest rate parity would hold. In effect, the simultaneous borrowing and lending transactions associated with a money-market hedge enable GE to create a "homemade" forward contract. The effective rate on this forward contract will equal the actual forward rate if interest rate parity holds. Otherwise, a covered interest arbitrage opportunity would exist.

In reality, there are transaction costs associated with hedging: the bid–ask spread on the forward contract and the difference between borrowing and lending rates. These transaction costs must be factored in when comparing a forward contract hedge with a money-market hedge. The key to making these comparisons, as shown in Chapter 7, is to ensure that the correct bid and ask and borrowing and lending rates are used.

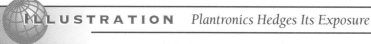

ILLUSTRATION *Plantronics Hedges Its Exposure*

Plantronics owes SKr 50 million, due in one year, for some electrical equipment it recently bought from ABB Asea Brown Boveri. At the current spot rate of $0.1480/SKr, this payable is $7.4 million. It wishes to hedge this payable but is undecided how to do it. The one-year forward rate is currently $0.1436. Plantronics' treasurer notes that the company has

EXHIBIT 10.10 • POSSIBLE OUTCOMES OF FORWARD MARKET HEDGE AS OF DECEMBER 31

Spot Exchange Rate	Value of Original Receivable (1)	+	Gain (Loss) on Money Market Hedge (2)	=	Total Cash Flow (3)
€1 = $1.00	$10,000,000		($430,000)		$9,570,000
€1 = $0.957	9,570,000		0		$9,570,000
€1 = $0.90	9,000,000		570,000		$9,570,000

$10 million in a marketable U.S. dollar CD yielding 7 percent per annum. At the same time, SE Banken in Stockholm is offering a one-year time deposit rate of 10.5 percent.

QUESTIONS

1. What is the low-cost hedging alternative for Plantronics? What is the cost?

Answer. Plantronics can use the forward market to lock in a cost for its payable of $7.18 million. Alternatively, Plantronics can use a money market hedge to lock in a lower dollar cost of $7,165,611 for its payable. Thus, the money market hedge is the low-cost hedge. To compute this cost, note that Plantronics must invest SKr 45,248,869 today at 10.5 percent to have SKr 50 million in one year (45,248,869 × 0.105 = 50 million). This amount is equivalent to $6,696,833 at the current spot of SKr $0.1480/SKr. The opportunity cost to Plantronics of taking this amount from its CD today and converting it into SKr is $7,165,611, which is the future value of $6,696,833 invested at 7 percent.

2. Suppose interest rate parity held. What would the one-year forward rate be?

Answer. Interest rate parity holds when the dollar return on investing dollars equals the dollar return on investing SKr, or $1.07 = (1/0.1480) \times 1.105 \times f_1$, where f_1 is the equilibrium one-year forward rate. The solution to this equation is $f_1 = $0.1433/SKr$. Because the actual one-year forward rate exceeds this number, interest rate parity does not hold and a forward hedge is more expensive than a money-market hedge.

Risk Shifting

MNCs can eliminate transaction risk by pricing all contracts in the home currency.

General Electric can avoid its transaction exposure altogether if Lufthansa allows it to price the sale of turbine blades in dollars. Dollar invoicing, however, does not eliminate currency risk; it simply shifts that risk from GE to Lufthansa, which now has dollar exposure. Lufthansa may or may not be better able, or more willing, to bear it. Despite the fact that this form of **risk shifting** is a zero-sum game, it is common in international business. Firms typically attempt to invoice exports in strong currencies and imports in weak currencies.

Is it possible to gain from risk shifting? Not if one is dealing with informed customers or suppliers. To see why, consider the GE–Lufthansa deal. If Lufthansa is willing to be invoiced in dollars for the turbine blades, that must be because Lufthansa calculates that its euro equivalent cost will be no higher than the €10 million price it was originally prepared to pay. Since Lufthansa does not have to pay for the turbine blades until December 31, its cost will be based on the spot price of the dollars as of that date. By buying dollars forward at the one-year forward rate of $0.9570/€, Lufthansa can convert a dollar price of *P* into a euro cost of *P*/0.9570. Thus, the maximum dollar price P_M that Lufthansa should be willing to pay for the turbine blades is the solution to

$$\frac{P_M}{0.9570} = €10 \text{ million}$$

or

$$P_M = $9.57 \text{ million}$$

Considering that GE can guarantee itself $9.57 million by pricing in euros and selling the resulting €10 million forward, it will not accept a lower dollar price. The bottom line is that both Lufthansa and General Electric will be indifferent between a U.S. dollar price and a euro price only if the two prices are equal at the forward exchange rate. Therefore, because the euro price arrived at through arm's-length negotiations is €10 million, the dollar price that is equally acceptable to Lufthansa and GE can only be $9.57 million. Otherwise, one or both of the parties involved in the negotiations has ignored the possibility of currency changes. Such naiveté is unlikely to exist for long in the highly competitive world of international business.

Pricing Decisions

Foreign currency contract prices should factor in possible exchange rate changes.

Notwithstanding the view just expressed, top management sometimes has failed to take anticipated exchange rate changes into account when making operating decisions, leaving financial management with the essentially impossible task, through purely financial operations, of recovering a loss already incurred at the time of the initial transaction. To illustrate this type of error, suppose that GE has priced Lufthansa's order of turbine blades at $10 million and then, because Lufthansa demands to be quoted a price in euro, converts the dollar price to a euro quote of €10 million, using the spot rate of $1.00/€.

In reality, the quote is worth only $9.57 million—even though it is booked at $10 million—because that is the risk-free price that GE can guarantee for itself by using the forward market. If GE management wanted to sell the blades for $10 million, it should have set a euro price equal to €10 million/0.957 = €10.45 million. Thus, GE lost $430,000 the moment it signed the contract (assuming that Lufthansa would have agreed to the higher price rather than turn to another supplier). This loss is not an exchange loss; it is a loss due to management inattentiveness.

The dollar price on foreign sales should be converted into a foreign currency price based on the forward rate, not the spot rate.

The general rule on credit sales overseas is to convert between the foreign currency price and the dollar price by using the forward rate, not the spot rate. If the dollar price is high enough, the exporter should follow through with the sale. Similarly, if the dollar price on a foreign-currency-denominated import is low enough, the importer should follow through on the purchase. All this rule does is to recognize that a euro (or any other foreign currency) tomorrow is not the same as a euro today. This rule is the international analogue to the insight that a dollar tomorrow is not the same as a dollar today. In the case of a sequence of payments to be received at several points in time, the foreign currency price should be a weighted average of the forward rates for delivery on those dates.

ILLUSTRATION *Weyerhaeuser Quotes a Euro Price for Its Lumber*

Weyerhaeuser is asked to quote a price in euros for lumber sales to a French company. The lumber will be shipped and paid for in four equal quarterly installments. Weyerhaeuser requires a minimum price of $1 million to accept this contract. If P_F is the euro price contracted for, then Weyerhaeuser will receive $0.25P_F$ every three months, beginning 90 days from now. Suppose the spot and forward rates for the euro are as follows:

Spot	90-Day	180-Day	270-Day	360-Day
$0.9772	$0.9767	$0.9761	$0.9758	$0.9751

On the basis of these forward rates, the certainty-equivalent dollar value of this euro revenue is $0.25P_F(0.9767 + 0.9761 + 0.9758 + 0.9751)$, or $0.25P_F(3.9037) = \$0.9759P_F$. In order for Weyerhaeuser to realize $1 million from this sale, the minimum euro price must be the solution to

$$\$0.9759P_F = \$1,000,000$$

or

$$P_F = €1,024,669$$

At any lower euro price, Weyerhaeuser cannot be assured of receiving the $1 million it demands for this sale. Note that the spot rate did not enter into any of these calculations.

Exposure Netting

Exposure netting involves offsetting exposure in one currency with exposure in the same or another currency.

As defined in Section 10.5, **exposure netting** involves offsetting exposures in one currency with exposures in the same or another currency, where exchange rates are expected to move in such a way that losses (gains) on the first exposed position should be offset by gains (losses) on the second currency exposure. Although simple conceptually, implementation of exposure netting can be more involved. It is easy to see, for example, that a €1 million receivable and €1 million payable cancel each other out, with no net (before-tax) exposure. Dow Chemical explained this basic form of exposure netting in its 1999 Annual Report when it stated that "Assets and liabilities denominated in the same currency are netted and only the net exposure is hedged." It may be less obvious that such exposure netting can also be accomplished by using positions in different currencies. However, companies practice multicurrency exposure netting all the time. According to one executive: "We might be willing to tolerate a short position in Swiss francs if we had a long position in Deutsche marks. They're fellow travelers. We look at our exposures as a portfolio."[9]

In practice, exposure netting involves one of three possibilities:

Exposure netting can be viewed in a portfolio context.

1. A firm can offset a long position in a currency with a short position in that same currency.
2. If the exchange rate movements of two currencies are positively correlated (for example, the Swiss franc and euro), then the firm can offset a long position in one currency with a short position in the other.
3. If the currency movements are negatively correlated, then short (or long) positions can be used to offset each other.

 ILLUSTRATION   *Using Exposure Netting to Manage Transaction Exposure*

Suppose that Apex Computers has the following transaction exposures:

Apex T-Account (millions)

Marketable securities	€2.4	Accounts payable	Mex$15.4
Accounts receivable	SFr 6.2	Bank loan	SFr 14.8
		Tax liability	€1.1

On a net basis, before taking currency correlations into account, Apex's transaction exposures—now converted into dollar terms—is:

Apex T-Account (millions)

Euro (1.3)	$1.2	Swiss franc (8.6)	$5.1
		Mexican peso (15.4)	$1.8

Given the historical positive correlation between the euro and Swiss franc, Apex decides to net out its euro long position from its franc short position, leaving it with a net short position in the Swiss franc of $3.9 million ($1.2 million – $5.1 million). Last, Apex takes into account the historical negative correlation between the Mexican peso and the Swiss franc and offsets these two short positions. The result is a net short position in Swiss francs of $2.1 million ($3.9 million – $1.8 million). By hedging only this residual transaction exposure, Apex can dramatically reduce the volume of its hedging transactions. The latter exposure netting—offsetting euro, Swiss franc, and Mexican peso exposures

---

[9] "How Corporations Are Playing the Currency Game," *Institutional Investor,* May 1976, p. 31.

with each other—depends on the strength of the correlations among these currencies. Specifically, Apex's offsetting its exposures on a dollar-for-dollar basis will be fully effective and appropriate only if the correlations are +1 for the €/SFr currency pair and –1 for the SFr/Mex$ currency pair.

Currency Risk Sharing

Companies can agree to share the exchange risk on their contracts.

In addition to, or instead of, a traditional hedge, General Electric and Lufthansa can agree to share the currency risks associated with their turbine blade contract. **Currency risk sharing** can be implemented by developing a customized hedge contract embedded in the underlying trade transaction. This hedge contract typically takes the form of a **price adjustment clause**, whereby a base price is adjusted to reflect certain exchange rate changes. For example, the base price could be set at €10 million, but the parties would share the currency risk beyond a neutral zone. The **neutral zone** represents the currency range in which risk is not shared.

Suppose the neutral zone is specified as a band of exchange rates: $0.98 – 1.02/€, with a base rate of $1.00/€. This means that the exchange rate can fall as far as $0.98/€ or rise as high as $1.02/€ without reopening the contract. Within the neutral zone, Lufthansa must pay GE the dollar equivalent of €10 million at the base rate of $1.00, or $10 million. Thus, Lufthansa's cost within the neutral zone can vary from €9.8 million to €10.2 million (10 million/1.02 to 10 million/0.98). However, if the euro depreciates from $1.00 to, say, $0.90, the actual rate will have moved $0.08 beyond the lower boundary of the neutral zone ($0.98/€). This amount is shared equally. Thus, the exchange rate actually used in settling the transaction is $0.96/€ ($1.00 – 0.08/2). The new price of the turbine blades becomes €10 million × 0.96, or $9.6 million. Lufthansa's cost rises to €10.67 million (9,600,000/0.90). In the absence of a risk-sharing agreement, the contract value to GE would have been $9.0 million. Of course, if the euro appreciates beyond the upper bound to, say, $1.10, GE does not get the full benefit of the euro's rise in value. Instead, the new contract exchange rate becomes $1.04 (1.00 + 0.08/2). GE collects €10 million × 1.04, or $10.4 million, and Lufthansa pays a price of €9.45 million (10,400,000/1.10).

Exhibit 10.11 compares the currency risk protection features of the currency risk-sharing arrangement with that of a traditional forward contract (at a forward rate of $0.957) and a no-hedge alternative. Within the neutral zone, the dollar value of GE's contract under the risk-sharing agreement stays at $10 million. This situation is equivalent to Lufthansa selling GE a forward contract at the current spot rate of $1.00. Beyond the neutral zone, the contract's dollar value rises or falls only half as much under the risk-sharing agreement as under the no-hedge alternative. The value of the hedged contract remains the same, regardless of the exchange rate.

Currency Collars

A currency collar is a contract that provides protection if the currency moves outside an agreed-on range.

Suppose that GE is prepared to take some but not all of the risk associated with its Euro receivable. In this case, it could buy a **currency collar**, which is a contract that provides protection against currency moves outside an agreed-upon range. For example, suppose that GE is willing to accept variations in the value of its euro receivable associated with fluctuations in the euro in the range of $0.95 to $1.05. Beyond that point, however, it wants protection. With a currency collar, also known as a **range forward**, GE will convert its euro receivable at the following range forward rate, RF, which depends on the actual future spot rate, e_1:

$$\text{If } e_1 < \$0.95, \text{ then } RF = \$0.95$$

$$\text{If } \$0.95 \leq e_1 \leq \$1.05, \text{ then } RF = e_1$$

$$\text{If } e_1 > \$1.05, \text{ then } RF = \$1.05$$

EXHIBIT 10.11 • CURRENCY RISK SHARING: GE AND LUFTHANSA

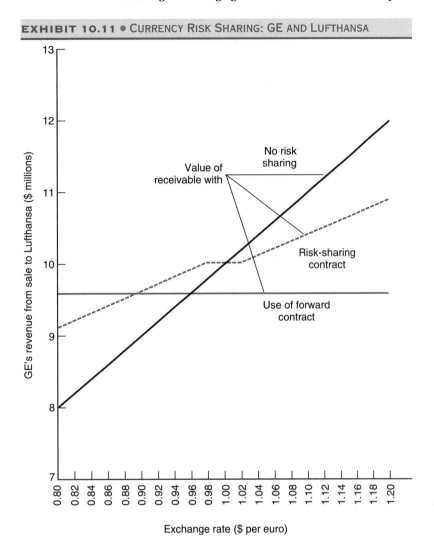

Exchange rate ($ per euro)

In effect, GE is agreeing to convert its euro proceeds at the future spot rate if that rate falls within the range $0.95–$1.05 and at the boundary rates beyond that range. Specifically, if the future spot rate exceeds $1.05, then it will convert the euro proceeds at $1.05, giving the bank a profit on the range forward. Alternatively, if the future spot rate falls below $0.95, then GE will convert the proceeds at $0.95 and the bank suffers a loss.

Exhibit 10.12 shows that with the range forward, GE has effectively collared its exchange risk (hence the term *currency collar*). Exhibit 10.12a shows the payoff profile of the euro receivable; Exhibit 10.12b shows the payoff profile for the currency collar; and Exhibit 10.12c shows the payoff profile for GE's receivable hedged with the collar. With the collar, GE is guaranteed a minimum cash flow of 10 million × $0.95, or $9,500,000. Its maximum cash flow with the collar is $10,500,000, which it receives for any exchange rate beyond $1.05. For exchange rates within the range, it receives 10 million × (actual spot rate).

Why would GE accept a contract that limits its upside potential? In order to lower its cost of hedging its downside risk. The cost saving can be seen by recognizing that a currency collar can be created by simultaneously buying an out-of-the-money put option and selling an out-of-the-money call option of the same size. In effect, the purchase of the put option is financed by the sale of the call option. By selling off the upside potential with

Currency collars trade off less protection for a lower cost.

the call option, GE can reduce the cost of hedging its downside risk with the put option. The payoff profile of the combined put purchase and call sale, also known as a **cylinder**, is shown in Exhibit 10.13. By adjusting the strike prices such that the put premium just

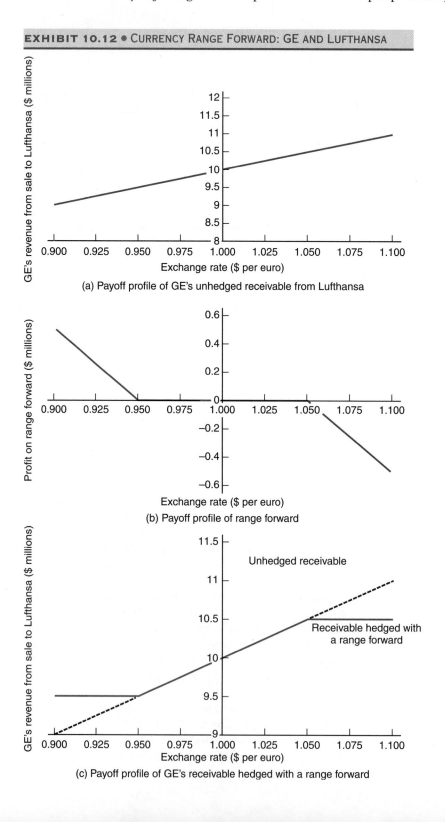

EXHIBIT 10.12 • CURRENCY RANGE FORWARD: GE AND LUFTHANSA

(a) Payoff profile of GE's unhedged receivable from Lufthansa

(b) Payoff profile of range forward

Unhedged receivable

Receivable hedged with a range forward

(c) Payoff profile of GE's receivable hedged with a range forward

EXHIBIT 10.13 • USE OF A CURRENCY CYLINDER TO HEDGE GE'S RECEIVABLE

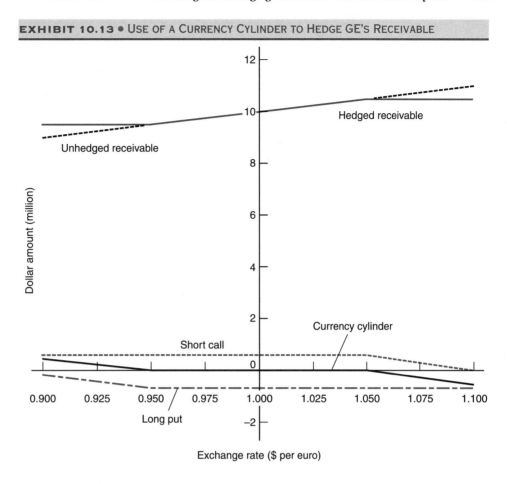

Exchange rate ($ per euro)

equals the call premium, you can always create a cylinder with a zero net cost, in which case you have a range forward. In this exhibit, it is assumed that the put premium at a strike price of $0.95 just equals the call premium at a strike price of $1.05.

Cross-Hedging

Hedging with futures is very similar to hedging with forward contracts. However, a firm that wants to manage its exchange risk with futures may find that the exact futures contract it requires is unavailable. In this case, it may be able to **cross-hedge** its exposure by using futures contracts on another currency that is correlated with the one of interest.

Cross-hedging involves hedging a given currency exposure by using a forward or futures contract on a related currency.

The idea behind cross-hedging is as follows: If we cannot find a futures/forward contract on the currency in which we have an exposure, we will hedge our exposure via a futures/forward contract on a related currency. Lacking a model or theory to tell us the exact relationship between the exchange rates of the two related currencies, we estimate the relationship by examining the historical association between these rates. The resulting regression coefficient tells us the sign and approximate size of the futures/forward position we should take in the related currency. However, the cross-hedge is only as good as the stability and economic significance of the correlation between the two currencies. A key output of the regression equation, such as the one between the Danish krone and euro, is the R^2, which measures the fraction of variation in the exposed currency that is explained by variation in the hedging currency. In general, the greater the R^2 of the regression of one exchange rate on the other, the better the cross-hedge will be.

I L L U S T R A T I O N   *Hedging a Danish Krone Exposure Using Euro Futures*

An exporter with a receivable denominated in Danish krone will not find krone futures available. Although an exact matching futures contract is unavailable, the firm may be able to find something that comes close. The exporter can cross-hedge his Danish krone position with euro futures, as the dollar values of those currencies tend to move in unison.

Suppose it is October 15 and our exporter expects to collect a DK 5 million receivable on December 15. The exporter can always sell the Danish kroner on the spot market at that time but is concerned about a possible fall in the krone's value between now and then. The exporter's treasurer has copied the spot prices of the Danish krone and euro from the *Wall Street Journal* every day for the past three months and has estimated the following regression relationship using this information:

$$\Delta DK/\$ = 0.8(\Delta €/\$)$$

where $\Delta = e_t - e_{t-1}$ and e_t is the spot rate for day t (that is, Δ is the change in the exchange rate). In addition, the R^2 of the regression is 0.91, meaning that 91 percent of the variation in the Danish krone is explained by movements in the euro. With an R^2 this high, the exporter can confidently use euro futures contracts to cross-hedge the Danish krone.

According to this relationship, a 1¢ change in the value of the euro leads to a 0.8¢ change in the value of the DK. To cross-hedge the forthcoming receipt of DK, 0.8 units of euro futures must be sold for every unit of DK to be sold on December 15. With a Danish krone exposure of DK 5 million, the exporter must sell euro futures contracts in the amount of €4 million (0.8 × 5 million). With a euro futures contract size of €125,000, this euro amount translates into 32 contracts (4 million/125,000). The example illustrates the idea that the euro futures can be used to effectively offset the risk posed by the DK receivable.

Foreign Currency Options

Companies often have contingent foreign currency cash flows that can't be hedged with forward contracts.

Thus far, we have examined how firms can hedge known foreign currency transaction exposures. Yet, in many circumstances, the firm is uncertain whether the hedged foreign currency cash inflow or outflow will materialize. For example, the previous assumption was that GE learned on January 1 that it had won a contract to supply turbine blades to Lufthansa. But suppose that, although GE's bid on the contract was submitted on January 1, the announcement of the winning bid would not be until April 1. During the three-month period from January 1 to April 1, GE does not know if it will receive a payment of €10 million on December 31. This uncertainty has important consequences for the appropriate hedging strategy.

GE would like to guarantee that the exchange rate does not move against it between the time it bids and the time it gets paid, should it win the contract. The danger of not hedging is that its bid will be selected and the euro will decline in value, possibly wiping out GE's anticipated profit margin. For example, if the forward rate on April 1 for delivery December 31 falls to €1 = $0.90, the value of the contract will drop from $9.57 million to $9 million, for a loss in value of $570,000.

The apparent solution is for GE to sell the anticipated €10 million receivable forward on January 1. However, if GE does that and loses the bid on the contract, it still has to sell the currency—which it will have to get by buying on the open market, perhaps at a big loss. For example, suppose the forward rate on April 1 for December 31 delivery has risen to $1.002. To eliminate all currency risk on its original forward contract, GE would have to buy €10 million forward at a price of $1.002. The result would be a loss of $450,000 [(0.957 − 1.002) × 10 million] on the forward contract entered into on January 1 at a rate of $0.9570.

Using Options to Hedge Bids   Until recently, GE, or any company that bid on a contract denominated in a foreign currency and was not assured of success, would be unable to resolve its foreign exchange risk dilemma. The advent of **currency options** has changed all that. Specifically, the solution to managing its currency risk in this case is for GE, at the time of its bid, to purchase an option to sell €10 million on December 31. For example, suppose that on January 1, GE can buy for $100,000 the right to sell Citigroup €10 million on December 31 at a price of $0.9570/€. If it enters into this put option contract with Citigroup, GE will guarantee itself a minimum price ($9.57 million) should its bid be selected, while simultaneously ensuring that if it lost the bid, its loss would be limited to the price paid for the option contract (the premium of $100,000). Should the spot price of the euro on December 31 exceed $0.9570, GE would let its option contract expire unexercised and convert the €10 million at the prevailing spot rate.

> Currency options can be used to hedge contingent foreign currency cash flows.

Instead of a straight put option, GE could use a futures put option. This would entail GE buying a put option on a December futures contract with the option expiring in April. If the put were in-the-money on April 1, GE would exercise it and receive a short position in a euro futures contract plus a cash amount equal to the strike price minus the December futures price as of April 1. Assuming it had won the bid, GE would hold on to the December futures contract. If it had lost the bid, GE would pocket the cash and immediately close out its short futures position at no cost.

As we saw in Chapter 8, two types of options are available to manage exchange risk. A **currency put option**, such as the one appropriate to GE's situation, gives the buyer the right, but not the obligation, to sell a specified number of foreign currency units to the option seller at a fixed dollar price, up to the option's expiration date. Alternatively, a **currency call option** is the right, but not the obligation, to buy the foreign currency at a specified dollar price, up to the expiration date.

A call option is valuable, for example, when a firm has offered to buy a foreign asset, such as another firm, at a fixed foreign currency price but is uncertain whether its bid will be accepted. By buying a call option on the foreign currency, the firm can lock in a maximum dollar price for its tender offer, while limiting its downside risk to the call premium in the event its bid is rejected.

 I L L U S T R A T I O N   *Air Products Lose Twice*

In May 2000, Air Products & Chemicals Inc. announced a $300 million after-tax charge. The bulk of this charge came about from currency losses associated with the acquisition of British pounds to be used in a failed attempt to buy BOC Group PLC. After Air Products bought the pounds, the currency fell in value. According to the *Wall Street Journal* (May 11, 2000, p. A4), "While it would have had losses from the hedge even if it were to have acquired BOC, it would have effectively paid less as well, because of the currency's decline." Purchase of a call option on pounds sterling instead of its outright currency purchase would have protected Air Products from the currency losses on its failed acquisition.

Using Options to Hedge Other Currency Risks   Currency options are a valuable risk-management tool in other situations as well. Conventional transaction-exposure management says you wait until your sales are booked or your orders are placed before hedging them. If a company does that, however, it faces potential losses from exchange rate movements because the foreign currency price does not necessarily adjust right away to changes in the value of the dollar. As a matter of policy, to avoid confusing customers and salespeople, most companies do not change their price list every time the exchange rate changes. Unless and until the foreign currency price changes, the unhedged company may suffer a decrease in its profit margin. Because of the uncertainty of anticipated sales or purchases, however, forward contracts are an imperfect tool to hedge the exposure.

For example, a company that commits to a foreign currency price list for, say, three months has a foreign currency exposure that depends on the unknown volume of sales at those prices during this period. Thus, the company does not know what volume of forward contracts to enter into to protect its profit margin on these sales. For the price of the premium, currency put options allow the company to insure its profit margin against adverse movements in the foreign currency while guaranteeing fixed prices to foreign customers. Without options, the firm might be forced to raise its foreign currency prices sooner than the competitive situation warranted.

 ILLUSTRATION *Hewlett-Packard Uses Currency Options to Protect Its Profit Margins*

Hewlett-Packard (HP), the California-based computer firm, uses currency options to protect its dollar profit margins on products built in the United States but sold in Europe. The firm needs to be able to lower local currency (LC) prices if the dollar weakens and hold LC prices steady for about three months (the price adjustment period) if the dollar strengthens.

Suppose HP sells anticipated euro sales forward at €1/$ to lock in a dollar value for those sales. If one month later the dollar weakens to €0.80/$, HP faces tremendous competitive pressure to lower its euro prices. HP would be locked into a loss on the forward contracts that would not be offset by a gain on its sales because it had to cut euro prices. With euro put options, HP would just let them expire, and it would lose only the put premium. Conversely, options help HP delay LC price increases when the dollar strengthens until it can raise them without suffering a competitive disadvantage. The reduced profit margin on local sales is offset by the gain on the put option.

Currency options can be used to hedge exposure to shifts in a competitor's currency.

Currency options also can be used to hedge exposure to shifts in a competitor's currency. Companies competing with firms from other nations may find their products at a price disadvantage if a major competitor's currency weakens, allowing the competitor to reduce its prices. Thus, the company will be exposed to fluctuations in the competitor's currency even if it has no sales in that currency. For example, a Swiss engine manufacturer selling in Germany will be placed at a competitive disadvantage if dollar depreciation allows its principal competitor, located in the United States, to sell at a lower price in Germany. Purchasing out-of-the-money put options on the dollar and selling them for a profit if they move into the money (which will happen if the dollar depreciates enough) will allow the Swiss firm to partly compensate for its lost competitiveness. The exposure is not contractually set, so forward contracts are again not as useful as options in this situation.

Options versus Forward Contracts The ideal use of forward contracts is when the exposure has a straight risk-reward profile: Forward contract gains or losses are exactly offset by losses or gains on the underlying transaction. If the transaction exposure is uncertain, however, because the volume or the foreign currency prices of the items being bought or sold are unknown, a forward contract will not match it. By contrast, currency options are a good hedging tool in situations in which the quantity of foreign exchange to be received or paid out is uncertain.

 ILLUSTRATION *How Cadbury Schweppes Uses Currency Options*

Cadbury Schweppes, the British candy manufacturer, uses currency options to hedge uncertain payables. The price of its key product input, cocoa, is quoted in sterling but is really a dollar-based product. That is, as the value of the dollar changes, the sterling price of cocoa changes as well. The objective of the company's foreign exchange strategy is to eliminate the currency element in the decision to purchase the commodity, thus leaving the company's buyers able to concentrate on fundamentals. However, this task is complicated by the fact that the company's projections of its future purchases are highly uncertain.

As a result, Cadbury Schweppes has turned to currency options. After netting its total exposure, the company covers with forward contracts a base number of exposed, known payables. It covers the remaining—uncertain—portion with options. The options act as an insurance policy.

A company could use currency options to hedge its exposure in lieu of forward contracts. However, each type of hedging instrument is more advantageous in some situations, and it makes sense to match the instrument to the specific situation. The general rules to follow when choosing between currency options and forward contracts for hedging purposes are summarized as follows:

Forward contracts can be used to hedge the known portion of foreign currency cash flows, and options the uncertain remainder.

1. When the quantity of a foreign currency cash outflow is known, buy the currency forward; when the quantity is unknown, buy a call option on the currency.

2. When the quantity of a foreign currency cash inflow is known, sell the currency forward; when the quantity is unknown, buy a put option on the currency.

3. When the quantity of a foreign currency cash flow is partially known and partially uncertain, use a forward contract to hedge the known portion and an option to hedge the maximum value of the uncertain remainder.[10]

These rules presume that the financial manager's objective is to reduce risk and not to speculate on the direction or volatility of future currency movements. They also presume that both forward and options contracts are fairly priced. In an efficient market, the expected value or cost of either of these contracts should be zero. Any other result would introduce the possibility of arbitrage profits. The presence of such profits would attract arbitrageurs as surely as bees are attracted to honey. Their subsequent attempts to profit from inappropriate prices would return these prices to their equilibrium values.

MINI-CASE   *Help DKNY Cover Up Its Mexican Peso Transaction Exposure*

DKNY, the apparel design firm, owes Mex$ 7 million in 30 days for a recent shipment of textiles from Mexico. DKNY's treasurer is considering hedging the company's peso exposure on this shipment and is looking for some help in figuring out what her different hedging options might cost and which option is preferable. You call up your favorite foreign exchange trader and receive the following interest rate and exchange rate quotes:

Spot rate:	*Mex$ 13.0/$*
Forward rate (30 days):	*Mex$ 13.1/$*
30-day put option on dollars at Mex$ 12.9/$	*1% premium*
30-day call option on dollars at Mex$ 13.1/$	*3% premium*
U.S. dollar 30-day interest rate (annualized)	*7.5%*
Peso 30-day interest rate (annualized)	*15%*

Based on these quotes, the treasurer presents you with a series of questions that she would like you to address.

---

[10] For elaboration, see Ian H. Giddy, "The Foreign Exchange Option as a Hedging Tool," *Midland Corporate Finance Journal,* Fall 1983, pp. 32–42.

QUESTIONS

1. What hedging options are available to DKNY?

2. What is the hedged cost of DKNY's payable using a forward market hedge?

3. What is the hedged cost of DKNY's payable using a money market hedge?

4. What is the hedged cost of DKNY's payable using a put option?

5. At what exchange rate is the cost of the put option just equal to the cost of the forward market hedge? To the cost of the money market hedge?

6. How can DKNY construct a currency collar? What is the net premium paid for the currency collar? Using this currency collar, what is the net dollar cost of the payable if the spot rate in 30 days is Mex$12.8/$? Mex$13.1/$? Mex$13.4/$?

7. What is the preferred alternative?

8. Suppose that DKNY expects the 30-day spot rate to be Mex$13.4/$. Should it hedge this payable? What other factors should go into DKNY's hedging decision?

10.8 SUMMARY AND CONCLUSIONS

In this chapter, we examined the concept of exposure to exchange rate changes from the perspective of the accountant. The accountant's concern is the appropriate way to translate foreign-currency–denominated items on financial statements to their home currency values. If currency values change, translation gains or losses may result. We surveyed the four principal translation methods available: the current/noncurrent method, the monetary/nonmonetary method, the temporal method, and the current rate method. In addition, we analyzed the present translation method mandated by the Financial Accounting Standards Board, FASB-52.

Regardless of the translation method selected, measuring accounting exposure is conceptually the same. It involves determining which foreign-currency-denominated assets and liabilities will be translated at the current (postchange) exchange rate and which will be translated at the historical (prechange) exchange rate. The former items are considered to be exposed, whereas the latter items are regarded as not exposed. Translation exposure is simply the difference between exposed assets and exposed liabilities.

Hedging this exposure is a complicated and difficult task. As a first step, the firm must specify an operational set of goals for those involved in exchange risk management. Failure to do so can lead to possibly conflicting and costly actions on the part of employees. We saw that the hedging objective that is most consistent with the overarching objective of maximizing shareholder value is to reduce exchange risk, where exchange risk is defined as that element of cash-flow variability attributable to currency fluctuations. This objective translates into the following exposure management goal: to arrange a firm's financial affairs in such a way that however the exchange rate may move in the future, the effects on dollar returns are minimized.

We saw that firms normally cope with anticipated currency changes by engaging in forward contracts, borrowing locally, and adjusting their pricing and credit policies. However, there is reason to question the value of much of this activity. In fact, in normal circumstances hedging cannot provide protection against expected exchange rate changes.

A number of empirical studies indicate that on average the forward rate appears to be an unbiased estimate of the future spot rate. On the other hand, the evidence also points to the possibility of bias in the forward rate at any point in time. However, trying to take advantage of this apparent bias via selective hedging is likely to expose the company to increased risk.

Furthermore, according to the international Fisher effect, in the absence of government controls, interest rate differentials among countries should equal anticipated currency devaluations or revaluations. Empirical research substantiates the notion that over time, gains or losses on debt in hard currencies tend to be offset by low interest rates; in soft currencies, they will be offset by higher interest rates unless, of course, there are barriers that preclude equalization of real interest rates. Again, to the extent that bias exists in the interest rate differential—because of a risk premium or other factor—the risk associated with selective hedging is likely to offset any expected gains.

The other hedging methods, which involve factoring anticipated exchange rate changes into pricing and credit decisions, can be profitable only at the expense of others. Thus, to consistently gain by these trade-term adjustments, it is necessary to deal continuously with less-knowledgeable people. Certainly, however, a policy predicated on the continued existence of naive firms is unlikely to be viable for very long in the highly competitive and well-informed world of international business. The real value to a firm of factoring currency change expectations into its pricing and credit decisions is to prevent others from profiting at its expense.

The basic value of hedging, therefore, is to protect a company against unexpected exchange rate changes; however, by definition, these changes are unpredictable and, consequently, impossible to profit from. To the extent that a government does not permit interest or forward rates to fully adjust to market expectations, a firm with access to these financial instruments can expect, on average, to gain from currency changes. Nevertheless, the very nature of these imperfections severely restricts a company's ability to engage in such profitable financial operations.

QUESTIONS

1. What is translation exposure? Transaction exposure?

2. What are the basic translation methods? How do they differ?

3. What factors affect a company's translation exposure? What can the company do to affect its degree of translation exposure?

4. What alternative hedging transactions are available to a company seeking to hedge the translation exposure of its German subsidiary? How would the appropriate hedge change if the German affiliate's functional currency were the U.S. dollar?

5. In order to eliminate all risk on its exports to Japan, a company decides to hedge both its actual and anticipated sales there. To what risk is the company exposing itself? How could this risk be managed?

6. Instead of its previous policy of always hedging its foreign currency receivables, Sun Microsystems has decided to hedge only when it believes the dollar will strengthen. Otherwise, it will go uncovered. Comment on this new policy.

7. Your bank is working with an American client who wishes to hedge its long exposure in the Malaysian ringgit. Suppose it is possible to invest in ringgit but not borrow in that currency. However, you can both borrow and lend in U.S. dollars.

   a. Assuming there is no forward market in ringgit, can you create a homemade forward contract that would allow your client to hedge its ringgit exposure?

   b. Several of your Malaysian clients are interested in selling their U.S. dollar export earnings forward for ringgit. Can you accommodate them by creating a forward contract?

8. Eastman Kodak gives its traders bonuses if their selective hedging strategies are less expensive than the cost of hedging all their transaction exposure on a continuous basis. What problems can you foresee from this bonus plan?

9. Many managers prefer to use options to hedge their exposure because it allows them the possibility of capitalizing on favorable movements in the exchange rate. In contrast, a company using forward contracts avoids the downside but also loses the upside potential as well. Comment on this strategy.

10. In January 1988, Arco bought a 24.3 percent stake in the British oil firm Britoil PLC. It intended to buy a further $1 billion worth of Britoil stock if Britoil was agreeable. However, Arco was uncertain whether Britoil, which had expressed a strong desire to remain independent, would accept its bid. To guard against the possibility of a pound appreciation in the interim, Arco decided to convert $1 billion into pounds and place them on deposit in London, pending the outcome of its discussions with Britoil's management. What exchange risk did Arco face, and did it choose the best way to protect itself from that risk?

PROBLEMS

1. Suppose that at the start and at the end of the year, Bell U.K., the British subsidiary of Bell U.S., has current assets of £1 million, fixed assets of £2 million, and current liabilities of £1 million. Bell has no long-term liabilities.

   a. What is Bell U.K.'s translation exposure under the current/noncurrent, monetary/nonmonetary, temporal, and current rate methods?

   b. Assuming the pound is the functional currency, if the pound depreciates during the year from $1.50 to $1.30, what will be the FASB-52 translation gain (loss) to be included in the equity account of Bell's U.S. parent?

   c. Redo part (b) assuming the dollar is the functional currency. Included in current assets is inventory of £0.5 million. The historical exchange rates for inventory and fixed assets are $1.45 and $1.65, respectively. If the dollar is the functional currency, where does Bell U.K.'s translation gain or loss show up on Bell U.S.'s financial statements?

2. Rolls-Royce, the British jet engine manufacturer, sells engines to U.S. airlines and buys parts from U.S. companies. Suppose it has accounts receivable of $1.5 billion and accounts payable of $740 million. It also has borrowed $600 million. The current spot rate is $1.5128/£.

   a. What is Rolls-Royce's dollar transaction exposure in dollar terms? In pound terms?

   b. Suppose the pound appreciates to $1.7642/£. What is Rolls-Royce's gain or loss, in pound terms, on its dollar transaction exposure?

3. Zapata Auto Parts, the Mexican affiliate of American Diversified, Inc., had the following balance sheet on January 1:

Assets (Mex$ millions)		Liabilities (Mex$ millions)	
Cash, marketable securities	Mex$1,000	Current liabilities	Mex$47,000
Accounts receivable	50,000	Long-term debt	12,000
Inventory	32,000	Equity	135,000
Net fixed assets	111,000		
Total assets	Mex$194,000	Liabilities plus equity	Mex$194,000

The exchange rate on January 1 was Mex$ 8,000 = $1.

   a. What is Zapata's FASB-52 peso translation exposure on January 1?

   b. Suppose the exchange rate on December 31 is Mex$ 12,000. What will be Zapata's translation loss for the year?

   c. Zapata can borrow an additional Mex$ 15,000 million. What will happen to its translation exposure if it uses the funds to pay a dividend to its parent? If it uses the funds to increase its cash position?

4. Walt Disney expects to receive a Mex$16 million theatrical fee from Mexico in 90 days. The current spot rate is $0.1321/Mex$, and the 90-day forward rate is $0.1242/Mex$.

   a. What is Disney's peso transaction exposure associated with this fee?

   b. If the spot rate expected in 90 days is $0.1305, what is the expected U.S. dollar value of the fee?

   c. What is the hedged dollar value of the fee?

   d. What factors will influence the hedging decision?

5. A foreign exchange trader assesses the euro exchange rate three months hence as follows:

   $1.11 with probability 0.25

   $1.13 with probability 0.50

   $1.15 with probability 0.25

   The 90-day forward rate is $1.12.

   a. Will the trader buy or sell euros forward against the dollar if she is concerned solely with expected values? In what volume?

   b. In reality, what is likely to limit the trader's speculative activities?

   c. Suppose the trader revises her probability assessment as follows:

   $1.09 with probability 0.33

   $1.13 with probability 0.33

   $1.17 with probability 0.33

   If the forward rate remains at $1.12, will this new assessment affect the trader's decision? Explain.

6. An investment manager hedges a portfolio of Bunds (German government bonds) with a six-month forward contract. The current spot rate is €1.64/$, and the 180-day forward rate is €1.61/$. At the end of the six-month period, the Bunds have risen in value by 3.75 percent (in euro terms), and the spot rate is now €1.46/$.

   a. If the Bunds earn interest at the annual rate of 5 percent, paid semiannually, what is the investment manager's total dollar return on the hedged Bunds?

   b. What would the return on the Bunds have been without hedging?

   c. What was the true cost of the forward contract?

7. Magnetronics, Inc., a U.S. company, owes its Taiwanese supplier NT$205 million in three months. The company wishes to hedge its NT$ payable. The current spot rate is NT$1 = U.S.$0.03987, and the three-month forward rate is NT$1 = U.S.$0.04051. Magnetronics can also borrow or lend U.S. dollars at an annualized interest rate of 12 percent and Taiwanese dollars at an annualized interest rate of 8 percent.

   a. What is the U.S. dollar accounting entry for this payable?

   b. What is the minimum U.S. dollar cost that Magnetronics can lock in for this payable? Describe the procedure it would use to get this price.

   c. At what forward rate would interest rate parity hold given the interest rates?

8. Cooper Inc., a U.S. firm, has just invested £500,000 in a note that will come due in 90 days and is yielding 9.5 percent annualized. The current spot value of the pound is $1.5612, and the 90-day forward rate is $1.5467.

   a. What is the hedged dollar value of this note at maturity?

   b. What is the annualized dollar yield on the hedged note?

   c. Cooper anticipates that the value of the pound in 90 days will be $1.5550. Should it hedge? Why or why not?

   d. Suppose that Cooper has a payable of £980,000 coming due in 180 days. Should this affect its decision of whether to hedge its sterling note? How and why?

9. American Airlines is trying to decide how to go about hedging SFr70 million in ticket sales receivable in 180 days. Suppose it faces the following exchange and interest rates.

Spot rate:	$0.6433–42/SFr
Forward rate (180 days):	$0.6578–99/SFr
Swiss franc 180-day interest rate (annualized):	4.01%–3.97%
U.S. dollar 180-day interest rate (annualized):	8.01%–7.98%

   a. What is the hedged value of American's ticket sales using a forward market hedge?

   b. What is the hedged value of American's ticket sales using a money-market hedge? Assume the first interest rate is the rate at which money can be borrowed and the second one the rate at which it can be lent.

   c. Which hedge is less expensive?

   d. Is there an arbitrage opportunity here?

   e. Suppose the expected spot rate in 180 days is $0.67/SFr, with a most likely range of $0.64–$0.70/SFr. Should American hedge? What factors should enter into its decision?

10. Madison Inc. imports olive oil from Chilean firms, and the invoices are always denominated in pesos (Ch$). It currently has a payable in the amount of Ch$250 million that it would like to hedge. Unfortunately, Madison is having difficulty arranging a peso forward contract. Its treasurer, who recently received her MBA, suggests using the Brazilian *real* to cross-hedge the peso exposure. She recently ran the following regression of the change in the exchange rate for the peso against the change in the *real* exchange rate:

$$\Delta Ch\$/US\$ = 1.6(\Delta R/\$)$$

   a. There is an active market in the forward *real*. To cross-hedge Madison's peso exposure, should the treasurer buy or sell the *real* forward?

   b. What is the risk-minimizing amount of reais that the treasurer would have to buy or sell forward to hedge Madison's drachma exposure?

BIBLIOGRAPHY

Bishop, Matthew. "A Survey of Corporate Risk Management." *The Economist*, February 10, 1996, special section.

Cornell, Bradford, and Alan C. Shapiro. "Managing Foreign Exchange Risks." *Midland Corporate Finance Journal*, Fall 1983, pp. 16–31.

Dufey, Gunter, and Sam L. Srinivasulu. "The Case for Corporate Management of Foreign Exchange Risk." *Financial Management*, Summer 1984, pp. 54–62.

Evans, Thomas G., and William R. Folks, Jr. "Defining Objectives for Exposure Management." *Business International Money Report*, February 2, 1979, pp. 37–39.

Folks, William R., Jr. "Decision Analysis for Exchange Risk Management." *Financial Management*, Winter 1972, pp. 101–112.

Giddy, Ian H. "The Foreign Exchange Option as a Hedging Tool." *Midland Corporate Finance Journal*, Fall 1983, pp. 32–42.

Goeltz, Richard K. *Managing Liquid Funds on an International Scope*. New York: Joseph E. Seagram and Sons, 1971.

Shapiro, Alan C., and David P. Rutenberg. "Managing Exchange Risks in a Floating World." *Financial Management*, Summer 1976, pp. 48–58.

Srinivasulu, Sam, and Edward Massura. "Sharing Currency Risks in Long-Term Contracts." *Business International Money Reports*, February 23, 1987, pp. 57–59.

Statement of Financial Accounting Standards No. 52. Stamford, Conn.: Financial Accounting Standards Board, December 1981.

Zenoff, David B. "Applying Management Principles to Foreign Exchange Exposure." *Euromoney*, September 1978, pp. 123–130.

INTERNET RESOURCES

www.fasb.org Web site of the Financial Accounting Standards Board. Provides information on FASB-52 and other FASB pronouncements on currency translation and hedge accounting.

www.florin.com/v4/valore4.html Web site that contains material discussing currency risk management.

www.reportgallery.com Web site that contains links to annual reports of over 2,200 companies, many of which are multinationals.

1. Go to General Electric's home page (www.ge.com) and find its latest annual report. What is General Electric's accumulated translation adjustment? Does General Electric use any functional currencies other than the dollar? What was GE's reported currency translation gain or loss during the year? What exchange rates (year-end or average) did GE use to translate its asset and liability accounts and revenue and expense items?

2. What are the latest FASB pronouncements dealing with currency translations?

3. Review the annual reports on the Web sites of three of the multinational companies listed in www.reportgallery.com.

    a.   What types of currency exposure are these companies hedging?

    b.   What hedging techniques are they using?

    c.   What hedging strategy (if any) appears to underlie their hedging activities?

MEASURING AND MANAGING ECONOMIC EXPOSURE

Let's face it. If you've got 75 percent of your assets in the U.S. and 50 percent of your sales outside it, and the dollar's strong, you've got problems.

Donald V. Fites
Executive Vice President
Caterpillar Inc.

CHAPTER LEARNING OBJECTIVES

- To define economic exposure and exchange risk and distinguish between the two
- To define operating exposure and distinguish between it and transaction exposure
- To identify the basic factors that determine the foreign exchange risk faced by a particular company or project
- To calculate economic exposure given a particular exchange rate change and specific cost and revenue scenarios
- To describe the marketing, production, and financial strategies that are appropriate for coping with the economic consequences of exchange rate changes
- To explain how companies can develop contingency plans to cope with exchange risk and the consequences of their ability to rapidly respond to currency changes
- To identify the role of the financial executive in facilitating the operation of an integrated exchange risk management program

KEY TERMS

competitive exposure
currency of denomination
currency of determination
differentiated products
economic exposure
exchange risk
flow-back effect
market selection
operating exposure
outsourcing
plant location

price elasticity of demand
pricing flexibility
pricing strategy
product cycles
product innovation
production shifting
product sourcing
product strategy
real exchange rate
transaction exposure

Chapter 10 focused on the accounting effects of currency changes. As we saw in that chapter, the adoption of FASB-52 has helped to moderate the wild swings in the translated earnings of overseas subsidiaries. Nevertheless, the problem of coping with volatile currencies remains essentially unchanged. Fluctuations in exchange rates will continue to have "real" effects on the cash profitability of foreign subsidiaries—complicating overseas selling, pricing, buying, and plant-location decisions.

This chapter develops an appropriate definition of foreign exchange risk. It discusses the *economic,* as distinguished from the accounting, consequences of currency changes on a firm's value and shows how economic exposure can be measured. This chapter also discusses the marketing, production, and financial management strategies that are appropriate for coping with the economic consequences of exchange rate changes.

11.1 FOREIGN EXCHANGE RISK AND ECONOMIC EXPOSURE

There is a major discrepancy between accounting practice and economic reality in terms of measuring exposure to exchange rate changes.

The most important aspect of foreign exchange risk management is to incorporate currency change expectations into *all* basic corporate decisions. In performing this task, the firm must know what is at risk. However, there is a major discrepancy between accounting practice and economic reality in terms of measuring *exposure,* which is the degree to which a company is affected by exchange rate changes.

As we saw in Chapter 10, those who use an accounting definition of exposure—whether FASB-52 or some other method—divide the balance sheet's assets and liabilities into those accounts that will be affected by exchange rate changes and those that will not. In contrast, economic theory focuses on the impact of an exchange rate change on future cash flows. That is, **economic exposure** is based on the extent to which the value of the firm—as measured by the present value of its expected future cash flows—will change when exchange rates change.

Companies should focus on the economic effects of currency changes rather than the accounting effects.

Specifically, if *PV* is the present value of a firm, then that firm is exposed to currency risk if $\Delta PV/\Delta e$ is not equal to zero, where ΔPV is the change in the firm's present value associated with an exchange rate change, Δe. **Exchange risk,** in turn, is defined as the variability in the firm's value that is caused by uncertain exchange rate changes. Thus, exchange risk is viewed as the possibility that currency fluctuations can alter the expected amounts or variability of the firm's future cash flows.

Economic exposure focuses on the cash flow effects of exchange rate changes.

Economic exposure can be separated into two components: transaction exposure and operating exposure. We saw that **transaction exposure** stems from exchange gains or losses on foreign-currency-denominated contractual obligations. Although transaction exposure is often included under accounting exposure, as it was in Chapter 10, it is more properly a cash-flow exposure and, hence, part of economic exposure. However, even if the company prices all contracts in dollars or otherwise hedges its transaction exposure, the residual exposure—longer-term operating exposure—still remains.

Operating exposure arises because currency fluctuations can alter a company's future revenues and costs—that is, its operating cash flows. Consequently, measuring a firm's operating exposure requires a longer-term perspective, viewing the firm as an ongoing concern with operations whose cost and price competitiveness could be affected by exchange rate changes.

Thus, the firm faces operating exposure the moment it invests in servicing a market subject to foreign competition or in sourcing goods or inputs abroad. This investment includes new-product development, a distribution network, foreign supply contracts, or production facilities. Transaction exposure arises later on and only if the company's commitments lead it to engage in foreign-currency-denominated sales or purchases. Exhibit 11.1 shows the time pattern of economic exposure.

EXHIBIT 11.1 • THE TIME PATTERN OF ECONOMIC EXPOSURE

Noncontractural	Quasi-Contractural	Contractural	
Investment in new product develop-ment, distribution facilities, brand name, marketing, foreign production capacity, foreign sup-plier relationships	Quote foreign currency price, receive a foreign currency price quote	Ship product/bill customers in foreign currency, receive bill for supplies in foreign currency	Collect foreign currency receivables, pay foreign currency liabilities

ILLUSTRATION *American Filmmakers Suffer When the Euro Slumps*

According to a recent story in the *Wall Street Journal* (May 19, 2000, p. B1), "The euro's plunge against the dollar is casting a pall over this year's Cannes Film Festival, forcing European distributors to curtail their purchases of American films and triggering concessions by U.S. producers of a sort once unheard of in this glitzy resort." The euro's decline by 24 percent against the dollar is a problem for European distributors because the international movie business is priced almost exclusively in dollars; it is a problem for U.S. producers because Europe is such a big market for American films. Before a film goes into production, a studio will usually "presell" the foreign rights to distributors and use these presale revenues to finance the film's production. The presale of rights to continental European distribution often accounts for about a third of a film's budget. The rise in the value of the dollar has hurt the prices that U.S. producers can get for these rights. At the same time, the higher euro prices for these rights has caused European distributors to seek better financing terms, such as stretching out payment for their acquired rights. Although some U.S. producers have talked about switching to pricing their rights in euros, the problem of a fallen euro would still remain: If the euro price is set at a level that yields the same dollar price, European distributors will face the same higher cost; if it is set at the same euro price as in the past, the U.S. producer will receive fewer dollars.

ILLUSTRATION *European Manufacturers Suffer When the Euro Soars*

At the beginning of 2002, the euro was about $0.86. By mid-2003, it had soared to $1.15, a rise of over 33 percent. European manufacturers suffered a profit squeeze on their exports as well as on goods competing against American imports. Consider, for example, the problems facing Head NV, the Dutch sporting-goods maker. The immediate impact of euro appreciation is to make dollar sales less valuable when converted into euros. For example, a tennis racket it might sell in the United States for $50 brought back €58.14 when the euro was at $0.86 (50/0.86) but would translate into only €43.48 at an exchange rate of $1.15 (50/1.15). With Head's costs set in euros, the result of euro appreciation is severe margin pressure on its U.S. exports. If Head decides to raise its dollar prices to improve its euro profit margin, it will lose export sales. European companies also face greater competitive pressure in their home markets as well as in third-country markets from U.S. companies selling in those markets. The reason: Given the large jump in the euro's value, U.S. exporters can offer foreign customers lower prices expressed in euros, while maintaining or improving their dollar profit margins.

Real Exchange Rate Changes and Exchange Risk

The exchange rate changes that give rise to operating exposure are real exchange rate changes. As presented in Chapter 4, the **real exchange rate** is defined as the nominal exchange rate (for example, the number of dollars per franc) adjusted for changes in the relative purchasing power of each currency since some base period. Specifically,

A company's operating exposure is only affected by changes in the real exchange rate.

$$e'_1 = e_1 \times \frac{1 + i_f}{1 + i_h} \tag{11.1}$$

where

e'_1 = the real exchange rate (home currency per one unit of foreign currency) at time 1

e_1 = the nominal exchange rate (home currency per one unit of foreign currency) at time 1

i_f = the amount of foreign inflation between times 0 and 1

i_h = the amount of domestic inflation between times 0 and 1

Given that the base period nominal rate, e_0, is also the real base period exchange rate, the change in the real exchange rate can be computed as follows:

$$\frac{e_1' - e_0}{e_0} \tag{11.2}$$

For example, suppose the Danish krone has devalued by 5 percent during the year. At the same time, Danish and U.S. inflation rates were 3 percent and 2 percent, respectively. Then, according to Equation 11.1, if e_0 is the exchange rate (dollar value of the krone) at the beginning of the year, the real exchange rate for the krone at year's end is

$$0.95e_0 \times \frac{1.03}{1.02} = 0.96e_0$$

Applying Equation 11.2, we can see that the real value of the krone has declined by 4 percent during the year:

$$\frac{0.96e_0 - e_0}{e_0} = -4\%$$

In effect, the krone's 5 percent nominal devaluation more than offset the 1 percent inflation differential between Denmark and the United States, leading to a 4 percent decline in the real value of the krone.

Importance of the Real Exchange Rate

The distinction between the nominal exchange rate and the real exchange rate is important because of their vastly different implications for exchange risk. A dramatic change in the nominal exchange rate accompanied by an equal change in the price level should have no effects on the relative competitive positions of domestic firms and their foreign competitors and, therefore, will not alter real cash flows. Alternatively, if the real exchange rate changes, it will cause relative price changes—changes in the ratio of domestic goods' prices to prices of foreign goods. In terms of currency changes affecting relative competitiveness, therefore, the focus must be not on nominal exchange rate changes, but instead on changes in the purchasing power of one currency relative to another. Put another way, it is impossible to assess the effects of an exchange rate change without simultaneously considering the impact on cash flows of the underlying relative rates of inflation associated with each currency.

Inflation and Exchange Risk

Let us begin by holding relative prices constant and looking only at the effects of general inflation. This condition means that if the inflation rate is 10 percent, the price of every good in the economy rises by 10 percent. In addition, we will initially assume that all goods are traded in a competitive world market without transaction costs, tariffs, or taxes of any kind. Given these conditions, economic theory tells us that the law of one price must prevail. That is, the price of any good, measured in a common currency, must be equal in all countries.

Companies face no operating exchange risk if exchange rate changes are fully off-set by differences in inflation rates.

If the law of one price holds and if there is no variation in the relative prices of goods or services, then the rate of change in the exchange rate must equal the difference between the inflation rates in the two countries. The implications of a constant real exchange rate—that is, that purchasing power parity (PPP) holds—are worth exploring further. To begin, purchasing power parity does not imply that exchange rate changes will necessarily be small or easy to forecast. If a country has high and unpredictable inflation (for example, Russia), then the country's exchange rate will also fluctuate randomly.

Nonetheless, without relative price changes, a multinational company faces no real operating exchange risk. As long as the firm avoids contracts fixed in foreign currency terms, its foreign cash flows will vary with the foreign rate of inflation. Because the exchange rate also depends on the difference between the foreign and the domestic rates of inflation, the movement of the exchange rate exactly cancels the change in the foreign price level, leaving real dollar cash flows unaffected.

 LLUSTRATION *Calculating the Effects of Exchange Rate Changes and Inflation on Apex Philippines*

Apex Philippines, the Philippine subsidiary of Apex Company, produces and sells medical imaging devices in the Philippines. At the current peso exchange rate of P1 = $0.01, the devices cost P40,000 ($400) to produce and sell for P100,000 ($1,000). The profit margin of P60,000 provides a dollar margin of $600. Suppose that Philippine inflation during the year is 20 percent, and the U.S. inflation rate is zero. All prices and costs are assumed to move in line with inflation. If we assume that purchasing power parity holds, the peso will devalue to $0.0083 [0.01 × (1/1.2)]. The real value of the peso stays at $0.01 [0.0083 × (1.2/1.0)], so Apex Philippines dollar profit margin will remain at $600. These effects are shown in Exhibit 11.2.

Of course, the conclusion in the Apex Philippines illustration does not hold if the firm enters into contracts fixed in terms of the foreign currency. Examples of such contracts are debt with fixed interest rates, long-term leases, labor contracts, and rent. However, if the real exchange rate remains constant, the risk introduced by entering into fixed price contracts is not exchange risk; it is inflation risk. For instance, a Mexican firm with fixed-rate debt in pesos faces the same risk as the subsidiary of an American firm with peso debt. If the rate of inflation declines, the real interest cost of the debt rises, and the real cash flow of both companies falls. The solution to the problem of inflation risk is to avoid writing contracts fixed in nominal terms in countries with unpredictable inflation. If the contracts are indexed and if the real exchange rate remains constant, exchange risk is eliminated.

EXHIBIT 11.2 • THE EFFECTS OF NOMINAL EXCHANGE RATE CHANGES AND INFLATION ON APEX PHILIPPINES

Price Level	Philippines	United States
Beginning of year	100	100
End of year	120	100

Exchange Rate	Beginning of Year	End of Year
Nominal rate	P1 = $0.01	P1 = $0.0083
Real Rate	P1 = $0.01	P1 = $0.0083 × 1.2/1
		= $0.01

Profit Impact	Beginning of Year		End of Year	
	Pesos	U.S. Dollars	Pesos	U.S. Dollars
Price*	P100,000	$1,000	P120,000	$1,000
Cost of production*	40,000	400	48,000	400
Profit margin	P60,000	$600	P72,000	$600

*Peso prices and costs are assumed to increase at the 20% rate of Philippine inflation.

Competitive Effects of Real Exchange Rate Changes

In general, a decline in the real value of a nation's currency makes its exports and import-competing goods more competitive. Conversely, an appreciating currency hurts the nation's exporters and those producers competing with imports.

When the real value of the dollar began rising against other currencies during the early 1980s. U.S. exporters found themselves with the unpleasant choice of either keeping dollar prices constant and losing sales volume (because foreign currency prices rose in line with the appreciating dollar), or setting prices in the foreign currency to maintain market share, with a corresponding erosion in dollar revenues and profit margins. At the same time, the dollar cost of American labor remained the same or rose in line with U.S. inflation. The combination of lower dollar revenues and unchanged or higher dollar costs resulted in severe hardship for those U.S. companies selling abroad. Similarly, U.S. manufacturers competing domestically with imports whose dollar prices were declining saw both their profit margins and sales volumes reduced. In a great reversal of fortune, Japanese firms then had to cope with a yen that appreciated by more than 150 percent in real terms between 1985 and 1995.

> An increase (decrease) in the real value of the dollar hurts (helps) U.S. companies facing foreign competition both at home and abroad.

ILLUSTRATION *Yen Appreciation Harms Japanese TV Producers*

For most of 1985, the yen traded at about ¥240 = $1. By 1995, the yen's value had risen to about ¥90 = $1, without a commensurate increase in U.S. inflation. This rise had a highly negative impact on Japanese television manufacturers. If it cost, say, ¥100,000 to build a color TV in Japan, ship it to the United States, and earn a normal profit, that TV could be sold in 1985 for about $417 (100,000/240). However, in 1995, the price would have had to be about $1,111 (100,000/90) for Japanese firms to break even, presenting them with the following dilemma. Because other U.S. prices had not risen much, as Japanese firms raised their dollar price to compensate for yen appreciation, Americans would buy fewer Japanese color TVs, and yen revenues would fall. If Japanese TV producers decided to keep their price constant at $417 to preserve market share in the United

States, they would have to cut their yen price to about ¥37,530 (417 × 90). In general, whether they held the line on yen prices or cut them, real yen appreciation was bad news for Japanese TV manufacturers. Subsequent yen depreciation eased the pressure on Japanese companies.

Alternatively, Industrias Penoles, the Mexican firm that is the world's largest refiner of newly mined silver, increased its dollar profits by more than 200 percent after the real devaluation of the Mexican peso relative to the dollar in 1982. Similarly, when the peso plunged in 1995, the company saw its profits rise again. The reason for the firm's success is that its costs, which are in pesos, declined in dollar terms, and the dollar value of its revenues, which are derived from exports, held steady.

A fixed exchange rate may lead to more, not less, exchange risk.

In summary, the economic impact of a currency change on a firm depends on whether the exchange rate change is fully offset by the difference in inflation rates or whether (because of price controls, a shift in monetary policy, or some other reason) the real exchange rate and, hence, relative prices, change. It is these relative price changes that ultimately determine a firm's long-run exposure.

A less obvious point is that a firm may face more exchange risk if nominal exchange rates do *not* change. The example involving Chile makes this point.

 ILLUSTRATION   *Chile Mismanages Its Exchange Rate*

A particularly dramatic illustration of the unfortunate effects of a fixed nominal exchange rate combined with high domestic inflation is provided by Chile. As part of its plan to bring down the rate of Chilean inflation, the government fixed the exchange rate in the middle of 1979 at 39 pesos to the U.S. dollar. Over the next two and a half years, the Chilean price level rose 60 percent, but U.S. prices rose by only about 30 percent. Thus, by early 1982, the Chilean peso had appreciated in real terms by approximately 23 percent (1.6/1.3 – 1) against the U.S. dollar. These data are summarized in Exhibit 11.3.

EXHIBIT 11.2 • NOMINAL AND REAL EXCHANGE RATES FOR CHILE, 1979–1982

Price Level		*Chile*	*United States*
1979		100	100
1982		160	130
Nominal Exchange Rate	1979	Ps. 1 = $0.02564	
	1982	Ps. 1 = $0.02564	
Real Exchange Rate	1979	Ps. 1 = $0.02564	
	1982	Ps. 1 = $0.02564 × $\frac{1.60}{1.30}$	
		= $0.03156	

Increase in Real Value of the $\dfrac{0.03156 - 0.02564}{0.02564}$ = 23.1%
    Chilean Peso

Result: Economic Devastation

—Loss of export markets

—Loss of domestic markets to imports

—Massive unemployment

—Numerous bankruptcies

—Numerous bank failures

An 18 percent "corrective" devaluation was enacted in June 1982. Overall, the peso fell 90 percent over the next twelve months. However, the artificially high peso had already done its double damage to the Chilean economy: It made Chile's manufactured products more expensive abroad, pricing many of them out of international trade; and it made imports cheaper, undercutting Chilean domestic industries. The effects of the over-valued peso were devastating. Banks became insolvent, factories and copper smelters were thrown into bankruptcy, copper mines were closed, construction projects were shut down, and farms were put on the auction block. Unemployment approached 25 percent, and some areas of Chile resembled industrial graveyards.

The implosion of the Chilean peso did have a silver lining: Chilean companies became dynamic exporters, which today sell chopsticks and salmon to Japan, wine to Europe, and machinery to the United States. It also sped the acceptance of free market economic policies, which have given Chile one of the strongest growth rates in the world.

An increase in the real value of a currency acts as a tax on exports and a subsidy on imports.

The Chilean example illustrates a critical point: *An increase in the real value of a currency acts as a tax on exports and a subsidy on imports.* Hence, firms that export or that compete with imports are hurt by an appreciating home currency. Conversely, such firms benefit from home-currency depreciation. These general principles identify a company's economic exposure.

11.2 THE ECONOMIC CONSEQUENCES OF EXCHANGE RATE CHANGES

We now examine more closely the specifics of a firm's economic exposure. Solely for the purpose of exposition, the discussion of exposure is divided into its component parts: transaction exposure and real operating exposure.

Transaction Exposure

Transaction exposure includes both on- and off-balance-sheet items.

Transaction exposure arises out of the various types of transactions that require settlement in a foreign currency. Examples are cross-border trade, borrowing and lending in foreign currencies, and the local purchasing and sales activities of foreign subsidiaries. Strictly speaking, of course, the items already on a firm's balance sheet, such as loans and receivables, capture some of these transactions. However, a detailed transaction exposure report must also contain a number of off-balance-sheet items as well, including future sales and purchases, lease payments, forward contracts, loan repayments, and other contractual or anticipated foreign currency receipts and disbursements.

In terms of measuring economic exposure, however, a transaction exposure report, no matter how detailed, has a fundamental flaw: the assumption that local currency cost and revenue streams remain constant following an exchange rate change.

That assumption does not permit an evaluation of the typical adjustments that consumers and firms can be expected to undertake under conditions of currency change. Hence, attempting to measure the likely exchange gain or loss by simply multiplying the projected pre-devaluation (pre-revaluation) local currency cash flows by the forecast devaluation (revaluation) percentage will lead to misleading results. Given the close relationship between nominal exchange rate changes and inflation as expressed in purchasing power parity, measuring exposure to a currency change without reference to the accompanying inflation is also a misguided task.

We will now take a closer look at the typical demand and cost effects that result from a real exchange rate change and show how these effects combine to determine a firm's true operating exposure. In general, an appreciating real exchange rate can be expected to have the opposite effects. The dollar is assumed to be the home currency (HC).

Operating Exposure

A real exchange rate change affects a number of aspects of the firm's operations. With respect to dollar (HC) appreciation, the key issue for a domestic firm is its degree of **pricing flexibility**—that is, can the firm maintain its dollar margins both at home and abroad? Can the company maintain its dollar price on domestic sales in the face of lower-priced foreign imports? In the case of foreign sales, can the firm raise its foreign currency selling price sufficiently to preserve its dollar profit margin?

The greater pricing flexibility held by companies with differentiated products reduces their exchange risk.

The answers to these questions depend largely on the **price elasticity of demand**. The less price elastic the demand, the more price flexibility a company will have to respond to exchange rate changes. Price elasticity, in turn, depends on the degree of competition and the location of key competitors. The more **differentiated** (distinct) a company's products are, the less competition it will face and the greater its ability will be to maintain its domestic currency prices both at home and abroad. Examples here are IBM and DaimlerChrysler (producer of Mercedes-Benz cars), both of which sell highly differentiated products whose demand has been relatively insensitive to price (at least historically, but competition is changing that). Similarly, if most competitors are based in the home country, then all will face the same change in their cost structure from home currency appreciation, and all can raise their foreign currency prices without putting any of them at a competitive disadvantage relative to their domestic competitors. Examples of this situation are in the precision instrumentation and high-end telecommunications industries, in which virtually all the important players are U.S.-based companies.

Conversely, the less differentiated a company's products are and the more internationally diversified its competitors (for example, the low-priced end of the auto industry) are, the greater the price elasticity of demand for its products will be and the less pricing flexibility it will have. These companies face the greatest amount of exchange risk. For example, in the wake of the Asian currency crisis, Chinese exporters suffered from intense price competition by Asian producers whose currencies had fallen by 40 percent or more against the yuan. The main culprit was the nature of the products they were producing—commodity-type products such as polyester fibers, steel, textiles, and ships that sell almost exclusively on the basis of price. On the other hand, when the yuan fell against other Asian currencies during 2003 (because it was tied to a falling dollar), Chinese manufacturers benefited greatly while other Asian manufacturers were hurt.[1]

 ILLUSTRATION *Product Differentiation and Susceptibility to Exchange Risk of the U.S. Apparel and Textile Industries*

The U.S. textile and apparel industries are highly competitive, with each composed of many small manufacturers. In addition, nearly every country has a textile industry, and apparel industries are also common to most countries.

Despite these similarities, the textile industry exists in a more competitive environment than the apparel industry because textile products are more standardized than apparel products. Buyers of textiles can easily switch from a firm that sells a standard good at a higher price to one that sells virtually the same good at a lower price. Because they are more differentiated, the products of competing apparel firms are viewed as more distinct and are less sensitive than textile goods to changes in prices. Thus, even though both textile and apparel firms operate in highly competitive industries, apparel firms—with their greater degree of pricing flexibility—are less subject to exchange risk than are textile firms.

[1] A falling dollar means that Asian exporters to the United States must either raise their dollar prices to maintain margins or accept lower revenues when converted into their home currencies. An added problem is that the costs of their Chinese competitors are denominated in yuan and the yuan is falling against other Asian currencies in line with the dollar's decline. At the same time, a yuan tied to the dollar means that U.S. manufacturers competing with Chinese firms get less of a boost from a falling dollar.

To cope with their currency risk, American textile manufacturers have slashed their production costs while concentrating on sophisticated textile materials such as industrial fabrics and on goods such as sheets and towels that require little direct labor and are less price sensitive.

American producers are also competing by developing a service edge in the domestic market, which enables them to differentiate even commodity products. For example, the industry developed a computerized inventory management and ordering program, called Quick Response, that provides close coordination among textile mills, apparel manufacturers, and retailers. The system cuts in half the time between a fabric order and delivery of the garment to a retailer and gives all the parties better information for planning, thereby placing foreign manufacturers at a competitive disadvantage. In response, Japanese companies—and even some Korean ones—are looking to set up U.S. factories.

Flexibility in shifting production and in sourcing inputs among countries lowers a firm's operating exposure.

Another important determinant of a company's susceptibility to exchange risk is its ability to shift production and the sourcing of inputs among countries. The greater a company's flexibility to substitute between home-country and foreign-country inputs or production, the less exchange risk the company will face. Other things being equal, firms with worldwide production systems can cope with currency changes by increasing production in a nation whose currency has undergone a real devaluation and decreasing production in a nation whose currency has revalued in real terms.

With respect to a multinational corporation's foreign operations, the determinants of its economic exposure will be similar to those just mentioned. A foreign subsidiary selling goods or services in its local market will generally be unable to raise its local currency (LC) selling price to the full extent of an LC devaluation, causing it to register a decline in its post-devaluation dollar revenues. However, because an LC devaluation will also reduce import competition, the more import competition the subsidiary was facing prior to the devaluation, the smaller its dollar revenue decline will be.

The harmful effects of LC devaluation will be mitigated somewhat since the devaluation should lower the subsidiary's dollar production costs, particularly those attributable to local inputs. However, the higher the import content of local inputs, the less dollar production costs will decline. Inputs used in the export or import-competing sectors will decline less in dollar price than other domestic inputs.

An MNC using its foreign subsidiary as an export platform will benefit from an LC devaluation since its export revenues should stay about the same, whereas its dollar costs will decline. The net result will be a jump in dollar profits for the exporter.

The major conclusion is that the sector of the economy in which a firm operates (export, import-competing, or purely domestic), the sources of the firm's inputs (imports, domestic traded or nontraded goods), and fluctuations in the real exchange rate are far more important in delineating the firm's true economic exposure than is any accounting definition. The economic effects are summarized in Exhibit 11.4.

Domestic facilities that supply foreign markets normally entail more exchange risk than do foreign facilities supplying local markets.

A surprising implication of this analysis is that domestic facilities that supply foreign markets normally entail much greater exchange risk than do foreign facilities that supply local markets. The explanation is that material and labor used in a domestic plant are paid for in the home currency, whereas the products are sold in a foreign currency. For example, take a Japanese company such as Nissan Motors that builds a plant to produce cars for export, primarily to the United States. The company will incur an exchange risk from the point at which it invests in facilities to supply a foreign market (the United States) because its yen expenses will be matched with dollar revenues rather than yen revenues. The point seems obvious; however, all too frequently, firms neglect those effects when analyzing a proposed foreign investment.

EXHIBIT 11.4 • CHARACTERISTIC ECONOMIC EFFECTS OF EXCHANGE RATE CHANGES ON MULTINATIONAL CORPORATIONS

Cash-Flow Categories	Relevant Economic Factors	Devaluation Impact	Revaluation Impact
Revenue		Parent-Currency Revenue Impact	Parent-Currency Revenue Impact
Export sales	Price-sensitive demand	Increase (+ +)	Decrease (− −)
	Price-insensitive demand	Slight increase (+)	Slight decrease (−)
Local sales	Weak prior import competition	Sharp decline (− −)	Increase (+ +)
	Strong prior import competition	Decrease (−) (less than devaluation %)	Slight increase (+)
Costs		Parent-Currency Cost Impact	Parent-Currency Cost Impact
Domestic inputs	Low import content	Decrease (− −)	Increase (+ +)
	High import content/ inputs used in export or import-competing sectors	Slight decrease (−)	Slight increase (+)
Imported inputs	Small local market	Remain the same (0)	Remain the same (0)
	Large local market	Slight decrease (−)	Slight increase (+)
Depreciation		Cash-Flow Impact	Cash-Flow Impact
Fixed assets	No asset valuation adjustment	Decrease by devaluation % (− −)	Increase by revaluation % (+ +)
	Asset valuation adjustment	Decrease (−)	Increase (+)

Note: To interpret the above chart, and taking the impact of a devaluation on local demand as an example, it is assumed that if import competition is weak, local prices will climb slightly, if at all; in such a case, there would be a sharp contraction in parent-company revenue. If imports generate strong competition, local-currency prices are expected to increase, although not to the full extent of the devaluation; in this instance, only a moderate decline in parent-company revenue would be registered.

Source: Alan C. Shapiro, "Developing a Profitable Exposure Management System," reprinted from p. 188 of the June 17, 1977, issue of *Business International Money Report,* with the permission of the Economist Intelligence Unit, NA, Incorporated.

Domestic facilities supplying the domestic market are subject to exchange risk if they face import competition.

Similarly, a facility producing solely for the domestic market and using only domestic sources of inputs can be strongly affected by currency changes, even though its accounting exposure is zero. Consider, for example, a Ford factory in Detroit that produces cars for sale only in the United States and uses only U.S. labor and materials. Because it buys and sells only in dollars, this factory has no accounting exposure. However, because its cars are subject to competition from foreign imports, this plant will be hurt by appreciation of the dollar. Conversely, a dollar depreciation will enhance its competitive position and boost its profits.

11.3 IDENTIFYING ECONOMIC EXPOSURE

At this point, it makes sense to illustrate some of the concepts just discussed by examining several firms to see in what ways they may be susceptible to exchange risk. The companies are Aspen Skiing Company, Petróleos Mexicanos, and Toyota Motor Company.

Aspen Skiing Company

Aspen Skiing Company owns and operates ski resorts in the Colorado Rockies, catering primarily to Americans. It buys all its supplies in dollars and uses only American labor and materials. All guests pay in dollars. Because it buys and sells only in dollars, by U.S. standards it has no accounting exposure. Yet, Aspen Skiing Company does face economic exposure because changes in the value of the dollar affect its competitive position. For example, the strong dollar in the early 1980s adversely affected the company because it led to bargains abroad that offered stiff competition for domestic resorts, including the Rocky Mountain ski areas.

Aspen Skiing Company faces exchange risk because changes in the value of the dollar affect its competitive position.

Despite record snowfalls in the Rockies during the early 1980s, many Americans decided to ski in the European Alps instead. Although airfare to the Alps cost much more than a flight to Colorado, the difference between expenses on the ground made a European ski holiday less expensive. For example, in January 1984, American Express offered a basic one-week ski package in Aspen for $439 per person, including double-occupancy lodging, lift ticket, and free rental car or bus transfer from Denver.[2] Throw in round-trip airfare between New York and Denver of $300 and the trip's cost totaled $739.

At the same time, skiers could spend a week in Chamonix in the French Alps for $234, including lodging, lift ticket, breakfast, and a bus transfer from Geneva, Switzerland. Adding in round-trip airfare from New York of $579 brought the trip's cost to $813. The Alpine vacation became less expensive than the one in the Rockies when the cost of meals was included: an estimated $50 a day in Aspen versus $30 a day in Chamonix.

In effect, Aspen Skiing Company is operating in a global market for skiing or, more broadly, vacation services. As the dollar appreciates in real terms, both foreigners and Americans find less-expensive skiing and vacation alternatives outside the United States. In addition, even if California and other West Coast skiers find that high transportation costs continue to make it more expensive to ski in Europe than in the Rockies, they are not restricted to the American Rockies. They have the choice of skiing in the Canadian Rockies, where the skiing is fine and their dollars go further.

Conversely, a depreciating dollar makes Aspen Skiing Company more competitive and should increase its revenues and profits. In either event, the use of American products and labor means that its costs will not be significantly affected by exchange rate fluctuations.

Petróleos Mexicanos

Petróleos Mexicanos, or Pemex, is the Mexican national oil company. It is the largest company in Mexico and ranks as one of the biggest non-U.S. industrial companies. Most of its sales are overseas. Suppose Pemex borrows U.S. dollars. If the peso devalues, is Pemex a better or worse credit risk?

Petróleos Mexicanos is helped by a peso devaluation because its revenues are in dollars and costs are in pesos.

The instinctive response of most people is that devaluation of the peso makes Pemex a poorer credit risk. This response is wrong. Consider Pemex's revenues. Assume that it exports all its oil. Because oil is priced in dollars, Pemex's dollar revenues will remain the same following peso devaluation. Its dollar costs, however, will change. Most of its operating costs are denominated in pesos. These costs include labor, local supplies, services, and materials. Although the peso amount of these costs may go up somewhat, they will not rise to the extent of the devaluation of the peso. Hence, the dollar amount of peso costs will decline. Pemex also uses a variety of sophisticated equipment and services to aid in oil exploration, drilling, and production. Because these inputs are generally from foreign sources, their dollar costs are likely to be unaffected by peso devaluation. Inasmuch as some costs will fall in dollar terms and other costs will stay the same, the overall effect of peso devaluation is a decline in Pemex's dollar costs.

Since its dollar revenue will stay the same while the dollar amount of its costs will fall, the net effect on Pemex of a peso devaluation is to increase its dollar cash flow. Hence, it becomes a better credit risk in terms of its ability to service dollar debt.

---

[2] Report in the *Wall Street Journal*, January 17, 1984, p. 1.

Might this conclusion be reversed if it turns out that Pemex sells much of its oil domestically? Surprisingly, the answer is no if we add the further condition that the Mexican government does not impose oil price controls. Suppose the price of oil is $20 a barrel. If the initial peso exchange rate is U.S.$0.16/Mex$, that means that the price of oil in Mexico must be Mex$125 (20/0.16) a barrel. Otherwise, there would be an arbitrage opportunity because oil transportation costs are a small fraction of the price of oil. If the peso now devalues to $0.08, the price of oil must rise to Mex$250. Consider what would happen if the price stayed at Mex$125. The dollar equivalent price would now be $10. But why would Pemex sell oil in Mexico for $10 a barrel when it could sell the same oil outside Mexico for $20 a barrel? It would not do so unless there were price controls in Mexico and the government prohibited foreign sales. Hence, in the absence of government intervention, the peso price of oil must rise to Mex$250 and Pemex's dollar profits will rise whether it exports all or part of its oil.

This situation points out the important distinction between the currency of denomination and the currency of determination. The **currency of denomination** is the currency in which prices are stated. For example, oil prices in Mexico are stated in pesos. However, although the currency of denomination for oil sales in Mexico is the peso, the peso price itself is determined by the dollar price of oil. That is, as the peso:dollar exchange rate changes, the peso price of oil changes to equate the dollar equivalent price of oil in Mexico with the dollar price of oil in the world market. Thus, the **currency of determination** for Pemex's domestic oil sales is the U.S. dollar.

Toyota Motor Company

Toyota is the largest Japanese auto company and the fourth largest non-U.S. industrial firm in the world. Over half of its sales are overseas, primarily in the United States. If the yen appreciates, Toyota has the choice of keeping its yen price constant or its dollar price constant. If Toyota holds its yen price constant, the dollar price of its auto exports will rise and sales volume will decline. On the other hand, if Toyota decides to maintain its U.S. market share, it must hold its dollar price constant. In either case, its yen revenues will fall.

If Toyota decides to focus on the Japanese market, it will face the **flow-back effect**, as previously exported products flow back into Japan. Flow-back occurs because other Japanese firms, finding that a high yen makes it difficult to export their cars, emphasize Japanese sales as well. The result is increased domestic competition and lower profit margins on domestic sales.

Toyota's yen production costs will also be affected by yen appreciation. Steel, copper, aluminum, oil (from which plastics are made), and other materials that go into making a car are all imported. As the yen appreciates, the yen cost of these imported materials will decline. Yen costs of labor and domestic services, products, and equipment will likely stay the same. The net effect of lower yen costs for some inputs and constant yen costs for other inputs is a reduction in overall yen costs of production.

The net effect on profits of lower yen revenues and lower yen costs is an empirical question. This question can be answered by examining the profit consequences of yen appreciation. Here, the answer is unambiguous: Yen appreciation hurts Toyota; the reduction in its revenues more than offsets the reduction in its costs.

These three examples illustrate a progression of ideas. Aspen Skiing Company's revenues were affected by exchange rate changes, but its costs were largely unaffected. By contrast, Pemex's costs, but not its revenues, were affected by exchange rate changes. Toyota had both its costs and its revenues affected by exchange rate changes. The process of examining these companies includes a systematic approach to identifying a company's exposure to exchange risk. Exhibit 11.5 summarizes this approach by presenting a series of questions that underlie the analysis of economic exposure.

Toyota Motors' yen revenues and yen costs will fall with yen appreciation.

EXHIBIT 11.5 • KEY QUESTIONS TO ASK THAT HELP IDENTIFY EXCHANGE RISK

1. Where is the company selling?
   Domestic versus foreign sales breakdown
2. Who are the company's key competitors?
   Domestic versus foreign companies
3. How sensitive is demand to price?
   Price-sensitive demand versus price-insensitive demand
4. Where is the company producing?
   Domestic production versus foreign production
5. Where are the company's inputs coming from?
   Domestic inputs versus foreign inputs
6. How are the company's inputs or outputs priced?
   Priced in a world market or in a domestic market; the currency of determination as opposed to the currency of denomination

---

11.4 CALCULATING ECONOMIC EXPOSURE

We will now work through a hypothetical, though comprehensive, example illustrating all the various aspects of exposure that have been discussed so far. This example emphasizes the quantitative, rather than qualitative, determination of economic exposure. It shows how critical the underlying assumptions are.

Calculating economic exposure depends critically on the assumptions as to the amounts and exchange rate sensitivities of future cash flows.

Spectrum Manufacturing AB is the wholly owned Swedish affiliate of a U.S. multinational industrial plastics firm. It manufactures patented sheet plastic in Sweden, with 60 percent of its output currently being sold in Sweden and the remaining 40 percent exported to other European countries. Spectrum uses only Swedish labor in its manufacturing process, but it uses both local and foreign sources of raw material. The effective Swedish tax rate on corporate profits is 40 percent, and the annual depreciation charge on plant and equipment, in Swedish kronor (SKr), is SKr 900,000. In addition, Spectrum AB has outstanding SKr 3 million in debt, with interest payable at 10 percent annually.

Exhibit 11.6 presents Spectrum's projected sales, costs, after-tax income, and cash flow for the coming year, based on the current exchange rate of SKr 4 = $1. All sales are invoiced in kronor (singular, krona).

Spectrum's Accounting Exposure

Exhibit 11.7 shows Spectrum's balance sheet before and after an exchange rate change. To contrast the economic and accounting approaches to measuring exposure, assume that the Swedish krona devalues by 20 percent, from SKr 4 = $1 to SKr 5 = $1. The third column of Exhibit 11.7 shows that under the current rate method mandated by FASB-52, Spectrum will have a translation loss of $685,000. Use of the monetary/nonmonetary method leads to a much smaller reported loss of $50,000.

Spectrum's Economic Exposure

On the basis of current information, it is impossible to determine the precise economic impact of the krona devaluation. Therefore, three different scenarios have been constructed, with varying degrees of plausibility, and Spectrum's economic exposure has been calculated under each scenario. The three scenarios are

1. All variables remain the same.
2. Krona sales prices and all costs rise; volume remains the same.
3. There are partial increases in prices, costs, and volume.

EXHIBIT 11.6 • SUMMARY OF PROJECTED OPERATIONS FOR SPECTRUM MANUFACTURING AB: BASE CASE

	Units (hundred thousands)	Unit Price (SKr)		Total
Domestic sales	6	20	(SKr) 12,000,000	
Export sales	4	20	8,000,000	
Total revenue				20,000,000
Total operating expenditures				10,800,000
Overhead expenses				3,500,000
Interest on krona debt @ 10%				300,000
Depreciation				900,000
Net profit before tax				(SKr) 4,500,000
Income tax @ 40%				1,800,000
Profit after tax				(SKr) 2,700,000
Add back depreciation				900,000
Net cash flow in kronor				(SKr) 3,600,000
Net cash flow in dollars (Skr 4 = $1)				$900,000

EXHIBIT 11.7 • IMPACT OF KRONA DEVALUATION ON SPECTRUM AB'S FINANCIAL STATEMENT UNDER FASB-52

	Kronor	U.S. Dollars before Krona Devaluation (SKr 4 = $1)	U.S. Dollars after Krona Devaluation (SKr 5 = $1)	
			Current Rate	Monetary/ Nonmonetary
Assets				
Cash	SKr 1,000,000	$ 250,000	$ 200,000	$ 200,000
Accounts receivable	5,000,000	$1,250,000	1,000,000	1,000,000
Inventory	2,700,000	$ 675,000	540,000	675,000
Net fixed assets	10,000,000	$2,500,000	2,000,000	2,500,000
Total assets	SKr 18,700,000	$4,675,000	$3,740,000	$4,375,000
Liabilities				
Accounts payable	2,000,000	500,000	400,000	400,000
Long-term debt	3,000,000	750,000	600,000	600,000
Equity	13,700,000	3,425,000	2,740,000	3,375,000
Total liabilities plus equity	SKr 18,700,000	$4,675,000	$3,740,000	$4,375,000
Translation gain (loss)			$ (685,000)	$ (50,000)

FASB-52 = Statement of Financial Accounting Standards No. 52.

Scenario 1: All Variables Remain the Same. If all prices remain the same (in kronor) and sales volume doesn't change, then Spectrum's krona cash flow will stay at SKr 3,600,000. At the new exchange rate, this amount will equal $720,000 (3,600,000/5). Then the net loss in dollar operating cash flow in year 1 can be calculated as follows:

First-year cash flow (SKr 4 = $1)		$900,000
First-year cash flow (SKr 5 = $1)		720,000
Net loss from devaluation		$180,000

Moreover, this loss will continue until relative prices adjust. Part of this loss, however, will be offset by the $150,000 gain that will be realized when the SKr 3 million loan is repaid (3 million × 0.05).[3] If a three-year adjustment process is assumed and the krona loan will be repaid at the end of year 3, then the present value of the economic loss from operations associated with the krona devaluation, using a 15 percent discount rate, equals $312,420:

Year	Postdevaluation Cash Flow (1)	−	Predevaluation Cash Flow (2)	=	Change in Cash Flow (3)	×	15% Present Value Factor (4)	=	Present Value (5)
1	$720,000		$900,000		−$180,000		0.870		−$156,600
2	720,000		900,000		− 180,000		0.756		− 136,080
3	870,000*		900,000		− 30,000		0.658		− 19,740
Net Loss									−$312,420

*Includes a gain of $150,000 on loan repayment.

This loss is due primarily to the inability to raise the sales price. The resulting constant krona profit margin translates into a 20 percent reduction in dollar profits. The economic loss of $312,420 contrasts with the accounting recognition of a $685,000 foreign exchange loss. In reality, of course, the prices, costs, volume, and input mix are unlikely to remain fixed. The discussion will now focus on the economic effects of some of these potential adjustments.

Scenario 2: Krona Sales Prices and All Costs Rise; Volume Remains the Same. It is assumed here that all costs and prices increase in proportion to the krona devaluation, but unit volume remains the same. However, the operating cash flow in kronor does not rise to the same extent because depreciation, which is based on historical cost, remains at SKr 900,000. As a potential offset, interest payments also hold steady at SKr 300,000. Working through the numbers in Exhibit 11.8 gives us an operating cash flow of $891,000.

The $9,000 reduction in cash flow equals the decreased dollar value of the SKr 900,000 depreciation tax shield less the decreased dollar cost of paying the SKr 300,000 in interest. Before devaluation, the depreciation tax shield was worth (900,000 × 0.4)/4 dollars, or $90,000. After devaluation, the dollar value of the tax shield declines to (900,000 × 0.4)/5 dollars = $72,000, or a loss of $18,000 in cash flow. Similarly, the dollar cost of paying SKr 300,000 in interest declines by $15,000 to $60,000 (from $75,000). After tax, this decrease in interest expense equals $9,000. Adding the two figures (−$18,000 + $9,000) yields a net loss of $9,000 annually in operating cash flow. The net economic gain over the coming three years, relative to pre-devaluation expectations, is $78,150.

Year	Postdevaluation Cash Flow (1)	−	Predevaluation Cash Flow (2)	=	Change in Cash Flow (3)	×	15% Present Value Factor (4)	=	Present Value (5)
1	$ 891,000		$900,000		−$9,000		0.870		− $7,830
2	891,000		900,000		− 9,000		0.756		− 6,800
3	1,041,000*		900,000		+141,000		0.658		92,780
Net Gain									$78,150

*Includes a gain of $150,000 on loan repayment.

---

[3] No Swedish taxes will be owed on this gain because SKr 3 million were borrowed and SKr 3 million were repaid.

EXHIBIT 11.8 • SUMMARY OF PROJECTED OPERATIONS FOR SPECTRUM MANUFACTURING AB: SCENARIO 2

	Units (hundred thousands)	Unit Price (SKr)	Total
Domestic sales	6	25	SKr 15,000,000
Export sales	4	25	10,000,000
Total revenue			25,000,000
Total operating expenditures			13,500,000
Overhead expenses			4,375,000
Interest on krona debt @ 10%			300,000
Depreciation			900,000
Net profit before tax			SKr 5,925,000
Income tax @ 40%			2,370,000
Profit after tax			SKr 3,555,000
Add back depreciation			900,000
Net cash flow in kronor			SKr 4,455,000
Net cash flow in dollars			$891,000
(SKr 5 = $1)			

All of this gain in economic value comes from the gain on repayment of the krona loan.

Scenario 3: Partial Increases in Prices, Costs, and Volume. In the most realistic situation, all variables will adjust somewhat. It is assumed here that the sales price at home rises by 10 percent to SKr 22 and the export price rises to SKr 24—still providing a competitive advantage in dollar terms over foreign products. The result is a 20 percent increase in domestic sales and a 15 percent increase in export sales.

Local input prices are assumed to go up, but the dollar price of imported material stays at its pre-devaluation level. As a result of the change in relative cost, some substitutions are made between domestic and imported goods. The result is an increase in SKr unit cost of approximately 17 percent. Overhead expenses rise by only 10 percent because some components of this account, such as rent and local taxes, are fixed in value. The net result of all these adjustments is an operating cash flow of $1,010,800, which is a gain of $110,800 over the pre-devaluation level of $900,000. The calculations are shown in Exhibit 11.9.

Over the next three years, cash flows and the firm's economic value will change as follows:

Year	Postdevaluation Cash Flow (1)	–	Predevaluation Cash Flow (2)	=	Change in Cash Flow (3)	×	15% Present Value Factor (4)	=	Present Value (5)
1	$1,010,800		$900,000		$110,800		0.870		$ 96,396
2	1,010,800		900,000		110,800		0.756		83,765
3	1,160,800*		900,000		260,800		0.658		171,606
Net Gain									$351,767

*Includes a gain of $150,000 on loan repayment.

Thus, under this scenario, the economic value of the firm will increase by $351,767. This gain reflects the increase in operating cash flow combined with the gain on loan repayment.

EXHIBIT 11.9 • SUMMARY OF PROJECTED OPERATIONS FOR SPECTRUM MANUFACTURING AB: SCENARIO 3

	Units (hundred thousands)	Unit Price (SKr)	Total	
Domestic sales	7.2	22	SKr 15,840,000	
Export sales	4.6	24	11,040,000	
Total revenue				26,880,000
Total operating expenditures				14,906,000
Overhead expenses				3,850,000
Interest on krona debt @ 10%				300,000
Depreciation				900,000
Net profit before tax				SKr 6,924,000
Income tax @ 40%				2,769,000
Profit after tax				SKr 4,154,000
Add back depreciation				900,000
Net cash flow in kronor				SKr 5,054,000
Net cash flow in dollars (SKr 5 = $1)				$1,010,800

Case Analysis   The three preceding scenarios demonstrate the sensitivity of a firm's economic exposure to assumptions concerning its price elasticity of demand, its ability to adjust its mix of inputs as relative costs change, its pricing flexibility, subsequent local inflation, and its use of local currency financing. Perhaps most important of all, this example makes clear the lack of any necessary relationship between accounting-derived measures of exchange gains or losses and the true impact of currency changes on a firm's economic value. The economic effects of this devaluation under the three alternative scenarios are summarized in Exhibit 11.10.

11.5 MANAGING OPERATING EXPOSURE

> Companies can manage their operating exposure by altering their marketing and production policies.

The basic message of this section is straightforward: Because currency risk affects all facets of a company's operations, it should not be the concern of financial managers alone. Operating managers, in particular, should develop marketing and production initiatives that help to ensure profitability over the long run. They should also devise anticipatory or proactive, rather than reactive, strategic alternatives in order to gain competitive leverage internationally.

EXHIBIT 11.10 • SUMMARY OF ECONOMIC EXPOSURE IMPACT OF KRONA DEVALUATION ON SPECTRUM MANUFACTURING AB

	Forecast Change in Cash Flows		
Year	Scenario 1	Scenario 2	Scenario 3
1	−$180,000	−$ 9,000	$110,800
2	− 180,000	− 9,000	110,800
3	− 30,000[*]	141,000[*]	260,800[*]
Change in present value (15% discount factor)	−$312,420	$ 78,220	$351,767

[*]Includes a gain of $150,000 on loan repayment.

The focus on the real (economic) effects of currency changes and how to cope with the associated risks suggests that a sensible strategy for exchange risk management is one that is designed to protect the dollar (HC) earning power of the company as a whole. But whereas firms can easily hedge transaction exposures, **competitive exposures**—those arising from competition with firms based in other currencies—are longer-term and cannot be dealt with solely through financial hedging techniques. Rather, they require making the longer-term operating adjustments described in this section.

Marketing Management of Exchange Risk

The international marketing manager should identify the likely effects of a currency change and then adjust pricing and product policies accordingly.

The design of a firm's marketing strategy under conditions of home currency (HC) fluctuation presents considerable opportunity for gaining competitive leverage. Thus, one of the international marketing manager's tasks should be to identify the likely effects of a currency change and then act on them by adjusting pricing and product policies.

Market Selection   Major strategic considerations for an exporter are the markets in which to sell—that is, **market selection**—and the relative marketing support to devote to each market. As a result of the strong dollar during the early 1980s, for example, some discouraged U.S. firms pulled out of markets that foreign competition made unprofitable. From the perspective of foreign companies, however, the strong U.S. dollar was a golden opportunity to gain market share at the expense of their U.S. rivals. Japanese and European companies also used their dollar cost advantage to carve out market share against American competitors in third markets. The subsequent drop in the dollar helped U.S. firms turn the tables on their foreign competitors, both at home and abroad.

An MNC must decide whether to go for market share or profit margin when coping with currency movements.

Pricing Strategy   The key issue that must be addressed when developing a **pricing strategy** in the face of currency volatility is whether to emphasize market share or profit margin. Following dollar depreciation, for example, U.S. exports will gain a competitive price advantage on the world market. A U.S. exporter now has the option of raising its dollar price and boosting its profit margins or keeping its dollar price constant and expanding its market share. The decision is influenced by such factors as whether this change is likely to persist, economies of scale, the cost structure of expanding output, consumer price sensitivity, and the likelihood of attracting competition if high unit profitability is obvious.

The greater the *price elasticity of demand*—the change in demand for a given change in price—the greater the incentive to hold down price and thereby expand sales and revenues. Similarly, if significant *economies of scale* exist, it generally will be worthwhile to hold down price, expand demand, and thereby lower unit production costs. The reverse is true if economies of scale are nonexistent or if price elasticity is low.

 ILLUSTRATION   *A.T. Cross Marks Down Its Pen Prices*

In February 1993, following a 10 percent decline in the dollar (from ¥123 to ¥111), A.T. Cross cut the yen prices of its pens by 20 percent. For example, a 10-carat gold Cross pen was marked down to ¥8,000 from ¥10,000. Suppose that the manufacturing and shipping costs of this Cross pen were $25 and distribution costs were ¥2,000, giving Cross a pre-exchange rate change contribution margin of $40 (¥10,000/123 – $25 – ¥2,000/123). Assuming these costs stay the same, how much additional volume must Cross generate in order to maintain its dollar profits on this pen?

Solution: The contribution margin given the new exchange rate and the price change equals $29 (¥8,000/111 – $25 – ¥2,000/111). In order to maintain dollar profits on this pen at its previous level, unit sales must rise by 38 percent (40/29). A sales increase of this magnitude implies a price elasticity of demand of 1.9 (38/20).

Price elasticity of demand and economies of scale are key factors in trading off market share for higher profit margins.

Turning now to domestic pricing after a fall in the home currency, a domestic firm facing strong import competition may have much greater latitude in pricing. It then has the choice of potentially raising prices consistent with import price increases or of holding prices constant in order to improve market share. Again, the strategy depends on such variables as economies of scale and the price elasticity of demand. For example, the sharp rise in the value of the yen and Deutsche mark during the 1990s led the German and Japanese automakers to raise their dollar prices and allowed Ford and General Motors to raise their prices on competing models. The price increases by the U.S. auto manufacturers, which were less than the sharp rise in import prices, improved their profit margins and kept U.S. cars competitive with their foreign rivals.

The competitive situation is reversed following appreciation of the dollar, which is equivalent to a foreign currency (FC) depreciation. In this case, a U.S. firm selling overseas should consider opportunities to increase the FC prices of its products. The problem, of course, is that local producers now will have a competitive cost advantage, limiting an exporter's ability to recoup dollar profits by raising FC selling prices.

At best, therefore, an exporter will be able to raise its product prices by the extent of the FC depreciation. For example, suppose Avon is selling cosmetics in England priced at £2.00 when the exchange rate is $1.80/£. This gives Avon revenue of $3.60 per unit. If the pound declines to $1.50/£, Avon's unit revenue will fall to $3.00, unless it can raise its selling price to £2.40 (2.40 × 1.50 = $3.60). At worst, in an extremely competitive situation, the exporter will have to absorb a reduction in HC revenues equal to the percentage decline in the value of the foreign currency. For example, if Avon cannot raise its pound price, its new dollar price of $3.00 represents a 16.7 percent drop in dollar revenue, the same percentage decline as the fall in the pound's value [(1.80 − 1.50)/1.80]. In the most likely case, FC prices can be raised somewhat, and the exporter will make up the difference through a lower profit margin on its foreign sales.

In coping with currency depreciation, companies must consider that raising prices today may lose them market share in the future.

In deciding whether to raise prices following a foreign currency depreciation, companies must consider not just sales that will be lost today but also the likelihood of losing future sales as well. For example, foreign capital goods manufacturers used the period when they had a price advantage to build strong U.S. distribution and service networks. U.S. firms that had not previously bought foreign-made equipment became loyal customers. When the dollar fell, foreign firms opened U.S. plants to supply their distribution systems and hold onto their customers.

The same is true in many other markets as well: *A customer who is lost may be lost forever.* For example, a customer who is satisfied with a foreign automobile may stick with that brand for a long time.

MINI-CASE   *Check the Euro and Ship the Boxes!*

In 2001, Kim Reynolds, president of Markel Corp., located in Plymouth Meeting, Pennsylvania, had to take a 40 percent pay cut to offset the effects of a skyrocketing dollar. Markel, which makes Teflon-based tubing and insulated wire used in the automotive, appliance, and water-purification industries, has developed a four-part strategy to cope with currency volatility: (1) Charge customers relatively stable prices in their own currencies to build overseas market share, while absorbing currency gains or losses; (2) use forward contracts to lock in dollar revenues for the next several months; (3) improve efficiency to survive when the dollar appreciates; and (4) pray. Mr. Reynolds believes his policy of keeping prices set in foreign currencies, mainly the euro, has helped Markel capture 70 percent of the world market for high-performance, Teflon-coated cable-control liners. However, it also means that Markel signs multiyear contracts denominated in euros. When he thinks the dollar will rise, Markel's CFO, James Hoban, might hedge the company's entire expected euro revenue stream for the next several months with a forward contract. If he thinks the dollar will fall, he will hedge perhaps 50 percent and take a chance that he will make more dollars by remaining exposed. Mr. Hoban sometimes guesses wrong, as when he sold euros forward assuming—incorrectly—that the euro would continue falling. To make matters worse, Markel entered a multiyear contract with a German firm in 1998 and set the sales price assuming that the euro would be at $1.18 for the next several years. In fact, the euro sank like a rock and Markel had over $625,000 in currency losses in 2001 and 2002 combined. One of Markel's responses was to buy new equipment that cut production down-time and waste material. By 2003, most of Markel's contracts outstanding were written assuming that the euro would be valued between 90 cents and 95 cents. The jump in the euro's dollar value thus created a currency windfall for Markel. To lock in his dollar costs and reduce his currency risk, Mr. Reynolds demands that his Japanese supplier of raw materials sign multiyear dollar contracts.

QUESTIONS

1. Why does a rise in the dollar hurt Markel? How does a falling dollar help Markel?

2. What does Markel do to hedge its currency risk? Can Markel use hedging to completely eliminate its currency risk?

3. Comment on Markel's policy of selective hedging. Are there any speculative elements involved in such a policy? Would you recommend Markel continue to follow a policy of selective hedging? Why or why not?

4. What are the basic elements of Markel's pricing policy? Does this pricing policy reduce its currency risk? Explain.

5. Does locking in Markel's dollar costs of raw materials through multiyear dollar contracts automatically reduce the company's currency exposure?

Currency movements may affect the timing of new product introductions.

Product Strategy   Companies often respond to exchange risk by altering their **product strategy**, which deals with such areas as new-product introduction, product line decisions, and product innovation. One way to cope with exchange rate fluctuations is to change the timing of the introduction of new products. For example, because of the competitive price advantage, the period after a home currency depreciation may be the ideal time to develop a brand franchise.

Exchange rate fluctuations also affect product line decisions. Following home currency devaluation, a firm will potentially be able to expand its product line and cover a wider spectrum of consumers both at home and abroad. Conversely, home currency appreciation may force a firm to reorient its product line and target it to a higher-income, more quality-conscious, less price-sensitive constituency. Volkswagen, for example, achieved its export prominence on the basis of low-priced, stripped-down, low-maintenance cars. The appreciation of the Deutsche mark in the early 1970s, however, effectively ended VW's ability to compete primarily on the basis of price. The company lost over $310 million in 1974 alone attempting to maintain its market share by lowering DM prices. To compete in the long run, Volkswagen was forced to revise its product line and sell relatively high-priced cars to middle-income consumers, from an extended product line, on the basis of quality and styling rather than cost.

The equivalent strategy for firms selling to the industrial rather than consumer market and confronting a strong home currency is **product innovation**, financed by an expanded research and development (R&D) budget. For example, Japanese exporters responded to the rising yen by shifting production from commodity-type goods to more sophisticated, high-value products. Demand for such goods, which embody advanced technology, high-quality standards, and other nonprice features, is less sensitive to price increases caused by yen appreciation.

ILLUSTRATION   *Automatic Feed Survives through Ingenuity*

The strong dollar of the late 1990s and early 2000s set off a small revolution in factories across America. Consider Automatic Feed Co. Located in Napoleon, Ohio, it makes machinery used in auto plants. To cope with the strong dollar, it undertook the most extensive product redesign in its fifty-two–year history. Its aim was to neutralize the cost advantages it foreign competitors enjoyed because of their weak home currencies. The company redesigned its machines to make them easier and less expensive to build and also modernized its production system to reduce the costs of manufacturing. By 2002, the production overhaul and redesign efforts had cut production costs by 20 percent. At the same time, Automatic Feed developed new software that allows customers to track such things as the productivity of a particular machine on a manufacturing line and to pinpoint exactly where a problem is when a line breaks down. By quickly flagging the source of a problem and displaying a digital rendering of it on a computer monitor, the software saves time and cost for customers. This ingenious software reduces the price elasticity of demand for the company's offerings, thereby making it less subject to currency risk.

Production Management of Exchange Risk

MNCs can cope with operating exposure through global sourcing and shifting production locations.

Sometimes exchange rates move so much that pricing or other marketing strategies cannot save the product. This was the case for U.S. firms in the early 1980s and for Japanese firms in the early 1990s. Firms facing this situation must either drop uncompetitive products or cut their costs.

Product sourcing and **plant location** are the principal variables that companies manipulate to manage competitive risks that cannot be dealt with through marketing changes alone. Consider, for example, the possible responses of U.S. firms to a strong dollar. The basic strategy would involve shifting the firm's manufacturing base overseas, but this can be accomplished in more than one way.

Foreign sourcing and outsourcing allow companies to take advantage of currency changes.

Input Mix   Outright additions to facilities overseas naturally accomplish a manufacturing shift. A more flexible solution is to change the *input mix* by purchasing more components overseas. Following the rise of the dollar in the early 1980s, most U.S. companies increased their global sourcing. For example, Caterpillar responded to the soaring U.S. dollar and a tenacious competitor, Japan's Komatsu, by "shopping the world" for components. More than 50 percent of the pistons that Caterpillar uses in the United States now come from abroad, mainly from a Brazilian company. Some work previously done by Caterpillar's Milwaukee plant was moved in 1984 to a subsidiary in Mexico. Caterpillar also stopped most U.S. production of lift trucks and began importing a new line—complete with Cat's yellow paint and logo—from South Korea's Daewoo.

ILLUSTRATION   *Japanese Automakers Outsource to Cope with a Rising Yen*

Japanese automakers have protected themselves against the rising yen by purchasing a significant percentage of intermediate components from independent suppliers. This practice, called **outsourcing**, gives them the flexibility to shift purchases of intermediate inputs toward suppliers with costs least affected by exchange rate changes. Some of these inputs come from South Korea and Taiwan, nations whose currencies have been closely linked to the U.S. dollar. Thus, even if such intermediate goods are not priced in dollars, their yen-equivalent prices tend to decline with the dollar and, thereby, lessen the impact of a falling dollar on the cost of Japanese cars sold in the United States.

Outsourcing in countries whose currencies are linked to the currency of the export market also creates competitive pressures on domestic suppliers of the same intermediate goods. To cope in such an environment, domestic suppliers must themselves have flexible arrangements with their own input suppliers. In many cases, these smaller firms can survive because they have greater ability to recontract their costs than do the larger firms specializing in assembly and distribution. When the suppliers are faced with the reality of an exchange rate change that reduces the competitive price of their outputs, they are able to recontract with their own inputs (typically by lowering wages) to reduce costs sufficiently to remain economically viable.

Shifting Production among Plants   Multinational firms with worldwide production systems can allocate production among their several plants in line with the changing dollar costs of production, increasing production in a nation whose currency has devalued and decreasing production in a country where there has been a revaluation. Contrary to conventional wisdom, therefore, multinational firms may well be subject to less exchange risk than an exporter, given the MNC's greater ability to adjust its production (and marketing) operations on a global basis, in line with changing relative production costs.

MNCs can reduce their exchange risk by allocating production among their several plants in line with changing costs.

A good example of this flexibility is provided by Westinghouse Electric Company of Pittsburgh, Pennsylvania (now a subsidiary of BNFL). Westinghouse can quote its customers prices from numerous foreign affiliates: gas turbines from Canada, generators from Spain, circuit breakers and robotics from Britain, and electrical equipment from Brazil. Its sourcing decisions take into account both the effect of currency values and subsidized export financing available from foreign governments.

The theoretical ability to shift production is more limited in reality, depending on many factors, not the least of which is the power of the local labor unions involved. However, the innovative nature of the typical MNC means a continued generation of new products. The sourcing of those new products among the firm's various plants can certainly be done with an eye to the costs involved.

A strategy of **production shifting** presupposes that the MNC has already created a portfolio of plants worldwide. For example, as part of its global sourcing strategy, Caterpillar now has dual sources, domestic and foreign, for some products. These sources allow Caterpillar to "load" the plant that offers the best economies of production, given exchange rates at any moment. But multiple plants also create manufacturing redundancies and impede cost cutting.

The benefits of a global portfolio of plants must be traded off against the potential loss of economies of scale.

The cost of multiple sourcing is especially great where there are economies of scale that would ordinarily dictate the establishment of only one or two plants to service the global market. But most firms have found that in a world of uncertainty, significant benefits may be derived from production diversification. In effect, having redundant capacity is the equivalent of buying an option to execute volume shifts fairly easily. As in the case of currency options, the value of such a real option increases with the volatility of the exchange rate. Hence, despite the higher unit costs associated with smaller plants and excess capacity, currency risk may provide one more reason for the use of multiple production facilities. Indeed, 63 percent of foreign exchange managers surveyed cited having locations "to increase flexibility by shifting plant loading when exchange rates changed" as a factor in international siting.[4]

The auto industry illustrates the potential value of maintaining a globally balanced distribution of production facilities in the face of fluctuating exchange rates. For Japanese and Swedish auto manufacturers, which historically located all their factories domestically, it has been feast or famine. When the home currency appreciates, as in the 1970s or

[4] Donald B. Lessard, "Survey on Corporate Responses to Volatile Exchange Rates," MIT Sloan School of Management Working Paper, 1990.

the late 1980s and early 1990s, the firms' exports suffer from a lack of cost competitiveness. On the other hand, a real depreciation of the home currency, as in the early 1980s, is a time of high profits.

By contrast, Ford and General Motors, with their worldwide manufacturing facilities, have substantial leeway in reallocating various stages of production among their several plants in line with relative production and transportation costs. For example, Ford can shift production among the United States, Spain, Germany, Great Britain, Brazil, and Mexico.

Plant Location   A firm without foreign facilities that is exporting to a competitive market whose currency has devalued may find that sourcing components abroad is insufficient to maintain unit profitability. Despite its previous hesitancy, the firm may have to locate new plants abroad. For example, the economic response by the Japanese to the strong yen has been to build new plants in the United States as opposed to expanding plants in Japan. For example, Honda now makes 75 percent of the cars it sells in the U.S. market in North American factories and Nissan recently doubled its production capacity in North America to 1.35 million vehicles a year with a $1 billion factory in Mississippi. Similarly, German automakers such as BMW (in South Carolina) and Mercedes-Benz (in Alabama) have built plants in the United States to shield themselves from currency fluctuations. By incurring costs in the United States, German and Japanese automakers have created natural hedges against their dollar sales revenue.

> *An exporter whose home currency has appreciated may be forced to locate plants overseas.*

Japan's big auto and electronics companies have gone even further and are increasingly moving development, engineering, and design operations overseas as well. Toyota, for example, announced it would open a design studio in Michigan in 2004, giving the company the ability to perform in the United States all the steps in the process of making new cars—from design to engineering to production. Similarly, Matsushita Electric, maker of Panasonic-brand equipment, began in 2003 to make its overseas divisions as self-sufficient as possible, reinvesting money earned abroad in local manufacturing and research facilities. By more closely matching costs with revenues denominated in the same currency, the Japanese companies can further reduce their foreign exchange risk.

Third-country plant locations are also a viable alternative in many cases, depending especially on the labor intensity of production or the projections for further monetary realignments. Many Japanese firms, for example, have shifted production offshore—to other Asian nations, such as Taiwan, South Korea, and increasingly to China, as well as to the United States—in order to cope with the high yen. Japanese automakers have been particularly aggressive in making these shifts. Moving production offshore can be a mixed blessing, however. Although it makes companies less vulnerable to a strong yen, it means less of a payoff if the yen declines. For example, when the yen weakened in 2001, Japanese manufacturers with foreign production facilities found they could not take full advantage of the yen's fall.

Raising Productivity   Many U.S. companies assaulted by foreign competition made prodigious efforts to improve their productivity—closing inefficient plants, automating heavily, and negotiating wage and benefit cutbacks and work-rule concessions with unions. Many also began programs to heighten productivity and improve product quality through employee motivation. These cost cuts stood U.S. firms in good stead as they tried to use the weaker dollar that began in 2002 to gain back market share lost to foreign competitors.

> *As an alternative to shifting production abroad, companies with a strong home currency can try to improve their productivity at home.*

Another way to improve productivity and lower cost structure is to revise product offerings. This is the route now being taken by the Japanese. Despite their vaunted super-lean production systems, many Japanese firms, in an attempt to gain market share, have created too much product variety and offered too many options to customers. The result is that parts makers and assembly plants have to accommodate very small and very rare

Companies can raise productivity by cutting back on their product offerings.

orders too frequently. This variety requires too much design work, too much capital investment for small-volume parts, too many parts inventories, and constant equipment setups and changeovers. By slashing variety to the 20 percent or so of models and product variations that account for 80 percent of sales and profits and by reducing unique parts by 30 percent to 50 percent for new models, Japanese companies are finding that they can dramatically reduce costs without sacrificing much in the way of market share.

 ILLUSTRATION   *Nissan Reverses Course*

In 1993, Nissan renounced a decade-long quest to build cars in ever more sizes, colors, and functions to cater to every conceivable consumer whim. That effort had spun out of control. For the 1993 model lineup alone, Nissan offered 437 different kinds of dashboard meters, 110 types of radiators, 1,200 types of floor carpets, and more than 300 varieties of ashtrays. Its Laurel model alone had 87 variations of steering wheels and 62 varieties of wiring harnesses (which link up electrical components in a car). To assemble these vehicles, Nissan used more than 6,000 different fasteners.

The payoff from this product proliferation was pathetic. Nissan engineers discovered that 70 of the 87 types of steering wheels accounted for just 5 percent of the Laurel's sales. Overall, 50 percent of Nissan's model variations contributed only about 5 percent of total sales.

Nissan ordered its designers to reduce the number of unique parts in its vehicles by 40 percent. Model variations, which had ballooned to more than 2,200, were rolled back 50 percent. The goal of this reformation was to reduce annual production costs by at least ¥200 billion ($2 billion at an exchange rate of ¥100/$1). These cost savings helped Nissan to maintain its profitability as it cut its prices in the United States to remain competitive in the face of a surging yen.

Planning for Exchange Rate Changes

Companies can use scenario analysis to plan for unpredictable currency movements.

The marketing and production strategies advocated thus far assume knowledge of exchange rate changes. Even if currency changes are unpredictable, however, contingency plans can be made. This planning involves developing several plausible currency scenarios (see Section 11.4), analyzing the effects of each scenario on the firm's competitive position, and deciding on strategies to deal with these possibilities.

When a currency change actually occurs, the firm is able to quickly adjust its marketing and production strategies in line with the plan. Given the substantial costs of gathering and processing information, a firm should focus on scenarios that have a high probability of occurrence and that also would have a strong impact on the firm.

 ILLUSTRATION   *Kodak Plans for Currency Changes*

Historically, Eastman Kodak focused its exchange risk management efforts on hedging near-term transactions. It now looks at exchange rate movements from a strategic perspective. Kodak's moment of truth came in the early 1980s when the strong dollar enabled overseas rivals such as Fuji Photo Film of Japan to cut prices and make significant inroads into its market share. This episode convinced Kodak that it had been defining its currency risk too narrowly. It appointed a new foreign exchange planning director, David Fiedler, at the end of 1985. According to Mr. Fiedler, "We were finding a lot of things that didn't fit our definition [of exposure] very well, and yet would have a real economic impact on the corporation."[5] To make sure such risks no longer go unrecognized, Mr. Fiedler now spends about 25 percent of his time briefing Kodak's operating managers on foreign exchange planning, advising them on everything from sourcing alternatives to market pricing. Kodak's new approach figured in a 1988 decision against putting in a factory in Mexico. Kodak decided to locate the plant elsewhere because of its assessment of the peso's relative strength. In the past, currency risk would have been ignored in such project assessments. According to Kodak's chief financial officer, before their reassessment of the company's foreign exchange risk management policy, its financial officers "would do essentially nothing to assess the possible exchange impact until it got to the point of signing contracts for equipment."[6]

The ability to plan for volatile exchange rates has fundamental implications for exchange risk management because there is no longer such a thing as the "natural" or "equilibrium" rate. Rather, there is a sequence of equilibrium rates, each of which has its own implications for corporate strategy. Success in such an environment—where change is the only constant—depends on a company's ability to react to change within a shorter time horizon than ever before. To cope, companies must develop competitive options—such as outsourcing, flexible manufacturing systems, a global network of production facilities, and shorter product cycles.

Investments in flexibility can reduce a company's operating exposure.

In a volatile world, these investments in flexibility are likely to yield high returns. For example, flexible manufacturing systems permit faster production response times to shifting market demand. Similarly, foreign facilities, even if they are uneconomical at the moment, can pay off by enabling companies to shift production in response to changing exchange rates or other relative cost shocks.

The greatest boost to competitiveness comes from compressing the time it takes to bring new and improved products to market. The edge a company gets from shorter **product cycles** is dramatic: not only can it charge a premium price for its exclusive products, but it can also incorporate more up-to-date technology in its goods and respond faster to emerging market niches and changes in taste.

Shortening the product cycle can greatly reduce a company's operating exposure.

With better planning and more competitive options, corporations can now change their strategies substantially before the impact of any currency change can make itself felt. As a result, the adjustment period following a large exchange rate change has been compressed dramatically. The 100 percent appreciation of the Japanese yen against the dollar from 1985 to 1988, for example, sparked some changes in Japanese corporate strategy that have proven to be long-lasting: increased production in the United States and East Asia to cope with the high yen and to protect their foreign markets from any trade backlash; purchase of more parts overseas to take advantage of lower costs; upscaling to reduce the price sensitivity of their products and broaden their markets; massive cost-reduction programs in their Japanese plants, with a long-term impact on production technology; and an increase in joint ventures between competitors.

ILLUSTRATION   *Toshiba Copes with a Rising Yen by Cutting Costs*

By 1988, Toshiba's cost cutting reduced its cost-to-sales ratio to where it was before the yen began rising. The company shifted production of low-tech products to developing nations and moved domestic production to high-value-added products. At a VCR plant outside of Tokyo, it halved the number of assembly-line workers by minimizing

---

[5] Quoted in Christopher J. Chipello, "The Market Watcher," *Wall Street Journal*, September 23, 1988, p. 14.
[6] Quoted in Chipello, "The Market Watcher."

inventories and simplifying operations. Other cost-reducing international activities included production of color picture tubes with Westinghouse in the United States, photocopier production in a joint venture with Rhone-Poulenc in France, assembly of videocassette recorders in Tennessee, production of similar VCRs in Germany, and establishment of a new plant in California for assembling and testing telephones and medical electronics equipment. Overall, Toshiba is estimated to have saved ¥115 billion—¥53 billion by redesigning products, ¥47 billion in parts cutbacks and lower raw material costs, and ¥15 billion in greater operating efficiency. Similarly, by 1989, with the dollar around ¥125, Fujitsu Fanuc, a robot maker, had streamlined itself so thoroughly and differentiated its products so effectively that it estimated it could break even with only a fifth of its plant in use and a dollar down to ¥70.

Financial Management of Exchange Risk

MNCs should structure their financing to give themselves breathing room while they undertake the necessary strategic marketing and production adjustments.

The one attribute that all the strategic marketing and production adjustments have in common is that accomplishing them in a cost-effective manner takes time. The role of financial management in this process is to structure the firm's liabilities in such a way that during the time the strategic operational adjustments are under way, the reduction in asset earnings is matched by a corresponding decrease in the cost of servicing these liabilities.

One possibility is to finance the portion of a firm's assets used to create export profits so that any shortfall in operating cash flows caused by an exchange rate change is offset by a reduction in debt-servicing expenses. For example, a firm that has developed a sizable export market should hold a portion of its liabilities in that country's currency. The portion to be held in the foreign currency depends on the size of the loss in profitability associated with a given currency change. No more-definite recommendations are possible, because the currency effects will vary from one company to another.

A company exporting to a foreign country should be partially financed in the currency of that country.

Volkswagen is a case in point. To hedge its operating exposure, VW should have used dollar financing in proportion to its net dollar cash flow from U.S. sales. This strategy would have cushioned the impact of the DM revaluation that almost brought VW to its knees. For the longer term, however, VW could manage its competitive exposure only by developing new products with lower price elasticities of demand and by establishing production facilities in lower-cost nations.

The implementation of a hedging policy is likely to be quite difficult in practice, if only because the specific cash-flow effects of a given currency change are hard to predict. Trained personnel are required to implement and monitor an active hedging program. Consequently, hedging should be undertaken only when the effects of anticipated exchange rate changes are expected to be significant.

A highly simplified example can illustrate the application of the financing rule developed previously, namely, that the liability structure of the combined MNC—parent and subsidiaries—should be set up in such a way that any change in the inflow on assets due to a currency change should be matched by a corresponding change in the outflow on the liabilities used to fund those assets. Consider the effect of a local currency (LC) change on the subsidiary depicted in Exhibit 11.11. In the absence of any exchange rate changes, the subsidiary is forecast to have an operating profit of $800,000. If a predicted 20 percent devaluation of the local currency from LC 1 = $0.25 to LC 1 = $0.20 occurs, the subsidiary's LC profitability is expected to rise to LC 3.85 million from LC 3.2 million because of price increases. However, that LC profit rise still entails a loss of $30,000, despite a reduction in the dollar cost of production.

Suppose the subsidiary requires assets equaling LC 20 million, or $5 million at the current exchange rate. It can finance these assets by borrowing dollars at 8 percent and converting them into their local currency equivalent, or it can use LC funds at 10 percent. How can the parent structure its subsidiary's financing in such a way that a 20 percent

EXHIBIT 11.11 • STATEMENT OF PROJECTED CASH FLOW

	Units (hundred thousands)	Unit Price (LC)	Total	
LC 1= $0.25				
Domestic sales	4	20	8,000,000	
Export sales	4	20	8,000,000	
Total revenue				16,000,000
Local labor (hours)	8	10	8,000,000	
Local material	8	3	2,400,000	
Imported material	6	4	2,400,000	
Total expenditures				12,800,000
Net cash flow from operations in LC				LC 3,200,000
Net cash flow from operations in U.S.$				$800,000
LC 1= $0.20				
Domestic sales	3	24	7,200,000	
Export sales	5	24	12,000,000	
Total revenue				19,200,000
Local labor (hours)	8	12	9,600,000	
Local material	10	3.5	3,500,000	
Imported material	4.5	5	2,250,000	
Total expenditures				15,350,000
Net cash flow from operations in LC				LC 3,850,000
Net cash flow from operations in U.S.$				$770,000

devaluation will reduce the cost of servicing the subsidiary's liabilities by $30,000 and thus balance operating losses with a decrease in cash outflows?

Actually, a simple procedure is readily available. If S is the dollar outflow on local debt service, then it is necessary that $0.2S$, the dollar gain on devaluation, equal $30,000, the operating loss on devaluation. Hence, $S = $150,000$, or LC 600,000 at the current exchange rate. At a local currency interest rate of 10 percent, that debt-service amount corresponds to local currency debt of LC 6 million. The remaining LC 14 million can be provided by borrowing $3.5 million. Exhibit 11.12 illustrates the offsetting cash effects associated with such a financial structure.

> The impact on debt servicing charges should offset the impact on operating cash flows.

This example would certainly become more complex if the effects of taxes, depreciation, and working capital were included. Although the execution becomes more difficult, a rough equivalence between operating losses (gains) and debt-service gains (losses) can still be achieved as long as all cash flows are accounted for. The inclusion of other foreign operations just requires the aggregation of the cash-flow effects over all affiliates because the MNC's total exchange risk is based on the sum of the changes of the profit contributions of each individual subsidiary.

 ILLUSTRATION   *DaimlerChrysler Hedges Its Operating Exposure*

In August 2003, DaimlerChrysler AG acknowledged that over half its second-quarter operating profit was generated by foreign-exchange hedging transactions. In July, the automaker had reported quarterly operating profit of €641 million, beating analyst expectations. At the time, the company said that currency trading activities to reduce the effect of the euro's rise against the dollar had had a positive effect but did not provide details. The August admission that €350 million of its operating profit came from currency trades indicated that the company made more money on foreign exchange than it did from selling cars. Analysts said that these hedging gains explained how DaimlerChrysler managed to hold its profit margins despite a brutal price war in North America and the euro's rise against the dollar, yen, and other currencies. Analysts said DaimlerChrysler deserved credit for managing the effects of the dollar's decline but that it was a worrying sign if 50 percent of your operating profit is coming from currency trading.

As mentioned earlier, this approach concentrates exclusively on risk reduction rather than on cost reduction. Where financial market imperfections are significant, a firm might consider exposing itself to more exchange risk in order to lower its expected financing costs.

ILLUSTRATION   *South Korean Companies and Banks Mismatch Their Currencies*

An important contributing factor to the magnitude of the collapse of the South Korean won was the currency mismatch faced by Korean companies and banks. Specifically, Korean banks lent huge amounts of won to the Korean *chaebol*, or conglomerates. The banks, in turn, financed their loans by borrowing dollars, yen, and other foreign currencies. The chaebol also borrowed large amounts of foreign currencies and invested the proceeds in giant industrial projects both at home and abroad. Considering how highly leveraged the chaebol were already, with debt-to-equity ratios on the order of 10:1, everything had to go right in order for them to be able to service their debts. When the won lost 40 percent of its value against the dollar during 1997, the chaebol had difficulty servicing their debts and many of them became insolvent. To the extent the Korean banks continued to receive won interest and debt repayments from the chaebol, devaluation of the won meant that the banks' won cash flows were insufficient to service their foreign debts. Similarly, although the chaebol's overseas projects were expected to generate foreign exchange to service their dollar debts, these projects turned out to be ill-conceived money losers. With both banks and chaebol scrambling to come up with dollars to service their foreign debts, the won was put under additional pressure and fell further, exacerbating the problems faced by Korean borrowers. In the last three months of 1997, eight out of the 30 largest chaebol went bankrupt.

EXHIBIT 11.12 • EFFECT OF FINANCIAL STRUCTURE ON NET CASH FLOW

	LC 1 = $0.25		LC 1 = $0.20	
	Local Currency	*Dollars*	*Local Currency*	*Dollars*
Operating cash flows	LC 3,200,000	$800,000	LC 3,850,000	$770,000
Debt service requirements:				
Local currency debt	600,000	150,000	600,000	120,000
Dollar debt	1,120,000	280,000	1,400,000	280,000
Total debt service outflow	1,720,000	430,000	2,000,000	400,000
Net cash flow	LC 1,480,000	$370,000	LC 1,850,000	$370,000

In August 2003, Empresa Brasileira de Aeronáutica SA (Embraer) of Brazil, the world's fourth-largest aircraft maker, reported that net income had fallen by 87 percent for the second quarter, despite recent multibillion orders from JetBlue and US Airways, due to Brazil's stronger currency and foreign-exchange hedging losses. Embraer President Maurício Botelho said that the company was "strongly hit by two factors beyond our control." He pointed out that the Brazilian *real* had appreciated by about 18 percent against the dollar during the quarter and that this had adversely affected Embraer. Embraer said that the appreciation raised its cost of goods sold, as well as its operating costs such as research and development and SG&A expenses. At the same time, nearly all of Embraer's revenue comes from exports. Its primary competitor in the regional jet market, Embraer's specialty, is Canada's Bombardier; to a lesser extent, Boeing and Airbus are also competitors. However, the biggest impact of the rising *real* came from $85 million in losses on currency swaps that Embraer used to convert its dollar-denominated liabilities into reais as a hedge. Embraer also lost money when Brazil's main export-credit agency, BNDES, delayed paying for $397 million in outstanding receivables. By the time BNDES made the payment, the *real's* strength meant that Embraer received fewer reais. In addition, BNDES had still not paid for $211 million of receivables for jets already delivered. Payments in reais are made at the spot rate in effect at the time of the payment.

QUESTIONS

1. What factors affect Embraer's operating exposure? Why did the *real's* appreciation reduce Embraer's operating profits?

2. Did Embraer decrease or increase its currency risk by hedging its dollar liabilities? Explain.

3. How can Embraer use financial hedging to reduce its currency risk?

4. Suppose that Embraer's $608 million in dollar receivables mentioned above were outstanding at the beginning of the second quarter and that payment for $397 million was not received until the end of the quarter. The remaining $211 million was still outstanding at the end of the quarter. With an 18 percent real appreciation during the quarter, how much of a dollar loss would Embraer take on these receivables? In performing this calculation, consider that Embraer must first translate its dollar receivables into reais and then convert any loss measured in reais back into dollars.

The currency turmoil in Asia in 1997 was unexpected, but Avon Products was prepared to deal with it. An examination of what Avon did before the crisis and how it responded afterward illustrates many of the principles of managing operating exposure. It also provides insights into the role of financial officers as key members of strategic management teams.

Avon has a long history of international operations. As a general rule, Avon tries to hedge its currency risk by buying almost all its raw materials and making nearly all its products in the markets in which they are sold. For example, Avon Asia-Pacific has factories that make cosmetics in its largest markets—China, Indonesia, the Philippines, and Japan—and contracts out production in six other Asian countries. It further hedged its currency risk by financing its local operations with local currency loans. Altogether, the ten Asian countries in which Avon operated accounted for $751 million of its $4.8 billion in revenue in 1996.

When the crisis began in Thailand in July 1997, Avon's executives did not anticipate that Thailand's problems would spread but as a precaution decided to further reduce currency risk by having the Asian units remit earnings weekly instead of monthly. By late August, however, the currency markets got nervous after the remarks of Malaysia's Prime Minister Mahathir Mohamad, who complained that Asia's economic crisis was provoked by an international cabal of Jewish financiers intent on derailing the region's growth. The head of Avon's Asia-Pacific region, Jose Ferriera, Jr., also considered the possibility that other Asian countries would have to allow their currencies to depreciate to maintain their export competitiveness. In response, Avon decided to sell about $50 million worth of five Asian currencies forward against the dollar for periods of up to fifteen months.

Having done what it could financially, Avon then turned to its operating strategy. Anticipating tough times ahead, Avon Asia-Pacific decided to redirect its marketing budget to hire more salespeople in Asia to bring in more customers rather than offering incentives to the existing sales force to get their current, cash-strapped customers to spend more money. Mr. Ferriera also urged his country managers to step up their purchase of local materials wherever possible and not allow local vendors to pass on all of their cost increases. At the same time, Avon began planning to compete more aggressively against disadvantaged competitors who have to import their products and raw materials. Finally, Avon began to analyze the incremental profits it could realize by using its Asian factories to supply more of the noncosmetic products sold in the United States. Avon Asia-Pacific was helped by a team of Latin American executives who traveled to Asia to share their experiences of how they had managed to cope in similar circumstances of currency turmoil in their countries. For example, during the Mexican crisis of 1994–1995, prices were raised slowly on price-sensitive brands aimed at low- and middle-income customers. Avon Mexico raised prices on premium brands much faster, since those brands were less price sensitive and competed with imports whose prices had doubled with the peso devaluation.

In all of these deliberations and decisions, Avon Treasurer Dennis Ling was a full and active participant. For example, he helped the head of Avon's jewelry business renegotiate the terms of its contract with a Korean company that supplies jewelry for sale in the United States. The result was a substantial price discount based on the won's steep decline against the dollar. According to Mr. Ling, "Part of my job is to help our managers of operations understand and take advantage of the impact of currencies on their business."[7]

11.6 SUMMARY AND CONCLUSIONS

In this chapter, we examined the concept of exposure to exchange rate changes from the perspective of the economist. We saw that the accounting profession's focus on the balance sheet impact of currency changes has led accountants to ignore the more important effect that these changes may have on future cash flows. We also saw that to measure exposure properly, we must focus on inflation-adjusted, or real, exchange rates instead of on nominal, or actual, exchange rates. Therefore, economic exposure has been defined as the extent to which the value of a firm is affected by currency fluctuations, inclusive of price-level changes. Thus, any accounting measure that focuses on the firm's past activities and decisions, as reflected in its current balance sheet accounts, is likely to be misleading.

Although exchange risk is conceptually easy to identify, it is difficult in practice to determine what the actual economic impact of a currency change will be. For a given firm, this impact

---

[7] Fred R. Bleakley, "How U.S. Firm Copes with Asian Crisis," *Wall Street Journal*, December 26, 1997, p. A2.

depends on a great number of variables, including the location of its major markets and competitors, supply and demand elasticities, substitutability of inputs, and offsetting inflation. Finally, we concluded that since currency risk affects all facets of a company's operations, it should not be the concern of financial managers alone. Operating managers, in particular, should develop marketing and production initiatives that help to ensure profitability over the long run. They should also devise anticipatory or proactive, rather than reactive, strategic alternatives in order to gain competitive leverage internationally.

The key to effective exposure management is to integrate currency considerations into the general management process. One approach that many MNCs use to develop the necessary coordination among executives responsible for different aspects of exchange risk management is to establish a committee for managing foreign currency exposure. Besides financial executives, such committees should—and often do—include the senior officers of the company such as the vice president-international, top marketing and production executives, the director of corporate planning, and the chief executive officer. This arrangement is desirable because top executives are exposed to the problems of exchange risk management, so they can incorporate currency expectations into their own decisions.

In this kind of integrated exchange risk program, the role of the financial executive is fourfold: (1) to provide local operating management with forecasts of inflation and exchange rates, (2) to identify and highlight the risks of competitive exposure, (3) to structure evaluation criteria so that operating managers are not rewarded or penalized for the effects of unanticipated currency changes, and (4) to estimate and hedge whatever operating exposure remains after the appropriate marketing and production strategies have been put in place.

QUESTIONS

1. a. Define exposure, differentiating between accounting and economic exposure. What role does inflation play?

   b. Describe at least three circumstances under which economic exposure is likely to exist.

   c. Of what relevance are the international Fisher effect and purchasing power parity to your answers to Parts a and b?

   d. What is exchange risk, as distinct from exposure?

   e. Under what circumstances might multinational firms be less subject to exchange risk than purely domestic firms in the same industry?

2. The sharp decline of the U.S. dollar between 1985 and 1995 significantly improved the profitability of U.S. firms both at home and abroad.

   a. In what sense was this profit improvement false prosperity?

   b. How would you incorporate the decline in the dollar in evaluating management performance? In making investment decisions?

   c. Comment on the following statement: "The sharp appreciation of the U.S. dollar during the early 1980s might have been the best thing that ever happened to American industry."

3. What marketing and production techniques can firms initiate to cope with exchange risk?

4. What is the role of finance in protecting against exchange risk?

5. E & J Gallo is the largest vintner in the United States. It gets its grapes in California (some of which it grows itself) and sells its wines throughout the United States. Does Gallo face currency risk? Why and how?

6. DaimlerChrysler's Chrysler division exports vans from the United States to Europe in competition with the Japanese. Similarly, Compaq exports computers to Europe. However, all of Compaq's biggest competitors are American companies—IBM, Hewlett-Packard, and Tandem. Assuming all else is equal, which of these companies—Chrysler or Compaq—is likely to benefit more from a weak dollar? Explain.

7. In 1994, the Singapore dollar rose by 9 percent in real terms against the U.S. dollar. What was the likely impact of the strong Singapore dollar on U.S. electronics manufacturers using Singapore as an export platform? Consider the following facts. On average, materials and components—85 percent of which are purchased abroad—account for about 60 percent of product costs; labor accounts for an additional 15 percent; and other operating costs account for the remaining 25 percent.

8. Di Giorgio International, a subsidiary of California-based Di Giorgio Corporation, processes fruit juices and packages condiments in Turnhout, Belgium. It buys Brazilian orange concentrate in dollars, German apples in marks, Italian peaches in lire, and cartons in Dutch guilders. At the same time, it exports 85 percent of its production. Assess Di Giorgio International's currency risk and determine how it can structure its financing to reduce this risk.

9. A U.S. company needs to borrow $100 million for a period of seven years. It can issue dollar debt at 7 percent or yen debt at 3 percent.

   a. Suppose the company is a multinational firm with sales in the United States and inputs purchased in Japan. How should this affect its financing choice?

   b. Suppose the company is a multinational firm with sales in Japan and inputs that are determined primarily in dollars. How should this affect its financing choice?

10. Huaneng Power International is a large Chinese company that runs coal-fired power plants in five provinces and in Shanghai. It has close to $1.2 billion in U.S. dollar debt whose proceeds it has used to purchase equipment abroad.

    a. What currency risks does Huaneng face?

    b. Do its lenders face any currency risks? Explain.

PROBLEMS

1. Hilton International is considering investing in a new Swiss hotel. The required initial investment is $1.5 million (or SFr 2.38 million at the current exchange rate of $0.63 = SFr 1). Profits for the first ten years will be reinvested, at which time Hilton will sell out to its partner. Based on projected earnings, Hilton's share of this hotel will be worth SFr 3.88 million in ten years.

   a. What factors are relevant in evaluating this investment?

   b. How will fluctuations in the value of the Swiss franc affect this investment?

   c. How would you forecast the $:SFr exchange rate ten years ahead?

2. A proposed foreign investment involves a plant whose entire output of 1 million units per annum is to be exported. With a selling price of $10 per unit, the yearly revenue from this investment equals $10 million. At the present rate of exchange, dollar costs of local production equal $6 per unit. A 10 percent devaluation is expected to lower unit costs by $0.30, while a 15 percent devaluation will reduce these costs by an additional $0.15. Suppose a devaluation of either 10 percent or 15 percent is likely, with respective probabilities of 0.4 and 0.2 (the probability of no currency change is 0.4). Depreciation at the current exchange rate equals $1 million annually, and the local tax rate is 40 percent.

   a. What will annual dollar cash flows be if no devaluation occurs?

   b. Given the currency scenario described above, what is the expected value of annual after-tax dollar cash flows assuming no repatriation of profits to the United States?

3. Mucho Macho is the leading beer in Patagonia, with a 65 percent share of the market. Because of trade barriers, it faces essentially no import competition. Exports account for less than 2 percent of sales. Although some of its raw material is bought overseas, the large majority of the value added is provided by locally supplied goods and services. Over the past five years, Patagonian prices have risen by 300 percent, and U.S. prices have risen by about 10 percent.

During this time period, the value of the Patagonian peso has dropped from P 1 = $1.00 to P 1 = $0.50.

   a. What has happened to the real value of the peso over the past five years? Has it gone up or down? A little or a lot?

   b. What has the high inflation over the past five years likely done to Mucho Macho's peso profits? Has it moved profits up or down? A lot or a little? Explain.

   c. Based on your answer to Part a, what has been the likely effect of the change in the peso's real value on Mucho Macho's peso profits converted into dollars? Have dollar-equivalent profits gone up or down? A lot or a little? Explain.

   d. Mucho Macho has applied for a dollar loan to finance its expansion. Were you to look solely at its past financial statements in judging its creditworthiness, what would be your likely response to Mucho Macho's dollar loan request?

   e. What foreign exchange risk would such a dollar loan face? Explain.

4. In 1990, General Electric acquired Tungsram Ltd., a Hungarian light bulb manufacturer. Hungary's inflation rate was 28 percent in 1990 and 35 percent in 1991, while the forint (Hungary's currency) was devalued 5 percent and 15 percent, respectively, during those years. Corresponding inflation for the United States was 6.1 percent in 1990 and 3.1 percent in 1991.

   a. What happened to the competitiveness of GE's Hungarian operations during 1990 and 1991? Explain.

   b. In early 1992, GE announced that it would cut back its capital investment in Tungsram. What might have been the purpose of GE's publicly announced cutback?

5. In 1985, Japan Airlines (JAL) bought $3 billion of foreign exchange contracts at ¥180/$1 over 11 years to hedge its purchases of U.S. aircraft. By 1994, with the yen at about ¥100/$1, JAL had incurred over $1 billion in cumulative foreign exchange losses on that deal.

a. What was the likely economic rationale behind JAL's hedges?

b. Did JAL's forward contracts constitute an economic hedge? That is, is it likely that JAL's losses on its forward contracts were offset by currency gains on its operations?

6. Nissan produces a car that sells in Japan for ¥1.8 million. On September 1, the beginning of the model year, the exchange rate is ¥150:$1. Consequently, Nissan sets the U.S. sticker price at $12,000. By October 1, the exchange rate has dropped to ¥125:$1. Nissan is upset because it now receives only $12,000 × 125 = ¥1.5 million per U.S. sale.

a. What scenarios are consistent with the U.S. dollar's depreciation?

b. What alternatives are open to Nissan to improve its situation?

c. How should Nissan respond in this situation?

d. Suppose that on November 1, the U.S. Federal Reserve intervenes to rescue the dollar, and the exchange rate adjusts to ¥220:$1 by the following July. What problems and/or opportunities does this situation present for Nissan and for General Motors?

7. Chemex, a U.S. maker of specialty chemicals, exports 40 percent of its $600 million in annual sales: 5 percent goes to Canada and 7 percent each to Japan, Britain, Germany, France, and Italy. It incurs all its costs in U.S. dollars, while most of its export sales are priced in the local currency.

a. How is Chemex affected by exchange rate changes?

b. Distinguish between Chemex's transaction exposure and its operating exposure.

c. How can Chemex protect itself against transaction exposure?

d. What financial, marketing, and production techniques can Chemex use to protect itself against operating exposure?

e. Can Chemex eliminate its operating exposure by hedging its position every time it makes a foreign sale or by pricing all foreign sales in dollars? Why or why not?

8. During 1993, the Japanese yen appreciated by 11 percent against the dollar. In response to the lower cost of the main imported ingredients—beef, cheese, potatoes, and wheat for burger buns—McDonald's Japanese affiliate reduced the price on certain set menus. For example, a cheeseburger, soda, and small order of french fries were marked down to ¥410 from ¥530. Suppose the higher yen lowered the cost of ingredients for this meal by ¥30.

a. How much of a volume increase is necessary to justify the price cut from ¥530 to ¥410? Assume

that the previous profit margin (contribution to overhead) for this meal was ¥220. What is the implied price elasticity of demand associated with this necessary rise in demand?

b. Suppose sales volume of this meal rises by 60 percent. What will be the percentage change in McDonald's dollar profit from this meal?

c. What other reasons might McDonald's have had for cutting price besides raising its profits?

9. In 1990, a Japanese investor paid $100 million for an office building in downtown Los Angeles. At the time, the exchange rate was ¥145/$. When the investor went to sell the building five years later, in early 1995, the exchange rate was ¥85/$ and the building's value had collapsed to $50 million.

a. What exchange risk did the Japanese investor face at the time of his purchase?

b. How could the investor have hedged his risk?

c. Suppose the investor financed the building with a 10 percent down payment in yen and a 90 percent dollar loan accumulating interest at the rate of 8 percent per annum. Since this is a zero-coupon loan, the interest on it (along with the principal) is not due and payable until the building is sold. How much has the investor lost in yen terms? In dollar terms?

d. Suppose the investor financed the building with a 10 percent down payment in yen and a 90 percent yen loan accumulating interest at the rate of 3 percent per annum. Since this is a zero-coupon loan, the interest on it (along with the principal) is not due and payable until the building is sold. How much has the investor lost in yen terms? In dollar terms?

10. Over the past year, China has experienced an inflation rate of about 22 percent, in contrast to U.S. inflation of about 3 percent. At the same time, the exchange rate has gone from Y8.7/U.S.$1 to Y8.3/U.S.$1.

a. What has happened to the real value of the yuan over the past year? Has it gone up or down? A little or a lot?

b. What are the likely effects of the change in the yuan's real value on the dollar profits of a multinational company like Procter & Gamble that sells in the local market? What can it do to cope with these effects?

c. What are the likely effects of the change in the yuan's real value on the dollar profits of a textile manufacturer that exports most of its output to the United States? What can it do to cope with these effects?

BIBLIOGRAPHY

Adler, Michael, and Bernard Dumas. "Exposure to Currency Risk: Definition and Measurement." *Financial Management,* Summer 1984, pp. 41–50.

Ankrom, Robert K. "Top Level Approach to the Foreign Exchange Problem." *Harvard Business Review,* July–August 1974, pp. 79–90.

Cornell, Bradford, and Alan C. Shapiro. "Managing Foreign Exchange Risks." *Midland Corporate Finance Journal,* Fall 1983, pp. 16–31.

Eaker, Mark R. "The Numeraire Problem and Foreign Exchange Risk." *Journal of Finance,* May 1981, pp. 419–426.

Garner, C. Kent, and Alan C. Shapiro. "A Practical Method of Assessing Foreign Exchange Risk." *Midland Corporate Finance Journal,* Fall 1984, pp. 6–17.

Giddy, Ian H. "Exchange Risk: Whose View?" *Financial Management,* Summer 1977, pp. 23–33.

Lessard, Donald R., and John B. Lightstone. "Volatile Exchange Rates Can Put Operations at Risk." *Harvard Business Review,* July–August 1986, pp. 107–114.

Shapiro, Alan C. "Exchange Rate Changes, Inflation, and the Value of the Multinational Corporation." *Journal of Finance,* May 1975, pp. 485–502.

_____, and Thomas S. Robertson. "Managing Foreign Exchange Risks: The Role of Marketing Strategy." Working Paper, The Wharton School, University of Pennsylvania, 1976.

INTERNET RESOURCES

www.reportgallery.com Web site that contains links to annual reports of over 2,200 companies, many of which are multinationals.

INTERNET EXERCISES

Review the annual reports of three MNCs found at www.reportgallery.com.

1. Is it obvious from their annual reports whether these companies are hedging their economic, transaction, or translation exposure?

2. Which currencies have these companies borrowed in besides the U.S. dollar? Do these foreign currency borrowings offset any obvious economic exposures they have in those currencies (e.g., because they have a subsidiary located in that country)?

PART III CASE STUDIES

CASE III.1
ROLLS-ROYCE LIMITED

Rolls-Royce Limited, the British aeroengine manufacturer, suffered a loss of £58 million in 1979 on worldwide sales of £848 million. The company's annual report for 1979 blamed the loss on the dramatic revaluation of the pound sterling against the dollar, from £1 = $1.71 in early 1977 to £1 = $2.12 by the end of 1979.

> *The most important reason for the loss was the effect of the continued weakness of the U.S. dollar against sterling. The large civil engines that Rolls-Royce produces are supplied to American air frames. Because of U.S. dominance in civil aviation, both as producer and customer, these engines are usually priced in U.S. dollars and escalated accordingly to U.S. indices. ...*

A closer look at Rolls-Royce's competitive position in the global market for jet engines reveals the sources of its dollar exposure. For the previous several years Rolls-Royce's export sales had accounted for a stable 40 percent of total sales and had been directed at the U.S. market. This market is dominated by two U.S. competitors, Pratt and Whitney Aircraft Group (United Technologies) and General Electric's aerospace division. As the clients of its mainstay engine, the RB 211, were U.S. aircraft manufacturers (Boeing's 747SP and 747, 00 and Lockheed's L1011), Rolls-Royce had little choice in the currency denomination of its export sales but to use the dollar.

Indeed, Rolls-Royce won some huge engine contracts in 1978 and 1979 that were fixed in dollar terms. Rolls-Royce's operating costs, on the other hand, were almost exclusively incurred in sterling (wages, components, and debt servicing). These contracts were mostly pegged to an exchange rate of about $1.80 for the pound, and Rolls-Royce officials, in fact, expected the pound to fall further to $1.65. Hence, they didn't cover their dollar exposures. If the officials were correct, and the dollar strengthened, Rolls-Royce would enjoy windfall profits. When the dollar weakened instead, the combined effect of fixed dollar revenues and sterling costs resulted in foreign exchange losses in 1979 on its U.S. engine contracts that were estimated by the *Wall Street Journal*

(March 11, 1980, p. 6) to be equivalent to as much as $200 million.

Moreover, according to that same *Wall Street Journal* article, "the more engines produced and sold under the previously negotiated contracts, the greater Rolls-Royce's losses will be."

QUESTIONS

1. Describe the factors you would need to know to assess the economic impact on Rolls-Royce of the change in the dollar:sterling exchange rate. Does inflation affect Rolls-Royce's exposure?

2. Given these factors, how would you calculate Rolls-Royce's economic exposure?

3. Suppose Rolls-Royce had hedged its dollar contracts. Would it now be facing any economic exposure? How about inflation risk?

4. What alternative financial management strategies might Rolls-Royce have followed that would have reduced or eliminated its economic exposure on the U.S. engine contracts?

5. What nonfinancial tactics might Rolls-Royce now initiate to reduce its exposure on the remaining engines to be supplied under the contracts? On future business (e.g., diversification of export sales)?

6. What additional information would you require to ascertain the validity of the statement that "the more engines produced and sold under the previously negotiated contracts, the greater Rolls-Royce's losses will be"?

CASE III.2
THE MEXICAN PESO

The basic purpose of this case is to have you conduct an in-depth analysis of government macroeconomic policies on firms and banks doing business with Mexico. The vehicle being used is the Mexican peso. See Exhibit III 2.1 for statistics related to exchange rates and price indexes in the United States and Mexico for the period 1976–1994. Using these data, please address the following questions.

EXHIBIT III 2.1 • THE MEXICAN PESO'S KEY STATISTICS: 1975–1997

Nominal Exchange Rates (period average)

Year:Quarter	Peso:Dollar	Dollar:Peso	CPI Mexico	CPI United States
75:1	12.5	$0.08000	100.0	100.0
75:2	12.5	$0.08000	103.2	101.9
75:3	12.5	$0.08000	107.0	104.1
75:4	12.5	$0.08000	110.4	105.8
76:1	12.5	$0.08000	115.2	106.8
76:2	12.5	$0.08000	118.2	108.2
76:3	19.9	$0.05038	122.0	109.8
76:4	20.0	$0.05013	137.3	111.0
77:1	22.7	$0.04407	149.1	113.0
77:2	23.0	$0.04348	155.7	115.5
77:3	22.7	$0.04407	162.4	117.1
77:4	22.7	$0.04399	168.6	118.5
78:1	22.7	$0.04398	177.7	120.4
78:2	22.8	$0.04384	183.9	123.6
78:3	22.7	$0.04399	191.4	126.5
78:4	22.7	$0.04401	197.6	129.0
79:1	22.8	$0.04380	209.5	132.3
79:2	22.8	$0.04378	217.0	136.8
79:3	22.8	$0.04390	225.2	141.3
79:4	22.8	$0.04386	235.6	145.4
80:1	22.9	$0.04376	256.8	151.1
80:2	22.9	$0.04361	271.5	156.6
80:3	23.1	$0.04337	289.3	159.4
80:4	23.3	$0.04301	303.9	163.7
81:1	23.8	$0.04209	328.5	168.0
81:2	24.4	$0.04103	348.4	171.9
81:3	25.2	$0.03968	365.9	176.9
81:4	26.3	$0.03804	389.4	179.3
82:1	45.5	$0.02198	435.0	180.9
82:2	48.0	$0.02082	501.5	183.5
82:3	50.0	$0.02000	606.1	187.0
82:4	96.5	$0.01036	730.8	187.5
83:1	102.0	$0.00980	926.2	187.3
83:2	120.0	$0.00833	1,076.9	189.7
83:3	132.0	$0.00758	1,217.2	191.9
83:4	143.9	$0.00695	1,369.6	193.6
84:1	155.8	$0.00642	1,601.9	195.7
84:2	167.6	$0.00597	1,807.3	197.9
84:3	179.6	$0.00557	1,987.7	200.1
84:4	192.6	$0.00519	2,196.5	201.5
85:1	208.9	$0.00479	2,552.7	202.8
85:2	228.0	$0.00439	2,800.9	205.3
85:3	305.1	$0.00328	3,097.0	206.7
85:4	371.7	$0.00269	3,527.5	212.6
86:1	473.6	$0.00211	4,254.7	213.1

(Continues)

Nominal Exchange Rates (period average) *(Continued)*

Year:Quarter	Peso:Dollar	Dollar:Peso	CPI Mexico	CPI United States
86:2	575.4	$0.00174	4,957.8	212.6
86:3	752.0	$0.00133	5,930.4	214.3
86:4	923.5	$0.00108	7,164.7	215.4
87:1	1,126.0	$0.00089	8,909.4	217.8
87:2	1,353.7	$0.00074	11,120.8	220.7
87:3	1,570.8	$0.00064	13,889.6	223.1
87:4	2,209.7	$0.00045	15,228.2	225.0
88:1	2,281.0	$0.00044	29,116.0	229.4
88:2	2,281.0	$0.00044	32,453.0	232.2
88:3	2,281.0	$0.00044	33,924.0	235.3
88:4	2,281.0	$0.00044	34,968.1	237.7
89:1	2,369.0	$0.00042	36,943.5	240.5
89:2	2,460.0	$0.00041	38,435.6	244.3
89:3	2,551.0	$0.00039	39,687.9	246.4
89:4	2,641.0	$0.00038	41,501.0	248.7
90:1	2,733.0	$0.00037	45,621.2	253.0
90:2	2,817.0	$0.00035	48,104.5	255.5
90:3	2,890.6	$0.00035	50,789.0	260.0
90:4	2,945.4	$0.00034	53,783.8	264.3
91:1	2,981.0	$0.00034	57,724.0	266.4
91:2	3,018.2	$0.00033	59,806.8	267.9
91:3	3,055.8	$0.00033	61,443.3	270.0
91:4	3,071.0	$0.00033	64,270.0	272.1
92:1	3,083.5	$0.00032	67,741.4	274.0
92:2	3,122.3	$0.00032	69,576.3	276.3
92:3	3,116.3	$0.00032	70,964.8	278.1
92:4	3,115.4	$0.00032	72,750.1	280.1
93:1	3,097.6	$0.00032	75,130.5	282.5
93:2	3,121.2	$0.00032	76,519.0	284.5
93:3	3,117.8	$0.00032	77,758.8	285.3
93:4	3,105.9	$0.00032	79,048.2	288.5
94:1	3,359.8	$0.00030	80,585.5	290.4
94:2	3,391.8	$0.00029	81,825.3	292.5
94:3	3,404.0	$0.00029	83,015.4	295.4
94:4	5,325.0	$0.00019	84,552.8	296.3
95:1	6,817.5	$0.00015	92,685.7	299.8
95:2	6,309.2	$0.00016	109,447.5	302.4
95:3	6,419.5	$0.00016	117,630.0	303.7
95:4	7,642.5	$0.00013	125,713.4	305.3
96:1	7,547.9	$0.00013	137,218.5	307.9
96:2	7,610.8	$0.00013	146,789.6	311.0
96:3	7,537.4	$0.00013	153,533.9	313.1
96:4	7,850.9	$0.00013	161,071.8	314.7
97:1	7,890.5	$0.00013	172,180.2	315.7
97:2	7,958.0	$0.00013	178,031.9	316.6
97:3	7,819.9	$0.00013	182,991.0	317.6
97:4	8,136.0	$0.00012	188,793.2	318.5

QUESTIONS

1. What are the causes of the continuing devaluation of the peso since August 1976? Analyze both the immediate causes (e.g., balance-of-payments deficits) and longer-term, more fundamental causes (e.g., inflation, the political and economic environment). Concentrate especially on the 1982 and 1994–1995 devaluations of the peso.

2. What role did oil price changes play in Mexico's difficulties?

3. What indicators of peso devaluation prior to 1982 and 1994 were there?

4. What were the likely effects of the peso devaluation between 1976 and January 1982 on

   a. Mexican companies?

   b. Foreign firms operating in Mexico?

   c. U.S. companies in border towns catering to Mexicans?

5. Redo question 4, focusing on the effects of peso devaluation subsequent to February 1982 and prior to December 1994.

6. In August 1982, the Mexican government devalued the peso, froze all dollar accounts in Mexican banks, and imposed currency controls. What are the government's objectives? How did these actions affect the black market value of the peso? Why?

7. How did the Mexican government's expropriation of Mexico City real estate, following the September 1985 earthquake, affect the value of the peso and why?

8. Consider the trust factor with respect to Mexican policies. What have been the probable effects of trust or its lack on investment in Mexico, Mexican citizens' investment choices, and the peso's value?

9. Are dollar loans to the Mexican government and Mexican companies exposed to exchange risk? Explain.

10. How did Mexico's economic policies contribute to its debt crisis? How have subsequent government policies affected Mexico's financial health?

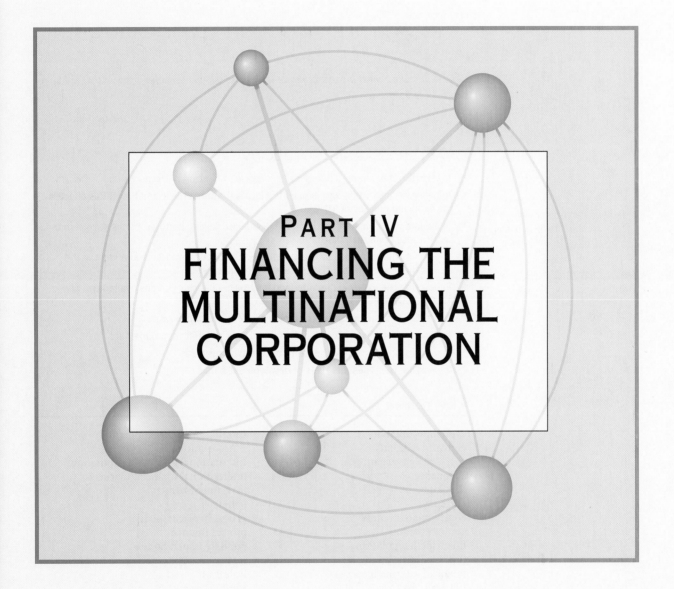

PART IV
FINANCING THE MULTINATIONAL CORPORATION

INTERNATIONAL FINANCING AND NATIONAL CAPITAL MARKETS

Money, like wine, must always be scarce with those who have neither wherewithal to buy it nor credit to borrow it.

Adam Smith (1776)

CHAPTER LEARNING OBJECTIVES

- To describe trends and differences in corporate financing patterns around the world
- To define securitization and explain the forces that underlie it and how it has affected the financing policies of MNCs
- To explain why bank lending is on the decline worldwide and how banks have responded to their loss of market share
- To explain what is meant by the globalization of financial markets and identify the factors that have affected the process of globalization
- To describe the external medium- and long-term financing options available to the multinational corporation
- To identify the functions and consequences of financial markets
- To describe the links between national and international capital markets
- To explain why firms may choose to raise capital overseas
- To describe the types and roles of development banks

KEY TERMS

capital productivity
convertible bonds
corporate governance
covenants
development bank
entrepôt
equity-related bonds
equity warrants
financial deregulation
financial innovation
financial intermediaries
fixed-rate issue
floating-rate note
foreign bank market
foreign bond market
foreign equity market
global bond issue
global shares
globalization of financial markets
International Bank for Reconstruction
    and Development

International Development
    Association
International Finance Corporation
international financial markets
investment banker
keiretsu
privately placed bonds
project finance
publicly issued bonds
regulatory arbitrage
Rule 144A
Samurai bond
securitization
Shogun bond
underwriting
universal banking
World Bank
World Bank Group
Yankee bond
Yankee stock issue

The growing internationalization of capital markets and the increased sophistication of companies means that the search for capital no longer stops at the water's edge. This reality is particularly true for multinational corporations. A distinctive feature of the financial strategy of MNCs is the wide range of external sources of funds that they use on an ongoing basis. General Motors packages car loans as securities and sells them in Europe and Japan. British Telecommunications offers stock in London, New York, and Tokyo, whereas Beneficial Corporation issues Euroyen notes that may not be sold in either the United States or Japan. Swiss Bank Corporation—aided by Italian, Belgian, Canadian, and German banks, as well as other Swiss banks—helps RJR Nabisco sell Swiss franc bonds in Europe and then swap the proceeds back into U.S. dollars.

This chapter and the next one explore the MNC's external medium- and long-term financing alternatives. These sources include both national and international capital markets. This chapter focuses on national capital markets along with specialized sources of capital, including development banks and project finance. Chapter 13 analyzes the international capital markets, particularly the Eurocurrency and Eurobond markets, which are increasingly important sources of funds for the MNC. We begin by discussing trends in corporate financing patterns.

12.1 CORPORATE SOURCES AND USES OF FUNDS

Firms can raise funds internally or externally.

Firms have three general sources of funds available: internally generated cash, short-term external funds, and long-term external funds. External finance can come from investors or lenders. Investors give a company money by buying the securities it issues in the financial markets. These securities, which are generally *negotiable* (tradable), usually take the form of publicly issued debt or equity. Debt is the preferred alternative: Regardless of the country studied, debt accounts for the overwhelming share of external funds. By contrast, new stock issues play a relatively small and declining role in financing investment. Regardless of whether debt or equity is offered to the public, the issuer will likely turn to a financing specialist—the **investment banker**—to assist in designing and marketing the issue. The latter function usually requires purchasing, or **underwriting**, the securities and then distributing them. Investment bankers are compensated by the *spread* between the price at which they buy the security and the price at which they can resell it to the public.

The main alternative to issuing public debt securities directly in the open market is to obtain a loan from a specialized financial intermediary that issues securities (or deposits) of its own in the market. These alternative debt instruments usually are commercial bank loans for short-term and medium-term credit or privately placed bonds for longer-term credit. Unlike **publicly issued bonds, privately placed bonds** are sold directly to only a limited number of sophisticated investors, usually life insurance companies and pension funds. Moreover, privately placed bonds are generally nonnegotiable and have complex, customized loan agreements—called **covenants.** The restrictions in the covenants range from limits on dividend payments to prohibitions on asset sales and new debt issues. They provide a series of checkpoints that permit the lender to review actions by the borrower that have the potential to impair the lender's position. These agreements have to be regularly renegotiated before maturity. As a result, privately placed bonds are much more like loans than like publicly issued and traded securities.

Financial Markets versus Financial Intermediaries

Companies in different countries exhibit different financing patterns.

Sources of external finance differ widely from country to country. German, French, and Japanese companies rely heavily on bank borrowing, whereas U.S. and British industry raise much more money directly from financial markets by the sale of securities. In all these countries, however, bank borrowing is on the decline. Corporate borrowing is increasingly taking the form of negotiable securities issued in the public capital markets rather than the form of nonmarketable loans provided by financial intermediaries.

This process, termed **securitization**, is most pronounced among Japanese companies. Securitization largely reflects a reduction in the cost of using financial markets at the same time that the cost of bank borrowing has risen. Until recently, various regulatory restrictions enabled banks to attract low-cost funds from depositors. With **financial deregulation**, which began in the United States in 1981 and in Japan in 1986 and is still ongoing, banks now must compete for funds with a wide range of institutions at market rates. In addition, regulatory demands for a stronger capital base have forced U.S. banks to use more equity financing, raising their cost of funds. Inevitably, these changes have pushed up the price of bank loans. Any top-flight company now can get money more cheaply by issuing commercial paper than it can from its banks. As a result, banks have a smaller share of the market for short-term business credit. Japanese companies also are finding that issuing bonds and leasing equipment are cheaper sources of medium-term and long-term money as well.

At the same time, the cost of accessing the public markets is coming down, especially for smaller and less well-known companies. Historically, these companies found it more economical to obtain loans from banks or to place private bond issues with life insurance companies. These **private placements** have proved cheaper because banks and life insurance companies specialize in credit analysis and assume a large amount of a borrower's debt. Consequently, they could realize important cost savings in several functions, such as gathering information about the condition of debtor firms, monitoring their actions, and renegotiating loan agreements.

Recent technological improvements in such areas as data manipulation and telecommunications have greatly reduced the costs of obtaining and processing information about the conditions that affect the creditworthiness of potential borrowers. Any analyst now has computerized access to a wealth of economic and financial information at a relatively low cost, along with programs to store and manipulate this information. Thus, investors are now more likely to find it cost-effective to lend directly to companies rather than indirectly through **financial intermediaries**, such as commercial banks.

Securitization, which involves replacing loans from banks with securities issued in the public markets, is increasing everywhere.

Securitization is replacing financial intermediation as the costs of gathering information on foreign firms declines.

Financial Systems and Corporate Governance

Despite the apparent convergence of financial systems, there are still some notable differences among countries in terms of **corporate governance**, which refers to the means whereby companies are controlled. The United States and United Kingdom are often viewed as prototypes of a market-oriented financial system (frequently referred to as the Anglo-Saxon, or AS, model), whereas Germany, France, and Japan are generally regarded as typical representatives of bank-centered finance (the Continental European and Japanese, or CEJ, type of financial system). In AS countries, institutional investors (pension funds, mutual funds, university and other nonprofit endowments, and insurance companies) make up an important part of the financial system. In CEJ countries, banks dominate the picture. Equity finance is important in AS countries and institutional shareholders exert a great deal of corporate control. The accepted objective is to maximize shareholder value, and boosting the return on capital employed is stressed. The emphasis on shareholder value has recently been endorsed by an international advisory panel to the Organization for Economic Cooperation and Development (OECD). According to the head of the panel, the Asian economic crisis can be traced to weak corporate governance: "Nobody was watching [Asian] management; they were growing for the sake of growth with no concern for shareholder value."[1] The crisis could most likely have been avoided, he said, had American-style corporate governance been in place.

Corporate governance differs significantly among countries, with equity finance very important in AS countries and bank finance being prominent in CEJ countries.

---

[1] Quoted in Robert L. Simison, "Firms Worldwide Should Adopt Ideas of U.S. Management, Panel Tells OECD," *Wall Street Journal,* April 2, 1998, p. A4.

Japanese and
German companies
have close relations
with their main
banks.

In CEJ countries, bank finance is prominent, share ownership and control are concentrated in banks and other firms, and corporate decision making is heavily influenced by close personal relationships between corporate leaders who sit on each other's boards of directors. Individual shareholders have little voice, resulting in much less concern for shareholder value and relatively low returns on capital. However, in all countries, competitive pressures and the threat of hostile takeovers of underperforming companies are forcing greater managerial accountability and an increased focus on shareholder value. For example, a number of Continental European companies are trying to make themselves more attractive to the growing ranks of international investors by improving their disclosure and corporate governance practices. The latter includes guarding the rights of shareholders, unraveling intricate takeover defenses designed to protect poorly performing management from the threat of a hostile bid, and improving the operations of their boards of directors by being clearer about how they function and by allowing shareholders (rather than other board members) to elect directors.

The difference in financial systems has real consequences for financial structures. For example, as already noted, large Japanese companies employ a high degree of leverage, particularly compared with U.S. companies. The ability to take on such large amounts of debt stems in part from the vast mutual-aid networks that most large Japanese firms can tap. These are the fabled **keiretsu**, the large industrial groupings—often with a major bank at the center—that form the backbone of corporate Japan. Keiretsu ties constitute a complex web of tradition, cross-shareholdings, trading relationships, management, cooperative projects, and information swapping. The keiretsu offer financial backing, management advice, and favorable contracts to their members and provide a safety net when corporate relatives get into trouble.

Partly because of the difference in industrial structures in the two countries, U.S. and Japanese firms relate to the banking system in a different way. Almost all big Japanese companies have one main bank—usually the bank around which the keiretsu is formed—that is their primary source of long-term loans. The main bank will have access to information about the company and have a say in its management that in most other countries would be unacceptable. Moreover, Japanese banks, unlike their U.S. counterparts, can hold industrial shares, so the main bank often holds a sizable amount of the equity of its borrowers. For example, until recently, Japanese banks owned almost 40 percent of the outstanding stock of Japanese manufacturing companies. Thus, for Japanese companies, the strong relation with one main bank—along with close ties to the other members of their keiretsu—is their main method of minimizing the risk of financial distress.[2]

The same is true of Germany, where so-called **universal banking** is practiced; German commercial banks not only perform investment banking activities but also take major equity positions in companies. As both stockholder and creditor, German banks can reduce the conflicts between the two classes of investors, leading to lower costs and speedier action in "workouts" of financial problems. The resulting increase in organizational efficiency should mean less risk for German companies in taking on large amounts of debt. In the United States, where corporate bank relations are less intimate, companies rely primarily on equity as a shock absorber. However, these cross-shareholdings have also created a highly stable corporate structure that sheltered German companies from competition and aggressive shareholders and resulted in underperforming operations.

---

[2] For a detailed analysis of the governance structure of the keiretsu, see Steven N. Kaplan and Bernadette A. Minton, "Appointments of Outsiders to Japanese Boards: Determinants and Implications for Managers," *Journal of Financial Economics,* October 1994, pp. 225–258; and Erik Berglöf and Enrico Perotti, "The Governance Structure of the Japanese Financial Keiretsu," *Journal of Financial Economics,* October 1994, pp. 259–284.

ILLUSTRATION   *Toyo Kogyo and Chrysler Experience Financial Distress*

The contrasting experiences of Toyo Kogyo (producer of Mazda cars) and Chrysler during recent periods of financial distress illustrate the unusual features of the Japanese financial system. In 1973, Toyo Kogyo (TK) was a successful producer of light and medium-sized cars. The energy crisis of 1974 precipitated a crisis at TK because of the high energy consumption of its rotary-engine, Wankel-powered Mazda models. Worldwide sales plunged 19 percent. To weather the storm, TK required a massive infusion of funds to develop new product offerings. Sumitomo Bank, its main bank, had the resources to rescue TK. On the basis of its thorough knowledge of TK's operations, Sumitomo decided that the company could be profitable with new product offerings and massive cost cutting. However, because it lacked confidence in TK's senior management, Sumitomo replaced them. With its own hand-picked executives in place, Sumitomo then financed the simultaneous development of three new models and the overhaul of TK's production system, extended credit to suppliers, and had the vast group of related Sumitomo companies buy Mazda vehicles. The new models were highly successful, and labor productivity grew by 118 percent over the next seven years.

In contrast to the situation at TK, Chrysler was able to persist with poor performance for over two decades because its investors had no effective remedies. Chrysler could ignore the need to restructure its operations because of its continued ability to borrow money; it still had a substantial, though dwindling, amount of shareholders' equity to support these loans. Despite the activities of some dissident shareholders, Chrysler continued under a self-perpetuating management until the crisis of 1979. Although Chrysler faced bankruptcy, its banks refused to lend it more money. In contrast to TK's Japanese banks, Chrysler's banks had an incomplete understanding of its plight and no way to obtain all the essential information. Even if they had, they could not have sent in the same type of rescue team that Sumitomo sent into TK. In the end, Chrysler was rescued by the U.S. government, which offered loan guarantees sufficient for the company's survival at about half its former size.

In a man-bites-dog turn of events, however, Chrysler eventually restructured to become the most profitable auto company in the world, and Mazda Motor Company once again got into deep trouble. Hurt by the strong yen and by a high-risk expansion strategy that backfired when global recession struck, by 1994 Mazda was stuck with $8 billion in debt and a main bank (still Sumitomo) that refused to bail it out. Instead, Sumitomo invited Ford Motor Company to take effective management control of Mazda, thereby entrusting Ford with the role that the bank itself played in the 1970s.

Competitive pressures are forcing a greater shareholder orientation in all countries, including Japan.

The price that Japanese and German companies pay for their heavy reliance on bank debt is less freedom of action. As the cost of accessing the capital markets directly has dropped, the main-bank relationship has gradually eroded in Japan and Germany, and Japanese and German companies have looked more to the equity market as their cushion against financial distress. The pace of change was accelerated in Japan when a law was passed that forced Japanese banks to reduce their shareholdings in individual companies to 5 percent or less. Similarly, intensifying foreign competition and the elimination of a steep capital gains tax are compelling German banks and insurance companies to unwind the complex system of interlocking shareholdings that has defined corporate Germany since World War II. In addition, in the wake of the Japanese stock market collapse and eroding corporate profits, some companies have begun to raise money by selling major chunks of their cross-shareholdings in the less important members of their keiretsu. Moreover, although relations between main banks and associated corporations remain intimate, companies are looking more carefully at second- and third-tier banks. Even main banks, however, are plagued with bad debts, declining bank capital, and a much higher cost of capital, forcing them to pay more attention to profitability and making them less reliable sources of capital for their corporate customers. In response, Japanese companies are turning increasingly to the corporate bond market to raise new capital.

In turning to the capital markets, German and Japanese firms are now confronting the same market pressures that U.S. companies have long faced. The result is a new shareholder-oriented management approach in many German and Japanese companies. With money being harder to come by, equity capital is forced to earn its keep. The result will be fewer poor investments and a greater focus on profits and shareholder value rather than on size and market share.

Globalization of Financial Markets

The globalization of financial markets stems from advances in communications and technology combined with financial deregulation.

The same advances in communications and technology that have lowered the cost of accessing financial markets directly, together with financial deregulation abroad—the lifting of regulatory structures that inhibit competition and protect domestic markets—have blurred the distinction between domestic and foreign financial markets. As the necessary electronic technology has been developed and transaction costs have plummeted, the world has become one vast, interconnected market. Markets for U.S. government securities and certain stocks, foreign exchange trading, and interbank borrowing and lending—to cite a few examples—operate continuously around the clock and around the world and in enormous size. The **globalization of financial markets** has brought about an unprecedented degree of competition among key financial centers and financial institutions that has further reduced the costs of issuing new securities.

Growing competition also has led to increasing deregulation of financial markets worldwide. Deregulation is hastened by the process of **regulatory arbitrage**, whereby the users of capital markets issue and trade securities in financial centers with the lowest regulatory standards and, hence, the lowest costs. In order to win back business, financial centers around the world are throwing off obsolete and costly regulations. For example, concerned that Tokyo had fallen behind London and New York as a global finance center, the Japanese government has developed a "Big Bang" financial reform program. This program would break down regulatory barriers between Japanese banks, insurance companies, and brokerage houses, and would also create opportunities in Japan for foreign financial companies by cutting red tape and barriers to the market. Deregulation—in Japan and elsewhere—is little more than an acknowledgment that the rules do not—and cannot—work.

ILLUSTRATION   *Capital Markets Compete for Business*

In mid-1989, Germany abolished its 10 percent withholding tax on interest income, less than six months after it took effect. The tax had triggered record capital flight from Germany, putting downward pressure on the Deutsche mark. Upon announcement of the repeal, German bonds jumped in value.

Similarly, in early 1990, Sweden announced that it would scrap a turnover tax on bond trading and halve a similar tax on trading in equities that had driven most international trading of Swedish shares abroad. The taxes had been imposed one year earlier as political concessions to powerful Swedish unions, which resented the large amounts of money being made in Swedish financial markets. Almost everyone else vehemently opposed the levies. The dire consequences predicted by critics were borne out in decimated trading volumes. For example, the tax on bond trading slashed the average daily trading volume of Swedish government securities by 78 percent from the year before. At the same time, volume on the Stockholm Stock Exchange plunged by 20 percent even though the market rose 119 percent in the period. The final straw was a study by the Finance Ministry showing that the various levies actually resulted in a net reduction in tax collections for Sweden as trades shifted abroad. On the day the tax cuts were announced, stocks of the largest Swedish companies rose almost 2.5 percent. By 1995, the 1 percent equity turnover tax had been removed entirely and the fraction of trades in Swedish equities done in Stockholm had risen to 60 percent from 40 percent in 1990.

Financial deregulation facilitates innovation and economic growth.

Financial deregulation also has been motivated by the growing recognition in nations with bank-centered financial systems that such systems are not providing adequately for the credit needs of the small and medium-sized firms that are the engines of growth and innovation. It has not escaped the notice of governments worldwide that the corporate success stories of the past twenty years—companies like Microsoft, Dell, Cisco, Amazon.com, 3Com, Yahoo!, Oracle, and Amgen—have come predominantly from the United States. Germany and Japan can boast of few Netscapes, AOLs, Iomegas, Suns, Compaqs, or Genentechs. By deregulating their financial markets, policymakers hope that their countries will emulate the results of the U.S. system of corporate finance.

The combination of freer markets with widely available information has laid the foundation for global growth. Fund raising is global now as well, with a growing amount of money being raised on the international capital markets. According to World Bank figures, the amount of money raised on the international capital markets has grown rapidly, rising to over $2.2 trillion in 1999. Treasurers are no longer confined to domestic markets as their source of funding and are now quick to exploit any attractive opportunity that occurs anywhere in the world.

Financial innovation segments, transfers, and diversifies risk.

Whereas competition drives the international financial system, innovation is its fuel. **Financial innovation** segments, transfers, and diversifies risk. It also enables companies to tap previously inaccessible markets and permits investors and issuers alike to take advantage of tax loopholes. More generally, financial innovation presents opportunities for value creation. To the extent that a firm can design a security that appeals to a special niche in the capital market, it can attract funds at a cost that is less than the market's required return on securities of comparable risk. However, such a rewarding situation is likely to be temporary because the demand for a security that fits a particular niche in the market is not unlimited. On the other hand, the supply of securities designed to tap that niche is likely to increase dramatically once the niche is recognized. Even though financial innovation may not be a sustainable form of value creation, it nonetheless can enable the initial issuers to raise money at a below-market rate.

 ILLUSTRATION *The Swedish Export Credit Corporation Innovates*

The Swedish Export Credit Corporation (SEK) borrows about $2 billion annually. To reduce its funding costs, SEK relies heavily on financial innovation. For example, SEK issued a straight bond, stripped it down to its two components—an annuity consisting of the interest payments and a zero-coupon bond consisting of the principal repayment at maturity—and sold the pieces to different investors. The annuity cash flow was tailored to meet the demands of a Japanese insurance company that was looking for an interest-only security, whereas the zero-coupon portion appealed to European investors who desired earnings taxed as capital gains rather than interest income. By unbundling the bond issue into separate parts that appealed to distinct groups of investors, SEK created a financial transaction whose parts were worth more than the whole.

Financial innovation has dramatically increased international capital mobility. As in the domestic case, cross-border financial transfers can take place through international securitization or international financial intermediation. The hypothetical case depicted in Exhibit 12.1 illustrates the distinction between these two mechanisms for international fund flows. A Belgian corporation with surplus funds seeks an investment outlet, and a Japanese corporation requires additional funds. International securitization might involve the Japanese firm issuing new bonds and selling them directly to the Belgian firm.

Alternatively, the Belgian firm's surplus funds could be transferred to the Japanese firm through international financial intermediation. This intermediation could involve three (or more) stages. First, the Belgian firm deposits its funds with a local Belgian bank. Second, the Belgian bank redeposits the money with an international money center bank in London that turns around and lends those funds to a Japanese bank. Third, the Japanese bank lends those funds to the Japanese corporation.

Whether international fund flows take place through financial intermediation or securitization depends on the relative costs and risks of the two mechanisms. The key determinant here is the cost of gathering information on foreign firms. As these costs continue to come down, international securitization should become increasingly more cost effective.

12.2 NATIONAL CAPITAL MARKETS AS INTERNATIONAL FINANCIAL CENTERS

Financial markets mobilize savings and allocate funds among potential users.

The principal functions of a financial market and its intermediaries are to mobilize savings (which involves gathering current purchasing power in the form of money from savers and transferring it to borrowers in exchange for the promise of greater future purchasing power) and to allocate those funds among potential users on the basis of expected risk-adjusted returns. Financial markets also facilitate both the transfer of risk (from companies to investors) and the reduction of risk (by investors holding a diversified portfolio of financial assets). Subsequent to the investment of savings, financial markets help

EXHIBIT 12.1 • SECURITIZATION VERSUS INTERMEDIATION

Securitization

| Nonbank corporation in Belgium | Belgian bank | International money center bank in London | Japanese bank | Nonbank corporation in Japan |

| Stage 1 | Stage 2 | Stage 3 |

Intermediation

Source: Anthony Saunders, "The Eurocurrency Interbank Market: Potential for International Crises?" Reprinted from *Business Review,* January/February 1988, p. 19. Used with permission of Federal Reserve Bank of Philadelphia.

to monitor managers (by gathering information on their performance) and exert corporate control (through the threat of hostile takeovers for underperforming firms and bankruptcy for insolvent ones). Financial markets also supply *liquidity* to investors by enabling them to sell their investments before maturity, thereby encouraging investment in worthwhile longer-term projects.

The consequences of well-functioning financial markets are as follows. More and better projects get financed (because of higher savings, a more realistic scrutiny of investment opportunities, and the lower cost of capital associated with risk diversification and increased liquidity); managers are compelled to run companies in accordance with the interests of investors (through active monitoring and the threat of bankruptcy or a hostile takeover for underperformers and by linking managerial compensation to stock prices); the rate of innovation is higher (by identifying and funding those entrepreneurs with the best chances of successfully initiating new goods and production processes); and individuals are able to select their preferred time pattern of consumption (saving consists of individuals deferring consumption in some periods so as to increase their consumption in later periods) and their preferred risk-return trade-off. The result is stronger economic growth and greater consumer satisfaction. These factors are summarized in Exhibit 12.2.

Financial markets work best when property rights are secure, contracts are easily enforceable, meaningful accounting information is available, and borrowers and investors are accountable for their decisions and bear the economic consequences of their behavior. In the absence of these conditions, markets cannot allocate capital efficiently and economic growth suffers.

The financial disaster in Asia points out the dangers of allocating capital by cronyism and bureaucratic dictate rather than through a rational process governed by realistic estimates of prospective risks and rewards. This command-and-control capitalism produced dysfunctional financial sectors that squandered hundreds of billions of dollars of hard-earned savings on unproductive investments and grandiose projects and begat corruption without end. The banking calamity in Japan bears continuing witness to the problems that can arise when the fundamental elements of openness and accountability are not just absent from a financial system but contrary to official policy.

Well-functioning financial markets lead to more and better projects being financed.

EXHIBIT 12.2 • THE ROLE AND CONSEQUENCES OF WELL-FUNCTIONING FINANCIAL MARKETS

Financial Functions
- Mobilize savings
- Allocate resources
- Facilitate risk transfer and risk management
- Monitor managers
- Exert corporate control
- Supply liquidity

Factors Promoting Well-Functioning Financial Markets
- Secure property rights
- Contracts easily enforceable
- Meaningful accounting information
- Transparent financial statements
- Accountability of borrowers and investors
- Borrowers and investors bear the consequences of their decisions

Consequences
- Greater capital accumulation
- Better projects
- More innovation
- Managerial accountability
- Preferred time pattern of consumption

Results
- Stronger economic growth
- Greater consumer satisfaction

ILLUSTRATION *Japanese Regulators Press Shinsei Bank to Make Bad Loans*

Even as the Japanese government has pledged to clean up its ravaged banking industry, Japanese regulators have pressured Shinsei Bank Ltd.—the first Japanese bank bought by foreigners—to continue lending to some of its shakiest customers. In meetings with Shinsei executives, top officials of Japan's Financial Services Agency directed Shinsei to loosen its credit policy and be more lenient to ailing borrowers. Shinsei was formed in March 2000 when a U.S. investor group, Ripplewood Holdings, acquired the failed Long Term Credit Bank of Japan Ltd (LTCB).

LTCB failed because it was unable—and unwilling—to follow the basic prescription for revitalizing a collapsing bank: Write off bad loans and cut credit to hopeless companies. That failure, and the difficulties faced by Shinsei, point up the clash between two visions of finance—a competitive, rational American one and Japan's longstanding system of entangled preferences and noneconomic motives. These conflicting visions are best expressed by the former head of LTCB, who said, "Perhaps the American way might be more efficient in a narrow economic sense, but it risked sacrificing the values that were most precious in Japan; ideas of harmony, respect and consensus." As Japan's property and stock markets collapsed during the 1990s, and bad loans proliferated, the Ministry of Finance quietly told banks to understate their bad debts and keep their borrowers on financial life support. LTCB followed this advice and kept growing, even showing profits by adopting ever more lenient loan classifications. Eventually, after several rescue plans fell through, LTCB was sold to Ripplewood.

Shinsei has stirred controversy since it opened under new management because it told its corporate borrowers that if loans did not meet new standards for profitability the borrowers had to repay them, pay higher interest, or offer collateral. Even more shocking to Japanese sensibilities, Shinsei has refused to help finance bailouts of delinquent borrowers and has cut off credit to risky customers. Such practices, standard among Western banks, are a novelty in Japan and have resulted in a spate of newspaper and magazine articles criticizing Shinsei for being tight-fisted. Foreign investors are closely watching Shinsei as a test of whether Japan will allow modern lending practices in its clubby banking world. Arm-twisting of bankers by politicians and regulators to support deadbeat borrowers is a major reason why Japan's banks have been crippled by bad loans for over a decade. Although Shinsei agreed to some of the FSA's changes to its lending policy, the bank said it would not make concessions that compromise its financial health.

Demanding investors and strong corporate governance improve capital productivity.

Conversely, a healthy dose of market discipline and the stringent credit standards it enforces can work wonders for an economy. A study by the McKinsey Global Institute examined **capital productivity**—the ratio of output (goods and services) to the input of physical capital (plant and equipment)—in Germany, Japan, and the United States.[3] Overall, U.S. capital productivity exceeded that of Japan and Germany by about 50 percent. As a result, the United States can simultaneously save less, consume more, and grow faster. This economic hat trick can be traced directly to activist shareholders demanding management accountability and paying for performance; tough disclosure rules and financial transparency in corporate accounts that allow investors to make informed decisions; rigorous credit analysis that helps screen out bad risks; and a willingness to inflict pain on imprudent lenders, cut off capital to less competitive companies, and allow inefficient companies to fail. Although many politicians and others claim that U.S. financial markets have hindered U.S. productivity by forcing American companies to be short-term

[3] McKinsey Global Institute, *Capital Productivity,* Washington, D.C., June 1996. This report is summarized in Raj Agrawal, Stephen Findley, Sean Greene, Kathryn Huang, Aly Jeddy, William W. Lewis, and Markus Petry, "Capital Productivity: Why the U.S. Leads and Why It Matters," *The McKinsey Quarterly,* 1996, No. 3, pp. 38–55.

oriented, the McKinsey report suggests exactly the opposite—that the focus of U.S. financial markets on financial performance, reinforced by strong corporate governance (the Enron and WorldCom scandals notwithstanding), leads directly to improved business performance. In the process of rewarding success and penalizing failure, financial virtue creates its own reward.

Good corporate governance also adds value for its practitioners. Another McKinsey study found that over 80 percent of potential investors would be willing to pay more for the shares of a well-governed company than for those of a poorly governed company with comparable financial performance. The actual premium investors say they would be willing to pay for a well-governed company differs by country: an 18 percent premium for a well-governed U.S. or U.K. company; a 20 percent premium for a well-governed German or Japanese company; a 22 percent premium for a well-governed Italian company; and a 27 percent premium for one in Venezuela or Indonesia.[4]

International Financial Markets

International financial centers develop where there is political stability, minimal government interference, and capital is well-treated.

Not surprisingly, most of the major financial markets attract both investors and fund raisers from abroad. That is, these markets are also **international financial markets**, where foreigners can both borrow and lend money. International financial markets can develop anywhere, provided that local regulations permit the market and that potential users are attracted to it. The most important international financial centers are London, Tokyo, and New York. All the other major industrial countries have important domestic financial markets as well, but only some, such as Germany and—recently—France, are also important international financial centers. On the other hand, some countries that have relatively unimportant domestic financial markets are important world financial centers. The markets of those countries, which include Switzerland, Luxembourg, Singapore, Hong Kong, the Bahamas, and Bahrain, serve as financial **entrepôts**, or channels through which foreign funds pass. That is, these markets serve as financial intermediaries between nonresident suppliers of funds and nonresident users of funds.

Political stability and minimal government intervention are prerequisites for becoming and remaining an important international financial center, especially an entrepôt center. Historically, London's preeminence as an entrepôt for international finance comes from its being a lightly regulated offshore market in a world of financial rigidities. That is why it became home to the Euromarkets about forty years ago. As financial markets deregulate, London's strength has shifted to its central location (including its central time zone) and financial infrastructure—its access to information by dint of its position astride huge international capital flows, its pool of financial talent, its well-developed legal system, and its telecommunications links. Even more important, financial firms need to be near big investors, and there is more money under management in London than anywhere else in Europe.

Foreign Access to Domestic Markets

Foreigners are often hampered in their ability to access domestic capital markets because of government regulations.

Despite the increasing liberalization of financial markets, governments are usually unwilling to rely completely on the market to perform the functions of gathering and allocating funds. Foreigners in particular are often hampered in their ability to gain access to domestic capital markets because of government-imposed or government-suggested restrictions relating to the maturities and amounts of money that they can raise. They are also hampered by the government-legislated extra costs, such as special

---

[4] *Investor Opinion Survey on Corporate Governance*, McKinsey & Company, June 2000. For the purpose of the country surveys, a well-governed company is defined as having a majority of outside directors on the board with no management ties; holding formal evaluations of directors; and being responsive to investor requests for information on governance issues. In addition, directors hold significant stockholdings in the company, and a large proportion of directors' pay is in the form of stock options.

taxes (for example, the U.S. interest equalization tax, or IET, in effect from 1963 to 1974), which they must bear on those funds that they can raise. Nonetheless, the financial markets of many countries are open wide enough to permit foreigners to borrow or invest.

As a citizen of many nations, the multinational firm has greater leeway in tapping a variety of local money markets than does a purely domestic firm, but it, too, is often the target of restrictive legislation aimed at reserving local capital for indigenous companies or the local government. The capital that can be raised is frequently limited to local uses through the imposition of exchange controls. As we have seen previously, however, multinationals are potentially capable of transferring funds, even in the presence of currency controls, by using a variety of financial channels. To the extent, therefore, that local credits substitute for parent- or affiliate-supplied financing, the additional monies are available for removal.

The Foreign Bond Market

The foreign bond market is that portion of the domestic bond market that represents issues floated by foreigners.

The **foreign bond market** is an important part of the international financial markets. It is simply that portion of the domestic bond market that represents issues floated by foreign companies or governments. As such, foreign bonds are subject to local laws and must be denominated in the local currency. At times, these issues face additional restrictions as well. For example, foreign bonds floated in Switzerland, Germany, and the Netherlands are subject to a queuing system, where they must wait for their turn in line.

The United States and Switzerland contain the most important foreign bond markets. (Dollar-denominated foreign bonds sold in the United States are called **Yankee bonds.**) Major foreign bond markets are also located in Japan and Luxembourg. (Yen bonds sold in Japan by a non-Japanese borrower are called **Samurai bonds**, in contrast to **Shogun bonds**, which are foreign currency bonds issued within Japan by Japanese corporations.)

In recent years, more of these foreign bond offerings have consisted of global bond issues. A **global bond issue** is an offering, usually denominated in dollars, that is registered in several national jurisdictions and marketed to investors around the world. A typical global issue is Philip Morris's $1 billion eight-year bond offering sold in 1997. The benefits of these global offerings are that issuing companies become better known overseas, broaden their investor base, and often save on financing costs.

Foreign bond issues, like their purely domestic counterpart, come in three primary flavors: fixed-rate issues, floating-rate notes (FRNs), and equity-related issues. **Fixed-rate issues** are similar to their domestic counterparts, with a fixed coupon, set maturity date, and full repayment of the principal amount at maturity. **Floating-rate notes** have variable coupons that are reset at fixed intervals, usually every three to six months. The new coupon is set at a fixed margin above a mutually agreed-upon reference rate such as the Treasury bill rate or the commercial paper rate.

Equity-related bonds combine features of the underlying bond and common stock. The two principal types of equity-related bonds are convertible bonds and bonds with equity warrants. **Convertible bonds** are fixed-rate bonds that are convertible into a given number of shares before maturity. **Equity warrants** give their holder the right to buy a specified number of shares of common stock at a specified price during a designated time period. The relative amount of foreign bonds issued in the three different categories varies from year to year depending on market conditions.

After the economic crisis in Asia, Asian corporations scrambled for new equity to recapitalize and shore up balance sheets overloaded with debt and unsupported by much remaining equity at the new exchange rates. The preferred method of providing new equity or its equivalent was through convertible bonds and preferred shares. Both give fresh money coming into a troubled company a higher claim on assets under liquidation than would straight equity, while at the same time providing a significant upside opportunity for investors who thought the markets had overreacted. The benefit for struggling companies is that convertibles reduce debt-service charges because they carry lower interest rates than the debt they replace. In addition, upon conversion (if it occurs), the debt becomes equity. Several such issues in 1998 included Singapore Telephone's $1 billion five-year convertible bond; New World Infrastructure's $250 million five-year convertible bond; COSCO (Hong Kong) Group's $150 million exchangeable bond; and Guangdong Investment's $125 million in convertible preferred.

The Foreign Bank Market   The **foreign bank market** represents that portion of domestic bank loans supplied to foreigners for use abroad. As in the case of foreign bond issues, governments often restrict the amounts of bank funds destined for foreign purposes. Foreign banks, particularly Japanese banks, have become an important funding source for U.S. corporations.

Foreign banks are an increasingly important source of funding.

One indication of the importance of foreign banks is the fact that only four out of the world's twenty-five largest banks ranked by assets as of the end of 2001 were American. Five of these banks were Japanese (including the largest, Mizuho Financial Group), five were British, four were German, three were French, with the Swiss and Dutch having two top–twenty-five banks apiece. The minimal representation by American banks among the world's largest can be attributed primarily to prohibitions on interstate banking in the United States. However, it should be noted that size is not everything. In terms of market capitalization, which reflects current and anticipated profitability, U.S. banks shine, accounting for five of the ten most valuable banks. Just one of the ten largest banks by market capitalization was Japanese, reflecting Japanese banks' dismal profit outlook and huge loan losses.

The Foreign Equity Market   The idea of placing stock in foreign markets has long attracted corporate finance managers. One attraction of the **foreign equity market** is the diversification of equity funding risk: A pool of funds from a diversified shareholder base insulates a company from the vagaries of a single national market. Some issues are too large to be taken up only by investors in the national stock market. For large companies located in small countries, foreign sales may be a necessity. When KLM, the Dutch airline, issued 50 million shares to raise $304 million, it placed 7 million shares in Europe, 7 million in the United States, and 1 million in Japan. According to a spokesman for the company, "The domestic market is too small for such an operation."[5]

Equity issues are increasingly being sold abroad.

Selling stock overseas also can increase the potential demand for the company's shares, and hence its price, by attracting new shareholders. For example, a study by Gordon Alexander, Cheol Eun, and S. Janakiramanan found that foreign companies that listed their shares in the United States experienced a decline in their required return, boosting their stock prices.[6] Similarly, Dennis Logue and Anant Sundaram found that cross-listing foreign companies in the United States enhances the valuations for the listing companies by up to 10 percent relative to country and industry benchmarks.[7] This evidence is consistent with the theoretical work of Robert Merton, who has shown that a company can lower its cost of equity capital and thereby increase its market value by expanding its investor base.[8]

For a firm that wants to project an international presence, an international stock offering can spread the firm's name in local markets. In the words of a London investment banker, "If you are a company with a brand name, it's a way of making your product known and your presence known in the financial markets, which can have a knock-off

[5] "International Equities: The New Game in Town," *Business International Money Report*, September 29, 1987, p. 306.
[6] Gordon J. Alexander, Cheol S. Eun, and S. Janakiramanan, "International Listings and Stock Returns: Some Empirical Evidence," *Journal of Financial and Quantitative Analysis* (June 1988), pp. 135–151.
[7] Dennis E. Logue and Anant K. Sundaram, "Valuation Effects of Foreign Company Listings on U.S. Exchanges," *Journal of International Business Studies* (1996), pp. 67–88.
[8] Robert C. Merton, "A Simple Model of Capital Market Equilibrium with Incomplete Information," *Journal of Finance* (July 1987), pp. 483–510.

effect on your overall business. A marketing exercise is done; it's just like selling soap."[9] According to Apple Computer's investor relations manager, Apple listed its shares on the Tokyo exchange and the Frankfurt exchange "to raise the profile of Apple in those countries to help us sell computers. In Japan, being listed there gets us more interest from the business press."[10]

 ILLUSTRATION   *Waste Management Lists Its Stock in Australia*

Chicago-based Waste Management has been operating in Australia since 1984 and has gained a leading share of the garbage-collection market through expansion and acquisition. In 1986, the firm issued shares in Australia and then listed those shares on the Australian exchanges. A principal reason for the listing was to enhance its corporate profile. According to a Waste Management spokesman, "We view Australia as a growth market, and what we really wanted was to increase our visibility."[11]

Listing gets Waste Management better known in the financial community as well. This visibility in turn aids the expansion program, which hinges largely on mergers and acquisitions, by increasing contacts with potential joint-venture or acquisition candidates. Listing also facilitates stock-for-stock swaps.

An Australian listing also enhances the local profit-sharing package. Waste Management uses an employee stock program as an integral feature of its compensation. By listing locally, the firm increases the prominence of its shares, and the program becomes more attractive to employees.

A growing number of foreign companies are listing their shares on the New York Stock Exchange and raising equity capital in the United States.

To capture some of these potential benefits, more companies are selling stock issues overseas. For example, the largest common stock offering in the United States in 1991 was a $1.2 billion issue by Telefonos de Mexico (Telmex), part of a $2.2 billion global offering. In all, **Yankee stock issues**—stock sold by foreign companies to U.S. investors—totaled almost $5 billion in 1991. That number has risen since then. For example, Deutsche Telekom's global equity offering (see Exhibit 12.3 for the announcement) included a $1.9 billion tranche to be sold in the United States because of its view that the size of its long-term capital needs required access to a larger and more liquid market than that provided by its German home market. Similarly, in October 1992, Roche Holding Ltd., the Swiss pharmaceutical giant, announced that it had completed a U.S. private placement of $275 million worth of stock. The move reflected Roche's desire to tap into the world's largest capital market because its rapid growth had "left Roche simply too big for the Swiss market."[12] Indeed, more foreign companies are selling their initial public offerings, or IPOs, in the United States because they "get a better price, a shareholder base that understands their business, and they can get publicity in a major market for their products."[13]

In 1993, Daimler-Benz (now DaimlerChrysler), the industrial conglomerate that makes the Mercedes-Benz, became the first German company to list its shares on the New York Stock Exchange. To qualify for the listing, Daimler-Benz had to provide an onerous, by German standards, level of financial disclosure and undertake a costly revision of its accounting practices to conform to U.S. generally accepted accounting principles (GAAP). The difference between GAAP and German accounting rules is apparent in

---

[9] "International Equities: The New Game in Town."

[10] Quoted in Kathleen Doler, "More U.S. Firms See Foreign Shareholdings as a Plus," *Investors Business Daily,* February 17, 1994, p. A4.

[11] "Waste Management Who? Why One U.S. Giant Is Now Listed Down Under," *Business International Money Report,* December 22, 1986, p. 403.

[12] Quoted in "Roche Sells 100,000 Shares in U.S. Market," *Wall Street Journal,* October 2, 1992, p. A7.

[13] Quoted in Michael R. Sesit, "Foreign Firms Flock to U.S. for IPOs," *Wall Street Journal,* June 23, 1995, p. C1.

EXHIBIT 12.3 • THE INTERNATIONAL EQUITY OFFERING BY DEUTSCHE TELEKOM

·· T Deutsche Telekom

Deutsche Telekom AG, Bonn, Germany

Global Initial Public Offering of 690,000,000 Ordinary Shares in the Form of Shares and American Depositary Shares at DM 28.50 per Share and at US$ 18.89 per ADS

Global Coordinators

Deutsche Bank
Aktiengesellschaft

Dresdner Bank
Aktiengesellschaft

Goldman, Sachs & Co.

The Shares were offered in the following regions

Germany – 462,300,000 Shares

Dresdner Bank
Aktiengesellschaft

Deutsche Bank
Aktiengesellschaft

DG BANK Deutsche Genossenschaftsbank	Westdeutsche Landesbank Girozentrale	Bayerische Landesbank Girozentrale	Commerzbank Aktiengesellschaft	Bayerische Hypotheken- und Wechsel-Bank Aktiengesellschaft	Bayerische Vereinsbank Aktiengesellschaft
	Helaba Landesbank Hessen-Thüringen Girozentrale	Bankgesellschaft Berlin Aktiengesellschaft	Norddeutsche Landesbank Girozentrale	SüdwestLB	
Baden-Württembergische Bank Aktiengesellschaft	BHF-BANK	CS First Boston Effectenbank Aktiengesellschaft	Goldman, Sachs & Co. oHG	Sal. Oppenheim jr. & Cie. Kommanditgesellschaft auf Aktien	M.M. Warburg & CO KGaA
Berenberg Bank Joh. Berenberg, Gossler & Co.	BfG Bank AG	Delbrück & Co. Privatbankiers	FLESSABANK Bankhaus Max Flessa & Co	Hamburgische Landesbank – Girozentrale –	Georg Hauck & Sohn Bankiers KGaA	IKB Deutsche Industriebank Aktiengesellschaft
Bankhaus Hermann Lampe Kommanditgesellschaft	Landesbank Rheinland-Pfalz –Girozentrale–	Landesbank Saar Girozentrale	Landesbank Sachsen Girozentrale	Landesbank Schleswig-Holstein Girozentrale	Landesgirokasse öffentliche Bank und Landessparkasse
	B. Metzler seel. Sohn & Co. Kommanditgesellschaft auf Aktien	SchmidtBank KGaA	Schröder Münchmeyer Hengst & Co	Trinkaus & Burkhardt Kommanditgesellschaft auf Aktien	

United Kingdom – 57,500,000 Shares

SBC Warburg
A DIVISION OF SWISS BANK CORPORATION

Dresdner Kleinwort Benson	NatWest Securities Limited	Deutsche Morgan Grenfell
ABN AMRO Rothschild	CS First Boston	Robert Fleming & Co. Limited
	Goldman Sachs International	
Bayerische Landesbank Girozentrale	Cazenove & Co.	Schroders

Americas – 97,750,000 Shares

Goldman, Sachs & Co.   **Deutsche Morgan Grenfell**   **Merrill Lynch & Co.**

Morgan Stanley & Co. Incorporated	Salomon Brothers Inc	
ABN AMRO Rothschild A Division of ABN AMRO Securities (USA) Inc.	CS First Boston	
	Dresdner Kleinwort Benson	
Bear, Stearns & Co. Inc.	Alex. Brown & Sons Incorporated	Dean Witter Reynolds Inc.
Donaldson, Lufkin & Jenrette Securities Corporation	A.G. Edwards & Sons, Inc.	Everen Securities, Inc. J.P. Morgan & Co.
PaineWebber Incorporated	Prudential Securities Incorporated	RBC Dominion Securities Corporation
Scotia Capital Markets	Smith Barney Inc.	Toronto Dominion Securities
Advest, Inc.	Arnhold and S. Bleichroeder, Inc.	Robert W. Baird & Co. Incorporated
Sanford C. Bernstein & Co., Inc.	Dain Bosworth Incorporated	Edward D. Jones & Co., L.P.
Legg Mason Wood Walker Incorporated	McDonald & Company Securities, Inc.	Principal Financial Securities, Inc.
Stephens Inc.	Stifel, Nicolaus & Company Incorporated	Sutro & Co. Incorporated

Rest of Europe – 37,950,000 Shares

Paribas Capital Markets

	UBS Limited	Dresdner Kleinwort Benson
ABN AMRO Rothschild	Banque Nationale de Paris	CS First Boston
	Deutsche Morgan Grenfell Goldman Sachs International	
BBV Interactivos, S.V.B.	Bayerische Vereinsbank Aktiengesellschaft	Banque Générale du Luxembourg S.A.
Creditanstalt Investment Bank	Commerzbank Aktiengesellschaft Den Danske Bank	Enskilda Securities Skandinaviska Enskilda Banken
KB-Securities	Mediobanca – Banca di Credito Finanziario SpA	Société Générale

Asia-Pacific/Rest of World – 34,500,000 Shares

Daiwa Europe Limited

Nomura International	Lehman Brothers	Deutsche Morgan Grenfell
ABN AMRO Rothschild		Dresdner Kleinwort Benson
	Goldman Sachs (Asia) L.L.C. HSBC Investment Banking	
Indosuez Capital	Nikko Europe Plc	WestLB Securities Pacific Ltd.
Yamaichi International (Europe) Limited	The Development Bank of Singapore Ltd	
	Rashid Hussain Securities Sdn Bhd	Securities One
Ssangyong Investment & Securities Co., Ltd.		J B Were & Son
Kankaku (Europe) Limited	KOKUSAI Europe Limited	New Japan Securities Europe Limited
	Universal (U.K.) Limited Wako International (Europe) Limited	

Employee Share Ownership Programme of 23,700,000 Shares

UBS
Schweizerische Bankgesellschaft (Deutschland) AG

DG BANK
Deutsche Genossenschaftsbank

Verband der Post-, Spar- und Darlehnsvereine e.V.

Advisors to the Company
NM Rothschild & Sons
Coopers & Lybrand/Sietz & Partner Ltd.

Advisor to the Government of the Federal Republic of Germany
CS First Boston
KPMG Deutsche Treuhand-Gesellschaft

Daimler-Benz's published results for fiscal 1994. Although Daimler showed a profit of $636 million under German rules, it reported a loss of $748 million after conforming to GAAP and eliminating the impact of drawing down hidden reserves (which is allowed in Germany). Daimler-Benz undertook the arduous task of revising its financial statements because the company wanted access to the large and liquid pool of capital represented by the U.S. market. Daimler also felt that the positive image of its Mercedes cars would help it raise capital at a lower price from wealthy Americans. During the six weeks between the announcement of its plans for a New York Stock Exchange (NYSE) listing and actually receiving the listing, Daimler-Benz's shares rose more than 30 percent, in contrast to an 11 percent rise for the German stock market overall.

It is not just large foreign companies that are issuing stock in the United States these days. The existence of numerous U.S. investment analysts, entrepreneurs, and investors familiar with the nature and needs of emerging firms means that many medium-sized European firms are now finding it easier and quicker to do IPOs on the Nasdaq exchange in the United States than to raise capital in their underdeveloped domestic capital markets. For example, in 1996, Genset, a French biotechnology company, raised $99 million on the Nasdaq in the largest biotechnology IPO that year.

An important new avenue for foreign equity (and debt) issuers, ranging from France's Rhone-Poulenc to Korea's Pohang Iron & Steel, to gain access to the U.S. market was opened up in 1990 when the Securities and Exchange Commission (SEC) adopted **Rule 144A**, which allows qualified institutional investors to trade in unregistered private placements, making them a closer substitute for public issues. This rule greatly increases the liquidity of the private placement market and makes it more attractive to foreign companies, who are frequently deterred from entering the U.S. market by the SEC's stringent disclosure and reporting requirements. An advantage of a private placement is that its total cost could be half of a public offering's cost. It also takes less time to do a private placement. However, pricing for private placements is not as competitive and the issuing company has limited ongoing access to U.S. securities markets compared to a public offering.

The desire to build a global shareholder base also is inducing many American companies—which until recently issued stock almost exclusively in the United States—to sell part of their issues overseas. For example, in May 1992, General Motors raised $2.1 billion by selling 40 million shares in the United States, 6 million in Britain, 4.5 million in Europe, and 4.5 million in the Far East. Exhibit 12.4 shows the announcement of that issue. As usual, the benefits of expanded ownership must be traded off against the added costs of inducing more investors to become shareholders.

Most major stock exchanges permit sales of foreign issues provided they satisfy all the listing requirements of the local market. Some of the major stock markets list large numbers of foreign stocks. For example, Black & Decker, Caterpillar, and General Motors are among the more than 200 foreign stocks listed on the German stock exchanges. Similarly, almost 500 foreign stocks—including ITT, Hoover, and Woolworth—are listed on the British exchanges. Although many foreign companies are listed on the NYSE, even more would be were it not for the SEC's demand that they first conform with tougher U.S. accounting and disclosure practices. The SEC, however, is under pressure to relax its stand by both foreign companies and the NYSE, the latter because it worries about falling behind in the race to list large non-U.S. companies. Nonetheless, in 1997, one out of every four new listings on the NYSE was a foreign company, and such listings almost quadrupled to 400 between 1992 and 2000.

The rise of electronic exchanges and the growing desire of investors and companies to move beyond national borders for trading shares and raising capital—and to do so more cheaply—has put pressure on national stock exchanges to internationalize. National exchanges are merging (or attempting to; the London Stock Exchange and the German Börse announced a merger in May 2000 that later fell apart) or entering into alliances (Nasdaq has formed affiliations with stock exchanges in Japan, Hong Kong, and Canada and the NYSE is exploring links with exchanges in Japan and France) in an attempt to capture more business or just to survive. The ultimate aim is to create a global stock market in which the shares of the world's largest companies can be traded 24 hours a day cheaply and efficiently. Such a market should bring greater liquidity and lower costs.

Rule 144A has improved foreign access to the U.S. equity market.

EXHIBIT 12.4 • GENERAL MOTORS' GLOBAL EQUITY ISSUE

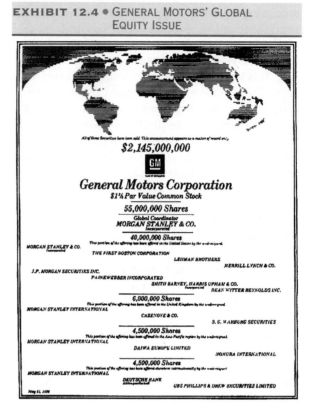

Source: Reprinted with permission from General Motors Corporation.

One outcome of the increasing globalization of stock markets is the global share. **Global shares** are the same as ordinary shares but trade in multiple currencies around the world. The first global share arose in late 1998 when the newly created DaimlerChrysler began trading as a global share in the United States, Germany, Japan, and five other countries. As of August 2001, only two other global shares existed, one by the Swiss financial services giant UBS and the other by the German chemical company Celanes.

Globalization of Financial Markets Has Its Downside

International financial markets reward countries following sound economic policies and are swift to punish countries following questionable economic policies.

The army of investors searching worldwide for the highest risk-adjusted returns wields a two-edged sword: It is likely to reward sound economic policies, and it is swift to abandon countries whose economic fundamentals are questionable. As a result, countries such as Italy, Spain, Sweden, and Mexico with large public sector or trade deficits or rapid money-supply growth have earned harsh treatment from financial markets. By demanding bigger premiums for the risk of holding these nations' currencies, the markets force *de facto* devaluations of their currencies, thereby serving to punish the profligate and reward the virtuous. In the eyes of many international economists, markets have replaced the International Monetary Fund as the disciplinary force for the global economy.

A devaluation raises the cost of imports for a country, boosts its interest rates (to lure investors back), and forces the government to take steps to address the monetary, budget, or trade problems that led to the capital flight and devaluation in the first place. Of course, changing the policies that created these problems can impose significant costs on favored political constituents, which is why these problems were not addressed earlier. For example, Japanese bureaucrats and politicians have long acted as if market forces exist only to be tamed or subverted. After a decade of Japanese economic stagnation, however, foreign investors pushed the stock and currency markets to levels so low that they threatened the existence of major Japanese banks and other corporations. The fear of further adverse financial market reaction has created a sense of crisis in Japan and pushed the nation's notoriously stodgy government to finally offer concrete plans to clean up its bankrupt financial sector and deregulate the economy.

Blaming financial markets for the political and economic disruptions caused by these policy changes misses the point. Financial markets are in the business of gathering and processing information from millions of savers and borrowers around the world in order to perform their real function, which is to price capital and allocate it to its most productive uses. In performing this function, markets reflect the perceptions of risk and reward of its participants. However, they do not create the underlying reality that caused those perceptions.

The long-run risk to the global economy caused by the abrupt shifts in capital flows and attendant waves of devaluations is that some politicians will seek to reimpose controls on capital and trade flows, particularly if the politicians manage to convince themselves that the markets are behaving in an irresponsible fashion. Such controls—whatever their motivation—would reverse the trend toward freer trade and capital markets and make the world worse off.

12.3 DEVELOPMENT BANKS

Development banks help finance projects that would not otherwise be funded by private capital.

To help provide the huge financial resources required to promote the development of economically backward areas, the United States and other countries have established a variety of **development banks**, whose lending is directed to investments that might not otherwise be funded by private capital. These investments include dams, roads, communication systems, and other infrastructure projects whose economic benefits cannot be completely captured by private investors, as well as projects such as steel mills or chemical plants whose value lies in perceived political and social advantages to the nation (or at least to its leaders). The loans generally are medium to long term and carry concessionary rates.

This type of financing has three implications for the private sector. First, the projects require goods and services, which corporations can provide. Second, establishing an infrastructure makes available new investment opportunities for multinational corporations. Third, even though most development bank lending is done directly to a government, multinationals find that these banks are potential sources of low-cost, long-term, fixed-rate funds for certain types of ventures. The time-consuming nature of arranging financing from them, however—in part due to their insistence on conducting their own in-house feasibility studies—usually leaves them as a secondary source of funds. Their participation may be indispensable, however, for projects that require heavy infrastructure investments such as roads, power plants, schools, communications facilities, and housing for employees. These infrastructure investments are the most difficult part of a project to arrange financing for because they generate no cash flow of their own. Thus, loans or grants from an international or regional development bank are often essential to fill a gap in the project financing plan.

There are three types of development banks: the World Bank Group, regional development banks, and national development banks.

The World Bank Group

The **World Bank Group** is a multinational financial institution that was established at the end of World War II to help provide long-term capital for the reconstruction and development of member countries. It comprises three related financial institutions: the

International Bank for Reconstruction and Development (IBRD), also known as the World Bank; the International Finance Corporation (IFC); and the International Development Association (IDA). The Group is important to multinational corporations because it provides much of the planning and financing for economic development projects involving billions of dollars for which private businesses can act as contractors and as suppliers of goods and engineering-related services.

The most important development bank is the World Bank Group, which consists of the IBRD, the IFC, and the IDA.

IBRD   The IBRD, or World Bank, makes loans at nearly conventional terms for projects of high economic priority. To qualify for financing, a project must have costs and revenues that can be estimated with reasonable accuracy. A government guarantee is a necessity for World Bank funding. The bank's main emphasis historically has been on large infrastructure projects such as roads, dams, power plants, education, and agriculture. In recent years, however, the bank has increasingly emphasized loans to help borrower countries alleviate their balance-of-payments problems. These loans are tied to the willingness of the debtor nations to adopt economic policies that will spur growth: freer trade, more open investment, lower budget deficits, and a more vigorous private sector. In addition to its members' subscriptions, the World Bank raises funds by issuing bonds to private sources.

IFC   The purpose of the IFC is to finance various projects in the private sector through loans and equity participations and to serve as a catalyst for flows of additional private capital investment to developing countries. In contrast to the World Bank, the IFC does not require government guarantees. It emphasizes providing risk capital for manufacturing firms that have a reasonable chance of earning the investors' required rate of return and that will provide economic benefits to the nation. However, instead of focusing on the small and medium-size firms that may really need its help, the IFC tends to concentrate the bulk of its lending and equity investments in investment-grade conglomerates that regularly tap public markets. One issue is whether the IFC should provide financing for private-sector companies that can presumably tap the capital markets to fund profitable projects. For example, the IFC has invested about $1.3 billion in more than fifty Chinese projects, even though China seems to have no trouble attracting foreign direct investment on its own, bringing in over $40 billion in 2002. IFC officials respond that their strategic investments will help prod Chinese companies and policy makers to conduct business in a more open and investor-friendly manner.

IDA   The World Bank concentrates on projects that have a high probability of being profitable; consequently, many of the poorest of the less-developed countries (LDCs) are unable to access its funds. IDA was founded in 1960 to remedy this shortcoming. As distinguished from the World Bank, IDA is authorized to make soft (highly concessionary) loans (for example, fifty-year maturity with no interest). It does require a government guarantee, however. The establishment of IDA illustrates a major unresolved issue for the World Bank Group: Should its emphasis be on making sound loans to developing countries, or should it concentrate on investing in those projects most likely to be of benefit to the host country? These goals are not necessarily in conflict, although many of a project's benefits may not be captured by the project itself but instead will appear elsewhere in the economy (for example, the benefits of an educational system).

Regional and National Development Banks

The past two decades have seen a proliferation of development banks. The functions of a development bank are to provide debt and equity financing to aid in the economic development of underdeveloped areas. This financing includes extending direct intermediate-to long-term capital, strengthening local capital markets, and supplying management consulting services to new companies. The professional guidance helps to safeguard, and thereby encourage, investments in a firm.

Regional Development Banks   Regional development banks provide funds for the financing of manufacturing, mining, agricultural, and infrastructure projects considered important to development. They tend to support projects that promote regional cooperation and economic integration. Repayment terms for the loans, in most cases, are over a five- to fifteen-year period at favorable interest rates. The leading regional development banks include the following:

Regional development ment banks finance industrial, agricultural, and infrastructure projects considered important to development.

1. *European Investment Bank (EIB):* The EIB offers funds for certain public and private projects in European and other nations associated with the Common Market. It emphasizes loans to the lesser-developed regions in Europe and to associated members in Africa.

2. *Inter-American Development Bank (IADB):* The IADB is a key source of long-term capital in Latin America. It lends to joint ventures, both minority and majority foreign-owned, and it provides small amounts of equity capital. A recent initiative is to act as a catalyst for further private-sector funding for Latin American infrastructure projects. By partially guaranteeing commercial bank loans and directly lending to infrastructure projects, the IADB aims to bring funding to many projects for which commercial bank loans might not otherwise be available. For example, it recently lent $75 million to a private consortium led by General Electric and Bechtel to build and lease the second stage of the Samalayuca power project in Mexico.

3. *Atlantic Development Group for Latin America (ADELA):* ADELA is an international private investment company dedicated to the socioeconomic development of Latin America. Its objective is to strengthen private enterprise by providing capital and entrepreneurial and technical services.

4. *Asian Development Bank (ADB):* The ADB guarantees or makes direct loans to member states and private ventures in Asian/Pacific nations and helps to develop local capital markets by underwriting securities issued by private enterprises.

5. *African Development Bank (ADB):* The ADB makes or guarantees loans and provides technical assistance to member states for various development projects. Beneficiaries of ADB loans and activities are normally governments or government-related agencies.

6. *Arab Fund for Economic and Social Development (AFESD):* The AFESD is a multilateral Arab fund that actively searches for projects (restricted to Arab League countries) and then assumes responsibility for project implementation by conducting feasibility studies, contracting, controlling quality, and supervising the work schedule.

7. *European Bank for Reconstruction and Development (EBRD):* The EBRD, which was founded in 1990 with an initial capital of about $13 billion, is supposed to finance the privatization of Eastern Europe. Many critics are skeptical of its chances, however. For example, the first person appointed to head it was a French socialist who masterminded the most sweeping program of nationalizations in French history. The EBRD's reputation was not helped when it was revealed in 1993 that in its first two years of operation, it had spent more than twice as much on its building, staff, and overhead (more than $300 million) as it had disbursed in loans (about $150 million) to its 25 client countries. Thanks to the nudging of the United States, one of the ground rules

for the EBRD is that it must make 60 percent of its loans to the private sector, a target it is now approaching after an early tilt toward the public sector.

National Development Banks Some national development banks concentrate on a particular industry or region; others are multipurpose. Although most are public institutions, there are several privately controlled development banks as well. The characteristics for success, however, are the same: They must attract capable, investment-oriented management; and they must have a large enough supply of economically viable projects to enable management to select a reasonable portfolio of investments.

National development ment banks include both publicly and privately controlled institutions.

Private-Sector Alternatives

Private-sector capital flows have replaced official flows as the major source of external infrastructure financing in developing countries.

A report by the International Finance Corporation states that private-sector infrastructure financing grew significantly in developing countries during the 1990s.[14] According to the IFC report, $26 billion in infrastructure projects that include at least some private funds have been completed in recent years, and another $100 billion in such projects is highly probable. These amounts represent huge increases over privately financed infrastructure spending since 1988, when such spending was less than $500 million. Current examples of the trend include telecommunications-privatization projects in Hungary and Latvia; private power-generation efforts in India and Pakistan; toll roads in Argentina; the reconstruction and management of a Bulgarian airport; management of Malaysia's national sewage system; and an elevated mass-transit rail system in Thailand.

The report noted that the main reason for the shift toward private infrastructure was growing disenchantment with public monopoly ownership and provision of infrastructure services such as power, waste disposal, roads, and telecommunications. Underinvestment by many state utilities has resulted in shortages of these services, leading to constraints on growth. The surge in private infrastructure financing also is being fed by fiscal constraints on governments and external aid agencies, which are forcing governments to turn to private capital despite their preference for public ownership. In spite of the large risks, the private sector has responded with tens of billions of dollars through the use of innovative financing techniques—such as project financing, securitization, and asset-backed financing—that permit efficient risk bearing. The result is a dramatic shift in the importance of private capital flows to developing nations relative to official flows. As recently as 1991, official flows made up more than 50 percent of long-term financial flows to developing countries; today, that figure is less than 15 percent. This evidence suggests that the proliferation of development banks and foreign aid may have actually stifled private infrastructure financing.

The World Bank and the IFC are attempting to reposition themselves in this changed environment, where private capital flows dominate official flows. For example, in 1996, the IFC announced a program expanding its reach into sixteen high-risk countries such as Cambodia, Guyana, Mongolia, Senegal, and Uzbekistan. Meanwhile, the World Bank is placing more emphasis on strengthening the legal and financial systems of developing countries so as to attract private investors. It is also seeking to stimulate private investment in these countries by providing more loan guarantees to businesses entering these markets.

12.4 PROJECT FINANCE

A frequently used mechanism for financing large-scale, long-term capital investments is **project finance.** For example, in 1998, $99.5 billion was raised in the global project

---

[14] Gary Bond and Laurence Carter, "Financing Private Infrastructure Projects," International Finance Corporation, 1994.

Project finance is often used to finance large-scale, long-term projects that are separable from their sponsors.

finance market.[15] Recent examples of project finance transactions include the $16 billion Channel Tunnel, or Chunnel, connecting France and England; the $5 billion Iridium global satellite project; and a $4 billion Venezuelan oil and gas refinery known as SINCOR.[16] Most project financings take the form of nonrecourse loans secured solely by the project and its cash flows. This mechanism helps shield the parent company from any financial obligations and risks associated with borrowings by the project. The ownership vehicle for a project is a single-purpose corporation that is legally independent of its sponsors.

This financial structure is consistent with the nature and purpose of project financing. Project financing can be defined as "the raising of funds to finance an economically separable capital investment project in which the providers of the funds look primarily to the cash flow from the project as the source of funds to service their loans and provide the return of and a return on their equity investment in the project."[17]

This definition highlights several key attributes of project financing. First, it focuses on the economically separable nature of investment projects suitable for project financing, such as power plants or pipelines. Second, because projects are set up as legally independent entities, nonrecourse lenders have resort only to project assets and cash flows; they have no recourse to the sponsors. Third, unlike the case for financial instruments such as mortgage-backed securities, the underlying assets in project finance are large, illiquid industrial assets. Finally, although not specified in the definition, projects have a finite life, at the end of which all debt and equity investors are repaid.

The projects' sponsors benefit from project finance by shielding themselves from the large risks they would otherwise have to bear. But project finance is not a free lunch. Because lenders rightly perceive that they cannot look to the parent to honor its projects' debts, they factor this greater degree of credit risk into the price at which they are willing to lend to these projects. The result is that the cost of project financing exceeds the parent's cost of borrowing. It is also expensive to arrange. Nonetheless, its widespread use indicates that project finance has net benefits to its sponsors.

Project finance can create value by resolving agency problems, reducing taxes, and improving risk management.

Project financing is likely to create value through its ability to resolve certain agency problems, reduce taxes and the costs of financial distress, and facilitate risk management.[18] For example, the relatively transparent nature of project finance, which stems from its single-purpose corporate structure and the fact that project assets are tangible (in contrast to, say, the value of an Internet strategy), improves credit risk analysis. The credit analyst need assess only the risk of the project, not the riskiness of the sponsor(s) as well. In addition, the project is insulated from problems that its sponsors may have: Its creditworthiness depends solely on the project's cash flows (which are dedicated to debt-service payments) and not on investment and other decisions made by the parent's management that might dissipate these cash flows. At the same time, the sponsor is relieved of the prospect of financial distress if the project goes bankrupt. The use of project finance may also help reduce corporate taxes by allowing the sponsors to take advantage of special tax holidays, tax rate reductions, and reduced royalty payments. Finally, project finance permits the allocation of specific risks and returns to those best able to bear those risks and influence the outcomes on which the returns depend. This careful alignment of risks and returns improves incentives and increases the likelihood that the project will be operated with maximum efficiency.

---

[15] This estimate appears in Exhibit 1 of "An Overview of the Project Finance Market," Harvard Business School, N9-200-028, written by Suzie Harris and Kathy Krueger under the supervision of Professor Benjamin C. Esty.

[16] These examples are given in "An Overview of the Project Finance Market."

[17] John D. Finnerty, *Project Finance: Asset-Based Financial Engineering* (New York: John Wiley & Sons, 1996).

[18] For a discussion and illustration of these advantages, see Benjamin C. Esty, "Petrozuata: A Case Study of the Effective Use of Project Finance," *Journal of Applied Corporate Finance,* Fall 1999, pp. 26–42.

12.5 SUMMARY AND CONCLUSIONS

Although there are significant differences among countries in their methods and sources of finance, corporate practice appears to be converging. Most significantly, more firms are bypassing financial intermediaries, mainly commercial banks, and are going directly to the financial markets for funds. The convergence of corporate financing practice largely reflects the globalization of financial markets, that is, the inextricable linkage—through arbitrage—of financial markets worldwide. In line with this trend, firms are finding that it pays to seek capital on a global basis rather than restricting their search to any one nation or capital market. These global sources include national capital markets, financial intermediaries, development banks, and project financing.

Competition among companies for capital is also forcing them to be more investor-friendly. The result is a trend toward more financial transparency and improved corporate governance with a greater focus on the rights of shareholders rather than managers.

QUESTIONS

1. What are some basic differences between the financing patterns of U.S. and Japanese firms? What might account for some of these differences?

2. What is securitization? What forces underlie it, and how has it affected the financing policies of multinational corporations?

3. Why is bank lending on the decline worldwide? How have banks responded to their loss of market share?

4. a. What is meant by the globalization of financial markets?

   b. How has technology affected the process of globalization?

   c. How has globalization affected government regulation of national capital markets?

5. Many financial commentators believe that bond owners and traders today have an enormous collective influence over a nation's economic policies. Explain why this might be correct.

6. Why are large multinational corporations located in small countries such as Sweden, Holland, and Switzerland interested in developing a global investor base?

7. Why are many U.S. multinationals seeking to improve their visibility with foreign investors, even going so far as to list their shares on foreign stock exchanges?

8. List some reasons why a U.S.-based corporation might issue debt denominated in a foreign currency.

9. In an attempt to regain business lost to foreign markets, Swiss authorities abolished stamp duties on transactions between foreigners as well as on new bond issues by foreign borrowers. However, transactions involving Swiss citizens will still incur a 0.15 percent tax, and bond issues by Swiss borrowers were also made more expensive. What are the likely consequences of these changes for Swiss financial markets?

10. On October 14, 1993, Portugal's Ministry of Finance announced that it would scrap the 20 percent withholding tax imposed on the interest payments due foreigners holding government bonds. At present, foreigners whose governments have a double-taxation treaty with Portugal wait up to two years to claim back a portion of the tax. What might have been Portugal's motivations for scrapping the tax? What are the likely consequences of eliminating the withholding tax?

PROBLEM

1. A European company issues common shares that pay taxable dividends and bearer shares that pay an identical dividend but offer an opportunity to evade taxes: Bearer shares come with a large supply of coupons that can be redeemed anonymously at banks for the current value of the dividend.

   a. Suppose taxable dividends are taxed at the rate of 10 percent. What is the ratio between market prices of taxable and bearer shares? If a new issue is planned, should taxable or bearer shares be sold?

   b. Suppose, in addition, that it costs 10 percent of proceeds to issue a taxable dividend, whereas it costs 20 percent of the proceeds to issue bearer stocks because of the expense of distribution and coupon printing. What type of share will the corporation prefer to issue?

   c. Suppose now that individuals pay 10 percent taxes on dividends, and corporations pay no taxes but bear an administrative cost of 10 percent of the value of any bearer dividends. Can you determine the relative market prices for the two types of shares?

BIBLIOGRAPHY

Agrawal, Raj, Stephen Findley, Sean Greene, Kathryn Huang, Aly Jeddy, William W. Lewis, and Markus Petry. "Capital Productivity: Why the U.S. Leads and Why It Matters." *The McKinsey Quarterly,* 1996, No. 3, pp. 38–55.

Alexander, Gordon J., Cheol S. Eun, and S. Janakiramanan. "International Listings and Stock Returns: Some Empirical Evidence." *Journal of Financial and Quantitative Analysis,* June 1988, pp. 135–151.

Berglöf, Erik, and Enrico Perotti. "The Governance Structure of the Japanese Financial Keiretsu." *Journal of Financial Economics,* October 1994, pp. 259–284.

Business International Corporation. *Financing Foreign Operations,* various issues.

Kaplan, Steven N., and Bernadette A. Minton. "Appointments of Outsiders to Japanese Boards: Determinants and Implications for Managers." *Journal of Financial Economics,* October 1994, pp. 225–258.

Logue, Dennis E., and Anant K. Sundaram. "Valuation Effects of Foreign Company Listings on U.S. Exchanges." *Journal of International Business Studies,* 1996, pp. 67–88.

Merton, Robert C. "A Simple Model of Capital Market Equilibrium with Incomplete Information." *Journal of Finance,* July 1987, pp. 483–510.

Solnik, Bruno H. *International Investments,* 4th ed. (Reading, Mass.: Addison-Wesley, 1996).

INTERNET RESOURCES

www.oecd.org/document/36/0,2340,en_2825_495635_1962020_1_1_1_1,00.html Web site for *Financial Market Trends.* This publication provides an up-to-date analysis of developments and trends in international and national capital markets. Each issue includes highlights of recent developments in financial markets; analysis of policy issues affecting financial markets; overviews of new statistical information from OECD countries in areas such as international direct investment, overall bank profitability, institutional investment, and privatization; and statistics and charts dealing with international financial markets.

www.standardandpoors.com Web site of Standard & Poor's. Contains information on various project financings and other international financings, along with country risk ratings.

www.bis.org Web site from the BIS that contains extensive information on the amounts and types of funds raised in the international banking and capital markets, including the Eurocurrency and Eurobond markets and the international equity markets.

INTERNET EXERCISES

1. What is the breakdown of currencies in which international borrowing has taken place in the past year?

2. How much money has been raised in the past year in the international bond market? Eurocurrency market? International equity market?

THE EUROMARKETS

The merchant has no country.

Thomas Jefferson

CHAPTER LEARNING OBJECTIVES

- To describe the Eurocurrency and Eurobond markets and explain why they exist
- To describe the characteristics and pricing of Eurocurrency loans, Eurobonds, Euronotes, and Euro-commercial paper
- To explain the links between the Euromarkets and their domestic counterparts

KEY TERMS

all-in cost	Eurocurrency market
Asiacurrency (Asiadollar) market	Eurodollar
basis points	Euro-medium term note (Euro-MTNs)
dragon bond	Euronote
drawdown	inverse floater
Eurobank	London interbank bid rate (LIBID)
Eurobond	London interbank offer rate (LIBOR)
Eurobond market	note issuance facility (NIF)
Euro-commercial paper (Euro-CP)	revolving underwriting facility (RUF)
Eurocurrency	swap

The most obvious example of the globalization of financial markets is the rise of the Euromarkets. This term encompasses the Eurocurrency and Eurobond markets as well as the Euronote and Euro-commercial paper markets. The major participants in these markets are large commercial and investment banks, multinational companies, central banks, and international financial organizations such as the IMF and World Bank. London is home to the most important Euromarket but smaller ones exist in Paris, Brussels, and Frankfurt. This chapter describes the functioning of these markets and then shows how each can be used to meet the multinational firm's financing requirements. It also discusses the links between these markets and their domestic counterparts.

13.1 THE EUROCURRENCY MARKET

The Eurocurrency market consists of banks that accept deposits and make loans in foreign currencies.

A **Eurocurrency** is a dollar or other freely convertible currency deposited in a bank outside its country of origin. Thus, U.S. dollars on deposit in London become **Eurodollars**. These deposits can be placed in a foreign bank or in the foreign branch of a domestic U.S. bank.[1] The **Eurocurrency market** then consists of those banks—called **Eurobanks**—that accept deposits and make loans in foreign currencies. Note that the prefix *Euro* as used here has nothing to do with the currency known as the euro.

The Eurobond and Eurocurrency markets are often confused with each other, but there is a fundamental distinction between the two. In the **Eurobond market, Eurobonds,** which are bonds sold outside the countries in whose currencies they are denominated, are issued directly by the final borrowers. The Eurocurrency market enables investors to hold short-term claims on commercial banks, which then act as intermediaries to transform these deposits into long-term claims on final borrowers. However, banks do play an important role in placing Eurobonds with the final investors.

The dominant Eurocurrency remains the U.S. dollar, but the importance of the Eurodollar waxes and wanes with the strength of the U.S. dollar. With dollar weakness in the latter parts of both the 1970s and 1980s, other currencies—particularly the Deutsche mark and the Swiss franc—increased in importance. Dollar strength in the 1990s again boosted the relative importance of the Eurodollar. The euro has now become an important currency for denominating Eurocurrency loans and Eurobonds.

Modern Origins

The origin of the post-World War II Eurodollar market is often traced to the fear of Soviet Bloc countries that their dollar deposits in U.S. banks might be attached by U.S. citizens with claims against communist governments. Therefore, they left their dollar balances with banks in France and England.

The Eurocurrency market thrives because of various government regulations.

Whatever its postwar beginnings, the Eurocurrency market has thrived for one reason: government regulation. By operating in Eurocurrencies, banks and suppliers of funds are able to avoid certain regulatory costs and restrictions that would otherwise be imposed. These costs and restrictions include:

1. Reserve requirements that lower a bank's earning asset base (that is, a smaller percentage of deposits can be lent out).

2. Special charges and taxes levied on domestic banking transactions, such as the requirement to pay Federal Deposit Insurance Corporation fees.

3. Requirements to lend money to certain borrowers at concessionary rates, thereby lowering the return on the bank's assets.

---

[1] The term *foreign* is relative to the operating unit's location, not to its nationality.

4. Interest rate ceilings on deposits or loans that inhibit the ability to compete for funds and lower the return on loans.

5. Rules or regulations that restrict competition among banks.

Continuing government regulations and taxes provide opportunities to engage in Eurocurrency transactions.

Although many of the most burdensome regulations and costs have been eased or abolished, the Eurocurrency market still exists. It will continue to exist as long as there are profitable opportunities to engage in offshore financial transactions. These opportunities persist because of continuing government regulations and taxes that raise costs and lower returns on domestic transactions. Because of the ongoing erosion of domestic regulations, however, these cost and return differentials are much less significant today than they were in the past. As a consequence, the domestic money market and Eurocurrency market are now tightly integrated for most of the major currencies, effectively creating a single worldwide money market for each participating currency.

Eurodollar Creation

The creation of Eurodollars can be illustrated by using a series of T-accounts to trace the movement of dollars into and through the Eurodollar market.

First, suppose that Leksell AB, a Swedish firm, sells medical diagnostic equipment worth $1 million to a U.S. hospital. It receives a check payable in dollars drawn on Citibank in New York. Initially, Leksell AB deposits this check in its Citibank checking account for dollar-working-capital purposes. This transaction would be represented on the firm's and Citibank's accounts as follows:

Citibank		Leksell AB	
	Demand deposit due Leksell AB +$1M	Demand deposit in Citibank +$1M	

In order to earn a higher rate of interest on the $1 million account (U.S. banks cannot pay interest on corporate checking accounts), Leksell decides to place the funds in a time deposit with Barclays Bank in London. This transaction is recorded as follows:

Citibank		Barclays	
	Demand deposit due Leksell AB −$1M Demand deposit due Barclays +$1M	Demand deposit in Citibank +$1M	Time deposit owed Leksell +$1M

Leksell AB	
Demand deposit in Citibank −$1M Demand deposit in Barclays +$1M	

One million Eurodollars have just been created by substituting a dollar account in a London bank for a dollar account held in New York. Notice that no dollars have left New York, although ownership of the U.S. deposit has shifted from a foreign corporation to a foreign bank.

Barclays could leave those funds idle in its account in New York, but the opportunity cost would be too great. If it cannot immediately lend those funds to a government or commercial borrower, Barclays will place the $1 million in the London interbank market. This involves lending the funds to another bank active in the Eurodollar market. We saw in Chapter 9 that the interest rate at which such interbank loans are made is called the **London interbank offered rate** (**LIBOR**). In this case, however, Barclays chooses to lend these funds to Ronningen SA, a Norwegian importer of fine wines. The loan is recorded as follows:

Citibank		Barclays	
Demand deposit due Barclays −$1M	Demand deposit in Citibank −$1M	Time deposit owed Leksell +$1M	
Demand deposit due Ronningen SA` +$1M	Loan to Ronningen SA +$1M		

Ronningen SA	
Demand deposit in Citibank +$1M	Eurodollar loan from Barclays +$1M

We can see from this example that the Eurocurrency market involves a chain of deposits and a chain of borrowers and lenders, not buyers and sellers. One does not buy or sell Eurocurrencies. Ordinarily, an owner of dollars will place them in a time-deposit or demand-deposit account in a U.S. bank, and the owner of a pound deposit will keep it in an account with a British bank. Until the dollar (or pound) deposit is withdrawn, control over its use resides with the U.S. (or British) bank. In fact, the majority of Eurocurrency transactions involve transferring control of deposits from one Eurobank to another Eurobank. Loans to non-Eurobanks account for fewer than half of all Eurocurrency loans. The net market size (subtracting off inter-Eurobank liabilities) is much smaller than the gross market size.

The example and data presented indicate that Eurocurrency operations differ from the structure of domestic banking operations in two ways:

1. There is a *chain of ownership* between the original dollar depositor and the U.S. bank.

2. There is a *changing control over the deposit* and the use to which the money is put.

Despite the chain of transactions, the total amount of foreign dollar deposits in the United States remains the same. Moreover, on the most fundamental level—taking in deposits and allocating funds—the Eurocurrency market operates much as does any other financial market, except for the absence of government regulations on loans that can be made and interest rates that can be charged. This section now examines some of the particular characteristics of Eurocurrency lending.

Eurocurrency Loans

The most important characteristic of the Eurocurrency market is that loans are made on a floating-rate basis. Interest rates on loans to governments and their agencies, corporations, and nonprime banks are set at a fixed margin above LIBOR for the given period and currency chosen. At the end of each period, the interest for the next period is calculated at the same fixed margin over the new LIBOR. For example, if the margin is 75 **basis**

Eurocurrency loans
are made on a
floating-rate basis.

points (100 basis points equal 1 percent) and the current LIBOR is 6 percent, then the borrower is charged 6.75 percent for the upcoming period. The reset period normally chosen is six months, but shorter periods such as one month or three months are possible. The LIBOR used corresponds to the maturity of the reset period (for example, six-month LIBOR, or LIBOR6, for a six-month reset period).

Terms   The *margin,* or spread between the lending bank's cost of funds and the interest charged the borrower, varies a good deal among borrowers and is based on the borrower's perceived riskiness. Typically, such spreads have ranged from as little as 15 basis points (0.15 percent) to more than 3 percent, with the median being somewhere between 1 percent and 2 percent.

Eurocurrency loans
are made by bank
syndicates.

The *maturity* of a loan can vary from approximately three to ten years. Maturities have tended to lengthen over time, from a norm of about five years originally to a norm of eight to ten years these days for prime borrowers. Lenders in this market are almost exclusively banks. In any single loan, there normally will be a number of participating banks that form a syndicate. The bank originating the loan usually will manage the syndicate. This bank, in turn, may invite one or two other banks to co-manage the loan. The managers charge the borrower a once-and-for-all syndication fee of 0.25 percent to 2 percent of the loan value, depending on the size and type of the loan. Part of this fee is kept by the managers, and the rest is divided up among all the participating banks (including the managing banks) according to the amount of funds each bank supplies.

The **drawdown**—the period over which the borrower may take down the loan—and the repayment period vary in accordance with the borrower's needs. A commitment fee of about 0.5 percent per annum is paid on the unused balance, and prepayments in advance of the agreed-upon schedule are permitted but are sometimes subject to a penalty fee. Borrowers in the Eurocurrency market are concerned about the effective interest rate on the money they have raised. This rate compares the interest rate paid to the net loan proceeds received by the borrower. Its computation is shown in the example "Calculating the Effective Annual Cost of a Eurocurrency Loan."

ILLUSTRATION   *Calculating the Effective Annual Cost of a Eurocurrency Loan*

San Miguel, the Filipino beer brewer, has arranged a €250 million, five-year, euro-denominated Eurocurrency (Euroeuro) loan with a syndicate of banks led by Credit Suisse and Deutsche Bank. With an up-front syndication fee of 2.0 percent, net proceeds to San Miguel are:

$$€250,000,000 - (0.02 \times €250,000,000) = €245,000,000$$

The interest rate is set at LIBOR + 1.75 percent, with LIBOR reset every six months. Assuming an initial LIBOR6 rate for euros of 5.5 percent, the first semiannual debt service payment is

$$\frac{0.055 + 0.0175}{2} \times €250,000,000 = €9,062,500$$

San Miguel's effective annual interest rate for the first six months is thus

$$\frac{€9,062,500}{€245,000,000} \times 2 \times 100 = 7.40\%$$

Every six months, this annualized cost will change with LIBOR6.

Multicurrency Clauses Borrowing can be done in many different currencies, although the dollar is still the dominant currency. Increasingly, Eurodollars have a multicurrency clause. This clause gives the borrower the right (subject to availability) to switch from one currency to another on any rollover (or reset) date. The multicurrency option enables the borrower to match currencies on cash inflows and outflows (a potentially valuable exposure management technique, as we saw in Chapter 10). Equally important, the option allows a firm to take advantage of its own expectations regarding currency changes (if they differ from the market's expectations) and shop around for those funds with the lowest effective cost.

An example of a typical multicurrency loan is a $100 million, ten-year revolving credit arranged by the Dutch firm Thyssen Bornemisza NV with nine Dutch, German, U.S., and Swiss banks, led by Amsterdam-Rotterdam Bank. Rates are fixed at the company's discretion at three-month, six-month, or twelve-month intervals. At each rollover date, the firm can choose from any freely available Eurocurrency except Eurosterling, but only four different Eurocurrencies may be outstanding at any one time.

Relationship between Domestic and Eurocurrency Money Markets

Interest rates in national and Eurocurrency markets are closely linked through arbitrage.

The presence of arbitrage activities ensures a close relationship between interest rates in national and international (Eurocurrency) money markets. Interest rates in the U.S. and Eurodollar markets, for example, can differ only to the extent that additional costs, controls, or risks are associated with moving dollars between, say, New York and London. Otherwise, arbitrageurs would borrow in the low-cost market and lend in the high-return market until any interest differential between the two was eliminated.

Interest Differentials Since the cost of shifting funds is relatively insignificant, we must look to currency controls or risk to explain any substantial differences between domestic and external rates. To the extent that exchange controls are effective, the national money market can be isolated or segmented from its international counterpart. In fact, the difference between internal and external interest rates can be taken as a measure of the effectiveness of the monetary authorities' exchange controls.

Interest differentials also can exist if there is a danger of future controls. The possibility that at some future time either the lender or borrower will not be able to transfer funds across a border—also known as sovereign risk—can help sustain persistent differences between domestic and external money market rates.

Eurocurrency Spreads In general, Eurocurrency spreads (a spread is the margin between lending and deposit rates) are narrower than domestic money market spreads (see Exhibit 13.1). Lending rates can be lower because:

1. The previously described regulatory expenses that raise costs and lower returns on domestic transactions are absent in Eurocurrency markets.
2. Most borrowers are well known, reducing the cost of information gathering and credit analysis.
3. Eurocurrency lending is characterized by high volumes, allowing for lower margins; transactions costs are reduced because most of the loan arrangements are standardized and conducted by telephone or telex.
4. Eurocurrency lending can and does take place out of tax-haven countries, providing for more favorable tax treatment and higher after-tax returns.

Eurocurrency deposit rates are higher than domestic rates for the following reasons:
1. They must be higher to attract domestic deposits.
2. Eurobanks can afford to pay higher rates based on their lower regulatory costs.

EXHIBIT 13.1 • INTEREST RATE RELATIONSHIPS BETWEEN DOMESTIC AND EUROCURRENCY CREDIT MARKETS

3. Eurobanks are able to pay depositors higher interest rates because they are not subject to the interest rate ceilings that prevail in many countries.

4. A larger percentage of deposits can be lent out.

Euromarket Trends

Creditworthy borrowers may be able to borrow below LIBOR.

In recent years, the London interbank offered rate has started to fade as a benchmark for lending money in the Eurocurrency market, in much the same way that the prime rate is no longer the all-important benchmark in the U.S. bank loan market. Although Eurocurrency rates are still computed off LIBOR, a number of creditworthy borrowers—including Denmark, Sweden, several major corporations, and some banks—are obtaining financing in the Euromarkets at interest rates well below LIBOR. For example, high-quality borrowers can borrow at the **London interbank bid rate** (**LIBID**), the rate paid by one bank to another for a deposit, which is about 12.5 basis points (1/8 of 1 percent) below LIBOR. The highest-quality borrowers, such as the World Bank, can raise funds at below LIBID.

This trend largely reflects the fact that the ability of banks to impose themselves as the credit yardstick by which all other international borrowers are measured has faltered. What the Euromarkets are saying in effect is that borrowers such as Denmark and the World Bank are considered better credit risks than are many banks.

Moreover, investor preferences for an alternative to bank Eurodollar certificates of deposit (whereby banks substitute their credit risk for their borrowers') have enabled investment banks to transform the usual bank-syndicated lending into securities offerings, such as floating-rate notes. This preference for the ultimate borrower's credit risk, rather than the bank's credit risk, has led to rapid growth in the Eurobond market, particularly the floating-rate segment of the market.

13.2 EUROBONDS

Eurobonds are similar in many respects to the public debt sold in domestic capital markets, consisting largely of fixed-rate, floating-rate, and equity-related debt. Unlike domestic bond

Eurobonds are bonds sold outside the country whose currency they are denominated in.

markets, however, the Eurobond market is almost entirely free of official regulation and is instead self-regulated by the Association of International Bond Dealers. The prefix *Euro* indicates that the bonds are sold outside the countries in whose currencies they are denominated. For example, the General Motors issue shown in Exhibit 13.2 is a Eurobond. You can tell that because the tombstone says, "These securities have not been registered under the United States Securities Act of 1933 and may not be offered or sold in the United States or to United States persons as part of the distribution."

The Eurobond market has grown dramatically during the past twenty years.

Borrowers in the Eurobond market are typically well known and have impeccable credit ratings (for example, developed countries, international institutions, and large multinational corporations like GM). Even then the amounts raised in the Eurobond market have historically been far less than those in the Eurocurrency market. However, the Eurobond market has grown dramatically during the past twenty years, and its size now exceeds that of the Eurocurrency market.

Swaps

The major catalyst for growth in the Eurobond market in the last twenty years has been the emergence of the **swap** transactions discussed in Chapter 9. Most Eurobond issues are now "swap-driven." These swaps allow the parties to the contract to arbitrage their relative access to different currency markets or differences in perceived credit quality.

Links between the Domestic and Eurobond Markets

The growing presence of sophisticated investors willing to arbitrage between the domestic dollar and Eurodollar bond markets—in part because the United States no longer imposes withholding taxes on foreign investors—has eliminated much of the interest disparity that once existed between Eurobonds and domestic bonds. Despite the closer alignment of the two markets, the Eurobond issuer may at any given time take advantage of Eurobond "windows" when a combination of domestic regulations, tax laws, and

EXHIBIT 13.2 ● ANNOUNCEMENT OF A GMAC EUROBOND ISSUE

General Motors Acceptance Corporation
(Incorporated in the State of New York, United States of America)

U.S.$200,000,000

7⅝ per cent. Notes due September 3, 1991

Swiss Bank Corporation International Limited

Credit Suisse First Boston Limited	Deutsche Bank Capital Markets Limited
Merrill Lynch Capital Markets	Morgan Stanley International
Nomura International Limited	Salomon Brothers International Limited

Union Bank of Switzerland (Securities) Limited

Algemene Bank Nederland N.V.	BankAmerica Capital Markets Group
Bankers Trust International Limited	Banque Bruxelles Lambert S.A.
Banque Générale du Luxembourg S.A.	Banque Nationale de Paris
Banque Paribas Capital Markets Limited	Commerzbank Aktiengesellschaft
Crédit Lyonnais	Creditanstalt-Bankverein
Daiwa Europe Limited	IBJ International Limited
Leu Securities Limited	The Nikko Securities Co., (Europe) Ltd.
Shearson Lehman Brothers International	Société Générale
Sumitomo Trust International Limited	Swiss Volksbank
S.G. Warburg Securities	Wood Gundy Inc.

Yamaichi International (Europe) Limited

Source: Reprinted with permission of General Motors Acceptance Corporation.

Arbitrage ensures
close links between
the Eurobond and
domestic bond
markets.

expectations of international investors enables the issuer to achieve a lower financing cost—often involving currency and interest swaps—than is available in domestic markets.[2] In addition to the possibility of reduced borrowing costs, the Eurobond issuer may diversify its investor base and funding sources by having access to the international Eurocapital markets of Western Europe, North America, and the Far East.

Placement   Issues are arranged through an underwriting group, often with a hundred or more underwriting banks involved for an issue as small as $25 million. A growing volume of Eurobonds is being placed privately because of the simplicity, speed, and privacy with which private placements can be arranged.

Most Eurobonds are
denominated in dol-
lars but other cur-
rencies are becoming
more important.

Currency Denomination   Historically, about 75 percent of Eurobonds have been dollar denominated. The most important nondollar currencies for Eurobond issues are the euro, the Japanese yen, and the pound sterling. The absence of Swiss franc Eurobonds is due to the Swiss Central Bank's ban on using the Swiss franc for Eurobond issues.

Interest Rates on Fixed-Rate Eurobonds   Fixed-rate Eurobonds ordinarily pay their coupons once a year, in contrast to bonds issued in the U.S. market, where interest is normally paid on a semiannual basis. Issuers, of course, are interested in their **all-in cost**—that is, the effective interest rate on the money they have raised. This interest rate is calculated as the discount rate that equates the present value of the future interest and principal payments to the net proceeds received by the issuer. In other words, it is the *internal rate of return* on the bond. To compare a Eurobond issue with a U.S. domestic issue, therefore, the all-in cost of funds on an annual basis must be converted to a semiannual basis or vice versa.

The annual yield can be converted to a semiannual rate by use of the following formula:

$$\text{Semiannual yield} = (1 + \text{Annual yield})^{1/2} - 1 \qquad (13.1)$$

Alternatively, a semiannual yield can be annualized by rearranging the terms in Equation 13.1 as follows:

Borrowers compare
the all-in costs of
Eurobonds and
domestic bonds.

$$\text{Annual yield} = (1 + \text{Semiannual yield})^{2} - 1 \qquad (13.2)$$

For example, suppose that Procter & Gamble plans to issue a five-year bond with a face value of $100 million. Its investment banker estimates that a Eurobond issue would have to bear a 7.5 percent coupon and that fees and other expenses will total $738,000, providing net proceeds to P&G of $99,262,000. Exhibit 13.3a shows the cash flows associated with the Eurobond issue. The all-in cost of this issue, which is an annual rate, is shown as 7.68 percent (rounded to the nearest basis point). The computation was done using an Excel spreadsheet. To ensure that we have the correct all-in cost of funds, the third column shows that the present values of the cash flows, using a discount rate of 7.68 percent, sum to P&G's net proceeds of $99,262,000.

Alternatively, its investment banker tells Procter & Gamble that it can issue a $100 million five-year bond in the U.S. market with a coupon of 7.4 percent. With estimated issuance costs of $974,000, P&G will receive net proceeds of $99,026,000. Exhibit 13.3b shows the cash flows associated with this issue and its all-in cost of 3.82 percent. Notice that the cash flows are semiannual, as is the all-in cost. The third column performs the same check on the present value of these cash flows to ensure that we have the correct all-in cost.

According to Equation 13.1, the equivalent semiannual all-in cost for the Eurobond issue is $(1.0768)^{1/2} - 1 = 3.77$ percent. These figures reveal that the all-in cost of the

[2] The existence of such windows is documented by Yong-Cheol Kim and René M. Stulz, "The Eurobond Market and Corporate Financial Policy: A Test of the Clientele Hypothesis," *Journal of Financial Economics* 22, (1988): 189–205; and Yong-Cheol Kim and René M. Stulz, "Is There a Global Market for Convertible Bonds?" *Journal of Business* 65 (1992): 75–91.

EXHIBIT 13.3 • COMPARISON OF ALL-IN COSTS OF A EUROBOND ISSUE AND A U.S. DOLLAR BOND ISSUE

a. Calculation of Eurobond all-in cost

Year	Cash Flows	Present Value at 7.68%
0[1]	99,262,000	99,262,000
1[2]	(7,500,000)	(6,964,868)
2	(7,500,000)	(6,467,919)
3	(7,500,000)	(6,006,427)
4	(7,500,000)	(5,577,864)
5[3]	(107,500,000)	(74,244,921)

Internal rate of return	7.68%	Sum	0

[1] Proceeds of $100 million net of $738,000 in expenses.
[2] Coupon of 7.5% applied to $100 million principal.
[3] Repayment of $100 million principal plus last interest payment.

b. Calculation of U.S. dollar bond all-in cost

Six-Month Period	Cash Flows	Present Value at 3.82%
0[1]	99,026,000	99,026,000
1[2]	-3,700,000	(3,563,895)
2	-3,700,000	(3,432,796)
3	-3,700,000	(3,306,520)
4	-3,700,000	(3,184,889)
5	-3,700,000	(3,067,732)
6	-3,700,000	(2,954,885)
7	-3,700,000	(2,846,189)
8	-3,700,000	(2,741,491)
9	-3,700,000	(2,640,644)
10[3]	-103,700,000	(71,286,961)

Internal rate of return	3.82%	Sum	0

[1] Proceeds of $100 million net of $974,000 in expenses.
[2] Semiannual coupon of 3.7% (7.4% annual) applied to $100 million principal.
[3] Repayment of $100 million principal plus last interest payment.

Eurobond is lower, making it the preferred issue assuming that other terms and conditions on the bonds are the same.

We could have converted the U.S. bond yield to its annual equivalent using Equation 13.2 and then compared that figure to the Eurobond yield of 7.68 percent. This computation would have yielded an annualized all-in cost of the U.S. bond issue equal to $(1.0382)^2 - 1 = 7.78$ percent. As before, the decision is to go with the Eurobond issue because its all-in cost is 10 basis points lower.

Interest Rates on Floating-Rate Eurobonds The interest rates on floating-rate Eurobonds (FRNs) are normally set in the same way as on Eurocurrency loans—as a fixed spread over a reference rate, usually LIBOR. The reset period is usually three months or six months, and the maturity of LIBOR corresponds to the reset period (for example, LIBOR6 for a six-month reset period). So, for example, if LIBOR3 on a reset date is 6.35

percent, an FRN that pays 50 basis points over LIBOR3 will bear an interest rate of 6.85 percent for the next three months.

Unlike the previous example, some FRNs have coupons that move opposite to the reference rate. Such notes are known as **inverse floaters.** An example would be a bond that pays 12 percent – LIBOR6. If LIBOR6 is, say, 7 percent on the reset date, the FRN's interest rate would be 5 percent (12 percent – 7 percent) for the coming six-month period. The risk to the issuer is that LIBOR will decline. Conversely, the investor's return suffers if LIBOR rises. There is a floor on the coupon at zero, meaning that the interest rate on an inverse floater is never negative.

Some floating-rate Eurobonds are inverse floaters.

Eurobond Retirement Sinking funds or purchase funds are usually required if a Eurobond is of more than seven years' maturity. A *sinking fund* requires the borrower to retire a fixed amount of bonds yearly after a specific number of years. By contrast, a *purchase fund* often starts in the first year, and bonds are retired only if the market price is below the issue price. The purpose of these funds is to support the market price of the bonds, as well as reduce bondholder risk by ensuring that not all the firm's debt will come due at once.

Most Eurobond issues carry *call provisions,* giving the borrower the option of retiring the bonds before maturity should interest rates decline sufficiently in the future. As with domestic bonds, Eurobonds with call provisions require both a call premium and higher interest rates relative to bonds without call provisions.

Ratings As noted earlier, Eurobond issuers are typically large multinational companies, government agencies, state-owned enterprises, or international organizations, all with familiar names and impeccable credit reputations. For this reason, in the past most Eurobonds carried no credit ratings, particularly because rating agencies charge a fee. But as the market has expanded to include newer issuers who are less well-known and with lesser credit reputations, investors have demanded ratings to better assess an issuer's credit risk. The majority of Eurobond ratings are provided by Moody's and Standard & Poor's, the dominant U.S. rating agencies. Euroratings is another agency that specializes in the Euromarkets, particularly in the dollar-denominated debt of non-U.S. issuers.

Eurobond issues are rated according to their relative degree of default risk. Note that interest rate changes or currency movements can make even default-free Eurobonds very risky. Bond raters, however, stick to just credit risk. Their focus is on the issuer's ability to generate sufficient quantities of the currency in which their debt is denominated. This element is particularly important for borrowers issuing foreign-currency-denominated debt (for example, the government of Mexico issuing debt denominated in U.S. dollars).

Rationale for Existence of Eurobond Market

The Eurobond market survives and thrives because, unlike any other major capital market, it remains largely unregulated and untaxed. Thus, big borrowers, such as Exxon, IBM, and Sears Roebuck, can raise money more quickly and more flexibly than they can at home. And because the interest investors receive is tax free, these companies have historically been able to borrow at a rate that is below the rate at which the U.S. Treasury could borrow.

The Eurobond market exists because it enables issuers and investors to avoid government regulations and taxes.

The tax-free aspect of Eurobonds is related to the notice in the tombstone for the GMAC Eurobond issue that it may not be offered to the U.S. public. U.S. tax law requires that for interest and principal to be payable in the United States, bonds must be in registered form. Eurobonds, however, are issued in bearer form, meaning they are unregistered, with no record to identify the owners. (Money can be considered to be a zero-coupon bearer bond.) This feature allows investors to collect interest in complete anonymity and, thereby, evade taxes. Although U.S. law discourages the sale of such bonds to U.S. citizens or residents, bonds issued in bearer form are common overseas.[3] As expected, investors are willing to accept lower yields on bearer bonds than on nonbearer bonds of similar risk.

Highly rated U.S. firms have long taken advantage of this opportunity to reduce their cost of funds by selling overseas Eurobonds in bearer form. Often, corporations can borrow abroad below the cost at which the U.S. government could borrow at home. Exxon's issue of zero-coupon Eurobonds shows how companies were able to exploit the arbitrage possibilities inherent in such a situation. Zero-coupon bonds pay no interest until maturity. Instead, they are sold at a deep discount from their par value.

 ILLUSTRATION   *Exxon Engages in International Tax Arbitrage*

In the fall of 1984, Exxon sold $1.8 billion principal amount of zero-coupon Eurobonds due November 2004 at an annual compounded yield of 11.65 percent, realizing net proceeds of about $199 million:

$$Bond\ value = \$1,800,000,000/(1.1165)^{20}$$
$$= \$199,000,000$$

It then used part of the proceeds to buy $1.8 billion principal amount of U.S. Treasury bonds maturing in November 2004 from which the coupons had been removed and sold separately. The yield on these "stripped" Treasuries, which are effectively zero-coupon Treasury bonds, was around 12.20 percent.[4] At this yield, it would have cost Exxon $180 million to purchase the $1.8 billion in stripped Treasury bonds:

$$Bond\ value = \$1,800,000,000/(1.1220)^{20}$$
$$= \$180,000,000$$

At this price, Exxon earned the difference of about $19 million.

A peculiar quirk in Japanese law was largely responsible for the big difference in yield between zero-coupon Eurobonds and stripped Treasuries: Japanese investors—who were the principal buyers of the Eurobonds—did not have to pay tax on a zero-coupon bond's accrued interest if they sold the bond prior to maturity. Because of this tax advantage, they were willing to pay a premium price for zeros (relative to coupon-bearing bonds). Although in principle the Japanese would have preferred to purchase the higher-yielding (and safer) stripped U.S. Treasury bonds, they are prohibited by Japanese law from doing so. The taxation of the accrued interest on zeros in Japan has eliminated this arbitrage opportunity.

Financial deregulation and the repeal of U.S. withholding tax on interest paid to foreigners is reducing the Eurobond market's appeal.

The Eurobond market, like the Eurocurrency market, exists because it enables borrowers and lenders alike to avoid a variety of monetary authority regulations and controls, as well as provides them with an opportunity to escape the payment of some taxes. As long as governments attempt to regulate domestic financial markets but allow a (relatively) free flow of capital among countries, the external financial markets will survive.

Recent years have seen a reduction in some of these regulatory costs. For example, the United States began permitting well-known companies—precisely the ones that would otherwise have used the Eurobond market—to bypass complex securities laws

---

[3] Americans can buy Eurobonds, but not until forty days after they have been issued, which cuts down on availability because many Eurobond issues are bought and stashed away.

[4] This case is discussed at greater length in John D. Finnerty, "Zero Coupon Bond Arbitrage: An Illustration of the Regulatory Dialectic at Work," *Financial Management*, Winter 1985, pp. 13–17.

when issuing new securities by using the *shelf registration* procedure. By lowering the cost of issuing bonds in the United States and dramatically speeding up the issuing process, shelf registration improved the competitive position of the U.S. capital market relative to the Eurobond market. More recently, the SEC's adoption of Rule 144A now enables companies to issue bonds simultaneously in Europe and the United States, further blurring the distinction between the U.S. bond market and its Eurobond equivalent. Other nations, such as Japan and England, are also deregulating their financial markets.

The Eurobond survives because of its adaptability.

With financial market deregulation in the United States and elsewhere, the Eurobond market lost some of the cost advantage that lured corporate borrowers in the past. Nonetheless, as long as Eurobond issuance entails low regulatory and registration costs relative to domestic bond issuance, the Eurobond market will continue to attract investors and borrowers from all over the world. Part of the lower registration costs stems from the less-stringent disclosure requirements in the Eurobond market, particularly as compared to the U.S. market. Even after the advent of shelf registration and Rule 144A, SEC disclosure requirements still are considered to be costly, time consuming, and burdensome by both U.S. and non-U.S. issuers.

Despite several forecasts of imminent death, the Eurobond market has survived, largely because its participants are so fleet of foot. As demand for one type of bond declines, quick-witted investment bankers seem to find other opportunities to create value for their customers. When the demand for fixed-rate Eurobonds fell, the Eurobond market led the boom in floating-rate note issues. When the FRN market collapsed in 1986, this business was replaced by issues of Japanese corporate bonds with equity warrants attached. In return for what is in effect a long-dated call option on the issuer's stock, the investor accepts a lower interest rate on the Eurobond to which the equity warrant is attached.

Demand for such issues soared as investors used the warrants to play Japan's rising stock market. In turn, Japanese companies found the Eurobond market easier and cheaper to use than the regulated domestic-yen market. However, the Tokyo stock market's plunge in 1990 triggered a steep decline in the Japanese equity-warrant issue market and in the Eurobond market overall. The equity-related Eurobond issue market has still not regained its former prominence.

The financial infrastructure in place in London should ensure the Eurobond market's survival. However, tax harmonization, financial deregulation, and the widespread loosening of capital controls mean that issuers have less incentive to borrow money offshore and some are returning to their domestic markets to raise capital. If these trends persist, the Eurobond market may never regain its preeminence. However, it can still preserve its basic role—as the nimblest intermediary for international capital flows between domestic markets.

Eurobonds versus Eurocurrency Loans

Both Eurocurrency and Eurobond financing have their advantages and disadvantages. Although many of these factors are reflected in the relative borrowing costs, not all factors are so reflected. For a given firm, therefore, and for a specific set of circumstances, one method of financing may be preferred to the other. The differences are categorized in five ways.

1. *Cost of borrowing:* Eurobonds are issued in both fixed-rate and floating-rate forms. Fixed-rate bonds are an attractive exposure-management tool because known long-term currency inflows can be offset with known long-term outflows in the same currency. In contrast, the interest rate on a Eurocurrency loan is variable, making Eurocurrency loans better hedges for noncontractual currency exposures. The variable interest rate benefits borrowers when rates decline, but it hurts them when rates rise. Arbitrage between Eurobonds and

Eurocurrencies, however, should not provide an automatic cost advantage to one or the other form of borrowing.

2. *Maturity:* Although the period of borrowing in the Eurocurrency market has tended to lengthen over time, Eurobonds still have longer maturities.

3. *Size of issue:* Historically, the amount of loanable funds available at any one time has been much greater in the interbank market than in the bond market. Now, however, the volume of Eurobond offerings exceeds global bank lending. In many instances, borrowers have discovered that the Eurobond market can easily accommodate financings of a size and at a price not previously thought possible. Moreover, although in the past the flotation costs of a Eurocurrency loan have been much lower than those on a Eurobond (about 0.5 percent of the total loan amount versus about 2.25 percent of the face value of a Eurobond issue), competition has worked to lower Eurobond flotation costs.

4. *Flexibility:* In the case of a Eurobond issue, the funds must be drawn down in one sum on a fixed date and repaid according to a fixed schedule unless the borrower pays an often substantial prepayment penalty. By contrast, the drawdown in a floating-rate loan can be staggered to suit the borrower's needs with a fee of about 0.5 percent per annum paid on the unused portion (normally much cheaper than drawing down and redepositing) and can be prepaid in whole or in part at any time, often without penalty. Moreover, a Eurocurrency loan with a multicurrency clause enables the borrower to switch currencies on any rollover date, whereas switching the denomination of a Eurobond from currency A to currency B would require a costly combined refunding and reissuing operation. A much cheaper and comparable alternative, however, would be to sell forward for currency B an amount of currency A equal to the value of the Eurobond issue still outstanding. There is a rapidly growing market in such currency swaps that enable the proceeds from bonds issued in one currency to be converted into money in another currency.

Eurocurrency loans tend to be more flexible than Eurobonds.

5. *Speed:* Internationally known borrowers can raise funds in the Eurocurrency market very quickly, often within two to three weeks of first request. A Eurobond financing generally takes more time to put together, although here again the difference is becoming less significant.

13.3 NOTE ISSUANCE FACILITIES AND EURONOTES

Euronote programs are of growing importance to financial executives.

Eurobanks have responded to the competition from the Eurobond market by creating a new instrument: the **note issuance facility** (NIF). The NIF, which is a low-cost substitute for syndicated credits, allows borrowers to issue their own short-term **Euronotes,** which are then placed or distributed by the financial institutions providing the NIF. NIFs—sometimes also called *short-term note issuance facilities,* or SNIFs—have some features of the U.S. commercial paper market and some features of U.S. commercial lines of credit. Like commercial paper, notes under NIFs are unsecured short-term debt generally issued by large corporations with excellent credit ratings. Indeed, notes issued under NIFs are sometimes referred to as Euro-commercial paper or Euro-CP. Typically, however, the name Euro-CP is reserved for those Euronotes that are not underwritten (see Section 13.4, "Euro-Commercial Paper"). Like loan commitments in the United States, NIFs generally include multiple pricing components for various contract features, including a market-based interest rate and one or more fees known as participation, facility, and underwriting fees. Participation fees are paid when the contract is formalized and are generally about 10 basis points times the facility size. Other fees are paid annually and sometimes are based on the full size of the facility, sometimes on the unused portions.

Many NIFs include underwriting services as part of the arrangements. When they are included, the arrangement generally takes the form of a **revolving underwriting facility (RUF)**. The RUF gives borrowers long-term continuous access to short-term money underwritten by banks at a fixed margin.

NIFs are more flexible than floating-rate notes and usually cheaper than syndicated loans. Banks eager to beef up their earnings without fattening their loan portfolios (which would then require them to add expensive equity capital) made NIFs an important new segment of the Euromarket. As in the case of floating-rate notes, the popularity of NIFs benefits from the market's preference for lending to high-grade borrowers through securities rather than bank loans.

Here's how the basic facility works (although alternate methods exist in abundance in the marketplace). A syndicate of banks underwrites an amount—usually between $50 million and $200 million—for a specified period, typically for five to seven years. A LIBOR-based underwriting margin is set, determined by the credit rating of the borrower, the size of the issue, and market conditions. When the borrower decides to draw on the facility, it will issue Euronotes, with one-month, three-month, six-month, or twelve-month maturities. A *tender panel* of banks is then established, whose members submit competitive bids. Any bids above the agreed underwriting margin are automatically purchased by the underwriters at the agreed-upon margin over LIBOR.

In effect, NIFs are put options. They give borrowers the right to sell their paper to the bank syndicate at a price that yields the prearranged spread over LIBOR. Borrowers will exercise this right only if they cannot place their notes at a better rate elsewhere, a plight most likely to occur if their creditworthiness deteriorates. The primary risk to the banks, therefore, is that they might someday have to make good on their pledge to buy paper at a spread that is too low for the credit risks involved. Although Euronote issuers generally are firms with sound credit standing, a NIF may oblige the banks to keep rolling the notes over for five to ten years—time enough for even the best credit risk to turn into a nightmare.

Note issuance are basically put options.

Most Euronotes are denominated in U.S. dollars and are issued with high face values (often $500,000 or more). They are intended for professional or institutional investors rather than private individuals.

The pricing of the Euronotes issued under NIFs depends on two conventions. First, instead of carrying a coupon rate, Euronotes are sold at a discount from face value. The return to the investor is the difference between the purchase price of the security and its face value. Second, the yield is usually quoted on a discount basis from its face value and is expressed in annual terms based on a 360-day year as shown in Equation 13.3:

$$\text{Discount rate} = \frac{\text{Discount}}{\text{Face value}} \times \frac{360}{n} \qquad (13.3)$$

where *n* is the number of days to maturity. For example, if a Euronote with a face value of $100,000 and 87 days to maturity is sold by the Export-Import Bank of Japan (JEXIM) at a discount of $1,600 from face value, its discount rate is computed as

$$\text{Discount rate} = \frac{1,600}{100,000} \times \frac{360}{87} = 6.62\%$$

Giving the discount pricing conventions for Euronotes, the market price of an issue is calculated as

$$\text{Market price} = \text{Face value} \times [1 - (\text{Discount rate} \times \frac{n}{360})] \qquad (13.4)$$

The application of Equation 13.4 would yield a market price of $98,400 for the JEXIM issue:

$$\text{Market price} = \$100,000 \times [1 - (0.0662 \times \frac{87}{360})] = \$98,400$$

To compute the annual yield on a basis comparable to interest-bearing securities that also use a 360-day year, the discount must be divided by the market price rather than the face value:

$$\text{Annual yield} = \frac{\text{Discount}}{\text{Market price}} \times \frac{360}{n} \quad (13.5)$$

In the case of the JEXIM issue, the annual yield would be 6.73 percent:

$$\text{Annual yield} = \frac{1,600}{98,400} \times \frac{360}{87} = 6.73\%$$

The relation between the annual yield and the discount rate, both based on a 360-day year, is as follows:

$$\text{Annual yield} = \text{Discount rate} \times \frac{\text{Face value}}{\text{Market price}} \quad (13.6)$$

Euronotes are sold at a discount to face value, so the annual yield will always exceed the discount rate.

The price of a Euronote issue can also be expressed in terms of its annual yield:

$$\text{Market price} = \frac{\text{Face value}}{1 + (\text{Annual yield} \times n/360)} \quad (13.7)$$

For example, the market price of a 114-day Euronote issue with a face value of $10,000 that is priced to yield 7.45 percent annually would be:

$$\text{Market price} = \frac{\$10,000}{1 + (0.0745 \times 114/360)} = \$9,769.52$$

The yields on some Euronotes, however, are based on a 365-day year. To reflect this difference, we would have to substitute 365 for 360 in the formula used to calculate the market price.

Note Issuance Facilities versus Eurobonds

In addition to their lower direct costs, NIFs offer several other benefits to the issuer relative to floating rate notes, their most direct competitor.

1. *Drawdown flexibility:* Note issuers usually can opt to draw down all or part of their total credit whenever their need arises, and they can roll over portions at will. This option is especially valuable for borrowers with seasonal or cyclical needs.

2. *Timing flexibility:* With FRNs, the borrower must live with the prevailing rate for the period's duration. By contrast, a Euronote borrower who thinks rates are going to fall can wait a month or so to issue. However, unless the financial director is better able to forecast interest rates, this option to wait is a dubious advantage.

3. *Choice of maturities:* FRN issuers are generally locked into one maturity setting—three months or six months—over the life of the deal. NIFs, on the other hand, give borrowers the choice of issuing notes with different maturities whenever they choose to draw down new debt or roll over old.

NIFs compete with FRNs.

Euro-Medium Term Notes

Securitization is rearing its head in the Euronote market too. A growing number of firms are now bypassing financial intermediaries and issuing **Euro-medium term notes (Euro-MTNs)** directly to the market. The Euro-MTN, which grew out of the medium-term notes issued in the U.S. market, is one of the most important developments in the Euromarkets in the past decade.

Reasons for Success   The three basic reasons for the success of the Euro-MTN market—speed, cost, and flexibility—ensure its continued growth and survival. Like their U.S. counterpart, Euro-MTNs are offered continuously rather than all at once like a bond issue. Euro-MTNs give issuers the flexibility to take advantage of changes in the shape and level of the yield curve and of the specific needs of investors with respect to amount, maturity, currency, and interest rate form (fixed or floating). They can be issued in maturities of as much as thirty years, although most are under five years, and in an ever-increasing range of currencies (including the Polish zloty, Czech koruna, Indonesian rupiah, and South African rand, in addition to the standards, such as the dollar, yen, euro, sterling, and Swiss franc). Unlike conventional underwritten debt securities, a program of medium-term notes can be offered in small amounts; in different maturities, currencies, seniority, and security; and on a daily basis, depending on the issuer's needs and the investors' appetites. By contrast, it is not customary to issue underwritten securities in batches of less than $50 million. In this way, Euro-MTNs bridge the maturity gap between Euro-CP and the longer-term international bond. However, with more Euro-MTNs being issued with maturities of less than one year, this has cut into the Euro-CP market.

Costs of a Euro-MTN Program   The costs of setting up a Euro-MTN program are estimated at $131,500.[5] In contrast, the estimated total cost of a Eurobond issue, including the printing and legal documentation associated with the prospectus (but excluding the underwriting fee), is about $100,000. Similar deals issued with Euro-MTN documentation incur only small one-time costs. Euro-MTN issuers thus save money after only two deals, and the savings increase with use.

Characteristics   Medium-term notes are not underwritten; securities firms place the paper as agents instead. Because issuers can change the price of their note offerings as often as several times a day, they can regularly fine-tune their liabilities to match the duration and amount of their assets and investors' demand. For example, a finance company that wants to match liabilities and assets could need, at a particular moment, $12 million of nine-month money, $15.3 million of fourteen-month money, and $19.1 million of twenty-two–month money. The bond market—with its high issuance costs—could not economically supply such small or precise amounts of debt, but a company with a Euro-MTN program could post appealing rates at those maturities to create the demand for its notes.

That is precisely what General Motors Acceptance Corporation (GMAC) does. Through its global MTN program GMAC shifts its borrowings between the United States and Europe, depending on which market is cheapest. Like many MTN borrowers with a voracious appetite for debt, GMAC publishes rates daily; that is, it advertises the interest rates at which it will issue notes over the full range of the MTN maturity spectrum. Investors are free to approach GMAC, through its dealers, to buy MTNs. Depending on its own particular requirements, GMAC will shift the rates it advertises to encourage investors to lend at the maturities it most needs.

Moreover, unlike public bond issues, the amounts and timing of medium-term note sales are not disclosed. Such a lack of visibility is just fine with many companies, for it

---

[5] This estimate appears in "A Vision of the Future," *Euromoney*, March 1996, p. 114.

allows them to raise funds quickly and discreetly without having to take the risk of a souring public offering. Euro-MTNs also can broaden an existing investor base to include bank trust departments, thrifts, and pension funds. Such a broadening of the investor base is not accidental. It is related to the most significant distinguishing feature of an MTN program—namely, that it is largely investor-driven, with notes tailored to meet the interests of particular investors.

Medium-term notes are not new, but for many years the market consisted almost exclusively of the auto companies' finance arms, particularly GMAC, which with more than $10 billion outstanding is still the largest issuer. Until 1983, however, secondary trading in the notes, a necessary part of a liquid market, languished. What apparently brought the market to life was GMAC's decision that year to issue notes through dealers rather than directly as it had been doing. The change convinced investors that there would be a strong secondary market, giving them the liquidity they sought.

Risks   The risk to the borrower of issuing Euro-MTNs rather than taking out a fixed-term Eurocurrency loan or Eurobond is that it might not be able to roll over its existing notes or place additional notes when necessary. This risk can be mitigated by extending the maturity of the MTNs issued or by issuing the notes under a revolving credit commitment, such as the note issuance facilities (NIFs) discussed earlier. In the event that market conditions at the time of any note issue are unfavorable and there is insufficient investor demand, the syndicate of banks underwriting the NIF provides the necessary funds by guaranteeing to purchase the notes or make advances in lieu of this, on pre-agreed terms. At maturity, the issuer repays the notes by either issuing new notes or drawing on other resources.

13.4 EURO-COMMERCIAL PAPER

Nonunderwritten short-term Euronotes bear a strong resemblance to commercial paper in the United States and are often called Euro-CP.

Another innovation in nonbank short-term credits that bears a strong resemblance to commercial paper is the nonunderwritten short-term Euronote, often called **Euro-commercial paper** (Euro-CP, for short). There are some differences between U.S. commercial paper and Euro-CP, however. For one thing, the average maturity of Euro-CP is about twice as long as the average maturity of U.S. CP. Also, Euro-CP is actively traded in a secondary market, but most U.S. CP is held to maturity by the original investors. Central banks, commercial banks, and corporations are important parts of the investor base for particular segments of the Euro-CP market; the most important holders of U.S. CP are money-market funds, which are not very significant in the Euro-CP market. In addition, the distribution of U.S. issuers in the Euro-CP market is of significantly lower quality than the distribution of U.S. issuers in the U.S.-CP market. An explanation of this finding may lie in the importance of banks as buyers of less-than-prime paper in the Euro-CP market.

Although similar, the U.S. CP and the Euro-CP markets differ in some important respects.

Another important difference between the two markets historically has been in the area of ratings. For example, at year end 1986, only about 45 percent of active Euro-CP issuers were rated. Credit ratings in the United States, on the other hand, are ubiquitous. This difference proved transitory, however, as investors became accustomed to the concept and the rating agencies facilitated the use of their services. For example, Standard & Poor's Corporation charges an entity with a U.S. rating only $5,000 for a Euro-CP rating on top of the $25,000 annual U.S. fee. Moody's has gone a step further by making its CP ratings global paper ratings that are applicable in any market or currency. Today, few Euro-CP issuers are unrated.

Although still dwarfed by the U.S. CP market, the Euro-CP market has grown rapidly since its founding in 1985. As one indication of its growing maturity, in September 1994, British Telecom took less than 48 hours to raise a record $635 million via Euro-CP.

Encouraged by such signs of the market's increasing depth and liquidity, many European companies have increased Euro-CP issuance. Moreover, despite their access to their huge domestic CP market, U.S. corporations have also started to take an interest. Two months after British Telecom broke Euro-CP records, AT&T extended the $200 million Euro-CP program it set up in 1987 to $1 billion. Despite these encouraging signs, most treasurers, whether or not in the United States, still regard the U.S. commercial paper market as their main source of low-cost funds to cover day-to-day working capital requirements because of its tremendous liquidity and depth.

A major advantage of the Euro-CP market is its flexibility.

The Euro-CP market has one advantage, however: flexibility. Unlike its U.S. counterpart, Euro-CP is multidenominational, allowing issuers to borrow in a range of currencies. For example, AT&T's $1 billion program allows it to issue CP in several currencies, including dollars, Swedish kronor, and euros. Although 77 percent of all Euro-CP are still denominated in dollars, the nondollar portion has been growing over time.

Aside from the obvious benefit of allowing overseas subsidiaries to borrow in their local currencies, a multicurrency Euro-CP program also allows considerable scope for swap arbitrage. By combining a commercial paper issue with a cross-currency swap (see Chapter 9), borrowers are able to achieve significant interest savings. About 40 percent of all Euro-CP issues are now swapped. The development of computer technology that permits both dealer and issuer easier access to swap arbitrage opportunities and investor demand presages more growth ahead for swap-driven Euro-CP programs.

13.5 THE ASIACURRENCY MARKET

Although dwarfed by its European counterpart, the **Asiacurrency** (or **Asiadollar**) **market** has been growing rapidly in terms of both size and range of services provided. Located in Singapore because of the lack of restrictive financial controls and taxes there, the Asiadollar market was founded in 1968 as a satellite market to channel to and from the Eurodollar market the large pool of offshore funds, mainly U.S. dollars, circulating in Asia. Its primary economic functions these days are to channel investment dollars to a number of rapidly growing Southeast Asian countries and to provide deposit facilities for those investors with excess funds. As with all such investments, credit analysis is critical. The example "Steady Safe Isn't" shows what could happen when lenders become too aggressive.

I L L U S T R A T I O N   *Steady Safe Isn't*

On January 12, 1998, the Asian financial crisis claimed another victim when Peregrine Investments Holdings Ltd., Hong Kong's premier investment bank and the largest Asian investment bank outside Japan, announced it would file for liquidation. Its collapse was triggered by the failure of a single large loan to an entrepreneur in Indonesia, where the dramatic decline of the rupiah brought a wave of loan defaults and bankruptcies and ultimately brought down President Suharto's authoritarian government. According to news reports, Peregrine lent $260 million—in the form of an unsecured bridge loan (a temporary loan to be repaid from the expected proceeds of a bond issue)—to a local taxicab operator named Yopie Widjara. Widjara, who reportedly enlisted President Suharto's eldest daughter as an equity investor, planned to create a system of car ferries linking the islands of Indonesia's sprawling archipelago. Peregrine's loan—which represented a third of its capital—was to be repaid through the sale of dollar-denominated bonds issued by Widjara's company, Steady Safe.

Peregrine's troubles started when the value of Asian currencies began falling during the summer of 1997, and it was unable to sell the Steady Safe bonds it had underwritten.

Then the Indonesian government lifted trading curbs on the rupiah and the bottom fell out of the currency. From Rp 2,400:$1 in July 1997, the rupiah exchange rate fell to more than Rp 8,000:$1 in January 1998. With the rupiah cost of servicing its debt rising by more than 200 percent, Steady Safe was unable (or unwilling—it is not clear what happened to the $260 million it borrowed) to repay its dollar-denominated bridge loan, and Peregrine collapsed.

The Asiabond counterpart to the Asiadollar market is the dragon bond. A **dragon bond** is debt denominated in a foreign currency, usually dollars, but launched, priced, and traded in Asia. The first dragon bond was issued in November 1991 by the Asian Development Bank. After growing rapidly in the early 1990s, however, the bond portion of the non-Japanese Asiabond market has slumped despite the existence of plentiful Asian savers and borrowers. The market's fundamental problem is that Asian borrowers with a good international credit rating can raise money for longer, and less, in Europe or the United States.

13.6 SUMMARY AND CONCLUSIONS

We saw that the growth of the international capital markets, specifically the Eurocurrency and Eurobond markets, is largely a response to the restrictions, regulations, and costs that governments impose on domestic financial transactions. At the same time, capital flows between the international capital markets and domestic markets have linked domestic markets in a manner that increasingly makes such government intervention irrelevant. A principal means whereby markets are linked is the use of interest rate and currency swaps, whereby two counterparties agree to exchange streams of payments over time in order to convert from one interest rate structure and/or currency to another.

As Eurobonds became a viable alternative to Eurocurrency loans, banks responded by creating note issuance facilities under which borrowers were able to issue their own Euronotes. Nonunderwritten short-term Euronotes, often termed Euro-commercial paper, is another important financial innovation in the Euromarkets. The Asiacurrency and Asiabond markets, located in Singapore, are the Asian counterparts to the Euromarkets.

QUESTIONS

1. What is the difference between a Eurocurrency loan and a Eurobond?

2. What is the difference between a foreign bond and a Eurobond?

3. What is the basic reason for the existence of the Eurodollar market? What factors have accounted for its growth over time?

4. Why have Eurobonds traditionally yielded less than comparable domestic issues?

5. a. What factors account for the growth of note issuance facilities?

   b. In what sense is the NIF part of the process of securitization?

   c. Why is the NIF described as a put option?

PROBLEMS

1. Suppose that the current 180-day interbank Eurodollar rate is 9 percent (all rates are stated on an annualized basis). If next period's rate is 9.5 percent, what will a Eurocurrency loan priced at LIBOR plus 1 percent cost?

2. Citibank offers to syndicate a Eurodollar credit for the government of Poland with the following terms:

Principal	U.S.$1,000,000,000
Maturity	7 years
Interest rate	LIBOR + 1.5%, reset every six months
Syndication fee	1.75%

a. What are the net proceeds to Poland from this syndicated loan?

b. Assuming that six-month LIBOR is currently at 6.35 percent, what is the effective annual interest cost to Poland for the first six months of this loan?

3. IBM wishes to raise $1 billion and is trying to decide between a domestic dollar bond issue and a Eurobond issue. The U.S. bond can be issued at a coupon of 6.75 percent, paid semiannually, with underwriting and other expenses totaling 0.95 percent of the issue size. The Eurobond would cost only 0.55 percent to issue but would bear an annual coupon of 6.88 percent. Both issues would mature in ten years.

   a. Assuming all else is equal, which is the less expensive issue for IBM?

   b. What other factors might IBM want to consider before deciding which bond to issue?

4. Daewoo Motors is about to issue $150 million face value in Euro-CP at a discount rate of 8.9 percent based on a 360-day year.

   a. If the maturity of Daewoo's Euro-CP is 91 days, what will be its proceeds from the issue?

   b. What will be its annual yield on this issue?

5. Commerzbank is seeking to invest $100 million short term. It has the choice between buying Euro-CP yielding 6.34 percent annually and a U.S. bank deposit yielding 6.36 percent annually, both maturing in 150 days. The Euro-CP yield is calculated on a 360-day year, whereas the U.S. bank-deposit yield is calculated on a 365-day year.

   a. How much Euro-CP in terms of face value can Commerzbank's $100 million buy?

   b. Assuming that all else is equal, which is Commerzbank's preferred investment? Explain.

   c. What would be the annual yield on the U.S. bank deposit if it were quoted on a 360-day year?

   d. What would be the annual Euro-CP yield if it were quoted on a 365-day year?

BIBLIOGRAPHY

Dufey, Gunter, and Ian H. Giddy. *The International Money Market.* Englewood Cliffs, N.J.: Prentice Hall, 1978.

Finnerty, John D. "Zero Coupon Bond Arbitrage: An Illustration of the Regulatory Dialectic at Work." *Financial Management,* Winter 1985, pp. 13–17.

Grabbe, Orlin J. *International Financial Markets,* 3rd ed. (Englewood Cliffs, N.J.: Prentice Hall, 1995).

Kim, Yong-Cheol, and René M. Stulz. "The Eurobond Market and Corporate Financial Policy: A Test of the Clientele Hypothesis." *Journal of Financial Economics* 22, 1988, pp. 189–205.

_____. "Is There a Global Market for Convertible Bonds?" *Journal of Business* 65, 1992, pp. 75–91.

INTERNET RESOURCES

www.oecd.org/document/36/0,2340,en_2825_495635_1962020_1_1_1_1,00.html Web site for *Financial Market Trends.* This publication provides an up-to-date analysis of developments and trends in international and national capital markets. Each issue includes highlights of recent developments in financial markets; analysis of policy issues affecting financial markets; overviews of new statistical information from OECD countries in areas such as international direct investment, overall bank profitability, institutional investment, and privatization; and statistics and charts dealing with international financial markets.

www.bis.org Web site from the BIS that contains extensive information on the amounts and types of funds raised in the international banking and capital markets, including the Eurocurrency and Eurobond markets and the international equity markets.

INTERNET EXERCISES

1. How much money has been raised in the past year in the Eurocurrency market? Eurobond market? Euronote market? Euro-commercial market?

2. What were the currency denominations of the past year's borrowings in the Euromarkets?

THE COST OF CAPITAL FOR FOREIGN INVESTMENTS

Traders and other undertakers may, no doubt, with great propriety, carry on a very consider-able part of their projects with borrowed money. In justice to their creditors, however, their own capital ought to be, in this case, sufficient to ensure, if I may say so, the capital of those creditors; or to render it extremely improbable that those creditors should incur any loss, even though the success of the project should fall very short of the expectations of the projectors.

Adam Smith (1776)

CHAPTER LEARNING OBJECTIVES

- To determine the cost of capital for foreign investments and identify those circumstances under which that cost should be higher, lower, or the same as that for comparable domestic projects
- To identify and address the key issues involved in applying the capital asset pricing model to estimate the cost of capital for foreign projects
- To illustrate the impact of globalization on the cost of capital
- To calculate the effective dollar costs of foreign currency borrowing taking into account interest rates, exchange rate changes, and taxes
- To identify the relevant factors and tradeoffs in establishing a company's worldwide capital structure
- To calculate the value of below-market financing opportunities

KEY TERMS

capital asset pricing model (CAPM)
corporate international diversification
cost of capital
cost of equity capital
domestic CAPM
global CAPM
home bias
international portfolio diversification
market risk premium

project beta
sovereign risk premium
systematic (nondiversifiable) risk
target capital structure
weighted average cost of capital
  (WACC)
worldwide capital structure
zero-coupon bond

A central question for the multinational corporation is whether the required rate of return on foreign projects should be higher, lower, or the same as that for domestic projects. To answer this question, we must examine the issue of cost of capital for multinational firms, one of the most complex issues in international financial management. Yet it is an issue that must be addressed because the foreign investment decision cannot be made properly without knowledge of the appropriate cost of capital.

In this chapter we seek to determine the cost-of-capital figure(s) that should be used in appraising the profitability of foreign investments. By definition, the **cost of capital** for a given investment is the minimum risk-adjusted return required by shareholders of the firm for undertaking that investment. As such, it is the basic measure of financial performance. Unless the investment generates sufficient funds to repay suppliers of capital, the firm's value will suffer. This return requirement is met only if the net present value of future project cash flows, using the project's cost of capital as the discount rate, is positive.

The development of appropriate cost-of-capital measures for multinational firms is closely bound to how those measures will be used. Because they are to be used as discount rates to aid in the global resource-allocation process, the rates must reflect the value to firms of engaging in specific activities. Thus, the emphasis here is on the cost of capital or required rate of return for a specific foreign project rather than for the firm as a whole. Unless the financial structures and commercial risks are similar for all projects engaged in, the use of a single overall cost of capital for project evaluation is incorrect. Different discount rates should be used to value projects that are expected to change the risk complexion of the firm.

This chapter also examines the factors that are relevant in determining the appropriate mix of debt and equity financing for the parent and its affiliates. In selecting financial structures for its various units, the multinational corporation must consider the availability of different sources of funds and the relative cost and effects of these sources on the firm's operating risks.

14.1 THE COST OF EQUITY CAPITAL

A company's cost of equity capital varies with the riskiness of its activities.

The **cost of equity capital** for a firm is the minimum rate of return necessary to induce investors to buy or hold the firm's stock. This required return equals a basic yield covering the time value of money plus a premium for risk. Because owners of common stock have only a residual claim on corporate income, their risk is the greatest, and so too are the returns they demand.

Alternatively, the cost of equity capital is the rate used to capitalize total corporate cash flows. As such, it is just the weighted average of the required rates of return on the firm's individual activities. From this perspective, the corporation is a mutual fund of specified projects, selling a compound security to capital markets. According to the principle of value additivity, the value of this compound security equals the sum of the individual values of the projects.

Although the two definitions are equivalent, the latter view is preferred from a conceptual standpoint because it focuses on the most important feature of the cost of equity capital—namely, that this cost is not an attribute of the firm per se but is a function of the riskiness of the activities in which it engages. Thus, the cost of equity capital for the firm as a whole can be used to value the stream of future equity cash flows—that is, to set a price on equity shares in the firm. It cannot be used as a measure of the required return on equity investments in future projects unless these projects are of a similar nature to the average of those already being undertaken by the firm.

One approach to determining the project-specific required return on equity is based on modern capital market theory. According to this theory, an equilibrium relationship exists between an asset's required return and its associated risk, which can be represented by the **capital asset pricing model (CAPM)**:

$$r_i = r_f + \beta_i (r_m - r_f) \tag{14.1}$$

The capital asset pricing model is a widely-used method for estimating a company's cost of capital.

where r_i = equilibrium expected return for asset i

r_f = rate of return on a risk-free asset, usually measured as the yield on a U.S. government Treasury bill or Treasury bond

r_m = expected return on the market portfolio consisting of all risky assets

$\beta_i = \rho_{im}\sigma_i/\sigma_m$, where ρ_{im} equals the correlation between returns on security i and the market portfolio, σ_i is the standard deviation of returns on asset i, and σ_m is the standard deviation of returns on the market portfolio

The CAPM is based on the notion that intelligent, risk-averse shareholders will seek to diversify their risks, and, as a consequence, the only risk that will be rewarded with a risk premium will be systematic risk. As can be seen from Equation 14.1, the risk premium associated with a particular asset i is assumed to equal $\beta_i(r_m - r_f)$, where β_i is the **systematic** or **nondiversifiable risk** of the asset. The term $r_m - r_f$ is known as the **market risk premium**.

The cost of capital for a project depends on the risk of that project.

Where the returns and financial structure of an investment are expected to be similar to those of the firm's typical investment, the corporatewide cost of equity capital may serve as a reasonable proxy for the required return on equity of the project. In this case, estimates of the value of the **project beta**—the beta for the project taken on its own—can be found either by direct computation using the CAPM or through professional investment companies that keep track of company betas.

It should be emphasized again that using a company beta to estimate the required return on a project's equity capital is valid only for investments with financial characteristics typical of the "pool" of projects represented by the corporation. This cost-of-equity-capital estimate is useless in calculating project-specific required returns on equity when the characteristics of the project diverge from the corporate norm.

14.2 THE WEIGHTED AVERAGE COST OF CAPITAL FOR FOREIGN PROJECTS

The weighted average cost of capital is appropriate only if the financial structures and commercial risks are similar for all new investments.

As commonly used, the required return on equity for a particular investment assumes that the financial structure and risk of the project is similar to that for the firm as a whole. This cost of equity capital, k_e, is then combined with the after-tax cost of debt, $k_d(1-t)$, to yield a **weighted average cost of capital (WACC)** for the parent and the project, k_0, computed as

$$k_0 = (1 - L)k_e + Lk_d (1 - t) \tag{14.2}$$

where L is the parent's debt ratio (debt to total assets). This cost of capital is then used as the discount rate in evaluating the specific foreign investment. It should be stressed that k_e is the required return on the firm's stock given the particular debt ratio selected.

Two caveats in employing the weighted average cost of capital are appropriate here. First, the weights must be based on the proportion of the firm's capital structure accounted for by each source of capital using *market,* not *book,* values. Second, in calculating the WACC, the firm's historical debt-equity mix is not relevant. Rather, the weights must be marginal weights that reflect the firm's **target capital structure**, that is, the proportions of debt and equity the firm plans to use in the future.

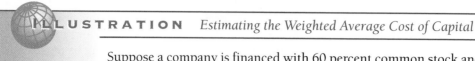

ILLUSTRATION *Estimating the Weighted Average Cost of Capital*

Suppose a company is financed with 60 percent common stock and 40 percent debt, with respective after-tax costs of 14 percent and 6 percent. Based on the financing proportions and the after-tax costs of the various capital components and Equation 14.2, the WACC for this firm is calculated as 10.8 percent ($0.6 \times 0.14 + 0.4 \times 0.06$). If the net present value of a project's cash flows—discounted at the weighted average cost of capital—is positive, and assuming that the risk of the project is the same as that of the firm, the project should be undertaken; if it is negative, the investment should be rejected.

Taxes and the project's risk characteristics affected its weighted average cost of capital.

Both project risk and project financial structure can vary from the corporate norm. For example, the project's capital structure can vary from the corporate norm because of its different debt capacity. It is necessary, therefore, to adjust the costs and weights of the different cost components to reflect their actual values. In particular, if the foreign project has a debt ratio of L', a cost of debt of k_d', and a cost of equity capital of k_e', the project's WACC will equal

$$k_0' = (1 - L')k_e' + L'k_d'(1 - t) \tag{14.3}$$

ILLUSTRATION *Estimating a Foreign Project's Weighted Average Cost of Capital*

Consider the company in the previous illustration. It is now planning a new foreign investment whose debt capacity can support a debt ratio of only 0.30 instead of the 0.40 debt ratio for the parent. Given the project's high degree of risk, its cost of equity equals 16 percent, and its after-tax cost of debt is 8 percent. Based on these parameters, k_0' equals 13.6 percent ($0.16 \times 0.7 + 0.08 \times 0.3$). This rate contrasts with the parent's previously estimated cost of capital of 10.8 percent.

14.3 DISCOUNT RATES FOR FOREIGN INVESTMENTS

The relevant component of risk in estimating a foreign project's cost of capital is its systematic risk.

The importance of the CAPM for the international firm is that the effect of a foreign project's risk on its cost of capital depends only on that project's systematic risk—that is, that portion of return variability that cannot be eliminated through diversification. As we saw earlier, a project's systematic risk is measured by its beta coefficient and is the factor that determines the risk premium associated with the project. The definition of beta is repeated here as Equation 14.4:

$$\beta_i = \frac{\rho_{im}\sigma_i}{\sigma_m} \tag{14.4}$$

where ρ_{im} equals the correlation between returns on project i and the market portfolio, σ_i is the standard deviation of returns on project i, and σ_m is the standard deviation of returns on the market portfolio. The correlation coefficient takes on values between -1 and $+1$. A positive correlation indicates that the project and market returns tend to move in the same direction; if the project and market are negatively correlated, their returns tend to move in opposite directions. A zero correlation means that the returns vary independently of each other.

The less positive or more negative the correlation between a foreign project's returns and returns on the market, the lower that project's systematic risk. However, we can see from Equation 14.4 that even if a foreign project's returns have a low correlation with market returns, the project can still have a high beta if the project risk, as measured by σ_i is sufficiently high.

Evidence suggests that much of the economic and political risk faced by MNCs is unsystematic risk, which therefore can be eliminated through diversification on the level of the individual investor. Although these risks may be quite large, they should not affect the discount rate to be used in valuing foreign projects. In other words, the low correlation between project and market returns offsets the effects of a high degree of project risk.

Many of the political and economic risks faced by MNCs are unsystematic in nature.

On the other hand, much of the systematic or general market risk affecting a company, at least as measured using a domestic stock index such as the Standard & Poor's 500, is related to the cyclical nature of the national economy in which the company is domiciled. Consequently, the returns on a project located in a foreign country whose economy is not perfectly synchronous with the home country's economy should be less highly correlated with domestic market returns than the returns on a comparable domestic project. If this is the case, then the systematic risk of a foreign project actually could be lower than the systematic risk of its domestic counterpart.

Paradoxically, it is the less-developed countries (LDCs), where political risks are greatest, that are likely to provide the largest diversification benefits. This is because the economies of LDCs are less closely tied to the economy of the United States or that of any other Western nation. By contrast, the correlation among the economic cycles of developed countries is considerably stronger, so the diversification benefits from investing in industrialized countries, from the standpoint of a Western investor, are proportionately less.

Yet the systematic risk of projects even in relatively isolated LDCs is unlikely to be far below the average for all projects because these countries are still tied into the world economy. The important point about projects in LDCs, then, is that their ratio of systematic to total risk generally is quite low; their systematic risk, though perhaps slightly lower, is probably not significantly less than that of similar projects located in industrialized countries (and could be somewhat more if their risk were sufficiently high to offset the effects of a low correlation with market returns).

Even if a nation's economy is not closely linked to the world economy, the systematic risk of a project located in that country might still be rather large. For example, a foreign copper-mining venture probably will face systematic risk very similar to that faced by an identical extractive project in the United States, whether the foreign project is located in Canada, Chile, or Zaire. The reason is that the major element of systematic risk in any extractive project is related to variations in the price of the mineral being extracted, which is set in a world market. The world market price, in turn, depends on worldwide demand, which itself is systematically related to the state of the world economy. By contrast, a market-oriented project in an LDC, whose risk depends largely on the evolution of the domestic market in that country, is likely to have a systematic risk that is small in both relative and absolute terms.

An example of a latter type of project would be a Ford plant in Brazil whose profitability is closely linked to the state of the Brazilian economy. The systematic risk of the project, therefore, largely depends on the correlation between the Brazilian economy and the U.S. economy. Although positive, this correlation is much less than 1.

Corporate international diversification should prove beneficial to shareholders.

Thus, **corporate international diversification** should prove beneficial to shareholders, particularly where there are barriers to **international portfolio diversification**. To the extent that multinational firms are uniquely able to supply low-cost international diversification, investors may be willing to accept a lower rate of return on shares of MNCs than on shares of single-country firms. By extension, the risk premium applied to foreign projects may be lower than the risk premium for domestic ones; that is, the required return on foreign projects may be less than the required return on comparable domestic projects. The net effect may be to enable MNCs to undertake overseas projects that would otherwise be unattractive.

However, if international portfolio diversification can be accomplished as easily and as cheaply by individual investors, then, although required rates of return on MNC securities would be lower to reflect the reduced covariability of MNC returns caused by international diversification, the discount rate would not be reduced further to reflect investors' willingness to pay a premium for the indirect diversification provided by the shares of MNCs. In fact, American investors actually undertake very little foreign portfolio investment. The lack of widespread international portfolio diversification has an important implication for estimating the beta coefficient.

Evidence from the Stock Market

Ali Fatemi has produced a useful study of the effects of foreign operations on the cost of equity capital.[1] That study compared the performance of two carefully constructed stock portfolios: a portfolio of 84 MNCs, each with at least 25 percent of its annual sales generated from international operations; and a portfolio of 52 purely domestic firms. Monthly performance comparisons were made over the five-year period January 1976–December 1980.

Although the validity of the study is limited by the relatively short time period involved, the difficulty in properly matching MNCs with their purely domestic counterparts (most firms do business in more than one industry), and the difficulty in calculating the degree of sales from abroad (consider the transfer pricing problem, for example), its conclusions are nonetheless of interest.

> Stock market data suggest that international diversification reduces a company's systematic risk.

1. The rates of return on the two portfolios are statistically identical. Ignoring risk, MNCs and uninational (purely domestic) corporations (UNCs) provide shareholders the same returns.

2. Consistent with our expectations, the rates of return on the MNC portfolio fluctuate less than those on the UNC portfolio. Thus, corporate international diversification seems to reduce shareholder total risk and may do the same for the firm's total risk.

3. The betas of the multinational portfolio are significantly lower and more stable than the betas of the purely domestic portfolio, indicating that corporate international diversification reduces the degree of systematic risk, at least if systematic risk is calculated relative to the domestic portfolio. It was also found that the higher the degree of international involvement, the lower the beta.

Key Issues in Estimating Foreign Project Discount Rates

Although the CAPM is the model of choice for estimating the cost of capital for foreign projects, the type of information that is needed to estimate foreign subsidiary betas directly—a history of past subsidiary returns or future subsidiary returns relative to predicted market returns—does not exist. About the only practical way to get around this problem is to find publicly traded firms that share similar risk characteristics and use the average beta for the portfolio of corporate surrogates to proxy for the subsidiary's beta. This approach, however, introduces four additional questions for a U.S. multinational:

> One way to estimate a foreign project's beta is to find publicly-traded proxy firms.

1. *Should the corporate proxies be U.S. or local (i.e., foreign) companies?* Although local companies should provide a better indication of risk, such companies may not exist. By contrast, selecting U.S. proxies ensures that such proxies and their data exist, but their circumstances—and hence their betas—may be quite different from those facing the foreign subsidiaries. In addition, it is important to differentiate between the unsystematic risks faced by a foreign project— which individual investors can eliminate through diversification—and the

[1] Ali M. Fatemi, "Shareholder Benefits from Corporate International Diversification," *Journal of Finance,* December 1984, pp. 1325–1344.

systematic risks affecting that project, which may be small relative to the project's total risk.

The relevant market portfolio for estimating a project's beta is debatable.

2. *Is the relevant base portfolio against which the proxy betas are estimated the U.S. market portfolio, the local portfolio, or the world market portfolio?* Selecting the appropriate portfolio matters because a risk that is systematic in the context of the local market portfolio may well be diversifiable in the context of the U.S. or world portfolio. If this is the case, using the local market portfolio to calculate beta will result in a higher required return—and a less desirable project—than if beta were calculated using the U.S. or world market portfolio.

3. *Should the market risk premium be based on the U.S. market or the local market?* One argument in favor of using the local-market risk premium is that this is the risk premium demanded by investors on investments in that market. On the other hand, estimates of the local-market risk premium may be subject to a good deal of statistical error. Moreover, such estimates may be irrelevant to the extent that an MNC's investors are not the same as the investors in the local market and the two sets of investors measure risk differently.

4. *How, if at all, should country risk be incorporated in the cost of capital estimates?* One approach to incorporating country risk that has been widely adopted in recent years is to add a country risk premium to the discount rate estimated using the CAPM. These premiums are often computed from the yield spread on dollar-denominated local government bonds versus U.S. Treasury bonds. However, such an approach may involve double counting of risks and be inconsistent with the theoretical foundations of the CAPM.

Let us now address these four questions and their related issues. As in any application of a theoretical model, the suggested answers are not precisely right, but are instead based on a mix of theory, empirical evidence, and judgment.

Proxy Companies

There are several alternative proxy betas.

Three alternatives for estimating proxy betas are proposed here. These alternatives are presented in the order of their desirability. Other approaches are also mentioned.[2]

Local Companies   As much as possible, the corporate proxies should be local companies. The returns on an MNC's local operations are likely to depend in large measure on the evolution of the local economy. Inevitably, therefore, the timing and magnitude of these returns will differ from those of the returns generated by comparable U.S. companies. This means that the degree of systematic risk for a foreign project, at least as measured from the perspective of an American investor, may well be lower than the systematic risk of comparable U.S. companies. Put differently, using U.S. companies and their returns to proxy for the returns of a foreign project will likely lead to an upward-biased estimate of the risk premium demanded by the MNC's investors.

Some indication of the upward bias in the estimate of beta imparted by using U.S. proxy companies to estimate the betas for foreign projects is provided by presenting the foreign market betas relative to the U.S. index for some foreign countries. The betas for the foreign markets from a U.S. perspective are calculated in the same way that individual asset betas are calculated:

$$\text{Foreign market beta} = \frac{\substack{\text{Correlation with} \\ \text{U.S. market}} \times \substack{\text{Standard deviation} \\ \text{of foreign market}}}{\text{Standard deviation of U.S. market}} \tag{14.5}$$

___

[2] This section has benefited from a discussion with René Stulz.

According to Equation 14.5, in conjunction with data from the 31-year period 1970–2000, the beta for the Australian market relative to the U.S. market was 0.76 (0.47 × 0.8635/0.5320). The corresponding betas for Hong Kong and Singapore were 0.85 and 0.94, respectively:

Country	Correlation with U.S. Market	Standard Deviation of Returns (%)	Beta from U.S. Perspective
Australia	0.47	86.35	0.76
Hong Kong	0.33	135.55	0.85
Singapore	0.47	106.09	0.94
United States	1.00	53.20	1.00

It may be that some U.S. companies operating overseas would have betas in the foreign markets in excess of 1.0, thereby raising their betas relative to the estimated foreign market betas. Nonetheless, this evidence does suggest the possibility that the average beta of U.S. proxy companies overstates the betas for foreign subsidiaries from a U.S. perspective.

Notice also that despite investment risks associated with the Hong Kong and Singapore markets (standard deviations of 135.55 percent and 106.09 percent, respectively), risks that are about twice that of the U.S. market (a standard deviation of 53.20 percent), both markets had betas that were substantially lower than the U.S. market beta of 1.0. The reason is that much of the risk associated with markets in individual countries is unsystematic and so can be eliminated by diversification, as indicated by the relatively low betas of these markets.

Proxy Industry   If foreign proxies are not directly available, a second alternative is to find a proxy industry in the local market, that is, one whose U.S. industry beta is similar to that of the project's U.S. industry beta. One way to analyze the empirical validity of this approach is to check whether the betas of the two industries (the project's and the proxy's) are also similar in other national markets that contain both industries (e.g., Britain, Germany, and Japan).

> A proxy industry is an alternative if local proxy companies are unavailable.

Adjusted U.S. Industry Beta   The third alternative is to estimate the foreign project's beta by computing the U.S. industry beta for the project, $\beta_{USPROXY}$, and multiplying it by the foreign market beta relative to the U.S. index. Specifically, suppose that β_{AUS} is the beta for the Australian market relative to the U.S. market. Then, under this proposed methodology, the beta for the Australian project, β_{AUSSUB}, would be estimated as

$$\beta_{AUSSUB} = \beta_{USPROXY} \times \beta_{AUS} \tag{14.6}$$

This approach is the least preferred of the three alternatives because implicit in it are two questionable assumptions:

1. *The beta for an industry in the United States will have the same relative beta in each foreign market.* In other words, the project has the same risk relative to the risk of the local market as a comparable project would have in the U.S. market. That is a large assumption considering that national markets have different industries and different weightings of industries in their indices.

2. *The only correlation with the U.S. market of a foreign company in the project's industry comes through its correlation with the local market and the local market's correlation with the U.S. market.* However, it is conceivable that, say, an oil firm could have a low correlation with the local market but a high correlation with the U.S. market.

That being said, to the extent that returns for a foreign project depend largely on the evolution of the local economy in which it operates, these two assumptions are likely to be satisfied. In that case, this approach would be an appropriate compromise.

Although these approaches to estimating foreign subsidiary betas involve a variety of assumptions, these assumptions appear to be no less plausible than the assumption that foreign operations are inherently riskier than comparable domestic operations and should be assessed an added risk premium.

The Relevant Base Portfolio

In employing the CAPM, the base portfolio against which the proxy betas are estimated can be the home portfolio or the global market portfolio. The resulting implementation of the CAPM depends on which base portfolio is selected. For a U.S. MNC evaluating a foreign investment opportunity, use of its home market portfolio would result in the following version of the CAPM:

$$r_i = r_f + \beta_{ius} (r_{us} - r_f) \tag{14.7}$$

where β_{ius} refers to the project beta when measured relative to the U.S. market (which is its home market) and r_{us} is the expected return on the U.S. market.

The global capital asset pricing model can be represented as

$$r_i = r_f + \beta_{ig} (r_g - r_f) \tag{14.8}$$

where β_{ig} refers to the project beta when measured relative to the global market and r_g is the expected return on the global market portfolio (which is measured by something like the Morgan Stanley Capital International, or MSCI, World Index).

The foreign project beta using the **global CAPM** is computed as follows:

$$\beta_{ig} = \frac{\begin{array}{c}\text{Correlation with} \\ \text{global market}\end{array} \times \begin{array}{c}\text{Standard deviation} \\ \text{of foreign project}\end{array}}{\text{Standard deviation of global market}} \tag{14.9}$$

The appropriate market portfolio depends on whether capital markets are integrated or segmented.

The appropriate market portfolio to use in measuring a foreign project's beta depends on one's view of world capital markets. More precisely, it depends on whether or not capital markets are globally integrated. If they are, then the world portfolio is the correct choice; if they are not, the correct choice is the home or domestic portfolio. The test of capital market integration depends on whether these assets are priced in a common context; that is, capital markets are integrated to the extent that security prices offer all investors worldwide the same tradeoff between systematic risk and real expected return. Conversely, if capital markets are segmented from each other, then risk is priced in a domestic context.

The truth probably lies somewhere in between. Capital markets now are integrated to a great extent, and they can be expected to become ever more so with time. However, because of various government regulations and other market imperfections, that integration is not complete. Unfortunately, it is not currently within our power, if indeed it ever will be, to empirically determine the relevant market portfolio and, hence, the correct beta to use in project evaluation. (The problem of determining the appropriate market portfolio to use in estimating beta arises domestically as well as internationally.)

The Impact of Globalization on the Cost of Capital   To the extent that a global CAPM is the appropriate model to use, it has important implications for companies. First, risk that is systematic in the context of the domestic economy may well be unsystematic in the context of the world economy. As long as the domestic economy is less than perfectly correlated with the world economy, the beta for a project that depends on the state of the local market will be less when measured against the global portfolio than when measured against the domestic portfolio. Other things being equal, the use of a global CAPM means a lower cost of capital for this company.

Another benefit of globally integrated markets is that investors are able to reduce some of the risk that they would otherwise have to bear in a segmented market. In particular, by diversifying across nations whose economic cycles are not perfectly in phase, a globally diversified portfolio will be less risky than a purely domestic portfolio. The reason is that risk which is systematic in the context of the U.S. economy may be unsystematic in the context of the global economy. For example, an oil price shock that hurts the U.S. economy helps the economies of oil-exporting nations, and vice versa. Thus, just as movements in different stocks partially offset one another in an all-U.S. portfolio, so also do movements in U.S. and non-U.S. stock portfolios cancel each other out somewhat.

Globally integrated financial markets reduce the cost of capital.

The lower risk of a globally diversified portfolio translates into a lower risk premium if markets are globally integrated. To understand this result, consider a segmented national market in which domestic securities can only be held by local investors and local investors cannot buy foreign assets. These investors will bear more risk than if they were free to invest internationally. Hence, they will demand a higher rate of return for holding domestic securities than would a globally diversified investor who can diversify away the country-specific risk. Once the domestic market is integrated into a global market, the purely domestic risk on local stocks will be diversified away in the global portfolio. With investors holding domestic stocks now bearing less risk, they will demand a lower risk premium.

The lower risk premium can be seen by recognizing that if the global CAPM holds, the market risk premium for the domestic market portfolio will equal the domestic market beta relative to the global market portfolio, β_d, multiplied by the global market risk premium. Given that β_d will usually be less than 1 and that the global market risk premium will be less than the domestic risk premium, the product of the two will also be smaller.

ILLUSTRATION   *How Globalization Affected Nestlé's Cost of Capital*

A striking example of the impact of globalization on the cost of capital is provided by the November 1988 decision of Nestlé, the giant Swiss foods conglomerate, to eliminate restrictions on foreign ownership of its shares.[3] Until that point, Nestlé had two classes of shares that differed only in who could own them. *Bearer* shares were available to both Swiss and foreign investors, whereas *registered* shares could be owned only by Swiss investors. Despite the fact that these shares had identical voting and dividend rights, registered shares were worth only about half as much as bearer shares. Once the restrictions on foreign ownership of registered shares were lifted, the price of registered shares rose by over 36 percent while the price of bearer shares fell by about 25 percent. Overall, the market value of Nestlé's equity rose by 10 percent. The explanations for these changes are straightforward.

Once the restrictions on registered shares were lifted, the Swiss could sell some of these shares to foreigners. As the Swiss better diversify their portfolios, they demand a lower risk premium for holding the remaining registered shares. The price of these shares will rise as their future cash flows are less heavily discounted.

With respect to bearer shares, the lifting of restrictions on registered shares meant that the supply of Nestlé shares available to foreign investors rose. With the supply of Nestlé shares exceeding the demand for these shares at the then existing price, the price of bearer shares fell.

Finally, the jump in the total value of Nestlé's equity is consistent with a decline in its cost of equity capital. We can illustrate this using some numbers provided by René Stulz.[4]

---

[3] This example and the data come from a widely cited article written by René Stulz ("Globalization of Capital Markets and the Cost of Capital: The Case of Nestlé," *Journal of Applied Corporate Finance*, Fall 1995, pp. 30–38).
[4] See *ibid.*

The estimated Swiss beta for Nestlé was 0.90. The fact that Nestlé's home beta is close to 1.0 is not surprising given that it comprises a large portion of the Swiss stock market.

The Swiss market risk premium is estimated at 5.2 percent based on the difference between the Swiss stock market's historical average return of 9.8 percent and the 4.6 percent historical return to Swiss government bonds. With a 4.5 percent risk-free rate, the home version of the CAPM yields an estimated cost of capital for Nestlé equal to 9.2 percent:

$$k_e(Nestlé) = r_f + \beta_{Nestlé(s)} (r_s - r_f) = 4.5\% + 0.90 \times 5.2\% = 9.2\%$$

where $\beta_{Nestlé(s)}$ is Nestlé's beta relative to the Swiss market and r_s is the expected return on the Swiss market.

Once Swiss shares are readily available to foreign investors, we might expect the global version of the CAPM to more accurately describe the pricing of risk for Nestlé and hence its cost of equity capital. The beta for Nestle relative to a global index of stocks is about 0.60. With an estimated world market risk premium of about 6 percent, Nestlé's estimated cost of capital using the global CAPM will be 8.1 percent, 110 basis points below its previously estimated cost of capital:

$$k_e(Nestlé) = r_f + \beta_{Nestlé(g)} (r_g - r_f) = 4.5\% + 0.60 \times 6.0\% = 8.1\%$$

where $\beta_{Nestlé(g)}$ is Nestlé's beta relative to the global market and r_g is the expected return on the global market portfolio. If we accept that an updated world risk premium would be on the order of 4 percent and that closer integration of the world stock markets would increase Nestlé's global beta to 0.70, then the global CAPM would yield an estimated cost of capital for Nestlé of 7.3 percent (4.5 percent + 0.70 × 4 percent), 190 basis points below the estimate using the local CAPM.

The impact of the lower cost of capital on the value of Nestlé's shares can be seen with the aid of the dividend growth model. According to this model, if a company's dividend is expected to grow at a constant rate g per annum, the price of that company's stock is determined as follows:

$$P_0 = \frac{DIV_1}{k_e - g} \tag{14.10}$$

where k_e is the cost of equity capital and DIV_1 is the expected dividend for the upcoming year. Suppose the dividend is set equal to SFr 1 and g is equal to 3 percent. According to Equation 14.10, the value of Nestlé's stock based on the home version of the CAPM will be 1/(0.092 − 0.03), or SFr 16.13. Using the global version of the CAPM and an 8.1 percent cost of capital yields a value for Nestlé shares of SFr 19.61 [1/(0.081 − 0.03)], or 22 percent higher than the previously calculated estimate (19.61/16.13 = 1.22). With a 7.3 percent cost of equity capital, Nestlé's price will jump by 44 percent, to SFr 23.26 [1/(0.073 − 0.03]. Thus, seemingly small changes in the cost of capital brought about by increased globalization can have large impacts on value.

Empirical Evidence   The evidence on asset pricing models is mixed, largely because of the statistical difficulty of testing any such model. For example, a substantial literature exists on the **home bias**—the tendency to hold domestic assets in one's investment portfolio—exhibited by investors.[5] This evidence shows that domestic residents hold a disproportionate share of the nation's stock market wealth. Such home bias leads to capital market segmentation and results in a preference for using the domestic or local version

[5] The home bias has been documented by Kenneth R. French and James M. Poterba, "Investor Diversification and International Equity Markets," *American Economic Review, Papers and Proceedings,* 1991, pp. 222–226; Ian Cooper and Evi Kaplanis, "What Explains the Home Bias in Portfolio Investment," *Review of Financial Studies,* 1994, 7, pp. 45–60; and Linda Tesar and Ingrid M. Werner, "Home Bias and High Turnover," *Journal of International Money and Finance,* 1995, 14, pp. 467–493.

of the CAPM rather than the global CAPM.[6] If the **domestic CAPM** is the appropriate model to use, the cost of capital for a foreign project is likely to be lower than the cost of capital for the same project undertaken in the home market, assuming that the total risks of the projects are the same.

A different stream of research supports the use of the global CAPM. In the most widely cited study on the use of a global CAPM, Campbell Harvey examined the historical returns of markets in seventeen countries over the period February 1970 to May 1989.[7] He found that the main prediction of the global CAPM (that the domestic market risk premium will equal the product of the domestic market beta computed relative to the global portfolio times the global market risk premium) held for fourteen of the seventeen countries studied. Other tests of the global CAPM are also supportive.[8]

A Recommendation   Despite the evidence in favor of the global CAPM, a pragmatic recommendation is for U.S. MNCs to measure the betas of international operations against the U.S. market portfolio. This recommendation is based on the following two reasons:

1. It ensures comparability of foreign with domestic investments, which are evaluated using betas that are calculated relative to a U.S. market index.

2. The relatively minor amount of international diversification attempted (as yet) by American investors suggests that the relevant portfolio from their standpoint is the U.S. market portfolio.

A foreign project's systematic risk, and hence its cost of capital, is unlikely to be higher than that of a comparable domestic project.

This reasoning suggests that the required return on a foreign project may well be lower, and is unlikely to be higher, than the required return on a comparable domestic project. Thus, applying the same discount rate to an overseas project as to a similar domestic project probably will yield a conservative estimate of the relative systematic riskiness of the project.

Using the domestic cost of capital to evaluate overseas investments also is likely to understate the benefits that stem from the ability of foreign activities to reduce the firm's total risk. As we saw in Chapter 1, reducing total risk can increase a firm's cash flows. By confining itself to its domestic market, a firm will be sensitive to periodic downturns associated with the domestic business cycle and other industry-specific factors. By operating in a number of countries, the MNC can trade off negative swings in some countries against positive ones in others. This option is especially valuable for non-U.S. firms whose local markets are small relative to the efficient scale of operation.

Despite the apparent benefits of corporate international diversification for shareholders, research by Bertrand Jacquillat and Bruno Solnik concluded that although multinational firms do provide some diversification for investors, they are poor substitutes for international portfolio diversification.[9] Their results indicate that an internationally diversified portfolio leads to a much greater reduction in variance than does one comprising firms with internationally diversified activities. Thus, the advantages of international portfolio diversification remain.

For non-U.S. companies, especially those from smaller countries whose markets are open to foreign investors, it would probably make more sense to use the global CAPM. This model should be used for both domestic and foreign investments to ensure comparability across projects.

---

[6] The use of the local version of the CAPM is recommended, for example, by Ian Cooper and Evi Kaplanis, "Home Bias in Equity Portfolios and the Cost of Capital for Multinational Companies," *Journal of Applied Corporate Finance,* Fall 1995, pp. 95–102.
[7] Campbell R. Harvey, "The World Price of Covariance Risk," *Journal of Finance,* 1991, pp. 111–158.
[8] See, for example, K.C. Chan, G. Andrew Karolyi, and René M. Stulz, "Global Financial Markets and the Risk Premium on U.S. Equity," *Journal of Financial Economics,* October 1992, pp. 137–167; and Giorgio DeSantis and Bruno Gerard, "International Asset Pricing and Portfolio Diversification with Time-Varying Risk," *Journal of Finance* 52, 1997, pp. 1881–1913.
[9] Bertrand Jacquillat and Bruno H. Solnik, "Multinationals Are Poor Tools for Diversification," *Journal of Portfolio Management,* Winter 1978, pp. 8–12.

The Relevant Market Risk Premium

A strong case can be made for using the U.S. market risk premium in computing the foreign project's risk premium.

In line with the basic premise that multinationals should use a methodology that is as consistent as possible with the methodology used to calculate the cost of capital for U.S. investments, the recommended market risk premium to be used is the U.S. market risk premium. This is the appropriate market risk premium to use for several reasons. First, the U.S. market risk premium is the one likely to be demanded by a U.S. company's mostly American investors. A second reason for preferring the U.S. market risk premium is the earlier recommendation that the betas of foreign subsidiaries be estimated relative to the U.S. market. Using the U.S. market risk premium will ensure consistency between the measure of systematic risk and price per unit of this systematic risk. Finally, the quality, quantity, and time span of U.S. capital market data are by far the best in the world, increasing the statistical validity of the estimated market risk premium.

Conversely, no other country has a stock market data series of the same time span and quality as that of the United States. In addition, virtually all foreign countries have undergone dramatic economic and political changes since the end of World War II— changes that inevitably will affect the required risk premium for those markets. To the extent that such regime changes have altered the market risk premium in foreign countries, estimates of these risk premiums based on historical data are less useful as forecasts of required risk premiums going forward.

The bottom line is that U.S. capital markets have the best data available on the required return that investors demand per unit of risk. Moreover, as national capital markets become increasingly integrated globally, the market price of risk becomes the same worldwide. Add to these points the fact that shareholders of U.S. firms are mostly American and a strong case can be made that the U.S. market risk premium is the appropriate price of risk for a foreign project.[10]

Recommendations

In summary, the recommended approach to estimating the cost of equity capital for the foreign subsidiary of a U.S. multinational is to find a proxy portfolio in the country in which that subsidiary operates and calculate its beta relative to the U.S. market. That beta should then be multiplied by the risk premium for the U.S. market. This estimated equity risk premium for the foreign subsidiary would then be added to the U.S. (home country) risk-free rate to compute a dollar (home currency) cost of equity capital.

An alternative, but problematic, approach used by many investment bankers these days is to estimate a **sovereign risk premium** for the foreign country (by taking the difference between the interest rate on U.S. dollar-denominated debt issued by the foreign government and the rate on U.S. government debt of the same maturity) and to add that figure to the estimated U.S. cost of equity capital. In particular, to the extent that the estimated sovereign risk premium measures risk (it may measure a liquidity premium), it is not systematic risk but rather default (or rescheduling) risk that is being measured. And default risk does not enter into the cost of equity capital. Of course, default risk is likely to be closely linked to political risk, but adjusting the cost of capital is not necessarily the best way to factor political risk into a foreign investment analysis. As recommended in Chapter 17, a better approach for dealing with political risk is to first identify its likely cash-flow consequences and then adjust projected cash flows to incorporate those consequences.

---

[10] René M. Stulz ("Globalization, Corporate Finance, and the Cost of Capital," *Journal of Applied Corporate Finance,* Fall 1999, pp. 8–25) argues for the use of the global market risk premium, which he estimates at about two-thirds of the historical U.S. market risk premium based on the assumption that the standard deviation of an internationally diversified portfolio is about 20 percent lower than that of a diversified portfolio invested only in U.S. stocks.

14.4 THE COST OF DEBT CAPITAL

This section shows how to compute the dollar costs of foreign currency debt that would enter into the weighted average cost of capital calculation. These costs take into account the interest rate on the debt, any currency gains or losses, and the effects of taxes.

To illustrate, suppose that Alpha S.A., the French subsidiary of a U.S.-based multinational, borrows €10 million for one year at an interest rate of 7 percent. This euro loan is equivalent to an $8.7 million loan at the current exchange rate of $0.87/€. In one year, Alpha will have to repay the principal plus interest, or €10.7 million. If the end-of-year exchange rate is $0.85/€, Alpha's loan will cost $9,095,000 to repay (10,700,000 × 0.85). Although the euro interest rate is 7 percent, the dollar cost of the loan is 4.54 percent:

$$\$9,095,000/\$8,700,000 = 1.0454$$

The dollar cost is less than 7 percent because of the depreciation of the euro. It combines the effects of the euro interest rate and the percentage change in the dollar value of the euro.

In general, the dollar cost of borrowing local currency (LC) at an interest rate of r_L and a currency change of c is the sum of the dollar interest cost plus the percentage change in the exchange rate:

The cost of a local currency loan equals the interest expense less the exchange gain (loss) on loan repayment.

$$\text{Dollar cost of LC loan} = \text{Interest cost} + \text{Exchange rate change}$$
$$= r_L(1 + c) + c \qquad (14.11)$$

The first term in Equation 14.11 is the dollar interest cost (paid at year end after an LC exchange rate change of c); the second term is the exchange gain or loss involved in repaying an LC loan valued at $1 at the beginning of the year with local currency worth $(1 + c)$ dollars at year end. The currency change c is computed as $c = (e_1 - e_0)/e_0$, where e_0 and e_1 are the beginning and ending exchange rates (LC 1 = e). For example, the change in the dollar value of the euro is calculated as $(0.85 - 0.87)/0.87 = -2.30$ percent.

We can employ Equation 14.11 to compute the dollar cost of Alpha's euro loan as follows:

$$0.07(1 - 0.0230) - 0.0230 = 4.54\%$$

Taxes complicate the calculation of various loan costs. Suppose Alpha's effective tax rate is 40 percent. Then the after-tax cost of paying the €700,000 in interest is €700,000 × (1 − 0.40), or €420,000. This figure translates into an after-tax interest expense of 4.2 percent. In dollar terms, the cost is even lower. Specifically, the net dollar cost of the loan equals the dollar cost of repaying the loan minus the dollar-equivalent value of the borrowed funds. Given that Alpha borrowed €10 million, the after-tax cost of repaying the principal plus interest is €10,420,000.[11] At the end-of-year exchange rate, this amount translates into $8,857,000. The net after-tax dollar cost of Alpha's loan then is $157,000 based on the difference between the $8.7 million value of its loan initially and the dollar cost of repaying the loan. This after-tax cost translates into an effective dollar interest rate of 1.80 percent ($157,000/$8,700,000).

In general, the after-tax dollar cost of borrowing in the local currency for a foreign affiliate equals the after-tax interest expense plus the change in the exchange rate, or

$$\text{After-tax dollar cost of LC loan} = \text{Interest cost} + \text{Exchange rate change}$$
$$= r_L(1 + c)(1 - t_a) + c \qquad (14.12)$$

where t_a is the affiliate's marginal tax rate. The first term in Equation 14.12 is the after-tax dollar interest cost paid at year end after an LC currency change of c; the second is the

Taxes complicate the calculation of borrowing costs in different currencies.

---

[11] Alpha borrowed €10 million and must repay €10.7 million. Given the tax deductibility of the interest expense, the after-tax cost of paying the €700,000 in interest is €700,000 × (1 − 0.40), or €420,000.

exchange gain or loss in dollars of repaying a local currency loan valued at one dollar with local currency worth $(1 + c)$ dollars at the end of the year. The gain or loss has no tax effect for the affiliate because the same amount of local currency was borrowed and repaid.

Using Sovereign Risk Spreads

Although the use of a sovereign risk premium was discouraged when computing the cost of equity capital, it is appropriate for estimating the cost of debt associated with a foreign project. This premium reflects the market's assessment of potential losses owing to various country risks noted above. These risks may not be perfectly correlated with the risks of a direct investment in that country, but they are probably representative of such risks. As such, the rate on dollar-denominated local government debt provides us with an objective estimate of the minimum return that investors demand for lending to a particular foreign country. Exhibit 14.1 presents sovereign spreads, expressed in basis points, for a group of developing countries in ascending order. According to this exhibit, if the Treasury bond yield was, say, 5.9 percent, the dollar cost of debt for Argentina would be 13.08 percent (5.9 percent + 7.18 percent).

14.5 ESTABLISHING A WORLDWIDE CAPITAL STRUCTURE

In establishing an MNC's capital structure, the focus must be on the MNC's consolidated worldwide financial structure.

In estimating the weighted average cost of capital for an MNC or its affiliates, we took the capital structure as given. However, the capital structure itself should be the outcome of an optimal global financial plan. This plan requires consideration not only of the component costs of capital, but also of how the use of one source affects the cost and availability of other sources. A firm that uses too much debt might find the cost of equity (and new debt) financing prohibitive. The capital structure problem for the multinational enterprise, therefore, is to determine the mix of debt and equity for the parent entity and for all consolidated and unconsolidated subsidiaries that maximizes shareholder wealth.

EXHIBIT 14.1 • SOVEREIGN RISK SPREADS AND THE DOLLAR COST OF DEBT IN SELECTED DEVELOPING COUNTRIES

Country	Spread over U.S. Treasuries	Treasury Bond Rate	Dollar Cost of Debt
South Africa	125	5.90%	7.15%
Poland	185	5.90%	7.75%
Philippines	226	5.90%	8.16%
Peru	434	5.90%	10.24%
Panama	514	5.90%	11.04%
Mexico	597	5.90%	11.87%
Brazil	610	5.90%	12.00%
Morocco	700	5.90%	12.90%
Argentina	718	5.90%	13.08%
Russia	765	5.90%	13.55%
Venezuela	811	5.90%	14.01%
Nigeria	1,087	5.90%	16.77%
Ecuador	1,113	5.90%	17.03%
Bulgaria	1,517	5.90%	21.07%

Source: Donald R. Lessard, "Incorporating Country Risk in the Valuation of Offshore Projects," *Journal of Applied Corporate Finance,* Fall 1996, p. 61. The original source of these data is J.P. Morgan.

The focus is on the consolidated, **worldwide capital structure** because suppliers of capital to a multinational firm are assumed to associate the risk of default with the MNC's worldwide debt ratio. This association stems from the view that bankruptcy or other forms of financial distress in an overseas subsidiary can seriously impair the parent company's ability to operate domestically. Any deviations from the MNC's target capital structure will cause adjustments in the mix of debt and equity used to finance future investments.

Another factor that may be relevant in establishing a worldwide debt ratio is the empirical evidence that earnings variability appears to be a decreasing function of foreign-source earnings. Because the risk of bankruptcy for a firm is dependent on its total earnings variability, the earnings diversification provided by its foreign operations may enable the multinational firm to leverage itself more highly than can a purely domestic corporation, without increasing its default risk.

Foreign Subsidiary Capital Structure

After a decision has been made regarding the appropriate mix of debt and equity for the entire corporation, questions about individual operations can be raised. How should MNCs arrange the capital structures of their foreign affiliates? And what factors are relevant in making this decision? Specifically, the problem is whether foreign subsidiary capital structures *should*

- Conform to the capital structure of the parent company
- Reflect the capitalization norms in each foreign country
- Vary to take advantage of opportunities to minimize the MNC's cost of capital

> Parents can finance their subsidiaries in different ways from different funding sources.

Disregarding public and government relations and legal requirements for the moment, we see that the parent company could finance its foreign affiliates by raising funds in its own country and investing these funds as equity. The overseas operations would then have a zero debt ratio (debt/total assets). Alternatively, the parent could hold only one dollar of share capital in each affiliate and require all to borrow on their own, with or without guarantees; in this case, affiliate debt ratios would approach 100 percent. Or the parent could itself borrow and relend the monies as intracorporate advances. Here again, the affiliates' debt ratios would be close to 100 percent. In all these cases, the total amount of borrowing and the debt/equity mix of the consolidated corporation are identical. Thus, the question of an optimal capital structure for a foreign affiliate is completely distinct from the corporation's overall debt/equity ratio.

> An individual subsidiary has no independent capital structure, unless the parent will allow its subsidiary to default.

Moreover, any accounting rendition of a separate capital structure for the subsidiary is wholly illusory *unless* the parent is willing to allow its affiliate to default on its debt.[12] As long as the rest of the MNC group has a legal or moral obligation or sound business reasons for preventing the affiliate from defaulting, the individual unit has no independent capital structure. Rather, its true debt/equity ratio is equal to that of the consolidated group. Exhibits 14.2 and 14.3 show the stated and the true debt-to-equity ratios for a subsidiary and its parent for four separate cases. In cases I, II, and III, the parent borrows $100 to invest in a foreign subsidiary, in varying portions of debt and equity. In case IV, the subsidiary borrows the $100 directly from the bank. Depending on what the parent calls its investment, the subsidiary's debt-to-equity ratio can vary from zero to infinity. Despite this variation, the consolidated balance sheet shows a debt-to-equity ratio after the foreign investment of 4:7, regardless of how the investment is financed and what it is called.

Exhibit 14.4 shows that the financing mechanism does affect the pattern of returns, whether they are called dividends or interest and principal payments. It also determines

---

[12] See, for example, Michael Adler, "The Cost of Capital and Valuation of a Two-Country Firm," *Journal of Finance*, March 1974, pp. 119–132; and Alan C. Shapiro, "Financial Structure and the Cost of Capital in the Multinational Corporation," *Journal of Financial and Quantitative Analysis*, June 1978, pp. 211–226.

EXHIBIT 14.2 • SUBSIDIARY CAPITAL STRUCTURE: DEBT-TO-EQUITY RATIOS

I. *100% Parent Financed*		II. *100% Parent Financed*	
$100	D = $50	$100	D = $100
	E = 50		E = 0
D/E = 1:1		D/E = Infinity	

III. *100% Parent Financed*		IV. *100% Bank Financed*	
$100	D = $ 0	$100	D = $100
	E = 100		E = 0
D/E = 0		D/E = Infinity	

EXHIBIT 14.3 • CONSOLIDATED PARENT BALANCE SHEET: DEBT-TO-EQUITY RATIOS

Before Foreign Investment

$1,000	D = $300
	E = 700
D/E = 3:7	

After Foreign Investment

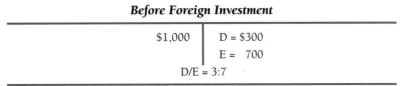

Case I, II, and III Parent Financed with 100% Bank Debt			Case IV Subsidiary Financed with 100% Bank Debt		
Domestic	$1,000	D = $400	Domestic	$1,000	D = $400
Foreign	100	E = 700	Foreign	100	E = 700
	D/E = 4:7			D/E = 4:7	

EXHIBIT 14.4 • SUBSIDIARY CAPITAL STRUCTURE DEPENDS ON WHAT ITS FUNDS ARE CALLED

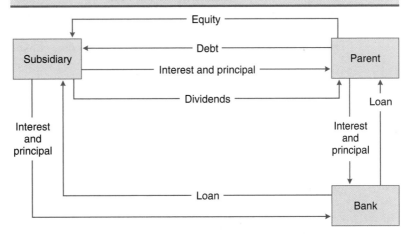

the initial recipient of the cash flows. Are the cash flows from the foreign unit paid directly to the outside investor (the bank), or are they first paid to the parent, which then turns around and repays the bank?

The point of this exercise is to show that unlike the case for the corporation as a whole, an affiliate's degree of leverage does not determine its financial risk. Therefore, the first two options—having affiliate financial structures conform to parent or local norms—are unrelated to shareholder wealth maximization.

The irrelevance of subsidiary capital structure is recognized by many multinationals.

Multinationals apparently recognize the irrelevance of subsidiary financial structures. In a 1979 survey by Business International of eight U.S.-based MNCs, most of the firms expressed little concern with the debt/equity mixes of their foreign affiliates.[13] (Admittedly, for most of the firms interviewed, the debt ratios of affiliates had not significantly raised the MNCs' consolidated indebtedness.) Their primary focus was on the worldwide, rather than individual, capital structure. The third option of varying affiliate financial structures to take advantage of local financing opportunities appears to be the appropriate choice. Thus, within the constraints set by foreign statutory or minimum equity requirements, the need to appear to be a responsible and good guest, and the requirements of a worldwide financial structure, a multinational corporation should finance its affiliates to minimize its incremental average cost of capital.

MNCs can use financing to reduce their susceptibility to political risk and exchange risk.

Political Risk Management A subsidiary with a capital structure similar to that of its parent may forgo profitable opportunities to lower its cost of funds or its risk. For example, rigid adherence to a fixed debt/equity ratio may not allow a subsidiary to take advantage of government-subsidized debt or low-cost loans from international agencies. Furthermore, it may hamper the subsidiary in designing a financing strategy to mitigate the effects of political risk. The use of financing to reduce political risks typically involves mechanisms to avoid or at least reduce the impact of certain risks, such as those of exchange controls. It may also involve financing mechanisms that actually change the risk itself, as in the case of expropriation or other direct political acts. For example, it may be worthwhile to raise funds locally if the country is politically risky. In the event the affiliate is expropriated, for instance, it would default on all loans from local financial institutions. Similarly, borrowing funds locally will decrease the company's vulnerability to exchange controls. Local currency profits can be used to service its LC debt.

Another approach used by multinational firms, especially those in the expropriation-prone extractive industries, is to finance their foreign investments with funds from the host and other governments, international development agencies, overseas banks, and customers—with payment to be provided out of production—rather than supplying their own capital. Because repayment is tied to the project's success, the firm(s) sponsoring the project can create an international network of banks, government agencies, and customers with a vested interest in the faithful fulfillment of the host government's contract with the sponsoring firm(s). Any expropriation threat is likely to upset relations with customers, banks, and governments worldwide. This strategy was employed successfully by Kennecott to finance a major copper mine expansion in Chile. Despite the subsequent rise to power of Salvador Allende—a politician who promised to expropriate all foreign holdings in Chile with "ni un centavo" in compensation—Chile was forced to honor all prior government commitments to Kennecott.

Currency Risk Management Borrowing in the local currency also can help a company to reduce its foreign exchange exposure. The basic rule is to finance assets that generate foreign-currency cash flows with liabilities denominated in those same foreign currencies. In the case of contractual items—those fixed in nominal terms—this structuring simply involves matching net positive positions (ones with net cash inflows) in each currency with

---

[13] "Policies of MNCs on Debt/Equity Mix," *Business International Money Report,* September 21, 1979, pp. 319–320.

borrowings of similar maturity. The goal here is to offset unanticipated changes in the dollar value of its cash flows with identical changes in the dollar cost of servicing its liabilities.

With noncontractual operating cash flows—those from future revenues and costs—the same financing principle applies: Finance assets that generate foreign currency cash flows with liabilities denominated in those same foreign currencies. Although it is impossible to perfectly hedge operating cash flows in this manner because of the many uncertainties concerning the effects of currency changes on operating flows, the hedging objective at least provides a clear-cut goal that firms should strive for.

On the other hand, forcing a subsidiary to borrow funds locally to meet parent norms may be quite expensive in a country with a high-cost capital market, or if the subsidiary is in a tax-loss-carryforward position. In the latter case, because the subsidiary cannot realize the tax benefits of the interest write-off, the parent should make an equity injection financed by borrowed funds. In this way, the interest deduction need not be sacrificed.

Tax factors complicate the financing decision for MNCs.

Leverage and Foreign Tax Credits   The choice of where to borrow to finance foreign operations is complicated because the distribution of debt between U.S. parents and their foreign subsidiaries affects the use of foreign tax credits. Foreign tax credits (FTCs) are credits that the United States and other home countries grant against domestic income tax for foreign income taxes already paid. The purpose of these FTCs is to eliminate double taxation of foreign-source earnings. In general, if the foreign tax on a dollar earned abroad and remitted to the United States is less than the U.S. corporate tax rate of 35 percent, then that dollar will be subject to additional tax in order to bring the total tax paid up to 35 cents. If the foreign tax rate is equal to or in excess of 35 percent, the United States will not impose additional taxes and, in fact, will allow the use of these excess taxes paid as an offset against U.S. taxes owed on other foreign-source income.

The problem for many U.S.-based MNCs is that they are in a position of excess foreign tax credits. One way to use up these FTCs is to push expenses overseas—and thus lower overseas profits—by increasing the leverage of foreign subsidiaries. In the aforementioned example, the U.S. parent may have one of its taxpaying foreign units borrow funds and use them to pay a dividend to the parent. The parent can then turn around and invest these funds as equity in the nontaxpaying subsidiary. In this way, the worldwide corporation can reduce its taxes without losing the benefits of its FTCs.

Leasing and Taxes   As an alternative to increasing the debt of foreign subsidiaries, U.S. multinationals could expand their use of leasing in the United States. Although leasing an asset is economically equivalent to using borrowed funds to purchase the asset, the international tax consequences differ. In the past, U.S. multinationals counted virtually all their interest expense as a fully deductible U.S. expense. Under current tax law, however, firms must allocate interest expense on general borrowings to match the location of their assets, even if all the interest is paid in the United States. This allocation has the effect of reducing the amount of interest expense that can be written off against U.S. income. Rental expense, on the other hand, can be allocated to the location of the leased property. Lease payments on equipment located in the United States, therefore, can be fully deducted.

At the same time, leasing equipment to be used in the United States, instead of borrowing to finance it, increases reported foreign income (because there is less interest expense to allocate against foreign income). The effect of leasing, therefore, is to increase the allowable foreign tax credit to offset U.S. taxes owed on foreign-source income, thereby providing another tax advantage of leasing for firms that owe U.S. tax on their foreign-source income.

Cost Minimizing Approach to Global Capital Structure   The cost-minimizing approach to determining foreign-affiliate capital structures would be to allow subsidiaries with access to low-cost capital markets to exceed the parent-company capitalization norm, while subsidiaries in higher-capital-cost nations would have lower target debt ratios. These costs must be figured on an after-tax basis, taking into account the company's worldwide tax position.

Some companies require their foreign units to be financially independent to motivate them.

The basic hypothesis proposed in this section is that a subsidiary's capital structure is relevant only insofar as it affects the parent's consolidated worldwide debt ratio. Nonetheless, some companies have a general policy of "every tub on its own bottom." Foreign units are expected to be financially independent after the parent's initial investment. The rationale for this policy is to "avoid giving management a crutch." By forcing foreign affiliates to stand on their own feet, affiliate managers presumably will be working harder to improve local operations, thereby generating the internal cash flow that will help replace parent financing. Moreover, the local financial institutions will have a greater incentive to monitor the local subsidiary's performance because they can no longer look to the parent company to bail them out if their loans go sour.

Companies that expect their subsidiaries to borrow locally had better be prepared to provide enough initial equity capital or subordinated loans. In addition, local suppliers and customers are likely to shy away from a new subsidiary operating on a shoestring if that subsidiary is not receiving financial backing from its parent. The foreign subsidiary may have to show its balance sheet to local trade creditors, distributors, and other stakeholders. Having a balance sheet that shows more equity demonstrates that the unit has greater staying power.

It also takes more staff time to manage a highly leveraged subsidiary in countries like Brazil and Mexico, where government controls and high inflation make local funds scarce. One treasury manager complained, "We spend 75–80 percent of management's time trying to figure out how to finance the company. Running around chasing our tails instead of attending to our basic business—getting production costs lower, sales up, and making the product better."[14]

Joint ventures complicate the financing decision.

Joint Ventures   Because many MNCs participate in joint ventures, either by choice or necessity, establishing an appropriate financing mix for this form of investment is an important consideration. The previous assumption that affiliate debt is equivalent to parent debt in terms of its impact on perceived default risk may no longer be valid. In countries such as Japan and Germany, increased leverage will not necessarily lead to increased financial risks, due to the close relationship between the local banks and corporations. Thus, debt raised by a joint venture in Japan, for example, may not be equivalent to parent-raised debt in terms of its impact on default risk. The assessment of the effects of leverage in a joint venture requires a qualitative analysis of the partner's ties with the local financial community, particularly with the local banks.

Unless the joint venture can be isolated from its partners' operations, some significant conflicts are likely to be associated with this form of ownership. Transfer pricing, setting royalty and licensing fees, and allocating production and markets among plants are just some of the areas in which each owner has an incentive to engage in activities that will harm its partners. These conflicts explain why bringing in outside equity investors is generally such an unstable form of external financing.

Because of their lack of complete control over a joint venture's decisions and its profits, most MNCs will, at most, guarantee joint-venture loans in proportion to their share of ownership. But where the MNC is substantially stronger financially than its partner, the MNC may wind up implicitly guaranteeing its weaker partner's share of any joint-venture borrowings, as well as its own. In this case, it makes sense to push for as large an equity base as possible; the weaker partner's share of the borrowings is then supported by its larger equity investment.

---

[14] "Determining Overseas Debt/Equity Ratios," *Business International Money Report,* January 27, 1986, p. 26.

14.6 VALUING LOW-COST FINANCING OPPORTUNITIES

Financing options at below-market rates are valuable.

So far, we have talked about the cost of capital assuming that companies are borrowing at market rates, that is, rates in line with their risks. However, sharp-eyed firms are always on the lookout for financing choices that are "bargains"—that is, financing options priced at below-market rates. The value of arranging such *below-market financing* can be illustrated by examining a case involving Sonat, the energy and energy services company based in Birmingham, Alabama. In late 1984, Sonat ordered from Daewoo Shipbuilding, a South Korean shipyard, six drilling rigs that can be partly submerged. Daewoo agreed to finance the $425 million purchase price with an 8.5-year loan at an annual interest rate of 9 percent paid semiannually. The loan is repayable in 17 equal semiannual installments. How much is this loan worth to Sonat? That is, what is its net present value?

At 9 percent interest paid semiannually, Sonat must pay interest equal to 4.5 percent of the loan balance plus $25 million in principal repayment every six months for the next 8.5 years. In return, Sonat receives $425 million today. Given these cash inflows and outflows, we can calculate the loan's NPV just as we would for any project analysis. Note, however, that unlike the typical capital-budgeting problem we looked at, the cash inflow occurs immediately and the cash outflows later, but the principle is the same. All we need now is the required return on this deal and Sonat's marginal tax rate.

The value of arranging low-cost financing can be computed using the net present value technique.

The required return is based on the opportunity cost of the funds provided, that is, the rate that Sonat would have to pay to borrow $425 million in the capital market. At the time the loan was arranged, in late 1984, the market interest rate on such a loan would have been about 16 percent. If the marginal tax rate at which the interest payments are written off is 50 percent (the federal plus state corporate tax rate at that time), then the after-tax semiannual required return is 4 percent (8 percent annually), and the after-tax semiannual interest payments are $0.0225 \times P_t$, where P_t is the loan balance in period t and 2.25 percent is the after-tax interest rate (0.5×4.5 percent). Now we can calculate the NPV of Sonat's financing bargain:

$$NPV = \$425,000,000 - \sum_{t=1}^{17} \frac{0.0225 P_t}{(1.04)^t} - \sum_{t=1}^{17} \frac{\$25,000,000}{(1.04)^t}$$

$$= \$425,000,000 - \$372,210,000$$

$$= \$52,790,000$$

These calculations are shown in Exhibit 14.5. You do not need a degree in financial economics to realize that borrowing money at 9 percent when the market rate is 16 percent is a good deal. However, what the NPV calculations tell you is just how much a particular below-market financing option is worth.

MNCs can raise funds at a below-market rate by taking advantage of financial market distortions.

Raising funds at a below-market rate is easier said than done, however. A company selling securities is competing for funds on a global basis, not only with other firms in its industry but with all firms, foreign and domestic, and with numerous government units and private individuals as well. The fierce competition for funds makes it highly unlikely that the firm can find bargain-priced funds. But, as we shall see, the task is not impossible. *Financial market distortions* arising from taxes, *government credit and capital controls,* and *government subsidies and incentives* sometimes enable firms to raise funds at below-market rates. Companies may also be able to raise low-cost money by devising securities for which specific investors are willing to pay a higher price.

Taxes

The asymmetrical tax treatment of various components of financial cost—such as dividend payments versus interest expenses and exchange losses versus exchange gains—often

EXHIBIT 14.5 • CALCULATING THE VALUE OF SONAT'S LOW-COST LOAN ARRANGEMENT (U.S. $ MILLIONS)

Period	Principal Balance (1)	Interest (1) × 0.225 (2)	Principal Repayment (3)	Total Payment (4)	PV Factor @ 4% (5)	Present Value (6)
1	$425	$9.56	$25	$34.56	0.962	$ 33.25
2	400	9.00	25	34.00	0.925	31.45
3	375	8.44	25	33.44	0.889	29.73
4	350	7.88	25	32.88	0.855	28.11
5	325	7.31	25	32.31	0.822	26.56
6	300	6.75	25	31.75	0.790	25.08
7	275	6.19	25	31.19	0.760	23.70
8	250	5.63	25	30.63	0.731	22.39
9	225	5.06	25	30.06	0.703	21.13
10	200	4.50	25	29.50	0.676	19.94
11	175	3.94	25	28.94	0.650	18.81
12	150	3.38	25	28.38	0.625	17.73
13	125	2.81	25	27.81	0.601	16.71
14	100	2.25	25	27.25	0.578	15.75
15	75	1.69	25	26.69	0.555	14.81
16	50	1.13	25	26.13	0.534	13.95
17	25	0.56	25	25.56	0.513	13.11
						Sum $372.21

causes equality of before-tax costs to lead to inequality in after-tax costs. This asymmetry holds out the possibility of reducing after-tax costs by judicious selection of securities. Yet, everything is not always what it seems.

For example, many firms consider debt financing to be less expensive than equity financing because interest expense is tax-deductible, whereas dividends are paid out of after-tax income. But this comparison is too limited. In the absence of any restrictions, the supply of corporate debt can be expected to rise. Yields also will have to rise in order to attract investors in higher and higher tax brackets. Companies will continue to issue debt up to the point at which the marginal investor tax rate will equal the marginal corporate tax rate.[15] At this point, the necessary yield would be such that there would no longer be a tax incentive for issuing more debt.

> Companies can take advantage of tax asymmetries.

The tax advantage of debt can be preserved only if the firm can take advantage of some tax distortion, issue tax-exempt debt, or sell debt to investors in marginal tax brackets below 34 percent. The example of zero-coupon bonds illustrates all of these categories.

Zero-Coupon Bonds In 1982, PepsiCo issued the first long-term **zero-coupon bond**. Although they have since become a staple of corporate finance, zero-coupon bonds initially were a startling innovation. They do not pay interest, but they are sold at a deep discount to their face value. For example, the price on PepsiCo's thirty-year bonds was around $60 for each $1,000 face amount of the bonds. Investors gain from the difference between the discounted price and the amount they receive at redemption.

Between 1982 and 1985, investors paid $4 billion for $18.9 billion worth of zero-coupon bonds, about half of which were purchased by Japanese investors. The offerings were attractive in Japan because the government does not tax the capital gain on bonds

---

[15] This insight first appeared in Merton Miller, "Debt and Taxes," *Journal of Finance*, May 1977, pp. 261–276.

sold before maturity. Catering to this tax break, a number of companies—including Exxon (see the illustration in Chapter 13) and IBM—were able to obtain inexpensive financing by targeting Japanese investors for zero-coupon bonds offered on international markets.

The ability to take advantage quickly of such tax windows is evident considering subsequent developments in Japan. Japan's Finance Ministry, embarrassed at this tax break, has effectively ended the tax exemption for zero-coupon bond gains. Japanese investors accordingly have demanded higher yields to compensate for their anticipated tax liability. The Japanese government's reaction to the proliferation of zero-coupon debt illustrates a key point: If one devises a legal way to engage in unlimited tax arbitrage through the financial markets, the government will change the law.

This example also points out that even though the world's capital markets are highly integrated, companies still can profit from tax differentials and government restrictions on capital flows between countries. However, the benefits go to those who are organized to quickly take advantage of such windows of opportunity.

Debt versus Equity Financing   Interest payments on debt extended by either the parent or a financial institution generally are tax-deductible by an affiliate, but dividends are not. In addition, principal repatriation is tax free, whereas dividend payments may lead to further taxation. As we will see in Chapter 20, parent company financing of foreign affiliates in the form of debt rather than equity has certain tax advantages. The consequences of these and other considerations for an MNC's cost of capital are discussed in Section 14.5, Establishing a Worldwide Capital Structure.

Government Credit and Capital Controls

Government credit and capital controls distort financial markets and may create financing bargains.

Governments intervene in their financial markets for a number of reasons: to restrain the growth of lendable funds, to make certain types of borrowing more or less expensive, and to direct funds to certain favored economic activities. In addition, corporate borrowing is often restricted in order to hold down interest rates (thereby providing the finance ministry with lower-cost funds to meet a budget deficit). When access to local-funds markets is limited, interest rates in them are usually below the risk-adjusted equilibrium level. There is often an incentive to borrow as much as possible where nonprice credit rationing is used.

Restraints on, or incentives to promote, overseas borrowing often are employed as well. We can point to numerous examples of restraints and incentives affecting overseas borrowing. Certain countries have limited the amount of local financing the subsidiary of a multinational firm can obtain to that required for working capital purposes; any additional needs will have to be satisfied from abroad. A prerequisite condition for obtaining official approval for a new investment or acquisition often is a commitment to inject external funds. Capital-exporting nations may attempt to control balance-of-payments deficits by restricting overseas investment flows—as the United States did from 1968 to 1974 under the Office of Foreign Direct Investment (OFDI) regulations.

Conversely, when a nation is concerned about excess capital inflows, a portion of any new foreign borrowing might have to be placed on deposit with the government, thereby raising the effective cost of external debt. Ironically, the effect of many of these government credit allocation and control schemes has been to hasten the development of the external financial markets—the Eurocurrency and Eurobond markets—further reducing government ability to regulate domestic financial markets.

The multinational firm with access to a variety of sources and types of funds and the ability to shift capital with its internal transfer system has more opportunities than does a single-nation company to secure the lowest risk-adjusted cost money and to circumvent credit restraints. These attributes should give it a substantial advantage over a purely domestic company.

Government Subsidies and Incentives

MNCs may be able to take advantage of financing bargains arising out of government subsidies and incentives.

Despite their often-hostile rhetoric directed against the multinational firm, many governments offer a growing list of incentives to MNCs to influence their production and export-sourcing decisions. Direct investment incentives include interest rate subsidies, loans with long maturities, official repatriation guarantees, grants related to project size, attractive prices for land, and favorable terms for the building of plants. For example, new investments located in Italy's Mezzogiorno can qualify for cash grants that cover up to 40 percent of the cost of plant and equipment, in addition to low-interest loans.

Governments sometimes will make the infrastructure investments as well by building the transportation, communication, and other links to support a new industrial project. Some indirect incentives include corporate income tax holidays, accelerated depreciation, and a reduction or elimination of the payment of other business taxes and import duties on capital equipment and raw materials.

In addition, all governments of developed nations have some form of export financing agency whose purpose is to boost local exports by providing loans with long repayment periods at interest rates below the market level and with low-cost political and economic risk insurance.

ILLUSTRATION   *Nestlé Keeps Finances Close to Home*

Nestlé, the Swiss foods conglomerate discussed earlier, is about as multinational as a company can be. About 98 percent of its sales take place overseas, and the group's diversified operations span 150 countries. Nestlé's numerous (and generally wholly owned) subsidiaries are operationally decentralized. However, finances are centralized in Vevey, Switzerland. Staffed by only twelve people, the finance department makes all subsidiary funding decisions, manages the resulting currency exposures, determines subsidiary dividend amounts, sets the worldwide debt/equity structure, and evaluates subsidiary performance.

Nestlé's centralized finance function plays the pivotal role in the firm's intricate web of subsidiary-to-headquarters profit remittances and headquarters-to-subsidiary investment flows. Profits and excess cash are collected by the treasury department in Vevey and then channeled back to overseas subsidiaries in the form of equity and debt investments. Nestlé considers this approach to be the best possible investment for the group's wealth.

When a subsidiary is first established, its fixed assets—which form about half of the total investment—are financed by the Nestlé group, generally with equity. Later on, the group may supply long-term debt as needed to support operations. The local subsidiary manager handles all the marketing and production decisions, but decisions regarding long-term debt and equity funding are managed solely by Vevey headquarters.

The other half of the investment—working capital—is then acquired locally, usually via bank credit or commercial paper. However, Nestlé varies this general approach to suit each country. In certain countries—those that permit free transfers of funds—Nestlé finances part of the working capital from Vevey instead of using local bank credits.

Central control over affiliate capital structures is facilitated by the policy of forcing local managers to dividend out almost 100 percent of their profits to Switzerland. The particular capital structure chosen for an affiliate depends on various considerations, including taxes, political risk, and currency risk.

To ensure that it borrows at the lowest possible cost, Nestlé takes considerable care to structure its capital base to keep a top credit rating. The desire for a low-risk capital structure is also consistent with Nestlé's business strategy. According to Senior Vice President, Finance, Daniel Regolatti, "Our basic strategy is that we are an industrial company. We have a lot of risks in a lot of countries, so we should not add high financial risks."[16]

---

[16] "The Nestlé Approach to Capital Markets and Innovation," *Business International Money Report*, October 27, 1986, p. 337.

14.7 SUMMARY AND CONCLUSIONS

Analysis of the available evidence on the impact of foreign operations on firm riskiness suggests that if there is an effect, that effect is generally to reduce both actual and perceived riskiness. These results indicate that corporations should continue investing abroad as long as there are profitable opportunities there. Retrenching because it is believed that investors desire smaller international operations is likely to lead to the forgoing of profitable foreign investments that would be rewarded, instead of penalized, by the firm's shareholders. At the very least, executives of multinational firms should seriously question the use of a higher risk premium to account for the added political and economic risks of overseas operations when evaluating prospective foreign investments.

The use of any added risk premium ignores the fact that the risk of an overseas investment in the context of the firm's other investments, domestic as well as foreign, will be less than the project's total risk. How much less depends on how highly correlated are the outcomes of the firm's different investments. Thus, the automatic inclusion of an added premium for risk when evaluating a foreign project is not a necessary element of conservatism; rather, it is a management shortcut that is unlikely to benefit the firm's shareholders. Some investments, however, are more risk-prone than others, and these risks must be accounted for. Chapter 17, on capital budgeting, presents a method for conducting the necessary risk analysis for foreign investments when the foreign risks are unsystematic. The present chapter showed how the necessary adjustments in project discount rates can be made, using the capital asset pricing model, when those additional foreign risks are systematic in nature. Specifically, the recommended approach to estimating the cost of equity capital for a foreign subsidiary is to find a proxy portfolio in the country in which that subsidiary operates and to calculate its beta relative to the U.S. market. That beta should then be multiplied by the risk premium for the U.S. market. This estimated equity risk premium for the foreign subsidiary would then be added to the U.S. (home country) risk-free rate to compute the dollar (home currency) cost of equity capital.

We also saw the consequences of globalizing the cost of capital by calculating the project beta relative to the global portfolio containing stocks in all readily accessible markets worldwide and using the global market risk premium. The typical result of using the global version of the CAPM is to estimate a lower cost of equity capital than when using the U.S. (home) market as the benchmark portfolio against which to estimate beta and the market risk premium.

We then assessed the factors that are relevant in determining appropriate parent, affiliate, and worldwide capital structures, taking into account the unique attributes of being a multinational corporation. We saw that the optimal global capital structure entails that mix of debt and equity for the parent entity and for all consolidated and unconsolidated subsidiaries that maximizes shareholder wealth. At the same time, affiliate capital structures should vary to take advantage of opportunities to minimize the MNC's cost of capital.

Many countries also provide subsidized financing for foreign investors or exporters. In addition, governments that impose interest rate and other capital controls or have unique tax rules create financial distortions that may enable multinational firms to arrange below-market financing. We saw how to value this low-cost financing. We also observed that such low-cost financing opportunities are fleeting.

QUESTIONS

1. What factors should be considered in deciding whether the cost of capital for a foreign affiliate should be higher, lower, or the same as the cost of capital for a comparable domestic operation?

2. According to an article in *Forbes,* "American companies can and are raising capital in Japan at relatively low rates of interest. Dow Chemical, for instance, has raised $500 million in yen. That cost the company over 50 percent less than it would have at home." Comment on this statement.

3. In early 1990, major Tokyo Stock Exchange issues sold for an average 60 times earnings, more than four times the 13.8 price/earnings ratio for the S&P 500 at that time. According to *BusinessWeek* (February 12, 1990, p. 76), "Since p-e ratios are a guide to a company's cost of equity capital, this valuation gap implies that raising new equity costs Japanese companies less than 2 percent a year, vs. an average 7 percent for the U.S." Comment on this statement.

4. What are some of the advantages and disadvantages of having highly leveraged foreign subsidiaries?

5. Compañía Troquelados ARDA is a medium-sized Mexico City auto parts maker. It is trying to decide whether to borrow dollars at 9 percent or Mexican

pesos at 75 percent. What advice would you give it? What information would you need before you gave the advice?

6. Boeing Commercial Airplane Company manufactures all its planes in the United States and prices them in dollars, even the 50 percent of its sales destined for overseas markets. What financing strategy would you recommend for Boeing? What data do you need?

7. United Airlines recently inaugurated service to Japan and now wants to finance the purchase of Boeing 747s to service that route. The CFO for United is attracted to yen financing because the interest rate on yen is 300 basis points lower than the dollar interest rate. Although he does not expect this interest differential to be offset by yen appreciation over the ten-year life of the loan, he would like an independent opinion before issuing yen debt.

   a. What are the key questions you would ask in responding to UAL's CFO?

   b. Can you think of any other reason for using yen debt?

   c. What would you advise him to do, given his likely responses to your questions and your answer to Part b?

8. The CFO of Eastman Kodak is thinking of borrowing Japanese yen because of their low interest rate, currently at 4.5 percent. The current interest rate on U.S. dollars is 9 percent. What is your advice to the CFO?

9. Rohm & Haas, a Philadelphia-based specialty chemicals company, traditionally finances its Brazilian operations from outside that country because it is "too expensive" to borrow local currency in Brazil. Brazilian interest rates vary from 50 percent to more than 100 percent. Rohm & Haas is now thinking of switching to *real* financing because of a pending *real* devaluation. Assess Rohm & Haas's financing strategy.

10. Nord Resources' Ramu River property in Papua New Guinea contains one of the world's largest deposits of cobalt and chrome outside of the Soviet Union and South Africa. The cost of developing a mine on this property is estimated to be around $150 million.

    a. Describe three major risks in undertaking this project.

    b. How can Nord structure its financing to reduce these risks?

    c. How can Nord use financing to add value to this project?

PROBLEMS

1. A firm with a corporatewide debt-to-equity ratio of 1:2, an after-tax cost of debt of 7 percent, and a cost of equity capital of 15 percent is interested in pursuing a foreign project. The debt capacity of the project is the same as for the company as a whole, but its systematic risk is such that the required return on equity is estimated to be about 12 percent. The after-tax cost of debt is expected to remain at 7 percent. What is the project's weighted average cost of capital? How does it compare with the parent's WACC?

2. Suppose that a foreign project has a beta of 0.85, the risk-free return is 12 percent, and the required return on the market is estimated at 19 percent. What is the cost of capital for the project?

3. IBM is considering having its German affiliate issue a ten-year, $100 million bond denominated in euros and priced to yield 7.5 percent. Alternatively, IBM's German unit can issue a dollar-denominated bond of the same size and maturity and carrying an interest rate of 6.7 percent.

   a. If the euro is forecast to depreciate by 1.7 percent annually, what is the expected dollar cost of the euro-denominated bond? How does this compare to the cost of the dollar bond?

   b. At what rate of euro depreciation will the dollar cost of the euro-denominated bond equal the dollar cost of the dollar-denominated bond?

   c. Suppose IBM's German unit faces a 35 percent corporate tax rate. What is the expected after-tax dollar cost of the euro-denominated bond?

4. Suppose that the cost of borrowing restricted euros is 7 percent annually, whereas the market rate for these funds is 12 percent. If a firm can borrow €10 million of restricted funds, how much will it save annually in before-tax euro interest expense?

5. Suppose that one of the inducements provided by Taiwan to woo Xidex into setting up a local production facility is a ten-year, $12.5 million loan at 8 percent interest. The principal is to be repaid at the end of the tenth year. The market interest rate on such a loan is about 15 percent. With a marginal tax rate of 40 percent, how much is this loan worth to Xidex?

BIBLIOGRAPHY

Adler, Michael, and Bernard Dumas. "International Portfolio Choice and Corporation Finance: A Synthesis." *Journal of Finance*, June 1983, pp. 925–984.

Agmon, Tamir, and Donald R. Lessard. "Investor Recognition of Corporate International Diversification." *Journal of Finance*, September 1977, pp. 1049–1056.

Black, Fischer. "International Capital Market Equilibrium with Investment Barriers." *Journal of Financial Economics,* December 1974, pp. 337–352.

Chan, K. C., G. Andrew Karolyi, and René M. Stulz. "Global Financial Markets and the Risk Premium on U.S. Equity." *Journal of Financial Economics,* October 1992, pp. 137–167.

Cho, Chinhyung D., Cheol S. Eun, and Lemma W. Senbet. "International Arbitrage Pricing Theory: An Empirical Investigation." *Journal of Finance* 41, 1986, pp. 313–330.

Cooper, Ian, and Evi Kaplanis. "What Explains the Home Bias in Portfolio Investment," *Review of Financial Studies,* 1994, 7, pp. 45–60.

Cooper, Ian, and Evi Kaplanis. "Home Bias in Equity Portfolios and the Cost of Capital for Multinational Companies." *Journal of Applied Corporate Finance,* Fall 1995, pp. 95–102.

DeSantis, Giorgio, and Bruno Gerard. "International Asset Pricing and Portfolio Diversification with Time-Varying Risk." *Journal of Finance* 52, 1997, pp. 1881–1913.

Fatemi, Ali M. "Shareholder Benefits from Corporate International Diversification." *Journal of Finance,* December 1984, pp. 1325–1344.

French, Kenneth R., and James M. Poterba. "Investor Diversification and International Equity Markets." *American Economic Review, Papers and Proceedings,* 1991, pp. 222–226.

Grauer, Frederick L. A., Robert H. Litzenberger, and Richard E. Stehle. "Sharing Rules and Equilibrium in an International Capital Market under Uncertainty." *Journal of Financial Economics,* June 1976, pp. 233–257.

Harvey, Campbell R. "The World Price of Covariance Risk." *Journal of Finance* 46, 1991, pp. 111–157.

Hughes, John S., Dennis E. Logue, and Richard J. Sweeney. "Corporate International Diversification and Market Assigned Measures of Risk and Diversification." *Journal of*

Financial and Quantitative Analysis, November 1975, pp. 627–637.

Jacquillat, Bertrand, and Bruno H. Solnik. "Multinationals Are Poor Tools for Diversification." *Journal of Portfolio Management,* Winter 1978, pp. 8–12.

Kester, W. Carl, and Timothy A. Luehrman. "The Myth of Japan's Low-Cost Capital." *Harvard Business Review,* May–June 1992, pp. 130–138.

Shapiro, Alan C. "The Impact of Taxation on the Currency-of-Denomination Decision for Long-Term Borrowing and Lending." *Journal of International Business Studies,* Spring–Summer 1984, pp. 15–25.

Shapiro, Alan C. "Financial Structure and the Cost of Capital in the Multinational Corporation." *Journal of Financial and Quantitative Analysis,* June 1978, pp. 211–226.

Solnik, Bruno H. "Testing International Asset Pricing: Some Pessimistic Views." *Journal of Finance,* May 1977, pp. 503–512.

Stonehill, Arthur I., and Kare B. Dullum. *Internationalizing the Cost of Capital.* New York: Wiley, 1982.

Stulz, René M. "A Model of International Asset Pricing." *Journal of Financial Economics,* December 1981, pp. 383–406.

Stulz, René M. "Globalization of Capital Markets and the Cost of Capital: The Case of Nestlé." *Journal of Applied Corporate Finance,* Fall 1995, pp. 30–38.

Stulz, René M. "Globalization, Corporate Finance, and the Cost of Capital." *Journal of Applied Corporate Finance,* Fall 1999, pp. 8–25.

Tesar, Linda, and Ingrid M. Werner. "Home Bias and High Turnover." *Journal of International Money and Finance,* 1995, 14, pp. 467–493.

Wheatley, Simon. "Some Tests of International Equity Integration." *Journal of Financial Economics* 21 (1988), pp. 177–212.

INTERNET RESOURCES

www.standardandpoors.com Web site of Standard & Poor's. Contains data on sovereign risk ratings and spreads.

www.bradynet.com/prices.html Contains information on emerging market debt prices and yields, particularly for Brady Bonds, the most widely traded emerging market debt instrument.

INTERNET EXERCISES

1. What are Standard & Poor's latest sovereign risk ratings for France, Japan, Argentina, Brazil, Mexico, South Korea, and Sweden?

2. Based on your review of the reports appearing on Standard & Poor's Web site, what factors does S&P appear to take into account in rating a country's debt?

3. Based on data appearing at www.bradynet.com/prices.html, describe the interest spreads over U.S. Treasury bonds at which various emerging market bonds are trading.

PART IV CASE STUDIES

 CASE IV.1

PLANO CRUZADO*

On February 28, 1986, President Jose Sarnay of Brazil announced the Plano Cruzado. At the time, Brazilian inflation was running at an annualized rate of more than 400 percent. The plan slashed inflation by freezing prices and wages. The purpose of the plan was to impose "shock treatment" on the economy and break the cycle of "inertial inflation" caused by high inflationary expectations. However, in a move that foreshadowed the splits that bedeviled the Plan, workers were granted pay hikes of 8 percent to 15 percent, just before the freeze. At the same time, government spending went largely unchecked, and the public-sector deficit—financed largely by printing more cruzados—grew to 4.5 percent of gross domestic product.

In November, the Plan achieved its first incontrovertible success: Government parties swept the congressional and gubernatorial races. Price controls were eased just after the election. However, the government found it politically impossible to remove subsidies to state industries because these industries formed the base for political power. Instead, large price hikes for state companies were granted by imposing huge increases in indirect taxes and tariffs on their products, and an attempt was made to disguise the effect of these increases on inflation by altering the basket of goods on which inflation was calculated. "They wanted me to tamper with inflation—simple as that," commented the head of the National Statistics Office, who immediately resigned.

QUESTIONS

1. What were the likely consequences for Brazil of controlling prices while gunning the money supply? Consider the effect on production and the availability of products in the stores.

2. How did the Plano Cruzado affect Brazil's huge trade surplus?

3. What would be your forecast of the Plan's effect on Brazil's ability to service its foreign debts?

4. President Sarnay terminated Plano Cruzado in February 1987, one year after it began. What impact do you think the Plan had in reducing inflation expectations? How would you go about measuring the effect of the Plan on inflation expectations?

5. What was the likely price response to the removal of price controls?

6. If you were a banker, how would seeing such a Plan put into effect your willingness to lend money to Brazil? Explain.

 CASE IV.2

MULTINATIONAL MANUFACTURING, INC.

PART I

Multinational Manufacturing, Inc. (MMI) is a large manufacturing firm engaged in the production and sale of a widely diversified group of products in a number of countries throughout the world. Some product lines enjoy outstanding success in new fields developed on the basis of an active research and development program; other product lines, whose innovative leads have disappeared, face very severe competition.

Each domestic product line and foreign affiliate is a separate profit center. Headquarters influences these centers primarily by evaluating their managers on the basis of certain financial criteria, including return on investment, return on sales, and growth in earnings.

Division and affiliate executives are held responsible for planning and evaluating possible new projects. Each project is expected to yield at least 15 percent. Projects requiring an investment below $250,000 (about one-third of the projects) are approved at the division or affiliate level without formal review by headquarters management. The present cutoff rate was established three years ago as part of a formal review of capital budgeting procedures. The conclusion at that time was that the company's weighted average cost of capital was 15 percent, and it should be applied when calculating net present values of proposed projects. In announcing the policy, Mr. Thomas Black, Vice President-Finance, said, "It's about time that we introduced some modern management techniques in allocating our capital resources."

Now Mr. Black is concerned that the policy introduced three years ago is having some unintended consequences. Specifically, top management gets to review only obvious investment candidates. Low-risk, low-return projects and high-risk, high-return projects seem to be systematically screened out along the way. The basis for this screening is not entirely clear, but it appears to be related to the way in which managerial performance is evaluated. Local executives seem to be concerned that low-potential projects will hurt their performance appraisal, while high-potential projects can turn out poorly. The president of one foreign affiliate said privately when asked why he never submitted projects at the extremes of risk and return, "Why should I take any chances? When headquarters says it wants 15 percent, it means 15 percent and nothing less. My crystal ball isn't good enough to allow me to accurately estimate sales and costs in this country, especially when I never know what the government is going to do."

QUESTIONS: PART I

Make recommendations to Mr. Black concerning the following points:

1. Should MMI lower the hurdle rate in order to encourage the submission of more proposals, or should it drop the hurdle rate concept completely?

2. Should MMI invest in lower-return projects that are less risky and/or in high-risk projects that appear promising? What is the relevant measure of risk?

3. How should MMI factor in the additional political and economic risks it faces overseas in conducting these project analyses?

4. Why are projects at the extremes of risk and return not reaching top management for review?

5. What actions, if any, should Mr. Black take to correct the situation?

PART II

In line with this current review of capital budgeting procedures, Mr. Black is also reconsidering certain financial policies that he recently recommended to MMI's board of directors. These policies include the maintenance of a debt/total assets ratio of 35 percent and a dividend payout rate equal to 60 percent of consolidated earnings. In order to achieve these ratios for the firm overall, each affiliate has been directed to use these ratios as guidelines in planning its own capital structure and payout rate.

This directive has been controversial. The executives of several foreign affiliates have raised questions about the appropriateness of applying these guidelines at the local level. The general managers of some of the largest affiliates have been particularly vocal in their objections, stating that it simply was not possible for overall policies relative to capital structure proportions to be given much consideration in financial planning at the local level. They pointed out that differences in the economic and political environment in which the various affiliates operate are far too great to force them into a financial straitjacket designed by headquarters. In their view, they must be left free to respond to their own unique set of circumstances.

The executives of the Brazilian affiliate, for example, felt that their financing should not follow the same pattern as that of the overall firm because inflationary conditions made local borrowing especially advantageous in Brazil. Executives of other foreign affiliates stressed the need for varying capital structures in order to cope with the exchange risks posed by currency fluctuations. The general manager of the Mexican affiliate, which is owned on a 50–50 basis with local investors, has argued forcefully that, despite effective headquarters control over the policies of this operation, joint ventures such as his cannot and should not be financed in the same manner as firms wholly owned by MMI. In addition, the tax manager of MMI has expressed his concern that implementing a rigid policy of repatriating 60 percent of each affiliate's earnings in the form of dividends will impose substantial tax costs on MMI. Moreover, Mr. Black recently attended a seminar at which it was pointed out that overseas affiliates can sometimes be financed in such a way that their susceptibility to political and economic risks is diminished.

QUESTIONS: PART II

Make recommendations to Mr. Black concerning the policies that should be adopted as guides in planning the capital structure and dividend payout policies of foreign affiliates, taking into account the following key questions:

1. What are the pros and cons of using the following sources of funds to finance the operations of the foreign affiliates: equity funds versus loans from MMI, retained earnings of

the affiliates, and outside borrowings? Consider cost, political and economic risks, and tax consequences in your answer.

2. Given these considerations, under what circumstances, if any, should the capital structure of foreign affiliates include more or less debt than the 35 percent considered desirable for the firm as a whole?

3. How will the resultant capital structures affect the required rates of return on affiliate projects? The actual rates of return?

4. How should MMI's dividend policy be implemented at the affiliate level?

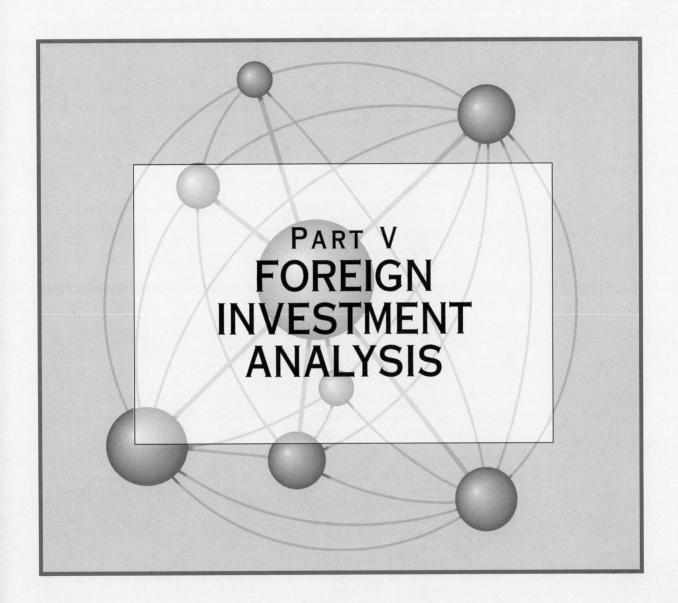

PART V
FOREIGN
INVESTMENT
ANALYSIS

INTERNATIONAL PORTFOLIO INVESTMENT

Capital now flows at the speed of light across national borders and into markets once deemed impregnable.

Citicorp Annual Report (1991)

CHAPTER LEARNING OBJECTIVES

- To calculate the return associated with investing in securities issued in different markets and denominated in various currencies
- To calculate the currency risk associated with investing in securities issued in different markets and denominated in various currencies
- To describe the advantages of international investing
- To explain how international investing can allow investors to achieve a better risk-return tradeoff than by investing solely in U.S. securities
- To identify the barriers to investing overseas
- To describe the various ways in which U.S. investors can diversify into foreign securities
- To explain why investing in foreign stocks and bonds provides a better risk-return trade-off than investing in either foreign stocks or bonds alone

KEY TERMS

American Depository Receipt (ADR)
American Depository Share (ADS)
efficient frontier
emerging markets
foreign market beta
Global Depository Receipt (GDR)
global fund
global registered share (GRS)
home bias
IFC Emerging Markets Index
international asset allocation
international diversification

international fund
international investing
liquidity
Morgan Stanley Capital International
    Europe, Australia, Far East (EAFE)
    Index
Morgan Stanley Capital International
    World Index
regional fund
risk-return tradeoff
single-country fund
total dollar return

There was a time when investors treated national boundaries as impregnable barriers, limiting their reach and financial options to predominantly domestic and regional markets. Times have changed. Just as companies and consumers are going global, so are increasing numbers of investors. American investors are buying foreign stocks and bonds, and foreign investors are purchasing U.S. securities. This chapter examines the nature and consequences of international portfolio investing. Although the focus is on international investing from an American perspective, the lessons drawn are applicable to investors from around the world.

15.1 THE BENEFITS OF INTERNATIONAL EQUITY INVESTING

International investing yields a better risk/return trade-off.

International investing offers several advantages. First, an international focus offers far more opportunity than a domestic focus. More than half of the world's stock market capitalization is in non-U.S. companies, and this fraction generally has increased over time. In fact, if you want to invest in certain products with huge global markets, you will find that most of the big, highly profitable manufacturers are overseas. For example, videotape recorders are the world's best-selling consumer electronics product, and 95 percent of them are made in Japan; more than 80 percent of all cars, 85 percent of all stereo systems, and 99 percent of all 35mm cameras are made abroad. The Japanese dominance of these and other consumer-product markets helps explain why by 1989 Japan's market capitalization actually exceeded that of the United States. The 67 percent plunge in the Tokyo Stock Exchange between 1990 and 2000 and the dramatic rise in the U.S. stock market during that same period once again gave the U.S. stock market—at about four times Japan's capitalization—the dominant share of the world's stock market capitalization. Japan's market capitalization has now fallen to third place, behind that of Great Britain.

International Diversification

The expanded universe of securities available internationally suggests the possibility of achieving a better **risk-return trade-off** than by investing solely in U.S. securities. That is, expanding the universe of assets available for investment should lead to higher returns for the same level of risk or less risk for the same level of expected return. This relation follows from the basic rule of portfolio diversification: *The broader the diversification, the more stable the returns and the more diffuse the risks.*

Domestic diversification reduces risk, but the degree of risk reduction is limited.

Prudent investors know that diversifying across industries leads to a lower level of risk for a given level of expected return. For example, a fully diversified U.S. portfolio is only about 27 percent as risky as a typical individual stock. Put another way, about 73 percent of the risk associated with investing in the average stock can be eliminated in a fully diversified U.S. portfolio. Ultimately, though, the advantages of such diversification are limited because all companies in a country are more or less subject to the same cyclical economic fluctuations. Through **international diversification**—that is, by diversifying across nations whose economic cycles are not perfectly in phase—investors should be able to reduce still further the variability of their returns. In other words, risk that is systematic in the context of the U.S. economy may be unsystematic in the context of the global economy. For example, an oil price shock that hurts the U.S. economy helps the economies of oil-exporting nations, and vice versa. Thus, just as movements in different stocks partially offset one another in an all-U.S. portfolio, so also do movements in U.S. and non-U.S. stock portfolios cancel each other out somewhat.

The possibility of achieving a better risk-return tradeoff by investing internationally is supported by Exhibit 15.1, which shows the annualized returns and standard deviations

EXHIBIT 15.1 • ANNUALIZED MONTHLY RETURNS AND STANDARD DEVIATION OF RETURNS: 1988–2000

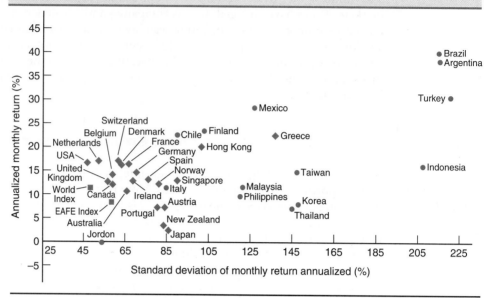

Note: Circles are emerging markets, diamonds are developed markets, and squares show MSCI EAFE and World Indices.

Source: Raw data from *Morgan Stanley Capital International,* www.msci.com.

of returns for a variety of developed and emerging stock markets over the thirteen-year period 1988–2000.[1] The exhibit illustrates four points:

1. Historically, national stock markets have wide differences in returns and risk (as measured by the standard deviation of annual returns).

2. **Emerging markets** (shown as circles)—a term that encompasses all of South and Central America; all of the Far East with the exception of Japan, Hong Kong, Singapore, Australia, and New Zealand; all of Africa; and parts of Southern Europe, as well as Eastern Europe and countries of the former Soviet Union—have generally had higher risk and return than the developed markets (shown as diamonds).

3. The **Morgan Stanley Capital International Europe, Australia, Far East (EAFE) Index** (which reflects all major stock markets outside of North America, twenty altogether) has had lower risk than most of its individual country components. The relatively low return for the EAFE Index reflects the dismal performance since 1989 of the Japanese stock market, which is a key component of the index.

4. The **Morgan Stanley Capital International World Index,** which combines the EAFE nations with North America, has lower risk than any of its component countries except for the United States.

Empirical research bears out the significant benefits from international equity diversification suggested by Exhibit 15.1. Bruno Solnik and Donald Lessard, among others, have presented evidence that national factors have a strong impact on security returns relative to that of any common world factor.[2] They also found that returns from the different

The value of international equity diversification appears to be substantial.

---

[1] The standard deviations used in this chapter are all monthly standard deviations annualized (multiplied by 12). They are significantly larger than annual standard deviations calculated using yearly data because monthly returns are more volatile than yearly returns. Monthly ups and downs often cancel each other out.

[2] Bruno H. Solnik, "Why Not Diversify Internationally Rather Than Domestically?" *Financial Analysts Journal,* July–August 1974, pp. 48–54; and Donald R. Lessard, "World, Country, and Industry Relationships in Equity Returns: Implications for Risk Reduction through International Diversification," *Financial Analysts Journal,* January–February 1976, pp. 32–38.

national equity markets have relatively low correlations with one another. More recent research shows that differences in industrial structure and currency movements account for very little of the low correlation between national stock market returns.[3] The more likely explanation for the low degree of international return correlation is that local monetary and fiscal policies, differences in institutional and legal regimes, and regional economic shocks induce large country-specific variation in returns.

Correlations and the Gains from Diversification   Exhibit 15.2 contains some data on correlations between the U.S. and non-U.S. stock markets. **Foreign market betas,** which are a measure of market risk derived from the capital asset pricing model (see Chapter 14), are calculated relative to the U.S. market in the same way that individual asset betas are calculated:

$$\frac{\text{Foreign market}}{\text{beta}} = \frac{\text{Correlation with}}{\text{U.S. market}} \times \frac{\text{Standard deviation of foreign market}}{\text{Standard deviation of U.S. market}}$$

For example, the Canadian market beta is $0.71 \times 66.53/53.20 = 0.89$. Market risk is also calculated from a world perspective, where the correlations are calculated relative to the

EXHIBIT 15.2 • How Foreign Markets Were Correlated with U.S. Market and World Index, 1970–2000

Country	Correlation with U.S. Market	Standard Deviation of Returns[1] (%)	Market Risk (Beta) from U.S. Perspective	Correlation with World Index	Market Risk (Beta) from World Perspective
United States	1.00	53.20	1.00	0.84	0.90
Canada	0.71	66.53	0.89	0.72	0.96
Australia	0.47	86.35	0.76	0.56	0.98
Hong Kong	0.33	135.55	0.85	0.44	1.19
Japan	0.29	79.49	0.43	0.68	1.09
Singapore	0.47	106.09	0.94	0.54	1.16
Austria	0.16	72.85	0.22	0.33	0.48
Belgium	0.42	65.68	0.52	0.61	0.81
Denmark	0.34	64.92	0.41	0.50	0.65
France	0.44	79.09	0.66	0.63	1.01
Germany	0.38	70.76	0.50	0.57	0.82
Italy	0.24	90.68	0.41	0.43	0.79
Netherlands	0.57	61.62	0.66	0.73	0.91
Norway	0.44	92.72	0.76	0.51	0.96
Spain	0.33	78.09	0.48	0.51	0.81
Sweden	0.42	78.46	0.61	0.57	0.90
Switzerland	0.49	65.82	0.60	0.67	0.88
United Kingdom	0.51	82.27	0.78	0.68	1.13
EAFE index[2]	0.50	58.10	0.54	0.88	1.03
World index	0.84	49.53	0.78	1.00	1.00

[1] Monthly standard deviation annualized.

[2] The Morgan Stanley Capital International Europe, Australia, Far East (EAFE) Index is the non-North American part of the world index and consists of 20 major stock markets from these parts of the world.

Source: Raw data from *Morgan Stanley Capital International,* www.msci.com.

[3] See Steven L. Heston and K. Geert Rouwenhorst, "Does Industrial Structure Explain the Benefits of International Diversification?" *Journal of Financial Economics,* August 1994, pp. 3–27, and Pierre Ruiz and Bruno Solnik, "Domestic and Global Factors in Individual Stock Returns," HEC School of Management Working Paper, November 2000.

world index. Notice that the betas calculated relative to the world index are higher than the betas calculated relative to the U.S. market for all but the U.S. market.

Measured for the thirty-one–year period 1970–2000, foreign markets in developed (EAFE) countries were correlated with the U.S. market from a high of 0.71 for Canada to a low of 0.16 for Austria. The relatively high correlation for Canada reveals that this market tracked the U.S. market's ups and downs. Austria's low correlation, on the other hand, indicates that the Austrian and U.S. markets have tended to move largely independently of each other.

Notice also that the investment risks associated with these different markets can be quite different; the Hong Kong market shows the highest level and the Dutch market the lowest. Indeed, all the markets had a higher level of risk, as measured by the standard deviation of returns, than the U.S. market. Yet the internationally diversified Morgan Stanley Capital International World Index had the lowest level of risk—lower even than the U.S. market. The reason is that much of the risk associated with markets in individual countries is unsystematic and so can be eliminated by diversification, as indicated by the relatively low betas of these markets.

These results imply that international diversification may significantly reduce the risk of portfolio returns. In fact, the standard deviation of an internationally diversified portfolio appears to be as little as 11.7 percent of that of individual securities. In addition, as shown in Exhibit 15.3, the benefits from international diversification are significantly greater than those that can be achieved solely by adding more domestic stocks to a portfolio. Specifically, an internationally diversified portfolio according to Exhibit 15.3 is less than half as risky as a fully diversified U.S. portfolio. However, the data from Exhibit 15.2 indicate that the risk reduction associated with an internationally diversified portfolio is now about 10 percent.

Moreover, as shown in Exhibit 15.4, historically the EAFE Index outpaced the U.S. market. However, the strong bull market in the United States since 1982, combined with the collapse of the Japanese market since 1989, had its inevitable result. By 1998, the U.S. index surpassed the EAFE Index. Overall, in the thirty-one years ended December 2000, the U.S. portion of Morgan Stanley Capital International's world stock index was up 3,702

> Much of the risk associated with individual markets is unsystematic and so can be diversified away.

EXHIBIT 15.3 • THE POTENTIAL GAINS FROM INTERNATIONAL DIVERSIFICATION

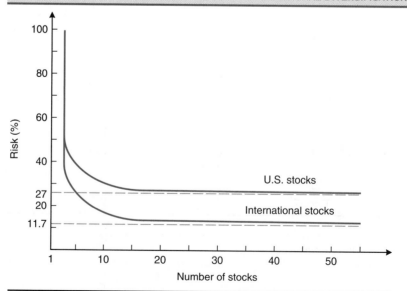

Source: Bruno H. Solnik, "Why Not Diversify Internationally Rather Than Domestically?" Reprinted with permission from Financial Analysts Federation, Charlottesville, VA. All rights reserved. *Financial Analysts Journal,* July–August 1974.

EXHIBIT 15.4 • THE U.S. MARKET OVERTAKES THE EAFE INDEX

Source: Raw data from *Morgan Stanley Capital International,* www.msci.com.

percent, and the cumulative return for the EAFE Index was 3,453 percent. These are extraordinary returns and unlikely to be repeated. Even more astounding, from 1949 to 1990, the Japanese market soared an incredible 25,000 percent. Even with the recent plunge in the Tokyo Stock Exchange, an investor in the Japanese stock market would still be way ahead. Taking a longer-term perspective, it should be noted that the EAFE Index outpaced the U.S. market twenty-two times during the forty-year period 1961–2000, indicating the advantages of international diversification. Moreover, anyone thinking of investing solely in the U.S. market because of its outstanding performance during the 1990s might consider the fact that Japanese investors likely felt justified in keeping their money at home when the Nikkei index hit a record high of 38,916 on December 31, 1989. In April 2003, it stood at under 7,800, less than 20 percent of its peak value.

> International diversification pushes out the efficient frontier.

The obvious conclusion is that international diversification pushes out the **efficient frontier**—the set of portfolios that has the smallest possible standard deviation for its level of expected return and has the maximum expected return for a given level of risk—allowing investors simultaneously to reduce their risk and increase their expected return. Exhibit 15.5 illustrates the effect of international diversification on the efficient frontier.

EXHIBIT 15.5 • INTERNATIONAL DIVERSIFICATION PUSHES OUT THE EFFICIENT FRONTIER

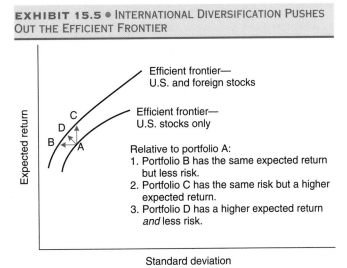

One way to estimate the benefits of international diversification is to consider the expected return and standard deviation of return for a portfolio consisting of a fraction α invested in U.S. stocks and the remaining fraction, $1 - \alpha$, invested in foreign stocks. Define r_{us} and r_{rw} to be the expected returns on the U.S. and rest-of-world stock portfolios, respectively. Similarly, let σ_{us} and σ_{rw} be the standard deviations of the U.S. and rest-of-world portfolios. The expected return on this internationally diversified portfolio, r_p, can be calculated as

$$r_p = \alpha r_{us} + (1 - \alpha)r_{rw} \tag{15.1}$$

To calculate the standard deviation of this portfolio, it helps to know that the general formula for the standard deviation of a two-asset portfolio with weights w_1 and w_2 ($w_1 + w_2 = 1$) is

$$\text{Portfolio standard deviation} = [w_1^2\sigma_1^2 + w_2^2\sigma_2^2 + 2w_1 w_2\sigma_{12}\sigma_1\sigma_2]^{1/2} \tag{15.2}$$

where σ_1^2 and σ_2^2 are the respective variances of the two assets, σ_1 and σ_2 are their standard deviations, and ρ_{12} is their correlation. We can apply Equation 15.2 to our internationally diversified portfolio by treating the domestic and foreign portfolios as separate assets. This operation yields a portfolio standard deviation σ_p equal to

$$\sigma_p = [\alpha^2\sigma_{us}^2 + (1 - \alpha)^2\sigma_{rw}^2 + 2\alpha(1 - \alpha)\sigma_{us}\sigma_{rw}\sigma_{us,rw}]^{1/2} \tag{15.3}$$

where $\rho_{us,rw}$ is the correlation between the returns on the U.S. and foreign stock portfolios.

To see the benefits of international diversification, assume that the portfolio is equally invested in U.S. and foreign stocks, where the EAFE Index represents the foreign stock portfolio. Using data from Exhibit 15.2, we see that σ_{us} = 53.2 percent, σ_{rw} = 58.1 percent, and $\rho_{us,rw}$ = 0.50. According to Equation 15.3, these figures imply that the standard deviation of the internationally diversified portfolio is

An internationally-diversified portfolio is less risky than a diversified U.S. stock portfolio.

$$\begin{aligned} \sigma_p &= [0.5^2(53.2)^2 + 0.5^2(58.1)^2 + 0.5^2 \times 2 \times 53.2 \times 58.1 \times 0.50]^{1/2} \\ &= 0.5(9,296.8)^{1/2} \\ &= 48.2\% \end{aligned}$$

Here the risk of the internationally diversified portfolio is about 10 percent below the risk of the U.S. portfolio.

Recent Correlations

Correlations between U.S. and non-U.S. markets have risen in recent years.

The benefits of diversification depend on relatively low correlations among assets. It is often assumed that, as their underlying economies become more closely integrated and cross-border financial flows accelerate, national capital markets will become more highly correlated, significantly reducing the benefits of international diversification. Indeed, the correlations between the U.S. and non-U.S. stock markets are generally higher today than they were during the 1970s. As Exhibit 15.6 shows, this pattern has persisted. Using five-year periods—1981–1985, say, versus 1996–2000—correlations are almost uniformly higher in more recent periods. Moreover, most of the rise in these correlations took place during the last five-year period, 1996–2000, indicating that economic integration and financial market integration increased significantly during the 1990s.

In addition to the higher correlations over time, the U.S. market has outperformed the Japanese and European markets in recent years (see Exhibit 15.4 over the period 1990–2000), reducing the expected return on the EAFE Index relative to the U.S. market.

Recent research points to another problematic aspect of international investing as well: When markets are the most volatile and investors most seek safety, global diversification is of limited value.[4] In particular, Exhibit 15.7 shows that the correlations among

---

[4] See Patrick Odier and Bruno Solnik, "Lessons for International Asset Allocation," *Financial Analysts Journal,* March–April 1993, pp. 63–77.

EXHIBIT 15.6 • CORRELATION OF MONTHLY RETURNS WITH THE U.S. MARKET: DEVELOPED COUNTRY MARKETS

	1981–2000	*1981–1985*	*1986–1990*	*1991–1995*	*1996–2000*
Canada	0.73	0.70	0.82	0.48	0.77
Australia	0.44	0.36	0.46	0.40	0.56
Hong Kong	0.39	0.14	0.54	0.33	0.56
Japan	0.31	0.31	0.25	0.20	0.50
Singapore	0.51	0.24	0.66	0.36	0.57
Austria	0.18	0.17	0.11	0.15	0.38
Belgium	0.43	0.27	0.49	0.56	0.47
Denmark	0.36	0.35	0.32	0.34	0.47
France	0.46	0.37	0.48	0.49	0.57
Germany	0.41	0.29	0.40	0.37	0.56
Italy	0.25	0.15	0.32	0.07	0.40
Netherlands	0.58	0.55	0.66	0.57	0.57
Norway	0.48	0.37	0.58	0.54	0.48
Spain	0.40	0.06	0.45	0.53	0.54
Sweden	0.43	0.33	0.48	0.49	0.47
Switzerland	0.50	0.47	0.57	0.50	0.44
United Kingdom	0.57	0.40	0.68	0.60	0.68
World Index	0.80	0.88	0.73	0.69	0.93

Source: Raw data from *Morgan Stanley Capital International*, www.msci.com.

EXHIBIT 15.7 • NO PLACE TO HIDE?

World markets seem to be most in step with each other when volatility is greatest. Correlation among markets is measured here on a scale of 0 to 1, where 1 indicates that markets track each other perfectly and 0 means they are completely independent. Volatility is measured on the basis of "standard deviation"—how much prices vary from the mean.

Source: Bruno Solnik. Hautes Etudes Commerciales in the *Wall Street Journal*, April 14, 1994, p. C1. Reprinted by permission of the *Wall Street Journal*, © 1994 Dow Jones & Company, Inc. All rights reserved worldwide.

International diversification is of limited value when financial markets are very volatile.

markets appear to increase when market volatility is at its highest. This effect suggests that the higher correlations seen in the latter half of the 1990s could reflect the impact of the Asian crisis, with its high degree of volatility. Even worse, the markets appear to move in synchrony only when they are falling, not when they are rising. In other words, only bear markets seem to be contagious, not bull markets. For example, immediately following the World Trade Center and Pentagon terrorist attacks of September 11, 2001, stock markets worldwide plunged in unison.

Taken together, these changes have diminished the risk-return benefits of international investing. Nonetheless, these benefits still exist, particularly for those who have patience to invest for the long term. Exhibit 15.8 calculates the standard deviations and annualized returns of different mixes of the U.S. (MSCI) Index and the EAFE Index using quarterly data for the thirty-one–year period 1970–2000. Shifting from a portfolio invested 100 percent in the EAFE Index to one that contains up to 60 percent invested in the U.S. Index reduces risk and at the same time increases return. As the percentage invested in the U.S. Index is increased past 60 percent, both portfolio risk and return rise. However, the change in return is minimal.

Investing in Emerging Markets

Emerging markets present attractive investment opportunities.

We have already seen in Exhibit 15.1 some of the high risks and rewards historically associated with investing in emerging markets. So it should perhaps come as no surprise that it is often these countries, with volatile economic and political prospects, that offer the greatest degree of diversification and the highest expected returns.[5] Exhibit 15.9 shows how some of these "emerging markets" performed over the twelve-year period ending December 31, 2000. As can be seen, historically no other stock markets so lavishly rewarded investors—and none penalized them so heavily either. Gains of 30 percent to 40 percent a year were not unusual, and neither were returns of close to zero. The low returns for the Asian markets reflect the effects of the Asian currency crisis.

In response to the high potential returns, since 1989 private capital flows to emerging stock markets expanded from less than $10 billion a year to between $60 billion and $80 billion a year by the mid-1990s. These flows have contracted in recent years because of the perceptions of increased risk associated with investments in emerging markets. Indeed, as can be seen in Exhibit 15.9, the high returns possible in emerging markets are matched by some breathtaking risks. To begin, these are small markets, representing in the aggregate less than 10 percent of the world's stock market capitalization. Hence, they are subject to the usual volatility and lack of liquidity associated with small markets. Yet they face some unique risks as well: relatively unstable governments, the risk of nationalization

EXHIBIT 15.8 ● AVERAGE RETURNS AND STANDARD DEVIATION OF RETURNS, 1970–2000

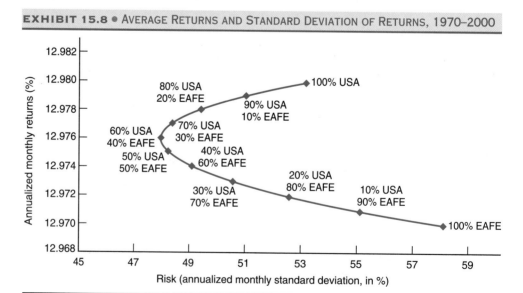

Source: Raw data from *Morgan Stanley Capital International* (MSCI), www.msci.com.

---

[5] See, for example, Vihang R. Errunza, "Gains from Portfolio Diversification into Less Developed Countries," *Journal of International Business Studies,* Fall–Winter 1977, pp. 83–99, and Warren Bailey and René M. Stulz, "Benefits of International Diversification: The Case of Pacific Basin Stock Markets," *Journal of Portfolio Management,* Summer 1990, pp. 57–62.

EXHIBIT 15.9 • RISK AND RETURN FOR EMERGING MARKETS, 1989–2000

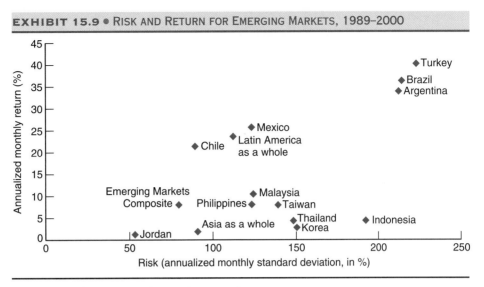

Source: Raw data from *Morgan Stanley Capital International,* www.msci.com.

of businesses, less protection of property rights, and the threat of abrupt price movements. For example, in February 1990, when the newly elected Brazilian president froze most personal bank accounts, the São Paulo exchange plummeted 70 percent in just a few days. Similarly, Taiwan's market rose more than 1,000 percent from January 1987 to its peak in February 1990. It then gave back most of these gains, falling nearly 80 percent by October 1990. The Indian stock market also has taken a roller coaster ride. In the euphoria that accompanied the liberalization of the Indian economy, the Bombay stock index rose 458 percent between June 1991 and April 1992. It then fell 30 percent in April and May after disclosure of a scandal in which a broker cheated financial institutions out of at least half a billion dollars to play the market. The more recent debacle in the Asian stock markets will remain fresh in the minds of investors for some time to come.

> Despite their high individual risks, emerging markets can reduce portfolio risk.

Despite their high investment risks, emerging markets can reduce portfolio risk because of their low correlations with returns elsewhere. That is, most of their high total risk is unsystematic in nature. For example, Exhibit 15.10 shows how some emerging markets were correlated with the U.S. market for the same four-year periods shown in Exhibit 15.6. For the four-year period 1997–2000, these correlations ranged from a high of 0.69 for Mexico to a low of –0.10 for Morocco. As the composite indices show, these correlations have generally risen in recent years. Nonetheless, these correlations are still relatively low, particularly as compared to the developed countries. Moreover, although not shown here, these emerging markets also have a low correlation with the MSCI World Index.

> Emerging markets tend to have low correlations with the U.S. market.

The fact that most of the emerging markets as a group as well as individually have low correlations with the U.S. market and the MSCI World Index indicates the potential for diversification benefits. Exhibit 15.11 shows for the thirteen-year period 1988–2000 the risk and return of a global portfolio that combines in varying proportions the MSCI World Index with the **IFC Emerging Markets Index,** published by the International Finance Corporation (an international lending organization discussed in Chapter 12).

We see that shifting from a portfolio invested 100 percent in the MSCI World Index to one that contains up to 10 percent invested in the IFC Emerging Markets Index reduces risk and at the same time increases expected return. Beyond that point, portfolio risk starts increasing as the higher volatility of the Emerging Markets Index more than offsets the benefits of diversification. Thus, even if one did not expect the emerging markets to outperform the developed country markets, risk reduction alone

EXHIBIT 15.10 • CORRELATIONS OF MONTHLY RETURNS WITH THE U.S. MARKET: EMERGING MARKETS

	1989–2000	*1989–1992*	*1993–1996*	*1997–2000*
Argentina	0.24	0.16	0.45	0.50
Chile	0.31	0.13	0.19	0.54
Colombia	N/A	N/A	−0.13	0.14
Czech Republic	N/A	N/A	N/A	0.21
Egypt	N/A	N/A	N/A	0.27
Hungary	N/A	N/A	N/A	0.56
India	N/A	N/A	−0.07	0.20
Indonesia	0.33	0.08	0.50	0.45
Israel	N/A	N/A	0.43	0.37
Jordan	0.15	0.23	−0.01	0.21
Korea	0.27	0.22	0.05	0.34
Malaysia	0.35	0.53	0.20	0.35
Mexico	0.45	0.35	0.22	0.69
Morocco	N/A	N/A	N/A	−0.06
Pakistan	N/A	N/A	−0.01	0.15
Peru	N/A	N/A	0.11	0.35
Philippines	0.40	0.40	0.16	0.51
Poland	N/A	N/A	0.20	0.40
Russia	N/A	N/A	N/A	0.58
South Africa	N/A	N/A	0.11	0.53
Taiwan	0.24	0.13	0.10	0.49
Thailand	0.45	0.40	0.29	0.54
Turkey	0.07	−0.19	0.09	0.29
Venezuela	N/A	N/A	−0.05	0.29
Composite	0.50	0.32	0.30	0.68
Asia	0.38	0.22	0.20	0.56
Latin America	0.44	0.30	0.27	0.64
Eastern Europe	N/A	N/A	N/A	0.59

Source: Raw data from *Morgan Stanley Capital International,* www.msci.com.

EXHIBIT 15.11 • RISK AND RETURN FOR VARIOUS MIXES OF MSCI WORLD AND EMERGING MARKETS INDICES, 1988–2000

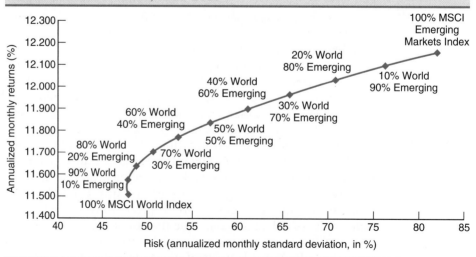

Source: Raw data from *Morgan Stanley Capital International,* www.msci.com.

would dictate an investment of up to 10 percent in the emerging markets. Because the emerging markets outperformed the developed country markets during this period, a 10 percent investment in the IFC Index would have reduced the annualized standard deviation while increasing the annual return as well. However, the gains are small, reflecting the weak performance of the emerging markets in the latter part of the 1990s.

ILLUSTRATION *Latin American Stocks Were Hotter than Salsa*

A conversion to free-market economics in much of Latin America did wonders for those countries' stock markets in the early 1990s. Investors expected that tighter monetary policies, lower tax rates, significantly lower budget deficits, and the sale of money-losing state enterprises would go a long way to cure the sickly Latin economies. These expectations, in turn, helped stock markets to soar during the early 1990s in all the countries shown in Exhibit 15.12 except Brazil—the one country that has backslid on instituting serious market-oriented reforms. Overall, from 1984 through 1996, the six Latin American stock markets depicted in Exhibit 15.12 rose an average 2,300 percent in dollar terms, far exceeding the returns available in any other region of the world. It should be noted, however, that these gains reflect the markets' low starting points as much as the success of the economic reforms. Most Latin American markets took a tumble in 1994, led by the Mexican market, as interest rates rose in the United States and it became obvious that the payoffs from these economic changes would take more time to be realized and would be riskier than expected.

EXHIBIT 15.12 • LATIN AMERICAN STOCK MARKETS TAKE OFF, 1985–1996

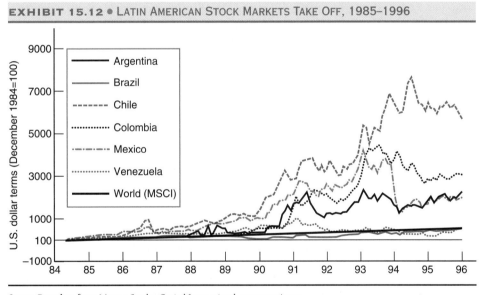

Source: Raw data from *Morgan Stanley Capital International*, www.msci.com.

One caveat with regard to the data presented on the low correlations between U.S. and emerging-country stock market returns, which are based on monthly data, is that monthly return correlations have tended to understate the long-run interrelatedness of emerging markets and their developed-country counterparts. A recent study shows that correlations between developed and developing country markets are much higher when these correlations are computed using yearly data instead of monthly data.[6] In contrast, correlations between developed-nation markets do not vary significantly when computed using yearly instead of monthly data. These results suggest that, because of various

---

[6] John Mullin, "Emerging Equity Markets in the Global Economy," *Federal Reserve Bank of New York Quarterly Review,* Summer 1993, pp. 54–83.

impediments to capital mobility in emerging markets, events that immediately affected developed country returns tended to affect emerging market returns with a lag. As these impediments to capital mobility—which include government restrictions on capital flows and a lack of liquidity—are reduced, the low monthly correlations between developed and developing markets are likely to rise in the future.

Estimated emerging market returns are subject to survivorship and selection bias.

Questions also exist as to the returns that can reliably be expected from emerging market investments. A number of researchers have suggested that these high measured returns may owe more to selection and survivorship bias than to economic reality.[7] In particular, given the way in which the IFC database is constructed, emerging markets that fail to reach a certain threshold capitalization are not included in the emerging market series. We do not observe emerging markets that fail to survive or to achieve the minimum size. Because high-return emerging markets are far more likely to survive and to reach the threshold, the IFC series is clearly biased against low-return markets. Similarly, emerging markets with historically low returns will enter the database if their recent returns are high, again biasing measured emerging-market returns. For example, a number of Latin American stock markets were in existence with low returns for many years before they entered the IFC database. These biases result in an overly optimistic picture of the future returns that can be expected from emerging-market investments.

Barriers to International Diversification

Barriers to investing overseas exist but they are being eroded.

Despite the demonstrated benefits to international diversification, these benefits will be limited because of barriers to investing overseas. Such barriers do exist. They include legal, informational, and economic impediments that serve to segment national capital markets, deterring investors seeking to invest abroad. The lack of **liquidity**—the ability to buy and sell securities efficiently—is a major obstacle on some overseas exchanges. Other barriers include currency controls, specific tax regulations, relatively less-developed capital markets abroad, exchange risk, and the lack of readily accessible and comparable information on potential foreign security acquisitions. The lack of adequate information can significantly increase the perceived riskiness of foreign securities, giving investors an added incentive to keep their money at home.

U.S. investors are not well diversified internationally.

Some of these barriers are apparently being eroded. Money invested abroad by both large institutions and individuals is growing dramatically. Despite the erosion in barriers to foreign investing and the consequent growth in the level of foreign investing, however, these investments still represent a relatively minor degree of international diversification. For example, in 1993, Americans held 94 percent of their equity investments in domestic stocks. Nonetheless, discussions with U.S. institutional investors indicate that many intend to have 20 percent to 25 percent of their funds invested overseas by the year 2000 (in contrast to only 7 percent in 1993).[8] This so-called **home bias**—the tendency to hold domestic assets in one's investment portfolio—is also apparent in other countries as well, with domestic residents holding a disproportionate share of the nation's stock market wealth.[9]

Several explanations for the home bias in portfolio investments have been put forth,[10] notably the existence of political and currency risks and the natural tendency to invest in the familiar and avoid the unknown. Whether these preferences are rational is another issue.

---

[7] See, for example, Stephen J. Brown, William N. Goetzmann, and Stephen A. Ross, "Survival," *Journal of Finance,* 50, pp. 853–873; Campbell Harvey, "Predictable Risk and Returns in Emerging Markets," *Review of Financial Studies,* 8, pp. 773–816; and William N. Goetzmann and Philippe Jorion, "Re-emerging Markets," Yale School of Management Working Paper, July 1996.

[8] These discussions were reported by Michael R. Sesit, "Foreign Investing Makes a Comeback," *Wall Street Journal,* September 1, 1989, pp. C1 and C14.

[9] The home bias has been documented by Kenneth R. French and James M. Poterba, "Investor Diversification and International Equity Markets," *American Economic Review, Papers and Proceedings,* 1991, pp. 222–226; Ian A. Cooper and Evi Kaplanis, "What Explains the Home Bias in Portfolio Investment," *Review of Financial Studies,* 1994, 7, pp. 45–60; and Linda Tesar and Ingrid M. Werner, "Home Bias and High Turnover," *Journal of International Money and Finance,* 1995, 14, pp. 467–493.

[10] See, for example, Jun-Koo Kang and René M. Stulz, "Why Is There a Home Bias? An Analysis of Foreign Portfolio Equity Ownership in Japan," *Journal of Financial Economics,* October 1997, pp. 3–28.

U.S. investors can diversify into foreign securities in several ways. A small number of foreign firms—fewer than 100—have listed their securities on the New York Stock Exchange (NYSE) or the American Stock Exchange. Historically, a major barrier to foreign listing has been the NYSE requirements for substantial disclosure and audited financial statements. For firms wishing to sell securities in the United States, the U.S. Securities and Exchange Commission's (SEC) disclosure regulations also have been a major obstruction. However, the gap between acceptable NYSE and SEC accounting and disclosure standards and those acceptable to European multinationals has narrowed substantially over the years. Moreover, Japanese and European multinationals that raise funds in international capital markets have been forced to conform to stricter standards. This change may encourage other foreign firms to list their securities in order to gain access to the U.S. capital market.

Investors can always buy foreign securities in their home markets. One problem with buying stocks listed on foreign exchanges is that it can be expensive, primarily because of steep brokerage commissions. Owners of foreign stocks also face the complications of foreign tax laws and the nuisance of converting dividend payments into dollars.

Instead of buying foreign stocks overseas, investors can buy foreign equities traded in the United States in the form of **American Depository Receipts (ADRs)**. An ADR is a negotiable certificate issued by a U.S. bank evidencing ownership of **American Depository Shares (ADSs)**.[11] An ADS is a U.S. dollar-denominated security representing shares of stock in a foreign company that are held on deposit on behalf of the ADS owner by a custodian bank in the issuing company's home country. The ADS owner is entitled to the corporate and economic rights of the foreign shares, subject to the terms specified on the ADR certificate. The ADR ratio gives the number of foreign shares represented by one ADS. For example, a 1:5 ratio means that one ADS represents ownership of five foreign shares.

ADRs provide U.S. investors with a convenient way to invest in and trade foreign shares in the United States. They are traded in the same way as shares in U.S. companies, on the New York Stock Exchange, the Nasdaq, and the American Stock Exchange. The investors in ADRs absorb the handling costs through transfer and handling charges. At the same time, they eliminate custodian safekeeping charges in the issuer's home country, reduce settlement delays, and facilitate prompt dividend payments. ADRs are estimated to save investors between 10 and 40 basis points annually as compared to the costs of investing in the underlying foreign shares directly.

Global depository receipts (GDRs) are similar to ADRs but differ in that they are generally traded on two or more markets outside the foreign issuer's home market. The GDR is generally structured as a combination of a Rule 144A ADR, which trades in the U.S. private placement market and can be sold only to Qualified Institutional Buyers, and a public offering outside the United States. A GDR program allows foreign companies to raise capital in two or more markets simultaneously and broaden their shareholder base.

As of June 2001, depository receipts (both ADRs and GDRs) for 615 companies from 33 foreign countries were listed on U.S. exchanges. Trading volume in 2000 for listed depository receipts exceeded $1.1 trillion.

An alternative to the ADR or GDR is the **global registered share (GRS)**, or **global share**. Unlike ADRs, which are dollar-denominated certificates traded in the United States, a GRS is similar to an ordinary share with the added benefit that investors can trade it on any stock exchange in the world where it is registered and in the local currency. Global shares are a response to the perceived need for a single class of security to be traded among investors worldwide owing to the globalization of financial markets, the increased operations of multinational companies in multiple markets around the world, and the explosion in cross-border merger-and-acquisition activity. However, before a global share can be launched, operators of the home country's clearing and settlement systems must work

U.S. investors have several ways to diversify into foreign securities.

U.S. investors can buy foreign equities traded in the United States in the form of ADRs.

---

[11] Although they represent distinct concepts, the terms ADR and ADS are often used interchangeably.

closely with their U.S. counterparts—as happened in Germany in 1998. Currently, there are only four global share issues, by DaimlerChrysler, Celanese, UBS, and Deutsche Bank.

MINI-CASE *Deutsche Bank Lists as a Global Share*

In August 2001, as Deutsche Bank was preparing its hotly anticipated U.S. share offering, it was pursuing a strategy that only three other foreign companies had tried before: listing as a global registered share. A global share from Deutsche Bank, Europe's largest bank, was a victory for the New York Stock Exchange. The NYSE has been a big promoter of the concept since its chairman hailed the first one as "the moment when globalization came to the U.S. markets." That moment was in November 1998, when DaimlerChrysler began trading as a global share in the United States, Germany, Japan, and five other countries.

One argument in favor of global shares is that they are less expensive to trade than ADRs. Specifically, while ADRs have been a widely accepted way to trade non-North American securities, fairly significant additional costs are associated with purchases and sales across markets. These costs arise from the need to convert ADRs to ordinary shares, and ordinary shares to ADRs with a cross-border transaction. The depositary bank executes the conversion and charges a fee each way, as much as 5 cents per share. By comparison, the NYSE charges a flat $5 per trade, no matter how many shares change hands. On the other hand, whereas the custodial bank that creates an ADR usually covers the listing costs, legal and other fees associated with global shares can run as much as $2 million. Moreover, a global share requires coordinating back-office systems and regulatory bodies. Creating such a global clearing and settlement system requires much more effort than issuing an ADR. However, as the world's markets edge closer to 24-hour trading, global shares will become increasingly convenient, as stock markets and clearing and settlement systems consolidate.

QUESTIONS

1. What are the pros and cons of Deutsche Bank listing on the NYSE as a global share instead of an ADR?

2. Are these pros and cons of a GRS issue likely to change over time? In which direction?

3. What changes would increase the desirability of issuing global shares?

The easiest approach to investing abroad is to buy shares in an internationally diversified mutual fund, of which a growing number are available. Four basic categories of mutual fund invest abroad:

1. **Global funds** can invest anywhere in the world, including the United States.

2. **International funds** invest only outside the United States.

3. **Regional funds** focus on specific geographical areas overseas, such as Asia or Europe.

4. **Single-country funds** invest in individual countries, such as Germany or Taiwan.

Internationally-diversified mutual funds provide a low-cost vehicle for international investing.

The greater diversification of the global and international funds reduces the risk for investors, but it also lessens the chances of a high return if one region (for example, Asia) or country (for example, Germany) suddenly gets hot. The problem with this approach is that forecasting returns is essentially impossible in an efficient market. This suggests that most investors would be better off buying an internationally diversified mutual fund. Of course, it is possible to construct one's own internationally diversified portfolio by buying shares in several different regional or country funds.

15.2 INTERNATIONAL BOND INVESTING

The benefits of international diversification extend to bond portfolios as well. G. Barnett and M. Rosenberg started with a portfolio fully invested in U.S. bonds and then replaced them, in increments of 10 percent, with a mixture of foreign bonds from seven markets.[12] They then calculated for the period 1973–1983 the risk and return of the ten portfolios they created. Their conclusions were as follows:

Internationally diversified bond portfolios offer superior investment performance.

1. As the proportion of U.S. bonds fell, the portfolio return rose. This result reflects the fact that foreign bonds outperformed U.S. bonds over this ten-year period.

2. As the proportion of U.S. bonds fell from 100 percent to 70 percent, the volatility of the portfolio fell. This fact reflects the low correlation between U.S. and foreign bond returns.

3. By investing up to 60 percent of their funds in foreign bonds, U.S. investors could have raised their return substantially while not increasing risk above the level associated with holding only U.S. bonds.

Other studies examining different time periods and markets have similarly found that an internationally diversified bond portfolio delivers superior performance.

15.3 OPTIMAL INTERNATIONAL ASSET ALLOCATION

Clearly, both international stock diversification and international bond diversification pay off. Not surprisingly, expanding the investment set to include stock and bonds, both domestic and foreign, similarly pays off in terms of an improved risk-return trade-off.

The most detailed study to date of the advantages of international stock and bond diversification is by Bruno Solnik and Bernard Noetzlin.[13] They compared the performances of various investment strategies over the period 1970–1980. The right-hand curve in Exhibit 15.13 is the efficient frontier when investments are restricted to stocks only. The left-hand curve is the efficient frontier when investors can buy both stocks and bonds. All returns are calculated in U.S. dollars. The conclusions of their study were as follows:

1. International stock diversification yields a substantially better risk-return trade-off than does holding purely domestic stock.

International stock and bond diversification together offers a better risk/return trade-off than either alone.

2. International diversification combining stock and bond investments results in substantially less risk than international stock diversification alone.

3. A substantial improvement in the risk-return tradeoff can be realized by investing in internationally diversified stock and bond portfolios whose weights do not conform to relative market capitalizations. In other words, the various market indices used to measure world stock and bond portfolios (e.g., Capital International's EAFE Index and World Index) do not lie on the efficient frontier.

As indicated by Exhibit 15.13, optimal **international asset allocation** makes it possible to double or even triple the return from investing in an index fund without taking on more risk. Although Solnik and Noetzlin had the enormous advantage of hindsight in constructing their efficient frontier, they concluded that the opportunities for increased risk-adjusted returns are sizable and that the performance gap between optimal international asset allocations and passive investing in simple index funds is potentially quite large.

---

[12] G. Barnett and M. Rosenberg, "International Diversification in Bonds," *Prudential International Fixed Income Investment Strategy,* Second Quarter 1983.
[13] Bruno H. Solnik and Bernard Noetzlin, "Optimal International Asset Allocation," *Journal of Portfolio Management,* Fall 1982, pp. 11–21.

EXHIBIT 15.13 • EFFICIENT FRONTIERS, DECEMBER 1970 TO DECEMBER 1980

Source: Bruno H. Solnik and Bernard Noetzlin, "Optimal International Asset Allocation," *Journal of Portfolio Management,* Fall 1982. This copyrighted material is reprinted with permission from Journal of Portfolio Management, Institutional Investor, Inc., 488 Madison Avenue, New York, NY 10022.

15.4 MEASURING THE TOTAL RETURN FROM FOREIGN PORTFOLIO INVESTING

This section shows how to measure the return associated with investing in securities issued in different markets and denominated in a variety of currencies. In general, the **total dollar return** on an investment can be divided into three separate elements: dividend/interest income, capital gains (losses), and currency gains (losses).

Bonds

The one-period total dollar return on a foreign bond investment $R_\$$ can be calculated as follows:

> The total dollar return on a foreign investment consists of dividend/interest income, capital gains, and currency gains.

$$\begin{matrix} \text{Dollar} \\ \text{return} \end{matrix} = \begin{matrix} \text{Foreign currency} \\ \text{return} \end{matrix} \times \begin{matrix} \text{Currency} \\ \text{gain (loss)} \end{matrix}$$

$$1 + R_\$ = [1 + \frac{B(1) - B(0) + C}{B(0)}](1 + g) \qquad (15.4)$$

where $B(t)$ = foreign currency (FC) bond price at time t

C = foreign currency coupon income

g = percent change in dollar value of the foreign currency

For example, suppose the initial bond price is FC 95, the coupon income is FC 8, the end-of-period bond price is FC 97, and the local currency appreciates by 3 percent against the dollar during the period. Then, according to Equation 15.4, the total dollar return is 13.8 percent:

$$R_\$ = [1 + (97 - 95 + 8)/95](1 + 0.03) - 1$$
$$= (1.105)(1.03) - 1$$
$$= 13.8\%$$

Note that the currency gain applies both to the local currency principal and to the local currency return.

Stocks

Using the same terminology, the one-period total dollar return on a foreign stock investment $R_\$$ can be calculated as follows:

$$
\begin{array}{ccc}
\text{Dollar} & \text{Foreign currency} & \text{Currency} \\
\text{return} & = \text{return} & \times \text{gain (loss)}
\end{array}
$$

$$1 + R_\$ = [1 + \frac{P(1) - P(0) + DIV}{P(0)}](1 + g)$$

(15.5)

where $P(t)$ = foreign currency stock price at time t

DIV = foreign currency dividend income

For example, suppose the beginning stock price is FC 50, the dividend income is FC 1, the end-of-period stock price is FC 48, and the foreign currency depreciates by 5 percent against the dollar during the period. Then, according to Equation 15.5, the total dollar return is –6.9 percent:

$$R_\$ = [1 + \frac{(48 - 50 + 1)}{50}](1 - 0.05) - 1$$

$$= (0.98)(0.95) - 1$$
$$= -6.9\%$$

In this case, the investor suffered both a capital loss on the FC principal and a currency loss on the investment's dollar value.

15.5 MEASURING EXCHANGE RISK ON FOREIGN SECURITIES

Currency fluctuations affect the risk of investing in foreign securities.

We have just seen that the dollar return on a foreign security can be expressed as

$$
\begin{array}{ccc}
\text{Dollar} & \text{Foreign currency} & \text{Currency} \\
\text{return} & = \text{return} & \times \text{gain (loss)}
\end{array}
$$

$$1 + R_\$ = (1 + R_f)(1 + g)$$

(15.6)

where R_f is the foreign currency rate of return. Ignoring the cross-product term, $R_f g$, which should be quite small relative to the other terms (because R_f and g are usually much less than 1), we can approximate Equation 15.6 by Equation 15.7:

$$R_\$ = R_f + g$$

(15.7)

Equation 15.7 states that the dollar rate of return is approximately equal to the sum of the foreign currency return plus the change in the dollar value of the foreign currency. Foreign currency fluctuations introduce exchange risk. The prospect of exchange risk is one of the reasons that investors have a preference for home country securities.

Using Equation 15.7, we can see how exchange rate changes affect the risk of investing in a foreign security (or a foreign market index). Specifically, we can write the standard deviation of the dollar return, $\sigma_\$$, as

$$\sigma_\$ = [\sigma_f^2 + \sigma_g^2 + 2\sigma_f\sigma_g\rho_{f,g}]^{1/2} \tag{15.8}$$

where σ_f^2 = the variance (the standard deviation squared) of the foreign currency return

σ_g^2 = the variance of the change in the exchange rate

$\rho_{f,g}$ = the correlation between the foreign currency return and the exchange rate change

Equation 15.8 shows that the foreign exchange risk associated with a foreign security depends on both the standard deviation of the foreign exchange rate change and the correlation between the exchange rate change and the foreign currency return on the security.

For example, suppose that the standard deviation of the return on Matsushita, a Japanese firm, in terms of yen is 23 percent and the standard deviation of the rate of change in the dollar:yen exchange rate is 17 percent. In addition, the estimated correlation between the yen return on Matsushita and the rate of change in the exchange rate is 0.31. Then, according to Equation 15.8, the standard deviation of the dollar rate of return on investing in Matsushita stock is 32.56 percent:

$$\sigma_\$(\text{Matsushita}) = (0.23^2 + 0.17^2 + 2 \times 0.23 \times 0.17 \times 0.31)^{1/2} = 0.3256$$

Clearly, foreign exchange risk increases risk in this case. However, the foreign exchange risk is not additive; that is, the standard deviation of the dollar return—32.56 percent—is less than the sum of the individual standard deviations—23 percent + 17 percent, or 40 percent. It is conceivable that exchange risk could lower the risk of investing overseas. Lowering risk would require a sufficiently large negative correlation between the rate of exchange rate change and the foreign currency return.

Hedging Currency Risk

Recent research indicates that hedging the currency risk of internationally diversified stock portfolios does not improve their risk-adjusted performance.

The existence of exchange risk leaves open the possibility of hedging to reduce it. Indeed, several studies have suggested that hedging currency risk can reduce the variability of returns on internationally diversified stock and bond portfolios while having little impact on or even enhancing expected returns.[14] These conclusions, however, rested mostly on data from the early 1980s. More recent data call these conclusions into question. These data show that although during the period 1980–1985—when the dollar was rising—the risk-adjusted returns on hedged stock portfolios dominated those on unhedged portfolios, this result is reversed for the period 1986–1996—when the dollar was generally falling.[15] These reversals in the dominance of unhedged versus hedged efficient frontiers for international stock portfolios occurred because of changes over time in the standard deviations and correlation coefficients of national stock market returns expressed in dollars. That is, the covariance structure of national stock market returns and currency movements is unstable.

In contrast, the returns of hedged, internationally diversified, bond portfolios exhibited dramatically lower volatility than the returns of unhedged bond portfolios over

[14] See, for example, André F. Perold and Evan C. Schulman, "The Free Lunch in Currency Hedging: Implications for Investment Policy and Performance Standards," *Financial Analysts Journal*, May/June 1988, pp. 45–50; Mark R. Eaker and Dwight M. Grant, "Currency Risk Management in International Fixed-Income Portfolios," *Journal of Fixed Income*, December 1991, pp. 31–37; Jack Glen and Philippe Jorion, "Currency Hedging for International Portfolios," *Journal of Finance*, December 1993, pp. 1865–1886; and Richard M. Levich and Lee R. Thomas III, "Internationally Diversified Bond Portfolios: The Merits of Active Currency Management," NBER Working Paper No. 4340, April 1993.

[15] These results are contained in Peter A. Abken and Milind M. Shrikhande, "The Role of Currency Derivatives in Internationally Diversified Portfolios," *Federal Reserve Bank of Atlanta Economic Review*, Third Quarter 1997, pp. 34–59.

both subperiods. Nonetheless, the case for hedging international bond portfolios is not decisive because the lower standard deviation of hedged bond returns is generally matched by lower returns. These results present investors with the familiar trade-off of risk versus return.

15.6 SUMMARY AND CONCLUSIONS

As the barriers to international capital flows come down and improved communications and data-processing technology provide low-cost information about foreign securities, investors are starting to realize the potential in international investing. We saw in this chapter that international stock and bond diversification can provide substantially higher returns with less risk than investment in a single market, particularly if the market in question is not the U.S. market. Even in a market as large as the United States, international investment offers a much broader range of opportunities than domestic investment alone. An investor restricted to the U.S. stock market, for example, is cut off, in effect, from more than half of the available investment opportunities.

Even though a passive international portfolio—one invested in an index fund based on market capitalization weights—improves risk-adjusted performance, an active strategy can do substantially better. The latter strategy bases the portfolio proportions of domestic and foreign investments on their expected returns and their correlations with the overall portfolio.

QUESTIONS

1. As seen in Exhibit 15.2, Hong Kong stocks are about twice as volatile as U.S. stocks. Does that mean that risk-averse American investors should avoid Hong Kong equities? Explain.

2. What characteristics of foreign securities lead to diversification benefits for American investors?

3. Will increasing integration of national capital markets reduce the benefits of international diversifications?

4. Studies show that the correlations between domestic stocks are greater than the correlations between domestic and foreign stocks. Explain why this is likely to be the case. What implications does this fact have for international investing?

5. Who is likely to gain more from investing overseas, a resident of the United States or of Mexico? Explain.

6. Suppose that Mexican bonds are yielding more than 100 percent annually. Does this high yield make them suitable for American investors looking to raise the return on their portfolios? Explain.

7. According to one investment adviser, "I feel more comfortable investing in Western Europe or Canada. I would not invest in South America or other regions

with a record of debt defaults and restructurings. The underwriters of large new issues of ADRs of companies from these areas assure us that things are different now. Maybe, but who can say that a government that has defaulted on debt won't change the rules again?" Comment on this statement.

8. Investors should avoid Hong Kong, given its problematic outlook now that Britain has surrendered the colony to China. Comment.

9. As noted in the chapter, from 1949 to 1990, the Japanese market rose 25,000 percent.
   a. Given these returns, does it make sense for Japanese investors to diversify internationally?
   b. What arguments would you use to persuade a Japanese investor to invest overseas?
   c. Why might Japanese (and other) investors still prefer to invest in domestic securities despite the potential gains from international diversification?

10. Because ADRs are denominated in dollars and are traded in the United States, they present less foreign exchange risk to U.S. investors than do the underlying foreign shares of stock. Comment.

PROBLEMS

1. During the year, the price of British gilts (government bonds) went from £102 to £106, while paying a coupon of £9. At the same time, the exchange rate went from £1:$1.76 to £1:$1.62. What was the total dollar return, in percent, on gilts for the year?

2. During the first half of 1990, Swiss government bonds yielded a local currency return of –1.6 percent. However, the Swiss franc rose by 8 percent

against the dollar over this six-month period. Corresponding figures for France were 1.8 percent and 2.6 percent. Which bond earned the higher U.S. dollar return? What was the return on the higher bond?

3. During the year, Toyota Motor Company shares went from ¥9,000 to ¥11,200, while paying a dividend of ¥60. At the same time, the exchange rate went from

$1 = ¥145 to $1 = ¥120. What was the total dollar return, in percent, on Toyota stock for the year?

4. During 1989, the Mexican stock market climbed 112 percent in peso terms, whereas the peso depreciated by 28.6 percent against the U.S. dollar. What was the dollar return on the Mexican stock market during the year?

5. a In 1992, the Brazilian market rose by 1,117 percent in cruzeiro terms, while the cruzeiro fell by 91.4 percent in dollar terms. Meanwhile, the U.S. market rose by 8.5 percent. Which market did better?

   b. In 1993, the Brazilian market rose by 4,190 percent in cruzeiro terms, while the cruzeiro fell by 95.9 percent in dollar terms. Did the Brazilian market do better in dollar terms in 1992 or in 1993?

6. Suppose that the dollar is now worth €1.1372. If one-year German bunds are yielding 9.8 percent and one-year U.S. Treasury bonds are yielding 6.5 percent, at what end-of-year exchange rate will the dollar returns on the two bonds be equal? What amount of euro appreciation or depreciation does this equilibrating exchange rate represent?

7. In 1990, Matsushita bought MCA Inc. for $6.1 billion. At the time of the purchase, the exchange rate was about ¥145/$. By the time that Matsushita sold an 80 percent stake in MCA to Seagram for $5.7 billion in 1995, the yen had appreciated to a rate of about ¥97/$.

   a. Ignoring the time value of money, what was Matsushita's dollar gain or loss on its investment in MCA?

   b. What was Matsushita's yen gain or loss on the sale?

   c. What did Matsushita's yen gain or loss translate into in terms of dollars? What accounts for the difference between this figure and your answer to Part a?

8. Suppose that the standard deviations of the British and U.S. stock markets have risen to 38 percent and 22 percent, respectively, and the correlation between the U.S. and British markets has risen to 0.67. What is the new beta of the British market from a U.S. perspective?

9. A portfolio manager is considering the benefits of increasing his diversification by investing overseas. He can purchase shares in individual country funds with the following characteristics:

	United States (%)	United Kingdom (%)	Spain (%)
Expected return	15	12	5
Standard deviation of return	10	9	4
Correlation with the United States	1.0	0.33	0.06

   a. What are the expected return and standard deviation of return of a portfolio with 25 percent invested in the United Kingdom and 75 percent in the United States?

   b. What are the expected return and standard deviation of return of a portfolio with 25 percent invested in Spain and 75 percent in the United States?

   c. Calculate the expected return and standard deviation of return of a portfolio with 50 percent invested in the United States and 50 percent in the United Kingdom. With 50 percent invested in the United States and 50 percent invested in Spain.

   d. Calculate the expected return and standard deviation of return of a portfolio with 25 percent invested in the United States and 75 percent in the United Kingdom; with 25 percent invested in the United States and 75 percent invested in Spain.

   e. Plot these two sets of risk-return combinations (Parts a through d), as in Exhibit 15.5. Which leads to a better set of risk-return choices, Spain or the United Kingdom?

   f. How can you achieve an even better risk-return combination?

10. Suppose that the standard deviation of the return on Nestlé, a Swiss firm, in terms of Swiss francs is 19 percent and the standard deviation of the rate of change in the dollar-franc exchange rate is 15 percent. In addition, the estimated correlation between the Swiss franc return on Nestlé and the rate of change in the exchange rate is 0.17. Given these figures, what is the standard deviation of the dollar rate of return on investing in Nestlé stock?

BIBLIOGRAPHY

Abken, Peter A., and Milind M. Shrikhande. "The Role of Currency Derivatives in Internationally Diversified Portfolios." *Federal Reserve Bank of Atlanta Economic Review,* Third Quarter 1997, pp. 34–59.

Bailey, Warren, and René M. Stulz. "Benefits of International Diversification: The Case of Pacific Basin Stock Markets." *Journal of Portfolio Management,* Summer 1990, pp. 57–62.

Barnett, G., and M. Rosenberg. "International Diversification in Bonds." *Prudential International Fixed Income Investment Strategy,* Second Quarter 1983.

Errunza, Vihang R. "Gains from Portfolio Diversification into Less Developed Countries." *Journal of International Business Studies,* Fall–Winter 1977, pp. 83–99.

Heston, Steven L., and K. Geert Rouwenhorst. "Does Industrial Structure Explain the Benefits of International Diversification?" *Journal of Financial Economics,* August 1994, pp. 3–27.

Ibbotson, Roger C., Richard C. Car, and Anthony W. Robinson. "International Equity and Bond Returns." *Financial Analysts Journal,* July–August 1982, pp. 61–83.

Kang, Jun-Koo, and René M. Stulz. "Why Is There a Home Bias? An Analysis of Foreign Portfolio Equity Ownership in Japan," *Journal of Financial Economics,* October 1997, pp. 3–28.

Lessard, Donald R. "World, Country, and Industry Relationships in Equity Returns: Implications for Risk Reduction through International Diversification." *Financial Analysts Journal,* January–February 1976, pp. 32–38.

Odier, Patrick, and Bruno Solnik. "Lessons for International Asset Allocation." *Financial Analysts Journal,* March–April 1993, pp. 63–77.

Solnik, Bruno H. *International Investments.* Reading, Mass.: Addison-Wesley, 1988.

————. "Why Not Diversify Internationally Rather Than Domestically?" *Financial Analysts Journal,* July–August 1974, pp. 48–54.

Solnik, Bruno H., and Bernard Noetzlin. "Optimal International Asset Allocation." *Journal of Portfolio Management,* Fall 1982, pp. 11–21.

INTERNET RESOURCES

quote.yahoo.com/m2?u Provides daily data on the performance of stock markets around the world.

biz.yahoo.com/reports/world.html Contains articles related to companies and stock markets worldwide.

www.msci.com Web site of Morgan Stanley Capital International. Contains downloadable data on the performance of a number of country indices, several regional indices, and a world index. It also contains data on several fixed income indices. A number of the time series go back to 1970.

www.adr.com Web site run by J.P. Morgan that contains detailed information and data on ADRs.

www.bankofny.com/adr Web site of the Bank of New York that contains a wealth of information on ADRs, including a complete listing of all ADRs and several regional ADR indexes along with an overall ADR index.

INTERNET EXERCISES

1. How has the MSCI World Index performed in dollar terms since the beginning of 1999? How has it performed in terms of the euro? What explains the difference in these returns?

2. What is the compound annual return on the Japanese stock market index since 1990 in yen terms? What is this same compound annual return expressed in dollar terms?

3. What was the return on the U.S. Treasury bond index over the last year? How does this compare to the dollar return on U.K. gilts?

4. Compare the dollar return on U.S. Treasury bonds to the hedged dollar return on Japanese government bonds. Which is higher? Why are they not the same?

5. These questions are based on the Bank of New York's ADR Web site.
   a. How many ADRs are currently trading in New York?
   b. How have Bank of New York's various ADR indexes performed so far this year?

CORPORATE STRATEGY AND FOREIGN DIRECT INVESTMENT

Luck. There isn't any. Just winners and losers.

The Silver Fox

CHAPTER LEARNING OBJECTIVES

- To identify the stages of corporate expansion overseas by which companies gradually become multinational corporations (MNCs)

- To identify the fundamental motives for companies to invest abroad in order to determine those foreign investments that are most likely to be successful

- To identify the competitive advantages that a firm must have to be a successful multinational

- To describe the strategies followed by MNCs in defending and exploiting barriers to entry created by product and factor market imperfections

- To identify the factors that help determine whether a firm will export its output, license foreign companies to manufacture its products, or set up its own production or service facilities abroad

- To explain why for many firms becoming multinational is a matter not of choice but of survival

- To assess the nature of global competition and be able to identify the key factors leading to globalization of markets and competition

- To specify a five-step approach to designing a global expansion strategy

KEY TERMS

competitive advantage	intangible capital
corporate international diversification	integration
cross investment	internalization
economic rent	international portfolio investment
economies of scale	learning curve
economies of scope	licensing
Europe 1992	market imperfections
foreign direct investment (FDI)	net present value (NPV)
global-scanning capability	rationalization
horizontal direct investment	vertical integration
industrial organization	world-scale

Although investors are buying an increasing amount of foreign stocks and bonds, most still invest overseas indirectly by holding shares of multinational corporations. MNCs create value for their shareholders by investing overseas in projects that have positive **net present values (NPVs)**—returns in excess of those required by shareholders. To continue to earn excess returns on foreign projects, multinationals must be able to transfer abroad their sources of domestic competitive advantage. This chapter discusses how firms create, preserve, and transfer overseas their competitive strengths.

The present focus on competitive analysis and value creation stems from the view that generating projects that are likely to yield **economic rent**—excess returns that lead to positive net present values—is a critical part of the capital budgeting process. This is the essence of corporate strategy—creating and then taking best advantage of imperfections in product and factor markets that are the precondition for the existence of economic rent.

This chapter examines the phenomenon of **foreign direct investment (FDI)**—the acquisition abroad of plant and equipment—and identifies those market imperfections that lead firms to become multinational. Only if these imperfections are well understood can a firm determine which foreign investments are likely *ex ante* to have positive NPVs. The chapter also analyzes corporate strategies for international expansion and presents a normative approach to global strategic planning and foreign investment analysis.

16.1 THE PROCESS OF OVERSEAS EXPANSION

The process of international expansion ordinarily evolves from a low risk-low return strategy to a higher risk-higher return strategy.

Studies of corporate expansion overseas indicate that firms become multinational by degree, with foreign direct investment being a late step in a process that begins with exports. For most companies, the *globalization process* does not occur through conscious design, at least in the early stages. It is the unplanned result of a series of corporate responses to a variety of threats and opportunities appearing at random abroad. From a broader perspective, however, the globalization of firms is the inevitable outcome of the competitive strivings of members of oligopolistic industries. Each member tries both to create and to exploit monopolistic product and factor advantages internationally while simultaneously attempting to reduce the competitive threats posed by other industry members.

To meet these challenges, companies gradually increase their commitment to international business, developing strategies that are progressively more elaborate and sophisticated. The sequence normally involves exporting, setting up a foreign sales subsidiary, securing licensing agreements, and eventually establishing foreign production. This evolutionary approach to overseas expansion is a risk-minimizing response to operating in a highly uncertain foreign environment. By internationalizing in phases, a firm can gradually move from a relatively low-risk, low-return, export-oriented strategy to a higher-risk, higher-return strategy emphasizing international production. In effect, the firm is investing in information, learning enough at each stage to improve significantly its chances for success at the next stage. Exhibit 16.1 depicts the usual sequence of overseas expansion.

EXHIBIT 16.1 ● TYPICAL FOREIGN EXPANSION SEQUENCE

Exporting

Firms facing highly uncertain demand abroad typically will begin by exporting to a foreign market. The advantages of exporting are significant: Capital requirements and start-up costs are minimal, risk is low, and profits are immediate. Furthermore, this initial step provides the opportunity to learn about present and future supply and demand conditions, competition, channels of distribution, payment conventions, financial institutions, and financial techniques. Building on prior successes, companies then expand their marketing organizations abroad, switching from using export agents and other intermediaries to dealing directly with foreign agents and distributors. As increased communication with customers reduces uncertainty, the firm might set up its own sales subsidiary and new service facilities, such as a warehouse, with these marketing activities culminating in the control of its own distribution system.

Overseas Production

A major drawback to exporting is the inability to realize the full sales potential of a product. By manufacturing abroad, a company can more easily keep abreast of market developments, adapt its products and production schedules to changing local tastes and conditions, fill orders faster, and provide more comprehensive after-sales service. Many companies also set up research and development (R&D) facilities along with their foreign operations; they aim to pick the best brains, wherever they are. The results help companies keep track of the competition and design new products. For example, the Japanese subsidiary of Loctite, a U.S. maker of engineering adhesives, devised several new applications for sealants in the electronics industry.

Setting up local production facilities also shows a greater commitment to the local market, a move that typically brings added sales and provides increased assurance of supply stability. Certainty of supply is particularly important for firms that produce intermediate goods for sale to other companies. A case in point is SKF, the Swedish ball-bearing manufacturer. It was forced to manufacture in the United States to guarantee that its product, a crucial component in military equipment, would be available when needed. The Pentagon would not permit its suppliers of military hardware to be dependent on imported ball bearings because imports could be halted in wartime and are always subject to the vagaries of ocean shipping.

Thus, most firms selling in foreign markets eventually find themselves forced to manufacture abroad. Foreign production covers a wide spectrum of activities from repairing, packaging, and finishing to processing, assembly, and full manufacture. Firms typically begin with the simpler stages—for example, packaging and assembly—and progressively integrate their manufacturing activities backward—to production of components and subassemblies.

Because the optimal entry strategy can change over time, a firm must continually monitor and evaluate the factors that bear on the effectiveness of its current entry strategy. New information and market perceptions change the risk-return trade-off for a given entry strategy, leading to a sequence of preferred entry modes, each adapted on the basis of prior experience to sustain and strengthen the firm's market position over time.

Associated with a firm's decision to produce abroad is the question of whether to *create* its own affiliates or to *acquire* going concerns. A major advantage of an acquisition is the capacity to effect a speedy transfer overseas of highly developed but underutilized parent skills, such as a novel production technology. Often the local firm also provides a ready-made marketing network. This network is especially important if the parent is a late entrant to the market. Many firms have used the acquisition approach to gain knowledge about the local market or a particular technology. The disadvantage is the cost of buying an ongoing company. In general, the larger and more experienced a firm becomes, the less frequently it uses acquisitions to expand overseas. Smaller and relatively less-experienced firms often turn to acquisitions.

Regardless of its preferences, a firm interested in expanding overseas may not have the option of acquiring a local operation. Michelin, the French manufacturer of radial tires, set up its own facilities in the United States because its tires are built on specially designed equipment; taking over an existing operation would have been out of the question.[1] Similarly, companies moving into developing countries often find they are forced to begin from the ground up because their line of business has no local counterpart.

Licensing

An alternative, and at times a precursor, to setting up production facilities abroad is to *license* a local firm to manufacture the company's products in return for royalties and other forms of payment. The principal advantages of **licensing** are the minimal investment required, faster market-entry time, and fewer financial and legal risks. But the corresponding cash flow is also relatively low, and there may be problems in maintaining product quality standards. The licensor may also face difficulty controlling exports by the foreign licensee, particularly when, as in Japan, the host government refuses to sanction restrictive clauses on sales to foreign markets. Thus, a licensing agreement may lead to the establishment of a competitor in third-country markets, with a consequent loss of future revenues to the licensing firm. The foreign licensee may even become such a strong competitor that the licensing firm will face difficulty entering the market when the agreement expires, leading to a further loss of potential profits.

For some firms, licensing alone is the preferred method of penetrating foreign markets. Other firms with diversified innovative product lines follow a strategy of trading technology for both equity in foreign joint ventures and royalty payments.

Foreign licensing tends to be a low-risk, low-return strategy.

16.2 THEORY OF THE MULTINATIONAL CORPORATION

It has long been recognized that all MNCs are oligopolists (although the converse is not true), but only recently have oligopoly and multinationality been explicitly linked via the notion of **market imperfections**. These imperfections can be related to product and factor markets or to financial markets.

Product and Factor Market Imperfections

The most promising explanation for the existence of multinationals relies on the theory of **industrial organization** (IO), which focuses on imperfect product and factor markets. *IO theory* points to certain general circumstances under which each approach—exporting, licensing, or local production—will be the preferred alternative for exploiting foreign markets.

According to this theory, multinationals have **intangible capital** in the form of trademarks, patents, general marketing skills, and other organizational abilities.[2] If this intangible capital can be embodied in the form of products without adaptation, then exporting generally will be the preferred mode of market penetration. Where the firm's knowledge takes the form of specific product or process technologies that can be written down and transmitted objectively, then foreign expansion usually will take the licensing route.

Often, however, this intangible capital takes the form of organizational skills that are inseparable from the firm itself. A basic skill involves knowing how best to service a market through new-product development and adaptation, quality control, advertising, distribution,

Multinationals owe their existence to product and factor market imperfections.

---

[1] Once that equipment became widespread in the industry, Michelin was able to expand through acquisition (which it did, in 1989, when it acquired Uniroyal Goodrich).

[2] Richard E. Caves, "International Corporations: The Industrial Economics of Foreign Investment," *Economica*, February 1971, pp. 1–27.

after-sales service, and the general ability to read changing market desires and translate them into salable products. Because it would be difficult, if not impossible, to unbundle these services and sell them apart from the firm, this form of market imperfection often leads to corporate attempts to exert control directly via the establishment of foreign affiliates. However, internalizing the market for an intangible asset by setting up foreign affiliates makes economic sense if—and only if—the benefits from circumventing market imperfections outweigh the administrative and other costs of central control.

A useful means to judge whether a foreign investment is desirable is to consider the type of imperfection that the investment is designed to overcome.[3] **Internalization,** and hence FDI, is most likely to be economically viable in those settings where the possibility of contractual difficulties make it especially costly to coordinate economic activities via arm's-length transactions in the marketplace.

Such "market failure" imperfections lead to both vertical and horizontal direct investment. **Vertical integration**—direct investment across industries that are related to different stages of production of a particular good—enables the MNC to substitute internal production and distribution systems for inefficient markets. For instance, vertical integration might allow a firm to install specialized cost-saving equipment in two locations without the worry and risk that facilities may be idled by disagreements with unrelated enterprises. **Horizontal direct investment**—investment that is cross-border but within an industry—enables the MNC to utilize an advantage such as know-how or technology and avoid the contractual difficulties of dealing with unrelated parties. Examples of contractual difficulties are the MNC's inability to price know-how or to write, monitor, and enforce use restrictions governing technology-transfer arrangements. Thus, foreign direct investment makes most sense when a firm possesses a valuable asset and is better off directly controlling use of the asset rather than selling or licensing it.

Yet the existence of market failure is not sufficient to justify FDI. Because local firms have an inherent cost advantage over foreign investors (who must bear, for example, the costs of operating in an unfamiliar, and possibly hostile, environment), multinationals can succeed abroad only if the production or marketing edge that they possess cannot be purchased or duplicated by local competitors. Eventually, however, all barriers to entry erode, and the firm must find new sources of **competitive advantage** or be driven back to its home country. Thus, to survive as multinational enterprises, firms must create and preserve effective barriers to direct competition in product and factor markets worldwide.

Financial Market Imperfections

An alternative, though not necessarily competing, hypothesis for explaining foreign direct investment relies on the existence of financial market imperfections. As we will see in Chapter 20, the ability to reduce taxes and circumvent currency controls may lead to greater project cash flows and a lower cost of funds for the MNC than for a purely domestic firm.

An even more important financial motivation for foreign direct investment is likely to be the desire to reduce risks through international diversification. This motivation may be somewhat surprising because the inherent riskiness of the multinational corporation is usually taken for granted. Exchange rate changes, currency controls, expropriation, and other forms of government intervention are some of the risks that purely domestic firms rarely, if ever, encounter. Thus, the greater a firm's international investment, the riskier its operations should be.

Yet, there is good reason to believe that being multinational may actually reduce the riskiness of a firm. Much of the systematic or general market risk affecting a company is related to the cyclical nature of the national economy in which the company is domiciled.

---

[3] These considerations are discussed by William Kahley, "Direct Investment Activity of Foreign Firms," *Economic Review,* Federal Reserve Bank of Atlanta, Summer 1987, pp. 36–51.

Hence, the diversification effect due to operating in a number of countries whose economic cycles are not perfectly in phase should reduce the variability of MNC earnings. Several studies indicate that this result, in fact, is the case.[4] Thus, because foreign cash flows generally are not perfectly correlated with those of domestic investments, the greater riskiness of individual projects overseas can well be offset by beneficial portfolio effects. Furthermore, because most of the economic and political risks specific to the multinational corporation are unsystematic, they can be eliminated through diversification.

The value of international diversification was made clear in Chapter 15. Thus, the ability of multinationals to supply an indirect means of international diversification should be advantageous to investors. However, this **corporate international diversification** will prove beneficial to shareholders only if there are barriers to direct **international portfolio investment** by individual investors. These barriers do exist and were described in Chapter 15. However, we also saw that many of these barriers are eroding.

Our present state of knowledge does not allow us to make definite statements about the relative importance of financial and nonfinancial market imperfections in stimulating foreign direct investment. Most researchers who have studied this issue, however, would probably agree that the nonfinancial market imperfections are much more important than the financial ones. In the remainder of this chapter, therefore, we will concentrate on the effects of nonfinancial market imperfections on overseas investment.

16.3 THE STRATEGY OF MULTINATIONAL ENTERPRISE

Linking strategic planning and capital allocation helps companies create positive NPV investments.

An understanding of the strategies followed by MNCs in defending and exploiting those barriers to entry created by product and factor market imperfections is crucial to any systematic evaluation of investment opportunities. For one thing, such an understanding would suggest those projects that are most compatible with a firm's international expansion. This ranking is useful because time and money constraints limit the investment alternatives that a firm is likely to consider. More important, a good understanding of multinational strategies should help to uncover new and potentially profitable projects; only in theory is a firm fortunate enough to be presented, with no effort or expense on its part, with every available investment opportunity. This creative use of knowledge about global corporate strategies is as important an element of rational investment decision making as is the quantitative analysis of existing project possibilities.

Linking strategic planning and capital allocation yields two other key advantages as well. First, the true economics of investments can be assessed more accurately for strategies than for projects. Second, the quality of the capital budgeting process typically improves greatly when capital expenditures are tied directly to the development and approval of business strategies designed to build or exploit competitive advantages.

Some MNCs rely on product innovation, others on product differentiation, and still others on cartels and collusion to protect themselves from competitive threats. We will now examine three broad categories of multinationals and their associated strategies.[5]

Innovation-Based Multinationals

Firms such as 3M (United States), N.V. Philips (Netherlands), and Sony (Japan) create barriers to entry by continually introducing new products and differentiating existing ones, both domestically and internationally. Firms in this category spend large amounts of

---

[4] See, for example, Benjamin I. Cohen, *Multinational Firms and Asian Exports* (New Haven, Conn.: Yale University Press, 1975); and Alan Rugman, "Risk Reduction by International Diversification," *Journal of International Business Studies,* Fall 1976, pp. 75–80.

[5] These categories are described by Raymond Vernon, *Storm over the Multinationals* (Cambridge, Mass.: Harvard University Press, 1977); and Ian H. Giddy, "The Demise of the Product Cycle Model in International Business Theory," *Columbia Journal of World Business,* Spring 1978, p. 93.

money on research and development (R&D) and have a high ratio of technical to factory personnel. Their products typically are designed to fill a need perceived locally that often exists abroad as well. Similarly, firms such as Wal-Mart, Toys 'R' Us, and Price/Costco take advantage of unique process technologies—largely in the form of superior information-gathering, organizational, and distribution skills—to sell overseas.

MNCs often create barriers to entry through product innovation and differentiation.

Technological leads have a habit of eroding, however. In addition, even the innovative multinationals retain a substantial proportion of standardized product lines. As the industry matures, other factors must replace technology as a barrier to entry; otherwise, local competitors may succeed in replacing foreign multinationals in their home markets.

The Mature Multinationals

What strategies have enabled the automobile, petroleum, paper and pulp, and packaged-foods industries, among others, to maintain viable international operations long after their innovative leads have disappeared and their products have become standardized? Simply put, these industries have maintained international viability by erecting the same barriers to entry internationally as those that allowed them to remain domestic oligopolists. A principal barrier is the presence of **economies of scale**, which exist whenever a given increase in the scale of production, marketing, or distribution results in a less-than-proportional increase in cost. The existence of scale economies means that there are inherent cost advantages to being large. The more significant these scale economies are, therefore, the greater will be the cost disadvantage faced by a new entrant to the market.

As an industry matures, economies of scale and scope often replace technology as a barrier to entry.

Some companies, such as Coca-Cola, McDonald's, Nestlé, and Procter & Gamble, take advantage of enormous advertising expenditures and highly developed marketing skills to differentiate their products and keep out potential competitors that are wary of the high marketing costs of new-product introduction. By selling in foreign markets, these firms can exploit the premium associated with their strong brand names. Increasingly, consumer goods firms that have traditionally stayed home also are going abroad in an attempt to offset slowing or declining domestic sales in a maturing U.S. market. Such firms, which include Anheuser-Busch (maker of Budweiser beer), Campbell Soup, and Philip Morris, find that selling overseas enables them to utilize their marketing skills and to take advantage of the popularity of American culture abroad.

Multinationals are now making major investments in emerging markets.

Both the established multinationals and the newcomers are now moving into the emerging markets of Eastern Europe, Latin America, and Asia in a big way. Companies such as Nestlé and Procter & Gamble expect sales of brand-name consumer goods to soar as disposable incomes rise in the developing countries in contrast to the mature markets of Europe and the United States. The costs and risks of taking advantage of these profitable growth opportunities are also lower today now that their more free-market-oriented governments have reduced trade barriers and cut regulations. In response, foreign direct investment in emerging markets by multinationals soared during the 1990s (see Exhibit 16.2). For example, Exhibit 16.3 shows the capital investments for soda production and bottling facilities in emerging markets announced in 1992 and early 1993 alone by PepsiCo and Coca-Cola as they raced to ensure that there would be a bottle of cola on every street corner around the world. Recession and hard economic times led to a sharp drop in emerging market FDI in the early years of the twenty-first century, although it has continued strong in the most promising market, China.

Other firms, such as Alcan and ExxonMobil, fend off new market entrants by exploiting economies of scale in production and transportation. Economies of scale also explain why so many firms invested in Western Europe in preparation for **Europe 1992**, when cross-border barriers to the movement of goods, services, labor, and capital were removed. Their basic rationale was that once Europe becomes a single market, the opportunities to exploit economies of scale will be greatly expanded. Companies that were not

EXHIBIT 16.2 • INFLOWS OF FOREIGN DIRECT INVESTMENT TO DEVELOPING COUNTRIES: 1970–2002

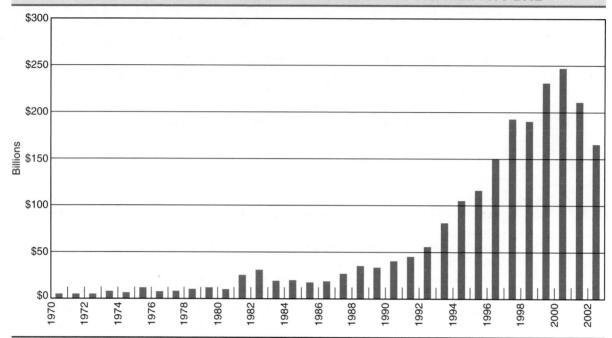

Source: UNCTAD at stats.unctad.org/fdi

EXHIBIT 16.3 • PLANNED CAPITAL INVESTMENTS FOR SODA PRODUCTION AND BOTTLING IN EMERGING MARKETS ANNOUNCED BY PEPSICO AND COCA-COLA IN 1992 AND 1993 (U.S. $ MILLIONS)

Country	PepsiCo	Coca-Cola
Chile	110	100
China	7.5	250
Czech Republic	N/A	28
Hungary	115	59
India	N/A	20
Mexico	750	195
Poland	560	300
Russia	N/A	65
Vietnam*	2	25
Total	$1,544.5	$1,042.0

*Pending removal of U.S. sanctions.
Source: Company reports. Data reported in *Business Week*, August 30, 1993, p. 46.

Economies of scope in research and development, marketing, and production are an important source of competitive advantage for many multinationals.

well positioned in the key European markets feared that they would be at a cost disadvantage relative to multinational rivals that were better able to exploit these scale economies.

Still other firms take advantage of economies of scope. **Economies of scope** exist whenever the same investment can support multiple profitable activities less expensively in combination than separately. Examples abound of the cost advantages to producing and selling multiple products related by a common technology, set of production facilities, or distribution network. For example, Honda has leveraged its investment in small-engine technology in the automobile, motorcycle, lawn mower, marine engine, chain saw, and generator businesses. Similarly, Matsushita has leveraged its investment in advertising and distribution of Panasonic products in a number of consumer and industrial markets, ranging from personal computers to VCRs. Each dollar invested in the Panasonic name or distribution system aids sales of dozens of different products.

Production economies of scope are becoming more prevalent as flexible manufacturing systems allow the same equipment to produce a variety of products more cheaply in combination than separately. The ability to manufacture a wide variety of products—with little cost penalty relative to large-scale manufacture of a single product—opens up new markets, customers, and channels of distribution, and with them, new routes to competitive advantage.

Many MNCs take advantage of the learning curve to cut costs and drive out competitors.

A strategy followed by Texas Instruments, Hewlett-Packard, Sony, and others is to take advantage of the **learning curve** in order to reduce costs and drive out actual and potential competitors. This latter concept is based on the old adage that you improve with practice. As production experience accumulates, costs can be expected to decrease because of improved production methods, product redesign and standardization, and the substitution of cheaper materials or practices. Thus, there is a competitive payoff from rapid growth. By increasing its share of the world market, a firm can lower its production costs and gain a competitive advantage over its rivals.

The consequences of disregarding these economic realities are illustrated by U.S. television manufacturers, who (to their sorrow) ignored the growing market for color televisions in Japan in the early 1960s. The failure of the U.S. manufacturers to preempt Japanese color-TV development spawned a host of Japanese competitors—such as Sony, Matsushita, and Hitachi—who not only came to dominate their own market but eventually took most of the U.S. market. The moral seems to be that to remain competitive at home, it is often necessary to challenge potential rivals in their local markets.

Cross investment can discourage rivals from launching price wars in foreign markets.

To counter the danger that a foreign multinational will use high home-country prices to subsidize a battle for market share overseas, firms often will invest in one another's domestic markets. This strategy is known as **cross-investment**. The implied threat is that "if you undercut me in my home market, I'll do the same in your home market." Firms with high domestic market share and minimal sales overseas are especially vulnerable to the strategic dilemma illustrated by the example of Fiat.

ILLUSTRATION   *Fiat's Strategic Dilemma*

Suppose Toyota, the Japanese auto company, cuts prices in order to gain market share in Italy. If Fiat, the dominant Italian producer with minimal foreign sales, responds with its own price cuts, it will lose profit on most of its sales. In contrast, only a small fraction of Toyota's sales and profits are exposed. Fiat is effectively boxed in: If it responds to the competitive intrusion with a price cut of its own, the response will damage it more than Toyota.

The correct competitive response is for the local firm (Fiat) to cut price in the intruder's (Toyota's) domestic market (Japan). Having such a capability will deter foreign competitors from using high home-country prices to subsidize marginal cost pricing overseas. However, this strategy necessitates investing in the domestic markets of potential competitors. The level of market share needed to pose a credible retaliatory threat depends on access to distribution networks and the importance of the market to the competitor's profitability. The easier distribution access is and the more important the market is to competitor profitability, the smaller the necessary market share.[6]

---

[6] The notion of undercutting competitors in their home market is explored in Gary Hamel and C. K. Prahalad, "Do You Really Have a Global Strategy?" *Harvard Business Review*, July–August 1985, pp. 139–148.

The Senescent Multinationals

Eventually, product standardization is far enough advanced or organizational and technological skills are sufficiently dispersed that all barriers to entry erode. What strategies do large multinationals follow when the competitive advantages in their product lines or markets become dissipated?

One possibility is to enter new markets where little competition currently exists. For example, Crown Cork & Seal, the Philadelphia-based maker of cans and bottle tops, reacted to slowing growth and heightened competition in its U.S. business by expanding overseas. It set up subsidiaries in such countries as Thailand, Malaysia, Zambia, Peru, and Ecuador, guessing—correctly, as it turned out—that in those developing and urbanizing societies, people would eventually switch from home-grown produce to food in cans and drinks in bottles. However, local firms are soon capable of providing stiff competition for those foreign multinationals that are not actively developing new sources of differential advantage.

> MNCs combine production rationalization with their global-scanning capability to minimize costs.

One strategy often followed when senescence sets in is to use the firm's **global-scanning capability** to seek out lower cost production sites. Costs can then be minimized by combining production shifts with **rationalization** and **integration** of the firm's manufacturing facilities worldwide. This strategy usually involves plants specializing in different stages of production—for example, in assembly or fabrication—as well as in particular components or products. Yet the relative absence of market imperfections confers a multinational production network with little, if any, advantage over production by purely local enterprises. For example, many U.S. electronics and textile firms shifted production facilities to Asian locations, such as Taiwan and Hong Kong, to take advantage of lower labor costs there. However, as more firms took advantage of this cost-reduction opportunity, competition in U.S. consumer electronics and textile markets—increasingly from Asian firms—intensified, causing domestic prices to drop and excess profits to be dissipated.

In general, the excess profits due to processing new information are temporary. Once new market or cost-reduction opportunities are recognized by other companies, the profit rate declines to its normal level. Hence, few firms rely solely on cost minimization or entering new markets to maintain competitiveness.

The more common choice is to drop old products and turn corporate skills to new products. Companies that follow this strategy of continuous product rollover are likely to survive as multinationals. Those who are unable to transfer their original competitive advantages to new products or industries must plan on divesting their foreign operations and returning home. But firms that withdraw from overseas operations because of a loss of competitive advantage should not count on a very profitable homecoming.

MINI-CASE   *The U.S. Tire Industry Gets Run Over*

The U.S. tire industry illustrates the troubles faced by multinational firms that have lost their source of differential advantage. Although Europe once was a profitable market for the Big Four U.S. tiremakers—Goodyear, Firestone, Goodrich, and Uniroyal—each of these firms has, by now, partially or completely eliminated its European manufacturing operations. The reason is the extraordinary price competition resulting from a lack of unique products or production processes and the consequent ease of entry into the market by new firms. Moreover, these firms then faced well-financed challenges in the U.S. market by, among others, the French tiremaker Michelin, the developer of the radial tire and its related production technology. Uniroyal responded by selling off its European tire-manufacturing operation and reinvesting its money in businesses that were less competitive there (and, hence, more profitable) than the tire industry. This reinvestment includes its chemical, plastics, and industrial-products businesses in Europe. Similarly, Goodrich stopped producing tires for new cars and expanded its operations in polyvinyl chloride resin and specialty chemicals. In 1986, Uniroyal and

Goodrich merged their tire units to become Uniroyal Goodrich Tire, selling only in North America. Late in 1989, its future in doubt, Uniroyal Goodrich sold out to Michelin. The previous year, in early 1988, Firestone sold out to the Japanese tiremaker Bridgestone. Goodyear is now the only one of the Big Four tiremakers that is still a U.S. company.

Goodyear, the world's number-one tire producer before Michelin's acquisition of Uniroyal Goodrich, has maintained its leadership by investing over $1 billion to build the most automated tire-making facilities in the world and is aggressively expanding its chain of wholly owned tire stores to maintain its position as the largest retailer of tires in the United States. It has also invested heavily in research and development to produce tires that are recognized as being at the cutting edge of world-class performance. Based on product innovation and high advertising expenditures, Goodyear dominates the high-performance segment of the tire market; it has captured nearly 90 percent of the market for high-performance tires sold as original equipment on American cars and is well represented on sporty imports. Geography has given Goodyear and other American tire manufacturers a giant assist in the U.S. market. Heavy and bulky, tires are expensive to ship overseas.

QUESTIONS

1. What barriers to entry has Goodyear created or taken advantage of?
2. Goodyear has production facilities throughout the world. What competitive advantages might global production provide Goodyear?
3. How do tire-manufacturing facilities in Japan fit in with Goodyear's strategy to create shareholder value?
4. How will Bridgestone's acquisition of Firestone affect Goodyear? How might Goodyear respond to this move by Bridgestone?

Foreign Direct Investment and Survival

For many firms, becoming multinational is not a matter of choice but one of survival.

Thus far we have seen how firms are capable of becoming and remaining multinationals. However, for many of these firms, becoming multinational is not a matter of choice but, rather, one of survival.

Cost Reduction   It is apparent that if competitors gain access to lower-cost sources of production abroad, following them overseas may be a prerequisite for domestic survival. One strategy that is often followed by firms for which cost is the key consideration is to develop a global-scanning capability to seek out lower-cost production sites or production technologies worldwide. In fact, firms in competitive industries have to continually seize new, nonproprietary, cost-reduction opportunities, not to earn excess returns but to make normal profits and survive.

Economies of Scale   A somewhat less obvious factor motivating foreign investment is the effect of economies of scale. In a competitive market, prices will be forced close to marginal costs of production. Hence, firms in industries characterized by high fixed costs relative to variable costs must engage in volume selling just to break even. A new term describes the size that is required in certain industries to compete effectively in the global marketplace: **world-scale**. These large volumes may be forthcoming only if the firms expand overseas. For example, companies manufacturing products such as computers that require huge R&D expenditures often need a larger customer base than that provided by even a market as large as the United States in order to recapture their investment in knowledge. Similarly, firms in capital-intensive industries with enormous production economies of scale may also be forced to sell overseas in order to spread their overhead over a larger quantity of sales.

L.M. Ericsson, the highly successful Swedish manufacturer of telecommunications equipment, is an extreme case. The manufacturer is forced to think internationally when designing new products because its domestic market is too small to absorb the enormous R&D expenditures involved and to reap the full benefit of production scale economies. Thus, when Ericsson developed its revolutionary AXE digital switching system, it geared its design to achieve global market penetration.

ILLUSTRATION   *Honda Builds an Asian Car Factory*

Honda and other automakers attempting to break into Asia's small but potentially fast-growing auto markets face a problem: It is tough to start small. Automakers need big volumes to take full advantage of economies of scale and justify the cost of building a modern car plant. But outside of Japan and China, few Asian countries offer such scale. Companies such as General Motors and Ford are relying on an export strategy in all but the largest Asian markets to overcome this hurdle. GM, for example, exports cars throughout Asia from a large plant in Thailand. However, the success of an export strategy depends on Asian countries fully embracing free trade, something that may not happen soon. Honda has decided to follow a different strategy. It is essentially building a car factory that spans all of Asia, putting up plants for different components in small Asian markets all at once: a transmission plant in Indonesia, engine-parts manufacturing in China, and other components operations in Malaysia. Honda assembles cars at its existing plants in the region. Its City subcompact, for example, is assembled in Thailand from parts made there and in nearby countries. By concentrating production of individual components in certain countries, Honda expects to reap economies of scale that are unattainable by setting up major factories in each of the small Asian markets. A sharp reduction in trade barriers across Asia that took effect in 2003 makes it easier for Honda to trade among its factories in Asia. Nonetheless, Asian countries are expected to still focus on balancing trade so that, in any given nation, an increase in imports is offset by an increase in exports. If so, Honda's web of Asian manufacturing facilities could give it an advantage over its rivals in avoiding trade friction.

Local production can expand a multinational's sales.

These firms may find a foreign market presence necessary in order to continue selling overseas. Local production can expand sales by providing customers with tangible evidence of the company's commitment to service the market. It also increases sales by improving a company's ability to service its local customers. For example, an executive from Whirlpool, explaining why the company decided to set up operations in Japan after exporting to it for twenty-five years, said, "You can only do so much with an imported product. We decided we needed a design, manufacturing, and corporate presence in Japan to underscore our commitment to the Japanese market and to drive our global strategy in Asia. You can't do that long distance."[7] Thus, domestic retrenchment can involve not only the loss of foreign profits but also an inability to price competitively in the home market because it no longer can take advantage of economies of scale.

ILLUSTRATION   *U.S. Chipmakers Produce in Japan*

Many U.S. chipmakers have set up production facilities in Japan. One reason is that the chipmakers have discovered they cannot expect to increase Japanese sales from halfway around the world. It can take weeks for a company without testing facilities in Japan to respond to customer complaints. A customer must send a faulty chip back to the maker for analysis. That can take up to three weeks if the maker's facilities are in the United

---

[7] "Whirlpool," *Fortune* (Special Advertising Section), March 18, 1993, p. S-21.

States. In the meantime, the customer will have to shut down its assembly line, or part of it. With testing facilities in Japan, however, the wait can be cut to a few days.

However, a testing operation alone would be inefficient; testing machines cost millions of dollars. Because an assembly plant needs the testing machines, a company usually moves in an entire assembly operation. Having the testing and assembly operations also reassures procurement officials about quality: They can touch, feel, and see tangible evidence of the company's commitment to service the market.

Multiple Sourcing   Once a firm has decided to produce abroad, it must determine where to do so. Although cost minimization will often dictate concentrating production in one or two plants, fear of strikes and political risks usually lead firms to follow a policy of multiple sourcing. For example, a series of strikes against British Ford in the late 1960s and early 1970s caused Ford to give lower priority to rationalization of supplies. Instead, it took a safer route, by a policy of double sourcing. Since that time, Ford has modified this policy, but many other firms still opt for several smaller plants in different countries instead of one large plant that could take advantage of scale economies but that would be vulnerable to disruptions.

> Multiple plants may provide multinationals with valuable options to reduce currency and political risks.

The costs of multiple sourcing are obvious; the benefits are less apparent, however. One benefit is the potential leverage that can be exerted against unions and governments by threatening to shift production elsewhere. For example, to reach settlement in the strikes against British Ford, Henry Ford II used the threat of withholding investments from England and placing them in Germany. Another, more obvious, benefit is the additional protection of having several plants capable of supplying the same product.

Having multiple facilities also gives the firm the option of switching production from one location to another to take advantage of transient unit-cost differences arising from, say, real exchange rate changes or new labor contracts. This option is enhanced, albeit at a price, by building excess capacity into the plants.

Knowledge Seeking   Some firms enter foreign markets in order to gain information and experience that is expected to prove useful elsewhere. For instance, Beecham, an English firm (now part of GlaxoSmithKline), deliberately set out to learn from its U.S. operations how to be more competitive, first in the area of consumer products and later in pharmaceuticals. This knowledge proved highly valuable in competing with American and other firms in its European markets. Similarly, in late 1992, the South Korean conglomerate Hyundai moved its PC division to the United States in order to keep up with the rapidly evolving personal computer market, whose direction was set by the U.S. market.

> MNCs can use foreign markets to gain information and experience that will prove useful elsewhere.

The flow of ideas is not all one-way, however. As Americans have demanded better-built, better-handling, and more fuel-efficient small cars, Ford of Europe has become an important source of design and engineering ideas and management talent for its U.S. parent, notably with the hugely successful Taurus.

In industries characterized by rapid product innovation and technical breakthroughs by foreign competitors, it is imperative to track overseas developments constantly. Japanese firms excel here, systematically and effectively collecting information on foreign innovation and disseminating it within their own research and development, marketing, and production groups. The analysis of new foreign products as soon as they reach the market is an especially long-lived Japanese technique. One of the jobs of Japanese researchers is to tear down a new foreign product and analyze how it works as a base on which to develop a product of their own that will outperform the original. In a bit of a switch, Data General's Japanese operation is giving the company a close look at Japanese technology, enabling it to quickly pick up and transfer back to the United States new information on Japanese innovations in the areas of computer design and manufacturing.

More firms are building labs in Japan and hiring its scientists and engineers in order to absorb Japan's latest technologies. For example, Texas Instruments works out production of new chips in Japan first because, an official says, "production technology is more advanced and Japanese workers think more about quality control."[8] A firm that remains at home can be blindsided by current or future competitors with new products, manufacturing processes, or marketing procedures.

Operating in a competitive market place often provides a valuable learning experience.

Tough competition in a foreign market is a valuable experience in itself. For many industries, a competitive home marketplace has proved to be as much of a competitive advantage as cheap raw materials or technical talent. Fierce domestic competition is one reason the U.S. telecommunications industry has not lost its lead in technology, R&D, design, software, quality, and cost. Japanese and European firms are at a disadvantage in this business because they do not have enough competition in their home markets. U.S. companies have been able to engineer a great leap forward because they saw firsthand what the competition could do. Thus, for telecommunications firms such as Germany's Siemens, Japan's NEC, and France's Alcatel, a position in the U.S. market has become mandatory.

Similarly, it has slowly dawned on consumer electronics firms that to compete effectively elsewhere, they must first compete in the toughest market of all: Japan. What they learn in the process—from meeting the extraordinarily demanding standards of Japanese consumers and battling a dozen relentless Japanese rivals—is invaluable and will possibly make the difference between survival and extinction.

ILLUSTRATION *A Savage Home Market Is Key to Japanese Automakers' Success*

By 2002, Japan's top automakers were nearly alone among its once-great industries in thriving in a country that was in the midst of a decade's long economic slump. This performance is all the more remarkable as it comes when Japan's automobile sales are shrinking and the auto market is crowded with nine domestic manufacturers, all fighting for a share of a market one-third as large as the U.S. market. Yet, it is that brutal competition that has enabled Toyota, Nissan, and Honda to post record profits, have the world's most efficient factories, and boast cars that top customer satisfaction lists. Toyota, Nissan, and Honda had combined net income for the fiscal year ended March 2002 of $11.64 billion, compared with a combined loss of $5.4 billion for General Motors, Ford, and DaimlerChrysler.

Japanese executives say that it is precisely their hypercompetitive home market that has forced them to overachieve. While much of their recent profit growth stems from strong sales in the U.S. market, Japanese automakers have remained killer competitors outside Japan largely because of the survival tactics they have developed to adapt to the free-for-all they face in their home market. With few high-volume models, the Japanese have learned how to make money on niche cars built in small numbers. Their tactics includes slashing the time they spend developing new vehicles and getting them into production and off the assembly line. Shorter lead times, in turn, enable them to jump on new design trends and respond to short-lived spikes in demand. It also reduces costs. Toyota brought one new model to market eighteen months after its design was approved, about seven months quicker than the fastest U.S. or European manufacturers. The payoff from reducing development time to eighteen months from twenty-five months was to shave 10 percent to 20 percent from development. That is a huge cost advantage considering that developing a new car costs from $500 million to over a billion dollars.

---

[8] *Wall Street Journal*, August 1, 1986, p. 6.

In contrast, protectionism has worked against Japanese pharmaceutical companies. Unlike U.S. pharmaceutical companies, which operate within a fiercely competitive home market that fosters an entrepreneurial spirit and scientific innovation, sheltered Japanese pharmaceutical companies have never had to adapt to international standards and competition, which has left them at a competitive disadvantage.

Although it may be stating the obvious to note that operating in a competitive marketplace is an important source of competitive advantage, this viewpoint appears to be a minority one today. Many companies prepared for Europe 1992 by seeking mergers, alliances, and collaboration with competitors. Some went further and petitioned their governments for protection from foreign rivals and assistance in R&D. However, to the extent that companies succeed in sheltering themselves from competition, they endanger the basis of true competitive advantage: dynamic improvement, which derives from continuous effort to enhance existing skills and learn new ones.

Subsidies and protectionism tend to make domestic industries less competitive.

This point is illustrated by the sorry experience of the European film industry. In order to preserve an indigenous industry, European governments have provided subsidies for local filmmakers and imposed restrictions on the showing of U.S. movies. Since 1980, however, cinema audiences for European-made films have collapsed—falling from 475 million in 1980 to 120 million in 1994. Meanwhile, the audience for American films has barely changed. In 1968, U.S. films took 35 percent of European box-office revenues; now, because European-made films have lost much of their audience, U.S. films take 80 percent, and in some countries 90 percent. One reason is the very subsidies and regulations intended to support Europe's filmmakers; they have spawned a fragmented industry, in which producers make films to show to each other rather than to a mass audience. In contrast, without subsidies and regulations to protect them, U.S. filmmakers have been forced to make films with global appeal rather than trying for art-house successes. Their achievement is reflected in the fact that Hollywood now earns over half its revenues from overseas and produced 88 of the 100 highest grossing movies in the world in 1997.

Keeping Domestic Customers   Suppliers of goods or services to multinationals often will follow their customers abroad in order to guarantee them a continuing product flow. Otherwise, the threat of a potential disruption to an overseas supply line—for example, a dock strike or the imposition of trade barriers—can lead the customer to select a local supplier, which may be a domestic competitor with international operations. Hence, comes the dilemma: Follow your customers abroad or face the loss of not only their foreign but also their domestic business. A similar threat to domestic market share has led many banks, advertising agencies, and accounting, law, and consulting firms to set up foreign practices in the wake of their multinational clients' overseas expansion.

Companies often follow their domestic customers overseas to provide uninterrupted service.

I L L U S T R A T I O N   *Bridgestone Buys Firestone*

As noted earlier, in March 1988, Bridgestone, the largest Japanese tiremaker, bought Firestone and its worldwide tire operations. Like other Japanese companies that preceded it to the United States, Bridgestone was motivated by a desire to circumvent potential trade barriers and soften the impact of the strong yen. The move also greatly expanded Bridgestone's customer base, allowing it to sell its own tires directly to U.S. automakers, and strengthened its product line. Bridgestone excelled in truck and heavy-duty-vehicle tires, whereas Firestone's strength was in passenger-car tires. But beyond these facts, a key consideration was Bridgestone's wish to reinforce ties with Japanese auto companies that had set up production facilities in the United States. By 1992, these companies, either directly or in joint ventures with U.S. firms, had the capacity to produce about 2 million vehicles annually in the United States.

Firestone also contributed plants in Spain, France, Italy, Portugal, Argentina, Brazil, and Venezuela. Thus, Bridgestone's purchase of Firestone has firmly established the company not only in North America, but in Europe and South America as well. Formerly, it had been primarily an Asian firm, but it had come to acknowledge the need to service Japanese automakers globally by operating closer to their customers' production facilities. The increasing globalization of the automobile market has prompted vehicle producers and tiremakers alike to set up production facilities in each of the three main markets: North America, Western Europe, and Japan.

Two main factors have been responsible for this trend toward globalization: First, transport costs are high for tires, and, as a result, exporting ceased to be a viable long-term strategy for supplying distant markets. Second, shifting manufacturing overseas was the only way for the tire companies to meet the logistic challenges posed by the adoption of just-in-time manufacturing and inventory systems by automakers.

A series of combinations in the tire industry—including Sumitomo Rubber's purchase of Dunlop Tire's European and U.S. operations, Pirelli's acquisition of Armstrong Tire and Rubber, and Continental AG's acquisition of General Tire and Rubber and its subsequent joint venture with two Japanese tiremakers—practically forced Bridgestone to have a major presence in the important American market if it were to remain a key player in the United States and worldwide. Without such a move, its Japanese competitors may have taken Bridgestone's share of the business of Japanese firms producing in the United States and Europe. This result would have affected its competitive stance in Japan as well.

A similar desire to increase its presence in the vital North American market was behind Michelin's 1989 acquisition of Uniroyal Goodrich. For Michelin, the addition of Uniroyal Goodrich provided entry into private-label and associate-label tire markets from which it had been absent, as well as added sales to U.S. automakers.

The benefits of a foreign investment may accrue elsewhere in the organization.

As is apparent, a foreign investment may be motivated by considerations other than profit maximization, and its benefits may accrue to an affiliate far removed from the scene. Moreover, these benefits may take the form of reduced risk or an increased cash flow, either directly or indirectly. Direct cash flows include those based on a gain in revenues or a cost savings. Indirect flows include those resulting from a competitor's setback or the firm's increased leverage to extract concessions from various governments or unions (for example, by having the flexibility to shift production to another location). In computing these indirect effects, a firm must consider what would have been the company's worldwide cash flows in the absence of the investment.

16.4 DESIGNING A GLOBAL EXPANSION STRATEGY

Although a strong competitive advantage today in, say, technology or marketing skills may give a company some breathing space, these competitive advantages will eventually erode, leaving the firm susceptible to increased competition both at home and abroad. The emphasis must be on systematically pursuing policies and investments congruent with worldwide survival and growth. This approach involves five interrelated elements.

1. Awareness of Profitable Investments

Firms must have an awareness of those investments that are likely to be most profitable. As we have previously seen, these investments are those that capitalize on and enhance the firm's differential advantage; that is, an investment strategy should focus explicitly on building competitive advantage. This strategy could be geared to building volume where economies of scale are all-important or to broadening the product scope where economies of scope are critical to success. Such a strategy is likely to encompass a sequence of tactical projects; projects may yield low returns when considered in isolation, but together they may either create valuable future investment opportunities or allow the firm to continue earning excess returns on existing investments. Proper evaluation of a sequence of tactical projects designed to achieve competitive advantage requires that the projects be analyzed jointly rather than incrementally.

An investment strategy should be geared toward building competitive advantage.

For example, if the key to competitive advantage is high volume, the initial entry into a market should be assessed on the basis of its ability to create future opportunities to build market share and the associated benefits thereof. Alternatively, market entry overseas may be judged according to its ability to deter a foreign competitor from launching a market-share battle by posing a credible retaliatory threat to the competitor's profit base. By reducing the likelihood of a competitive intrusion, foreign market entry may lead to higher future profits in the home market.

In designing and valuing a strategic investment program, a firm must be careful to consider the ways in which the investments interact. For example, where economies of scale exist, investment in large-scale manufacturing facilities may be justified only if the firm has made supporting investments in foreign distribution and brand awareness. Investments in a global distribution system and a global brand franchise, in turn, are often economical only if the firm has a range of products (and facilities to supply them) that can exploit the same distribution system and brand name.

Developing a broad product line usually requires and facilitates (by enhancing economies of scope) investment in critical technologies that cut across products and businesses. Investments in R&D also yield a steady stream of new products that raises the return on the investment in distribution. At the same time, a global distribution capability may be critical in exploiting new technology.

The return to an investment in R&D is largely determined by the size of the market in which the firm can exploit its innovation and the durability of its technological advantage. As the technology-imitation lag shortens, a company's ability to fully exploit a technological advantage may depend on its being able to quickly push products embodying that technology through distribution networks in each of the world's critical national markets.

Investments in large-scale production facilities, worldwide distribution, a global brand franchise, and new technology may help achieve global competitive advantage.

Individually or in pairs, investments in large-scale production facilities, worldwide distribution, a global brand franchise, and new technology are likely to be negative net present value projects. Together, however, they may yield a highly positive NPV by forming a mutually supportive framework for achieving global competitive advantage.

2. Selecting a Mode of Entry

This global approach to investment planning necessitates systematic evaluation of individual entry strategies in foreign markets, comparison of the alternatives, and selection of the optimal mode of entry. For example, in the absence of strong brand names or distribution capabilities but with a labor-cost advantage, Japanese television manufacturers entered the U.S. market by selling low-cost, private-label, black-and-white TVs.

A recent entry mode is the acquisition of a state-owned enterprise. In pursuit of greater economic efficiency or to raise cash, governments around the world are *privatizing* (selling to the private sector) many of their companies. Since 1985, governments have sold off over half a trillion dollars in state-owned firms. Many of the firms being privatized come from the same industries: airlines, utilities (telecommunications, gas, electric, water), oil, financial services (banking, insurance), and manufacturing (petrochemicals, steel, autos). These privatizations present new opportunities for market entry in areas traditionally closed to multinationals.

3. Auditing the Effectiveness of Entry Modes

A key element is a continual audit of the effectiveness of current entry modes, bearing in mind that a market's sales potential is at least partially a function of the entry strategy. As

Over time, the optimal foreign market penetration strategy will likely change.

knowledge about a foreign market increases or as sales potential grows, the optimal market-penetration strategy will likely change. By the late 1960s, for example, the Japanese television manufacturers had built a large volume base by selling private-label TVs. Using this volume base, they invested in new process and product technologies, from which came the advantages of scale and quality. Recognizing the transient nature of a competitive advantage built on labor and scale advantages, Japanese companies, such as Matsushita and Sony, strengthened their competitive position in the U.S. market by investing throughout the 1970s to build strong brand franchises and distribution capabilities. The new-product positioning was facilitated by large-scale investments in R&D. By the 1980s, the Japanese competitive advantage in TVs and other consumer electronics had switched from being cost-based to being based on quality, features, strong brand names, and distribution systems.[9]

 ILLUSTRATION   *Canon Doesn't Copy Xerox*

The tribulations of Xerox illustrate the dynamic nature of Japanese competitive advantage.[10] Xerox dominates the U.S. market for large copiers. Its competitive strengths—a large direct sales force that constitutes a unique distribution channel, a national service network, a wide range of machines using custom-made components, and a large installed base of leased machines—defeated attempts by IBM and Kodak to replicate its success by creating matching sales and service networks. Canon's strategy, by contrast, was simply to sidestep these barriers to entry by (1) creating low-end copiers that it sold through office-product dealers, thereby avoiding the need to set up a national sales force; (2) designing reliability and serviceability into its machines, so users or nonspecialist dealers could service them; (3) using commodity components and standardizing its machines to lower costs and prices and boost sales volume; and (4) selling rather than leasing its copiers. By 1986, Canon and other Japanese firms had more than 90 percent of copier sales worldwide. And having ceded the low end of the market to the Japanese, Xerox soon found those same competitors flooding into its stronghold sector in the middle and upper ends of the market.

Canon's strategy points out an important distinction between *barriers to entry* and *barriers to imitation*.[11] Competitors, such as IBM and 3M, that tried to imitate Xerox's strategy had to pay a matching entry fee. Through competitive innovation, Canon avoided these costs and, in fact, stymied Xerox's response. Xerox realized that the more quickly it responded—by downsizing its copiers, improving reliability, and developing new distribution channels—the more quickly it would erode the value of its leased machines and cannibalize its existing high-end product line and service revenues. Hence, what were barriers to entry for imitators became barriers to retaliation for Xerox.

4. Using Appropriate Evaluation Criteria

A systematic investment analysis requires the use of appropriate evaluation criteria. Nevertheless, despite (or perhaps because of) the complex interactions between investments or corporate policies and the difficulties in evaluating proposals, most firms still use simple rules of thumb in selecting projects to undertake. Analytical techniques are used only as a rough screening device or as a final checkoff before project approval. Although simple rules of thumb are obviously easier and cheaper to implement, there is a danger of obsolescence and consequent misuse as the fundamental assumptions underlying their

---

[9] For an excellent discussion of Japanese strategy in the U.S. TV market and elsewhere, see Hamel and Prahalad, "Do You Really Have a Global Strategy?"

[10] This example appears in Gary Hamel and C. K. Prahalad, "Strategic Intent," *Harvard Business Review,* May–June 1989, pp. 63–76.

[11] This distinction is emphasized by Hamel and Prahalad in *ibid.*

Investments should be evaluated based on their underlying strategic rationale.

applicability change. On the other hand, use of the theoretically sound and recommended present value analysis is anything but straightforward. The strategic rationale underlying many investment proposals can be translated into traditional capital-budgeting criteria, but it is necessary to look beyond the returns associated with the project itself to determine its true impact on corporate cash flows and riskiness. For example, an investment made to save a market threatened by competition or trade barriers must be judged on the basis of the sales that would otherwise have been lost. In addition, export creation and direct investment often go hand in hand. In the case of ICI, the British chemical company, its exports to Europe were enhanced by its strong market position there in other product lines, a position due mainly to ICI's local manufacturing facilities.

We saw earlier that some foreign investments are designed to improve the company's competitive posture elsewhere. For example, Air Liquide, the world's largest industrial-gas maker, opened a facility in Japan because Japanese factories make high demands of their gas suppliers and keeping pace with them ensures that the French company will stay competitive elsewhere. In the words of the Japanese unit's president, "We want to develop ourselves to be strong wherever our competitors are."[12] Similarly, a spokesperson said that Air Liquide expanded its U.S. presence because the United States is "the perfect marketing observatory."[13] U.S. electronics companies and paper-makers have found new uses for the company's gases, and Air Liquide has brought back the ideas to European customers.

Applying this concept of evaluating an investment on the basis of its global impact will force companies to answer tough questions: How much is it worth to protect our reputation for prompt and reliable delivery? What effect will establishing an operation here have on our present and potential competitors or on our ability to supply competitive products, and what will be the profit impact of this action? One possible approach is to determine the incremental costs associated with, say, a defensive action such as building multiple plants (as compared with several larger ones) and then use that number as a benchmark against which to judge how large the present value of the associated benefits (e.g., greater bargaining leverage vis-à-vis host governments) must be to justify the investment.

5. Estimating the Longevity of a Competitive Advantage

Competitive advantages erode over time and must be continually recreated.

The firm must estimate the longevity of its particular form of competitive advantage. If this advantage is easily replicated, both local and foreign competitors will soon apply the same concept, process, or organizational structure to their operations. The resulting competition will erode profits to a point where the MNC can no longer justify its existence in the market. For this reason, the firm's competitive advantage should be constantly monitored and maintained to ensure the existence of an effective barrier to entry into the market. Should these entry barriers break down, the firm must be able to react quickly and either reconstruct them or build new ones. But no barrier to entry can be maintained indefinitely; to remain multinational, firms must continually invest in developing new competitive advantages that are transferable overseas and that are not easily replicated by the competition.

16.5 SUMMARY AND CONCLUSIONS

For many firms, becoming multinational was the end result of an apparently haphazard process of overseas expansion. However, as international operations provide a more important source of profit and as competitive pressures increase, these firms are trying to develop global strategies that will enable them to maintain their competitive edge both at home and abroad.

---

[12] *Wall Street Journal,* November 12, 1987, p. 32.
[13] *Wall Street Journal,* February 23, 1988, p. 20.

The key to developing a successful strategy is to understand and then capitalize on those factors that have led to success in the past. In this chapter, we saw that the rise of the multinational firm can be attributed to a variety of market imperfections that prevent the completely free flow of goods and capital internationally. These imperfections include government regulations and controls, such as tariffs and capital controls, that impose barriers to free trade and private portfolio investment. More significant as a spawner of multinationals are market failures in the areas of firm-specific skills and information. There are various transaction, contracting, and coordinating costs involved in trying to sell a firm's managerial skills and knowledge apart from the goods it produces. To overcome these costs, many firms have created an internal market, one in which these firm-specific advantages can be embodied in the services and products they sell.

Searching for and utilizing those sources of differential advantage that have led to prior success is clearly a difficult process. This chapter sketched some of the key factors involved in conducting an appropriate global investment analysis. Essentially, such an analysis requires the establishment of corporate objectives and policies that are congruent with each other and with the firm's resources and that lead to the continual development of new sources of differential advantage as the older ones reach obsolescence.

Such a comprehensive investment approach requires large amounts of time, effort, and money; yet competitive pressures and increasing turbulence in the international environment are forcing firms in this direction. Fortunately, the supply of managers qualified to deal with such complex multinational issues is rising to meet the demand for their services.

QUESTIONS

1. Why do firms from each of the following categories become multinational? Identify the competitive advantages that a firm in each category must have to be a successful multinational.
   a. Raw-materials seekers
   b. Market seekers
   c. Cost minimizers

2. a. Why do companies generally follow a sequential strategy in moving overseas?
   b. What are the pluses and minuses of exporting? Of licensing? Of foreign production?

3. What factors help determine whether a firm will export its output, license foreign companies to manufacture its products, or set up its own production or service facilities abroad? Identify the competitive advantages that lead companies to prefer one mode of international expansion over another.

4. Time Warner is trying to decide whether to license foreign companies to produce its films and records or to set up foreign sales affiliates to sell its products directly. What factors might determine whether it expands abroad via licensing or by investing in its own sales force and distribution network?

5. Given the added political and economic risks that appear to exist overseas, are multinational firms more or less risky than purely domestic firms in the same industry? Consider whether a firm that decides not to operate abroad is insulated from the effects of economic events that occur outside the home country.

6. How is the nature of IBM's competitive advantages related to its becoming a multinational firm?

7. Black & Decker, the maker of small, hand-held power tools, finds that when it builds a plant in a foreign country, sales of both its locally manufactured products and its exports to that country grow. What could account for this boost in sales? Consider the likely reactions of customers, distributors, and retailers to the fact that Black & Decker is producing there.

8. What was the Japanese strategy for penetrating the TV market? What similarities are there between it and the Japanese strategy for entering the U.S. car market? The photocopier market?

9. The value of a particular foreign subsidiary to its parent company may bear little relationship to the subsidiary's profit-and-loss statement. The strategic purpose or nature of a foreign unit may dictate that some of the value of the unit will show up in the form of higher profits in other affiliates.
   a. Describe three ways in which the incremental cash flows associated with a foreign unit can diverge from its actual cash flows.
   b. Describe two strategic rationales for establishing and maintaining a foreign subsidiary that will lead to higher profits elsewhere in the corporation but will not be reflected in the subsidiary's profit-and-loss statement.

10. In 1989, the British company Beecham Group merged with the U.S. company SmithKline Beckman. What economic advantages might the two drug companies be expecting from their marriage? More generally, what economic forces underlie the ongoing process of consolidation and globalization in the world pharmaceutical industry? Consider the merger's impact in the areas of R&D, marketing, and production.

PROBLEMS

1. Suppose the worldwide profit breakdown for General Motors is 85 percent in the United States, 3 percent in Japan, and 12 percent in the rest of the world. Its principal Japanese competitors earn 40 percent of their profits in Japan, 25 percent in the United States, and 35 percent in the rest of the world. Suppose further that through diligent attention to productivity and substitution of enormous quantities of capital for labor (for example, Project Saturn), GM manages to get its automobile production costs down to the level of the Japanese.

   a. Who is likely to have the global competitive advantage? Consider, for example, the ability of GM to respond to a Japanese attempt to gain U.S. market share through a sharp price cut.

   b. How might GM respond to the Japanese challenge?

   c. Which competitive response would you recommend to GM's CEO?

2. Airbus Industrie, the European consortium of aircraft manufacturers, buys jet engines from U.S. companies. According to a recent story in *The Wall Street Journal,* "As a result of the weaker dollar, the cost of a major component (jet engines) is declining for Boeing's biggest competitor." The implication is that the lower price of engines for Airbus gives it a competitive advantage over Boeing. Will Airbus now be more competitive relative to Boeing? Explain.

3. Tandem Computer, a U.S. maker of fault-tolerant computers, is thinking of shifting virtually all the labor-intensive portion of its production to Mexico. What risks is Tandem likely to face if it goes ahead with this move?

4. Germany's $28 billion electronics giant, Siemens AG, sells medical and telecommunications equipment, power plants, automotive products, and computers. Siemens has been operating in the United States since 1952, but its U.S. revenues account for only about 10 percent of worldwide revenues. It intends to expand further in the U.S. market.

   a. According to the head of its U.S. operation, "The United States is a real testing ground. If you make it here, you establish your credentials for the rest of the world." What does this statement mean? How would you measure the benefits flowing from this rationale for investing in the United States?

   b. What other advantages might Siemens realize from a larger American presence?

5. Kao Corporation is a highly innovative and efficient Japanese company that has managed to take on and beat Proctor & Gamble in Japan. Two of Kao's revolutionary innovations include disposable diapers with greatly enhanced absorption capabilities and concentrated laundry detergent. However, Kao has had difficulty in establishing the kind of market-sensitive foreign subsidiaries that P&G has built.

   a. What competitive advantages might P&G derive from its global network of market-sensitive subsidiaries?

   b. What competitive disadvantages does Kao face if it is unable to replicate P&G's global network of subsidiaries?

BIBLIOGRAPHY

Caves, Richard E. "International Corporations: The Industrial Economics of Foreign Investment." *Economica,* February 1971, pp. 1–27.

Giddy, Ian H. "The Demise of the Product Cycle Model in International Business Theory." *Columbia Journal of World Business,* Spring 1978, p. 93.

Hamel, Gary, and C. K. Prahalad. "Do You Really Have a Global Strategy?" *Harvard Business Review,* July–August 1985, pp. 139–148.

_____. "Strategic Intent." *Harvard Business Review,* May–June 1989, pp. 63–76.

Kahley, William. "Direct Investment Activity of Foreign Firms." *Economic Review,* Federal Reserve Bank of Atlanta, Summer 1987, pp. 36–51.

Rugman, Alan M. "Motives for Foreign Investment: The Market Imperfections and Risk Diversification Hypothesis." *Journal of World Trade Law,* September–October 1975, pp. 567–573.

Shapiro, Alan C. "Capital Budgeting and Corporate Strategy." *Midland Corporate Finance Journal,* Spring 1985, pp. 22–36.

_____. "Economic Import of Europe 1992." *Journal of Applied Corporate Finance,* Winter 1991, pp. 25–36.

Vernon, Raymond. *Storm over the Multinationals.* (Cambridge, Mass.: Harvard University Press, 1977).

INTERNET RESOURCES

globaledge.msu.edu/ibrd/ibrd.asp Web site run by Michigan State University (MSU) that contains links to various country information helpful for making investment decisions.

www.bea.doc.gov/bea/di1.htm Web site run by the Bureau of Economic Analysis (BEA) that contains data on U.S. foreign direct investment (FDI) and on FDI in the United States.

1. Based on information gathered from MSU's Web site, analyze the investment climate in a particular country of your choosing. Describe the economic and political environments in that country and how they would affect your investment decision.

2. The following questions are based on data from the BEA Web site.

    a. List the largest recipients of U.S. FDI in the past year. What factors do you think account for these countries being large recipients of U.S. FDI? How have these recipients changed in the past ten years? What might account for these changes?

    b. List the largest countries of origin of foreign direct investment in the United States. What factors do you think account for companies in these countries being such large direct investors in the United States?

    c. What U.S. industries are the largest investors overseas? Which foreign industries are the largest investors in the United States? What might account for these industries being such large sources of FDI?

CAPITAL BUDGETING FOR THE MULTINATIONAL CORPORATION

Nobody can really guarantee the future. The best we can do is size up the chances, calculate the risks involved, estimate our ability to deal with them, and then make our plans with confidence.

Henry Ford II

CHAPTER LEARNING OBJECTIVES

- To assess the profitability of foreign investments by identifying the incremental cash flows generated by these investments
- To explain the various ways in which incremental cash flow can differ from total project cash flow
- To contrast the net present value approach using a weighted cost of capital with the adjusted present value approach for valuing foreign projects and explain when each method is most appropriate
- To compute the unlevered equity beta in order to calculate the all-equity cost of capital
- To identify the differences between foreign project and parent cash flows and describe a three-stage approach to account for these differences in a capital-budgeting analysis
- To describe the three main methods for incorporating political and economic risks into foreign investment analysis and determine the circumstances (if any) under which each of these methods is most appropriate
- To describe a two-step procedure for incorporating exchange rate changes and inflation into a foreign investment analysis
- To show how foreign project cash-flow adjustments can be carried out, especially in the case of political risk
- To explain what growth options are, why they are of great importance to multinational firms, what factors affect their value, and how to incorporate them in a capital-budgeting analysis

KEY TERMS

adjusted present value (APV)
all-equity beta
all-equity rate
blocked funds
cannibalization
depreciation tax shield
expropriation
growth option
incremental cash flows

interest tax shield
net present value (NPV)
opportunity cost
sales creation
systematic risk
total corporate risk
true profitability
value additivity principle
weighted average cost of capital (WACC)

Multinational corporations evaluating foreign investments find their analyses complicated by a variety of problems that domestic firms rarely, if ever, encounter. This chapter examines several such problems, including differences between project and parent company cash flows, foreign tax regulations, expropriation, blocked funds, exchange rate changes and inflation, project-specific financing, and differences between the basic business risks of foreign and domestic projects. The purpose of this chapter is to develop a framework that allows measuring, and reducing to a common denominator, the effects of these complex factors on the desirability of the foreign investment opportunities under review. In this way, projects can be compared and evaluated on a uniform basis. The major principle behind methods proposed to cope with these complications is to maximize the use of available information while reducing arbitrary cash flow and cost of capital adjustments.

17.1 BASICS OF CAPITAL BUDGETING

The net present value criterion is the most appropriate one to use in selecting foreign investments.

Once a firm has compiled a list of prospective investments, it must then select from among them that combination of projects that maximizes the firm's value to its shareholders. This selection requires a set of rules and decision criteria that enable managers to determine, given an investment opportunity, whether to accept or reject it. The criterion of net present value is generally accepted as being the most appropriate one to use because its consistent application will lead the company to select the same investments the shareholders would make themselves, if they had the opportunity.

Net Present Value

The **net present value** (**NPV**) is defined as the present value of future cash flows discounted at the project's cost of capital minus the initial net cash outlay for the project. Projects with a positive NPV should be accepted; projects with a negative NPV should be rejected. If two projects are mutually exclusive, the one with the higher NPV should be accepted. As discussed in Chapter 14, the cost of capital is the expected rate of return on projects of similar risk. In this chapter, we take its value as given.

In mathematical terms, the formula for net present value is

$$NPV = -I_0 + \sum_{t=1}^{n} \frac{X_t}{(1 + k)^t} \tag{17.1}$$

where I_0 = the initial cash investment
X_t = the net cash flow in period t
k = the project's cost of capital
n = the investment horizon

To illustrate the NPV method, consider a plant expansion project with the following stream of cash flows and their present values:

Year	Cash Flow	×	Present Value Factor (10%)	=	Present Value	Cumulative Present Value
0	−$4,000,000		1.00000		−$4,000,000	−$4,000,000
1	1,200,000		0.9091		1,091,000	−2,909,000
2	2,700,000		0.8264		2,231,000	− 678,000
3	2,700,000		0.7513		2,029,000	1,351,000

Assuming a 10 percent cost of capital, the project is acceptable.

The net present
value criterion is
consistent with
shareholder wealth
maximization.

The most desirable property of the NPV criterion is that it evaluates investments in the same way that the company's shareholders do; the NPV method properly focuses on cash rather than on accounting profits and emphasizes the opportunity cost of the money invested. Thus, it is consistent with shareholder wealth maximization.

Another desirable property of the NPV criterion is that it obeys the **value additivity principle.** That is, the NPV of a set of independent projects is simply the sum of the NPVs of the individual projects. This property means that managers can consider each project on its own. It also means that when a firm undertakes several investments, its value increases by an amount equal to the sum of the NPVs of the accepted projects. Thus, if the firm invests in the previously described plant expansion, its value should increase by $1,351,000, the NPV of the project.

Incremental Cash Flows

The distinction
between a project's
total and incremen-
tal cash flows is a
crucial one.

The most important as well as the most difficult part of an investment analysis is to calculate the cash flows associated with the project: the cost of funding the project; the cash inflows during the life of the project; and the terminal, or ending, value of the project. Shareholders are interested in how many additional dollars they will receive in the future for the dollars they lay out today. Hence, what matters is not the project's total cash flow per period, but the **incremental cash flows** generated by the project.

The distinction between total and incremental cash flows is a crucial one. Incremental cash flow can differ from total cash flow for a variety of reasons. We now examine some of the reasons.

Cannibalization   When Honda introduced its Acura line of cars, some customers switched their purchases from the Honda Accord to the new models. This example illustrates the phenomenon known as **cannibalization**, a new product taking sales away from the firm's existing products. Cannibalization also occurs when a firm builds a plant overseas and winds up substituting foreign production for parent company exports. To the extent that sales of a new product or plant just replace other corporate sales, the new project's estimated profits must be reduced by the earnings on the lost sales.

Foreign production
facilities may canni-
balize existing sales
or create additional
sales for existing
products.

The previous examples notwithstanding, it is often difficult to assess the true magnitude of cannibalization because of the need to determine what would have happened to sales in the absence of the new product or plant. Consider Motorola's construction of a plant in Japan to supply chips to the Japanese market previously supplied via exports. In the past, Motorola got Japanese business whether or not it manufactured in Japan. But now Japan is a chip-making dynamo whose buyers no longer have to depend on U.S. suppliers. If Motorola had not invested in Japan, it might have lost export sales anyway. Instead of losing these sales to local production, however, it would have lost them to one of its rivals. The *incremental* effect of cannibalization—the relevant measure for capital-budgeting purposes—equals the lost profit on lost sales *that would not otherwise have been lost* had the new project not been undertaken. Those sales that would have been lost anyway should not be counted a casualty of cannibalization.

Sales Creation   Black & Decker, the U.S. power tool company, significantly expanded its exports to Europe after investing in European production facilities that gave it a strong local market position in several product lines. Similarly, GM's auto plants in Britain use parts made by its U.S. plants, parts that would not otherwise be sold if GM's British plants disappeared.

In both cases, an investment either created or was expected to create additional sales for existing products. Thus, **sales creation** is the opposite of cannibalization. In calculations of the project's cash flows, the additional sales and associated incremental cash flows should be attributed to the project.

Opportunity Cost   Suppose IBM decides to build a new office building in São Paulo on some land it bought ten years ago. IBM must include the cost of the land in calculating the value of undertaking the project. Also, this cost must be based on the current market value of the land, not the price it paid ten years ago.

   This example demonstrates a more general rule. Project costs must include the true economic cost of any resource required for the project, regardless of whether the firm already owns the resource or has to go out and acquire it. This true cost is the **opportunity cost**, the maximum amount of cash the asset could generate for the firm should it be sold or put to some other productive use. It would be foolish for a firm that acquired oil at $3 a barrel and converted it into petrochemicals to sell those petrochemicals based on $3 a barrel oil if the price of oil has risen to $30 per barrel. So, too, it would be foolish to value an asset used in a project at other than its opportunity cost, regardless of how much cash changes hands.

Transfer prices can distort the true profitability of a proposed investment.

Transfer Pricing   By raising the price at which a proposed Ford plant in Dearborn, Michigan, will sell engines to its English subsidiary, Ford can increase the apparent profitability of the new plant but at the expense of its English affiliate. Similarly, if Matsushita lowers the price at which its Panasonic division buys microprocessors from its microelectronics division, the latter's new semiconductor plant will show a decline in profitability.

   These examples demonstrate that the transfer prices at which goods and services are traded internally can significantly distort the profitability of a proposed investment. Where possible, the prices used to evaluate project inputs or outputs should be market prices. If no market exists for the product, then the firm must evaluate the project based on the cost savings or additional profits to the corporation of going ahead with the project. For example, when Atari decided to switch most of its production to Asia, its decision was based solely on the cost savings it expected to realize. This approach was the correct one to use because the stated revenues generated by the project were meaningless, an artifact of the transfer prices used in selling its output back to Atari in the United States.

Fees and Royalties   Often companies will charge projects for various items such as legal counsel, power, lighting, heat, rent, research and development, headquarters staff, management costs, and the like. These charges appear in the form of fees and royalties. They are costs to the project, but they are a benefit from the standpoint of the parent firm. From an economic standpoint, the project should be charged only for the additional expenditures that are attributable to the project; those overhead expenses that are unaffected by the project should not be included in estimates of project cash flows.

In performing an incremental analysis, managers must ask, "What will happen if we don't make this investment?"

Getting the Base Case Right   In general, a project's incremental cash flows can be found only by subtracting worldwide corporate cash flows without the investment—the *base case*—from postinvestment corporate cash flows. To come up with a realistic base case, and thus a reasonable estimate of incremental cash flows, managers must ask the key question, "What will happen if we *don't* make this investment?" Failure to heed this question led General Motors during the 1970s to slight investment in small cars despite the Japanese challenge; small cars looked less profitable than GM's then-current mix of cars. As a result, Toyota, Nissan, and other Japanese automakers were able to expand and eventually threaten GM's base business. Similarly, many American companies—such as Kodak and Zenith—that thought overseas expansion too risky or unattractive today find their domestic competitive positions eroding. They did not adequately consider the consequences of *not* building a strong global position.

   The critical error made by these and other companies is to ignore competitor behavior and assume that the base case is the status quo. In a competitive world economy, however, the least likely future scenario is the status quo. A company that opts not to come out with a new product because it is afraid that the product will cannibalize its existing product line is most likely leaving a profitable niche for some other company to exploit. Sales will be lost anyway, but now they will be lost to a competitor. Similarly, a company that chooses not to invest in a new process technology because it calculates that the higher quality is not worth the added cost may discover that it is losing sales to competitors who have made the investment. In a competitive market, the rule is simple: *If you must be the victim of a cannibal, make sure the cannibal is a member of your family.*

 ILLUSTRATION   *Investing in Memory Chips*

Since 1984, the intense competition from Japanese firms has caused most U.S. semiconductor manufacturers to lose money in the memory chip business. The only profitable part of the chip business for them is in making microprocessors and other specialized chips. Why did U.S. companies continue investing in facilities to produce memory chips (the DRAMs) despite their losses in this business?

Historically, U.S. companies cared so much about memory chips because of their importance in fine-tuning the manufacturing process. Memory chips are manufactured in huge quantities and are fairly simple to test for defects, which makes them ideal vehicles for refining new production processes. Having worked out the bugs by making memories, chip companies apply an improved process to hundreds of more complex products. Until recently, without manufacturing some sort of memory chip, it was very difficult to keep production technology competitive. Thus, making profitable investments elsewhere in the chip business was contingent on producing memory chips. As manufacturing technology has changed, diminishing the importance of memory chips as process technology drivers, U.S. chipmakers such as Intel have stopped producing DRAMs.

Accounting for Intangible Benefits   Related to the choice of an incorrect base case is the problem of incorporating intangible benefits in the capital-budgeting process. Intangibles such as better quality, faster time to market, quicker and less error-prone order processing, and higher customer satisfaction can have a very tangible impact on corporate cash flows, even if they cannot be measured precisely. Similarly, many investments provide intangible benefits in the form of valuable learning experiences and a broader knowledge base. For example, investing in foreign markets can sharpen competitive skills: It exposes companies to tough foreign competition; it enables them to size up new products being developed overseas and figure out how to compete with them before these products show up in the home market; and it can aid in tracking emerging technologies to transfer back home. Adopting practices, products, and technologies discovered overseas can improve a company's competitive position worldwide.

> Foreign projects often yield intangible benefits that are difficult to value.

 ILLUSTRATION   *Intangible Benefits from Investing in Japan*

The prospect of investing in Japan scares many foreign companies. Real estate is prohibitively expensive. Customers are extraordinarily demanding. The government bureaucracy can seem impenetrable at times, and Japanese competitors fiercely protect their home market.

An investment in Japanese operations provides a variety of intangible benefits, however. More companies are realizing that to compete effectively elsewhere, they must first compete in the toughest market of all: Japan. What they learn in the process—from meeting the stringent standards of Japanese customers and battling a dozen relentless Japanese rivals—is invaluable and will possibly make the difference between survival and extinction. At the same time, operating in Japan helps a company such as IBM keep up the pressure on some of its most potent global competitors in their home market. A position in the Japanese market also gives a company an early look at new products and technologies originating in Japan, enabling it to quickly pick up and transfer back to the United States information on Japanese advances in manufacturing technology and product development. And monitoring changes in the Japanese market helps boost sales there as well.

Although the principle of incremental analysis is a simple one to state, its rigorous application is a complicated undertaking. However, this rule at least points in the right direction those executives responsible for estimating cash flows. Moreover, when estimation shortcuts or simplifications are made, it provides those responsible with some idea of what they are doing and how far they are straying from a thorough analysis.

Alternative Capital-Budgeting Frameworks

As we have just seen, the standard capital-budgeting analysis involves first calculating the expected after-tax values of all cash flows associated with a prospective investment and then discounting those cash flows back to the present, using an appropriate discount rate. Typically, the discount rate used is the **weighted average cost of capital** (WACC), introduced in Chapter 14, where the weights are based on the proportion of the firm's capital structure accounted for by each source of capital.

An Adjusted Present Value Approach The weighted average cost of capital is simple in concept and easy to apply. A single rate is appropriate, however, only if the financial structures and commercial risks are similar for all investments undertaken. Projects with different risks are likely to possess differing debt capacities with each project, therefore necessitating a separate financial structure. Moreover, the financial package for a foreign investment may include project-specific loans at concessionary rates or higher-cost foreign funds because of home country exchange controls, leading to different component costs of capital for foreign investments.

The weighted average cost of capital figure can be modified to reflect these deviations from the firm's typical investment, but for some companies, such as those in extractive industries, there is no norm. Project risks and financial structure vary by country, raw material, production stage, and position in the life cycle of the project. An alternative approach is to discount cash flows using the **all-equity rate**, k^*. This rate abstracts from the project's financial structure and is based solely on the riskiness of the project's anticipated cash flows. In other words, the all-equity cost of capital equals the company's cost of capital if it were all-equity financed, that is, with no debt.

To calculate the all-equity rate, we rely on the capital asset pricing model (CAPM) introduced in Chapter 14:

$$k^* = r_f + \beta^*(r_m - r_f) \tag{17.2}$$

where β^* is the **all-equity beta**—that is, the beta associated with the unleveraged cash flows.

> Project risks and financial structures often vary by country, production stage, and position in the product life cycle.

> The all-equity cost of capital abstracts from leverage and is based solely on the riskiness of the project's anticipated cash flows.

ILLUSTRATION *Estimating a Foreign Project's Cost of Capital*

Suppose that a foreign project has an all-equity beta of 1.15, the risk-free return is 7 percent, and the required return on the market is estimated at 15 percent. Then based on Equation 17.2, the project's cost of capital is

$$k^* = 0.07 + 1.15(0.15 - 0.07) = 16.2\%$$

In reality, the firm will not be able to estimate β^* with the degree of precision implied here. Instead, it will have to use guesswork based on theory. The considerations involved in the estimation process are discussed in the following section.

If the project is of similar risk to the average project selected by the firm, it is possible to estimate β^* by reference to the firm's stock price beta, β_e. In other words, β_e is the beta that appears in the estimate of the firm's cost of equity capital, k_e, given its current capital structure.

To transform β_e into β^*, we must separate out the effects of debt financing. This operation is known as *unlevering,* or converting a levered equity beta to its unlevered or all-equity value. Unlevering can be accomplished by using the following approximation:

The all-equity beta abstracts from the effects of financing.

$$\beta^* = \frac{\beta_e}{1 + (1-t)D/E} \tag{17.3}$$

where t is the firm's marginal tax rate, and D/E is its current debt-to-equity ratio. Thus, for example, if a firm has a stock price beta of 1.1, a debt/equity ratio of 0.6, and a marginal tax rate of 35 percent, Equation 17.3 estimates its all-equity beta as 0.79 [1.1/(1 + 0.65 × 0.6)].

The adjusted present value framework incorporates the effects of financing subsidies and interest tax shields in separate terms.

The all-equity rate k^* can be used in capital budgeting by viewing the value of a project as being equal to the sum of the following components: (1) the present value of project cash flows after taxes but before financing costs, discounted at k^*; (2) the present value of the tax savings on debt financing, which is also known as the **interest tax shield**; and (3) the present value of any savings (penalties) on interest costs associated with project-specific financing.[1] This latter differential would generally be due to government regulations and/or interest subsidies that caused interest rates on restricted funds to diverge from domestic interest payable on unsubsidized, arm's-length borrowing. The **adjusted present value (APV)** with this approach is

APV =	Present value of investment outlay	+	Present value of operating cash flows	+	Present value of interest tax shield	+	Present value of interest subsidies

$$V = -I_0 + \sum_{t=1}^{n} \frac{X_t}{(1+k^*)^1} + \sum_{t=1}^{n} \frac{T_t}{(1+i_d)^t} + \sum_{t=1}^{n} \frac{S_t}{(1+i_d)} \tag{17.4}$$

where T_t = tax savings in year t due to the specific financing package

S_t = before-tax dollar (home currency) value of interest subsidies (penalties) in year t due to project-specific financing

i_d = before-tax cost of dollar (home currency) debt

The last two terms in Equation 17.4 are discounted at the before-tax cost of dollar debt to reflect the relatively certain value of the cash flows due to tax shields and interest savings (penalties). The interest tax shield in period t, T_t, equals $\tau i_d D_t$, where τ is the corporate tax rate and D_t is the incremental debt supported by the project in period t.

It should be emphasized that the all-equity cost of capital equals the required rate of return on a specific project—that is, the riskless rate of interest plus an appropriate risk premium based on the project's particular risk. Thus, k^* varies by project as project risks vary.

According to the CAPM, the market prices only **systematic risk** relative to the market rather than **total corporate risk**. In other words, only interactions of project returns with overall market returns are relevant in determining project riskiness; interactions of

---

[1] This material is based on Donald R. Lessard, "Evaluating Foreign Projects: An Adjusted Present Value Approach," in *International Financial Management,* 2nd ed., edited by Donald R. Lessard. (Boston: Warren, Gorham & Lamont), 1985.

project returns with total corporate returns can be ignored. Thus, each project has its own required return and can be evaluated without regard to the firm's other investments. If a project-specific approach is not used, the primary advantage of the CAPM is lost—the concept of value additivity, which allows projects to be considered independently.

17.2 ISSUES IN FOREIGN INVESTMENT ANALYSIS

The analysis of a foreign project raises two additional issues other than those dealing with the interaction between the investment and financing decisions:

1. Should cash flows be measured from the viewpoint of the project or that of the parent?
2. Should the additional economic and political risks that are uniquely foreign be reflected in cash-flow or discount rate adjustments?

Parent versus Project Cash Flows

Parent and project cash can diverge significantly because of tax regulations, currency controls, and other factors.

A substantial difference can exist between the cash flow of a project and the amount that is remitted to the parent firm because of tax regulations and exchange controls. In addition, project expenses such as management fees and royalties are returns to the parent company. Furthermore, the incremental revenue contributed to the parent of the multinational corporation (MNC) by a project can differ from total project revenues if, for example, the project involves substituting local production for parent company exports or if transfer price adjustments shift profits elsewhere in the system.

Given the differences that are likely to exist between parent and project cash flows, the question arises as to the relevant cash flows to use in project evaluation. Economic theory has the answer to this question. According to economic theory, the value of a project is determined by the net present value of future cash flows back to the investor. Thus, the parent MNC should value only those cash flows that are, or can be, repatriated net of any transfer costs (such as taxes) because only accessible funds can be used for the payment of dividends and interest, for amortization of the firm's debt, and for reinvestment.

A Three-Stage Approach   A three-stage analysis is recommended for simplifying project evaluation. In the first stage, project cash flows are computed from the subsidiary's standpoint, exactly as if the subsidiary were a separate national corporation. The perspective then shifts to the parent company. This second stage of analysis requires specific forecasts concerning the amounts, timing, and form of transfers to headquarters, as well as information about what taxes and other expenses will be incurred in the transfer process. Finally, the firm must take into account the indirect benefits and costs that this investment confers on the rest of the system, such as an increase or decrease in export sales by another affiliate.

Estimating Incremental Project Cash Flows   Essentially, the company must estimate a project's true profitability. **True profitability** is an amorphous concept, but basically it involves determining the marginal revenue and marginal costs associated with the project. In general, as mentioned earlier, incremental cash flows to the parent can be found only by subtracting worldwide parent company cash flows (without the investment) from postinvestment parent company cash flows. This estimating entails the following:

Estimating a project's true profitability requires various adjustments to the project's cash flows.

1. Adjust for the effects of transfer pricing and fees and royalties.
   a. Use market costs/prices for goods, services, and capital transferred internally.

    b. Add back fees and royalties to project cash flows, because they are benefits to the parent.

    c. Remove the fixed portions of such costs as corporate overhead.

2. Adjust for global costs/benefits that are not reflected in the project's financial statements. These costs/benefits include

    a. Cannibalization of sales of other units

    b. Creation of incremental sales by other units

    c. Additional taxes owed when repatriating profits

    d. Foreign tax credits usable elsewhere

    e. Diversification of production facilities

    f. Market diversification

    g. Provision of a key link in a global service network

    h. Knowledge of competitors, technology, markets, and products

> A foreign investment analysis should incorporate the project's strategic purpose and its impact on other units.

The second set of adjustments involves incorporating the project's strategic purpose and its impact on other units. These strategic considerations embody the factors that were discussed in Chapter 16. For example, AT&T is investing heavily in the ability to provide multinational customers with seamless global telecommunications services.

    Although the principle of valuing and adjusting incremental cash flows is itself simple, it can be complicated to apply. Its application is illustrated in the case of taxes.

> Only after-tax cash flows are relevant.

Tax Factors   Because only after-tax cash flows are relevant, it is necessary to determine when and what taxes must be paid on foreign-source profits. The following example illustrates the calculation of the incremental tax owed on foreign-source earning. Suppose an affiliate remits after-tax earnings of $150,000 to its U.S. parent in the form of a dividend. Assume that the foreign tax rate is 25 percent, the withholding tax on dividends is 4 percent, and excess foreign tax credits are unavailable. The marginal rate of additional taxation is found by adding the withholding tax that must be paid locally to the U.S. tax owed on the dividend. Withholding tax equals $6,000 ($150,000 \times 0.04$), and U.S. tax owed equals $14,000. This latter tax is calculated as follows. With a before-tax local income of $200,000 ($200,000 \times 0.75 = 150,000$), the U.S. tax owed would equal $200,000 \times 0.35$, or $70,000. The firm then receives foreign tax credits equal to $56,000—the $50,000 in local tax paid and the $6,000 dividend withholding tax—leaving a net of $14,000 owed the IRS. This calculation yields a marginal tax rate of 13.33 percent on remitted profits, as follows:

$$\frac{6,000 + 14,000}{150,000} = 0.1333$$

If excess foreign tax credits are available to offset the U.S. tax owed, then the marginal tax rate on remittances is just the dividend withholding tax rate of 4 percent.

Political and Economic Risk Analysis

All else being equal, firms prefer to invest in countries with stable currencies, healthy economies, and minimal political risks, such as expropriation. All else is usually not equal, however, and so firms must assess the consequences of various political and economic risks for the viability of potential investments.

    The three main methods for incorporating the additional political and economic risks, such as the risks of currency fluctuation and expropriation, into foreign investment analysis are (1) shortening the minimum payback period, (2) raising the required rate of return of the investment, and (3) adjusting cash flows to reflect the specific impact of a given risk.

There are three main methods for incorporating political and economic risks into a foreign investment analysis.

Adjusting the Discount Rate or Payback Period   The additional risks confronted abroad are often described in general terms instead of being related to their impact on specific investments. This rather vague view of risk probably explains the prevalence among multinationals of two unsystematic approaches to account for the added political and economic risks of overseas operations. One is to use a higher discount rate for foreign operations; another is to require a shorter payback period. For instance, if exchange restrictions are anticipated, a normal required return of 15 percent might be raised to 20 percent, or a five-year payback period might be shortened to three years.

Neither of the aforementioned approaches, however, lends itself to a careful evaluation of the actual impact of a particular risk on investment returns. Thorough risk analysis requires an assessment of the magnitude and timing of risks and their implications for the projected cash flows. For example, an expropriation five years hence is likely to be much less threatening than one expected next year, even though the probability of its occurring later may be higher. Thus, using a uniformly higher discount rate simply distorts the meaning of the present value of a project by penalizing future cash flows relatively more heavily than current ones, without obviating the necessity for a careful risk evaluation. Furthermore, the choice of a risk premium is an arbitrary one, whether it is 2 percent or 10 percent. Instead, adjusting cash flows makes it possible to fully incorporate all available information about the impact of a specific risk on the future returns from an investment.

Adjusting the discount rate for the added risks abroad can distort the meaning of a project's NPV.

Adjusting Expected Values   The recommended approach is to adjust the cash flows of a project to reflect the specific impact of a given risk, primarily because there is normally more and better information on the specific impact of a given risk on a project's cash flows than on its required return. The cash-flow adjustments presented in this chapter employ only expected values; that is, the analysis reflects only the first moment of the probability distribution of the impact of a given risk. Although this procedure does not assume that shareholders are risk-neutral, it does assume either that risks such as expropriation, currency controls, inflation, and exchange rate changes are unsystematic or that foreign investments tend to lower a firm's systematic risk. In the latter case, adjusting only the expected values of future cash flows will yield a lower bound on the value of the investment to the firm.

Although the suggestion that cash flows from politically risky areas should be discounted at a rate that ignores those risks is contrary to current practice, the difference is more apparent than real: Most firms evaluating foreign investments discount most likely (modal) rather than expected (mean) cash flows at a risk-adjusted rate. If an expropriation or currency blockage is anticipated, then the mean value of the probability distribution of future cash flows will be significantly below its mode. From a theoretical standpoint, of course, cash flows should always be adjusted to reflect the change in expected values caused by a particular risk; however, only if the risk is systematic should these cash flows be further discounted.

Exchange Rate Changes and Inflation

Exchange rate changes and inflation can be analyzed separately when estimating a foreign project's cash flows.

The present value of future cash flows from a foreign project can be calculated using a two-stage procedure: (1) Convert nominal foreign currency cash flows into nominal home currency terms, and (2) discount those nominal cash flows at the nominal domestic required rate of return. In order to properly assess the effect of exchange rate changes on expected cash flows from a foreign project, one must first remove the effect of offsetting inflation and exchange rate changes. It is worthwhile to analyze each effect separately because different cash flows may be differentially affected by inflation. For example, the **depreciation tax shield** will not rise with inflation, while revenues and variable costs are likely to rise in line with inflation. Or local price controls may not permit internal price adjustments. In practice, correcting for these effects means first adjusting the foreign currency cash flows for inflation and then converting the projected cash flows back into dollars using the forecast exchange rate.

ILLUSTRATION *Factoring in Currency Depreciation and Inflation*

Suppose that with no inflation the cash flow in year 2 of a new project in France is expected to be €1 million, and the exchange rate is expected to remain at its current value of €1 = $0.85. Converted into dollars, the €1 million cash flow yields a projected cash flow of $850,000. Now suppose that French inflation is expected to be 6 percent annually, but project cash flows are expected to rise only 4 percent annually because the depreciation tax shield will remain constant. At the same time, because of purchasing power parity (and U.S. inflation of 1 percent), the euro is expected to depreciate at the rate of 5 percent annually—giving rise to a forecast exchange rate in year 2 of $0.85 \times (1 - 0.05)^2 = 0.7671. Then the forecast cash flow in year 2 becomes €1 million $\times 1.04^2 = $€1,081,600, with a forecast dollar value of $829,722 ($0.7671 \times 1,081,600$).

An alternative approach to valuing a foreign project's future cash flows is to (1) discount the nominal foreign currency cash flows at the nominal foreign currency required rate of return and (2) convert the resulting foreign currency present value into the home currency using the current spot rate. These two different approaches to valuing project cash flows should give the same results if the international Fisher effect is assumed to hold.

17.3 FOREIGN PROJECT APPRAISAL: THE CASE OF INTERNATIONAL DIESEL CORPORATION

This section illustrates how to deal with some of the complexities involved in foreign project analysis by considering the case of a U.S. firm with an investment opportunity in England. International Diesel Corporation (IDC-U.S.), a U.S.-based multinational firm, is trying to decide whether to establish a diesel manufacturing plant in the United Kingdom (IDC-U.K.). IDC-U.S. expects to significantly boost its European sales of small diesel engines (40–160 hp) from the 20,000 it is currently exporting there. At the moment, IDC-U.S. is unable to increase exports because its domestic plants are producing to capacity. The 20,000 diesel engines it is currently shipping to Europe are the residual output that it is not selling domestically.

IDC-U.S. has made a strategic decision to significantly increase its presence and sales overseas. A logical first target of this international expansion is the European Community (EC). Market growth seems assured by recent large increases in fuel costs and the advent of Europe 1992 and the European Monetary Union. IDC-U.S. executives believe that manufacturing in England will give the firm a key advantage with customers in England and throughout the rest of the EC.

England is the most likely production location because IDC-U.S. can acquire a 1.4-million-square-foot plant in Manchester from British Leyland (BL), which used it to assemble gasoline engines before its recent closing. As an inducement to locate in this vacant plant and thereby ease unemployment among autoworkers in Manchester, the National Enterprise Board (NEB) will provide a five-year loan of £5 million ($10 million) at 3 percent interest, with interest paid annually at the end of each year and the principal to be repaid in a lump sum at the end of the fifth year. Total acquisition, equipment, and retooling costs for this plant are estimated to equal $50 million.

Full-scale production can begin six months from the date of acquisition because IDC-U.S. is reasonably certain it can hire BL's plant manager and about 100 other former employees. In addition, conversion of the plant from producing gasoline engines to producing diesel engines should be relatively simple.

The parent will charge IDC-U.K. licensing and overhead allocation fees equal to 7 percent of sales in pounds sterling. In addition, IDC-U.S. will sell its English affiliate valves, piston rings, and other components that account for approximately 30 percent of the total amount of materials used in the manufacturing process. IDC-U.K. will be billed in dollars at the current market price for this material. The remaining components will be purchased locally. IDC-U.S. estimates that its all-equity nominal required rate of return for the project will equal 12 percent, based on an anticipated 3 percent U.S. rate of inflation and the business risks associated with this venture. The debt capacity of such a project is judged to be about 20 percent—that is, a debt-to-equity ratio for this project of about 1:4 is considered reasonable.

To simplify its investment analysis, IDC-U.S. uses a five-year capital-budgeting horizon and then calculates a terminal value for the remaining life of the project. If the project has a positive net present value for the first five years, there is no need to engage in costly and uncertain estimates of future cash flows. If the initial net present value is negative, then IDC-U.S. can calculate a break-even terminal value at which the net present value will just be positive. This break-even value is then used as a benchmark against which to measure projected cash flows beyond the first five years.

We now apply the three-stage investment analysis outlined in the preceding section: (1) Estimate project cash flows; (2) forecast the amounts and timing of cash flows to the parent; and (3) add to, or subtract from, these parent cash flows the indirect benefits or costs that this project provides the remainder of the multinational firm.

Estimation of Project Cash Flows

A principal cash outflow associated with the project is the initial investment outlay, consisting of the plant purchase, equipment expenditures, and working-capital requirements. Other cash outflows include operating expenses, later additions to working capital as sales expand, and taxes paid on its net income.

IDC-U.K. has cash inflows from its sales in England and other EC countries. It also has cash inflows from three other sources:

- The tax shield provided by depreciation and interest charges
- Interest subsidies
- The terminal value of its investment, net of any capital gains taxes owed upon liquidation

Recapture of working capital is not assumed until eventual liquidation because this working capital is necessary to maintain an ongoing operation after the fifth year.

Initial Investment Outlay Total plant acquisition, conversion, and equipment costs for IDC-U.K. were previously estimated at $50 million. The plant and equipment will be depreciated on a straight-line basis over a five-year period, with a zero salvage value.

Of the $50 million in net plant and equipment costs, $10 million will be financed by NEB's loan of £5 million at 3 percent. The remaining $40 million will be supplied by the parent in the form of equity capital.

Working-capital requirements—comprising cash, accounts receivable, and inventory—are estimated at 30 percent of sales, but this amount will be partially offset by accounts payable to local firms, which are expected to average 10 percent of sales. Therefore, net investment in working capital will equal approximately 20 percent of sales. The transfer price on the material sold to IDC-U.K. by its parent includes a 25 percent contribution to IDC-U.S.'s profit and overhead. That is, the variable cost of production equals 75 percent of the transfer price. Lloyds Bank is providing an initial working-capital loan of £1.5 million ($3 million). All future working-capital needs will be financed out of internal cash flow. Exhibit 17.1 summarizes the initial investment.

Financing IDC-U.K.   Based on the information just provided, IDC-U.K.'s initial balance sheet, in both pounds and dollars, is presented in Exhibit 17.2. The debt ratio (debt to total assets) for IDC-U.K. is 33:53, or 62 percent. Note that this debt ratio could vary from 25 percent, if the parent's total investment was in the form of equity, all the way up to 100 percent, if IDC-U.S. provided all of its $40 million investment for plant and equipment as debt. In other words, as discussed in Chapter 14, an affiliate's capital structure is not independent; rather, it depends on its parent's investment policies.

As discussed in Section 17.1 (see Equation 17.4), the tax shield benefits of interest write-offs are represented separately. Assume that IDC-U.K. contributes $10.6 million to its parent's debt capacity (0.2 × $53 million), the dollar market rate of interest for IDC-U.K. is 8 percent, and the U.K. tax rate is 40 percent. This calculation translates into a cash flow in the first and subsequent years equal to $10.6 million × 0.08 × 0.40, or $339,000. Discounted at 8 percent, this cash flow provides a benefit equal to $1.4 million over the next five years.

EXHIBIT 17.1 • INITIAL INVESTMENT OUTLAY IN IDC-U.K. (£1 = $2)

	£ *(millions)*	$ *(millions)*
Plant purchase and retooling expense	17.5	35
Equipment		
Supplied by parent (used)	2.5	5
Purchased in the United Kingdom	5	10
Working capital		
Bank financing	1.5	3
Total initial investment	£26.5	$53

EXHIBIT 17.2 • INITIAL BALANCE SHEET OF IDC-U.K. (£1 = $2)

	£ *(millions)*	$ *(millions)*
Assets		
Current assets	1.5	3
Plant and equipment	25	50
Total assets	26.5	53
Liabilities		
Loan payable (to Lloyds)	1.5	3
Total current liabilities	1.5	3
Loan payable (to NEB)	5	10
Loan payable (to IDC-U.S.)	10	20
Total liabilities	16.5	33
Equity	10	20
Total liabilities plus equity	£26.5	$53

Interest Subsidies   Based on a 5 percent anticipated rate of inflation in England and on an expected annual 2 percent depreciation of the pound relative to the dollar, the market rate on the pound loan to IDC-U.K. would equal about 10 percent. Thus, the 3 percent interest rate on the loan by the National Enterprise Board represents a 7 percent subsidy to IDC-U.K. The cash value of this subsidy equals £350,000 (£5 million × 0.07, or approximately $700,000) annually for the next five years, with a present value of $2.7 million.[2]

Sales and Revenue Forecasts   At a profit-maximizing price of £250 per unit in the first year ($490 at the projected year 1 exchange rate), demand for diesel engines in England and the other EC countries is expected to increase by 10 percent annually, from 60,000 units in the first year to 88,000 units in the fifth year. It is assumed here that purchasing power parity holds with no lag and that real prices remain constant in both absolute and relative terms. Hence, the sequences of nominal pound prices and exchange rates, reflecting anticipated annual rates of inflation equaling 5 percent and 3 percent for the pound and dollar, respectively, are

			Year			
	0	*1*	*2*	*3*	*4*	*5*
Price (pounds)	—	250	278	308	342	380
Exchange rate (dollars)	2.00	1.96	1.92	1.89	1.85	1.82

It is also assumed here that purchasing power parity holds with respect to the euro and other currencies of the various EC countries to which IDC-U.K. exports. These exports account for about 60 percent of total IDC-U.K. sales. Disequilibrium conditions in the currency markets or relative price changes can be dealt with using an approach similar to that taken in the exposure measurement example (Spectrum Manufacturing) in Chapter 11.

In the first year, although demand is at 60,000 units, IDC-U.K. can produce and supply the market with only 30,000 units (because of the six-month start-up period). IDC-U.S. exports another 20,000 units to its English affiliate at a unit transfer price of £250, leading to no profit for IDC-U.K. Because these units would have been exported anyway, IDC-U.K. is not credited from a capital-budgeting standpoint with any profits on these sales. IDC-U.S. ceases its exports of finished products to England and the EC after the first year. From year 2 on, IDC-U.S. is counting on an expanding U.S. market to absorb the 20,000 units. Based on these assumptions, IDC-U.K.'s projected sales revenues are shown in Exhibit 17.3, line C.

In nominal terms, IDC-U.K.'s pound sales revenues are projected to rise at a rate of 15.5 percent annually, based on a combination of the 10 percent annual increase in unit demand and the 5 percent annual increase in unit price (1.10 × 1.05 = 1.155). Dollar revenues will increase at about 13 percent annually, due to the anticipated 2 percent annual rate of pound depreciation.

Production Cost Estimates   Based on the assumptions that relative prices will remain constant and that purchasing power parity will hold continually, variable costs of production, stated in real terms, are expected to remain constant, whether denominated in pounds or in dollars. Hence, the pound prices of both labor and material sourced in

---

[2] The present value of this subsidy is found by discounting it at 10 percent and then converting the resulting pound present value into dollars at the current spot rate of $2/£. The appropriate discount rate is 10 percent because this is a pound loan. The exact present value of this subsidy is given by the difference between the present value of debt service on the 3 percent loan discounted at 10 percent and the face value of the loan.

EXHIBIT 17.3 • PRESENT VALUE OF IDC-U.K.: PROJECT VIEWPOINT

				Year			
	0	*1*	*2*	*3*	*4*	*5*	*5+*
A. Sales (units)		30,000	66,000	73,000	80,000	88,000	
B. Price per unit (£)		250	263	276	289	304	
C. Sales revenue (£ millions)		7.5	17.3	20.1	23.2	26.7	
D. Variable cost per unit (£)		140	147	154	162	170	
E. Total variable cost (£ millions)		4.2	9.7	11.3	13.0	15.0	
F. Licensing fees and royalties (0.07 × line C, in £ millions)		0.5	1.2	1.4	1.6	1.9	
G. Overhead expenses (£ millions)		0.6*	1.2	1.3	1.4	1.5	
H. Depreciation (£ millions)		5.0	5.0	5.0	5.0	5.0	
I. Total expenses (E + F + G + H, in £ millions)		10.3	17.1	19.0	21.0	23.3	
J. Profit before tax (C – I, in £ millions)		–2.8	0.2	1.2	2.2	3.4	
K. U.K. corporate income taxes @ 40% = 0.40 × J**		0.0	0.0	0.0	0.3	1.4	
L. Net profit after tax (J – K, in £ millions)		–2.8	0.2	1.2	1.9	2.0	
M. Terminal value for IDC-U.K. [2.7 × (L + H), for year 5, in £ millions]							19.0
N. Initial investment, including working capital (£ millions)	–26.5						
O. Working capital investment at 20% of revenue (0.2 × C, in £ millions)		1.5	3.5	4.0	4.6	5.3	
P. Required addition to working capital (line O for year t – line O for year t – 1; t = 2, …, 5, in £ millions)	0.0	2.0	0.6	0.6	0.7		
Q. IDC-U.K. net cash flow (L + H + M + N – P, in £ millions)	–26.5	2.2	3.3	5.6	6.3	6.3	19.0
R. £ exchange rate ($)	$2.00	$1.96	$1.92	$1.89	$1.85	$1.82	$1.82
S. IDC-U.K. cash flow (Q × R, in $ millions)	–53.0	4.3	6.3	10.6	11.6	11.5	34.5
T. Present value factor at 12%	1.0	0.8929	0.7972	0.7118	0.6355	0.5674	0.5674
U. Present value (S × T, in $ millions)	–53.0	3.8	5.0	7.5	7.4	6.5	19.6
V. Cumulative present value ($ millions)	–$53.0	–$49.2	–$44.2	–$36.7	–$29.3	–$22.8	–$3.2

* Represents overhead for less than one full year.
** Loss carryforward from year 1 of £2.8 million eliminates tax for years 2 and 3 and reduces tax for year 4.

England and components imported from the United States are assumed to increase by the rate of British inflation, or 5 percent annually. Unit variable costs in the first year are expected to equal £140, including £30 ($60) in components purchased from IDC-U.S.

In addition, the license fees and overhead allocations, which are set at 7 percent of sales, will rise at an annual rate of 15.5 percent because pound revenues are rising at that rate. With a full year of operation, initial overhead expenses would be expected to equal £1.1 million. Actual overhead expenses incurred, however, are only £600,000 because the plant does not begin operation until midyear. These expenses are partially fixed, so their rate of increase should be about 8 percent annually.

The plant and equipment, valued at £25 million, can be written off over five years, yielding an annual depreciation charge against income of £5 million. The cash flow associated with this tax shield remains constant in nominal pound terms but declines in nominal dollar value by 2 percent annually. With a 3 percent rate of U.S. inflation, its real value is, therefore, reduced by 5 percent annually, the same as its loss in real pound terms.

Annual production costs for IDC-U.K. are estimated in Exhibit 17.3, lines D-I. It should be realized, of course, that some of these expenses, like depreciation, are a non-cash charge or, like licensing fees, a benefit to the overall corporation.

Total production costs rise less rapidly each year than the 15.5 percent annual increase in nominal revenue. This situation is due both to the fixed depreciation charge and to the semifixed nature of overhead expenses. Thus, the profit margin should increase over time.

Projected Net Income   Net income for years 1 through 5 is estimated on line L of Exhibit 17.3. The effective tax rate on corporate income faced by IDC-U.K. in England is estimated to be 40 percent. The £2.8 million loss in the first year is applied against income in years 2, 3, and 4, reducing corporate taxes owed in those years.

Additions to Working Capital   One of the major outlays for any new project is the investment in working capital. IDC-U.K. begins with an initial investment in working capital of £1.5 million ($3 million). Working-capital requirements are projected at a constant 20 percent of sales. Thus, the necessary investment in working capital will increase by 15.5 percent annually, the rate of increase in pound sales revenue. These calculations are shown on lines O and P of Exhibit 17.3.

Terminal Value   Calculating a terminal value is a complex undertaking, given the various possible ways to treat this issue. Three different approaches are pointed out. One approach is to assume that the investment will be liquidated after the end of the planning horizon and to use this value. However, this approach just takes the question one step further: What would a prospective buyer be willing to pay for this project? The second approach is to estimate the market value of the project, assuming that it is the present value of remaining cash flows. Again, however, the value of the project to an outside buyer may differ from its value to the parent firm, owing to parent profits on sales to its affiliate, for instance. The third approach is to calculate a break-even terminal value at which the project is just acceptable to the parent and then use that as a benchmark against which to judge the likelihood of the present value of future cash flows exceeding that value.

Most firms try to be quite conservative in estimating terminal values. IDC-U.K. calculates a terminal value based on the assumption that the market value of the project will be 2.7 times the net cash flow in year 5 (net income plus depreciation), or £19.0 million.

Estimated Project Present Value   We are now ready to estimate the net present value of IDC-U.K. from the viewpoint of the project. As shown in Exhibit 17.3, line V, the NPV of project cash flows equals –$3.2 million. Adding to this amount the $2.7 million value of interest subsidies and the $1.4 million present value of the tax shield on interest payments yields an overall positive project net present value of $0.9 million. The estimated value of the interest tax shield would be correspondingly greater if this analysis were to incorporate benefits derived over the full ten-year assumed life of the project, rather than including benefits from the first five years only. Over ten years, the present value of the tax shield would equal $2.3 million, bringing the overall project net present value to $1.8 million. The latter approach is the conceptually correct one.

Despite the favorable net present value for IDC-U.K., it is unlikely a firm would undertake an investment that had a positive value only because of interest subsidies or the interest tax shield provided by the debt capacity of the project. However, this is exactly what most firms do if they accept a marginal project, using a weighted cost of capital. Based on the debt capacity of the project and its subsidized financing, IDC-U.K. would have a weighted cost of capital of approximately 10 percent. At this discount rate, IDC-U.K. would be marginally profitable.

It would be misleading, however, to conclude the analysis at this point without recognizing and accounting for differences between project and parent cash flows and their impact on the worth of investing in IDC-U.K. Ultimately, shareholders in IDC-U.S. will benefit from this investment only to the extent that it generates cash flows that are, or can be, transferred out of England. The value of this investment is now calculated from the viewpoint of IDC-U.S.

Estimation of Parent Cash Flows

From the parent's perspective, additional cash outflows are recorded for any taxes paid to England or the United States on remitted funds. IDC-U.S. has additional cash inflows as well. It receives licensing and overhead allocation fees each year for which it incurs no additional expenses. If it did, the expenses would have to be charged against the fees. IDC-U.S. also profits from exports to its English affiliate.

Loan Payments   IDC-U.K. first will make all necessary loan repayments before paying dividends. Specifically, IDC-U.K. will repay the £1.5 million working-capital loan from Lloyds at the end of year 2 and NEB's loan of £5 million at the end of the fifth year. Their dollar repayment costs are estimated at $2.9 million and $9.3 million, respectively, based on the forecasted exchange rates. These latter two loan repayments are counted as parent cash inflows because they reduce the parent's outstanding consolidated debt burden and increase the value of its equity by an equivalent amount. Assuming that the parent would repay these loans regardless, having IDC-U.K. borrow and repay funds is equivalent to IDC-U.S. borrowing the money, investing it in IDC-U.K., and then using IDC-U.K.'s higher cash flows (because it no longer has British loans to service) to repay IDC-U.S.'s debts.

Remittances to IDC-U.S.   IDC-U.K. is projected to pay dividends equal to 100 percent of its remaining net cash flows after making all necessary loan repayments. It also pays licensing and overhead allocation fees equal, in total, to 7 percent of gross sales. On both of these forms of transfer, the English government will collect a 10 percent withholding tax. These remittances are shown in Exhibit 17.4. IDC-U.S., however, will not owe any further tax to the IRS because the company is assumed to have excess foreign tax credits. Otherwise, IDC-U.S. would have to pay U.S. corporate income taxes on the dividends and fees it receives, less any credits for foreign income and withholding taxes already paid. In this case, IDC-U.K. losses in the first year, combined with the higher British corporate tax rate, will assure that IDC-U.S. would owe minimal taxes to the IRS even if it did not have any excess foreign tax credits.

EXHIBIT 17.4 • Dividends and Fees and Royalties Received by IDC-U.S. (U.S. $ Millions)

			Year			
	1	*2*	*3*	*4*	*5*	*5+*
A. Net cash flow to IDC-U.K. (from Exhibit 17.3, line S)	4.3	6.3	10.6	11.6	11.5	34.5
B. Loan repayments by IDC-U.K.		2.9			9.3	
C. Dividend paid to IDC-U.S. (A–B)	4.3	3.3	10.6	11.6	2.2	34.5
D. Fees and royalties (Exhibit 17.3, line F × line G)	1.0	2.3	2.7	3.0	3.4	15.5*
E. Withholding tax paid to England @ 10% = $0.10 \times (C + D)$	0.5	0.6	1.3	1.5	0.6	5.0
F. Net income received by IDC-U.S. (C + D – E, in $ millions)	$4.8	$5.1	$11.9	$13.1	$5.1	$45.0
G. Exchange rate	$1.96	$1.92	$1.89	$1.85	$1.82	$1.82

* Estimated present value of future fees and royalties. These were not incorporated in the terminal value figure of $25 million.

Earnings on Exports to IDC-U.K.   With a 25 percent margin on its exports, and assuming it has sufficient spare-parts manufacturing capacity, IDC-U.S. has incremental earnings on sales to IDC-U.K. equaling 25 percent of the value of these shipments. After U.S. corporate tax of 35 percent, IDC-U.S. generates cash flows valued at 16.5 percent (25 percent × 65 percent) of its exports to IDC-U.K. These cash flows are presented in Exhibit 17.5.

Estimated Present Value of Project to IDC-U.S.   In Exhibit 17.6, all the various cash flows are added up, net of tax and interest subsidies on debt; and their present value is calculated at $13.0 million. Adding the $5 million in debt-related subsidies ($2.4 million for the interest tax shield and $2.6 million for the NEB loan subsidy) brings this value up to $18.0 million. It is apparent that, despite the additional taxes that must be paid to England and the United States, IDC-U.K. is more valuable to its parent than it would be to another owner on a stand-alone basis. This situation is due primarily to the various licensing and overhead allocation fees received and the incremental earnings on exports to IDC-U.K.

Lost Sales   There is a circumstance, however, that can reverse this conclusion. This discussion has assumed that IDC-U.S. is now producing at capacity and that the 20,000 diesels currently being exported to the EC can be sold in the United States, starting in year 2. Should this assumption not be the case (that is, should 20,000 units of IDC-U.K. sales

EXHIBIT 17.5 • Net Cash Flows from Exports to IDC-U.K.

			Year			
	1	*2*	*3*	*4*	*5*	*5+*
A. Sales (units)	30,000	66,000	73,000	80,000	88,000	88,000
B. Components purchased from IDC-U.S.						
1. Unit price ($)	60.0	61.8	63.7	65.6	67.5	67.5
2. Total export revenue (A × B1 in $ millions)	1.8	4.1	4.6	5.2	5.9	5.9
C. After-tax cash flow (0.165 × B2 in $ millions)	$0.3	$0.7	$0.8	$0.9	$1.0	$1.0

EXHIBIT 17.6 • PRESENT VALUE OF IDC-U.K.: PARENT VIEWPOINT (U.S. $ MILLIONS)

				Year			
	0	1	2	3	4	5	5+
A. Cash inflows							
1. Loan repayments by IDC-U.K. (from Exhibit 17.4, line B)			2.9			9.3	
2. Dividends paid to IDC-U.S. (from Exhibit 17.4, line C)		4.3	3.3	10.6	11.6	2.2	34.5
3. Fees and royalties paid to IDC-U.S. (from Exhibit 17.4, line D)		1.0	2.3	2.7	3.0	3.4	15.5
4. Net cash flows from exports (from Exhibit 17.5, line C)		0.3	0.7	0.8	0.9	1.0	4.1*
5. Total cash inflows		5.6	9.3	14.0	15.4	15.9	54.1
B. Cash outflows							
1. Plant and equipment	50.0						
2. Working capital	3.0						
3. Withholding tax paid to U.K. (from Exhibit 17.4, line E)		0.5	0.6	1.3	1.5	0.6	5.0
4. Total cash outflows	53.0	0.5	0.6	1.3	1.5	0.6	5.0
C. Net cash flow (A5 – B4)	–53.0	5.1	8.7	12.7	14.0	15.3	49.1
D. Present-value factor at 12%	1.0	0.8929	0.7972	0.7118	0.6355	0.5674	0.5674
E. Present value (C × D)	–53.0	4.5	6.9	9.0	8.9	8.7	27.9
F. Cumulative present value ($ millions)	–$53.0	–$48.5	–$41.5	–$32.5	–$23.6	–$14.9	$13.0

* Estimated present value of future earnings on export sales to IDC-U.K.

just replace 20,000 units of IDC-U.S. sales), then the project would have to be charged with the incremental cash flow that IDC-U.S. would have earned on these lost exports. We now see how to incorporate this effect in a capital-budgeting analysis.

Suppose the incremental after-tax cash flow per unit to IDC-U.S. on its exports to the EC equals $180 at present, and that this contribution is expected to maintain its value in current dollar terms over time. Then, in nominal dollar terms, this margin grows by 3 percent annually. If we assume lost sales of 20,000 units per year, beginning in year 2 and extending through year 10, and a discount rate of 12 percent, the present value associated with these lost sales equals $19.5 million. The calculations are presented in Exhibit 17.7. Subtracting the present value of lost sales from the previously calculated present value of $18.0 million yields a net present value of IDC-U.K. to its parent equal to –$1.5 million (–$6.5 million ignoring the interest tax shield and subsidy).

This example points up the importance of looking at incremental cash flows generated by a foreign project rather than total cash flows. An investment that would be marginally profitable on its own, and quite profitable when integrated with parent activities, becomes unprofitable when taking into account earnings on lost sales.

17.4 POLITICAL RISK ANALYSIS

It is apparent from the figures in Exhibit 17.6 that IDC-U.S.'s English investment is quite sensitive to the potential political risks of currency controls and expropriation. The net

EXHIBIT 17.7 • VALUE OF LOST EXPORT SALES

	Year								
	2	3	4	5	6	7	8	9	10
A. Lost unit sales	20,000	20,000	20,000	20,000	20,000	20,000	20,000	20,000	20,000
B. Cash flow per unit*	185.4	191.0	196.7	202.6	208.7	214.9	221.4	228.0	234.9
C. Total cash flow from exports (A × B)	3.7	3.8	3.9	4.1	4.2	4.3	4.4	4.6	4.7
D. Present value factor at 12%	0.7972	0.7118	0.6355	0.5674	0.5066	0.4523	0.4039	0.3606	0.3220
E. Present value (C × D)	3.0	2.7	2.5	2.5	2.1	1.9	1.8	1.6	1.5
F. Cumulative present value	$3.0	$5.7	$8.2	$8.2	$12.6	$14.5	$16.3	$18.0	$19.5

* The figures in this row grow by 3 percent each year. So, 185.4 = 180(1.03), and so on.

present value of the project does not turn positive until well after its fifth year of operation (assuming there are no lost sales). Should expropriation occur or exchange controls be imposed at some point during the first five years, it is unlikely that the project will ever be viable from the parent's standpoint. Only if compensation is sufficiently great in the event of expropriation, or if unremitted funds can earn a return reflecting their opportunity cost to IDC-U.S. with eventual repatriation in the event of exchange controls, can this project still be viable in the face of these risks.

> Political risks can be incorporated into an NPV analysis by adjusting expected project cash flows to reflect these risks.

The general approach recommended previously for incorporating political risk in an investment analysis usually involves adjusting the cash flows of the project (rather than its required rate of return) to reflect the impact of a particular political event on the present value of the project to the parent. This section shows how these cash-flow adjustments can be made for the cases of expropriation and exchange controls.

Expropriation

The extreme form of political risk is **expropriation**. Expropriation is an obvious case where project and parent company cash flows diverge. The approach suggested here examines directly the impact of expropriation on the present value of the project to the parent. The example of United Fruit Company shows how the technique of adjusting expected cash flows can be used to evaluate how expropriation affects the value of specific projects.

 ILLUSTRATION   *United Fruit Company Calculates the Consequences of Expropriation*

Suppose that United Fruit Company (UFC) is worried that its banana plantation in Honduras will be expropriated during the next twelve months.[3] The Honduran government has promised, however, that compensation of $100 million will be paid at the year's end if the plantation is expropriated. UFC believes that this promise would be kept. If expropriation does not occur this year, it will not occur any time in the foreseeable future.

[3] Illustration suggested by Richard Roll.

The plantation is expected to be worth $300 million at the end of the year. A wealthy Honduran has just offered UFC $128 million for the plantation. If UFC's risk-adjusted discount rate is 22 percent, what is the probability of expropriation at which UFC is just indifferent between selling now or holding onto its plantation?

Exhibit 17.8 displays UFC's two choices and their consequences. If UFC sells out now, it will receive $128 million today. Alternatively, if it chooses to hold on to the plantation, its property will be worth $300 million if expropriation does not occur, and worth only $100 million in the event the Honduran government expropriates its plantation and compensates UFC. If the probability of expropriation is p, then the expected end-of-year value of the plantation to UFC (in millions of dollars) is $100p + 300(1 - p) = 300 - 200p$. The present value of the amount, using UFC's discount rate of 22 percent, is $(300 - 200p)/1.22$. Setting this equal to the $128 million offer by the wealthy Honduran yields a value of $p = 72$ percent. In other words, if the probability of expropriation is at least 72 percent, UFC should sell out now for $128 million. If the probability of expropriation is less than 72 percent, it would be more worthwhile for UFC to hold on to its plantation.

EXHIBIT 17.8 • UNITED FRUIT COMPANY'S CHOICES (U.S. $ MILLIONS)

	Expropriation	*No Expropriation*	*Expected Present Value*
Sell out now	128	128	128
Wait	100	300	$[100p + 300(1 - p)]/1.22$

Blocked Funds

The same method of adjusting expected cash flows can be used to analyze the effects of various exchange controls which lead to **blocked funds**. This methodology is illustrated by the example of Brascan. In any discussion of blocked funds, it must be pointed out that if all funds are expected to be blocked in perpetuity, then the value of the project is zero.

ILLUSTRATION   *Brascan Calculates the Consequences of Currency Controls*

On January 1, 1981, the Indonesian electrical authority expropriated a power-generating station owned by Brascan, Inc., a Canadian operator of foreign electric facilities.[4] In compensation, a perpetuity of C$50 million will be paid annually at the end of each year. Brascan believes, however, that the Indonesian Central Bank may block currency repatriations during the calendar year 1983, allowing only 75 percent of each year's payment to be repatriated (and no repatriation of reinvestments from the other 25 percent). Assuming a cost of capital of 20 percent and a probability of currency blockage of 40 percent, what is the current value (on January 1, 1981) of Indonesia's compensation?

Exhibit 17.9 displays the two possibilities and their consequences for the cash flows Brascan expects to receive. If currency controls are not imposed, Brascan will receive C$50 million annually, with the first payment due December 31, 1981. The present value of this stream of cash equals C$250 million (50/0.2). Alternatively, if controls are imposed, Brascan will receive C$50 million at the end of the first two years and C$37.5 million (50 × 0.75) on each December 31 thereafter. The present value of these cash flows is C$206.6 million [$50/1.2 + 50/(1.2)^2 + (37.5/0.2)/(1.2)^2$].[5] Weighting these present values by the probability that each will come to pass yields an expected present value (in millions of Canadian dollars) of $0.6 × 250 + 0.4 × 206.6 = C232.6 million.

---

[4] Illustration suggested by Richard Roll.

[5] As of the end of year 2 the $37.5 million annuity beginning in year 3 has a present value equal to 37.5/0.2. The present value of this annuity as of today equals $[37.5/0.2]/(1.2)^2$.

EXHIBIT 17.9 • CASH FLOWS TO BRASCAN (C$ MILLIONS)

	Cash Flow at Year End		
	1981	1982	1983 and On
Currency controls	50.0	50.0	37.5
No currency controls	50.0	50.0	50.0

17.5 GROWTH OPTIONS AND PROJECT EVALUATION

The discounted cash flow (DCF) analysis presented so far treats a project's expected cash flows as given at the outset. This approach presupposes a static approach to investment decision making: It assumes that all operating decisions are set in advance. In reality, however, the opportunity to make decisions contingent on information to become available in the future is an essential feature of many investment decisions.

Options are an important component of many investment decisions.

Consider the decision of whether to reopen a gold mine. The cost of doing so is expected to be $1 million. There are an estimated 40,000 ounces of gold remaining in the mine. If the mine is reopened, the gold can be removed in one year at a variable cost of $390 per ounce. Assuming an expected gold price in one year of $400/ounce, the expected profit per ounce mined is $10. Clearly, the expected cash inflow (ignoring taxes) of $400,000 next year ($10 × 40,000) is far below that necessary to recoup the $1 million investment in reopening the mine, much less to pay the 15 percent yield required on such a risky investment. However, intuition—which suggests a highly negative project NPV of –$652,174 (–$1 million + 400,000/1.15)—is wrong in this case. The reason is that the cash-flow projections underlying the classical DCF analysis ignore the option *not* to produce gold if it is unprofitable to do so.

Here is a simple example that demonstrates the fallacy of always using expected cash flows to judge an investment's merits. Suppose there are only two possible gold prices next year: $300/ounce and $500/ounce, each with probability 0.5. The expected gold price is $400/ounce, but this expected price is irrelevant to the optimal mining decision rule: Mine gold if, and only if, the price of gold at year's end is $500/ounce. Exhibit 17.10 shows the cash-flow consequences of that decision rule. Closure costs are assumed to be zero.

Incorporating the mine owner's option *not* to mine gold when the price falls below the cost of extraction reveals a positive net present value of $913,043 for the decision to reopen the gold mine:

$$\frac{\text{NPV of gold mine}}{\text{investment}} = -\$1,000,000 + \frac{\$2,200,000}{1.15}$$

$$= \$913,043$$

Ignoring the options associated with an investment will understate the NPV of that investment.

As the example of the gold mine demonstrates, the ability to alter decisions in response to new information may contribute significantly to the value of a project. Such investments bear the characteristics of options on securities and should be valued accordingly. As we saw in the case of foreign exchange, a call option gives the holder the right, but not the obligation, to buy a security at a fixed, predetermined price (called the exercise price) on or before some fixed future date. By way of analogy, the opportunities a firm may have to invest capital to increase the profitability of its existing product lines and benefit from expanding into new products or markets may be thought of as **growth options**.[6] Similarly, a firm's ability to capitalize on its managerial talent, experience in a particular product line, its brand name, technology, or its other resources may provide valuable but uncertain future prospects.

---

[6] A good discussion of growth options is contained in W. Carl Kester, "Today's Options for Tomorrow's Growth," *Harvard Business Review,* March–April 1984, pp. 153–160.

EXHIBIT 17.10 • THE GOLD MINE OPERATING DECISION

Growth options are
of great importance
to multinational
firms and requires
an expanded NPV
rule.

Growth options are of great importance to multinational firms. Consider the value of IDC-U.K.'s production and market positions at the end of its planning horizon. IDC-U.S. may increase or decrease the diesel plant's output depending on current market conditions, expectations of future demand, and relative cost changes, such as those due to currency movements. The plant can be expanded; it can be shut down and then reopened when production and market conditions are more favorable; or it can be abandoned permanently. Each decision is an option from the viewpoint of IDC-U.S. The value of these options, in turn, affects the value of the investment in IDC-U.K.

Moreover, by producing locally, IDC-U.S. will have an enhanced market position in the EC that may enable the company to expand its product offerings at a later date. The ability to exploit this market position depends on the results of IDC-U.S.'s R&D efforts and the shifting pattern of demand for its products. In all these cases, the optimal operating policy depends on outcomes that are not known at the project's inception.

Investments in
emerging markets
can be viewed as
growth options.

Similarly, the investments that many Western firms are now considering in Eastern Europe can also be thought of as growth options. Some view investments there as a way to gain entry into a potentially large market. Others see Eastern Europe as an underdeveloped area with educated and skilled workers but low wages, and they view such investments as a low-cost backdoor to Western European markets. In either case, companies that invest there are buying an option that will pay off in the event that Eastern European markets boom, or that Eastern European workers turn out to be much more productive with the right technology and incentives than they were under Communism. Other investments are undertaken, in part, to gain knowledge that can later be capitalized on elsewhere. For example, in announcing its plans to build in Alabama, Mercedes officials said the factory would serve as a laboratory for learning to build cars more efficiently. Similarly, several Regional Bell Operating Companies (RBOCs) such as SBC Communications and USWest Communications established operations in Great Britain to learn how—and whether—to provide services such as cable TV, combined cable TV and telephone service, and personal communications services (PCS) that were prohibited to RBOCs in the U.S. market. By failing to take into account the benefits of operating flexibility, learning, and potentially valuable add-on projects, the traditional DCF will tend to understate project values.

The problem of undervaluing investment projects using the standard DCF analysis is particularly acute for strategic investments. Many strategically important investments, such as investments in R&D, factory automation, a brand name, or a distribution network, provide growth opportunities because they are often only the first link in a chain of subsequent investment decisions.

Valuing investments that embody discretionary follow-up projects requires an expanded net present value rule that considers the attendant options. More specifically, the value of an option to undertake a follow-up project equals the expected project NPV using the conventional discounted cash-flow analysis plus the value of the discretion associated with undertaking the project. This relation is shown in Exhibit 17.11. Based on the discussion of currency options in Chapter 8, the latter element of value (the discretion to invest or not invest in a project) depends on the following.

1. *The length of time the project can be deferred:* The ability to defer a project gives the firm more time to examine the course of future events and to avoid costly errors if unfavorable developments occur. A longer time interval also raises the odds that a positive turn of events will dramatically boost the project's profitability and turn even a negative NPV project into a positive one.

2. *The risk of the project:* Surprisingly, the riskier the investment, the more valuable is an option on it. The reason is the asymmetry between gains and losses. A large gain is possible if the project's NPV becomes highly positive, whereas losses are limited by the option not to exercise when the project NPV is negative. The riskier the project, the greater the odds of a large gain without a corresponding increase in the size of the potential loss. Thus, growth options are likely to be especially valuable for MNCs because of the large potential variation in costs and the competitive environment.

Options on riskier projects are more valuable.

3. *The level of interest rates:* Although a high discount rate lowers the present value of a project's future cash flows, it also reduces the present value of the cash outlay needed to exercise an option. The net effect is that high interest rates generally raise the value of projects that contain growth options.

4. *The proprietary nature of the option:* An exclusively owned option is clearly more valuable than one that is shared with others. The latter might include the chance to enter a new market or to invest in a new production process. Shared options are less valuable because competitors can replicate the investments and drive down returns. For the multinational firm, however, most growth options arise out of its intangible assets. These assets, which take the form of skills, knowledge, brand names, and the like, are difficult to replicate and so are likely to be more valuable.

EXHIBIT 17.11 • VALUING A GROWTH OPTION TO UNDERTAKE A FOLLOW-UP PROJECT

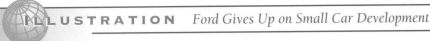

ILLUSTRATION   *Ford Gives Up on Small Car Development*

In late 1986, Ford gave up on small-car development in the United States and handed over the job to Japan's Mazda, in which Ford owned a 25 percent stake. Although seemingly cost-effective in the short run (Ford should save about $500 million in development costs for one car model alone), such a move—which removed a critical mass from Ford's own engineering efforts—could prove dangerous in the longer term. Overcoming engineering obstacles unique to subcompact cars—for example, the challenges of miniaturization—enhances engineers' skills and allows them to apply innovations to all classes of vehicles. By eroding its technological base, Ford may have yielded the option of generating ideas that can be applied elsewhere in its business. Moreover, the cost of reentering the business of in-house design can be substantial. The abandonment option is not one to be exercised lightly.

Some American consumer-electronics companies, for example, are learning the penalties of ceding major technologies and the experiences that come from working with these technologies on a day-to-day basis. Westinghouse Electric (now CBS), after quitting the development and manufacture of color television tubes in 1976, later decided to get back into the color-video business. However, because it lost touch with the product, Westinghouse was able to reenter only by way of a joint venture with Japan's Toshiba.

Similarly, RCA and other U.S. manufacturers years ago conceded to the Japanese development of videocassette recorders and laser video disc players. Each technology has since spawned entirely new, popular product lines—from video cameras to compact disc players—in which U.S. companies are left with nothing to do beyond marketing Japanese-made goods.

To take another example, RCA and Westinghouse first discovered the principles of liquid crystal displays (LCDs) in the 1960s. But where the Americans did not follow up with investment and development, Japanese companies did. Sharp, Seiko, and Casio used LCDs in calculators and digital watches. That gave them knowledge of the technology so that later, when laptop computers developed needs for sophisticated graphics and color pictures, Japanese manufacturers could deliver increasingly capable screens.

Even those companies that merely turn to outside partners for technical help could nevertheless find their skills atrophying over the years as their partners handle more of the complex designing and manufacturing. Such companies range from Boeing, which has enlisted three Japanese firms to help engineer a new plane, to Honeywell, which is getting big computers from NEC. The corresponding reduction in in-house technological skills decreases the value of the option these firms have to develop and apply new technologies in novel product areas.

17.6 SUMMARY AND CONCLUSIONS

Capital budgeting for the multinational corporation presents many elements that rarely, if ever, exist in domestic capital budgeting. The primary thrust of this chapter has been to adjust project cash flows instead of the discount rate to reflect the key political and economic risks that MNCs face abroad. Tax factors are also incorporated via cash-flow adjustments. Cash-flow adjustments are preferred on the pragmatic grounds that more and better information is available on the effect of such risks on future cash flows than on the required discount rate. Furthermore, adjusting the required rate of return of a project to reflect incremental risk does not usually allow for adequate consideration of the time pattern and magnitude of the risk being evaluated. Using a uniformly higher discount rate to reflect additional risk involves penalizing future cash flows relatively more heavily than present ones.

This chapter showed how these cash-flow adjustments can be carried out by presenting a lengthy numerical example. It also discussed the significant differences that can exist between project and parent cash flows and showed how these differences can be accounted for when estimating the value to the parent firm of a foreign investment. The chapter also pointed out that failure to take into account the options available to managers to adjust the scope of a project will lead to a downward bias in estimating project cash flows. These options include the possibility of expanding or contracting the project or abandoning it, the chance to employ radical new process technologies by utilizing skills developed from implementing the project, and the possibility of entering the new lines of business to which a project may lead.

QUESTIONS

1. A foreign project that is profitable when valued on its own will always be profitable from the parent firm's standpoint. True or false. Explain.

2. What are the principal cash outflows associated with the IDC-U.K. project?

3. What are the principal cash inflows associated with the IDC-U.K. project?

4. In what ways do parent and project cash flows differ on the IDC-U.K. project? Why?

5. Why are loan repayments by IDC-U.K. to Lloyds and NEB treated as a cash inflow to the parent company?

6. How sensitive is the value of the project to the threat of currency controls and expropriation? How can the financing be structured to make the project less sensitive to these political risks?

7. What options does investment in the new British diesel plant provide to IDC-U.S.? How can these options be accounted for in the traditional capital-budgeting analysis?

8. Early results on the Lexus, Toyota's upscale car, showed it was taking the most business from customers changing from BMW (15 percent), Mercedes (14 percent), Toyota (14 percent), General Motors' Cadillac (12 percent), and Ford's Lincoln (6 percent). With what in the auto business is considered a high percentage of sales coming from its own customers (14 percent), how badly is Toyota hurting itself with the Lexus?

9. Comment on the following statement that appeared in *The Economist* (August 20, 1988, p. 60): "Those oil producers that have snapped up overseas refineries—Kuwait, Venezuela, Libya and, most recently, Saudi Arabia—can feed the flabbiest of them with dollar-a-barrel crude and make a profit. ... The majority of OPEC's existing overseas refineries would be scrapped without its own cheap oil to feed them. Both Western European refineries fed by Libyan oil (in West Germany and Italy) and Kuwait's two overseas refineries (in Holland and Denmark) would almost certainly be idle without it."

10. In December 1989, General Electric spent $150 million to buy a controlling interest in Tungsram, the Hungarian state-owned light bulb maker. Even in its best year, Tungsram earned less than a 4 percent return on equity (based on the price GE paid).

    a. What might account for GE's decision to spend so much money to acquire such a dilapidated, inefficient manufacturer?

    b. A Hungarian lighting worker earns about $170 a month in Hungary, compared with about $1,700 a month in the United States. Do these figures indicate that Tungsram will be a low-cost producer? Explain.

PROBLEMS

1. Suppose England raised its corporate tax rate by 1 percentage point. How would this increase affect the economics of the IDC-U.K. project?

2. Suppose a firm projects a $5 million perpetuity from an investment of $20 million in Spain. If the required return on this investment is 20 percent, how large does the probability of expropriation in year 4 have to be before the investment has a negative NPV? Assume that all cash inflows occur at the end of each year and that the expropriation, if it occurs, will occur just before the year-4 cash inflow or not at all. There is no compensation in the event of expropriation.

3. Suppose a firm has just made an investment in France that will generate $2 million annually in depreciation, converted at today's spot rate. Projected annual rates of inflation in France and in the United States are 7 percent and 4 percent, respectively. If the real exchange rate is expected to remain constant and the French tax rate is 50 percent, what is the expected real value (in terms of today's dollars) of the depreciation charge in year 5, assuming that the tax write-off is taken at the end of the year?

4. Jim Toreson, chairman and CEO of Xebec Corporation, a Sunnyvale, California, manufacturer of disk-drive controllers, is trying to decide whether

to switch to offshore production. Given Xebec's well-developed engineering and marketing capabilities, Toreson could use offshore manufacturing to ramp up production, taking full advantage of both low-wage labor and a grab bag of tax holidays, low-interest loans, and other government largess. Most of his competitors seem to be doing it. The faster he follows suit, the better off Xebec would be according to the conventional discounted cash-flow analysis, which shows that switching production offshore is clearly a positive NPV investment. However, Toreson is concerned that such a move would entail the loss of certain intangible strategic benefits associated with domestic production.

a. What might be some strategic benefits of domestic manufacturing for Xebec? Consider the fact that its customers are all U.S. firms and that manufacturing technology—particularly automation skills—is key to survival in this business.

b. What analytic framework can be used to factor these intangible strategic benefits of domestic manufacturing (which are intangible costs of offshore production) into the factory location decision?

c. How would the possibility of radical shifts in manufacturing technology affect the production location decision?

d. Xebec is considering producing more sophisticated drives that require substantial customization. How does this possibility affect its production decision?

e. Suppose the Taiwan government is willing to provide a loan of $10 million at 5 percent to Xebec to build a factory there. The loan would be paid off in equal annual installments over a five-year period. If the market interest rate for such an investment is 14 percent, what is the before-tax value of the interest subsidy?

f. Projected before-tax income from the Taiwan plant is $1 million annually, beginning at the end of the first year. Taiwan's corporate tax rate is 25 percent, and there is a 20 percent dividend withholding tax. However, Taiwan will exempt the plant's income from corporate tax (but not withholding tax) for the first five years. If Xebec plans to remit all income as dividends back to the United States, how much is the tax holiday worth?

g. An alternative sourcing option is to shut down all domestic production and contract to have Xebec's products built for it by a foreign supplier in a country such as Japan. What are some of the potential advantages and disadvantages of foreign contracting vis-à-vis manufacturing in a wholly owned foreign subsidiary?

BIBLIOGRAPHY

Kester, W. Carl. "Today's Options for Tomorrow's Growth." *Harvard Business Review,* March–April 1984, pp. 153–160.

Lessard, Donald R. "Evaluating Foreign Projects: An Adjusted Present Value Approach." In *International Financial Management,* 2nd ed., edited by Donald R. Lessard. New York: John Wiley & Sons, 1985.

Shapiro, Alan C. "Capital Budgeting for the Multinational Corporation." *Financial Management,* Spring 1978, pp. 7–16.

_____. "International Capital Budgeting." *Midland Journal of Corporate Finance,* Spring 1983, pp. 26–45.

INTERNET RESOURCES

globaledge.msu.edu/ibrd/ibrd.asp Web site run by Michigan State University (MSU) that contains links to various country information helpful for making investment decisions.

www.bloomberg.com Web site of Bloomberg. Contains a wealth of financial and economic information on financial markets and countries worldwide.

www.economist.com Web site of *The Economist.* Contains stories on the economic and political situations of countries and international business developments, along with various national and international economic and financial data.

INTERNET EXERCISES

1. Given exchange rate changes over the past month, how would you revise cash-flow projections for a planned project in Mexico? How would the nature of the project—export-oriented versus producing for the Mexican market—affect your revised cash flows?

2. Based on recent political and economic changes in Mexico gleaned from the MSU, Bloomberg, and/or *The Economist* Web sites, how would you revise cash flows for the project mentioned in the previous question?

PART V CASE STUDIES

CASE V.1
THE INTERNATIONAL MACHINE CORPORATION*

The International Machine Corporation (IMC) is a large, well-established manufacturer of a wide variety of food processing and packaging equipment. Total revenue for last year was $12 billion, of which 45 percent was generated outside of the United States. IMC has subsidiaries in twenty-three countries, with licensing arrangements in eight others.

The management of IMC is currently contemplating the establishment of a subsidiary in Mexico. IMC has been exporting products to Mexico for several years, and its international division believes there is sufficient demand for the product and that a Mexican investment might be appropriate at this time. More important, management believes that the Mexican market is expanding, that the economy is growing, and that producing such products locally appears to be consistent with the national aspirations of the Mexican government.

Mexican inflation is projected to be 20 percent annually, and the U.S. inflation rate is expected to be 10 percent annually. The current exchange rate is $1 = Ps 7.2 and is expected to remain fixed in real terms over the life of the investment. The following list contains details of the contemplated investment.

1. Initial investment
   a. It is estimated that it would take one year to purchase and install plant and equipment.
   b. Imported machinery and equipment will cost $9 million. No import duties will be levied by the Mexican government. With a small allowance for banking fees, the bill will come to Ps 65.5 million.
   c. The plant would be set up on government-owned land that will be sold to the project for Ps 6.5 million.
   d. IMC plans to maintain effective control of the subsidiary with ownership of 60 percent of equity. The remaining 40 percent is to be distributed widely among Mexican financial institutions and private investors.

Accordingly, IMC needs to invest U.S. $6 million in the project.

2. Working capital
   a. The company plans to maintain 5 percent of annual sales as a minimum cash balance.
   b. Accounts receivable are estimated to be 73 days of annual sales.
   c. Inventory is estimated to be 20 percent of annual sales.
   d. Accounts payable are estimated to be 10 percent of annual sales.
   e. Other payables are estimated to be 5 percent of annual sales.
   f. Licensing and overhead allocation fees are paid annually at the end of the year.

3. Sales volume
   a. Sales volume for the first year is estimated to be 200 units.
   b. Selling price in the first year will be Ps 458,000 per unit.
   c. Unit sales growth of 10 percent is expected during the project life.
   d. An annual price increase of 20 percent is expected.

4. Cost of goods sold
   a. The U.S. parent company is expected to provide parts and components adding up to Ps 59,000 per unit in the first year of operation. These costs (in U.S. dollars) are expected to rise on an average of 10 percent annually, in line with the projected U.S. inflation rate.
   b. Local material and labor costs are expected to be Ps 137,000 per unit, with an annual rate of increase of 20 percent.
   c. Manufacturing overhead (without depreciation) is expected to be Ps 9.2 million the first year of operation. An average rate of increase of 15 percent is expected.
   d. Depreciation of manufacturing equipment is to be computed on a straightline basis, with a projected life of ten years and zero salvage value to be assumed.

---

* *Source:* This is an edited version of "The International Machine Corporation: An Analysis of Investment in Mexico," by Vinod B. Bavishi, University of Connecticut, and Haney A. Shawkey, State University of New York at Albany. Permission to use this case was provided by Professors Bavishi and Shawkey.

5. Selling and administrative costs

   a. The variable portion of selling and administrative costs are expected to equal 10 percent of annual sales revenue.

   b. Semifixed selling costs are expected to equal 5 percent of the first year's sales. These costs will then rise at 15 percent annually.

6. Licensing and overhead allocation fees

   a. The parent company will levy Ps 23,000 per unit as licensing and overhead allocation fees, payable at year end in U.S. dollars.

   b. This fee will increase 20 percent per year to compensate for Mexican inflation.

7. Interest expense

   a. Local borrowings can be obtained for working capital purposes at 15 percent. Borrowing will occur at the end of the year with the full year's interest budgeted in the following year.

   b. Any excess funds can be invested in Mexican marketable securities with an annual rate of return of 15 percent. Investment will be made at the end of the year, with the full year's interest to be received in the following year.

8. Income taxes

   a. Corporate income taxes in Mexico are 42 percent of taxable income.

   b. Withholding taxes on licensing and overhead allocation fees are 20 percent.

   c. The parent company's effective U.S. tax rate is 35 percent, which is the rate used in analyzing investment projects. It can be assumed that the parent company can take appropriate credits for taxes paid to, or withheld by, the Mexican government.

9. Dividend payments

   a. No dividends will be paid for the first three years.

   b. Dividends equal to 70 percent of earnings will be paid to the shareholders, beginning in the fourth year.

10. Terminal payment

    It is assumed that, at the end of the tenth year of operation, IMC's share of net worth in the Mexican subsidiary will be remitted in the form of a terminal payment.

11. Parent company's capital structure

    a. Domestic debt equals U.S. $1 billion with an average before-tax cost of 12 percent. The cost of new long-term debt is estimated at 14 percent before tax.

    b. An amount equivalent to $600 million of parent debt is denominated in various foreign currencies, and after adjusting for previous exchange gains/losses the cost (or effective cost) of this debt has averaged 16 percent.

    c. Shareholder equity (capital, surplus, and retained earnings) equals U.S. $1.5 billion. The company plans to pay U.S. $3.20 in dividends per share during the coming year. Over the last ten years, earnings and dividends have grown at a compounded rate of 7 percent. The market price of common stock was $40, and number of shares outstanding were 60 million as of last December 31.

12. Exports lost

    At present IMC is exporting about 25 units per year to Mexico. If IMC decides to establish the Mexican subsidiary, it is expected that the after-tax effects on income due to the lost exports sales would be $648,000, $742,000, and $930,000 in the first three years of operation, respectively. IMC assumes it cannot count on these export sales for more than three years because the Mexican government is determined to see that such machinery is manufactured locally in the near future.

QUESTIONS

1. Should IMC make this investment?
2. What is IMC's required rate of return for this project?
3. What factors and assumptions are critical to your project analysis?

 CASE V.2
EURO DISNEYLAND

It is 1987, and in a muddy sugar-beet field twenty miles east of Paris, Walt Disney Co. is creating Euro Disneyland. By the time of its scheduled opening in 1992, Euro Disneyland (EDL) is expected to cost FF 15 billion ($2.5 billion based on an exchange rate of FF 6 = $1). Most signs point to the park's success. Two million Europeans already visit its American parks every year. And Paris demographics look great: In two hours, 17 million people could drive to the park and 310 million people could fly to the park.

Disney's risk appears to be modest. It has invested $350 million in planning the park but has put up just $145 million for 49 percent of EDL's equity. Public investors will pay $1 billion for the other 51 percent in a stock offering in October 1989. The public company, through its traded shares, will give Europeans a chance to participate in the success of the project once the gates open in 1992. (When the stock begins trading on the Paris Bourse in October 1989, Disney's stake will be valued at $1 billion—an $855 million gain in value.)

Even if profits are weak, Disney will rake in fat management fees. And it could clean up just on the land: It has rights to buy 4,800 acres from the government at just $7,500 an acre—compared with $750,000 an acre for similar land in the area. Disney can resell chunks to other developers for any price it can get. The acreage should jump in value once high-speed rail lines from Paris and London (via the Chunnel, the tunnel under the English Channel) are in place.

But there is risk nonetheless. The most critical variable is attendance. Many experts think surprises may await Disney. They doubt that attendance will meet Disney's expectations. Others think that the crowds will come but will spend less than Disney projects. Disney faces other unknowns as well. MCA/Universal, which will be bought by Matsushita in 1990, is thinking of building a park in London, which would cannibalize Euro Disneyland's attendance. There's also the grim winter weather, which prompts European parks to close until spring. Then there's the challenge of training 12,000 Europeans, half of them French, to be Disney "cast members." Bowing to French individualism, Disney will relax its personal grooming code a bit. Disney may also decide to change its ban on booze if customers call loudly enough for wine and beer. Disney claims that its experience with Tokyo Disneyland, its last major development project, shows that it can deal with non-American culture and bad weather. Tokyo Disneyland was completed on time and within 1 percent of budget. It has also been a huge commercial success.

FINANCING

In March 1987, Disney and the French government sign a "Master Agreement" for Euro Disneyland. In accordance with that agreement, Disney forms a holding company to control development of the entire site. It pays $145 million for 49 percent of the holding company's shares and sells 51 percent of EDL to European investors for a little over $1 billion; of the latter shares, around half are sold to the French.

The holding company set up as an SCA (*Societé Commanditeé par Actions*), a unique French corporate form that is very similar to an American limited partnership. Disney is the *gerant,* or general partner. The SCA structure allows Disney to control management, even with a minority shareholding. Thus, even though the holding company owns EDL, Disney will manage it and collect an estimated $35 million a year in royalties on sales of admission tickets, food, and souvenirs.

The master agreement is basically an inducement for Disney to bring Euro Disneyland to Paris rather than to Spain's Mediterranean coast. The inducements include the following:

- Loans of up to FF 4.8 billion are available from a French government agency. The loans carry a fixed interest rate of 7.85 percent, in contrast to a normal commercial rate of 9.25 percent.

- EDL can use accelerated depreciation to write off the construction costs of its extravaganza over a ten-year period.

- The French government will invest $350 million in park-related infrastructure. This includes sewer and telephone trunk lines, subway and road links to Paris, and a new line of its 156-mile-per-hour *train a grande vitesse* (TGV) that will link EDL to the Chunnel (and thence to London), Brussels, and Lyons.

- Disney is allowed to buy 4,800 acres of land at 1971 prices. The average cost is FF 11.1 per square meter compared with FF 1,000 per square meter for development land in the Paris suburbs.

- The French government agrees to cut the value-added tax (VAT) on ticket sales to just 7 percent instead of the usual 18.5 percent.

Disney will structure the $2.5 billion Euro Disneyland project so that the operating losses created during construction can be used, along with the accelerated depreciation benefits, as tax shelters. These tax benefits will be sold to a group of French companies for $200 million. Equity contributions include the $1.15 billion stock sale plus Disney's $350 million investment in project planning. The remaining $800 million of project financing will come from loans subsidized by the French government. The repayment schedule on these loans is as follows (in FF millions):

1992–1996	1997	1998	1999	2000	2001
0	FF 960	FF 960	FF 960	FF 960	FF 960

Euro Disneyland will also require about $115 million in working capital initially, and this amount is expected to grow at the rate of sales revenue. The working capital will be financed by French franc bank loans carrying an interest rate expected to average about 9.5 percent annually.

FINANCIAL PROJECTIONS

Disney's projections assume a minimum 1992 attendance rate at Euro Disneyland of 11 million visitor-days and maximum of 16 million. These numbers compare with 1988 attendance at the domestic U.S. parks of 25.1 million for Orlando's Disney World and 13 million for Anaheim's Disneyland. In projections of future years' attendance, a conservative 3 percent annual growth rate is reasonable. The range of EDL attendance figures based on these assumptions is shown in Exhibit V2.1.

EXHIBIT V2.1 • PROJECTED NUMBER OF VISITOR DAYS AT EURO DISNEYLAND (MILLIONS)

1992	1993	1994	1995	1996
11	11.3	11.7	12.0	12.4
12	12.4	12.7	13.1	13.5
13	13.4	13.8	14.2	14.6
14	14.4	14.9	15.3	15.8
15	15.5	15.9	16.4	16.9
16	16.5	17.0	17.5	18.0

Source: Liz Buyer, "EuroDisney: As Close to Risk Free as a Deal Can Get," *The Journal of European Business* March/April 1992, p. 27. Reprinted with permission of *Journal of European Business* and Faulkner and Gray.

The next step is to forecast individual expenditures at the park on a daily basis, for admission as well as for food and merchandise. Disney's projections assume that each visitor will spend FF 78.6 on merchandise, FF 59.5 on food and beverages, and FF 5.5 on parking and other items (e.g., stroller rentals). Admission fees are estimated at FF 144.4 apiece.

These estimates are based on 1989 francs. French inflation is expected to increase these figures by 5 percent each year. As of late 1989, the French franc:dollar exchange rate was about FF 6 = $1, but this rate could obviously vary considerably. For example, U.S. inflation is expected to average about 4 percent annually, about 1 percent below the expected French inflation rate.

Euro Disneyland will also collect "participation fees" from various corporate sponsors, such as Kodak and Renault. These fees are payment for the privilege of sponsoring specific attractions in return for promotional considerations (e.g., Kraft's "The Land") and are expected to approximate $35 million in 1992.

EDL's pretax operating margin is expected to be about 35 percent. That money will not all flow into the hands of EDL shareholders. EDL must pay interest on its debt and French tax. The effective tax rate is estimated at 55 percent. In addition, EDL must pay Disney royalties, a base management fee, and an incentive-based bonus fee. Under the master agreement, Disney will collect 10 percent of the revenues generated by ticket sales and 5 percent of all expenditures on food, beverage, and merchandise. Disney also can collect significantly higher fees from EDL if the park exceeds certain operating cash flow (OCF) targets. Specifically, Disney will collect 30 percent of the park's OCF in the range of FF 1.4–2.1 billion; 40 percent of all OCF between FF 2.1 and 2.8 billion; and 50 percent of all OCF above FF 2.8 billion. Disney will receive no incentive fee if the park's OCF is less than FF 1.4 billion. In this case, the operating cash flow will equal operating income as Disney has sold its depreciation tax benefits.

In November 1989, Walt Disney Co. announced plans to add a movie studio theme park as the second gated attraction to Euro Disneyland. The movie studio theme park is expected to open in 1996. In addition to strengthening Disney's film production capabilities in Europe (where the movement to enforce geographic quotas continues to gain momentum), the second attraction could add as much as FF 3.3 billion to 1996 operating revenues.

QUESTIONS

1. These questions are related to the $800 million (FF 4.8 billion at FF 6 = $1) in French government-subsidized loans.

   a. What is the value to Disney of the French government's loan subsidies?

   b. What exchange risk is this project subject to from the standpoint of Disney? How can financing be used to mitigate this exchange risk?

   c. Suppose it turns out that having $800 million in French franc financing actually adds to Disney's economic exposure. How should this affect Disney's willingness to accept the full amount of financing offered by the French government?

2. Based on purchasing power parity, project the dollar:franc exchange rate from 1989 through 1996.

3. What is the range of projected dollar net income for Euro Disneyland for the years 1992–1996?

4. Suppose the terminal value at the end of 1996 is estimated at seven times net income for 1996. Using a 15 percent cost of capital, what is the range of net present values of Euro Disneyland as a stand-alone project?

5. Using the same 15 percent cost of capital, what is the range of net present values of Walt Disney's investment in Euro Disneyland?

6. Should Walt Disney go ahead with this project? What other factors might you consider in estimating the value of Euro Disneyland to Walt Disney?

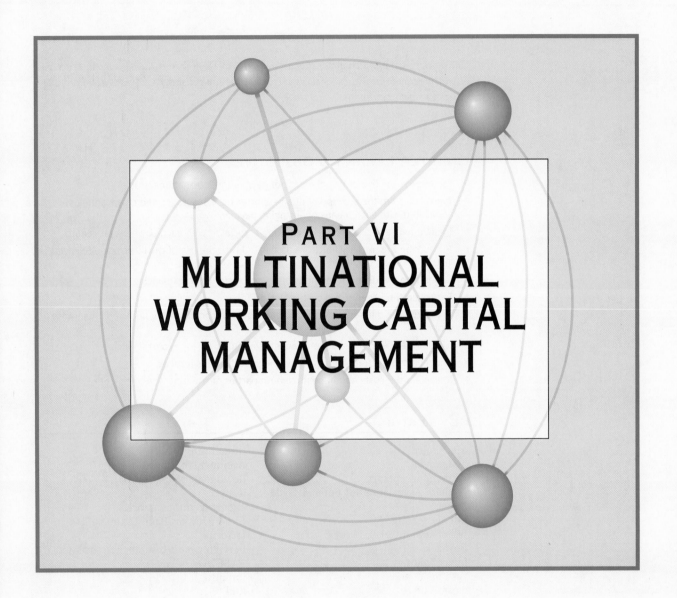

PART VI
MULTINATIONAL WORKING CAPITAL MANAGEMENT

FINANCING FOREIGN TRADE

The development of a new product is a three-step process: first, a U.S. firm announces an invention; second, the Russians claim they made the same discovery 20 years ago; third, the Japanese start exporting it.

Anonymous

CHAPTER LEARNING OBJECTIVES

- To describe the five principal means of payment in international trade
- To explain from the standpoint of an exporter the advantages and disadvantages associated with each means of arranging payment
- To identify the necessary documentation associated with each payment procedure
- To describe the primary functions associated with the use of the basic trade-financing instruments and documents
- To describe the different methods of private sector export financing
- To explain the benefits and costs of factoring
- To identify the different government-sponsored export-financing and credit insurance programs
- To describe the trends and consequences of public sector export financing
- To define countertrade and describe the specific forms it takes
- To explain the costs and benefits to both parties of countertrade transactions

KEY TERMS

acceptance
assignment
bankers' acceptance
Bankers' Association for Foreign Trade
barter
bill of exchange
bill of lading (B/L)
buyback
buyer credits
cash in advance
clean B/L
clean draft
clean (nondocumentary) L/C
commercial invoice
commercial paper
confirmed L/C
consignment
consular invoice
counterpurchase
countertrade

discounting
documentary draft
documentary L/C
draft
export-credit insurance
Export-Import Bank (Eximbank)
factoring
Foreign Credit Insurance Association
  (FCIA)
forfaiting
foul B/L
insurance certificate
irrevocable L/C
letter of credit (L/C)
mixed-credit financing
nonrecourse
on-board B/L
open account selling
order B/L
preliminary commitment

Private Export Funding Corporation
  (PEFCO)
received-for-shipment B/L
recourse
revocable L/C
sight draft

straight B/L
supplier credits
time draft
trade acceptance
transferable L/C
unconfirmed L/C

Most multinational corporations are heavily involved in foreign trade in addition to their other international activities. The financing of trade-related working capital requires large amounts of money as well as financial services such as letters of credit and acceptances. It is vital, therefore, that the multinational financial executive have knowledge of the institutions and documentary procedures that have evolved over the centuries to facilitate the international movement of goods. Much of the material in this chapter is descriptive in nature, but interspersed throughout will be discussions of the role of these special financial techniques and their associated advantages and disadvantages.

This chapter describes and analyzes the various payment terms possible in international trade, along with the necessary documentation associated with each procedure. It also examines the different methods and sources of export financing and credit insurance that are available from the public sector. The final section discusses the rise of counter-trade, a sophisticated word for barter.

18.1 PAYMENT TERMS IN INTERNATIONAL TRADE

Every shipment abroad requires some kind of financing while in transit. The exporter also needs financing to buy or manufacture its goods. Similarly, the importer has to carry these goods in inventory until the goods are sold. Then, it must finance its customers' receivables.

A financially strong exporter can finance the entire trade cycle out of its own funds by extending credit until the importer has converted these goods into cash. Alternatively, the importer can finance the entire cycle by paying cash in advance. Usually, however, some in-between approach is chosen, involving a combination of financing by the exporter, the importer, and one or more financial intermediaries.

The various means of payment in international trade impose different risks on the exporter.

The five principal means of payment in international trade, ranked in terms of increasing risk to the exporter, are

- Cash in advance
- Letter of credit
- Draft
- Consignment
- Open account

As a general rule, the greater the protection afforded the exporter, the less convenient are the payment terms for the buyer (importer). Some of these methods, however, are designed to protect both parties against commercial and/or political risks. It is up to the exporter when choosing among these payment methods to weigh the benefits in risk reduction against the cost of lost sales. The five basic means of payment are discussed in the following paragraphs.

Cash in Advance

Cash in advance affords the exporter the greatest protection because payment is received either before shipment or upon arrival of the goods. This method also allows the exporter to avoid tying up its own funds. Although less common than in the past, cash payment upon presentation of documents is still widespread.

Cash terms are used when there is political instability in the importing country or when the buyer's credit is doubtful. Political crises or exchange controls in the purchaser's country may cause payment delays or even prevent fund transfers, leading to a demand for cash in advance. In addition, where goods are made to order, prepayment is usually demanded, both to finance production and to reduce marketing risks.

Letter of Credit

Importers often will balk at paying cash in advance and will demand credit terms instead. When credit is extended, the **letter of credit (L/C)** offers the exporter the greatest degree of safety.

If the importer is not well known to the exporter or if exchange restrictions exist or are possible in the importer's country, the exporter selling on credit may wish to have the importer's promise of payment backed by a foreign or domestic bank. On the other hand, the importer may not wish to pay the exporter until it is reasonably certain that the merchandise has been shipped in good condition. A letter of credit satisfies both of these conditions.

In essence, the letter of credit is a letter addressed to the seller, written and signed by a bank acting on behalf of the buyer. In the letter, the bank promises it will honor drafts drawn on itself if the seller conforms to the specific conditions set forth in the L/C. (The draft, which is a written order to pay, is discussed in the next part of this section.) Through an L/C, the bank substitutes its own commitment to pay for that of its customer (the importer). The letter of credit, therefore, becomes a financial contract between the issuing bank and a designated beneficiary that is separate from the commercial transaction.

The advantages to the exporter are as follows:

1. Most important, an L/C eliminates credit risk if the bank that opens it is of undoubted standing. Therefore, the firm need check only on the credit reputation of the issuing bank.

2. An L/C also reduces the danger that payment will be delayed or withheld because of exchange controls or other political acts. Countries generally permit local banks to honor their letters of credit. Failure to honor them could severely damage the country's credit standing and credibility.

3. An L/C reduces uncertainty. The exporter knows all the requirements for payment because they are clearly stipulated on the L/C.

4. The L/C can also guard against preshipment risks. The exporter who manufactures under contract a specialized piece of equipment runs the risk of contract cancellation before shipment. Opening a letter of credit will provide protection during the manufacturing phase.

5. Last, and certainly not least, the L/C facilitates financing because it ensures the exporter a ready buyer for its product. It also becomes especially easy to create a banker's acceptance—a draft accepted by a bank.

Most advantages of an L/C are realized by the seller; nevertheless, there are some advantages to the buyer as well.

1. Because payment is only in compliance with the L/C's stipulated conditions, the importer is able to ascertain that the merchandise is actually shipped on, or before, a certain date by requiring an on-board bill of lading. The importer also can require an inspection certificate.

2. Any documents required are carefully inspected by clerks with years of experience. Moreover, the bank bears responsibility for any oversight.

3. An L/C is about as good as cash in advance, so the importer usually can command more advantageous credit terms and/or prices.

4. Some exporters will sell only on a letter of credit. Willingness to provide one expands a firm's sources of supply.

5. L/C financing may be cheaper than the alternatives. There is no tie-up of cash if the L/C substitutes for cash in advance.

6. If prepayment is required, the importer is better off depositing its money with a bank than with the seller because it is then easier to recover the deposit if the seller is unable or unwilling to make a proper shipment.

The mechanics of letter-of-credit financing are quite simple, as illustrated by the case of U.S.A. Importers, Inc., of Los Angeles. The company is buying spare auto parts worth $38,000 from Japan Exporters, Inc., of Tokyo, Japan. U.S.A. Importers applies for, and receives, a letter of credit for $38,000 from its bank, Wells Fargo. The actual L/C is shown in Exhibit 18.1. Exhibit 18.2, in turn, shows the relationships between the three parties to the letter of credit.

After Japan Exporters has shipped the goods, it draws a draft against the issuing bank (Wells Fargo) and presents it, along with the required documents, to its own bank, the Bank of Tokyo-Mitsubishi. The Bank of Tokyo-Mitsubishi, in turn, forwards the bank draft and attached documents to Wells Fargo; Wells Fargo pays the draft upon receiving evidence that all conditions set forth in the L/C have been met. Exhibit 18.3 details the sequence of steps in the L/C transaction.

Most L/Cs issued in connection with commercial transactions are **documentary**—that is, the seller must submit, together with the draft, any necessary invoices and the like. The documents required from Japan Exporters are listed on the face of the letter of credit in Exhibit 18.1 following the words "accompanied by." A **nondocumentary**, or **clean**, **L/C** is normally used in other than commercial transactions.

The letter of credit can be revocable or irrevocable. A **revocable L/C** is a means of arranging payment, but it does not carry a guarantee. It can be revoked, without notice, at any time up to the time a draft is presented to the issuing bank. An **irrevocable L/C**, on the other hand, cannot be revoked without the specific permission of all parties concerned, including the exporter. Most credits between unrelated parties are irrevocable; otherwise, the advantage of commitment to pay is lost. In the case of Japan Exporters, the L/C is irrevocable.

Although the essential character of a letter of credit—the substitution of the bank's name for the merchant's—is absent with a revocable credit, this type of L/C is useful in some respects. The fact that a bank is willing to open a letter of credit for the importer is in itself an indication of the customer's creditworthiness. Thus, it is safer than sending goods on a collection basis, where payment is made by a draft only after the goods have been shipped. Of equal, if not greater, importance is the probability that imports covered by letters of credit will be given priority in the allocation of foreign exchange should currency controls be imposed.

A letter of credit can also be confirmed or unconfirmed. A **confirmed L/C** is an L/C issued by one bank and confirmed by another, obligating both banks to honor any drafts drawn in compliance. An **unconfirmed L/C** is the obligation of only the issuing bank.

An exporter will prefer an irrevocable letter of credit by the importer's bank with confirmation by a domestic bank. In this way, the exporter need look no further than a bank in its own country for compliance with terms of the letter of credit. For example, if the Bank of Tokyo-Mitsubishi had confirmed the letter of credit issued by Wells Fargo, and Wells Fargo, for whatever reason, failed to honor its irrevocable L/C, Japan Exporters could collect $38,000 from the Bank of Tokyo-Mitsubishi, assuming that Japan Exporters met all the necessary conditions. This arrangement serves two purposes. Most exporters are not in a position to evaluate or deal with a foreign bank directly should difficulties arise. Domestic confirmation avoids this problem. In addition, should the foreign bank be

---

An irrevocable L/C provides the exporter with a stronger guarantee of payment.

The essential feature of the irrevocable L/C is that it substitutes the bank's name for the importer's.

The confirmed L/C protects the exporter against problems with the bank that issued the L/C.

EXHIBIT 18.1 • LETTER OF CREDIT

IRREVOCABLE
COMMERCIAL
LETTER OF
CREDIT

Since 1852

WELLS FARGO BANK N.A.

☐ 475 SANSOME STREET, SAN FRANCISCO, CALIFORNIA 94111

☐ 770 WILSHIRE BLVD. LOS ANGELES, CALIFORNIA 90017

INTERNATIONAL DIVISION   **COMMERCIAL L/C DEPARTMENT**   CABLE ADDRESS: **WELLS**

**OUR LETTER
OF CREDIT NO.** XYZ9000   AMOUNT US$38,000   DATE MAY 6, 20XX
THIS NUMBER MUST BE MENTIONED
ON ALL DRAFTS AND CORRESPONDENCE

. JAPAN EXPORTERS INC.   . BANK OF TOKYO
. TOKYO, JAPAN   . TOKYO, JAPAN
.   .
.   .

GENTLEMEN:

   BY ORDER OF   U.S.A. IMPORTERS INC.

AND FOR ACCOUNT OF   SAME

WE HEREBY AUTHORIZE YOU TO DRAW ON OURSELVES

UP TO AN AGGREGATE AMOUNT OF THIRTY EIGHT THOUSAND AND NO/100 U.S. DOLLARS

AVAILABLE BY YOUR DRAFTS AT ON OURSELVES, IN DUPLICATE, AT 90 DAYS SIGHT
ACCOMPANIED BY
SIGNED INVOICE IN TRIPLICATE
PACKING LIST IN DUPLICATE
FULL SET OF CLEAN OCEAN BILLS OF LADING, MADE OUT TO ORDER OF SHIPPER,
   BLANK ENDORSED, MARKED FREIGHT PREPAID AND NOTIFY: U.S.A. IMPORTERS,
   INC., LOS ANGELES, DATED ON BOARD NOT LATER THAN MAY 30, 19XX.
INSURANCE POLICY/CERTIFICATE IN DUPLICATE FOR 110% OF INVOICE VALUE,
   COVERING ALL RISKS.

COVERING: SHIPMENT OF AUTOMOBILE SPARE PARTS, AS PER BUYER'S ORDER NO.
   900 DATED MARCH 15, 20XX FROM ANY JAPANESE PORT C.I.F.
   LOS ANGELES, CALIFORNIA
PARTIAL SHIPMENTS ARE PERMITTED.
TRANSHIPMENT IS NOT PERMITTED.
DOCUMENTS MUST BE PRESENTED WITHIN 7 DAYS AFTER THE BOARD DATE OF
   THE BILLS OF LADING, BUT IN ANY EVENT NOT LATER THAN JUNE 6, 20XX.

SPECIMEN

DRAFTS MUST BE DRAWN AND NEGOTIATED NOT LATER THAN   JUNE 6, 20XX
ALL DRAFTS DRAWN UNDER THIS CREDIT MUST BEAR ITS DATE AND NUMBER AND THE AMOUNTS
MUST BE ENDORSED ON THE REVERSE SIDE OF THIS LETTER OF CREDIT BY THE NEGOTIATING BANK.
WE HEREBY AGREE WITH THE DRAWERS, ENDORSERS, AND BONA FIDE HOLDERS OF ALL DRAFTS
DRAWN UNDER AND IN COMPLIANCE WITH THE TERMS OF THIS CREDIT, THAT SUCH DRAFTS WILL
BE DULY HONORED UPON PRESENTATION TO THE DRAWEE.
THIS CREDIT IS SUBJECT TO THE UNIFORM CUSTOMS AND PRACTICE FOR DOCUMENTARY CREDITS
(1974 REVISION). INTERNATIONAL CHAMBER OF COMMERCE PUBLICATION NO. 290.

SPECIMEN
AUTHORIZED SIGNATURE

Used by permission of Wells Fargo Bank, N.A.

unable to fulfill its commitment to pay, whether because of foreign exchange controls or political directives, that is of no concern to the exporter. The domestic confirming bank still must honor all drafts in full.

Thus, the three main types of L/C, in order of safety for the exporter, are (1) the irrevocable, confirmed L/C; (2) the irrevocable, unconfirmed L/C; and (3) the revocable L/C. Selecting the type of L/C to use depends on an evaluation of the risks associated with the transaction and the relative costs involved. One of the costs is the possibility of lost sales if the importer can get better credit terms elsewhere.

EXHIBIT 18.2 • RELATIONSHIPS AMONG THE THREE PARTIES TO A LETTER OF CREDIT

EXHIBIT 18.3 • EXAMPLE OF LETTER OF CREDIT FINANCING OF U.S. IMPORTS

An exporter who acts as an intermediary may have to provide some assurance to its supplier that the supplier will be paid. It can provide this assurance by transferring or assigning the proceeds of the letter of credit opened in its name to the manufacturer.

A **transferable L/C** is one under which the beneficiary has the right to instruct the paying bank to make the credit available to one or more secondary beneficiaries. No L/C is transferable unless specifically authorized in the credit; moreover, it can be transferred only once. The stipulated documents are transferred along with the L/C.

An **assignment**, in contrast to a transfer, assigns part or all of the proceeds to another party but does not transfer the required documents to the party. This provision is not as safe to the assignee as a transfer because the assignee does not have control of the required merchandise and documentation.

Draft

Commonly used in international trade, a **draft** is an unconditional order in writing—usually signed by the exporter (seller) and addressed to the importer (buyer) or the importer's agent—ordering the importer to pay on demand, or at a fixed or determinable future date, the amount specified on its face. Such an instrument, also known as a **bill of exchange**, serves three important functions:

- It provides written evidence, in clear and simple terms, of a financial obligation.
- It enables both parties to potentially reduce their costs of financing.
- It provides a negotiable and unconditional instrument. (That is, payment must be made to any holder in due course despite any disputes over the underlying commercial transaction.)

Using a draft also enables an exporter to employ its bank as a collection agent. The bank forwards the draft or bill of exchange to the foreign buyer (either directly or through a branch or correspondent bank), collects on the draft, and then remits the proceeds to the exporter. The bank has all the necessary documents for control of the merchandise and turns them over to the importer only when the draft has been paid or accepted in accordance with the exporter's instructions.

The conditions for a draft to be negotiable under the U.S. Uniform Commercial Code are that it must be

- In writing
- Signed by the issuer (drawer)
- An unconditional order to pay
- A certain sum of money
- Payable on demand or at a definite future time
- Payable to order of bearer

There are usually three parties to a draft. The party who signs and sends the draft to the second party is called the *drawer*; payment is made to the third party, the *payee*. Normally, the drawer and payee are the same person. The party to whom the draft is addressed is the *drawee*, who may be either the buyer or, if a letter of credit was used, the buyer's bank. In the case of a confirmed L/C, the drawee would be the confirming bank.

In the previous example, Japan Exporters is the drawer, and the Bank of Tokyo-Mitsubishi is the payee. The drawee is Wells Fargo under the terms of the L/C. This information is included in the draft shown in Exhibit 18.4.

Drafts may be either sight or time drafts. **Sight drafts** must be paid on presentation or else dishonored. **Time drafts** are payable at some specified future date and as such become a useful financing device. The maturity of a time draft is known as its *usance* or *tenor*. As mentioned earlier, for a draft to qualify as a negotiable instrument, the date of payment must be determinable. For example, a time draft payable "upon delivery of goods" is not specific enough, given the vagaries of ocean freight; the vague date of payment will likely nullify its negotiability. As shown in Exhibit 18.4, the draft drawn under the letter of credit by Japan Exporters is a time draft with a tenor of ninety days, indicated by the words "at ninety days sight." Thus, the draft will mature on August 24, ninety days after it was drawn (May 26).

A time draft becomes an **acceptance** after being accepted by the drawee. Accepting a draft means writing *accepted* across its face, followed by an authorized person's signature and the date. The party accepting a draft incurs the obligation to pay it at maturity. A draft accepted by a bank becomes a **bankers' acceptance**; one drawn on and accepted by a commercial enterprise is termed a **trade acceptance**. Exhibit 18.5 is the time draft in Exhibit 18.4 after being accepted by Wells Fargo.

EXHIBIT 18.4 • TIME DRAFT

TOKYO, JAPAN	MAY 26	, 20 XX No. 712

AT NINETY DAYS _____ SIGHT OF THIS **ORIGINAL** OF EXCHANGE (DUPLICATE UNPAID)

PAY TO THE ORDER OF __BANK OF TOKYO_____ U.S. $ __38,000.00__

THE SUM OF __THIRTY EIGHT THOUSAND AND NO/100 * * * * * * * * * * * * * * * * * *__ U.S. Dollars

DRAWN UNDER LETTER OF CREDIT NO.	DATED	ISSUED BY
X Y Z 9000	MAY 6, 20XX	WELLS FARGO BANK

To   WELLS FARGO BANK   *SPECIMEN*

770 WILSHIRE BLVD.

LOS ANGELES, CALIFORNIA   JAPAN EXPORTERS INC.

Used by permission of Wells Fargo Bank.

The exporter can hold the acceptance or sell it at a discount from face value to its bank, to some other bank, or to an acceptance dealer. The discount normally is less than the prevailing prime rate for bank loans. These acceptances enjoy a wide market and are an important tool in the financing of international trade. They are discussed in more detail in the next section. An acceptance can be transferred from one holder to another simply by endorsement.

Drafts can be clean or documentary. A **clean draft**, one unaccompanied by any other papers, normally is used only for nontrade remittances. Its primary purpose is to put pressure on a recalcitrant debtor that must pay or accept the draft or else face damage to its credit reputation.

Most drafts used in international trade are documentary. A **documentary draft**, which can be either sight or time, is accompanied by documents that are to be delivered to the drawee on payment or acceptance of the draft. Typically, these documents include the bill of lading in negotiable form, the commercial invoice, the consular invoice where required, and an insurance certificate. The bill of lading in negotiable form is the most important document because it gives its holder the right to control the goods covered. A documentary sight draft is also known as a D/P (documents against payment) draft; if documents are delivered on acceptance, it is a D/A draft.

> Most drafts used in international trade are accompanied by documents to be delivered to the drawee on payment or acceptance of the draft.

EXHIBIT 18.5 • BANKER'S ACCEPTANCE

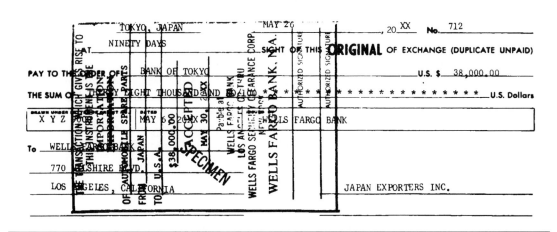

Used by permission of Wells Fargo Bank.

There are two significant aspects to shipping goods under documentary time drafts for acceptance. First, the exporter is extending credit to the importer for the usance of the draft. Second, the exporter is relinquishing control of the goods in return for a signature on the acceptance to assure it of payment.

Sight drafts are not always paid at presentation, nor are time drafts always paid at maturity. Firms can get bank statistics on the promptness of sight and time draft payments, by country, from bank publications such as Chase Manhattan's *Collection Experience* bulletin.

Unless a bank has accepted a draft, the exporter ultimately must look to the importer for payment. Thus, use of a sight or accepted time draft is warranted only when the exporter has faith in the importer's financial strength and integrity.

Consignment

Goods that are shipped to the importer with payment to be made later are subject to the risk of currency controls.

Goods sent on **consignment** are only shipped, but not sold, to the importer. The exporter (consignor) retains title to the goods until the importer (consignee) has sold them to a third party. This arrangement is normally made only with a related company because of the large risks involved. There is little evidence of the buyer's obligation to pay, and should the buyer default, it will prove difficult to collect.

The seller must carefully consider the credit risks involved as well as the availability of foreign exchange in the importer's country. Imports covered by documentary drafts receive priority to scarce foreign exchange over imports shipped on consignment.

Open Account

Open account selling is shipping goods first and billing the importer later. The credit terms are arranged between the buyer and the seller, but the seller has little evidence of the importer's obligation to pay a certain amount at a certain date. Sales on open account, therefore, are made only to a foreign affiliate or to a customer with which the exporter has a long history of favorable business dealings. However, open account sales have greatly expanded because of the major increase in international trade, the improvement in credit information about importers, and the greater familiarity with exporting in general. The benefits include greater flexibility (no specific payment dates are set) and involve lower costs, including fewer bank charges than with other methods of payment. As with shipping on consignment, the possibility of currency controls is an important factor because of the low priority in allocating foreign exchange normally accorded this type of transaction.

Exhibit 18.6 summarizes some of the advantages and disadvantages associated with the various means of arranging payment in international trade.

Banks and Trade Financing

Historically, banks have been involved in only a single step in international trade transactions such as providing a loan or a letter of credit. However, as financing has become an integral part of many trade transactions, U.S. banks—especially major money center banks—have evolved as well. They have gone from financing individual trade deals to providing comprehensive solutions to trade needs. Such comprehensive services include combining bank lending with subsidized funds from government export agencies, international leasing, and other nonbank financing sources, along with political and economic risk insurance.

Collecting Overdue Accounts

Typically, 1 percent to 3 percent of a company's export sales go uncollected. Small businesses, however, take more risks than do large ones, often selling on terms other than a confirmed

EXHIBIT 18.6 • INTERNATIONAL METHODS OF PAYMENT: ADVANTAGES AND DISADVANTAGES (RANKED BY RISK)

Method	Risk*	Chief Advantage	Chief Disadvantage
Cash in advance	L	No credit extension required	Can limit sales potential, disturb some potential customers
Sight draft	M/L	Retains control and title; ensures payment before goods are delivered	If customer does not or cannot accept goods, goods remain at port of entry and no payment is due
Letters of credit		Banks accept responsibility to pay; payment upon presentation of papers; costs go to buyer	If revocable, terms can change during contract work
Irrevocable	M		
Revocable	M/H		
Time draft	M/H	Lowers customer resistance by allowing extended payment after receipt of goods	Same as sight draft, plus goods are delivered before payment is due or received
Consignment sales	M/H	Facilitates delivery; lowers customer resistance	Capital tied up until sales; must establish distributor's creditworthiness; need political risk insurance in some countries; increased risk from currency controls
Open account	H	Simplified procedure; no customer resistance	High risk; seller must finance production; increased risk from currency controls

*L: low risk; M: medium risk; H: high risk.

letter of credit. One reason is that they are eager to develop a new market opportunity; another reason is that they are not as well versed in the mechanics of foreign sales. Thus, their percentage of uncollected export sales may be higher than that of large companies.

Once an account becomes delinquent, sellers have three options: (1) They can try to collect the account themselves; (2) they can hire an attorney who is experienced in international law; or (3) they can engage the services of a collection agency.

The first step is for sellers to attempt to recover the money themselves. Turning the bill over to a collection agency or a lawyer too quickly will hurt the customer relationship. However, after several telephone calls, telexes, and/or personal visits, the firm must decide whether to write the account off or pursue it further.

Collecting overdue accounts in a foreign country is a frustrating and expensive process.

The cost of hiring a high-priced U.S. lawyer, who then contacts an expensive foreign lawyer, is a deterrent to following the second option for receivables of less than $100,000. With such a relatively small amount, a collection agency usually would be more appropriate. Unlike lawyers, who charge by the hour for their services, regardless of the amount recovered, collection agencies work on a percentage basis. A typical fee is 20 percent to 25 percent of the amount collected, but if the claim is more than $25,000 or so, the agency will often negotiate a more favorable rate.

Even with professional help, there are no guarantees of collecting on foreign receivables. This reality puts a premium on checking a customer's credit before filling an order. But getting credit information on specific foreign firms is often difficult.

One good source of credit information is the U.S. Department of Commerce's International Trade Administration (ITA). Its *World Data Trade Reports* covers nearly 200,000 foreign establishments and can be obtained from district offices of ITA for $75. Other places to check on the creditworthiness of foreign companies and governments are export management companies and the international departments of commercial banks. Also, Dun & Bradstreet International publishes *Principal International Businesses,* a book with information on about 50,000 foreign enterprises in 133 countries.

The National Association of Credit Management collects data on how much time it takes to collect on the average bill from importers in various foreign countries. Exhibit 18.7, which contains these data for the second quarter of 1992, shows the wide variation in collection times by country.

18.2 DOCUMENTS IN INTERNATIONAL TRADE

The most important supporting document required in commercial bank financing of exports is the bill of lading. Of secondary importance are the commercial invoice, insurance certificate, and consular invoice.

Bill of Lading

Of the shipping documents, the **bill of lading (B/L)** is the most important. It serves three main and separate functions:

The bill of lading is the document covering actual shipment of the merchandise by a common carrier and title.

1. It is a contract between the carrier and shipper (exporter) in which the carrier agrees to carry the goods from port of shipment to port of destination.
2. It is the shipper's receipt for the goods.
3. The *negotiable B/L*, its most common form, is a document that establishes control over the goods.

A bill of lading can be either a straight or an order B/L. A **straight B/L** consigns the goods to a specific party, normally the importer, and is not negotiable. Title cannot be transferred to a third party merely by endorsement and delivery; therefore, a straight B/L is not good collateral and is used only when no financing is involved.

Most trade transactions do involve financing, which requires transfer of title, so the vast majority of bills of lading are order B/Ls. Under an **order B/L**, the goods are consigned to the order of a named party, usually the exporter. In this way, the exporter retains title to the merchandise until it endorses the B/L on the reverse side. The exporter's representative may endorse to a specific party or endorse it in blank by simply signing his or her name. The shipper delivers the cargo in the port of destination to the bearer of the endorsed order B/L, who must surrender it.

EXHIBIT 18.7 • YOUR CHECK IS NOT IN THE MAIL YET: LENGTH OF TIME REQUIRED FOR U.S. COMPANIES TO COLLECT ON THE AVERAGE BILL FROM CONCERNS IN SELECTED FOREIGN COUNTRIES IN THE SECOND QUARTER OF 1992

Country	*Number of Days*
Iran	337
Kenya	129
Argentina	123
Brazil	119
Italy	90
India	80
Mexico	74
Taiwan	73
United Kingdom	70
Japan	58
Germany	54

Source: Michael Selz, "Small Firms Hit Foreign Obstacles in Billing Overseas," *Wall Street Journal*, December 18, 1992, p. B2. Reprinted by permission of the *Wall Street Journal*, © Dow Jones & Company, Inc. 1992. All rights reserved worldwide.

An order B/L represents goods in transit that are probably readily marketable and fully insured, so this document is generally considered to be good collateral by banks. It is required under L/C financing and for discounting of drafts.

Bills of lading also can be classified in several other ways. An **on-board B/L** certifies that the goods have actually been placed on board the vessel. By contrast, a **received-for-shipment B/L** merely acknowledges that the carrier has received the goods for shipment. It does not state that the ship is in port or that space is available. The cargo can, therefore, sit on the dock for weeks, or even months, before it is shipped. When goods are seasonal or perishable, therefore, the received-for-shipment B/L is never satisfactory to either the shipper or the importer. A received-for-shipment B/L can easily be converted into an on-board B/L by stamping it "on-board" and supplying the name of the vessel, the date, and the signature of the captain or the captain's representative.

A **clean B/L** indicates that the goods were received in apparently good condition. However, the carrier is not obligated to check beyond the external visual appearance of the boxes. If boxes are damaged or in poor condition, this observation is noted on the B/L, which then becomes a **foul B/L**. It is important that the exporter get a clean B/L—that is, one with no such notation—because foul B/Ls generally are not acceptable under a letter of credit.

Commercial Invoice

Trade documents that are necessary but of lesser importance include commercial and consular invoices and the insurance receipts.

A **commercial invoice** contains an authoritative description of the merchandise shipped, including full details on quality, grades, price per unit, and total value. It also contains the names and addresses of the exporter and importer, the number of packages, any distinguishing external marks, the payment terms, other expenses such as transportation and insurance charges, any fees collectible from the importer, the name of the vessel, the ports of departure and destination, and any required export or import permit numbers.

Insurance Certificate

All cargoes going abroad are insured. Most of the insurance contracts used today are under an *open, or floating, policy*. This policy automatically covers all shipments made by the exporter, thereby eliminating the necessity of arranging individual insurance for each shipment. To evidence insurance for a shipment under an open policy, the exporter makes out an **insurance certificate** on forms supplied by the insurance company. This certificate contains information on the goods shipped. All entries must conform exactly with the information on the B/L, on the commercial invoice and, where required, on the consular invoice.

Consular Invoice

Exports to many countries require a special **consular invoice**. This invoice, which varies in its details and information requirements from nation to nation, is presented to the local consul in exchange for a visa. The form must be filled out very carefully, for even trivial inaccuracies can lead to substantial fines and delays in customs clearance. The consular invoice does not convey any title to the goods being shipped and is not negotiable.

18.3 FINANCING TECHNIQUES IN INTERNATIONAL TRADE

In addition to straight bank financing, several other techniques are available for trade financing: bankers' acceptances, discounting, factoring, and forfaiting.

Bankers' Acceptances

Bankers' acceptances have played an important role in financing international trade for many centuries. As we saw in the previous section, a banker's acceptance is a time draft drawn on a bank. By "accepting" the draft, the bank makes an unconditional promise to pay the holder of the draft a stated amount on a specified day. Thus, the bank effectively substitutes its own credit for that of a borrower, and in the process it creates a negotiable instrument that may be freely traded.

Creating an Acceptance A typical acceptance transaction is shown in Exhibit 18.8. An importer of goods seeks credit to finance its purchase until the goods can be resold. If the importer does not have a close relationship with and cannot obtain financing from the exporter it is dealing with, it may request acceptance financing from its bank. Under an acceptance agreement, the importer will have its bank issue a letter of credit on its behalf, authorizing the foreign exporter to draw a time draft on the bank in payment for the goods. On the basis of this authorization, the exporter ships the goods on an order B/L made out to itself and presents a time draft and the endorsed shipping documents to its bank. The foreign bank then forwards the draft and the appropriate shipping documents to the importer's bank; the importer's bank accepts the draft and, by so doing, creates a banker's acceptance. The exporter discounts the draft with the accepting bank and receives payment for the shipment. The shipping documents are delivered to the importer, and the importer now may claim the shipment. The accepting bank may either buy (discount) the B/A and hold it in its own portfolio or sell (rediscount) the B/A in the money market. In Exhibit 18.8, the bank sells the acceptance in the money market.

Acceptances also are created to finance the shipment of goods within the United States and to finance the storage of goods in the United States and abroad. However, domestic shipment and storage acceptances have been a small part of the market in recent years. Most acceptances arise from imports into the United States, U.S. exports, and the storage of goods or shipment of goods between foreign countries.

Terms of Acceptance Financing Typical maturities on bankers' acceptances are 30 days, 90 days, and 180 days, with the average being 90 days. Maturities can be tailored, however, to cover the entire period needed to ship and dispose of the goods financed.

For an investor, a banker's acceptance is a close substitute for other bank liabilities, such as certificates of deposit (CDs). Consequently, bankers' acceptances trade at rates very close to those on CDs. Market yields, however, do not give a complete picture of the costs of acceptance financing to the borrower because the accepting bank levies a fee, or commission, for accepting the draft. The fee varies depending on the maturity of the draft as well as the creditworthiness of the borrower, but it averages less than 1 percent per annum. The bank also receives a fee if a letter of credit is involved. In addition, the bank may hope to realize a profit on the difference between the price at which it purchases and the price at which it resells the acceptance.

On the maturity date of the acceptance, the accepting bank is required to pay the current holder the amount stated on the draft. The holder of a bank acceptance has recourse for the full amount of the draft from the last endorser in the event of the importer's unwillingness or inability to pay at maturity. The authenticity of an accepted draft is separated from the underlying commercial transaction and may not be dishonored for reason of a dispute between the exporter and importer. This factor significantly enhances its marketability and reduces its riskiness.

In recent years, the demand for acceptance financing has fallen off. One factor has been the increased availability of funding from nonbank investors in the U.S. commercial paper market. **Commercial paper** (CP) is a short-term unsecured promissory note that is

EXHIBIT 18.8 • EXAMPLE OF BANKER'S ACCEPTANCE FINANCING OF U.S. IMPORTS: CREATED, DISCOUNTED, SOLD, AND PAID AT MATURITY

Source: Instruments of the Money Market. Federal Reserve Bank of Richmond, 1981, p. 116. Used with permission.

In recent years, commercial paper has provided a highly competitive alternative to bankers' acceptances in financing trade.

generally sold by large corporations on a discount basis to institutional investors and to other corporations. Prime commercial paper generally trades at rates near those on acceptance liabilities of prime banks; for firms with access to this market, the overall cost—including placement fees charged by dealers and fees for back-up line of credit—is usually below the all-in cost of acceptance financing.

Evaluating the Cost of Acceptance Financing   Suppose that the discount rate on a $1 million acceptance for 90 days is 9.8 percent per annum and the acceptance fee is 2 percent per annum. If the exporter chooses to hold the acceptance, then in 90 days it will receive the face amount less the acceptance fee:

Face amount of acceptance	$1,000,000
Less 2% per annum commission for 90 days	−5,000
Amount received by exporter in 90 days	$995,000

Alternatively, the exporter can sell the acceptance at a 2.45 percent discount (9.8 percent/4) and receive $970,500 immediately:

Face amount of acceptance	$1,000,000
Less 2% per annum commission for 90 days	−5,000
Less 9.8% per annum discount for 90 days	−24,500
Amount received by exporter immediately	$970,500

Whether the exporter should discount the acceptance or wait depends on the opportunity cost of money. Suppose that the exporter's opportunity cost of money is 10.2 percent. Then the present value of holding onto the acceptance is $995,000/[1 + (0.102/4)], or $970,258. In this case, the exporter would come out ahead by selling the acceptance.

Discounting

A trade draft can be converted into cash by means of discounting.

Even if a trade draft is not accepted by a bank, the exporter still can convert the trade draft into cash by means of **discounting.** The exporter places the draft with a bank or other financial institution and, in turn, receives the face value of the draft less interest and commissions. By insuring the draft against both commercial and political risks, the exporter often will pay a lower interest rate. If losses covered by the insurer do occur, the insuring agency will reimburse the exporter or any institution to which the exporter transfers the draft.

The discount rate for trade paper is often lower than interest rates on overdrafts, bank loans, and other forms of local funding. This lower rate is usually a result of export promotion policies that lead to direct or indirect subsidies of rates on export paper.

Discounting may be done with or without **recourse.** With recourse, the bank can collect from the exporter if the importer fails to pay the bill when due. The bank bears the collection risk if the draft is sold without recourse.

Factoring

Firms with a substantial export business can sell their receivables to a factor for cash.

Firms with a substantial export business and companies too small to afford a foreign credit and collections department can turn to a *factor.* Factors buy a company's receivables at a discount, thereby accelerating their conversion into cash. Most **factoring** is done on a **nonrecourse** basis, which means that the factor assumes all the credit and political risks except for those involving disputes between the transacting parties. In order to avoid being stuck with only receivables of risky customers (with good credits not being factored), factors usually insist on handling most or all sales. This selection bias is not an issue in factoring *with recourse,* where the exporter assumes all risks.

Factoring is becoming increasingly popular as a trade financing vehicle. The value of world exports financed through factoring now exceeds $10 billion. By using a factor, a firm can ensure that its terms are in accord with local practice and are competitive. For instance, customers can be offered payment on open account rather than being asked for a letter of credit or stiffer credit requirements. If the margin on its factored sales is not sufficiently profitable, then the firm can bear the credit risks itself or forgo that business. Even if an exporter chooses not to discount its foreign receivables with a factor, it still can use the factor's extensive credit information files to ascertain the creditworthiness of prospective customers.

An exporter that has established an ongoing relationship with a factor will submit new orders directly to the factor. After evaluating the creditworthiness of the new claim, the factor will make a recourse/nonrecourse decision within two days to two weeks, depending on the availability of information.

Although the factors may consider their fees to be nominal considering the services provided, they are not cheap. Export factoring fees are determined on an individual company basis and are related to the annual turnover (usually a minimum of $500,000 to $1 million is necessary), the average invoice size (smaller invoices are more expensive because of the fixed information-gathering costs), the creditability of the claims, and the terms of sale. In general, these fees run from 1.75 percent to 2 percent of sales.

Evaluating the Cost of Factoring   Suppose that a factor will buy an exporter's receivables at a 2.5 percent per *month* discount. In addition, the factor will charge an extra 1.75 percent fee for nonrecourse financing. If the exporter decides to factor $1 million in 90-day receivables without recourse, then it will receive $907,500 today:

Face amount of receivable	$1,000,000
Less 1.75% nonrecourse fee	–17,500
Less 2.5% monthly factoring fee	–75,000
Amount received by exporter	$907,500

On an annualized basis, factoring is costing this company 41.34 percent:

$$\text{Annual percentage rate (APR)} = \frac{17,500 + 75,000}{1,000,000 - 17,500 - 75,000} \times \frac{365}{90}$$
$$= 41.34\%$$

Factoring is expensive but may be of great value to the occasional exporter.

Despite these high costs, factoring can be quite worthwhile to many firms for one principal reason: The cost of bearing the credit risk associated with a given receivable can be substantially lower to a factor than to the selling firm. First, the factor's greater credit information makes it more knowledgeable about the actual, as opposed to the perceived, risks involved and thereby reduces its required risk premium. Second, by holding a well-diversified portfolio of receivables, the factor can eliminate some of the risks associated with individual receivables.

Factors are often better able to assess and bear credit risk.

In general, factoring is most useful for (1) the occasional exporter and (2) the exporter having a geographically diverse portfolio of accounts receivable. In both cases, it would be organizationally difficult and expensive to internalize the accounts-receivable collection process. Such companies generally would be small or else would be involved on a limited scale in foreign markets.

Forfaiting

The specialized factoring technique known as forfaiting is sometimes used in the case of extreme credit risk. **Forfaiting** is the discounting—at a fixed rate without recourse—of medium-term export receivables denominated in fully convertible currencies (U.S. dollar, Swiss franc, euro). This technique is generally used in the case of capital-goods exports with a five-year maturity and repayment in semiannual installments. The discount is set at a fixed rate: about 1.25 percent above the local cost of funds.

Forfaiting is especially popular in Western Europe (primarily in Switzerland and Austria), and many forfaiting houses are subsidiaries of major international banks, such as Credit Suisse. These houses also provide help with administrative and collection problems.

18.4 GOVERNMENT SOURCES OF EXPORT FINANCING AND CREDIT INSURANCE

In the race for export orders, particularly for capital equipment and other big-ticket items requiring long repayment arrangements, most governments of developed countries have attempted to provide their domestic exporters with a competitive edge in the form of low-cost export financing and concessionary rates on political and economic risk insurance. Nearly every developed nation has its own export-import agency for development and trade financing.

Governments often provide subsidized export credits to boost exports.

Export Financing

Procedures for extending credit vary greatly among agencies. Many agencies offer funds in advance of the actual export contract, whereas private sources extend financing only after the sale has been made. Some programs extend credit only to the supplier—called **supplier credits**—to pass on to the importer; others grant credit directly to the buyer—called **buyer credits**—who then pays the supplier. The difference is that in the first arrangement, the supplier bears the credit risk, whereas in the latter case, the government is the risk bearer. The government often provides credit insurance in conjunction with supplier credits.

The Export-Import Bank (Eximbank) is a U.S. government agency dedicated to financing and facilitating U.S. exports.

Export-Import Bank   The **Export-Import Bank (Eximbank)** is the only U.S. government agency dedicated solely to financing and facilitating U.S. exports. Eximbank loans provide competitive, fixed-rate financing for U.S. export sales facing foreign competition backed with subsidized official financing. Evidence of foreign competition is not required for exports produced by small businesses where the loan amount is $2.5 million or less. Eximbank also provides guarantees of loans made by others. The loan and guarantee programs cover up to 85 percent of the U.S. export value and have repayment terms of one year or more.

Eximbank operations generally conform to five basic principles:

The Eximbank provides loans and loan guarantees to help U.S. exporters more effectively compete in world markets.

1. Loans are made for the specific purpose of financing U.S. exports of goods and services. If a U.S. export item contains foreign-made components, Eximbank will cover up to 100 percent of the U.S. content of exports provided that the total amount financed or guaranteed does not exceed 85 percent of the total contract price of the item and that the total U.S. content accounts for at least half of the contract price.

2. Eximbank will not provide financing unless private capital is unavailable in the amounts required. It supplements, rather than competes with, private capital.

3. Loans must have reasonable assurance of repayment and must be for projects that have a favorable impact on the country's economic and social well-being. The host government must be aware of, and not object to, the project.

4. Fees and premiums charged for guarantees and insurance are based on the risks covered.

5. In authorizing loans and other financial assistance, Eximbank is obliged to take into account any adverse effects on the U.S. economy or balance of payments that might occur.

In recent years, the Eximbank has become very aggressive in financing U.S. trade with China. Indeed, China—already the bank's biggest lending market in Asia—had become its biggest lending market in the world by the year 2000.

The interest rates on Eximbank's loans are based on an international arrangement among the twenty-nine members of the Organization for Economic Cooperation and

Development (OECD). The purpose of the arrangement, which sets minimum rates that an official export finance agency must charge on export credits, is to limit the interest subsidies used by many industrial countries to gain competitive advantage vis-à-vis other nations. The OECD minimum rates are based on the weighted average interest rate on government bond issues denominated in the U.S. dollar, euro, British pound, and Japanese yen. In this way, rates on export credits are brought closer to market interest rates.

Eximbank extends direct loans to foreign buyers of U.S. exports and intermediary loans to financial institutions that extend loans to the foreign buyers. Both direct and intermediary loans are provided when U.S. exporters face officially subsidized foreign competition.

Eximbank extends direct loans to foreign buyers of U.S. exports.

Eximbank's medium-term loans to intermediaries (where the loan amount is $10 million or less and the term is seven years or less) are structured as "standby" loan commitments. The intermediary may request disbursement by Eximbank at any time during the term of the underlying debt obligation.

Eximbank guarantees provide repayment protection for private-sector loans to creditworthy buyers of exported U.S. goods and services. The guarantees are available alone or may be combined with an intermediary loan. Most guarantees provide comprehensive coverage of both political and commercial risks. Eximbank also will guarantee payments on cross-border or international leases.

Exporters may also have access to an Eximbank program that guarantees export-related working-capital loans to creditworthy small and medium-sized businesses. All Eximbank guarantees carry the full faith and credit of the U.S. government, so loans provided under these guarantee programs are made at nearly the risk-free interest rate. In effect, low-cost guarantees are another form of government-subsidized export financing.

Repayment terms vary with the project and type of equipment purchased. For capital goods, long-term credits are normally provided for a period of five to ten years. Loans for projects and large product acquisitions are eligible for longer terms, whereas lower-unit-value items receive shorter terms. Loan amortization is made in semiannual installments, beginning six months after delivery of the exported equipment.

Another program run by Eximbank provides a **preliminary commitment** that outlines the amount, terms, and conditions of financing it will extend to importers of U.S. goods and services. This commitment gives U.S. firms a competitive advantage in bidding on foreign projects because it enables the firms to offer financing along with their equipment proposals. Preliminary commitments are issued without cost (there is a $100 processing fee) or obligation to applicants.

Eximbank terms depend on the risk of the transaction and the degree of competition from foreign export financing agencies.

Eximbank charges a front-end *exposure fee,* assessed on each disbursement of a loan by Eximbank or the guaranteed or intermediary lender. Exposure fees, which are adjusted periodically, vary according to the term of the loan, the classification of the borrower or guarantor, and the borrower's country. For exposure-fee purposes, Eximbank classifies countries in five country categories according to risk. Under each country category, there are three borrower/guarantor classifications:

- Class I: Sovereign borrowers or guarantors, or for political-risks-only coverage
- Class II: Creditworthy nonsovereign public institutions or banks, or highly creditworthy private buyers
- Class III: Other creditworthy private buyers

In recent years, Eximbank has become more aggressive in fighting perceived abuses by foreign export-credit agencies. One area that Eximbank has targeted is foreign **mixed-credit financing**—the practice of tying grants and low-interest loans to the acceptance of specific commercial contracts. For years, U.S. capital-equipment exporters, engineering firms, and high-tech producers have lost overseas bids to foreign firms backed by government mixed credits. Eximbank now offers its own mixed credits. It will even offer mixed-credit deals before the fact. Any deal that has a chance of attracting a foreign mixed-credit bid is considered. However, an Eximbank spokesperson noted, "This is not an export promotion. We are not out there to match every mixed credit. We're out to end mixed credits, and will only offer one if it helps us to make a specific negotiating point."[1]

Private Export Funding Corporation   The **Private Export Funding Corporation (PEFCO)** was created in 1970 by the **Bankers' Association for Foreign Trade** to mobilize private capital for financing the export of big-ticket items by U.S. firms. It purchases the medium- to long-term debt obligations of importers of U.S. products at fixed interest rates. PEFCO finances its portfolio of foreign importer loans through the sale of its own securities. Eximbank fully guarantees repayment of all PEFCO foreign obligations.

PEFCO normally extends its credits jointly with one or more commercial banks and Eximbank. The maturity of the importers' notes purchased by PEFCO varies from 2.5 years to 12 years; the banks take the short-term maturity and Eximbank takes the long-term portion of a PEFCO loan. Much of this money goes to finance purchases of U.S.-manufactured jet aircraft and related equipment such as jet engines.

Trends   There are several trends in public-source export financing, including:

> Government export financing agencies are shifting to buyer credits and are acting as catalysts to attract private capital.

1. *A shift from supplier to buyer credits:* Many capital goods exports that cannot be financed under the traditional medium-term supplier credits become feasible under buyer credits, where the payment period can be stretched up to 20 years.

2. *A growing emphasis on acting as catalysts to attract private capital:* This action includes participating with private sources, either as a member of a financial consortium or as a partner with an individual private investor, in supplying export credits.

3. *Public agencies as a source of refinancing:* Public agencies are becoming an important source for refinancing loans made by bankers and private financiers. Refinancing enables a private creditor to discount its export loans with the government.

4. *Attempts to limit competition among agencies:* The virtual export-credit war among governments has led to several attempts to agree upon and coordinate financing terms. These attempts, however, have been honored more in the breach than in the observance.

Export-Credit Insurance

> Subsidized government export-credit insurance enables exporters to borrow from banks at below-market rates.

Export financing covered by government credit insurance, also known as **export-credit insurance**, provides protection against losses from political and commercial risks. It serves as collateral for the credit and is often indispensable in making the sale. The insurance does not usually provide an ironclad guarantee against all risks, however. Having this insurance results in lowering the cost of borrowing from private institutions because the government agency is bearing those risks set forth in the insurance policy. The financing is nonrecourse to the extent that risks and losses are covered. Often, however, the insurer requires additional security in the form of a guarantee by a foreign local bank or a certificate from the foreign central bank that foreign exchange is available for repayment of the interest and principal.

---

[1] "How U.S. Firms Benefit from Eximbank's War on Foreign Mixed Credits," *Business International Money Report*, February 10, 1986, p. 41.

The purpose of export-credit insurance is to encourage a nation's export sales by protecting domestic exporters against nonpayment by importers. The existence of medium- and long-term credit insurance policies makes banks more willing to provide nonrecourse financing of big-ticket items that require lengthy repayment maturities, provided the goods in question have been delivered and accepted.

The FCIA insures against commercial and political risks.

Foreign Credit Insurance Association   In the United States, the export-credit insurance program is administered by the **Foreign Credit Insurance Association (FCIA)**. The FCIA is a cooperative effort of Eximbank and a group of approximately fifty of the leading marine, casualty, and property insurance companies. FCIA insurance offers protection from political and commercial risks to U.S. exporters: The private insurers cover commercial risks, and the Eximbank covers political risks. The exporter (or the financial institution providing the loan) must self-insure that portion not covered by the FCIA.

Short-term insurance is available for export credits up to 180 days (360 days for bulk agricultural commodities and consumer durables) from the date of shipment. Coverage is of two types: comprehensive (90–100 percent of political and 90–95 percent of commercial risks) and political only (90–100 percent coverage). Coinsurance is required presumably because of the element of moral hazard: the possibility that exporters might take unreasonable risks knowing that they would still be paid in full.

Rather than sell insurance on a case-by-case basis, the FCIA approves discretionary limits within which each exporter can approve its own credits. Insurance rates are based on terms of sale, type of buyer, and country of destination and can vary from a low of 0.1 percent to a high of 2 percent. The greater the loss experience associated with the particular exporter and the countries and customers it deals with, the higher the insurance premium charged. The FCIA also offers preshipment insurance up to 180 days from the time of sale.

Medium-term insurance, guaranteed by Eximbank and covering big-ticket items sold on credit usually from 181 days to five years, is available on a case-by-case basis. As with short-term coverage, the exporter must reside in, and ship from, the United States. However, the FCIA will provide medium-term coverage for that portion only of the value added that originated in the United States. As before, the rates depend on the terms of sale and the destination.

Under the FCIA lease insurance program, lessors of U.S. equipment and related services can cover both the stream of lease payments and the fair market value of products leased outside the United States. The FCIA charges a risk-based premium that is determined by country, lease term, and the type of lease.

Taking Advantage of Government-Subsidized Export Financing

Government-subsidized export-credit programs often can be employed advantageously by multinationals. The use will depend on whether the firm is seeking to export or import goods or services, but the basic strategy remains the same: Shop around among the various export-credit agencies for the best possible financing arrangement.

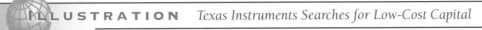

ILLUSTRATION   *Texas Instruments Searches for Low-Cost Capital*

Texas Instruments (TI) is seeking to finance an aggressive capital spending program through a series of joint ventures and other cooperative arrangements with foreign governments and corporations. In Italy, TI received a package of development grants and low-cost loans from the government that offset more than half of TI's investment in a state-of-the-art semiconductor plant there—an investment expected to total more than $1 billion over many years. TI was able to negotiate the incentive package because the Italian government was seeking to improve its technological infrastructure in the area selected by TI for the new plant.

In Taiwan, TI and a Taiwanese customer, Acer Computer Company, established a joint venture in which Acer's majority stake is financed with Taiwanese equity capital that would be unavailable to a U.S. company acting alone. In Japan, TI entered into a joint venture with Kobe Steel, a company seeking diversification. Here, too, TI relies on its foreign partner to supply a majority of the equity. In both Asian joint ventures, however, TI has an option to convert its initial minority stake into a majority holding.

Export Financing Strategy   Massey-Ferguson (now Varity Corporation), the multinational Canadian farm-equipment manufacturer, illustrates how MNCs are able to generate business for their foreign subsidiaries at minimum expense and risk by playing off national export-credit programs against each other.

> MNCs can get better financing terms by playing off export-credit agencies against each other.

The key to this *export financing strategy* is to view the foreign countries in which the MNC has plants not only as markets but also as potential sources of financing for exports to third countries. For example, in early 1978, Massey-Ferguson was looking to ship 7,200 tractors (worth $53 million) to Turkey, but it was unwilling to assume the risk of currency inconvertibility.[2] Turkey at that time already owed $2 billion to various foreign creditors, and it was uncertain whether it would be able to come up with dollars to pay off its debts (especially because its reserves were at about zero).

Massey solved this problem by manufacturing the tractors at its Brazilian subsidiary, Massey-Ferguson of Brazil, and selling them to Brazil's Interbras—the trading-company arm of Petrobras, the Brazilian national oil corporation. Interbras, in turn, arranged to sell the tractors to Turkey and pay Massey in cruzeiros. The cruzeiro financing for Interbras came from Cacex, the Banco do Brazil department that is in charge of foreign trade. Cacex underwrote all the political, commercial, and exchange risks as part of the Brazilian government's intense export promotion drive. Before choosing Brazil as a supply point, Massey made a point of shopping around to get the best export-credit deal available.

Import Financing Strategy   Firms engaged in projects that have sizable import requirements may be able to finance these purchases on attractive terms. A number of countries, including the United States, make credit available to foreign purchasers at low (below-market) interest rates and with long repayment periods. These loans are almost always tied to procurement in the agency's country; thus, the firm must compile a list of goods and services required for the project and relate them to potential sources by country. Where there is overlap among the potential suppliers, the purchasing firm may have leverage to extract more favorable financing terms from the various export-credit agencies involved. This strategy is illustrated by the hypothetical example of a copper mining venture in Exhibit 18.9.

Perhaps the best-known application of this *import financing strategy* in recent years was the financing of the Soviet gas pipeline to Western Europe. The former Soviet Union played off various European and Japanese suppliers and export financing agencies against each other and managed to get extraordinarily favorable credit and pricing terms.

18.5 COUNTERTRADE

In recent years, more and more multinationals have had to resort to **countertrade** to sell overseas: purchasing local products to offset the exports of their own products to that market. Countertrade transactions often can be complex and cumbersome. They may involve two-way or three-way transactions, especially where a company is forced to accept unrelated goods for resale by outsiders.

---

[2] "Massey-Ferguson's No-Risk Tractor Deal," *Business International Money Report*, February 3, 1978, pp. 35–36.

EXHIBIT 18.9 • ALTERNATIVE SOURCES OF PROCUREMENT: HYPOTHETICAL COPPER MINE (U.S. $ MILLION)

Item	Total Project	United States	France	Germany	Japan	United Kingdom	Sweden	Italy
Mine Equipment								
Shovels	$12	$12	$ 8	$12	$12	$12	$10	—
Trucks	20	20	—	20	20	10	20	12
Other	8	8	5	3	6	8	—	4
Mine Facilities								
Shops	7	7	7	7	3	7	5	6
Offices	3	3	3	3	2	3	3	2
Preparation Plant								
Crushers	11	11	8	11	11	11	—	—
Loading	15	15	10	10	15	12	15	7
Environmental	13	13	5	8	5	10	7	5
Terminal								
Ore Handling	13	13	10	13	13	13	8	9
Shiploader	6	6	6	6	6	6	2	4
Bulk Commodities								
Steel	20	20	20	20	20	15	8	20
Electrical	17	17	12	14	10	15	5	8
Mechanical	15	15	8	—	12	10	6	—
Total potential foreign purchases	$160	$160	$102	$127	$135	$132	$89	$77

More and more MNCs have resorted to countertrade in recent years to sell overseas.

If swapping goods for goods sounds less efficient than using cash or credit, that is because it is less efficient, but it is preferable to having no sales in a given market. More firms are finding it increasingly difficult to conduct business without being prepared to countertrade. Although precise numbers are impossible to come by, this transaction is growing in importance. One estimate placed countertrade volume at from 20 percent to 30 percent of all international trade.[3]

Countertrade is viewed as a necessary evil by the firms involved.

When a company exports to a nation requiring countertrade, it must take back goods that the country cannot (or will not try to) sell in international markets. To unload these goods, the company usually has to cut the prices at which the goods are nominally valued in the barter arrangement. Recognizing this necessity, the firm typically will pad the price of the goods it sells to its countertrade customer. When a German machine-tool maker sells to Romania, for instance, it might raise prices by 20 percent. Then, when it unloads the blouses it gets in return, the premium covers the reduction in price.

Usually, an exporting company wants to avoid the trouble of marketing those blouses, so it hands over the 10 percent premium to a countertrade specialist. This middleman splits the premium with a blouse buyer, keeping perhaps 2 percent and passing the remaining 8 percent along in price cuts. The result: Romania pays above the market for imports, making international trade less attractive than it should be, and dumps its own goods through back-door price shaving. In the long run, however, the practice is self-defeating. Having failed to set up continuing relationships with customers, Romania never learns what the market really wants—what style blouses, for instance—or how it might improve its competitiveness.

Countertrade takes several specific forms.

1. **Barter** is a direct exchange of goods between two parties without the use of money. For example, Iran might swap oil for guns.

---

[3] Thomas R. Hofstedt, "An Overview of Countertrade," July 29, 1987, unpublished.

2. **Counterpurchase**, also known as parallel barter, is the sale and purchase of goods that are unrelated to each other. For example, PepsiCo sold soft drinks to the former Soviet Union for vodka.

3. **Buyback** is repayment of the original purchase price through the sale of a related product. For example, Western European countries delivered various pipeline materials to the former Soviet Union for construction of a gas pipeline from Siberian gas fields and in return agreed to purchase 28 billion cubic meters of gas per year.

The unanswered question in countertrade is: Why go through such a convoluted sales process? Why not sell the goods directly at their market price (which is what ultimately happens anyway) using experts to handle the marketing? One argument is that countertrade enables members of cartels such as OPEC to undercut an agreed-upon price without formally doing so. Another argument is that countertrade keeps bureaucrats busy in centrally planned economies. Countertrade also may reduce the risk faced by a country that contracts for a new manufacturing facility. If the contractor's payment is received in the form of goods supplied by the facility, the contractor has an added incentive to do quality work and to ensure that the plant's technology is suitable for the skill levels of the available workers.

Regardless of its reason for being, countertrading is replete with problems for the firms involved. First, the goods that can be taken in countertrade are usually undesirable. Those that could be readily converted into cash have already been converted, so, although a firm shipping computers to Brazil might prefer to take coffee beans in return, the only goods available might be Brazilian shoes. Second, the trading details are difficult to work out. (How many tons of naphtha is a pile of Romanian blouses worth?) The inevitable result is a very high ratio of talk to action, with only a small percentage of deals that are talked about getting done. And lost deals cost money.

Until recently, most countertrade centered on the government foreign trade organizations (FTOs) of Eastern European countries. In order to sell a machine or an entire plant to an FTO, a Western firm might be required to take at least some of its pay in goods (for example, tomatoes, linen, and machine parts). Sometimes these deals will stretch over several years. Centered in Vienna, the countertrade experts in this business use their contacts with Eastern European officials and their knowledge of available products to earn their keep. However, the restructuring currently taking place in Eastern Europe has eliminated most FTOs and thereby reduced the scale and profitability of the countertrade business.

The loss of Eastern European business, however, has been more than offset by the explosive growth in countertrade with Third World countries. The basis for the new wave of countertrade is the cutting off of bank credit to developing nations. Third World countertrade involves more commodities and fewer hard-to-sell manufactured goods. A typical deal, arranged by Sears World Trade, involved bartering U.S. breeding swine for Dominican sugar. Another countertrader swapped BMWs for Ecuadorian tuna fish. The dissolution of the former Soviet Union also has created new opportunities for countertrade, as the convoluted example of Marc Rich & Co. illustrates.

As Eastern European countries have reduced counter-trading, Third World countries have filled the gap.

ILLUSTRATION   *Marc Rich & Co. Recreates the Former Soviet Union's Supply System*

In 1992, Marc Rich & Co., a giant Swiss-based commodity trader, engineered a remarkable $100 million deal involving enterprises and governments in five newly independent countries. This deal essentially pieced together shattered supply links that Moscow controlled when the U.S.S.R. was one giant planned economy.

Here's how the deal worked. Marc Rich bought 70,000 tons of raw sugar from Brazil on the open market. The sugar was shipped to Ukraine, where, through a "tolling contract," it was processed at a local refinery. After paying the sugar refinery with part of the sugar, Marc Rich sent 30,000 tons of refined sugar east to several huge Siberian oil refineries, which need sugar to supply their vast workforces.

Strapped for hard currency, the oil refineries paid instead with oil products, much of it low-grade A-76 gasoline, which has few export markets. But one market is Mongolia, with which Marc Rich has long traded. The company shipped 130,000 tons of oil products there; in payment, the Mongolians turned over 35,000 tons of copper concentrate. The company sent most of that back across the border to Kazakhstan, where it was refined into copper metal. Then the metal was shipped westward to a Baltic seaport and out to the world market where, several months after the deal began, Marc Rich earned a hard currency profit.

In an effort to make it easier for Third World countries to buy their products, big manufacturers—including General Motors, General Electric, and Caterpillar—have set up countertrading subsidiaries. Having sold auto and truck parts to Mexico, for example, GM's countertrade subsidiary, Motors Trading Corporation, arranged tour groups to the country and imported Mexican slippers and gloves. Similarly, arms manufacturers selling to developing countries are often forced to accept local products in return—for example, Iraqi oil for French Exocet missiles or Peruvian anchovies for Spanish Piranha patrol boats.

Authorities in countertrading countries are concerned that goods taken in countertrade will cannibalize their existing cash markets. Proving that countertrade goods go to new markets is difficult enough in the area of manufactured goods; it's impossible for commodities, whose ultimate use cannot be identified with its source. For example, some Indonesian rubber taken in countertrade inevitably will displace rubber that Indonesia sells for cash.

> *Countertrading countries try to ensure that goods taken in countertrade will not cannibalize their existing cash exports.*

Interest in countertrade and its variations appears to be growing, even among developed countries, despite the obvious difficulties it presents to the firms and countries involved. For example, in order for McDonnell Douglas to sell F-15s to the Japanese air force, it had to offset the cost to Japan in currency and jobs by agreeing to teach Japanese manufacturers to make military aircraft.

The growth in countertrade is reflected in the scramble for experienced specialists. It has been said that a good countertrader combines the avarice and opportunism of a commodities trader, the inventiveness and political sensitivity of a crooked bureaucrat, and the technical knowledge of a machine-tool salesperson.

18.6 SUMMARY AND CONCLUSIONS

In this chapter, we examined different financing arrangements and documents involved in international trade. The most important documents encountered in bank-related financing are the draft, which is a written order to pay; the letter of credit, which is a bank guarantee of payment provided that certain stipulated conditions are met; and the bill of lading, the document covering actual shipment of the merchandise by a common carrier and title. Documents of lesser importance include commercial and consular invoices and the insurance certificate.

These instruments serve four primary functions. They

- Reduce both buyer and seller risk
- Define who bears those risks that remain
- Facilitate the transfer of risk to a third party
- Facilitate financing

Each instrument evolved over time as a rational response to the additional risks in international trade posed by the greater distances, lack of familiarity between exporters and importers, possibility of government imposition of exchange controls, and greater costs involved in bringing suit against a party domiciled in another nation. Were it not for the latter two factors and publicly financed export-promotion programs, we might expect that, with the passage of time, the financial arrangements in international trade would differ little from those encountered in purely domestic commercial transactions.

We also examined some of the government-sponsored export-financing programs and credit-insurance programs. The number of these institutions and their operating scope have grown steadily, in line with national export drives. From the standpoint of international financial managers, the most significant difference between public and private sources of financing is that public lending agencies offer their funds and credit insurance at lower-than-normal commercial rates. The multinational firm can take advantage of these subsidized rates by structuring its marketing and production programs in accord with the different national financial programs.

QUESTIONS

1. What are the basic problems arising in international trade financing, and how do the main financing instruments help solve those problems?

2. The different forms of export financing distribute risks differently between the exporter and the importer. Analyze the distribution of risk in the following export-financing instruments.
   a. Confirmed, revocable letter of credit
   b. Confirmed, irrevocable letter of credit
   c. Open account credit
   d. Time draft, D/A
   e. Cash with order
   f. Cash in advance
   g. Consignment
   h. Sight draft

3. Describe the different steps and documents involved in exporting motors from Kansas to Hong Kong using a confirmed letter of credit, with payment terms of 90 days sight. What alternatives are available to the exporter to finance this shipment?

4. Explain the advantages and disadvantages of each of the following forms of export financing:
   a. Bankers' acceptances
   b. Discounting
   c. Factoring
   d. Forfaiting

5. What are the potential advantages and disadvantages of countertrade for the parties involved?

PROBLEMS

1. Texas Computers (TC) recently has begun selling overseas. It currently has thirty foreign orders outstanding, with the typical order averaging $2,500. TC is considering the following three alternatives to protect itself against credit risk on these foreign sales:

   • *Request a letter of credit from each customer.* The cost to the customer would be $75 plus 0.25 percent of the invoice amount. To remain competitive, TC would have to absorb the cost of the letter of credit.

   • *Factor the receivables.* The factor would charge a nonrecourse fee of 1.6 percent.

   • *Buy FCIA insurance.* The FCIA would charge a 1 percent insurance premium.

   a. Which of these alternatives would you recommend to Texas Computers? Why?

   b. Suppose that TC's average order size rose to $250,000. How would that affect your decision?

2. L.A. Cellular has received an order for phone switches from Singapore. The switches will be exported under the terms of a letter of credit issued by Sumitomo Bank on behalf of Singapore Telecommunications. Under the terms of the L/C, the face value of the export order, $12 million, will be paid six months after Sumitomo accepts a draft drawn by L.A. Cellular. The current dis-count rate on six-month acceptances is 8.5 percent per annum, and the acceptance fee is 1.25 percent per annum. In addition, there is a flat commission, equal to 0.5 percent of the face amount of the accepted draft, that must be paid if it is sold.

   a. How much cash will L.A. Cellular receive if it holds the acceptance until maturity?

   b. How much cash will it receive if it sells the acceptance at once?

   c. Suppose L.A. Cellular's opportunity cost of funds is 8.75 percent per annum. If it wishes to maximize the present value of its acceptance, should it discount the acceptance?

3. Suppose Minnesota Machines (MM) is trying to price an export order from Russia. Payment is due nine months after shipping. Given the risks involved, MM would like to factor its receivable without recourse. The factor will charge a monthly discount of 2 percent plus a fee equal to 1.5 percent of the face value of the receivable for the nonrecourse financing.

   a. If Minnesota Machines desires revenue of $2.5 million from the sale, after paying all factoring charges, what is the minimum acceptable price it should charge?

   b. Alternatively, CountyBank has offered to discount the receivable, but with recourse, at an annual rate of

14 percent plus a 1 percent fee. What price will net MM the $2.5 million it desires to clear from the sale?

c. On the basis of your answers to Parts a and b, should Minnesota Machines discount or factor its Russian receivables? MM is competing against Nippon Machines for the order, so the higher MM's price, the lower the probability that its bid will be accepted. What other considerations should influence MM's decision?

d. What other alternatives might be available to MM to finance its sale to Russia?

BIBLIOGRAPHY

Business International Corporation. *Financing Foreign Operations.* New York: BIC, various issues.

Chase World Information Corporation. *Methods of Export Financing,* 2nd ed. New York: Chase World Information Corporation, 1976.

Schneider, Gerhard W. *Export-Import Financing.* New York: The Ronald Press, 1974.

INTERNET RESOURCES

www.export.gov/ Web site that is dedicated to helping U.S. firms learn the costs and risks associated with exporting and develop a strategy for exporting. Contains detailed information on all aspects of exporting, including setting payment terms, financing, logistics, and so on.

www.exim.gov Web site of the U.S. Export-Import Bank (Eximbank). Contains detailed information on the Eximbank and its various programs.

www.countertrade.org Web site of the American Countertrade Association (ACA). Contains information on countertrade and links to other relevant Web sites.

INTERNET EXERCISES

1. What programs does the U.S. Eximbank have available to help U.S. exporters?

2. What issues are countertraders currently grappling with?

3. Go to the Web site of a major international bank such as Citigroup (www.citigroup.com) or Bank of America (www.bankofamerica.com). What international trade financing services does this bank provide? How can these services be of value to a multinational company?

CURRENT ASSET MANAGEMENT AND SHORT-TERM FINANCING

A penny saved is a penny earned.

Benjamin Franklin

CHAPTER LEARNING OBJECTIVES

- To describe the basic objectives of international cash management
- To identify the advantages of a centralized international cash management program
- To describe the techniques that multinational corporations (MNCs) can use to expedite the collection of funds both within a foreign country and across borders, and to more effectively manage their disbursements
- To define payments netting and explain its benefits
- To identify the basic techniques and guidelines for globally managing a marketable securities portfolio
- To describe the techniques available to an MNC with operating subsidiaries in many countries to economize on cash and marketable securities
- To describe the techniques companies can use for international cash planning and budgeting
- To identify the basic problems MNCs have in managing their bank relations and describe how MNCs can cope with these problems
- To describe the circumstances under which an MNC may benefit by easing its credit terms on foreign sales
- To describe a five-step approach that firms can use to compare the expected benefits and costs associated with extending credit internationally
- To identify the inventory management problems faced by MNCs and the techniques that they can use to deal with these problems
- To identify the key factors associated with developing a short-term overseas financing strategy
- To describe and evaluate the objectives that a firm might use to arrive at its borrowing strategy, including deciding where and in which currencies to borrow
- To describe the available short-term borrowing options

KEY TERMS

bankers' acceptance
bilateral netting
cable remittances
cash pool
cleanup clause
cleared funds
collections
commercial paper (CP)

compensating balance requirements
credit terms
current assets
current liabilities
disbursements
discounting
good funds
interaffiliate fund flows

intercompany loan	payments netting
internal interest rates	political risk
international cash management	revolving credit agreement
inventory stockpiling	same-day value
line of credit	SWIFT
lock box	term loan
multilateral netting	treasury workstation
multinational cash mobilization	value-dating
netting center	working capital
overdraft	

The management of **working capital** in the multinational corporation is similar to its domestic counterpart. Both are concerned with selecting that combination of **current assets**—cash, marketable securities, accounts receivable, and inventory—and **current liabilities**—short-term funds to finance those current assets—that will maximize the value of the firm. The essential differences between domestic and international working-capital management include the impact of currency fluctuations, potential exchange controls, and multiple tax jurisdictions on these decisions, in addition to the wider range of short-term financing and investment options available.

Chapter 20 discusses the mechanisms by which the multinational firm can shift liquid assets among its various affiliates; it also examines the tax and other consequences of these maneuvers. This chapter deals with the management of working-capital items available to each affiliate. The focus is on international cash, accounts receivable, and inventory management and short-term financing.

19.1 INTERNATIONAL CASH MANAGEMENT

The principals of domestic and international cash management are the same, but the latter is a more complicated exercise.

International money managers attempt to attain on a worldwide basis the traditional domestic objectives of cash management: (1) bringing the company's cash resources within control as quickly and efficiently as possible and (2) achieving the optimum conservation and utilization of these funds. Accomplishing the first goal requires establishing accurate, timely forecasting and reporting systems, improving cash collections and disbursements, and decreasing the cost of moving funds among affiliates. The second objective is achieved by minimizing the required level of cash balances, making money available when and where it is needed, and increasing the risk-adjusted return on those funds that can be invested.

This section is divided into seven key areas of **international cash management**: (1) organization, (2) collection and disbursement of funds, (3) netting of interaffiliate payments, (4) investment of excess funds, (5) establishment of an optimal level of worldwide corporate cash balances, (6) cash planning and budgeting, and (7) bank relations.

Organization

When compared with a system of autonomous operating units, a fully centralized international cash management program offers a number of advantages:

- The corporation is able to operate with a smaller amount of cash; pools of excess liquidity are absorbed and eliminated; each operation will maintain transactions balances only and not hold speculative or precautionary ones.
- By reducing total assets, profitability is enhanced and financing costs are reduced.

- The headquarters staff, with its purview of all corporate activity, can recognize problems and opportunities that an individual unit might not perceive.
- All decisions can be made using the overall corporate benefit as the criterion.
- By increasing the volume of foreign exchange and other transactions done through headquarters, firms encourage banks to provide better foreign exchange quotes and better service.
- Greater expertise in cash and portfolio management exists if one group is responsible for these activities.
- Less can be lost in the event of an expropriation or currency controls restricting the transfer of funds because the corporation's total assets at risk in a foreign country can be reduced.

There is a growing tendency by MNCs to centralize their international cash management.

Many experienced multinational firms have long understood these benefits. Today the combination of volatile currency and interest rate fluctuations, questions of capital availability, increasingly complex organizations and operating arrangements, and a growing emphasis on profitability virtually mandates a highly centralized international cash management system. There is also a trend to place much greater responsibility in corporate headquarters.

Centralization does not necessarily mean that corporate headquarters has control of all facets of cash management. Instead, a concentration of decision making at a sufficiently high level within the corporation is required so that all pertinent information is readily available and can be used to optimize the firm's position.

Collection and Disbursement of Funds

Accelerating collections to reduce float is a key element of international cash management.

Accelerating **collections** both within a foreign country and across borders is a key element of international cash management. Material potential benefits exist because long delays often are encountered in collecting receivables, particularly on export sales, and in transferring funds among affiliates and corporate headquarters. Allowing for mail time and bank processing, delays of eight to ten business days are common from the moment an importer pays an invoice to the time when the exporter is credited with **good funds**—that is, when the funds are available for use. Given high interest rates, wide fluctuations in the foreign exchange markets, and the periodic imposition of credit restrictions that have characterized financial markets in some years, cash in transit has become more expensive and more exposed to risk.

With increasing frequency, corporate management is participating in the establishment of an affiliate's credit policy and the monitoring of collection performance. The principal goals of this intervention are to minimize **float**—that is, the transit time of payments—to reduce the investment in accounts receivable and to lower banking fees and other transaction costs. By converting receivables into cash as rapidly as possible, a company can increase its portfolio or reduce its borrowing and thereby earn a higher investment return or save interest expense.

Considering either national or international collections, accelerating the receipt of funds usually involves: (1) defining and analyzing the different available payment channels, (2) selecting the most efficient method, which can vary by country and by customer, and (3) giving specific instructions regarding procedures to the firm's customers and banks.

In addressing the first two points, the full costs of using the various methods must be determined, and the inherent delay of each must be calculated. Two main sources of delay in the collections process are (1) the time between the dates of payment and of receipt and (2) the time for the payment to clear through the banking system. Inasmuch as banks will be as "inefficient" as possible to increase their float, understanding the subtleties of domestic and international money transfers is requisite if a firm is to reduce the time that funds are held and extract the maximum value from its banking relationships. Exhibit 19.1 lists the different methods multinationals use to expedite their collection of receivables.

With respect to payment instructions to customers and banks, the use of **cable remittances** is a crucial means for companies to minimize delays in receipt of payments and in conversion of payments into cash, especially in Europe because European banks tend to defer the value of good funds when the payment is made by check or draft.

In the case of international cash movements, having all affiliates transfer funds by telex enables the corporation to better plan because the vagaries of mail time are eliminated. Third parties, too, will be asked to use wire transfers. For most amounts, the fees required for telex are less than the savings generated by putting the money to use more quickly.

One of the cash manager's biggest problems is that bank-to-bank wire transfers do not always operate with great efficiency or reliability. Delays, crediting the wrong account, availability of funds, and many other operational problems are common. One solution to these problems is to be found in the **SWIFT** (Society for Worldwide Interbank Financial Telecommunications) network, first mentioned in Chapter 7. SWIFT has standardized international message formats and employs a dedicated computer network to support funds transfer messages.

The SWIFT network connects more than 7,000 banks and broker-dealers in 192 countries and processes more than five million transactions a day, representing about $5 trillion in payments. Its mission is to quickly transmit standard forms to allow its member banks to automatically process data by computer. All types of customer and bank transfers are transmitted, as well as foreign exchange deals, bank account statements, and administrative messages. To use SWIFT, the corporate client must deal with domestic banks that are subscribers and with foreign banks that are highly automated. Like many other proprietary data networks, SWIFT is facing growing competition from Internet-based systems that allow both banks and nonfinancial companies to connect to a secure payments network.

To cope with some of the transmittal delays associated with checks or drafts, customers are instructed to remit to "mobilization" points that are centrally located in regions with large sales volumes. These funds are managed centrally or are transmitted to the selling subsidiary. For example, European customers may be told to make all payments to Switzerland, where the corporation maintains a staff specializing in cash and portfolio management and collections.

Sometimes customers are asked to pay directly into a designated account at a branch of the bank that is mobilizing the MNC's funds internationally. This method is particularly useful when banks have large branch networks. Another technique used is to have customers remit funds to a designated **lock box**, which is a postal box in the company's name. One or more times daily, a local bank opens the mail received at the lock box and deposits any checks immediately.

Multinational banks now provide firms with rapid transfers of their funds among branches in different countries, generally giving their customers **same-day value**—that is,

> The SWIFT network improves the efficiency and reliability of international fund transfers among member banks.

EXHIBIT 19.1 • HOW MULTINATIONALS EXPEDITE THEIR COLLECTION OF RECEIVABLES

Procedures for Expediting Receipt of Payment	Procedures for Expediting Conversion of Payments into Cash
Cable remittances	Cable remittances
Mobilization centers	Establishing accounts in customers' banks
Lock boxes	Negotiations with banks on value-dating
Electronic fund transfers	

funds are credited that same day. Rapid transfers also can be accomplished through a bank's correspondent network, although it becomes somewhat more difficult to arrange same-day value for funds.

Chief financial officers are increasingly relying on computers and worldwide telecommunications networks to help manage the company cash portfolio. Many multinational firms will not deal with a bank that does not have a leading-edge electronic banking system.

At the heart of today's high-tech corporate treasuries are the **treasury workstation** software packages that many big banks sell as supplements to their cash management systems. Linking the company with its bank and branch offices, the workstations let treasury personnel compute a company's worldwide cash position on a real-time basis. Thus, the second a transaction is made in, say, Rio de Janeiro, it is electronically recorded in Tokyo as well. This simultaneous recordkeeping lets companies keep their funds active at all times. Treasury personnel can use their workstation to initiate fund transfers from units with surplus cash to those units that require funds, thereby reducing the level of bank borrowings.

MNCs today insist that their banks have leading-edge electronic banking systems.

ILLUSTRATION   *International Cash Management at National Semiconductor*

After computerizing its cash management system, National Semiconductor was able to save significant interest expenses by quickly transferring money from locations with surplus cash to those needing money. In a typical transaction, the company shifted a surplus $500,000 from its Japanese account to its Philippine operations—avoiding the need to borrow the half-million dollars and saving several thousand dollars in interest expense. Before computerization, it would have taken five or six days to discover the surplus.

Management of **disbursements** is a delicate balancing act: holding onto funds versus staying on good terms with suppliers. It requires a detailed knowledge of individual country and supplier nuances, as well as the myriad payment instruments and banking services available around the world. Exhibit 19.2 presents some questions that corporate treasurers should address in reviewing their disbursement policies.

Payments Netting in International Cash Management

Many multinational corporations are now in the process of rationalizing their production on a global basis. This process involves a highly coordinated international interchange of

EXHIBIT 19.2 • REVIEWING DISBURSEMENTS: AUDITING PAYMENT INSTRUMENTS

1. What payment instruments are you using to pay suppliers, employees, and government entities (e.g., checks, drafts, wire transfers, direct deposits)?
2. What are the total disbursements made through each of these instruments annually?
3. What is the mail and clearing float for these instruments in each country?
4. What techniques, such as remote disbursement, are being used to prolong the payment cycle?
5. How long does it take suppliers to process the various instruments and present them for payment?
6. What are the bank charges and internal processing costs for each instrument?
7. Are banking services such as controlled disbursement and zero-balance accounts used where available?

The high volume of interaffiliate trade leads to substantial interaffiliate fund flows.

materials, parts, subassemblies, and finished products among the various units of the MNC, with many affiliates both buying from and selling to each other.

The importance of these physical flows to the international financial executive is that they are accompanied by a heavy volume of **interaffiliate fund flows**. Of particular importance is the fact that a measurable cost is associated with these cross-border fund transfers, including the cost of purchasing foreign exchange (the foreign exchange spread), the opportunity cost of float (time in transit), and other transaction costs, such as cable charges. These transaction costs are estimated to vary from 0.25 percent to 1.5 percent of the volume transferred. Thus, there is a clear incentive to minimize the total volume of intercompany fund flows. This can be achieved by payments netting.

Payments netting reduces the volume and cost of intercompany fund flows.

Bilateral and Multilateral Netting The idea behind a **payments netting** system is very simple: Payments among affiliates go back and forth, whereas only a netted amount need be transferred. Suppose, for example, the German subsidiary of an MNC sells goods worth $1 million to its Italian affiliate that in turn sells goods worth $2 million to the German unit. The combined flows total $3 million. On a net basis, however, the German unit need remit only $1 million to the Italian unit. This type of **bilateral netting** is valuable, however, only if subsidiaries sell back and forth to each other.

Bilateral netting would be of less use where there is a more complex structure of internal sales, such as in the situation depicted in Exhibit 19.3A, which presents the payment flows (converted first into a common currency, assumed here to be the dollar) that take place among four European affiliates, located in France, Belgium, Sweden, and the Netherlands. On a multilateral basis, however, there is greater scope for reducing cross-border fund transfers by netting out each affiliate's inflows against its outflows.

Multilateral netting can lead to dramatic reductions in intercompany fund flows.

Since a large percentage of multinational transactions are internal, leading to a relatively large volume of interaffiliate payments, the payoff from **multilateral netting** can be large relative to the costs of such a system. Many companies find they can eliminate 50 percent or more of their intercompany transactions through multilateral netting, with annual savings in foreign exchange transactions costs and bank-transfer charges that average between 0.5 percent and 1.5 percent per dollar netted. For example, SmithKline Beckman (now part of GlaxoSmithKline) estimates that it saves $300,000

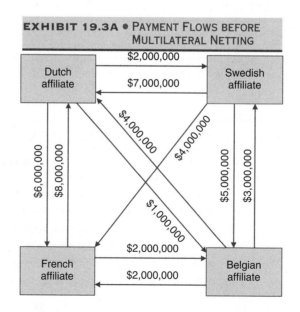

EXHIBIT 19.3A • PAYMENT FLOWS BEFORE MULTILATERAL NETTING

annually in foreign exchange transactions costs and bank transfer charges by using a multilateral netting system.[1] Similarly, Baxter International estimates that it saves $200,000 per year by eliminating approximately 60 percent of its intercompany transactions through netting.[2]

Information Requirements   Essential to any netting scheme is a centralized control point that can collect and record detailed information on the intracorporate accounts of each participating affiliate at specified time intervals. The control point, called a **netting center**, is a subsidiary company set up in a location with minimal exchange controls for trade transactions.

The netting center will use a matrix of payables and receivables to determine the net payer or creditor position of each affiliate at the date of clearing. An example of such a matrix is provided in Exhibit 19.3B, which takes the payment flows from Exhibit 19.3a and shows the amounts due to and from each of the affiliated companies. Note that in an intercompany system, the payables will always equal the receivables on both a gross basis and a net basis. Typically, the impact of currency changes on the amounts scheduled for transfer is minimized by fixing the exchange rate at which these transactions occur during the week that netting takes place.

Without netting, the total payments in the system would equal $44 million and the number of separate payments made would be 11. Multilateral netting will pare these transfers to $12 million, a net reduction of 73 percent, and the number of payments can be reduced to three, a net reduction of 73 percent as well. One possible set of payments is shown in Exhibit 19.3C. Assuming foreign exchange and bank-transfer charges of 0.75 percent, this company will save $240,000 through netting (0.0075 × $32 million).

Notice that alternative sets of multilateral payments were also possible in this example. For example, the Swedish unit could have paid $11 million to the Dutch unit, with the Dutch and Belgian units then sending $1 million each to the French unit. The choice of which affiliate(s) each payer pays depends on the relative costs of transferring funds between each pair of affiliates. The per-unit costs of sending funds between two affiliates can vary significantly from month to month because one subsidiary may receive payment from a third party in a currency that the other subsidiary needs. Using this currency for payment can eliminate one or more foreign exchange conversions. This conclusion implies that the cost of sending funds from Germany to France, for example, can differ greatly from the cost of moving money from France to Germany.

The netting center coordinates payment flows among the MNC's various units.

EXHIBIT 19.3B • INTERCOMPANY PAYMENTS MATRIX (U.S.$ MILLIONS)

	Paying Affiliates					
Receiving Affiliates	*Netherlands*	*France*	*Sweden*	*Belgium*	*Total Receipts*	*Net Receipt (Payment)*
Netherlands	—	8	7	4	19	10
France	6	—	4	2	12	2
Sweden	2	0	—	3	5	(11)
Belgium	1	2	5	=	8	(1)
Total payments	9	10	16	9	44	

[1] "How Centralized Systems Benefit Managerial Control: SmithKline Beckman," *Business International Money Report,* June 23, 1986, p. 198.
[2] Business International Corporation, *Solving International Financial and Currency Problems* (New York: BIC, 1976), p. 29.

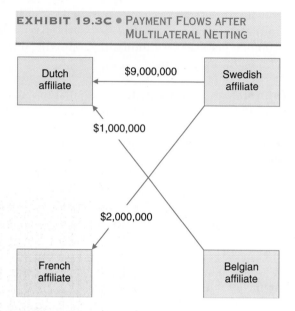

EXHIBIT 19.3C • PAYMENT FLOWS AFTER MULTILATERAL NETTING

For example, Volvo has a policy of transferring a currency, without conversion, to a unit needing that currency to pay a creditor.[3] To see how this policy works, suppose that Volvo Sweden buys automotive components from a German manufacturer and Volvo Belgium purchases automotive kits from Volvo Sweden. At the same time, a German dealer buys automobiles from Volvo Belgium and pays in euros. Volvo Belgium will then use these euros to pay Volvo Sweden, which in turn will use them to pay its German creditor.

Foreign Exchange Controls   Before implementing a payments netting system, a company needs to know whether any restrictions on netting exist. Firms sometimes may be barred from netting or be required to obtain permission from the local monetary authorities.

The value of netting rise with the volume of intercompany transactions.

Analysis   The higher the volume of intercompany transactions and the more back-and-forth selling that takes place, the more worthwhile netting is likely to be. A useful approach to evaluating a netting system would be to establish the direct cost savings of the netting system and then use this figure as a benchmark against which to measure the costs of implementation and operation. These setup costs have been estimated at less than $20,000.[4]

An additional benefit from running a netting system is the tighter control that management can exert over corporate fund flows. The same information required to operate a netting system also will enable an MNC to shift funds in response to expectations of currency movements, changing interest differentials, and tax differentials.

ILLUSTRATION   *Cost/Benefit Analysis of an International Cash Management System*

Although company A already operates a multilateral netting system, it commissioned a study to show where additional improvements in cash management could be made.[5] The firm proposed to establish a finance company (FINCO) in Europe. FINCO's primary function would be to act as a collecting and paying agent for divisions of company A that export to third parties. All receivables would be gathered into the international branch

---

[3] Ibid, p. 32.

[4] Business International Corporation, "The State of the Art," in *New Techniques in International Exposure and Cash Management*, vol. 1 (New York: BIC, 1977), p. 244.

[5] This illustration appears in "Cost/Benefit Analysis of One Company's Cash Management System," *Business International Money Report*, April 14, 1986, pp. 119–120.

network of bank X. Each branch would handle receivables denominated in the currency of its country of domicile. These branch accounts would be monitored by both FINCO and the exporting unit via the bank's electronic reporting facility.

Intercompany payments and third-party collection payments from FINCO to each exporter would be included in the existing multilateral netting system, which would be administered by FINCO. Payments for imports from third-party suppliers also would be included. Finally, the netting system would be expanded to include intercompany payments from operations in the United States, Canada, and one additional European country.

The feasibility study examined six basic savings components and two cost components. The realizable, annualized savings are summarized as follows:

Savings Component	Cost Savings
1. Optimized multilateral netting	$ 29,000
2. Reduced remittance-processing time by customer and remitting bank	26,000
3. Reduction in cross-border transfer float by collecting currencies in their home country	46,000
4. Reduction in cross-border transfer commissions and charges by collecting currencies in their home country	41,000
5. Use of incoming foreign currencies to source outgoing foreign payments in the same currencies	16,000
6. Use of interest-bearing accounts	8,000
Total estimated annual savings	$166,000

Cost Component	Cost
1. Computer time-sharing charges for accessing Bank X's system	$ 17,000
2. Communications charges for additional cross-border funds transfers	13,000
Total estimated annual costs	$ 30,000
Total net savings	$136,000

Management of the Short-Term Investment Portfolio

Companies must decide where to invest their cash balances.

A major task of international cash management is to determine the levels and currency denominations of the multinational group's investment in cash balances and money-market instruments. Firms with seasonal or cyclical cash flows have special problems, such as spacing investment maturities to coincide with projected needs. To manage this investment properly requires (1) a forecast of future cash needs based on the company's current budget and past experience and (2) an estimate of a minimum cash position for the coming period. These projections should take into account the effects of inflation and anticipated currency changes on future cash flows.

Successful management of an MNC's required cash balances and of any excess funds generated by the firm and its affiliates depends largely on the astute selection of appropriate short-term money market instruments. Rewarding opportunities exist in many countries, but the choice of an investment medium depends on government regulations, the structure of the market, and the tax laws, all of which vary widely. Available money instruments differ among the major markets, and at times, foreign firms are denied access to existing investment opportunities. Only a few markets, such as the broad and diversified U.S. market and the Eurocurrency markets, are truly free and international. Capsule summaries of key money market instruments are provided in Exhibit 19.4.

Once corporate headquarters has fully identified the present and future needs of its affiliates, it must then decide on a policy for managing its liquid assets worldwide. This policy must recognize that the value of shifting funds across national borders to earn the highest possible risk-adjusted return depends not only on the risk-adjusted yield differential, but also on the transaction costs involved. In fact, the basic reason for holding cash in several currencies simultaneously is the existence of currency conversion costs. If these costs are zero and government regulations permit, all cash balances should be held in the currency having the highest effective risk-adjusted return net of withdrawal costs.

Given that transaction costs do exist, the appropriate currency denomination mix of an MNC's investment in money and near-money assets is probably more a function of the

> The value of taking advantage of higher investment returns overseas must be traded off against the transaction costs involved.

EXHIBIT 19.4 ● KEY MONEY-MARKET INSTRUMENTS

Instrument	Borrower	Maturities	Comments
Treasury bills (T-bills)	Central governments of many countries	Up to 1 year	Safest and most liquid short-term investment
Federal funds (U.S.)	U.S. commercial banks temporarily short of legal reserve requirements	Overnight to 3 days	Suitable for very short-term investment of large amounts ($1 million or more)
Government agency notes (U.S.)	Issued by U.S. government agencies such as Federal National Mortgage Association	30 days to 270 days	Similar to local authority notes in the United Kingdom; both offer slightly higher yields than T-bills
Demand deposits	Commercial banks	On demand	Governments sometimes impose restrictions on interest rates banks can offer (as in the U.S.)
Time deposits	Commercial banks	Negotiable but advance notice usually required	Governments sometimes regulate interest rates and/or maturities.
Deposits with nonbank financial institutions	Nonbank financial institutions	Negotiable	Usually offer higher yields than banks do
Certificates of deposit (CDs)	Commercial banks	Negotiable but normally 30, 60, or 90 days	Negotiable papers representing a term bank deposit; more liquid than straight deposits because they can be sold
Bankers' acceptances	Bills of exchange guaranteed by a commercial bank	Up to 180 days	Highest-quality investment next to T-bills
Commercial paper (also known as trade paper or, in the United Kingdom, fine trade bills)	Large corporations with high credit ratings	30 days to 270 days	Negotiable, unsecured promissory notes; available in all major money markets
Temporary corporate loans	Corporations	Negotiable	Usually offer higher returns than those available from financial institutions but are not liquid because they must be held to maturity

currencies in which it has actual and projected inflows and outflows than of effective yield differentials or government regulations. The reason why is simple: Despite government controls, it would be highly unusual to see an annualized risk-adjusted interest differential of even 2 percent. Although seemingly large, a 2 percent annual differential yields only an additional 0.167 percent for a 30-day investment or 0.5 percent extra for a 90-day investment. Such small differentials can easily be offset by foreign exchange transaction costs. Thus, even large annualized risk-adjusted interest spreads may not justify shifting funds for short-term placements.

Portfolio Guidelines   Common-sense guidelines for globally managing the marketable securities portfolio are as follows:

1. Diversify the instruments in the portfolio to maximize the yield for a given level of risk. Don't invest only in government securities. Eurodollar and other instruments may be nearly as safe.

2. Review the portfolio daily to decide which securities should be liquidated and what new investments should be made.

3. In revising the portfolio, make sure that the incremental interest earned more than compensates for such added costs as clerical work, the income lost between investments, fixed charges such as the foreign exchange spread, and commissions on the sale and purchase of securities.

4. If rapid conversion to cash is an important consideration, then carefully evaluate the security's marketability (liquidity). Ready markets exist for some securities, but not for others.

5. Tailor the maturity of the investment to the firm's projected cash needs, or be sure a secondary market for the investment with high liquidity exists.

6. Carefully consider opportunities for covered or uncovered interest arbitrage.

Optimal Worldwide Cash Levels

Centralized cash management typically involves the transfer of an affiliate's cash in excess of minimal operating requirements into a centrally managed account, or **cash pool.** Some firms have established a special corporate entity that collects and disburses funds through a single bank account.

Cash pooling enables the MNC to minimize its level of cash reserves to achieve a given financial safety level.

With cash pooling, each affiliate need hold locally only the minimum cash balance required for transactions purposes. All precautionary balances are held by the parent or in the pool. As long as the demands for cash by the various units are reasonably independent of each other, centralized cash management can provide an equivalent degree of protection with a lower level of cash reserves.

Another benefit from pooling is that either less borrowing need be done or more excess funds are available for investment where returns will be maximized. Consequently, interest expenses are reduced or investment income is increased. In addition, the larger the pool of funds, the more worthwhile it becomes for a firm to invest in cash management expertise. Furthermore, pooling permits exposure arising from holding foreign currency cash balances to be centrally managed.

Evaluation and Control   Taking over control of an affiliate's cash reserves can create motivational problems for local managers unless some adjustments are made to the way in which these managers are evaluated. One possible approach is to relieve local managers of profit responsibility for their excess funds. The problem with this solution is that it provides no incentive for local managers to take advantage of specific opportunities of which only they may be aware.

An alternative approach is to present local managers with interest rates for borrowing or lending funds to the pool that reflect the opportunity cost of money to the parent corporation. In setting these **internal interest rates** (IIRs), the corporate treasurer, in effect, is acting as a bank, offering to borrow or lend currencies at given rates. By examining these IIRs, local treasurers will be more aware of the opportunity cost of their idle cash balances, as well as having an added incentive to act on this information. In many instances, they will prefer to transfer at least part of their cash balances (where permitted) to a central pool in order to earn a greater return. To make pooling work, managers must have access to the central pool whenever they require money.

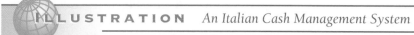

ILLUSTRATION *An Italian Cash Management System*

An Italian firm has created a centralized cash management system for its 140 operating units within Italy. At the center is a holding company that manages banking relations, borrowings, and investments. In the words of the firm's treasurer, "We put ourselves in front of the companies as a real bank and say, 'If you have a surplus to place, I will pay you the best rates.' If the company finds something better than that, they are free to place the funds outside the group. But this doesn't happen very often."[6] In this way, the company avoids being overdrawn with one bank while investing with another.

Cash Planning and Budgeting

A good reporting system is the key to successful global coordination of a firm's cash and marketable securities.

The key to the successful global coordination of a firm's cash and marketable securities is a good reporting system. Cash receipts must be reported and forecast in a comprehensive, accurate, and timely manner. If the headquarters staff is to use the company's worldwide cash resources fully and economically, they must know the financial positions of affiliates, the forecast cash needs or surpluses, the anticipated cash inflows and outflows, local and international money market conditions, and likely currency movements.

As a result of rapid and pronounced changes in the international monetary arena, the need for more frequent reports has become acute. Firms that had been content to receive information quarterly now require monthly, weekly, or even daily data. Key figures are often transmitted by email or via a corporate intranet.

Multinational Cash Mobilization A **multinational cash mobilization** system is designed to optimize the use of funds by tracking current and near-term cash positions. The information gathered can be used to aid a multilateral netting system, to increase the operational efficiency of a centralized cash pool, and to determine more effective short-term borrowing and investment policies.

Cash reporting should be done in cleared funds, which is money that is available for immediate use.

The operation of a multinational cash mobilization system is illustrated here with a simple example centered around a firm's four European affiliates. Assume that the European headquarters maintains a regional cash pool in London for its operating units located in England, France, Germany, and Italy. Each day, at the close of banking hours, every affiliate reports to London its current cash balances in **cleared funds**—that is, its cash accounts net of all receipts and disbursements that have cleared during the day. All balances are reported in a common currency, which is assumed here to be the U.S. dollar, with local currencies translated at rates designated by the manager of the central pool.

One report format is presented in Exhibit 19.5. It contains the end-of-day balance as well as a revised five-day forecast. According to the report for July 12, the Italian affiliate has a cash balance of $400,000. This balance means the affiliate could have disbursed an additional $400,000 that day without creating a cash deficit or having to use its overdraft facilities. The French affiliate, on the other hand, has a negative cash balance of $150,000, which it is presumably covering with an overdraft. Alternatively, it might have

---

[6] "Central Cash Management Step by Step: The European Approach," *Business International Money Report,* October 19, 1984, p. 331.

EXHIBIT 19.5 • DAILY CASH REPORTS OF EUROPEAN CENTRAL CASH POOL (U.S. $ THOUSANDS)

Date: July 12, 200X
Affiliate: France
Cash Position: –150
Five-Day Forecast:

Date: July 12, 200X
Affiliate: Germany
Cash Position: +350
Five-Day Forecast:

Day	Deposit	Disburse	Net	Day	Deposit	Disburse	Net
1	400	200	+200	1	430	50	+380
2	125	225	–100	2	360	760	–400
3	300	700	–400	3	500	370	+130
4	275	275	0	4	750	230	+520
5	250	100	150	5	450	120	+330
		Net for period	–150			Net for period	+960

Date: July 12, 200X
Affiliate: Italy
Cash Position: +400
Five-Day Forecast:

Date: July 12, 200X
Affiliate: England
Cash Position: +100
Five-Day Forecast:

Day	Deposit	Disburse	Net	Day	Deposit	Disburse	Net
1	240	340	–100	1	100	50	+ 50
2	400	275	+125	2	260	110	+150
3	480	205	+275	3	150	350	–200
4	90	240	–150	4	300	50	+250
5	300	245	+ 55	5	200	300	–100
		Net for period	+205			Net for period	+150

borrowed funds from the pool to cover this deficit. The British and German subsidiaries report cash surpluses of $100,000 and $350,000, respectively.

The manager of the central pool can then assemble these individual reports into a more usable form, such as that depicted in Exhibit 19.6. This report shows the cash balance for each affiliate, its required minimum operating cash balance, and the resultant cash surplus or deficit for each affiliate individually and for the region as a whole. According to the report, both the German and Italian affiliates ended the day with funds in excess of their operating needs, whereas the English unit wound up with $25,000 less than it normally requires in operating funds (even though it had $100,000 in cash). The

EXHIBIT 19.6 • AGGREGATE CASH POSITION OF EUROPEAN CENTRAL CASH POOL (U.S. $ THOUSANDS)

	Daily Cash Position, July 12, 200X		
Affiliate	Closing Balance	Minimum Required	Cash Balance Surplus (Deficit)
France	–150	100	–250
Germany	+350	250	100
Italy	+400	150	250
England	+100	125	– 25
Regional surplus (deficit)			+ 75

French affiliate was short $250,000, including its operating deficit and minimum required balances. For the European region as a whole, however, there was excess cash of $75,000.

The information contained in these reports can be used to decide how to cover any deficits and where to invest temporary surplus funds. Netting also can be facilitated by breaking down each affiliate's aggregate inflows and outflows into their individual currency components. This breakdown will aid in deciding what netting operations to perform and in which currencies.

The cash forecasts contained in the daily reports can help determine when to transfer funds to or from the central pool and the maturities of any borrowings or investments. For example, although the Italian subsidiary currently has $250,000 in excess funds, it projects a deficit tomorrow of $100,000. One possible strategy is to have the Italian unit remit $250,000 to the pool today and, in turn, have the pool return $100,000 tomorrow to cover the projected deficit. However, unless interest differentials are large and/or transaction costs are minimal, it may be preferable to instruct the Italian unit to remit only $150,000 to the pool and invest the remaining $100,000 overnight in Italy.

Similarly, the five-day forecast shown in Exhibit 19.7, based on the data provided in Exhibit 19.6, indicates that the $75,000 European regional surplus generated today can be invested for at least two days before it is required (because of the cash deficit forecasted two days from today).

The cash mobilization system illustrated here has been greatly simplified in order to bring out some key details. In reality, such a system should include longer-term forecasts of cash flows broken down by currency, forecasts of intercompany transactions (for netting purposes), and interest rates paid by the pool (for decentralized decision making).

Bank Relations

Good bank relations are central to a company's international cash management effort. Although some companies may be quite pleased with their banks' services, others may not even realize that they are being poorly served by their banks. Poor cash management services mean lost interest revenues, overpriced services, and inappropriate or redundant services. Some common problems in bank relations are

1. *Too many relations:* Many firms that have conducted a bank relations audit find that they are dealing with too many banks. Using too many banks invariably generates idle balances, higher compensating balances, more check-clearing float, suboptimal rates on foreign exchange and loans, a heavier administrative workload, and diminished control over every aspect of banking relations.

2. *High banking costs:* To keep a lid on bank expenses, treasury management must carefully track not only the direct costs of banking services—including rates,

EXHIBIT 19.7 • FIVE-DAY CASH FORECAST OF EUROPEAN CENTRAL CASH POOL (U.S. $ THOUSANDS)

	Days from July 12, 200X					
Affiliate	+1	+2	+3	+4	+5	Five-Day Total
France	+200	−100	−400	0	+150	− 150
Germany	+380	−400	+130	+520	+330	+ 960
Italy	−100	+125	+275	−150	+ 55	+ 205
England	+ 50	+150	−200	+250	−100	+ 150
Forecast regional surplus (deficit) by day	+530	−225	−195	+620	+435	+1,165

spreads, and commissions—but also the indirect costs rising from check float, **value-dating**—that is, when value is given for funds—and compensating balances. This monitoring is especially important in developing countries of Latin America and Asia. In these countries, compensating balance requirements—the fraction of an outstanding loan balance required to be held on deposit in a non-interest-bearing account—may range as high as 30–35 percent, and check-clearing times may drag on for days or even weeks. It also pays off in such European countries as Italy, where banks enjoy value-dating periods of as long as twenty to twenty-five days.

3. *Inadequate reporting:* Banks often do not provide immediate information on collections and account balances. This delay can cause excessive amounts of idle cash and prolonged float. To avoid such problems, firms should instruct their banks to provide daily balance information and to clearly distinguish between *ledger* and *collected balances*—that is, posted totals versus immediately available funds.

4. *Excessive clearing delays:* In many countries, bank float can rob firms of funds availability. In such nations as Mexico, Spain, Italy, and Indonesia, checks drawn on banks located in remote areas can take weeks to clear to headquarters accounts in the capital city. Fortunately, firms that negotiate for better float times often meet with success. Whatever method is used to reduce clearing time, it is crucial that companies constantly check up on their banks to ensure that funds are credited to accounts as expected.

MNCs should determine the value of the bank services they receive and the value of the business they generate for each bank they deal with.

Negotiating better service is easier if the company is a valued customer. Demonstrating that it is a valuable customer requires the firm to have ongoing discussions with its bankers to determine the precise value of each type of banking activity and the value of the business it generates for each bank. Armed with this information, the firm should make up a monthly report that details the value of its banking business. By compiling this report, the company knows precisely how much business it is giving to each bank it uses. With such information in hand, the firm can negotiate better terms and better service from its banks.

ILLUSTRATION *How Morton Thiokol Manages Its Bank Relations*

Morton Thiokol, a Chicago-based manufacturer with international sales of about $300 million, centralizes its banking policy for three main reasons: Cash management is already centralized; small local staffs may not have time to devote to bank relations; and overseas staffs often need the extra guidance of centralized bank relations. Morton Thiokol is committed to trimming its overseas banking relations to cut costs and streamline cash management. A key factor in maintaining relations with a bank is a bank's willingness to provide the firm with needed services at reasonable prices. Although Morton Thiokol usually tries to reduce the number of banks with which it maintains relations, it will sometimes add banks to increase competition and thereby improve its chances of getting quality services and reasonable prices.

19.2 ACCOUNTS RECEIVABLE MANAGEMENT

Firms grant trade credit to customers, both domestically and internationally, because they expect the investment in receivables to be profitable, either by expanding sales volume or by retaining sales that otherwise would be lost to competitors. Some companies also earn a profit on the financing charges they levy on credit sales.

The need to scrutinize **credit terms** is particularly important in countries experiencing rapid rates of inflation. The incentive for customers to defer payment, liquidating their debts with less valuable money in the future, is great. Furthermore, credit standards abroad are often more relaxed than standards in the home market, especially in countries lacking alternative sources of credit for small customers. To remain competitive, MNCs may feel compelled to loosen their own credit standards. Finally, the compensation system in many companies tends to reward higher sales more than it penalizes an increased investment in accounts receivable. Local managers frequently have an incentive to expand sales even if the MNC overall does not benefit.

To better manage receivables overseas, salespeople must understand how credit and collection affect company profits.

The effort to better manage receivables overseas will not get far if finance and marketing do not coordinate their efforts. In many companies, finance and marketing work at cross purposes. Marketing thinks about selling, and finance thinks about speeding up cash flows. One way to ease the tensions between finance and marketing is to educate the sales force on how credit and collection affect company profits. Another way is to tie bonuses for salespeople to *collected* sales or to adjust sales bonuses for the interest cost of credit sales. Forcing managers to bear the opportunity cost of working capital ensures that their credit, inventory, and other working-capital decisions will be more economical.

ILLUSTRATION   *Nestlé Charges for Working Capital*

Nestlé charges local subsidiary managers for the interest expense of net working capital using an internally devised standard rate. The inclusion of this finance charge encourages country managers to keep a tight rein on accounts receivable and inventory because the lower the net working capital, the lower the theoretical interest charge, and the higher their profits.

Credit Extension

Companies selling abroad must decide in which currencies to extend credit.

A firm selling abroad faces two key credit decisions: the amount of credit to extend and the currency in which credit sales are to be billed. Nothing need be added here to Chapter 10's discussion (see Chapter 10, Section 10.7: Managing Transaction Exposure) of the latter decision except to note that competitors will often resolve the currency-of-denomination issue.

The easier the credit terms are, the more sales are likely to be made. But generosity is not always the best policy. Balanced against higher revenues must be the risk of default, increased interest expense on the larger investment in receivables, and the deterioration (through currency devaluation) of the dollar value of accounts receivable denominated in the buyer's currency. These additional costs may be partly offset if liberalized credit terms enhance a firm's ability to raise its prices.

One way to better manage receivables overseas is to adjust sales bonuses for the interest and currency costs of credit sales.

The bias of most personnel evaluation systems is in favor of higher revenues, but another factor often tends to increase accounts receivable in foreign countries. An uneconomic expansion of local sales may occur if managers are credited with dollar sales when accounts receivable are denominated in the local currency. Sales managers should be charged for the expected depreciation in the value of local currency accounts receivable. For instance, if the current exchange rate is LC 1 = $0.10, but the expected exchange rate 90 days hence (or the three-month forward rate) is $0.09, managers providing three-month credit terms should be credited with only $0.90 for each dollar in sales booked at the current spot rate.

The following five-step approach enables a firm to compare the expected benefits and costs associated with extending credit internationally:

1. Calculate the current cost of extending credit.

Firms should com-
pare the expected
costs and benefits of
extending credit
internationally.

2. Calculate the cost of extending credit under the revised credit policy.
3. Using the information from steps 1 and 2, calculate incremental credit costs under the revised credit policy.
4. Ignoring credit costs, calculate incremental profits under the new credit policy.
5. If, and only if, incremental profits exceed incremental credit costs, select the new credit policy.

ILLUSTRATION   *Evaluating Credit Extension Overseas*

Suppose a subsidiary in France currently has annual sales of $1 million with 90-day credit terms. It is believed that sales will increase by 6 percent, or $60,000, if terms are extended to 120 days. Of these additional sales, the cost of goods sold is $35,000. Monthly credit expenses are 1 percent in financing charges. In addition, the euro is expected to depreciate an average of 0.5 percent every 30 days.

If we ignore currency changes for the moment, but consider financing costs, the value today of $1 of receivables to be collected at the end of 90 days is approximately $0.97. When the expected euro depreciation of 1.5 percent (3×0.5 percent) over the 90-day period is taken into account, this value declines to $0.97(1 - 0.015)$, or $0.955, imply-ing a 4.5 percent cost of carrying euro receivables for three months. Similarly, $1 of receivables collected 120 days from now is worth $(1 - 4 \times 0.01)(1 - 0.02)$ today, or $0.941. Then the incremental cost of carrying euro receivables for the fourth month equals 0.955 – 0.941 dollars, or 1.4 percent.

Applying the five-step evaluation approach and using the information generated in this illustration yields current 90-day credit costs of $1 million $\times$ 0.045 = $45,000. Lengthening the terms to 120 days will raise this cost to $1 million $\times$ 0.059 = $59,000. The cost of carrying for 120 days the incremental sales of $60,000 is $60,000 $\times$ 0.059 = $3,540. Thus, incremental credit costs under the new policy equal $59,000 + $3,540 – $45,000 = $17,540. Since this amount is less than the incremental profit of $25,000 (60,000 – 35,000), it is worthwhile to provide a fourth month of credit.

19.3 INVENTORY MANAGEMENT

Inventory in the form of raw materials, work in process, or finished goods is held (1) to facilitate the production process by both ensuring that supplies are at hand when needed and allowing a more even rate of production, and (2) to make certain that goods are avail-able for delivery at the time of sale.

MNCs typically find
it more difficult to
control their over-
seas inventory and
to realize inventory
turnover objectives.

Although, conceptually, the inventory management problems faced by multina-tional firms are not unique, they may be exaggerated in the case of foreign operations. For instance, MNCs typically find it more difficult to control their inventory and realize inventory turnover objectives in their overseas operations than in domestic ones. There are a variety of reasons: long and variable transit times if ocean transportation is used, lengthy customs proceedings, dock strikes, import controls, high duties, supply disrup-tion, and anticipated changes in currency values.

Production Location and Inventory Control

Many U.S. companies have eschewed domestic manufacturing for offshore production to take advantage of low-wage labor and a grab bag of tax holidays, low-interest loans, and other government largess. However, a number of firms have found that low manu-facturing cost is not everything. Aside from the strategic advantages associated with U.S.

Overseas production locations often lead to higher inventories.

production, such as maintaining close contact with domestic customers, onshore manufacturing allows for a more efficient use of capital. In particular, because of the delays in international shipment of goods and potential supply disruptions, firms producing abroad typically hold larger work-in-process and finished goods inventories than do domestic firms. The result is higher inventory-carrying costs.

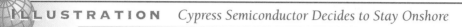

ILLUSTRATION *Cypress Semiconductor Decides to Stay Onshore*

The added inventory expenses that foreign manufacture would entail is an important reason that Cypress Semiconductor decided to manufacture integrated circuits in San Jose, California, instead of going abroad. Cypress makes relatively expensive circuits (they average around $8 apiece), so time-consuming international shipments would have tied up the company's capital in a very expensive way. Even though offshore production would save about $0.032 per chip in labor costs, the company estimated that the labor saving would be more than offset by combined shipping and customs duties of $0.025 and an additional $0.16 in the capital cost of holding inventory.

According to Cypress Chairman L. J. Sevin, "Some people just look at the labor rates, but it's inventory cost that matters. It's simply cheaper to sell a part in one week than in five or six. You have to figure out what you could have done with the inventory or the money you could have made simply by pulling the interest on the dollars you have tied up in the part."[7]

The estimate of $0.16 in carrying cost can be backed out as follows: As the preceding quotation indicates, parts manufactured abroad were expected to spend an extra five weeks or so in transit. This means that parts manufactured abroad would spend five more weeks in work-in-process inventory than would parts manufactured domestically. Assuming an opportunity cost of 20 percent (not an unreasonable number considering the volatility of the semiconductor market) and an average cost per chip of $8 yields the following added inventory-related interest expense associated with overseas production:

$$\text{Added interest expense} = \text{Opportunity cost of funds} \times \text{Added time in transit} \times \text{Cost per part}$$

$$= 0.20 \times 5/52 \times \$8 = \$0.154$$

Advance Inventory Purchases

Companies can partially hedge their currency risk, albeit at a cost, by buying imported goods in advance.

In many developing countries, forward contracts for foreign currency are limited in availability or are nonexistent. In addition, restrictions often preclude free remittances, making it difficult, if not impossible, to convert excess funds into a hard currency. One means of hedging is to engage in anticipatory purchases of goods, especially imported items. The trade-off involves owning goods for which local currency prices may be increased, thereby maintaining the dollar value of the asset even if devaluation occurs, versus forgoing the return on local money market investments.

Inventory Stockpiling

Because of long delivery lead times, the often limited availability of transport for economically sized shipments, and currency restrictions, the problem of supply failure is of particular importance for any firm that is dependent on foreign sources. These conditions may make the knowledge and execution of an optimal stocking policy, under a threat of a disruption to supply, more critical in the MNC than in the firm that purchases domestically.

---

[7] Joel Kotkin, "The Case for Manufacturing in America," *Inc.,* March 1985, p. 54.

MNCs can protect against supply disruptions by advance purchases of imported goods, but stockpiling inventory is very expensive.

Charging managers for the cost of stockpiling inventory will make them more sensitive to the tradeoffs involved.

The traditional response to such risks has been advance purchases. Holding large amounts of inventory can be quite expensive, however. The high cost of **inventory stockpiling**—including financing, insurance, storage, and obsolescence—has led many companies to identify low inventories with effective management. In contrast, production and sales managers typically desire a relatively large inventory, particularly when a cutoff in supply is anticipated. One way to get managers to consider the trade-offs involved—the costs of stockpiling versus the costs of shortages—is to adjust the profit performances of those managers who are receiving the benefits of additional inventory on hand to reflect the added costs of stockpiling.

As the probability of disruption increases or as holding costs go down, more inventory should be ordered. Similarly, if the cost of a stock-out rises or if future supplies are expected to be more expensive, it will pay to stockpile additional inventory. Conversely, if these parameters were to move in the opposite direction, less inventory should be stockpiled.

19.4 SHORT-TERM FINANCING

Financing the working capital requirements of a multinational corporation's foreign affiliates poses a complex decision problem. This complexity stems from the large number of financing options available to the subsidiary of an MNC. Subsidiaries have access to funds from sister affiliates and the parent, as well as from external sources. This section is concerned with the following four aspects of developing a short-term overseas financing strategy: (1) identifying the key factors, (2) formulating and evaluating objectives, (3) describing available short-term borrowing options, and (4) developing a methodology for calculating and comparing the effective dollar costs of these alternatives.

Key Factors in Short-Term Financing Strategy

Five key factors influence the expected cost and risk of a short-term financing strategy.

Expected costs and risks, the basic determinants of any funding strategy, are strongly influenced in an international context by six key factors.

1. If forward contracts are unavailable, the crucial issue is whether differences in nominal interest rates among currencies are matched by anticipated changes in the exchange rate. For example, is the difference between an 8 percent dollar interest rate and a 3 percent Swiss franc interest rate due solely to expectations that the dollar will devalue by 5 percent relative to the franc? The key issue here, in other words, is whether there are deviations from the international Fisher effect. If deviations do exist, then expected dollar borrowing costs will vary by currency, leading to a decision problem. Trade-offs must be made between the expected borrowing costs and the exchange risks associated with each financing option.

2. The element of exchange risk is the second key factor. Many firms borrow locally to provide an offsetting liability for their exposed local currency assets. On the other hand, borrowing a foreign currency in which the firm has no exposure will increase its exchange risk. That is, the risks associated with borrowing in a specific currency are related to the firm's degree of exposure in that currency.

3. The third essential element is the firm's degree of risk aversion. The more risk averse the firm (or its management) is, the higher the price it should be willing to pay to reduce its currency exposure. Risk aversion affects the company's risk-cost trade-off and consequently, in the absence of forward contracts, influences the selection of currencies it will use to finance its foreign operations.

4. If forward contracts are available, however, currency risk should not be a factor in the firm's borrowing strategy. Instead, relative borrowing costs, calculated on a

covered basis, become the sole determinant of which currencies to borrow in. The key issue here is whether the nominal interest differential equals the forward differential—that is, whether interest rate parity holds. If it does hold, then the currency denomination of the firm's debt is irrelevant. Covered costs can differ among currencies because of government capital controls or the threat of such controls. Because of this added element of risk, the annualized forward discount or premium may not offset the difference between the interest rate on the LC loan versus the dollar loan—that is, interest rate parity will not hold.

5. Even if interest rate parity does hold before tax, the currency denomination of corporate borrowings does matter where tax asymmetries are present. These tax asymmetries are based on the differential treatment of foreign exchange gains and losses on either forward contracts or loan repayments. For example, English firms or affiliates have a disincentive to borrow in strong currencies because Inland Revenue, the British tax agency, taxes exchange gains on foreign currency borrowings but disallows the deductibility of exchange losses on the same loans. An opposite incentive (to borrow in stronger currencies) is created in countries such as Australia that may permit exchange gains on forward contracts to be taxed at a lower rate than the rate at which forward contract losses are deductible. In such a case, even if interest parity holds before tax, after-tax forward contract gains may be greater than after-tax interest costs. Such tax asymmetries lead to possibilities of borrowing arbitrage, even if interest rate parity holds before tax. The essential point is that, in comparing relative borrowing costs, firms must compute these costs on an after-tax covered basis.

6. A final factor that may enter into the borrowing decision is **political risk.** Even if local financing is not the minimum cost option, multinationals often will still try to maximize their local borrowings if they believe that expropriation or exchange controls are serious possibilities. If either event occurs, an MNC has fewer assets at risk if it has used local, rather than external, financing.

Short-Term Financing Objectives

Four possible objectives can guide a firm in deciding where and in which currencies to borrow.

1. *Minimize expected cost:* By ignoring risk, this objective reduces information requirements, allows borrowing options to be evaluated on an individual basis without considering the correlation between loan cash flows and operating cash flows, and lends itself readily to break-even analysis (see Chapter 14, Section 14.4: The Cost of Debt Capital).

2. *Minimize risk without regard to cost:* A firm that followed this advice to its logical conclusion would dispose of all its assets and invest the proceeds in government securities. In other words, this objective is impractical and contrary to shareholder interests.

3. *Trade off expected cost and systematic risk:* The advantage of this objective is that, like the first objective, it allows a company to evaluate different loans without considering the relationship between loan cash flows and operating cash flows from operations. Moreover, it is consistent with shareholder preferences as described by the capital asset pricing model. In practical terms, however, there is probably little difference between expected borrowing costs adjusted for systematic risk and expected borrowing costs without that adjustment. The reason for this lack of difference is that the correlation

between currency fluctuations and a well-diversified portfolio of risky assets is likely to be quite small.

4. *Trade off expected cost and total risk:* The theoretical rationale for this approach was described in Chapter 1. Basically, it relies on the existence of potentially substantial costs of financial distress. On a more practical level, management generally prefers greater stability of cash flows (regardless of investor preferences). Management typically will self-insure against most losses but might decide to use the financial markets to hedge against the risk of large losses. To implement this approach, it is necessary to take into account the covariances between operating and financing cash flows. This approach (trading off expected cost and total risk) is valid only where forward contracts are unavailable. Otherwise, selecting the lowest-cost borrowing option, calculated on a covered after-tax basis, is the only justifiable objective (for the reason why, see Chapter 10, Section 10.5: Designing a Hedging Strategy).[8]

Short-Term Financing Options

Firms typically prefer to finance the temporary component of current assets with short-term funds. The three principal short-term financing options that may be available to an MNC include (1) the intercompany loan, (2) the local currency loan, and (3) commercial paper.

The parent or a sister affiliate may provide short-term financing in the form of an intercompany loan.

Intercompany Financing A frequent means of affiliate financing is to have either the parent company or sister affiliate provide an **intercompany loan**. At times, however, these loans may be limited in amount or duration by official exchange controls. In addition, interest rates on intercompany loans are frequently required to fall within set limits. The relevant parameters in establishing the cost of such a loan include the lender's opportunity cost of funds, the interest rate set, tax rates and regulations, the currency of denomination of the loan, and expected exchange rate movements over the term of the loan.

Local Currency Financing Like most domestic firms, affiliates of multinational corporations generally attempt to finance their working capital requirements locally, for both convenience and exposure management purposes. All industrial nations and most LDCs have well-developed commercial banking systems, so firms desiring local financing generally turn there first. The major forms of bank financing include overdrafts, discounting, and term loans. Nonbank sources of funds include commercial paper and factoring (see Chapter 18, Section 18.3: Financing Techniques in International Trade).

Bank Loans

Bank loans are the dominant form of short-term financing used around the world.

Loans from commercial banks are the dominant form of short-term interest-bearing financing used around the world. These loans are described as *self-liquidating* because they are generally used to finance temporary increases in accounts receivable and inventory. These increases in working capital soon are converted into cash, which is used to repay the loan.

Short-term bank credits are typically unsecured. The borrower signs a note evidencing its obligation to repay the loan when it is due, along with accrued interest. Most notes are payable in 90 days; the loans must, therefore, be repaid or renewed every 90 days. The need to periodically roll over bank loans gives a bank substantial control over the use of its funds, reducing the need to impose severe restrictions on the firm. To further ensure that short-term credits are not being used for permanent financing, a bank will usually

---

[8] These possible objectives are suggested by Donald R. Lessard, "Currency and Tax Considerations in International Financing," Teaching Note No. 3, Massachusetts Institute of Technology, Spring 1979.

insert a **cleanup clause** requiring the company to be completely out of debt to the bank for a period of at least thirty days during the year.

Forms of Bank Credit   Bank credit provides a highly flexible form of financing because it is readily expandable and, therefore, serves as a financial reserve. Whenever the firm needs extra short-term funds that cannot be met by trade credit, it is likely to turn first to bank credit. Unsecured bank loans may be extended under a line of credit, under a revolving credit arrangement, or on a transaction basis. Bank loans can be originated in either the domestic or the Eurodollar market.

Bank loans are very flexible and come in several different varieties.

1. *Term loans:* **Term loans** are straight loans, often unsecured, that are made for a fixed period of time, usually ninety days. They are attractive because they give corporate treasurers complete control over the timing of repayments. A term loan typically is made for a specific purpose with specific conditions and is repaid in a single lump sum. The loan provisions are contained in the promissory note that is signed by the customer. This type of loan is used most often by borrowers who have an infrequent need for bank credit.

2. *Line of credit:* Arranging separate loans for frequent borrowers is a relatively expensive means of doing business. One way to reduce these transaction costs is to use a **line of credit.** This informal agreement permits the company to borrow up to a stated maximum amount from the bank. The firm can draw down its line of credit when it requires funds and pay back the loan balance when it has excess cash. Although the bank is not legally obligated to honor the line-of-credit agreement, it almost always does so unless it or the firm encounters financial difficulties. A line of credit is usually good for one year, with renewals renegotiated every year.

3. *Overdrafts:* In countries other than the United States, banks tend to lend through overdrafts. An **overdraft** is simply a line of credit against which drafts (checks) can be drawn (written) up to a specified maximum amount. These overdraft lines often are extended and expanded year after year, thus providing, in effect, a form of medium-term financing. The borrower pays interest on the debit balance only.

4. *Revolving credit agreement:* A **revolving credit agreement** is similar to a line of credit except that now the bank (or syndicate of banks) is *legally committed* to extend credit up to the stated maximum. The firm pays interest on its outstanding borrowings plus a commitment fee, ranging between 0.125 percent and 0.5 percent per annum, on the *unused* portion of the credit line. Revolving credit agreements are usually renegotiated every two or three years.

   The danger that short-term credits are being used to fund long-term requirements is particularly acute with a revolving credit line that is continuously renewed. Inserting an out-of-debt period under a cleanup clause validates the temporary need for funds.

5. *Discounting:* The **discounting** of trade bills is the preferred short-term financing technique in many European countries—especially in France, Italy, Belgium, and, to a lesser extent, Germany. It is also widespread in Latin America, particularly in Argentina, Brazil, and Mexico. These bills often can be rediscounted with the central bank.

Discounting is the preferred short-term financing technique in many European countries.

Discounting usually results from the following set of transactions. A manufacturer selling goods to a retailer on credit draws a bill on the buyer, payable in, say, thirty days. The buyer endorses (accepts) the bill or gets his or her bank to accept it, at which point it becomes a **bankers' acceptance.** The manufacturer then takes the bill to his or her bank, and the bank accepts it for a fee if the buyer's bank has not already accepted it. The bill is then sold at a discount to the manufacturer's bank or to a money-market dealer. The rate of interest varies with the term of the bill and the general level of local money-market interest rates.

The popularity of discounting in European countries stems from the fact that according to European commercial law, which is based on the Code Napoleon, the claim of the bill holder is independent of the claim represented by the underlying transaction. (For example, the bill holder must be paid even if the buyer objects to the quality of the merchandise.) This right makes the bill easily negotiable and enhances its liquidity (or tradability), thereby lowering the cost of discounting relative to other forms of credit.

Interest Rates on Bank Loans The interest rate on bank loans is based on personal negotiation between the banker and the borrower. The loan rate charged to a specific customer reflects that customer's creditworthiness, previous relationship with the bank, maturity of the loan, and other factors. Ultimately, bank interest rates are based on the same factors as the interest rates on the financial securities issued by a borrower: the risk-free return, which reflects the time value of money, plus a risk premium based on the borrower's credit risk. However, there are certain bank-loan pricing conventions that you should be familiar with.

Interest on a loan can be paid at maturity or in advance. Each payment method gives a different effective interest rate, even if the quoted rate is the same. The **effective interest rate** is defined as follows:

> The effective interest rate on a bank loan typically exceeds the stated interest rate.

$$\text{Effective interest rate} \ = \ \frac{\text{Annual interest paid}}{\text{Funds received}}$$

Suppose you borrow $10,000 for one year at 11 percent interest. If the interest is paid at maturity, you owe the lender $11,100 at the end of the year. This payment method yields an effective interest rate of 11 percent, the same as the stated interest rate:

$$\text{Effective interest rate when interest is paid at maturity} = \frac{\$1,100}{\$10,000} = 11\%$$

If the loan is quoted on a *discount basis,* the bank deducts the interest in advance. On the $10,000 loan, you will receive only $8,900 and must repay $10,000 in one year. The effective rate of interest exceeds 11 percent because you are paying interest on $10,000 but have the use of only $8,900:

$$\text{Effective interest rate on discounted loan} = \frac{\$1,100}{\$8,900} = 12.4\%$$

An extreme illustration of the difference in the effective interest rate between paying interest at maturity and paying interest in advance is provided by the Mexican banking system. In 1985, the nominal interest rate on a peso bank loan was 70 percent, about 15 percentage points higher than the inflation rate. But high as it was, the nominal figure did not tell the whole story. By collecting interest in advance, Mexican banks boosted the effective rate dramatically. Consider, for example, the cost of a Ps 10,000 loan. By collecting interest of 70 percent, or Ps 7,000, in advance, the bank actually loaned out only Ps 3,000 and received Ps 10,000 at maturity. The effective interest rate on the loan was 233 percent:

$$\text{Effective interest rate on Mexican loan} = \frac{\text{Ps } 7,000}{\text{Ps } 3,000} = 233\%$$

Many banks require borrowers to hold from 10 percent to 20 percent of their outstanding loan balance on deposit in a noninterest-bearing account. These **compensating balance require-ments** raise the effective cost of a bank credit because not all of the loan is available to the firm:

$$\text{Effective interest rate with compensating balance requirement} = \frac{\text{Annual interest paid}}{\text{Usable funds}}$$

Usable funds equal the net amount of the loan less the compensating balance requirement.

Returning to the previous example, suppose you borrow $10,000 at 11 percent interest paid at maturity, and the compensating balance requirement is 15 percent, or $1,500. Thus, the $10,000 loan provides only $8,500 in usable funds for an effective interest rate of 12.9 percent:

$$\text{Effective interest rate when interest is paid at maturity} = \frac{\$1,100}{\$8,500} = 12.9\%$$

If the interest is prepaid, the amount of usable funds declines by a further $1,100—that is, to $7,400—and the effective interest rate rises to 14.9 percent:

$$\text{Effective interest rate on discounted loan} = \frac{\$1,100}{\$7,400} = 14.9\%$$

In both instances, the compensating balance requirement raises the effective interest rate above the stated interest rate. This higher rate is the case even if the bank pays interest on the compensating balance deposit because the loan rate invariably exceeds the deposit rate.

Commercial Paper   One of the most favored alternatives for MNCs to borrowing short term from a bank is to issue commercial paper. As defined in Chapter 18, **commercial paper** (CP) is a short-term unsecured promissory note that is generally sold by large corporations on a discount basis to institutional investors and to other corporations. Because commercial paper is unsecured and bears only the name of the issuer, the market has generally been dominated by the largest, most creditworthy companies.

Commercial paper is a favorite short-term nonbank financing method for MNCs.

Available maturities are fairly standard across the spectrum, but average maturities—reflecting the terms that companies actually use—vary from twenty to twenty-five days in the United States to more than three months in the Netherlands. The minimum denomination of paper also varies widely: In Australia, Canada, Sweden, and the United States, firms can issue CP in much smaller amounts than in other markets. In most countries, the instrument is issued at a discount, with the full face value of the note redeemed upon maturity. In other markets, however, interestbearing instruments are also offered.

MNCs are substituting commercial paper for bank loans because of the interest savings.

By going directly to the market rather than relying on a financial intermediary such as a bank, large, well-known corporations can save substantial interest costs, often on the order of 1 percent or more. In addition, because commercial paper is sold directly to large institutions, U.S. CP is exempt from SEC registration requirements. This exemption reduces the time and expense of readying an issue of commercial paper for sale.

Commercial paper entails several non-interest costs.

There are three major noninterest costs associated with using commercial paper as a source of short-term funds: (1) backup lines of credit, (2) fees to commercial banks, and (3) rating service fees. In most cases, issuers back their paper 100 percent with lines of credit from commercial banks. Because its average maturity is very short, commercial paper poses the risk that an issuer might not be able to pay off or roll over maturing paper. Consequently, issuers use backup lines as insurance against periods of financial stress or tight money, when lenders ration money directly rather than raise interest rates. For example, the market for Texaco paper, which provided the bulk of its short-term financing, disappeared after an $11.1 billion judgment against the company. Texaco replaced these funds by drawing on its bank lines of credit.

Backup lines usually are paid for through compensating balances, typically about 10 percent of the unused portion of the credit line plus 20 percent of the amount of credit actually used. As an alternative to compensating balances, issuers sometimes pay straight fees ranging from 0.375 percent to 0.75 percent of the line of credit; this explicit pricing procedure has been used increasingly in recent years.

Another cost associated with issuing commercial paper is fees paid to the large commercial and investment banks that act as issuing and paying agents for the paper issuers and handle all the associated paperwork. Finally, rating services charge fees ranging from $5,000 to $25,000 per year for ratings, depending on the rating service. Credit ratings are not legally required by any nation, but they are often essential for placing paper.

In Chapter 13, we saw that alternatives to commercial paper issued in the local market are Euronotes and Euro-commercial paper (Euro-CP). The Euronotes are typically underwritten, whereas Euro-CP is not.

Calculating the Dollar Costs of Alternative Financing Options

The cost of a local currency loan equals the interest expense less the exchange gain (loss) on loan repayment.

This section presents explicit formulas to compute the effective dollar costs of a local currency loan and a dollar loan.[9] These cost formulas can be used to calculate the least expensive financing source for each future exchange rate. A computer can easily perform this analysis—called *break-even analysis*—and determine the range of future exchange rates within which each particular financing option is cheapest.

With this break-even analysis, the treasurer can readily see the amount of currency appreciation or depreciation necessary to make one type of borrowing less expensive than another. The treasurer will then compare the firm's actual forecast of currency change, determined objectively or subjectively, with this benchmark.

Break-even analysis can establish the amount of currency change that equates the costs of local currency and dollar financing.

To illustrate break-even analysis and show how to develop cost formulas, suppose that Du Pont's Mexican affiliate requires funds to finance its working capital needs for one year. It can borrow pesos at 45 percent or dollars at 11 percent. To determine an appropriate borrowing strategy, this section will develop explicit cost expressions for each of these loans using the numbers just given. Expressions then will be generalized to obtain analytical cost formulas that are usable under a variety of circumstances.

Case 1: No Taxes　Absent taxes and forward contracts, costing these loans is relatively straightforward.

1. *Local currency loan:* We saw in Chapter 14 (see Section 14.4, The Cost of Debt Capital) that, in general, the dollar cost of borrowing local currency (LC) at an interest rate of r_L and a currency change of c, is the sum of the dollar interest cost plus the percentage change in the exchange rate:

$$\begin{aligned}\frac{\textit{Dollar cost}}{\textit{of LC loan}} &= \textit{Interest cost} + \textit{Exchange gain (loss)} \\ &= r_L(1 + c) + c \end{aligned} \tag{19.1}$$

Employing Equation 19.1, we compute an expected dollar cost of borrowing pesos for Du Pont's Mexican affiliate of $0.45 \times (1 + c) + c$, or $0.45 + 1.45c$. For example, if the peso is expected to fall by 20 percent ($c = -0.20$), then the effective dollar interest rate on the peso loan will be 16 percent ($0.45 - 1.45 \times -0.20$).

2. *Dollar loan:* The Mexican affiliate can borrow dollars at 11 percent. In general, the cost of a dollar (HC) loan to the affiliate is the interest rate on the dollar (HC) loan r_H.

[9] This section draws on material in Alan C. Shapiro, "Evaluating Financing Costs for Multinational Subsidiaries," *Journal of International Business Studies*, Fall 1975, pp. 25–32.

Analysis   The peso loan costs $0.45(1 + c) + c$, and the dollar loan costs 11 percent. To find the break-even rate of currency depreciation at which the dollar cost of peso borrowing is just equal to the cost of dollar financing, equate the two costs—$0.45(1 + c) + c = 0.11$—and solve for c:

$$c = \frac{(0.45 - 0.11)}{1.45} = -0.2345$$

In other words, the Mexican peso must devalue by 23.45 percent before it is less expensive to borrow pesos at 45 percent than dollars at 11 percent. Ignoring the factor of exchange risk, the borrowing decision rule is as follows:

> If $c < -23.45\%$, borrow pesos.
> If $c > -23.45\%$, borrow dollars.

In the general case, the break-even rate of currency change is found by equating the dollar costs of dollar and local currency financing—that is, $r_H = r_L(1 + c) + c$—and solving for c:

$$c^* = \frac{r_H - r_L}{1 + r_L} \tag{19.2}$$

Dollar and local currency financing costs will be equal if the international Fisher effect holds.

If the international Fisher effect holds, then we saw in Chapter 4 (Equation 4.11) that c^*, the break-even amount of currency change, also equals the expected LC devaluation (revaluation); that is, the expected peso devaluation should equal 23.45 percent unless there is reason to believe that some form of market imperfection is not permitting interest rates to adjust to reflect anticipated currency changes.

Case 2: Taxes   Taxes complicate the calculating of various loan costs. Suppose the effective tax rate on the earnings of Du Pont's Mexican affiliate is 40 percent.

   1. *Local currency loan:* Chapter 14 presented the after-tax dollar cost of borrowing in the local currency for a foreign affiliate as equaling the after-tax interest expense plus the change in the exchange rate, or

$$\text{After-tax dollar cost of LC loan} = \text{Interest cost} - \text{Exchange rate change} \tag{19.3}$$
$$= r_L(1 + c)(1 - t_a) + c$$

where t_a is the affiliate's marginal tax rate. Employing Equation 19.3, we can calculate the after-tax dollar cost of borrowing pesos as equaling $0.45 \times (1 + c)(1 - 0.40) + c$, or $0.27 + 1.27c$.

   2. *Dollar loan:* The after-tax cost of a dollar loan equals the Mexican affiliate's after-tax interest expense, $0.11(1 - 0.40)$, minus the dollar value to the Mexican affiliate of the tax write-off on the increased number of pesos necessary to repay the dollar principal following a peso devaluation, $0.4c$.

   In general, the total cost of the dollar loan is the after-tax interest expense less the tax write-off associated with the dollar principal repayment, or

$$\text{After-tax cost of dollar loan} = \text{Interest cost to subsidiary} - \text{Tax gain (loss)}$$
$$= r_H(1 - t_a) + c t_a \tag{19.4}$$

Substituting in the relevant parameters to Equation 19.4 yields an after-tax cost of borrowing dollars equal to $0.11 \times (1 - 0.40) + 0.4c$, or $0.066 + 0.4c$.

Analysis   As in case 1, we will set the cost of dollar financing, $0.066 + 0.4c$, equal to the cost of local currency financing, $0.27(1 + c) + c$, in order to find the break-even rate of peso depreciation necessary to leave the firm indifferent between borrowing in dollars or pesos. The break-even value of c occurs when $0.066 + 0.4c = 0.27(1 + c) + c$, or

$$c^* = -0.2345$$

Thus, the peso must devalue by 23.45 percent before it is cheaper to borrow pesos at 45 percent than dollars at 11 percent. This is the same break-even exchange rate as in the before-tax case. Although taxes affect the after-tax costs of the dollar and LC loans, they do not affect the relative desirability of the two loans. That is, if one loan has a lower cost before tax, it will also be less costly on an after-tax basis.

In general, the breakeven rate of currency appreciation or depreciation can be found by equating the dollar costs of local currency and dollar financing and solving for c:

$$r_H(1 - t_a) + ct_a = r_L(1 + c)(1 - t_a) + c$$

Taxes affect the absolute costs of borrowing but not the relative costs.

or

$$c^* = \frac{r_H(1 - t_a) - r_L(1 - t_a)}{(1 + r_L)(1 - t_a)} = \frac{r_H - r_L}{1 + r_L} \tag{19.5}$$

The tax rates cancel out and we are left with the same break-even value for c as in the before-tax case (see Equation 19.2).

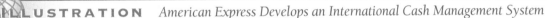

ILLUSTRATION   *American Express Develops an International Cash Management System*

In early 1980, American Express (Amex) completed an eight-month study of the cash cycles of its travel, credit card, and traveler's check businesses operating in seven European countries.[10] On the basis of that project, Amex developed an international cash management system that was expected to yield cash gains—increased investments or reduced borrowing—of about $35 million in Europe alone. About half of these savings were projected to come from accelerated collection of receipts and better control of disbursements. The other half of projected gains represented improved bank-balance control, reduced bank charges, improved value-dating, and better control of foreign exchange.

The components of the system are collection and disbursement methods, bank-account architecture, balance targeting, and foreign exchange management. The world-wide system is controlled on a regional basis, with some direction from the corporate treasurer's office in New York. A regional treasurer's office in Brighton, England, controls cash, financing, and foreign exchange transactions for Europe, the Middle East, and Africa.

The most advantageous collection and disbursement method for every operating division in each country was found by analyzing the timing of mail and clearing floats. This analysis involved

- Establishing what payment methods were used by customers in each country, because checks are not necessarily the primary method of payment in Europe
- Measuring the mail time between certain sending and receiving points
- Identifying clearing systems and practices, which vary considerably among countries
- Analyzing for each method of payment the value-dating practice, the times for processing check deposits, and the bank charges per item

---

[10] This section is adapted from Lars H. Thunell, "The American Express Formula," *Euromoney*, March 1980, pp. 121–127.

Using these data, Amex changed some of its collection and disbursement methods. For example, it installed interception points in Europe to minimize the collection float.

Next, Amex centralized the management of all its bank accounts in Europe on a regional basis. Allowing each subsidiary to set up its own independent bank account has the merit of simplicity, but it leads to a costly proliferation of different pools of funds. Amex restructured its bank accounts, eliminating some and ensuring that funds could move freely among the remaining accounts. By pooling its surplus funds, Amex can invest them for longer periods and also cut down on the chance that one subsidiary will be borrowing funds while another has surplus funds. Conversely, by combining the borrowing needs of various operations, Amex can use term financing and dispense with more expensive overdrafts. Reducing the number of accounts made cash management less complicated and also reduced banking charges.

The particular form of bank-account architecture used by Amex is a modular account structure that links separate accounts in each country with a master account. Management, on a daily basis, has only to focus on the one account through which all the country accounts have access to borrowing and investment facilities.

Balance targeting is used to control bank-account balances. The target is an average balance set for each account that reflects compensating balances, goodwill funds kept to foster the banking relationship, and the accuracy of cash forecasting. Aside from the target balance, the minimum information needed each morning to manage an account by balance targeting is the available opening balance and expected debits and credits.

Foreign exchange management in Amex's international cash management system focuses on its transaction exposure. This exposure, which is due to the multicurrency denomination of traveler's checks and credit card charges, fluctuates on a daily basis.

Procedures to control these exposures and to coordinate foreign exchange transactions center on how Amex finances its working capital from country to country, as well as the manner in which interaffiliate debts are settled. For example, if increased spending by cardholders creates the need for more working capital, Amex must decide whether to raise funds in local currency or in dollars. As a general rule, day-to-day cash is obtained at the local level through overdrafts or overnight funds.

To settle indebtedness among divisions, Amex uses interaffiliate settlements. For example, if a Swiss cardholder uses her card in Germany, the Swiss credit card office pays the German office, which in turn pays the German restaurant or hotel in euros. Amex uses netting, coordinated by the regional treasurer's office in Brighton, to reduce settlement charges. For example, suppose that a German cardholder used his card in Switzerland at the same time the Swiss cardholder charged with her card in Germany. Instead of two transactions, one foreign exchange transaction settles the differences between the two offices.

19.5 SUMMARY AND CONCLUSIONS

This chapter examined the diverse elements involved in international cash, accounts receivable, and inventory management, as well as the short-term financing of foreign affiliates. With regard to cash management, we saw that although the objectives are the same for the MNC as for the domestic firm—to accelerate the collection of funds and optimize their use—the key ingredients to successful management differ. The wider investment options available to the multinational firm were discussed, as were the concepts of multilateral netting, cash pooling, and multinational cash mobilization. As multinational firms develop more efficient and comprehensive information-gathering systems, the international cash management options available to them will increase. Accompanying these options will be even more sophisticated management techniques than currently exist.

Similarly, we saw that inventory and receivable management in the MNC involve the familiar cost-minimizing strategy of investing in these assets up to the point at which the marginal cost of extending another dollar of credit or purchasing one more unit of inventory is just equal to the additional expected benefits to be derived. These benefits accrue in the form of maintaining or increasing the value of other current assets—such as cash and marketable securities—increasing sales revenue, or reducing inventory stock-out costs.

We also have seen that most of the inventory and receivables management problems that arise internationally have close parallels in the purely domestic firm. Currency changes have effects that are similar to those of inflation, and supply disruptions are not unique to international business. The differences that do exist are more in degree than in kind.

The major reason why inflation, currency changes, and supply disruptions generally cause more concern in the multinational than in the domestic firm is that multinationals often are restricted in their ability to deal with these problems because of financial market constraints or import controls. Where financial markets are free to reflect anticipated economic events, there is no need to hedge against the loss of purchasing power by inventorying physical assets; financial securities or forward contracts are cheaper and more effective hedging media. Similarly, there is less likelihood that government policies will disrupt the flow of supplies among regions within a country than among countries.

We also examined the various short-term financing alternatives available to a firm, focusing on parent company loans, local currency bank loans, and commercial paper. We saw how factors such as relative interest rates, anticipated currency changes, the existence of forward contracts, and economic exposure combine to affect a firm's short-term borrowing choices. Various objectives that a firm might use to arrive at its borrowing strategy were evaluated. It was concluded that if forward contracts exist, the only valid objective is to minimize covered interest costs. In the absence of forward contracts, firms can either attempt to minimize expected costs or establish some trade-off between reducing expected costs and reducing the degree of cash-flow exposure. The latter goal involves offsetting operating cash inflows in a currency with financing cash outflows in that same currency.

This chapter also developed formulas to compute effective dollar costs of loans denominated in dollars (home currency) or local currency. These formulas were then used to calculate the break-even rates of currency appreciation or depreciation that would equalize the costs of borrowing in the local currency or in the home currency.

QUESTIONS

1. High interest rates put a premium on careful management of cash and marketable securities.
   a. What techniques are available to an MNC with operating subsidiaries in many countries to economize on these short-term assets?
   b. What are the advantages and disadvantages of centralizing the cash management function?
   c. What can the firm do to enhance the advantages and reduce the disadvantages described in Part b?

2. Standard advice given to firms exporting to soft-currency countries is to invoice in their own currency. Critically analyze this recommendation and suggest a framework that will help a financial manager decide whether to stipulate hard-currency invoicing in export contracts.
   a. Under what circumstances does this advice make sense?
   b. Are these circumstances consistent with market efficiency?

   c. Are there any circumstances under which importer and exporter will mutually agree on an invoicing currency?

3. Comment on the following statement: "One should borrow in those currencies expected to depreciate and invest in those expected to appreciate."

4. What are the three basic types of bank loans? Describe their differences.

5. How does each of the following affect the relationship of stated and effective interest rates?
   a. The lending bank requires the borrower to repay principal and interest at the end of the borrowing period only.
   b. Interest is deducted from the amount borrowed before the borrower receives the proceeds.
   c. What is the likely ranking of the above from least to most expensive?

PROBLEMS

1. A $1.5 billion Italian multinational manufacturing company has a total of $600 million in intercompany trade flows and settles accounts in thirteen currencies. It also has about $400 million in third-party trade flows. Intercompany settlements are all made manually, there are no predefined remittance channels for either intercompany or third-party payments, and the methods and currencies of payment are determined

by each unit independently of the other units. Payment terms for intercompany and third-party accounts are identical. What techniques might help this company better manage its affairs?

2. SmithKline Beckman, the health-care products multinational (now part of GlaxoSmithKline), has 105 affiliates worldwide. There is a great deal of intercompany sales, dividend flows, and fee and royalty payments. Each unit makes its intercompany credit, payments, and hedging decisions independently. What advantages might SKB realize from centralizing international cash management and foreign exchange management?

3. A major food and beverage manufacturer with three major divisions, 150 countries of operation, and international revenues accounting for 15 percent of total revenues of $6 billion conducted a treasury audit. It gathered data in the following areas: (a) local reports put out by the subsidiaries; (b) cross-border reports prepared by regional headquarters; (c) the system's organization; (d) transmission of data between subsidiaries, regional headquarters, and parent headquarters; (e) possible computerization of local reporting systems; (f) local bank-balance reports; and (g) the accuracy of cash forecasts. What information should the company be looking for in each of these areas and why?

4. Twenty different divisions of Union Carbide sell to thousands of customers in more than fifty countries throughout the world. The proceeds are received in the form of drafts, checks, and letters of credit. Controlling the flow of funds from each transaction is an extremely complex task. Union Carbide wants to reduce the collection float to improve its cash flow. What are some techniques that might help to achieve this objective?

5. Newport Circuits is trying to decide whether to shift production overseas of its relatively expensive integrated circuits (they average around $11 each). Offshore assembly would save about 11.1¢ per chip in labor costs. However, by producing offshore, it would take about five weeks to get the parts to customers, in contrast to one week with domestic manufacturing. Thus, offshore production would force Newport to carry another four weeks of inventory. In addition, offshore production would entail combined shipping and customs duty costs of 3.2¢. Suppose Newport's cost of funds is 15 percent. Will it save money by shifting production offshore?

6. Tiger Car Corporation, a leading Japanese automaker, is considering a proposal to locate a factory abroad in Tennessee. Although labor costs would rise by ¥33,000 per car, the time in transit for the cars (to be sold in the United States) would be reduced by 65 days. Tigers sell for ¥825,000, and TCC's cost of funds is 12.5 percent. Should TCC locate the plant in Tennessee?

7. Apex Supplies borrows £1 million at 12 percent, payable in one year. If Apex is required to maintain a compensating balance of 20 percent, what is the effective percentage cost of its loan (in pounds)?

8. The Olivera Corporation, a manufacturer of olive oil products, needs to acquire €1 million in funds today to expand a pimiento-stuffing facility. Banca di Roma has offered the company a choice of an 11 percent loan payable at maturity or a 10 percent loan on a discount basis. Which loan should Olivera choose?

9. If Consolidated Corporation issues a Eurobond denominated in yen, the 7 percent interest rate on the $1 million, one-year borrowing will be 2 percent less than rates in the United States. However, ConCorp would have to pay back the principal and interest in Japanese yen. Currently, the exchange rate is ¥183 = $1. By how much could the yen rise against the dollar before the Euroyen bond would lose its advantage to ConCorp?

10. Ford can borrow dollars at 12 percent or pesos at 80 percent for one year. The peso:dollar exchange rate is expected to move from $1 = Ps 3300 currently to $1 = Ps 4500 by year's end.

    a. What is the expected after-tax dollar cost of borrowing dollars for one year if the Mexican corporate tax rate is 53 percent?

    b. What is Ford's expected after-tax dollar cost of borrowing pesos for one year?

    c. At what end-of-year exchange rate will the after-tax peso cost of borrowing dollars equal the after-tax peso cost of borrowing pesos?

BIBLIOGRAPHY

Business International Corporation. *Financing Foreign Operations.* New York: BIC, various issues.

Goeltz, Richard K. "Managing Liquid Funds Internationally." *Columbia Journal of World Business,* July–August 1972, pp. 59–65.

Lessard, Donald R. "Currency and Tax Considerations in International Financing." Teaching Note No. 3, Massachusetts Institute of Technology, Spring 1979.

Prindl, Andreas R. "International Money Management II: Systems and Techniques." *Euromoney,* October 1971.

Shapiro, Alan C. "Evaluating Financing Costs for Multinational Subsidiaries." *Journal of International Business Studies,* Fall 1975, pp. 25–32.

_____. "International Cash Management: The Determination of Multicurrency Cash Balances." *Journal of Financial and Quantitative Analysis,* December 1976, pp. 893–900.

_____. "Payments Netting in International Cash Management." *Journal of International Business Studies,* Fall 1978, pp. 51–58.

INTERNET RESOURCES

www.bloomberg.com Web site of Bloomberg. Contains a wealth of financial and economic information on financial markets and countries worldwide.

INTERNET EXERCISES

1. Using data from Bloomberg, what is the relative cost of short-term borrowing for the countries listed there? Which country has the highest interest rates? Which has the lowest rates? What might account for the differences in interest rates among these countries?

2. Based on the interest rates found on the Bloomberg Web site, where would you invest excess cash for the next three months? What other factors would you want to take into account besides relative interest rates?

3. Go to the Web site of a major international bank such as Citigroup (www.citigroup.com) or Bank of America (www.bankofamerica.com). What treasury services does this bank provide? How can these services be of value to a multinational company?

MANAGING THE MULTINATIONAL FINANCIAL SYSTEM

An injudicious tax offers a great temptation to smuggling. But the penalties of smuggling must rise in proportion to the temptation. The law, contrary to all the ordinary principles of justice, first creates the temptation, and then punishes those who yield to it.

Adam Smith (1776)

The Eiffel Tower is the Empire State Building after taxes.

Anonymous

CHAPTER LEARNING OBJECTIVES

- To identify the principal transfer mechanisms that multinational corporations (MNCs) can use to move money and profits among their various affiliates and to describe their tax, currency control, and cash management implications
- To identify the three principal arbitrage opportunities available to MNCs that stem from their ability to shift profits and funds internally
- To describe the costs and benefits associated with each transfer mechanism, as well as the constraints on their use
- To identify the factors that affect a multinational firm's ability to benefit from its internal financial transfer system
- To describe the information an MNC needs to take full advantage of its internal financial system

KEY TERMS

ad valorem tariff
advance pricing agreement (APA)
arm's-length prices
back-to-back loan
dividends
exchange controls
fees and royalties
financial channels
financial market arbitrage
foreign tax credit (FTC)
interaffiliate trade credit

intercompany fund flows
intercompany loan
leading and lagging
multinational financial system
parallel loan
regulatory system arbitrage
Section 482
Subpart F income
tax arbitrage
transfer prices

From a financial management standpoint, one of the distinguishing characteristics of the multinational corporation, in contrast to a collection of independent national firms dealing at arm's length with one another, is its ability to move money and profits among its affiliated companies through internal financial transfer mechanisms. Collectively, these mechanisms make up the **multinational financial system.** These mechanisms include transfer prices on goods and services traded internally, intercompany loans, dividend payments, leading (speeding up) and lagging (slowing down) intercompany payments, and fee and royalty charges. Together, they lead to patterns of profits and movements of funds that would be impossible in the world of Adam Smith.

These internal financial transfers are inherent in the MNC's global approach to international operations, specifically the highly coordinated international interchange of goods (material, parts, subassemblies, and finished products), services (technology, management skills, trademarks, and patents), and capital (equity and debt) that is the hallmark of the modern multinational firm. Indeed, almost 40 percent of U.S. imports and exports are transactions between U.S. firms and their foreign affiliates or parents. Intercompany trade is not confined to U.S. multinationals. Nearly 80 percent of the two-way trade between the United States and Japan goes from parent to foreign subsidiary or vice versa. So too does 40 percent of U.S.-European Community trade and 55 percent of EC-Japan trade.

This chapter analyzes the benefits, costs, and constraints associated with the multinational financial system. This analysis includes (1) identifying the conditions under which use of this system will increase the value of the firm relative to what it would be if all financial transactions were made at arm's length (that is, between unrelated entities) through external financial channels, (2) describing and evaluating the various channels for moving money and profits internationally, and (3) specifying the design principles for a global approach to managing international fund transfers. We will examine the objectives of such an approach and the various behavioral, informational, legal, and economic factors that help determine its degree of success.

20.1 THE VALUE OF THE MULTINATIONAL FINANCIAL SYSTEM

The multinational firm can control the mode and timing of internal financial transfers and thereby maximize global profits.

Financial transactions within the MNC result from the internal transfer of goods, services, technology, and capital. These product and factor flows range from intermediate and finished goods to less tangible items such as management skills, trademarks, and patents. Those transactions not liquidated immediately give rise to some type of financial claim, such as royalties for the use of a patent or accounts receivable for goods sold on credit. In addition, capital investments lead to future flows of dividends and interest and principal repayments. Exhibit 20.1 depicts some of the myriad financial linkages possible in the MNC.

Although all the links portrayed in Exhibit 20.1 can and do exist among independent firms, the MNC has greater control over the mode and timing of these financial transfers.[1]

Mode of Transfer

The MNC has considerable freedom in selecting the **financial channels** through which funds, allocated profits, or both are moved. For example, patents and trademarks can be sold outright or transferred in return for a contractual stream of royalty payments. Similarly, the MNC can move profits and cash from one unit to another by adjusting

[1] See Donald R. Lessard, "Transfer Prices, Taxes, and Financial Markets: Implications of Internal Financial Transfers within the Multinational Firm," in *The Economic Effects of Multinational Corporations*, edited by Robert G. Hawkins. (Greenwich, Conn.: JAI Press, 1979); and David P. Rutenberg, "Maneuvering Liquid Assets in a Multinational Company," *Management Science,* June 1970, pp. B671–B684. This section draws extensively from Lessard's article.

EXHIBIT 20.1 • THE MULTINATIONAL CORPORATE FINANCIAL SYSTEM

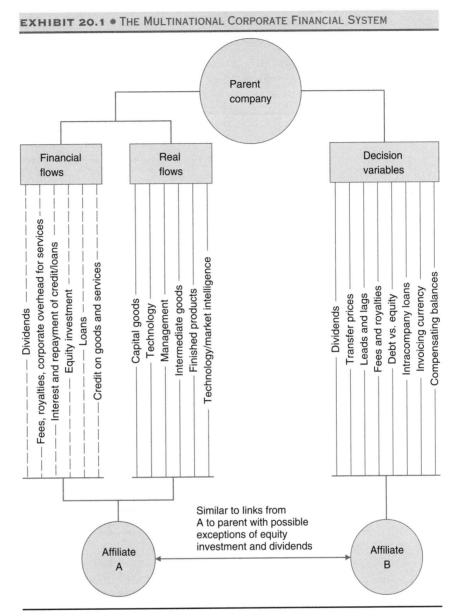

Source: Adapted from Figure 1 in Donald R. Lessard, "Transfer Prices, Taxes, and Financial Markets: Implications of Internal Financial Transfers within the Multinational Firm," in *The Economic Effects of Multinational Corporations,* edited by Robert G. Hawkins (Greenwich, Conn.: JAI Press, 1979), by permission of the author and the publisher.

transfer prices on intercompany sales and purchases of goods and services. With regard to investment flows, capital can be sent overseas as debt with at least some choice of interest rate, currency of denomination, and repayment schedule, or as equity with returns in the form of **dividends.** Multinational firms can use these various channels, singly or in combination, to transfer funds internationally, depending on the specific circumstances encountered. Furthermore, within the limits of various national laws and with regard to the relations between a foreign affiliate and its host government, these flows may be more advantageous than those that would result from dealings with independent firms.

Timing Flexibility

Some of the internally generated financial claims require a fixed payment schedule; others can be accelerated or delayed. This **leading and lagging** is most often applied to **inter-affiliate trade credit**, where a change in open account terms, say from 90 to 180 days, can involve massive shifts in liquidity. (Some nations have regulations about the repatriation of the proceeds of export sales. Thus, typically they do not have complete freedom to move funds by leading and lagging.) In addition, the timing of fee and royalty payments may be modified when all parties to the agreement are related. Even if the contract cannot be altered once the parties have agreed, the MNC generally has latitude when the terms are initially established.

In the absence of **exchange controls**—government regulations that restrict the transfer of funds to nonresidents—firms have the greatest amount of flexibility in the timing of equity claims. The earnings of a foreign affiliate can be retained or used to pay dividends that in turn can be deferred or paid in advance.

Despite the frequent presence of government regulations or limiting contractual arrangements, most MNCs have some flexibility in the timing of fund flows. This latitude is enhanced by the MNC's ability to control the timing of many of the underlying real transactions. For instance, shipping schedules can be altered so that one unit carries additional inventory for a sister affiliate.

MNCs often have flexibility in terms of timing their fund flows.

Value

The value of the MNC's network of financial linkages stems from the wide variations in national tax systems and significant costs and barriers associated with international financial transfers. Exhibit 20.2 summarizes the various factors that enhance the value of internal, relative to external, financial transactions. These restrictions are usually imposed to allow nations to maintain artificial values (usually inflated) for their currencies. In addition, capital controls are necessary when governments set the cost of local funds at a lower-than-market rate when currency risks are accounted for—that is, when government regulations do not allow the international Fisher effect or interest rate parity to hold.

EXHIBIT 20.2 ● MARKET IMPERFECTIONS THAT ENHANCE THE VALUE OF INTERNAL FINANCIAL TRANSACTIONS

Formal Barriers to International Transactions
Quantitative restrictions (exchange controls) and direct taxes on international movements of funds
Differential taxation of income streams according to nationality and global tax situation of the owners
Restrictions by nationality of investor and/or investment on access to domestic capital markets

Informal Barriers to International Transactions
Costs of obtaining information
Difficulty of enforcing contracts across national boundaries
Transaction costs
Traditional investment patterns

Imperfections in Domestic Capital Markets
Ceilings on interest rates
Mandatory credit allocations
Limited legal and institutional protection for minority shareholders
Limited liquidity due to thinness of markets
High transaction costs due to small market size and/or monopolistic practices of key financial institutions
Difficulty of obtaining information needed to evaluate securities

Source: Donald R. Lessard, "Transfer Prices, Taxes and Financial Markets: Implications of Internal Financial Transfers within the Multinational Firm," in *The Economic Effects of Multinational Corporations,* ed. Robert G. Hawkins (Greenwich, CT: JAI Press, 1979). Reprinted with permission by Donald R. Lessard and JAI Press.

Consequently, the ability to transfer funds and to reallocate profits internally presents multinationals with three different types of arbitrage opportunities.

1. **Tax arbitrage:** MNCs can reduce their global tax burden by shifting profits from units located in high-tax nations to those in lower-tax nations. Or they may shift profits from units in a taxpaying position to those with tax losses.

2. **Financial market arbitrage:** By transferring funds among units, MNCs may be able to circumvent exchange controls, earn higher risk-adjusted yields on excess funds, reduce their risk-adjusted cost of borrowed funds, and tap previously unavailable capital sources.

3. **Regulatory system arbitrage:** When subsidiary profits are a function of government regulations (for example, when a government agency sets allowable prices on the firm's goods) or union pressure, rather than the marketplace, the ability to disguise true profitability by reallocating profits among units may give the multinational firm a negotiating advantage.[2]

A fourth possible arbitrage opportunity is the ability to permit an affiliate to negate the effect of credit restraint or controls in its country of operation. If a government limits access to additional borrowing locally, then the firm able to draw on external sources of funds may not only achieve greater short-term profits, but also a more powerful market position over the long term.

At the same time, we must recognize that because most of the gains derive from the MNC's skill at taking advantage of openings in tax laws or regulatory barriers, governments do not always appreciate the MNC's capabilities and global profit-maximizing behavior. MNCs must be aware of the potentially controversial nature of some of these maneuvers and not put themselves in a position where they lose the goodwill necessary to make them welcome citizens of their host countries.

20.2 INTERCOMPANY FUND-FLOW MECHANISMS: COSTS AND BENEFITS

The MNC can be visualized as *unbundling* the total flow of funds between each pair of affiliates into separate components that are associated with resources transferred in the form of products, capital, services, and technology. For example, dividends, interest, and loan repayments can be matched against capital invested as equity or debt; fees, royalties, or corporate overhead can be charged for various corporate services, trademarks, or licenses.

The different channels available to the multinational enterprise for moving money and profits internationally include transfer pricing, fee and royalty adjustments, leading and lagging, intercompany loans, dividend adjustments, and investing in the form of debt versus equity. This section examines the costs, benefits, and constraints associated with each of these methods of effecting **intercompany fund flows:** It begins by sketching out some of the tax consequences for U.S.-based MNCs of interaffiliate financial transfers.

Tax Factors

Total tax payments on intercompany fund transfers are dependent on the tax regulations of both the host and recipient nations. The host country ordinarily has two types of taxes that directly affect tax costs: corporate income taxes and withholding taxes on dividend, interest, and fee remittances. In addition, several countries, such as Germany and Japan, tax retained earnings at a different (usually higher) rate than earnings paid out as dividends.

Many recipient nations, including the United States, tax income remitted from abroad at the regular corporate tax rate. Where this rate is higher than the foreign tax rate,

---

[2] See *ibid.*

dividend and other payments will normally entail an incremental tax cost. A number of countries, however—such as Canada, the Netherlands, and France—do not impose any additional taxes on foreign-source income.

As an offset to these additional taxes, most countries, including the United States, provide tax credits for affiliate taxes already paid on the same income. For example, if a subsidiary located overseas has $100 in pretax income, pays $30 in local tax, and then remits the remaining $70 to its U.S. parent in the form of a dividend, the U.S. Internal Revenue Service (IRS) will impose a $35 tax (0.35 × $100) but will then provide a dollar-for-dollar **foreign tax credit (FTC)** for the $30 already paid in foreign taxes, leaving the parent with a bill for the remaining $5. Excess foreign tax credits from other remittances can be used to offset these additional taxes. For example, if a foreign subsidiary earns $100 before tax, pays $45 in local tax, and then remits the remaining $55 in the form of a dividend, the parent will wind up with an excess FTC of $10, the difference between the $35 U.S. tax owed and the $45 foreign tax paid.

Transfer Pricing

MNCs can reduce taxes by using transfer prices to shift profits from the high-tax to the low-tax nation.

The pricing of goods and services traded internally is one of the most sensitive of all management subjects, and executives typically are reluctant to discuss it. Each government normally presumes that multinationals use *transfer pricing* to its country's detriment. For this reason, a number of home and host governments have set up policing mechanisms to review the transfer pricing policies of MNCs.

The most important uses of transfer pricing include (1) reducing taxes, (2) reducing tariffs, and (3) avoiding exchange controls. Transfer prices also may be used to increase the MNC's share of profits from a joint venture and to disguise an affiliate's true profitability.

Tax Effects   The following scenario illustrates the tax effects associated with a change in transfer price. Suppose that affiliate A produces 100,000 circuit boards for $10 apiece and sells them to affiliate B. Affiliate B, in turn, sells these boards for $22 apiece to an unrelated customer. As shown in Exhibit 20.3, pretax profit for the consolidated company is $1 million regardless of the price at which the goods are transferred from affiliate A to affiliate B.

EXHIBIT 20.3 • TAX EFFECT OF HIGH VERSUS LOW TRANSFER PRICE ($ THOUSANDS)

	Affiliate A	Affiliate B	Affiliates A + B
Low-Markup Policy			
Revenue	1,500	2,200	2,200
Cost of goods sold	1,000	1,500	1,000
Gross profit	500	700	1,200
Other expenses	100	100	200
Income before taxes	400	600	1,000
Taxes (30%/50%)	120	300	420
Net income	280	300	580
High-Markup Policy			
Revenue	1,800	2,200	2,200
Cost of goods sold	1,000	1,800	1,000
Gross profit	800	400	1,200
Other expenses	100	100	200
Income before taxes	700	300	1,000
Taxes (30%/50%)	210	150	360
Net income	490	150	640

Nevertheless, because affiliate A's tax rate is 30 percent whereas affiliate B's tax rate is 50 percent, consolidated after-tax income will differ depending on the transfer price used. Under the low-markup policy, in which affiliate A sets a unit transfer price of $15, affiliate A pays taxes of $120,000 and affiliate B pays $300,000, for a total tax bill of $420,000 and a consolidated net income of $580,000. Switching to a high-markup policy (a transfer price of $18), affiliate A's taxes rise to $210,000 and affiliate B's decline to $150,000, for combined tax payments of $360,000 and consolidated net income of $640,000. The result of this transfer price increase is to lower total taxes paid by $60,000 and raise consolidated income by the same amount.

In effect, profits are being shifted from a higher to a lower tax jurisdiction. In the extreme case, an affiliate may be in a loss position because of high start-up costs, heavy depreciation charges, or substantial investments that are expensed. Consequently, it has a zero effective tax rate, and profits channeled to that unit can be received tax-free. The basic rule of thumb to follow if the objective is to minimize taxes is as follows: If affiliate A is selling goods to affiliate B, and t_A and t_B are the marginal tax rates of affiliate A and affiliate B, respectively, then

If $t_A > t_B$, set the transfer price as low as possible.

If $t_A < t_B$, set the transfer price as high as possible.

Tariffs   The introduction of tariffs complicates this decision rule. Suppose that affiliate B must pay **ad valorem tariffs**—import duties that are set as a percentage of the value of the imported goods—at the rate of 10 percent. Then, raising the transfer price will increase the duties that affiliate B must pay, assuming that the tariff is levied on the invoice (transfer) price. The combined tax-plus-tariff effects of the transfer price change are shown in Exhibit 20.4.

Under the low-markup policy, import tariffs of $150,000 are paid. Affiliate B's taxes will decline by $75,000 because tariffs are tax-deductible. Total taxes plus tariffs paid are

Tariff considerations complicate the optimal transfer price decision.

EXHIBIT 20.4 • TAX-PLUS-TARIFF EFFECT OF HIGH VERSUS LOW TRANSFER PRICE ($ THOUSANDS)

	Affiliate A	*Affiliate B*	*Affiliates A + B*
Low-Markup Policy			
Revenue	1,500	2,200	2,200
Cost of goods sold	1,000	1,500	1,000
Import duty (10%)	—	150	150
Gross profit	500	550	1,050
Other expenses	100	100	200
Income before taxes	400	450	850
Taxes (30%/50%)	120	225	345
Net income	280	225	505
High-Markup Policy			
Revenue	1,800	2,200	2,200
Cost of goods sold	1,000	1,800	1,000
Import duty	—	180	180
Gross profit	800	220	1,020
Other expenses	100	100	200
Income before taxes	700	120	820
Taxes (30%/50%)	210	60	270
Net income	490	60	550

$495,000. Switching to the high-markup policy raises import duties to $180,000 and simultaneously lowers affiliate B's income taxes by half that amount, or $90,000. Total taxes plus tariffs rise to $450,000. The high-markup policy is still desirable, but its benefit has been reduced by $15,000 to $45,000. In general, the higher the ad valorem tariff relative to the income tax differential, the more likely it is that a low transfer price is desirable.

There are some costs associated with using transfer prices for tax reduction. If the price is too high, tax authorities in the purchaser's (affiliate B's) country will see revenues forgone; if the price is too low, both governments might intervene. Affiliate A's government may view low transfer prices as tax evasion at the same time that the tariff commission in affiliate B's country sees dumping or revenue foregone, or both. These costs must be paid for in the form of legal fees, executive time, and penalties.

Most countries have specific regulations governing transfer prices. For instance, **Section 482** of the U.S. Revenue Code calls for **arm's-length prices**—prices at which a willing buyer and a willing unrelated seller would freely agree to transact. The four alternative methods for establishing an arm's-length price, in order of their general acceptability to tax authorities, are as follows:

> Most governments regulate the transfer prices MNCs can use.

1. *Comparable uncontrolled price method:* Under this method, the transfer price is set by direct references to prices used in comparable bona fide transactions between enterprises that are independent of each other or between the multinational enterprise group and unrelated parties. In principle, this method is the most appropriate to use, and the easiest. In practice, however, it may be impractical or difficult to apply. For example, differences in quantity, quality, terms, use of trademarks or brand names, time of sale, level of the market, and geography of the market may be grounds for claiming that the sale is not comparable. There is a gradation of comparability: Adjustments can be made easily for freight and insurance but cannot be made accurately for trademarks.

2. *Resale price method:* Under this method, the arm's-length price for a product sold to an associate enterprise for resale is determined by reducing the price at which it is resold to an independent purchaser by an appropriate markup (that is, an amount that covers the reseller's costs and profit). This method is probably most applicable to marketing operations. However, determining an appropriate markup can be difficult, especially where the reseller adds substantially to the value of the product. Thus, there is often quite a bit of leeway in determining a standard markup.

3. *Cost-plus method:* This method adds an appropriate profit markup to the seller's cost to arrive at an arm's-length price. This method is useful in specific situations, such as where semifinished products are sold between related parties or where one entity is essentially acting as a subcontractor for a related entity. However, ordinarily it is difficult to assess the cost of the product and to determine the appropriate profit markup. In fact, no definition of full cost is given, nor is there a unique formula for prorating shared costs over joint products. Thus, the markup over cost allows room for maneuver.

4. *Another appropriate method:* In some cases, it may be appropriate to use a combination of the above methods, or still other methods (e.g., comparable profits and net yield methods) to arrive at the transfer price. In addition, the U.S. Treasury regulations are quite explicit that while a new market is being established, it is legitimate to charge a lower transfer price.

In light of Section 482 (and the U.S. government's willingness to use it) together with similar authority by most other nations, the current practice of MNCs appears to be setting standard prices for standardized products. However, the innovative nature of the typical multinational ensures a continual stream of new products for which no market equivalent exists. Hence, some leeway is possible on transfer pricing. In addition, although finished products do get traded among affiliates, trade between related parties increasingly is in high-tech, custom-made components and subassemblies (for example, automobile transmissions and circuit boards) where there are no comparable sales to unrelated buyers. Firms also have a great deal of latitude in setting prices on rejects, scrap, and returned goods. Moreover, as trade in intangible services becomes more important, monitoring transfer prices within MNCs has become extraordinarily complex, creating plentiful opportunities for multinationals to use transfer pricing to shift their overall taxable income from one jurisdiction to another.

ILLUSTRATION   *President Clinton Seeks $45 Billion from Foreign Companies*

One of the linchpins of President Bill Clinton's economic revival plan was a proposal to extract billions from foreign companies doing business in the United States. By closing loopholes and instituting more vigorous enforcement, Clinton said he believed that the federal government could raise $45 billion over four years from foreign companies, which take in nearly $1 trillion in U.S. revenue annually. Clinton's contention was based on a view prevalent in the IRS that foreign multinationals were manipulating their transfer prices on goods they sold to their U.S. subsidiaries to avoid paying U.S. tax. For example, IRS data for 1989 showed that the 44,480 domestic companies controlled by foreign entities generated $1 trillion of worldwide sales and had total assets of $1.4 trillion but reported net income of only $11.2 billion, a return on assets of under 1 percent. However, many analysts are skeptical that much is to be gained by tougher enforcement of Section 482. For example, one government study reportedly found that the IRS had only limited success in recovering additional taxes in transfer pricing cases involving foreign MNCs. From 1987 through 1989, the IRS got only 26.5 percent of the $757 million it sought.

In addition, the circumstantial evidence the IRS relied on to support its case was suspect. For example, in 1990, the IRS cited as evidence of transfer pricing manipulation the fact that, over a ten-year period, foreign-controlled companies' (1) gross income had more than doubled and (2) the taxes paid by these companies had hardly changed. However, this argument made no sense because on U.S. tax returns, "gross income" is "sales" less "cost of sales"; thus transfer price manipulation, if any, would reduce "gross income" (by raising the cost of goods sold). Therefore, a doubling of "gross income" could not indicate transfer price manipulation.

One means of dealing with the U.S. government's crackdown on alleged transfer pricing abuses is greater reliance on **advance pricing agreements (APAs)**. The APA procedure allows the multinational firm, the IRS, and the foreign tax authority to work out, in advance, a method to calculate transfer prices. APAs are expensive, can take quite a while to negotiate, and involve a great deal of disclosure on the part of the MNC, but if a company wants assurance that its transfer pricing is in order, the APA is a useful tool.

Transfer pricing can be used to avoid currency controls.

Exchange Controls   Another important use of transfer pricing is to avoid currency controls. For example, in the absence of offsetting foreign tax credits, a U.S. parent will wind up with 0.65Q_0$ after tax for each dollar increase in the price at which it sells Q_0 units of a product to an affiliate with blocked funds (based on a U.S. corporate tax rate of 35 percent). Hence, a transfer price change from P_0 to P_1 will lead to a shift of $0.65(P_1 - P_0)Q_0$ dollars to the parent. The subsidiary, of course, will show a corresponding reduction in its cash balances and taxes, due to its higher expenses.

Bypassing currency restrictions appears to explain the seeming anomaly whereby subsidiaries operating in less-developed countries (LDCs) with low tax rates are sold overpriced goods by other units. In effect, companies appear to be willing to pay a tax penalty to access otherwise unavailable funds.

Joint Ventures   Conflicts over transfer pricing often arise when one of the affiliates involved is owned jointly by one or more other partners. The outside partners are often suspicious that transfer pricing is being used to shift profits from the joint venture, where they must be shared, to a wholly owned subsidiary. Although there is no pat answer to this problem, the determination of fair transfer prices should be resolved before the establishment of a joint venture. Continuing disputes may still arise, however, over the pricing of new products introduced to an existing venture.

Disguising Profitability   Many LDCs erect high tariff barriers in order to develop import-substituting industries. However, because they are aware of the potential for abuse, many host governments simultaneously attempt to regulate the profits of firms operating in such a protected environment. When confronted by a situation in which profits depend on government regulations, the MNC can use transfer pricing (buying goods from sister affiliates at a higher price) to disguise the true profitability of its local affiliate, enabling it to justify higher local prices. Lower reported profits also may improve a subsidiary's bargaining position in wage negotiations. It is probably for this reason that several international unions have called for fuller disclosure by multinationals of their worldwide accounting data.

Evaluation and Control   Transfer price adjustments will distort the profits of reporting units and create potential difficulties in evaluating managerial performance. In addition, managers evaluated on the basis of these reported profits may have an incentive to behave in ways that are suboptimal for the corporation as a whole.

Reinvoicing Centers

One approach used by some multinationals to disguise profitability, avoid the scrutiny of governments, and coordinate transfer pricing policy is to set up reinvoicing centers in low-tax nations. The reinvoicing center takes title to all goods sold by one corporate unit to another affiliate or to a third-party customer, although the goods move directly from the factory or warehouse location to the purchaser. The center pays the seller and, in turn, is paid by the purchasing unit.

With price quotations coming from one location, it is easier and quicker to implement decisions to have prices reflect changes in currency values. The reinvoicing center also provides a firm with greater flexibility in choosing an invoicing currency. Affiliates can be ordered to pay in other than their local currency if required by the firm's external currency obligations. In this way, the MNC can avoid the costs of converting from one currency to another and then back again.

Having a reinvoicing center can be expensive, however. There are increased communications costs due to the geographical separation of marketing and sales from the production centers. In addition, tax authorities may be suspicious of transactions with an affiliated trading company located in a tax haven.

Before 1962, many U.S. multinationals had reinvoicing companies located in low- or zero-tax countries. By buying low and selling high, U.S. MNCs could siphon off most of the profit on interaffiliate sales with little or no tax liability because the U.S. government at that time did not tax unremitted foreign earnings. This situation changed with passage of the U.S. Revenue Act of 1962, which declared that reinvoicing-center income is Subpart F income. **Subpart F income** is a category of foreign-source income that is subject to U.S. taxation immediately, whether or not remitted to the United States. For most

U.S.-based multinationals, this situation negated the tax benefits associated with a reinvoicing center.

A 1977 ruling by the IRS, however, has increased the value of tax havens in general and reinvoicing centers in particular. That ruling, which allocates to a firm's foreign affiliates certain parent expenses that previously could be written off in the United States, has generated additional foreign tax credits that can be utilized only against U.S. taxes owed on foreign-source income, increasing the value of tax-haven subsidiaries.

A reinvoicing center, by channeling profits overseas, can create Subpart F income to offset these excess FTCs. In effect, foreign tax credits can be substituted for taxes that would otherwise be owed to the United States or to foreign governments. Suppose a firm shifts $100 in profit from a country with a 50 percent tax rate to a reinvoicing center where the tax rate is only 10 percent. If this $100 is deemed Subpart F income by the IRS, the U.S. parent will owe an additional $25 in U.S. tax (based on the U.S. corporate tax rate of 35 percent and the $10 foreign tax credit). However, if the company has excess foreign tax credits available, then each $100 shift in profits can reduce total tax payments by $25, until the excess FTCs are all expended.

Fees and Royalties

Fees and royalties are often a more convenient way of accessing subsidiary profits.

Management services such as headquarters advice, allocated overhead, patents, and trademarks are often unique and, therefore, are without a reference market price. The consequent difficulty in pricing these corporate resources makes them suitable for use as additional routes for international fund flows by varying the **fees and royalties** charged for using these intangible factors of production.

Transfer prices for services or intangible assets have the same tax and exchange control effects as those for transfer prices on goods. However, host governments often look with more favor on payments for industrial know-how than for profit remittances. Where restrictions do exist, they are more likely to be modified to permit a fee for technical knowledge than to allow for dividends.

For MNCs, these charges have assumed a somewhat more important role as a conduit for funneling remittances from foreign affiliates. To a certain extent, this trend reflects the fact that many of these payments are tied to overseas sales or assets that increased very rapidly over the past fifty years, as well as the growing importance of tax considerations and exchange controls. For example, by setting low transfer prices on intangibles to manufacturing subsidiaries in low-tax locations such as Puerto Rico or Singapore, multinationals can receive profits essentially tax free.

In recognition of this possibility, the United States in 1986 amended Section 482 to provide that the transfer price of an intangible must be "commensurate with the income" the intangible generates. This means in practice that the IRS will not consider a related-party transfer price for an intangible arm's length unless it produces a split in profits between transferor and transferee that falls within the range of profits that unrelated parties realize (1) on similar intangibles and (2) in similar circumstances. Armed with this amendment, the IRS now carefully scrutinizes the pricing of intangibles.

MNCs tend to follow a stable remittance policy for fees and royalties.

The most common approach to setting fee and royalty charges is for the parent to decide on a desired amount of total fee remittances from the overseas operations, usually based on an allocation of corporate expenses, and then to apportion these charges according to subsidiary sales or assets. This method, which sometimes involves establishing identical licensing agreements with all units, gives these charges the appearance of a legitimate and necessary business expense, thereby aiding in overcoming currency restrictions.

Governments typically prefer prior agreements and steady and predictable payment flows; a sudden change in licensing and service charges is likely to be regarded with suspicion. For this reason, firms try to avoid abrupt changes in their remittance policies.

However, where exchange controls exist or are likely, or if there are significant tax advantages, many firms will initially set a higher level of fee and royalty payments while still maintaining a stable remittance policy.

Special problems exist with joint ventures because the parent company will have to obtain permission from its partner(s) to be able to levy charges for its services and licensing contributions. These payments ensure the parent of receiving at least some compensation for the resources it has invested in the joint venture, perhaps in lieu of dividends over which it may have little or no control.

Leading and Lagging

Leading and lagging of interaffiliate payments is a common method of shifting money from one unit to another.

A highly favored means of shifting liquidity among affiliates is an acceleration (**leading**) or delay (**lagging**) in the payment of interaffiliate accounts by modifying the credit terms extended by one unit to another. For example, suppose affiliate A sells goods worth $1 million monthly to affiliate B on 90-day credit terms. Then, on average, affiliate A has $3 million of accounts receivable from affiliate B and is, in effect, financing $3 million of working capital for affiliate B. If the terms are changed to 180 days, there will be a one-time shift of an additional $3 million to affiliate B. Conversely, reducing credit terms to 30 days will create a flow of $2 million from affiliate B to affiliate A, as shown in Exhibit 20.5.

The value of leading and lagging depends on the opportunity cost of funds to both the paying unit and the recipient.

Shifting Liquidity The value of leading and lagging depends on the opportunity cost of funds to both the paying unit and the recipient. When an affiliate already in a surplus position receives payment, it can invest the additional funds at the prevailing local lending rate; if it requires working capital, the payment received can be used to reduce its borrowings at the borrowing rate. If the paying unit has excess funds, it loses cash that it would have invested at the lending rate; if it is in a deficit position, it has to borrow at the borrowing rate. Assessment of the benefits of shifting liquidity among affiliates requires that these borrowing and lending rates be calculated on an after-tax dollar (HC) basis.

Suppose, for example, that a multinational company faces the following effective, after-tax dollar borrowing and lending rates in Germany and the United States:

	Borrowing Rate (%)	Lending Rate (%)
United States	3.8	2.9
Germany	3.6	2.7

EXHIBIT 20.5 • FUND-TRANSFER EFFECTS OF LEADING AND LAGGING

Affiliate A Sells $1 Million in Goods Monthly to Affiliate B

	Credit Terms		
Balance Sheet Accounts	*Normal (90 days)*	*Leading (30 days)*	*Lagging (180 days)*
Affiliate A			
Accounts receivable from B	$3,000,000	$1,000,000	$6,000,000
Affiliate B			
Accounts payable to A	$3,000,000	$1,000,000	$6,000,000
Net Cash Transfers			
From B to A		$2,000,000	—
From A to B		—	$3,000,000

Both the U.S. and German units can have either a surplus (+) or deficit (−) of funds. The four possibilities, along with the domestic interest rates (U.S./German) and interest differentials (U.S. rate − German rate) associated with each state, are as follows:

		Germany	
		+	−
United States	+	2.9%/2.7% (0.2%)	2.9%/3.6% (−0.7%)
	−	3.8%/2.7% (1.1%)	3.8%/3.6% (0.2%)

For example, if both units have excess funds, then the relevant opportunity costs of funds are the U.S. and German lending rates of 2.9 percent and 2.7 percent, respectively, and the associated interest differential (in parentheses) is 0.2 percent. Similarly, if the U.S. unit requires funds while the German affiliate has a cash surplus, then the relevant rates are the respective U.S. borrowing and German lending rates of 3.8 percent and 2.7 percent and the interest differential is 1.1 percent.

If the interest rate differential is positive, the corporation as a whole—by moving funds to the United States—will either pay less on its borrowing or earn more interest on its investments. This move can be made by leading payments to the United States and lagging payments to Germany. Shifting money to Germany—by leading payments to Germany and lagging them to the United States—will be worthwhile if the interest differential is negative.

Based on the interest differentials in this example, all borrowings should be done in Germany, and surplus funds should be invested in the United States. Only if the U.S. unit has excess cash and the German unit requires funds should money flow into Germany.

For example, suppose the German unit owes $2 million to the U.S. unit. The timing of this payment can be changed by up to 90 days in either direction. Assume that the U.S. unit is borrowing funds, and the German unit has excess cash available. According to the prevailing interest differential of 1.1 percent, given the current liquidity status of each affiliate, the German unit should speed up, or lead, its payment to the U.S. unit. The net effect of these adjustments is that the U.S. firm can reduce its borrowing by $2 million, and the German unit has $2 million less in cash—all for 90 days. Borrowing costs for the U.S. unit are pared by $19,000 ($2 million × 0.038 × 90/360), and the German unit's interest income is reduced by $13,500 ($2 million × 0.027 × 90/360). There is a net savings of $5,500. The savings could be computed more directly by using the relevant interest differential of 1.1 percent as follows: $2 million × 0.011 × 90/360 = $5,500.

Advantages   A leading and lagging strategy has several advantages over direct intercompany loans.

> Leading and lagging has several advantages over intercompany loans.

1. No formal note of indebtedness is needed, and the amount of credit can be adjusted up or down by shortening or lengthening the terms on the accounts. Governments do not always allow such freedom on loans.

2. Governments are less likely to interfere with payments on intercompany accounts than on direct loans.

3. Section 482 allows intercompany accounts up to six months to be interest free. In contrast, interest must be charged on all intercompany loans. The ability to set a zero interest rate is valuable if the host government does not allow interest payments on parent company loans to be tax deductible, or if there are withholding taxes on interest payments.

Government Restrictions   As with all other transfer mechanisms, government controls on intercompany credit terms are often tight and are given to abrupt changes. Although appearing straightforward on the surface, these rules are subject to different degrees of government interpretation and sanction. For example, in theory, Japan permits firms to employ leads and lags. In reality, however, leading and lagging is very difficult because regulations require that all settlements be made in accordance with the original trade documents unless a very good reason exists for an exception. On the other hand, Sweden, which prohibits import leads, will often lift this restriction for imports of capital goods.

Intercompany Loans

A principal means of financing foreign operations and moving funds internationally is to engage in intercompany lending activities. The making and repaying of **intercompany loans** is often the only legitimate transfer mechanism available to the MNC.

> Intercompany loans add value to the MNC if credit rationing, currency controls, or differences in national tax rates exist.

Intercompany loans are more valuable to the firm than arm's-length transactions only if at least one of the following market distortions exist: (1) credit rationing (due to a ceiling on local interest rates), (2) currency controls, or (3) differential tax rates among countries. This list is not particularly restrictive because it is the rare MNC that faces none of these situations in its international operations.

Although various types of intercompany loans exist, the most important methods at present are direct loans, back-to-back financing, and parallel loans. *Direct loans* are straight extensions of credit from the parent to an affiliate or from one affiliate to another. The other types of intercompany loans typically involve an intermediary.

> Back-to-back loans can be used to avoid currency controls and reduce taxes.

Back-to-Back Loans   **Back-to-back loans**, also called *fronting loans* or *link financing,* are often employed to finance affiliates located in nations with high interest rates or restricted capital markets, especially when there is a danger of currency controls or when different rates of withholding tax are applied to loans from a financial institution. In the typical arrangement, the parent company deposits funds with a bank in country A that in turn lends the money to a subsidiary in country B. These transactions are shown in Exhibit 20.6. By contrasting these transactions with a direct intercompany loan, the figure reveals that, in effect, a back-to-back loan is an intercompany loan channeled through a bank. From the bank's point of view, the loan is risk free because the parent's deposit fully collateralizes it. The bank simply acts as an intermediary or a front; compensation is provided by the margin between the interest received from the borrowing unit and the rate paid on the parent's deposit.

A back-to-back loan may offer several potential advantages when compared with a direct intercompany loan. Two of the most important advantages are as follows:

1. Certain countries apply different withholding-tax rates to interest paid to a

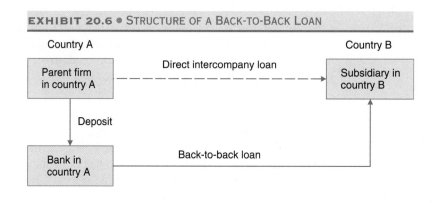

EXHIBIT 20.6 ● STRUCTURE OF A BACK-TO-BACK LOAN

foreign parent and interest paid to a financial institution. A cost saving in the form of lower taxes may be available with a back-to-back loan.

MNCs can use back-to-back loans to recycle funds tax free.

2. If currency controls are imposed, the government usually will permit the local subsidiary to honor the amortization schedule of a loan from a major multinational bank; to stop payment would hurt the nation's credit rating. Conversely, local monetary authorities would have far fewer reservations about not authorizing the repayment of an intercompany loan. In general, back-to-back financing provides better protection than does a parent loan against expropriation and/or exchange controls.

Some financial managers argue that a back-to-back loan conveys another benefit: The subsidiary seems to have obtained credit from a major bank on its own, possibly enhancing its reputation. However, this appearance is unlikely to be significant in the highly informed international financial community.

The costs of a back-to-back loan are evaluated in the same way as any other financing method (i.e., by considering relevant interest and tax rates and the likelihood of changes in currency value). To see how these calculations should be made, assume that the parent's opportunity cost of funds is 10 percent, and the parent's and affiliate's marginal tax rates are 34 percent and 40 percent, respectively. Then, if the parent earns 8 percent on its deposit, the bank charges 9 percent to lend dollars to the affiliate, and the local currency devalues by 11 percent during the course of the loan, the effective cost of this back-to-back loan equals

Interest cost to parent	−	Interest income to parent	+	Interest cost to subsidiary	−	Tax gain on exchange loss		
0.10(0.66)	−	0.08(0.66)	+	0.09(0.6)	−	0.40(0.11)	=	2.32%

Variations on the back-to-back loan include the parent depositing dollars while the bank lends out local currency, or a foreign affiliate placing the deposit in any of several currencies with the bank loan being denominated in the same or a different currency. To calculate the costs of these variations would require modifying to the methodology shown previously, but the underlying rationale is the same: Include all interest, tax, and currency effects that accrue to both the borrowing and the lending units and convert these costs to the home currency.

Users of the fronting technique include U.S. companies that have accumulated sizable amounts of money in "captive" insurance firms and holding companies located in low-tax nations. Rather than reinvesting this money overseas (assuming that is the intent) by first paying dividends to the parent company and incurring a large tax liability, some of these companies attempt to recycle their funds indirectly via back-to-back loans.

For example, suppose affiliate A, wholly owned and located in a tax haven, deposits $2 million for one year in a bank at 7 percent; the bank, in turn, lends this money to affiliate B at 9 percent. If we assume that there are no currency changes, and if B has an effective tax rate of 50 percent, then its after-tax interest expense equals $90,000 ($2 million × 0.09 × 0.5). The return to A equals $140,000 ($2 million × 0.07), assuming that A pays no taxes. The net result of this transaction has been to shift $2 million from A to B while realizing a net gain to A + B combined of $50,000 (A's interest income of $140,000 less the after-tax cost to B of $90,000).

Back-to-back arrangements also can be used to access blocked currency funds without physically transferring them. Suppose Xerox wishes to use the excess reais (the plural of *real,* the Brazilian currency) being generated by its Brazilian operation to finance a needed plant expansion in the Philippines, where long-term money is virtually unobtainable. Xerox prefers not to invest additional dollars in the Philippines because of the high probability of a Philippine peso devaluation. Because of stringent Brazilian exchange controls, however, this movement of reais cannot take place directly. However, Xerox may be able to use the worldwide branching facilities of an international bank as a substitute for an internal transfer. For example, suppose the Brazilian branch of J.P. Morgan Chase Bank needs deposits of reais to continue funding its loans in a restrictive credit environment. Chase may be willing to lend Xerox long-term pesos through its branch in the Philippines in return for a *real* deposit of equivalent maturity of reais in Brazil.

In this way, Xerox gets the use of its funds in Brazil and at the same time receives locally denominated funds in the Philippines. Protection is provided against a peso devaluation, although Xerox's funds in reais are, of course, still exposed. The value of this arrangement is based on the relative interest rates involved, anticipated currency changes, and the opportunity cost of the funds being utilized. Given the exchange and credit restrictions and other market imperfections that exist, it is quite possible that both the bank and its client can benefit from this type of arrangement. Negotiation between the two parties will determine how these benefits are to be shared.

Parallel Loans   A **parallel loan** is a method of effectively repatriating blocked funds (at least for the term of the arrangement), circumventing exchange control restrictions, avoiding a premium exchange rate for investments abroad, financing foreign affiliates without incurring additional exchange risk, or obtaining foreign currency financing at attractive rates. As shown in Exhibit 20.7, it consists of two related but separate—that is, parallel—borrowings and usually involves four parties in at least two different countries. In Exhibit 20.7a, a U.S. parent firm wishing to invest in Spain lends dollars to the U.S. affiliate of a Spanish firm that wants to invest in the United States. In return, the Spanish parent lends euros in Spain to the U.S. firm's Spanish subsidiary. Drawdowns, payments of interest, and repayments of principal are made simultaneously. The differential

> A parallel loan consists of two related but separate borrowings, usually involving four parties in two different countries.

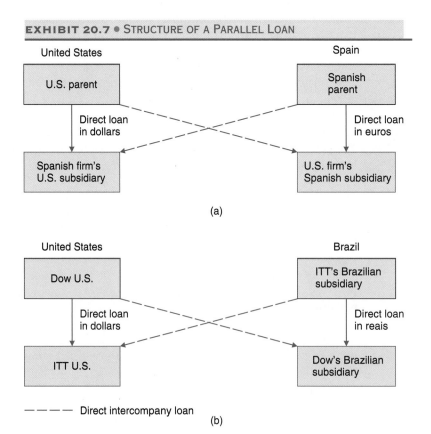

EXHIBIT 20.7 • STRUCTURE OF A PARALLEL LOAN

(a)

(b)

– – – – – Direct intercompany loan

between the rates of interest on the two loans is determined, in theory, by the cost of money in each country and anticipated changes in currency values.

Exhibit 20.7b shows how a parallel loan can be used to access blocked funds. In this instance, the Brazilian affiliate of ITT is generating reais that it is unable to repatriate. It lends this money to the local affiliate of Dow Chemical; in turn, Dow lends dollars to ITT in the United States. Hence, ITT would have the use of dollars in the United States and Dow would obtain reais in Brazil. In both cases, the parallel transactions are the functional equivalent of direct intercompany loans.

Fees to banks brokering these arrangements usually run from 0.25 percent to 0.5 percent of the principal for each side. (Chapter 9 discussed currency swaps, which are an outgrowth of parallel loans.)

Dividends

Dividends are by far the most important means of transferring funds from foreign affiliates to the parent company, typically accounting for more than 50 percent of all remittances to U.S. firms. Among the various factors that MNCs consider when deciding on dividend payments by their affiliates are taxes, financial statement effects, exchange risk, currency controls, financing requirements, availability and cost of funds, and the parent's dividend payout ratio. Firms differ, however, in the relative importance they place on these variables, as well as in how systematically the variables are incorporated in an overall remittance policy.

Dividends are the most important means of transferring funds from foreign affiliates to the parent company.

The parent company's *dividend payout ratio* often plays an important role in determining the dividends to be received from abroad. Some firms require the same payout percentage as the parent's rate for each of their subsidiaries; others set a target payout rate as a percentage of overall foreign-source earnings without attempting to receive the same percentage from each subsidiary. The rationale for focusing on the parent's payout ratio is that the subsidiaries should contribute their share of the dividends paid to the stockholders. Thus, if the parent's payout rate is 60 percent, then foreign operations should contribute 60 percent of their earnings toward meeting this goal. Establishing a uniform percentage for each unit, rather than an overall target, is explained as an attempt to persuade foreign governments, particularly those of less-developed countries, that these payments are necessary rather than arbitrary.

Tax Effects   A major consideration behind the dividend decision is the effective tax rate on payments from different affiliates. By varying payout ratios among its foreign subsidiaries, the corporation can reduce its total tax burden.

By varying dividend payout rates among its foreign units, the MNC can reduce its total taxes.

Once a firm has decided on the amount of dividends to remit from overseas, it can then reduce its tax bill by withdrawing funds from those locations with the lowest transfer costs. Here is a highly simplified example. Suppose a U.S. company, International Products, wishes to withdraw $1 million from abroad in the form of dividends. Each of its three foreign subsidiaries—located in Germany, the Republic of Ireland, and France—has earned $2 million before tax this year and, hence, all are capable of providing the funds. The problem for International Products is to decide on the dividend strategy that will minimize the firm's total tax bill.

The German subsidiary is subject to a split corporate tax rate of 50 percent on undistributed gross earnings and 36 percent on dividends, as well as a dividend withholding tax of 10 percent. As an export incentive, the Republic of Ireland grants a fifteen-year tax holiday on all export profits. Because the Irish unit receives all its profits from exports, it pays no taxes. There are no dividend withholding taxes. The French affiliate is taxed at a rate of 45 percent and must also pay a 10 percent withholding tax on its dividend remittances. It is assumed that there are no excess foreign tax credits available and that any credits generated cannot be used elsewhere. The U.S. corporate tax rate is 35 percent. Exhibit 20.8 summarizes the relevant tax consequences of remitting $1 million from each affiliate in turn.

These calculations indicate that it would be cheapest to remit dividends from Germany. By paying this $1 million dividend with its associated total worldwide tax cost of $1.86 million, International Products is actually reducing its worldwide tax costs by $40,000, compared with its total tax bill of $1.9 million in the absence of any dividend.[3] This result is due to the tax penalty that the German government imposes on retained earnings.

Financing Requirements   In addition to their tax consequences, dividend payments lead to liquidity shifts. The value of moving these funds depends on the different opportunity costs of money among the various units of the corporation. For instance, an affiliate that must borrow funds will usually have a higher opportunity cost than a unit with excess cash available. Moreover, some subsidiaries will have access to low-cost financing sources, whereas others have no recourse but to borrow at a relatively high interest rate.

> An MNC can exploit yield differences among its affiliates by varying its dividend payout rate.

All else being equal, a parent can increase its value by exploiting yield differences among its affiliates—that is, setting a high dividend payout rate for subsidiaries with relatively low opportunity costs of funds while requiring smaller dividend payments from those units facing high borrowing costs or having favorable investment opportunities.

Exchange Controls   Exchange controls are another major factor in the dividend decision. Nations with balance-of-payments problems are apt to restrict the payment of dividends to foreign companies. These controls vary by country, but in general they limit the size of dividend remittances, either in absolute terms or as a percentage of earnings, equity, or registered capital.

> A record of consistent dividend payments reduces the threat of government interference with these payments.

Many firms try to reduce the danger of such interference by maintaining a record of consistent dividends. The record is designed to show that these payments are part of an established financial program rather than an act of speculation against the host country's currency. Dividends are paid every year, whether or not they are justified by financial and tax considerations, just to demonstrate a continuing policy to the local government and central bank. Even when they cannot be remitted, dividends are sometimes declared for the same reason, namely, to establish grounds for making future payments when these controls are lifted or modified.

Some companies even set a uniform dividend payout ratio throughout the corporate system to set a global pattern and maintain the principle that affiliates have an obligation to pay dividends to their stockholders. If challenged, the firm then can prove that its French or Brazilian or Italian subsidiaries must pay an equivalent percentage dividend. MNCs often are willing to accept higher tax costs to maintain the principle that dividends are a necessary and legitimate business expense. Many executives believe that a record of paying dividends consistently (or at least declaring them) helps in getting approval for further dividend disbursements.

Joint Ventures   The presence of local stockholders may constrain an MNC's ability to adjust its dividend policy in accordance with global factors. In addition, to the extent that multinationals have a longer-term perspective than their local partners, conflicts might arise, with local investors demanding a shorter payback period and the MNC insisting on a higher earnings-retention rate.

---

[3] In fact, paying a dividend from Germany could reduce International Products' tax bill even further. As shown in Exhibit 20.8, International Products will receive a foreign tax credit of $240,351 on the German dividend. To the extent that International Products can use this credit, it can reduce its worldwide tax bill by an additional $240,351.

EXHIBIT 20.8 • TAX EFFECTS OF DIVIDEND REMITTANCES FROM ABROAD

Location of Foreign Affiliate	Dividend Amount	Host Country Income Tax if Dividend Paid	Host Country Withholding Tax	U.S. Income Tax	Total Taxes if Dividend Paid	Host Country Income Tax if No Dividend Paid	Worldwide Tax Liability if Dividend Paid*
Germany	$1,000,000	$360,000 500,000 $860,000	$100,000	0[1]	$ 960,000	$1,000,000	$1,860,000
Republic of Ireland	$1,000,000	0	0	$350,000	$350,000	0	$2,250,000
France	$1,000,000	$900,000	$100,000	0	$1,000,000	$900,000	$2,000,000

[1]Computation of U.S. tax owed

Profit before tax	$2,000,000
Tax ($1,000,000 × 0.50 + $1,000,000 × 0.36)	860,000
Profit after tax	$1,140,000
Dividend paid to U.S. parent company	1,000,000
Less withholding tax @ 10%	100,000
Net dividend received in United States	$900,000
Include in U.S. income	
Gross dividend received	$1,000,000
Foreign indirect tax deemed paid[2]	754,386
U.S. gross dividend included	$1,754,386
U.S. tax @ 35%	614,035
Less foreign tax credit[2]	854,386
Net U.S. tax cost (credit)	$–240,351
U.S. tax payable	0

[2]Computation of indirect and total foreign tax credit

(a) Direct credit for withholding tax	$100,000
(b) Indirect foreign tax credit	

$$\frac{\text{Dividend paid}}{\text{Profit after tax}} \times \text{Foreign tax} = \frac{1,000,000}{1,140,000} \times 860,000 = 754,386$$

Total tax credit	$854,386

* Worldwide tax liability if dividend paid equals tax liability for foreign affiliate paying the dividend plus tax liabilities of nondividend-paying affiliates plus any U.S. taxes owed.

Equity versus Debt

Corporate funds invested overseas, whether they are called debt or equity, require the same rate of return, namely, the firm's marginal cost of capital. Nonetheless, MNCs generally prefer to invest in the form of loans rather than equity for several reasons.

MNCs can realize several advantages by investing overseas in the form of debt rather than equity.

First, a firm typically has wider latitude to repatriate funds in the form of interest and loan repayments than as dividends or reductions in equity because the latter fund flows are usually more closely controlled by governments. In addition, a reduction in equity may be frowned on by the host government and is likely to pose a real problem for a firm trying to repatriate funds in excess of earnings. Withdrawing these funds by way of dividend payments will reduce the affiliate's capital stock, whereas applying this money toward repayment of a loan will not affect the unit's equity account. Moreover, if the firm ever desired to increase its equity investment, it could relatively easily convert the loan into equity.

A second reason for the use of intercompany loans over equity investments is the possibility of reducing taxes. The likelihood of a tax benefit is due to two factors: (1) Interest paid on a loan is ordinarily tax-deductible in the host nation, whereas dividend payments are not; and (2) unlike dividends, principal repayments on the loan do not normally constitute taxable income to the parent company.

For example, suppose General Foods Corporation (GFC) is looking for a way to finance a $1 million expansion in working capital for its Danish affiliate, General Foods Denmark (GFD). The added sales generated by this increase in working capital promise to yield 20 percent after local tax (but before interest payments), or $200,000 annually, for the foreseeable future. GFC has a choice between investing the $1 million as debt, with an interest rate of 10 percent, or as equity. GFD pays corporate income tax at the rate of 50 percent as well as a 10 percent withholding tax on all dividend and interest payments. Other assumptions are that the parent expects all available funds to be repatriated and that any foreign tax credits generated are unusable.

If the $1 million is financed as an equity investment, the Danish subsidiary will pay the full return as an annual dividend to GFC of $200,000—of which GFC will receive $180,000 net of the withholding tax. Alternatively, if structured as a loan, the investment will be repaid in ten annual installments of $100,000 each with interest on the remaining balance. Interest is tax-deductible, so the net outflow of cash from GFD is only half the interest payment. It is assumed that the parent does not have to pay additional tax to the United States on dividends received because of the high tax rate on GFD's income. In addition, the interest is received tax-free because of the availability of excess foreign tax credits. All funds remaining after interest and principal repayments are remitted as dividends. In year 5, for example, $100,000 of the $200,000 cash flow is sent to GFC as a loan repayment and $60,000 as interest (on a balance of $600,000). The $30,000 tax saving on the interest payment and the remaining $40,000 on the $200,000 profit are remitted as dividends. Hence, GFC winds up with $217,000 after the withholding tax of $13,000 (on total dividend plus interest payments of $130,000).

The evaluation of these financing alternatives is presented in Exhibit 20.9. If we assume a 15 percent discount rate, the present value of cash flows under the debt financing plan is $1,102,695. This amount is $199,275 more over the first ten years of the investment's life than the $903,420 present value using equity financing. The reason for this disparity is the absence of withholding tax on the loan repayments and the tax deductibility of interest expenses. It is apparent that the higher the interest rate that can be charged on the loan, the larger the cash flows will be. After ten years, of course, the cash flows are the same under debt and equity financing because all returns will be in the form of dividends.

Alternatively, suppose the same investment and financing plans are available in a country having no income or withholding taxes. This situation increases annual project

EXHIBIT 20.9 • DOLLAR CASH FLOWS UNDER DEBT AND EQUITY FINANCING

	Debt					**Equity**		
	(1)	**(2)**	**(3)**	**(4)**	**(5)**	**(6)**	**(7)**	**(8)**
Year	**Principal Repayment**	**Interest**	**Dividend**	**Withholding Tax**	**Cash Flow to Parent (1 + 2 + 3 − 4)**	**Dividend**	**Withholding Tax**	**Cash Flow to Parent (6 − 7)**
1	100,000	100,000	50,000	15,000	235,000	200,000	20,000	180,000
2	100,000	90,000	55,000	14,500	230,500	200,000	20,000	180,000
3	100,000	80,000	60,000	14,000	226,000	200,000	20,000	180,000
4	100,000	70,000	65,000	13,500	221,500	200,000	20,000	180,000
5	100,000	60,000	70,000	13,000	217,000	200,000	20,000	180,000
6	100,000	50,000	75,000	12,500	212,500	200,000	20,000	180,000
7	100,000	40,000	80,000	12,000	208,000	200,000	20,000	180,000
8	100,000	30,000	85,000	11,500	203,500	200,000	20,000	180,000
9	100,000	20,000	90,000	11,000	199,000	200,000	20,000	180,000
10	100,000	10,000	95,000	10,500	194,500	200,000	20,000	180,000
Present Value Discounted at 15%					$1,102,695			$903,420

Subsidiary debt-to-equity ratios are often a subject of negotiation with host governments.

returns to $400,000. Because no excess foreign tax credits are available, the U.S. government will impose corporate tax at the rate of 35 percent on all remitted dividends and interest payments. The respective cash flows are presented in Exhibit 20.10. In this situation, the present value under debt financing is $175,657 more ($1,480,537 − $1,304,880) than with equity financing.

Firms do not, however, have complete latitude in choosing their debt-to-equity ratios abroad, though. This subject is frequently open for negotiation with the host governments. In addition, dividends and local borrowings often are restricted to a fixed

EXHIBIT 20.10 • DOLLAR CASH FLOWS UNDER DEBT AND EQUITY FINANCING

	Debt					**Equity**		
	(1)	**(2)**	**(3)**	**(4)**	**(5)**	**(6)**	**(7)**	**(8)**
Year	**Principal Repayment**	**Interest**	**Dividend**	**U.S. Tax (2 + 3) × 0.35**	**Cash Flow to Parent (1 + 2 + 3 − 4)**	**Dividend**	**U.S. Tax (6 × 0.35)**	**Cash Flow to Parent (6 − 7)**
1	100,000	100,000	200,000	105,000	295,000	400,000	140,000	260,000
2	100,000	90,000	210,000	105,000	295,000	400,000	140,000	260,000
3	100,000	80,000	220,000	105,000	295,000	400,000	140,000	260,000
4	100,000	70,000	230,000	105,000	295,000	400,000	140,000	260,000
5	100,000	60,000	240,000	105,000	295,000	400,000	140,000	260,000
6	100,000	50,000	250,000	105,000	295,000	400,000	140,000	260,000
7	100,000	40,000	260,000	105,000	295,000	400,000	140,000	260,000
8	100,000	30,000	270,000	105,000	295,000	400,000	140,000	260,000
9	100,000	20,000	280,000	105,000	295,000	400,000	140,000	260,000
10	100,000	10,000	290,000	105,000	295,000	400,000	140,000	260,000
Present Value Discounted at 15%					$1,480,537			$1,304,880

percentage of equity. A small equity base also can lead to a high return on equity, exposing a company to charges of exploitation.

Another obstacle to taking complete advantage of parent company loans is the U.S. government. The IRS may treat loan repayments as constructive dividends and tax them if it believes the subsidiary is too thinly capitalized. Many executives and tax attorneys feel that the IRS is satisfied as long as the debt-to-equity ratio does not exceed 4 to 1.

Firms normally use guidelines such as 50 percent of total assets or fixed assets in determining the amount of equity to provide their subsidiaries. These guidelines usually lead to an equity position greater than that required by law, causing MNCs to sacrifice flexibility and pay higher taxes than necessary.

The IRS also has gone after foreign companies operating in the United States that it accuses of "earnings stripping." Earnings stripping occurs when a foreign company uses parent loans instead of equity capital to fund its U.S. activities. The resulting interest payments, particularly on loans used to finance acquisitions in the United States, are deducted from pretax income, leaving minimal earnings to tax.

Congress tried to control earnings stripping with a law that took effect in 1989. Under this law, if a heavily indebted U.S. unit pays interest to its foreign parent, the interest deduction is limited to 50 percent of the unit's taxable income. But that still left a large loophole. The foreign-owned companies continued to take big interest deductions by arranging loans through banks rather than through their parent companies. To reassure the banks, the parent companies provided guarantees.

A law that took effect in 1994 attempts to close this loophole by treating guaranteed loans as if they were loans from the parent company. U.S. officials expected that foreign companies would convert their loans to their U.S. units into equity, thus generating taxable dividends. But most companies seem to have found new ways to avoid taxes. Some sold assets and leased them back, replacing loans with leases. Others factored accounts receivable or turned mortgages into securities. The net result so far has been few new taxes collected.

20.3 DESIGNING A GLOBAL REMITTANCE POLICY

To effectively utilize its internal financial system, the MNC must consider four interrelated factors.

The task facing international financial executives is to coordinate the use of the various financial linkages in a manner consistent with value maximization for the firm as a whole. This task requires the following four interrelated decisions: (1) how much money (if any) to remit, (2) when to do so, (3) where to transmit these funds, and (4) which transfer method(s) to use.

In order to take proper advantage of its internal financial system, the firm must conduct a systematic and comprehensive analysis of the available remittance options and their associated costs and benefits. It also must compare the value of deploying funds in affiliates other than just the remitting subsidiary and the parent. For example, rather than simply deciding whether to keep earnings in Germany or remit them to the U.S. parent, corporate headquarters must consider the possibility and desirability of moving those funds to, say, Italy or France via leading and lagging or transfer price adjustments. In other words, the key question to be answered is: Where and how in the world can available funds be deployed most profitably? Most multinationals, however, make their dividend remittance decision independently of, say, their royalty or leading and lagging decision rather than considering what mix of transfer mechanisms would be best for the company overall.

In part, the decision to "satisfice" rather than optimize is due to the complex nature of the financial linkages in a typical multinational corporation. For instance, if there are ten financial links connecting each pair of units in a multinational enterprise, then a firm consisting of a parent and two subsidiaries will have thirty intercompany links, three times as many as a parent with just one affiliate. A parent with three subsidiaries will have sixty links; a company with n units will have $10n(n + 1)/2$ financial linkages.

A real-life firm will have many more than three affiliates, so the exponential growth of potential intercompany relationships means that, unless the options are severely limited, system optimization will be impossible. It is not surprising, therefore, that surveys by David Zenoff and by Sidney Robbins and Robert Stobaugh found that few firms seemed to think in terms of a worldwide pool of funds to be allocated in accordance with global profit maximization.[4] Instead, most parents allowed their affiliates to keep just enough cash on hand to meet their fund requirements and required them to send the rest back home.

This limited approach to managing international financial transactions is understandable in view of the tangled web of interaffiliate connections that already has been depicted. Still, compromising with complexity ought not to mean ignoring the system's profit potential. A hands-off policy is not the only alternative to system optimization. Instead, the MNC should search for relatively high-yield uses of its internal financial system. This task often is made easier by choices that are generally more limited in practice than in theory.

First of all, many of the potential links will be impossible to use because of government regulations and the specifics of the firm's situation. For example, two affiliates might not trade with each other, eliminating the transfer pricing link. Other channels will be severely restricted by government controls.

Furthermore, in many situations, it is not necessary to develop an elaborate mathematical model to figure out the appropriate policy. For example, where a currency is blocked and investment opportunities are lacking or local tax rates are quite high, it normally will be in the company's best interest to shift its funds and profits elsewhere. Where credit rationing exists, a simple decision rule usually suffices: Maximize local borrowing. Moreover, most MNCs already have large staffs for data collection and planning, as well as some form of computerized accounting system. These elements can form the basis for a more complete overseas-planning effort.

The more limited, though still numerous, real-life options facing a firm and the existing nucleus of a planning system can significantly reduce the costs of centralizing the management of a firm's intercompany transactions. In addition, for most multinationals, fewer than ten affiliates account for an overwhelming majority of intercompany fund flows. Recognizing this situation, several firms have developed systems to optimize flows among this limited number of units. The lack of global optimization (interactions with other affiliates are taken as given, rather than treated as decision variables) is not particularly costly because most of the major fund flows are already included. Realistically, the objective of such an effort should be profit improvement rather than system optimization.

Prerequisites

A number of factors strongly affect an MNC's ability to benefit from its internal financial transfer system. These include the (1) number of financial links, (2) volume of interaffiliate transactions, (3) foreign-affiliate ownership pattern, (4) degree of product and service standardization, and (5) government regulations.

Because each channel has different costs and benefits associated with its use, the wider the range of choice, the greater a firm's ability to achieve specific goals. For example, some links are best suited to avoiding exchange controls, and others are most efficiently employed in reducing taxes. In this vein, a two-way flow of funds will give a firm greater flexibility in deploying its money than if all links are in only one direction. Of

The complexity of the MNC's internal financial transfer system often leads managers to satisfice rather than optimize.

The value of an MNC's internal financial system depends on the number of financial links and the volume of intercompany transactions.

[4] David B. Zenoff, "Remitting Funds from Foreign Affiliates," *Financial Executive*, March 1968, pp. 46–63; and Sidney M. Robbins and Robert B. Stobaugh, *Money in the Multinational Enterprise* (New York: Basic Books, 1973), p. 86.

course, the larger the volume of flows through these financial arteries, the more funds that can be moved by a given adjustment in intercompany terms. A 1 percent change in the transfer price on goods flowing between two affiliates will have a ten times greater absolute effect if annual sales are $10 million rather than $1 million. Similarly, altering credit terms by thirty days will become a more effective means of transferring funds as the volume of intercompany payables and receivables grows.

A large volume of intercompany transactions is usually associated with the world-wide dispersal and rationalization of production activities. As plants specialize in different components and stages of production, interaffiliate trade increases, as do the accompanying financial flows. Clearly, 100 percent ownership of all foreign affiliates removes a major impediment to the efficient allocation of funds worldwide. The existence of joint ventures is likely to confine a firm's transfer activities to a set of mutually agreed-upon rules, eliminating its ability to react swiftly to changed circumstances.

The more standardized its products and services are, the less latitude an MNC has to adjust its transfer prices and fees and royalties. Conversely, a high-technology input, strong product differentiation, and short product life cycle enhance a company's ability to make use of its mechanisms for transfer pricing and fee adjustments. The latter situation is more typical of the MNC, so it is not surprising that the issue of transfer pricing is a bone of contention between multinationals and governments.

Last, and most important, government regulations exert a continuing influence on international financial transactions. It is interesting to consider that government tax, credit allocation, and exchange control policies provide the principal incentives for firms to engage in international fund maneuvers at the same time that government regulations most impede these flows.

> Government regulations simultaneously motivate and constrain the use of intercompany financial maneuvers by MNCs.

Information Requirements

In order to take full advantage of its global financial system, a multinational firm needs detailed information on affiliate financing requirements, sources and costs of external credit, local investment yields, available financial channels, volume of interaffiliate transactions, all relevant tax factors, and government restrictions and regulations on fund flows.

Without belaboring the points already made, it is clear that the costs and benefits of operating an integrated financial system depend on the funds and transfer options available, as well as on the opportunity costs of money for different affiliates and the tax effects associated with these transfer mechanisms. Hence, the implementation of centralized decision making requires information concerning all these factors.

Behavioral Consequences

> Companies that shift profits and cash among their various affiliates must consider the behavioral consequences.

Manipulating transfer prices on goods and services, adjusting dividend payments, and leading and lagging remittances lead to a reallocation of profits and liquidity among a firm's affiliates. Although the aim of this corporate intervention is to boost after-tax global profits, the actual result may be to destroy incentive systems based on profit centers and to cause confusion and computational chaos. Subsidiaries may rebel when asked to undertake actions that will benefit the corporation as a whole but will adversely affect their own performance evaluations. To counter this reaction, a firm must clearly spell out the rules and adjust profit center results to reflect true affiliate earnings rather than the distorted remnants of a global profit-maximizing exercise.

 ILLUSTRATION   *Transfer Pricing and Tax Evasion*

On September 19, 1983, the Swiss-based commodities trading firm Marc Rich & Co. (the same one mentioned in Chapter 18 under countertrade), its U.S. unit, and its two principal officers, Marc Rich and Pincus Green, were indicted by the U.S. government for allegedly evading more than $100 million in U.S. taxes, making it the biggest tax-evasion case in U.S. history. The U.S. government charged that Marc Rich, his companies, and Pincus Green had the U.S. unit transfer profit to the Swiss parent by having the U.S. affiliate pay the Swiss company artificially high prices for oil. Both men fled to Switzerland and later were the subjects of highly controversial last-minute pardons by President Clinton when he left office in January 2001.

In 1982, the United States subpoenaed from the Swiss parent documents that it thought would buttress its case—and that would make public a great deal of information about the company. Despite its size—annual revenue exceeding $10 billion—Marc Rich & Co. has a penchant for secrecy. Because of its refusal to give the documents to a grand jury, the company was cited in contempt of court and made subject to a $50,000-a-day fine while it appealed a federal judge's refusal to vacate the contempt order. In September 1983, the Swiss government seized Marc Rich's internal documents on the ground that releasing them to U.S. authorities would violate Swiss secrecy laws.

Marc Rich & Co. settled with the U.S. government in October 1984. The back taxes plus interest, penalties, fines, and seized assets made the settlement worth almost $200 million—the most ever recovered in a criminal tax-evasion case.

Except for its magnitude, however, the Rich case is not unique. Since the late 1960s, the Department of Justice has been cracking down on the use of transfer pricing to evade U.S. taxes. One case was U.S. Gypsum Company. Strange things were happening to the price of gypsum rock that the company mined in Canada and shipped to the United States. The rock was sold by the company's Canadian unit at a low price, keeping Canadian profit and taxes down, and was resold to the U.S. unit at a high price, keeping U.S. profit and taxes down. The profit was siphoned into another U.S. Gypsum subsidiary that owned the rock only while it fell through the air from the Canadian conveyor belt down to the hold of a U.S. ship. This intermediate subsidiary was a paper company and was in a low-tax bracket. The Department of Justice challenged this arrangement in court and won in a civil case.

In June 1983, the American sales subsidiary of Toyota Motor Company was ordered by a federal judge to turn over to the Internal Revenue Service information about the prices its parent firm charged its car dealers in Japan. The IRS maintained that the Japanese data were necessary for it to determine whether the transfer prices it charged Toyota Motor Sales U.S.A. for Toyota products in the United States were being used to reduce its U.S. tax liability. The IRS claimed that the U.S. sales unit of Toyota trimmed its taxable U.S. income by paying its Japanese parent higher-than-reasonable prices for the vehicles sold in the United States. This case and a similar one brought against Nissan Motor Company were settled in late 1987 when the U.S. sales units of both companies paid undisclosed amounts of additional income taxes to the IRS. Reportedly, the combined payments exceeded $600 million. These taxes were offset by tax refunds of an equivalent (though lesser) amount received from Japan's national tax agency for taxes paid on the income previously recorded in Japan but now reallocated to the United States. Currently, the IRS has cases pending against a number of Japanese and South Korean companies, including Hitachi, Mitsubishi Electric, Tokai Bank, and Daewoo.

Sometimes it is not the U.S. government that feels cheated. Amway of Canada and its U.S. parent, Amway Corporation, were fined $25 million in November 1983 after pleading guilty in Ontario Supreme Court to using a complex transfer pricing scheme to undervalue goods they were exporting to Canada, defrauding the Canadian government of more than $28 million in customs duties and sales tax.

20.4 SUMMARY AND CONCLUSIONS

This chapter examined a variety of fund-shifting mechanisms. Corporate objectives associated with the use of these techniques include financing foreign operations, reducing interest costs, reducing tax costs, and removing blocked funds.

It is apparent after examining these goals that there are trade-offs involved. For instance, removing blocked funds from a low-tax nation is likely to raise the firm's worldwide tax bill. Similarly, reducing exchange risk often results in higher interest expenses and adds to the financing needs of affiliates in soft-currency nations. The realistic weight that should be assigned to each of these goals depends on the individual impact of each goal on corporate profitability. Focusing on just one or two of these goals, such as avoiding exchange risk or minimizing taxes, to the exclusion of all others will probably lead to suboptimal decisions.

The recommended global approach to managing fund transfers is best illustrated by the creative use of financial linkages, whereby one unit becomes a conduit for the movement of funds elsewhere. For example, requiring affiliate A to remit dividends to its parent while financing this withdrawal by lowering transfer prices on goods sold to affiliate A by affiliate B will reduce income taxes and/or customs duties in the process. Or cash can be shifted from A to B through leading and lagging, with these same funds moved on to affiliate C by adjusting royalties or repaying a loan. Taking advantage of being multinational means remitting funds to the parent and other affiliates via royalties and licensing fees from some countries, dividend payments from other nations, and loan repayments from still others. All these maneuvers are to be coordinated with an eye toward maximizing corporate benefits.

It is apparent that the major benefit expected from engaging in these maneuvers comes from government actions that distort the risk-return trade-offs associated with borrowing or lending in different currencies or that alter after-tax returns because of tax asymmetries. The fact that a particular action is legal and profitable, however, does not necessarily mean it should be undertaken. When devising currency, credit, and tax regulations, governments obviously have other goals in mind besides creating profitable arbitrage opportunities for multinational firms. A company that consistently attempts to apply a "sharp pencil" and take maximum advantage of these arbitrage opportunities may optimize short-run profits, but this "penciling" is likely to be done at the expense of long-run profits.

The notion of being a good corporate citizen may be an amorphous concept, but firms that are perceived as being short-run profit-oriented may face questions regarding their legitimacy. More and more, multinationals are dependent on the goodwill of home and host governments, and actions that undermine this key factor may reduce the viability of their foreign operations.

Thus, it may well be worthwhile to pass up opportunities to make higher profits today if those profits are gained at the expense of the corporation's long-run international existence. As in all business decisions, of course, it is important to evaluate the costs and benefits associated with particular actions. Such evaluation has been the goal of this chapter in the area of intercompany fund flows.

QUESTIONS

1. a. What is the internal financial transfer system of the multinational firm?

   b. What are its distinguishing characteristics?

   c. What are the different modes of internal fund transfers available to the MNC?

2. How does the internal financial transfer system add value to the multinational firm?

3. California, like several other states, applies the unitary method of taxation to firms doing business within the state. Under the unitary method, a state determines the tax on a company's worldwide profit through a formula based on the share of the company's sales, assets, and payroll falling within the state. In California's case, the share of worldwide profit taxed is calculated as the average of these three factors.

   a. What are the predictable corporate responses to the unitary tax?

   b. What economic motives might help explain why Oregon, Florida, and several other states have eliminated their unitary tax schemes?

4. In comparisons of a multinational firm's reported foreign profits with domestic profits, caution must be exercised. This same caution must also be applied when analyzing the reported profits of the firm's various subsidiaries. Only coincidentally will these reported profits correspond to actual profits.

a. Describe five different means that MNCs use to manipulate reported profitability among their various units.

b. What adjustments to its reported figures would be required to compute the true profitability of a firm's foreign operations so as to account for these distortions?

c. Describe at least three reasons that might explain some of these manipulations.

5. In 1987, U.S.-controlled companies earned an average 2.09 percent return on assets, nearly four times their foreign-controlled counterparts. A number of American politicians have used these figures to argue that there is widespread tax cheating by foreign-owned multinationals.

a. What are some economically plausible reasons (other than tax evasion) that would explain the low rates of return earned by foreign-owned companies in the United States? Consider the consequences of the debt-financed U.S.-investment binge that foreign companies went on during the 1980s and the dramatic depreciation of the U.S. dollar beginning in 1985.

b. What are some of the mechanisms that foreign-owned companies can use to reduce their tax burden in the United States?

c. The corporate tax rate in Japan is 60 percent, whereas it is 35 percent in the United States. Are these figures consistent with the argument that big Japanese companies are overcharging their U.S. subsidiaries in order to avoid taxes? Explain.

PROBLEMS

1. Suppose Navistar's Canadian subsidiary sells 1,500 trucks monthly to the French affiliate at a transfer price of $27,000 per unit. Assume that the Canadian and French marginal tax rates on corporate income equal 45 percent and 50 percent, respectively.

a. Suppose the transfer price can be set at any level between $25,000 and $30,000. At what transfer price will corporate taxes paid be minimized? Explain.

b. Suppose the French government imposes an ad valorem tariff of 15 percent on imported tractors. How would this tariff affect the optimal transfer pricing strategy?

c. If the transfer price of $27,000 is set in euros and the euro revalues by 5 percent, what will happen to the firm's overall tax bill? Consider the tax consequences both with and without the 15 percent tariff.

d. Suppose the transfer price is increased from $27,000 to $30,000 and credit terms are extended from 90 days to 180 days. What are the fund-flow implications of these adjustments?

2. Suppose a U.S. parent owes $5 million to its English affiliate. The timing of this payment can be changed by up to 90 days in either direction. Assume the following effective annualized after-tax dollar borrowing and lending rates in England and the United States.

	Lending (%)	Borrowing (%)
United States	3.2	4.0
England	3.0	3.6

a. If the U.S. parent is borrowing funds while the English affiliate has excess funds, should the parent speed up or slow down its payment to England?

b. What is the net effect of the optimal payment activities in terms of changing the units' borrowing costs and/or interest income?

3. Suppose that DMR SA, located in Switzerland, sells $1 million worth of goods monthly to its affiliate DMR GmbH, located in Germany. These sales are based on a unit transfer price of $100. Suppose the transfer price is raised to $130 at the same time that credit terms are lengthened from the current 30 days to 60 days.

a. What is the net impact on cash flow for the first 90 days? Assume that the new credit terms apply only to new sales already booked but uncollected.

b. Assume that the tax rate is 25 percent in Switzerland and 50 percent in Germany and that revenues are taxed and costs deducted upon sale or purchase of goods, not upon collection. What is the impact on after-tax cash flows for the first 90 days?

4. Suppose a firm earns $1 million before tax in Spain. It pays Spanish tax of $0.52 million and remits the remaining $0.48 million as a dividend to its U.S. parent. Under current U.S. tax law, how much U.S. tax will the parent owe on this dividend?

5. Suppose a French affiliate repatriates as dividends all the after-tax profits it earns. If the French income tax rate is 50 percent and the dividend withholding tax is 10 percent, what is the effective tax rate on the French affiliate's before-tax profits, from the standpoint of its U.S. parent?

BIBLIOGRAPHY

Arpan, Jeffrey S. *International Intracorporate Pricing*. New York: Praeger, 1972.

Lessard, Donald R. "Transfer Prices, Taxes, and Financial Markets: Implications of International Financial Transfers within the Multinational Firm." In *The Economic Effects of Multinational Corporations*, edited by Robert G. Hawkins. Greenwich, Conn.: JAI Press, 1979.

Obersteiner, Erich. "Should the Foreign Affiliate Remit Dividends or Reinvest?" *Financial Management,* Spring 1973, pp. 88–93.

Robbins, Sidney M., and Robert B. Stobaugh. *Money in the Multinational Enterprise.* New York: Basic Books, 1973.

Rutenberg, David P. "Maneuvering Liquid Assets in a Multinational Company." *Management Science,* June 1970, pp. B671–B684.

Zenoff, David B. "Remitting Funds from Foreign Affiliates." *Financial Executive,* March 1968, pp. 46–63.

INTERNET RESOURCES

www.kpmg.com Web site of KPMG, the global accounting and consulting company. Contains information on the various international tax and transfer pricing services it provides.

www.deloitte.com/dtt/section_node/0%2C2332%2Csid%25253D1005%2C00.html
Web site run by Deloitte Touche Tohmatsu (Deloitte), another global accounting and consulting firm, that contains information on international tax issues as well as information about the tax and investment climate in over 60 countries.

www.taxsites.com/international.html Web site that contains links to tax authorities worldwide as well as to other international tax information.

INTERNET EXERCISES

1. Based on materials found at the KPMG and Deloitte Web sites, what are some international tax issues that multinationals are concerned about? Which tax issues are the national tax authorities concerned about?

2. Go to the Web site of a major international bank such as Citigroup (www.citigroup.com) or Bank of America (www.bankofamerica.com). What financial services does this bank provide that would be of value to an MNC in managing its multinational financial system?

PART VI CASE STUDIES

CASE VI.1
XEROX MISCOPIES FOREIGN INTEREST RATE DATA

On May 31, 2001, Xerox disclosed in a filing with the Securities and Exchange Commission (SEC) that several years earlier it had changed the way in which some of its foreign affiliates booked revenues from copiers leased to customers. The company said that the effect of this change in accounting practices, which involved changing the discount-rate assumptions on its leases, was to add $253 million to Xerox's pretax income over the past three years. In response, the SEC launched an investigation to determine if Xerox changed its lease-accounting assumptions in order to artificially boost revenues and profits in Latin America and elsewhere. A Xerox spokesman stated that the company had used proper accounting assumptions in booking lease revenues and that it only disclosed this practice because it was already under scrutiny for misapplying other accepted accounting rules related to its copier business.

Xerox typically leases copiers to customers for periods of three to five years. The accounting assumptions in question relate to the discount rate Xerox used to value the future stream of lease payments. For example, a customer who buys a copier priced at $10,000 on a five-year lease will pay a fixed monthly lease payment for the next sixty months. The size of the monthly payment depends on the implicit interest rate associated with the lease (which takes into account the time value of money and risk) and the assumed residual value of the copier when the lease expires. In general, the lease payment is the solution L to the following equation:

$$P = \sum_{t=1}^{n} \frac{L}{(1+r)^t} + R$$

where

P = the price of the copier

R = the residual value in present value terms

n = the number of months in the lease

r = the monthly interest rate imbedded in the lease

To illustrate, suppose the implicit interest rate is 12 percent (1 percent monthly), the lease term is five years, the price is $10,000, and the residual value in present value terms is $2,000. Substituting these

numbers into the equation yields a monthly lease payment of $178. The value of the lease receivable given the lease payments and assumed residual value in this illustration is $8,000. However, if the interest rate used to value the lease payments for accounting purposes differs from the interest rate used to set the lease payments in the first place, then the booked value of the lease will differ from its economic value. In particular, if the interest rate for valuation purposes is below the interest rate used to set lease payments, the value of the lease receivable will be overstated.

According to the *Wall Street Journal* (June 1, 2001, p. C1), this is what happened. In the late 1990s, senior executives at Xerox ordered the company's Mexican subsidiary to use a discount rate well below local interest rates to value the peso lease receivables it was generating. For example, in 1996, Xerox Mexico booked leases using a discount rate of 20 percent. That rate was progressively lowered over the next three years, to 18 percent in 1997, 10 percent in 1998, and 6 percent in 1999. Comparable Mexican interest rates during this period were 34.4 percent in 1996, 22.5 percent in 1997, 24.5 percent in 1998, and 24.1 percent in 1999. Similar aggressive interest rate assumptions were used in other foreign units as well to book revenues and value their lease receivables.

Managers at Xerox's business units were given bonuses for meeting or exceeding aggressive revenue targets. Evidently, managers at these units figured out how to get their bonuses.

QUESTIONS

1. What is the purpose and consequence of using a discount rate that is close to the market interest rate in valuing lease rentals?

2. Why were interest rates so high in Mexico in the late 1990s? What factors were built into these interest rates?

3. Assuming a $10,000 copier price, $3,500 residual value in present value terms, and a five-year lease, what was the consequence of Xerox Mexico booking peso revenues using interest rates of 20 percent in 1996, 18 percent in 1997, 10 percent in 1998, and 6 percent in 1999 instead of the comparable Mexican interest rates during this period of 34.4 percent in

1996, 22.5 percent in 1997, 24.5 percent in 1998, and 24.1 percent in 1999? That is, on each $10,000 copier lease for each year, how much revenue did Xerox Mexico book? Compare those figures to their present values using the market rates.

4. Apparently, Xerox used similarly rosy assumptions in Brazil as well. Instead of using a discount rate on the order of 30 percent, Xerox used a 6 percent discount rate to record *real* revenues. Assuming the same $10,000 copier price and $3,500 residual value in present value terms, how much revenue was booked by using a 6 percent discount rate on a 60-month lease? Compare this figure to its present value using a 30 percent discount rate.

5. How did the use of low discount rates help managers at Xerox Mexico get their bonuses? How might these low discount rates affect the amount of exchange risk that managers were willing to tolerate?

6. Suppose Xerox tried to sell its foreign lease receivables to an investor. What could you say about the price it would likely receive as compared to their book values? Explain.

7. Do you agree or disagree with Xerox's claim that it used proper accounting assumptions in booking its revenues and recording asset values for foreign lease receivables? Explain.

Acceptance   A time draft that is accepted by the drawee. Accepting a draft means writing *accepted* across its face, followed by an authorized person's signature and the date. The party accepting a draft incurs the obligation to pay it at maturity.

Accounting Exposure   The change in the value of a firm's foreign-currency-denominated accounts due to a change in exchange rates.

Act of State Doctrine   This doctrine says that a nation is sovereign within its own borders and its domestic actions may not be questioned in the courts of another nation.

Adjusted Present Value   The net present value of a project using the all-equity rate as a discount rate. The effects of financing are incorporated in separate terms.

Administrative Pricing Rule   IRS rules used to allocate income on export sales to a foreign sales corporation.

Advance Pricing Agreement (APA)   Procedure that allows the multinational firm, the IRS, and the foreign tax authority to work out, in advance, a method to calculate transfer prices.

Adverse Incentives   *See* moral hazard.

Adverse Selection   The possibility that only the highest-risk customers will seek insurance.

African Development Bank (ADB)   The ADB makes or guarantees loans and provides technical assistance to member states for various development projects.

Agency Costs   Costs that stem from conflicts between managers and stockholders and between stockholders and bondholders.

All-Equity Beta   The beta associated with the unleveraged cash flows of a project or company.

All-Equity Rate   The discount rate that reflects only the business risks of a project and abstracts from the effects of financing.

All-In Cost   The effective interest rate on a loan, calculated as the discount rate that equates the present value of the future interest and principal payments to the net proceeds received by the borrower; it is the internal rate of return on the loan.

American Depository Receipt (ADR)   A certificate of ownership issued by a U.S. bank as a convenience to investors in lieu of the underlying foreign corporate shares it holds in custody.

American Option   An option that can be exercised at any time up to the expiration date.

American Shares   Securities certificates issued in the United States by a transfer agent acting on behalf of the foreign issuer. The certificates represent claims to foreign equities.

American Terms   Method of quoting currencies; it is expressed as the number of U.S. dollars per unit of foreign currency.

Appreciation   *See* revaluation.

Arab Fund for Economic and Social Development (AFESD)   A multilateral Arab fund that actively searches for projects in Arab League countries and then assumes responsibility for project implementation.

Arbitrage   The purchase of securities or commodities on one market for immediate resale on another in order to profit from a price discrepancy.

Arm's-Length Price   Price at which a willing buyer and a willing unrelated seller would freely agree to transact (i.e., a market price).

Asiacurrency (or Asiadollar) Market   Offshore financial market located in Singapore that channels investment dollars to a number of rapidly growing Southeast Asian countries and provides deposit facilities for those investors with excess funds.

Asian Development Bank (ADB)   The ADB guarantees or makes direct loans to member states and private ventures in Asian/Pacific nations and helps to develop local capital markets by underwriting securities issued by private enterprises.

Ask   The price at which one can sell a currency. Also known as the offer price.

Atlantic Development Group for Latin America (ADELA)   An international private investment company dedicated to the socioeconomic development of Latin America. Its objective is to strengthen private enterprise by providing capital and entrepreneurial and technical services.

At-the-Money   An option whose exercise price is the same as the spot exchange rate.

Back-to-Back Loan   An intercompany loan, also known as a *fronting loan* or *link financing,* that is channeled through a bank.

Baker Plan   A plan by U.S. Treasury Secretary James Baker under which 15 principal middle-income debtor countries (the "Baker countries") would undertake growth-oriented structural reforms, to be supported by increased financing from the World Bank and continued lending from commercial banks.

Balance of Payments   Net value of all economic transactions—including trade in goods and services, transfer payments, loans, and investments—between residents of the same country and those of all other countries.

Balance of Trade   Net flow of goods (exports minus imports) between countries.

Balance-Sheet Exposure   *See* accounting exposure.

Bank Capital   The equity capital and other reserves available to protect bank depositors against credit losses.

Bank Draft   A draft addressed to a bank. *See also* draft.

Bankers' Acceptance   Draft accepted by a bank: *See also* draft.

Bank for International Settlements (BIS)   Organization headquartered in Basle that acts as the central bank for the industrial countries' central banks. The BIS helps central banks manage and invest their foreign exchange reserves and also holds deposits of central banks so that reserves are readily available.

Bank Loan Swap   *See* debt swap.

Barrier Option   *See* knockout option.

Basis Point   One hundred basis points equal one percent of interest.

Basis Swap   Swap in which two parties exchange floating interest payments based on different reference rates.

Bearer Securities   Securities that are unregistered.

Bear Spread   A currency spread designed to bet on a currency's decline. It involves buying a put at one strike price and selling another put at a lower strike price.

Beggar-Thy-Neighbor Devaluation   A devaluation that is designed to cheapen a nation's currency and thereby increase its exports at others' expense and reduce imports. Such devaluations often led to trade wars.

Beta   A measure of the systematic risk faced by an asset or project. Beta is calculated as the covariance between returns on the asset and returns on the market portfolio divided by the variance of returns on the market portfolio.

Bid   The price at which one can buy a currency.

Bid-Ask Spread   The difference between the buying and selling rates.

Bill of Exchange   *See* bank draft.

Bill of Lading   A contract between a carrier and an exporter in which the former agrees to carry the latter's goods from port of shipment to port of destination. It is also the exporter's receipt for the goods.

Black Market   An illegal market that often arises when price controls or official rationing lead to shortages of goods, services, or assets.

Black-Scholes Option Pricing Model   The most widely used model for pricing options. Named after its creators, Fischer Black and Myron Scholes.

Blocked Currency   A currency that is not freely convertible to other currencies due to exchange controls.

Brady Bonds   New government securities issued under the Brady Plan whose interest payments were backed with money from the International Monetary Fund.

Brady Plan   Plan developed by U.S. Treasury Secretary Nicholas Brady in 1989 that emphasized LDC debt relief through forgiveness instead of new lending. It gave banks the choice of either making new loans or writing off portions of their existing loans in exchange for Brady Bonds.

Branch A foreign operation incorporated in the home country.

Bretton Woods System International monetary system established after World War II under which each government pledged to maintain a fixed, or pegged, exchange rate for its currency vis-à-vis the dollar or gold. As one ounce of gold was set equal to $35, fixing a currency's gold price was equivalent to setting its exchange rate relative to the dollar. The U.S. government pledged to maintain convertibility of the dollar into gold for foreign official institutions.

Bull Spread A currency spread designed to bet on a currency's appreciation. It involves buying a call at one strike price and selling another call at a higher strike price.

Call Provision Clause giving the borrower the option of retiring the bonds before maturity should interest rates decline sufficiently in the future.

Capital Account Net result of public and private international investment and lending activities.

Capital Asset Pricing Model (CAPM) A model for pricing risk. The CAPM assumes that investors must be compensated for the time value of money plus systematic risk, as measured by an asset's beta.

Capital Flight The transfer of capital abroad in response to fears of political risk.

Capital Market Imperfections Distortions in the pricing of risk, usually attributable to government regulations and asymmetries in the tax treatment of different types of investment income.

Capital Market Integration The situation that exists when real interest rates are determined by the global supply and global demand for funds.

Capital Market Segmentation The situation that exists when real interest rates are determined by local credit conditions.

Capital Productivity The ratio of output (goods and services) to the input of physical capital (plant and equipment).

Cash-Flow Exposure Used synonymously with economic exposure, it measures the extent to which an exchange rate change will change the value of a company through its impact on the present value of the company's future cash flows.

Cash Pooling *See* pooling.

Central Bank The nation's official monetary authority.

Chicago Mercantile Exchange (CME) The largest market in the world for trading standardized futures and options contracts on a wide variety of commodities, including currencies and bonds.

CHIPS *See* Clearing House Interbank Payments System.

Clean Draft A draft unaccompanied by any other papers; it is normally used only for nontrade remittances.

Clean Float *See* free float.

Cleanup Clause A clause inserted in a bank loan requiring the company to be completely out of debt to the bank for a period of at least 30 days during the year.

Clearing House Interbank Payments System (CHIPS) A computerized network for transfer of international dollar payments, linking about 140 depository institutions that have offices or affiliates in New York City.

Commercial Invoice A document that contains an authoritative description of the merchandise shipped, including full details on quality, grades, price per unit, and total value, along with other information on terms of the shipment.

Commercial Paper (CP) A short-term unsecured promissory note that is generally sold by large corporations on a discount basis to institutional investors and to other corporations.

Compensating Balance The fraction (usually 10% to 20%) of an outstanding loan balance that a bank requires borrowers to hold on deposit in a noninterest-bearing account.

Concession Agreement An understanding between a company and the host government that specifies the rules under which the company can operate locally.

Consignment Under this selling method, goods are only shipped, but not sold, to the importer. The exporter (consignor) retains title to the goods until the importer (consignee) has sold them to a third party. This arrangement is normally made only with a related company because of the large risks involved.

Consular Invoice   An invoice, which varies in its details and information requirements from nation to nation, that is presented to the local consul in exchange for a visa.

Controlled Foreign Corporation (CFC)   A foreign corporation whose voting stock is more than 50% owned by U.S. stockholders, each of whom owns at least 10% of the voting power.

Convertible Bonds   Fixed-rate bonds that are convertible into a given number of shares prior to maturity.

Corporate Governance   The means whereby companies are controlled.

Correspondent Bank   A bank located in any other city, state, or country that provides a service for another bank.

Cost of Equity Capital   The minimum rate of return necessary to induce investors to buy or hold a firm's stock. It equals a basic yield covering the time value of money plus a premium for risk.

Countertrade   A sophisticated form of barter in which the exporting firm is required to take the countervalue of its sale in local goods or services instead of in cash.

Country Risk   General level of political and economic uncertainty in a country affecting the value of loans or investments in that country. From a bank's standpoint, it refers to the possibility that borrowers in a country will be unable to service or repay their debts to foreign lenders in a timely manner.

Coupon Swap   Swap in which one party pays a *fixed rate* calculated at the time of trade as a spread to a particular Treasury bond, and the other side pays a *floating rate* that resets periodically throughout the life of the deal against a designated index.

Covered Interest Arbitrage   Movement of short-term funds between two currencies to take advantage of interest differentials with exchange risk eliminated by means of forward contracts.

Covered Interest Differential   The difference between the domestic interest rate and the hedged foreign interest rate.

Cross-Default Clause   Clause in a loan agreement which says that a default by a borrower to one lender is a default to all lenders.

Cross-Hedge   Hedging exposure in one currency by the use of futures or other contracts on a second currency that is correlated with the first currency.

Cross-Rate   The exchange rate between two currencies, neither of which is the U.S. dollar, calculated by using the dollar rates for both currencies.

Currency Arbitrage   Taking advantage of divergences in exchange rates in different money markets by buying a currency in one market and selling it in another.

Currency Call Option   A financial contract that gives the buyer the right, but not the obligation, to buy a specified number of units of foreign currency from the option seller at a fixed dollar price, up to the option's expiration date.

Currency Collar   A contract that provides protection against currency moves outside an agreed-upon range. It can be created by simultaneously buying an out-of-the-money put option and selling an out-of-the-money call option of the same size. In effect, the purchase of the put option is financed by the sale of the call option.

Currency Controls   *See* exchange controls.

Currency Futures Contract   Contract for future delivery of a specific quantity of a given currency, with the exchange rate fixed at the time the contract is entered. Futures contracts are similar to forward contracts except that they are traded on organized futures exchanges and the gains and losses on the contracts are settled each day.

Currency of Denomination   Currency in which a transaction is stated.

Currency of Determination   Currency whose value determines a given price.

Currency Option   A financial contract that gives the buyer the right, but not the obligation, to buy (call) or sell (put) a specified number of foreign currency units to the option seller at a fixed dollar price, up to the option's expiration date.

Currency Put Option   A financial contract that gives the buyer the right, but not the obligation, to sell a specified number of foreign currency units to the option seller at a fixed dollar price, up to the option's expiration date.

Currency Risk Sharing   An agreement by the parties to a transaction to share the currency risk associated with the transaction. The arrangement involves a customized hedge contract imbedded in the underlying transaction.

Currency Spread   An options position created by buying an option at one strike price and selling a similar option at a different strike price. It allows speculators to bet on the direction of a currency at a lower cost than buying a put or a call option alone but at the cost of limiting the position's upside potential.

Currency Swap   A simultaneous borrowing and lending operation whereby two parties exchange specific amounts of two currencies at the outset at the spot rate. They also exchange interest rate payments in the two currencies. The parties undertake to reverse the exchange after a fixed term at a fixed exchange rate.

Current Account   Net flow of goods, services, and unilateral transactions (gifts) between countries.

Current Assets   Short-term assets, including cash, marketable securities, accounts receivable, and inventory.

Current Exchange Rate   Exchange in effect today.

Current Liabilities   Short-term liabilities, such as accounts payable and loans expected to be repaid within one year.

Current/Noncurrent Method   Under this currency translation method, all of a foreign subsidiary's current assets and liabilities are translated into home currency at the current exchange rate while noncurrent assets and liabilities are translated at the historical exchange rate (that is, at the rate in effect at the time the asset was acquired or the liability incurred).

Current Rate Method   Under this currency translation method, all foreign currency balance-sheet and income items are translated at the current exchange rate.

Cylinder   The payoff profile of a currency collar created through a combined put purchase and call sale.

Debt Relief   Reducing the principal and/or interest payments on LDC loans.

Debt Swap   A set of transactions (also called a debt-equity swap) in which a firm buys a country's dollar bank debt at a discount and swaps this debt with the central bank for local currency that it can use to acquire local equity.

Depreciation   *See* devaluation.

Depreciation Tax Shield   The value of the tax write-off on depreciation of plant and equipment.

Derivatives   Contracts that derive their value from some underlying asset (such as a stock, bond, or currency), reference rate (such as a 90-day Treasury bill rate), or index (such as the S&P 500 stock index). Popular derivatives include swaps, forwards, futures, and options.

Devaluation   A decrease in the spot value of a currency.

Direct Quotation   A quote that gives the home currency price of a foreign currency.

"Dirty" Float   *See* managed float.

Discount Basis   Means of quoting the interest rate on a loan under which the bank deducts the interest in advance.

Discounting   A means of borrowing against a trade or other draft. The exporter or other borrower places the draft with a bank or other financial institution and, in turn, receives the face value of the draft less interest and commissions.

Doctrine of Sovereign Immunity   Doctrine that says a nation may not be tried in the courts of another country without its consent.

Documentary Draft   A draft accompanied by documents that are to be delivered to the drawee on payment or acceptance of the draft. Typically, these documents include the bill of lading in negotiable form, the commercial invoice, the consular invoice where required, and an insurance certificate.

Domestic International Sales Corporation (DISC)   A domestic U.S. corporation that receives a tax incentive for export activities.

Double Dip Lease   A cross-border lease in which the disparate rules of the lessor's and lessee's countries let both parties be treated as the owner of the leased equipment for tax purposes.

Down-and-In Option   An option that comes into existence if and only if the currency weakens enough to cross a preset barrier.

Down-and-Out Call   A knockout option that has a positive payoff to the option holder if the underlying currency strengthens but is canceled if it weakens sufficiently to hit the outstrike.

Down-and-Out Put   A knockout option that has a positive payoff if the currency weakens but is canceled if it weakens beyond the outstrike.

Draft   An unconditional order in writing—signed by a person, usually the exporter, and addressed to the importer—ordering the importer or the importer's agent to pay, on demand (sight draft) or at a fixed future date (time draft), the amount specified on its face. Accepting a draft means writing *accepted* across its face, followed by an authorized person's signature and the date. The party accepting a draft incurs the obligation to pay it at maturity.

Dragon Bond   Debt denominated in a foreign currency, usually dollars, but launched, priced, and traded in Asia.

Drawdown   The period over which the borrower may take down the loan.

Dual Currency Bond   Bond that has the issue's proceeds and interest payments stated in foreign currency and the principal repayment stated in dollars.

Dual Syndicate Equity Offering   An international equity placement where the offering is split into two tranches—domestic and foreign—and each tranche is handled by a separate lead manager.

EAFE Index   The Morgan Stanley Capital International Europe, Australia, Far East Index, which reflects the performance of all major stock markets outside of North America.

Economic Exposure   The extent to which the value of the firm will change due to an exchange rate change.

Economies of Scale   Situation in which increasing production leads to a less-than-proportionate increase in cost.

Economies of Scope   Scope economies exist whenever the same investment can support multiple profitable activities less expensively in combination than separately.

Edge Act Corporation   A subsidiary, located in the United States, of a U.S. bank that is permitted to carry on international banking and investment activities.

Effective Interest Rate   The true cost of a loan; it equals the annual interest paid divided by the funds received.

Efficient Frontier   The set of portfolios that has the smallest possible standard deviation for its level of expected return and has the maximum expected return for a given level of risk.

Efficient Market   One in which new information is readily incorporated in the prices of traded securities.

Electronic Trading System   A system used in the foreign exchange market that offers automated matching. Traders can enter buy and sell orders directly into their terminals on an anonymous basis, and these prices will be visible to all market participants. Another trader, anywhere in the world, can execute a trade by simply hitting two buttons.

Emerging Markets   A term that encompasses the stock markets in all of South and Central America; all of the Far East with the exception of Japan, Australia, and New Zealand; all of Africa; and parts of Southern Europe, as well as Eastern Europe and countries of the former Soviet Union.

Equity-Related Bonds   Bonds that combine features of the underlying bond and common stock. The two principal types of equity-related bonds are convertible bonds and bonds with equity warrants.

Equity Warrants   Securities that give their holder the right to buy a specified number of shares of common stock at a specified price during a designated time period.

Euro   New currency created for members of the European Monetary Union and issued by the European Central Bank. Coins and bills denominated in the euro will be unavailable until 2002.

Eurobank   A bank that accepts and makes loans in Eurocurrencies.

Eurobond   A bond sold outside the country in whose currency it is denominated.

Eurobond Market   Market in which Eurobonds are issued and traded.

Euro-Commercial Paper (Euro-CP)   Euronotes that are not underwritten.

Eurocurrency   A currency deposited in a bank outside the country of its origin.

Eurocurrency Market   The set of banks that accept deposits and make loans in Eurocurrencies.

Eurodollar   A U.S. dollar on deposit outside the United States.

Eurodollar Future   A cash-settled futures contract on a three-month, $1,000,000 Eurodollar deposit that pays LIBOR.

Euroequity Issue   A syndicated equity offering placed throughout Europe and handled by one lead manager.

Euro-Medium Term Note (Euro-MTN)   A nonunder-written Euronote issued directly to the market. Euro-MTNs are offered continuously rather than all at once like a bond issue. Most Euro-MTN maturities are under five years.

Euronote   A short-term note issued outside the country of the currency it is denominated in.

Europe, Australia, Far East (EAFE) Index   An index put out by Morgan Stanley Capital International which tracks the performance of the 20 major stock markets outside of North America.

European Bank for Reconstruction and Development (EBRD)   A development bank supposed to finance the privatization of Eastern Europe.

European Central Bank   The central bank for the European Monetary Union. It has the sole power to issue a single European currency called the **euro**.

European Currency Unit (ECU)   A composite currency, consisting of fixed amounts of 12 European currencies.

European Investment Bank (EIB)   A development bank that offers funds for certain public and private projects in European and other nations associated with the European Community.

European Monetary System (EMS)   Monetary system formed by the major European countries under which the members agree to maintain their exchange rates within a specific margin around agreed-upon, fixed central exchange rates. These central exchange rates are denominated in currency units per ECU.

European Monetary Union   Eleven members of the European Community who have joined together to establish a single central bank (the European Central Bank) that issues a common European currency (usually referred to as the euro).

European Option   An option that can be exercised only at maturity.

European Terms   Method of quoting currencies; it is expressed as the number of foreign currency units per U.S. dollar.

European Union   Organization of fifteen European nations whose purpose is to promote economic harmonization and tear down barriers to trade and commerce within Europe.

Exchange Controls   Restrictions placed on the transfer of a currency from one nation to another.

Exchange Rate Mechanism (ERM)   Arrangement at the heart of the European Monetary System which allows each member of the EMS to determine a mutually agreed-on central exchange rate for its currency; each rate is denominated in currency units per ECU.

Exchange Risk   The variability of a firm's (or asset's) value that is due to uncertain exchange rate changes.

Exercise Price   The price at which an option is exercised. Also known as **strike price**.

Export-Import Bank (Eximbank)   U.S. government agency dedicated to facilitating U.S. exports, primarily through subsidized export financing.

Exposure Netting   Offsetting exposures in one currency with exposures in the same or another currency, where exchange rates are expected to move in such a way that losses (gains) on the first exposed position should be offset by gains (losses) on the second currency exposure.

Expropriation   The taking of foreign property, with or without compensation, by a government.

Factor   Specialized buyer, at a discount, of company receivables.

FASB No. 8   *See* Statement of Financial Accounting Standards No. 8

FASB No. 52   *See* Statement of Financial Accounting Standards No. 52.

FedWire   The Federal Reserve' network for transferring fed funds.

Fiat Money   Nonconvertible paper money.

Financial Accounting Standards Board
Organization in the United States that sets the rules that govern the presentation of financial statements and resolves other accounting issues.

Financial Channels   The various ways in which funds, allocated profits, or both are transferred within the multinational corporation.

Financial Deregulation   The dismantling of various regulations that restrict the nature of financial contracts that consenting parties, such as borrowers and lenders, could enter into.

Financial Economics   A discipline that emphasizes the use of economic analysis to understand the basic workings of financial markets, particularly the measurement and pricing of risk and the intertemporal allocation of funds.

Financial Innovation   The process of segmenting, transferring, and diversifying risk to lower the cost of capital as well as creating new securities that avoid various tax and regulatory costs.

Fisher Effect   States that the nominal interest differential between two countries should equal the inflation differential between those countries.

Fixed Exchange Rate   An exchange rate whose value is fixed by the governments involved.

Fixed-Rate Bonds   Bonds that have a fixed coupon, set maturity date, and full repayment of the principal amount at maturity.

Floating Currency   A currency whose value is set by market forces.

Floating Exchange Rate   An exchange rate whose value is determined in the foreign exchange market.

Floating-Rate Bond   A bond whose interest rate is reset every three to six months, or so, at a fixed margin above a mutually agreed-upon interest rate

"index" such as LIBOR for Eurodollar deposits, the corresponding Treasury bill rate, or the prime rate.

Foreign Bank Market   That portion of domestic bank loans supplied to foreigners for use abroad.

Foreign Bond Market   That portion of the domestic bond market that represents issues floated by foreign companies or governments.

Foreign Credit Insurance Association   The FCIA is a cooperative effort of Eximbank and a group of approximately 50 of the leading marine, casualty, and property insurance companies that administers the U.S. government's export-credit insurance program. FCIA insurance offers protection from political and commercial risks to U.S. exporters: The private insurers cover commercial risks, and the Eximbank covers political risks.

Foreign Direct Investment   The acquisition abroad of physical assets such as plant and equipment, with operating control residing in the parent corporation.

Foreign Equity Market   That portion of the domestic equity market that represents issues floated by foreign companies.

Foreign Exchange Brokers   Specialists in matching net supplier and demander banks in the foreign exchange market.

Foreign Exchange Market Intervention   Official purchases and sales of foreign exchange that nations undertake through their central banks to influence their currencies.

Foreign Exchange Risk   *See* exchange risk.

Foreign Market Beta   A measure of foreign market risk that is derived from the capital asset pricing model and is calculated relative to the U.S. market in the same way that individual asset betas are calculated.

Foreign Sales Corporation (FSC)   A special type of corporation created by the Tax Reform Act of 1986 that is designed to provide a tax incentive for exporting U.S.-produced goods.

Foreign Tax Credit   Home country credit against domestic income tax for foreign taxes already paid on foreign-source earnings.

Forfaiting   The discounting—at a fixed rate without recourse—of medium-term export receivables denominated in fully convertible currencies (e.g., U.S. dollar, Swiss franc, Deutsche mark).

Forward Contract   Agreement between a bank and a customer (which could be another bank) that calls for delivery, at a fixed future date, of a specified amount of one currency against dollar payment; the exchange rate is fixed at the time the contract is entered into.

Forward Differential   The forward discount or premium on a currency expressed as an annualized percentage of the spot rate.

Forward Discount   A situation that pertains when the forward rate expressed in dollars is below the spot rate.

Forward Forward   A contract that fixes an interest rate today on a future loan or deposit.

Forward Market Hedge   The use of forward contracts to fix the home currency value of future foreign currency cash flows. Specifically, a company that is long a foreign currency will sell the foreign currency forward, whereas a company that is short a foreign currency will buy the currency forward.

Forward Premium   A situation that pertains when the forward rate expressed in dollars is above the spot rate.

Forward Rate   The rate quoted today for delivery at a fixed future date of a specified amount of one currency against dollar payment.

Forward Rate Agreement (FRA)   A cash-settled, over-the-counter forward contract that allows a company to fix an interest rate to be applied to a specified future interest period on a notional principal amount.

Free Float   An exchange rate system characterized by the absence of government intervention. Also known as a **clean float**.

Functional Currency   As defined in FASB No. 52, an affiliate's functional currency is the currency of the primary economic environment in which the affiliate generates and expends cash.

Fundamental Analysis   An approach to forecasting asset prices that relies on painstaking examination of the macroeconomic variables and policies that are likely to influence the asset's prospects.

Funds Adjustment   A hedging technique designed to reduce a firm's local currency accounting exposure by altering either the amounts or the currencies (or both) of the planned cash flows of the parent or its subsidiaries.

Futures Contracts   Standardized contracts that trade on organized futures markets for specific delivery dates only.

Futures Option   An option contract calling for delivery of a standardized IMM futures contract in the currency rather than the currency itself.

G-5 Nations   The United States, France, Japan, Great Britain, and Germany.

G-7 Nations   The G-5 nations plus Italy and Canada.

Global Fund   A mutual fund that can invest anywhere in the world, including the United States.

Gold Standard   A system of setting currency values whereby the participating countries commit to fix the prices of their domestic currencies in terms of a specified amount of gold.

Good Funds   Funds that are available for use.

Government Budget Deficit   A closely watched figure that equals government spending minus taxes.

Growth Options   The opportunities a company may have to invest capital so as to increase the profitability of its existing product lines and benefit from expanding into new products or markets.

Hard Currency   A currency expected to maintain its value or appreciate.

Hedge   To enter into a forward contract in order to protect the home currency value of foreign-currency-denominated assets or liabilities.

Herstatt Risk   Named after a German bank that went bankrupt, this is the risk that a bank will deliver currency on one side of a foreign exchange deal only to find that its counterparty has not sent any money in return. Also known as **settlement risk**.

Historical Exchange Rate   In accounting terminology, it refers to the rate in effect at the time a foreign currency asset was acquired or a liability incurred.

Home Bias   The tendency of investors to hold domestic assets in their investment portfolios.

Hyperinflationary Country   Defined in FASB No. 52 as one that has cumulative inflation of approximately 100% or more over a three-year period.

IFC Emerging Markets Index   An index of developing country stock markets published by the International Finance Corporation.

Implied Volatility   The volatility that, when substituted in the Black-Scholes option pricing formula, yields the market price of the option.

Import-Substitution Development Strategy   A development strategy followed by many Latin American countries and other LDCs that emphasized import substitution—accomplished through protectionism—as the route to economic growth.

Indexed Bond   Bond that pays interest tied to the inflation rate. The intent is to fix the real interest rate on the bond.

Indirect Quotation   A quote that gives the foreign currency price of the home currency.

Inflation   Change in the general level of prices.

Inflation Risk   Refers to the divergence between actual and expected inflation.

Inter-American Development Bank (IADB)   A source of long-term capital in Latin America.

Interbank Market   The wholesale foreign exchange market in which major banks trade currencies with each other.

Intercompany Loan   Loan made by one unit of a corporation to another unit of the same corporation.

Intercompany Transaction   Transaction, such as a loan. carried out between two units of the same corporation.

Interest Rate/Currency Swap   Swap that combines the features of both a currency swap and an interest rate swap. It converts a liability in one currency with a stipulated type of interest payment into one denominated in another currency with a different type of interest payment.

Interest Rate Parity   A condition whereby the interest differential between two currencies is (approximately) equal to the forward differential between two currencies.

Interest Rate Swap   An agreement between two parties to exchange interest payments for a specific maturity on an agreed upon principal amount. The most common interest rate swap involves exchanging fixed interest payments for floating interest payments.

Interest Tax Shield   The value of the tax write-off on interest payments (analogous to the depreciation tax shield).

International Bank for Reconstruction and Development (IBRD)   Also known as the World Bank, the IBRD is owned by its member nations and makes loans at nearly conventional terms to countries for projects of high economic priority.

International Banking Facility (IBF)   A bookkeeping entity of a U.S. financial institution that is permitted to conduct international banking business (such as receiving foreign deposits and making foreign loans) largely exempt from domestic regulatory constraints.

International Diversification   The attempt to reduce risk by investing in more than one nation. By diversifying across nations whose economic cycles are not perfectly in phase, investors can typically reduce the variability of their returns.

International Finance Subsidiary   A subsidiary incorporated in the United States (usually in Delaware) whose sole purpose was to issue debentures overseas and invest the proceeds in foreign operations, with the interest paid to foreign bondholders not subject to U.S. withholding tax. The elimination of the corporate withholding tax has ended the need for this type of subsidiary.

International Fisher Effect   States that the interest differential between two countries should be an unbiased predictor of the future change in the spot rate.

International Fund   A mutual fund that can invest only outside the United States.

International Monetary Fund (IMF)   International organization created at Bretton Woods, N.H., in 1944 to promote exchange rate stability, including the provision of temporary assistance to member nations trying to defend their currencies against transitory phenomena.

International Monetary Market (IMM)   The IMM is a market created by the Chicago Mercantile Exchange for the purpose of trading currency futures.

International Monetary System   The set of policies, institutions, practices, regulations, and mechanisms that determine the rate at which one currency is exchanged for another.

In-the-Money   An option that would be profitable to exercise at the current price.

Intrinsic Value   The value of an option that is attributable to its being in-the-money. An out-of-the money option has no intrinsic value.

Inverse Floaters   Floating-rate notes with coupons that move opposite to the reference rate.

Investment Banker   A financing specialist who assists organizations in designing and marketing security issues.

Irrevocable Letter of Credit   An L/C that cannot be revoked without the specific permission of all parties concerned, including the exporter.

J-Curve   Theory that says a country's trade deficit will initially worsen after its currency depreciates because higher prices on foreign imports will more than offset the reduced volume of imports in the short run.

Keiretsu   The large industrial groupings—often with a major bank at the centers—that form the backbone of corporate Japan.

Knockout Option   An option that is similar to a standard option except that it is canceled—that is, knocked out—if the exchange rate crosses, even briefly, a pre-defined level called the outstrike. If the exchange rate breaches this barrier, the holder cannot exercise this option, even if it ends up in-the-money. Also known as **barrier options.**

Law of One Price   The theory that exchange-adjusted prices on identical tradeable goods and financial assets must be within transaction costs of equality worldwide.

L/C   *See* letter of credit.

LDC Debit-Equity Swap   *See* debt swap.

LDC Debt Swap   *See* debt swap.

Leading and Lagging   A means of shifting liquidity by accelerating (leading) and delaying (lagging) international payments by modifying credit terms, normally on trade between affiliates.

Lean Production   Ultra-efficient manufacturing techniques pioneered by Japanese industry that gave it a formidable competitive edge over U.S. rivals.

Lender of Last Resort   Official institution that lends funds to countries or banks that get into financial trouble. It is designed to avert the threat of a financial panic.

Letter of Credit   A letter addressed to the seller, written and signed by a bank acting on behalf of the buyer, in which the bank promises to honor drafts drawn on itself if the seller conforms to the specific conditions contained in the letter.

Line of Credit   An informal agreement that permits a company to borrow up to a stated maximum amount from a bank. The firm can draw down its line of credit when it requires funds and pay back the loan balance when it has excess cash.

Link Financing   *See* back-to-back loan.

Liquidity   The ability to readily exchange an asset for goods or other assets at a known price, thereby facilitating economic transactions. It is usually measured by the difference between the rates at which dealers can buy and sell that asset.

Listed Options   Option contracts with prespecified terms (amount, strike price, expiration date, fixed maturity) that are traded on an organized exchange.

Loan Syndication   Group of banks sharing a loan.

Lock Box   A postal box in a company's name to which customers remit their required payments.

London Interbank Bid Rate (LIBID)   The rate paid by one bank to another for a deposit.

London Interbank Offer Rate (LIBOR)   The deposit rate on interbank transactions in the Eurocurrency market.

Long Position   In the foreign exchange market, it means that one has more assets in a particular currency than liabilities.

Look-Thru   A method for calculating U.S. taxes owed on income from controlled foreign corporations that was introduced by the Tax Reform Act of 1986.

Louvre Accord   Named for the Paris landmark where it was negotiated, this accord called for the G-7 nations to support the falling dollar by pegging exchange rates within a narrow, undisclosed range, while they also moved to bring their economic policies into line.

Maastricht Criteria   Tough standards on inflation, currency stability, and deficit spending established in the Maastricht Treaty that European nations must meet in order to join EMU.

Maastricht Treaty Agreement under which the EC nations would establish a European Monetary Union with a single central bank having the sole power to issue a single European currency called the euro.

Managed Float Also known as a "dirty" float, this is a system of floating exchange rates with central bank intervention to reduce currency fluctuations.

Market Efficiency A market in which the prices of traded securities readily incorporate new information.

Market Risk Premium The difference between the required return on a particular stock market and the risk-free interest rate.

Marking to Market A daily settlement feature in which profits and losses of futures contracts are paid over every day at the end of trading. More generally, this term refers to pricing assets at their market value rather than their book value.

Monetary/Nonmonetary Method Under this translation method, monetary items (for example, cash, accounts payable and receivable, and long-term debt) are translated at the current rate while nonmonetary items (for example, inventory, fixed assets, and longterm investments) are translated at historical rates.

Monetary Union A group of states that join together to have a single central bank that issues a common currency.

Money-Market Hedge The use of simultaneous borrowing and lending transactions in two different currencies to lock in the home currency value of a foreign currency transaction.

Moral Hazard The tendency to incur risks that one is protected against.

Morgan Stanley Capital International World Index An internationally diversified index of developed country stock markets that combines the EAFE index with the U.S. market index.

Multicurrency Clause This clause gives a Eurocurrency borrower the right to switch from one currency to another when the loan is rolled over.

Multinational Cash Mobilization A system designed to optimize the use of funds by tracking current and near-term cash positions and redeploying those funds in an efficient manner.

Multinational Financial System The aggregate of the internal transfer mechanisms available to the MNC to shift profits and money among its various affiliates. These transfer mechanisms include transfer price adjustments, leading and lagging interaffiliate payments, dividend payments, fees and royalties, intercompany loans, and intercompany equity investments.

Nationalization The taking of property, with or without compensation, by a government.

Net Liquidity Balance The change in private domestic borrowing or lending that is required to keep payments in balance without adjusting official reserves. Nonliquid, private, short-term capital flows and errors and omissions are included in the balance; liquid assets and liabilities are excluded.

Netting *See* exposure netting; payments netting.

No-Arbitrage Condition The relationship between exchange rates such that profitable arbitrage opportunities don't exist. If this condition is violated on an ongoing basis, we would wind up with a money machine.

Nominal Exchange Rate The actual exchange rate; it is expressed in current units of currency.

Nominal Interest Rate The price quoted on lending and borrowing transactions. It is expressed as the rate of exchange between current and future units of currency unadjusted for inflation.

Nonrecourse Method of borrowing against an asset, such as a receivable, under which the lender assumes all the credit and political risks except for those involving disputes between the transacting parties. The lender has no recourse to the borrower.

Note Issuance Facility (NIF) A facility provided by a syndicate of banks that allows borrowers to issue short-term notes, which are then placed by the syndicate providing the NIF. Borrowers usually have the right to sell their notes to the bank syndicate at a price that yields a prearranged spread over LIBOR.

Notional Principal A reference amount against which the interest on a swap is calculated.

Official Reserves Holdings of gold and foreign currencies by official monetary institutions.

Official Reserve Transactions Balance The adjustment required in official reserves to achieve balance-of-payments equilibrium.

Offshore Finance Subsidiary   A wholly owned affiliate incorporated overseas, usually in a tax-haven country, whose function is to issue securities abroad for use in either the parent's domestic or foreign business.

Open Account Selling   This selling method involves shipping goods first and billing the importer later.

Open Interest   The number of futures contracts out-standing at any one time.

Open-Market Operation   Purchase or sale of government securities by the monetary authorities to increase or decrease the domestic money supply.

Operating Exposure   Degree to which an exchange rate change, in combination with price changes, will alter a company's future operating cash flows.

Optimum Currency Area   Largest area in which it makes sense to have only one currency. It is defined as that area for which the cost of having an additional currency—higher costs of doing business and greater currency risk—just balances the benefits of another currency—reduced vulnerability to economic shocks associated with the option to change the area's exchange rate.

Option   A financial instrument that gives the holder the right—but not the obligation—to sell (put) or buy (call) another financial instrument at a set price and expiration date.

Out-of-the-Money   An option that would not be profitable to exercise at the current price.

Outright Rate   Actual forward rate expressed in dollars per currency unit, or vice versa.

Outsourcing   The practice of purchasing a significant percentage of intermediate components from outside suppliers.

Outstrike   Pre-defined exchange rate at which a knockout option is canceled if the spot rate crosses this price even temporarily.

Overdraft   A line of credit against which drafts (checks) can be drawn (written) up to a specified maximum amount.

Overseas Private Investment Corporation (OPIC)   Agency of the U.S. government that provides political risk insurance coverage to U.S. multinationals. Its purpose is to encourage U.S. direct investment in less-developed countries.

Over-the-Counter Market (OTC)   A market in which the terms and conditions on contracts are negotiated between the buyer and seller, in contrast to an organized exchange where contractual terms are fixed by the exchange.

Over-the-Counter Options   Option contracts whose specifications are generally negotiated as to the amount, exercise price, underlying instrument, and expiration. They are traded by commercial and investment banks.

Parallel Loan   Simultaneous borrowing and lending operation usually involving four related parties in two different countries.

Payments Netting   Reducing fund transfers between affiliates to only a netted amount. Netting can be done on a bilateral basis (between pairs of affiliates) or on a multilateral basis (taking all affiliates together).

Pegged Currency   A currency whose value is set by the government.

Peso Problem   Reference to the possibility that during the time period studied investors anticipated significant events that didn't materialize, thereby invalidating statistical inferences based on data drawn from that period.

Plaza Agreement   A coordinated program agreed to in September 1985 that was designed to force down the dollar against other major currencies and thereby improve American competitiveness.

Political Risk   Uncertain government action that affects the value of a firm.

Pooling   Transfer of excess affiliate cash into a central account (pool), usually located in a low-tax nation, where all corporate funds are managed by corporate staff.

Possession Corporation   A U.S. corporation operating in a U.S. possession. Such companies are entitled to certain tax breaks.

Price Elasticity of Demand   Percentage change in the quantity demanded of a particular good or service for a given percentage change in price.

Price-Specie-Flow Mechanism   Adjustment mechanism under the classical gold standard whereby disturbances in the price level in one country would be wholly or partly offset by a countervailing flow of specie (gold coins) that would act to equalize prices across countries and automatically bring international payments back in balance.

Private Export Funding Corporation (PEFCO) Company that mobilizes private capital for financing the export of big-ticket items by U.S. firms by purchasing at fixed interest rates the medium- to long-term debt obligations of importers of U.S. products.

Private Placements   Securities that are sold directly to only a limited number of sophisticated investors, usually life insurance companies and pension funds.

Privatization   The act of returning state-owned or state-run companies back to the private sector, usually by selling them off.

Product Cycle   The time it takes to bring new and improved products to market. Japanese companies have excelled in compressing product cycles.

Property Rights   Rights of individuals and companies to own and utilize property as they see fit and to receive the stream of income that their property generates.

Protectionism   Protecting domestic industry from import competition by means of tariffs, quotas, and other trade barriers.

Purchasing Power Parity   The notion that the ratio between domestic and foreign price levels should equal the equilibrium exchange rate between domestic and foreign currencies.

Put-Call Option Interest Rate Parity   A parity condition that relates put and call currency options prices to the interest differential between two currencies and, by extension, to their forward differential.

Quota   Government regulation specifying the quantity of particular products that can be imported to a country.

Range Forward   *See* currency collar.

Rational Expectations   The idea that people rationally anticipate the future and respond to what they see ahead.

Real Exchange Rate   The spot rate adjusted for relative price level changes since a base period.

Real Interest Rate   The nominal interest rate adjusted for expected inflation over the life of the loan; it is the exchange rate between current and future goods.

Real or Inflation-Adjusted Exchange Rate Measured as the nominal exchange rate adjusted for changes in relative price levels.

Regional Fund   A mutual fund that invests in a specific geographic areas overseas, such as Asia or Europe.

Regulatory Arbitrage   The process whereby the users of capital markets issue and trade securities in financial centers with the lowest regulatory standards and, hence, the lowest costs.

Reinvoicing Center   A subsidiary that takes title to all goods sold by one corporate unit to another affiliate or to a third-party customer. The center pays the seller and in turn is paid by the buyer.

Reporting Currency   The currency in which the parent firm prepares its own financial statements; that is, U.S. dollars for a U.S. company.

Revaluation   An increase in the spot value of a currency.

Revolving Credit Agreement   A line of credit under which a bank (or syndicate of banks) is *legally committed* to extend credit up to the stated maximum.

Revolving Underwriting Facility (RUF)   A note issuance facility that includes underwriting services. The RUF gives borrowers long-term continuous access to short-term money underwritten by banks at a fixed margin.

Right of Offset   Clause that gives each party to a swap or parallel loan arrangement the right to offset any nonpayment of principal or interest with a comparable nonpayment.

Risk Arbitrage   The process that leads to equality of risk-adjusted returns on different securities, unless market imperfections that hinder this adjustment process exist.

Rollover Date   Date on which the interest rate on a floating-rate loan is reset based on current market conditions.

Rule 144A   Rule adopted by the Securities and Exchange Commission (SEC) in 1990 that allows qualified institutional investors to trade in unregistered private placements, making them a closer substitute for public issues.

Same-Day Value   Funds that are credited and available for use the same day they are transferred.

Samurai Bonds   Yen bonds sold in Japan by a non-Japanese borrower.

Secondary Market   The market where investors trade securities already bought.

Section 482   United States Department of Treasury regulations governing transfer prices.

Securitization   The matching up of borrowers and lenders wholly or partly by way of the financial markets. This process usually refers to the replacement of nonmarketable loans provided by financial intermediaries with negotiable securities issued in the public capital markets.

Seigniorage   The profit to the central bank from money creation; it equals the difference between the cost of issuing the money and the value of the goods and services that money can buy.

Settlement Risk   *See* Herstatt risk.

Shogun Bonds   Foreign currency bonds issued within Japan by Japanese corporations.

Shogun Lease   Yen-based international lease.

Short Position   In the foreign exchange market, it means that one has more liabilities in a particular currency than assets.

Sight Draft   A draft that must be paid on presentation or else dishonored.

Single-Country Fund   A mutual fund that invests in individual countries outside the United States, such as Germany or Thailand.

Smithsonian Agreement   After the currency turmoil of August 1971, the United States agreed in December 1971 to devalue the dollar to 1/38 of an ounce of gold, and other countries agreed to revalue their currencies by negotiated amounts vis-à-vis the dollar.

Society for Worldwide Interbank Financial Telecommunications (SWIFT)   A dedicated computer network to support funds transfer messages internationally between more than 900 member banks worldwide.

Soft Currency   A currency expected to depreciate.

Sovereign Risk   The risk that the country of origin of the currency a bank is buying or selling will impose foreign exchange regulations that will reduce or negate the value of the contract; also refers to the risk of government default on a loan made to it or guaranteed by it.

Special Drawing Rights (SDR)   A new form of international reserve assets, created by the IMF in 1967, whose value is based on a portfolio of widely used currencies.

Spot Rate   The price at which foreign exchange can be bought or sold with payment set for the same day.

Statement of Financial Accounting Standards No. 8   This is the currency translation standard previously in use by U.S. firms.

Statement of Financial Accounting Standards No. 52   This is the currency translation standard currently in use by U.S. firms. It basically mandates the use of the current rate method.

Statistical Discrepancy   A number on the balance-of-payments account that reflects errors and omissions in collecting data on international transactions.

Step-Down Note   A debt instrument with a high coupon in earlier payment periods and a lower coupon in later payment periods.

Step-Up Note   A callable debt issue that features one or more increases in a fixed rate or a step-up in a spread over LIBOR during the life of the note.

Sterilized Intervention   Foreign exchange market intervention in which the monetary authorities have insulated their domestic money supplies from the foreign exchange transactions with offsetting sales or purchases of domestic assets.

Strike Price   *See* exercise price.

Structured Notes   Interest-bearing securities whose interest payments are determined by reference to a formula set in advance and adjusted on specified reset dates.

Subpart F   Special category of foreign-source "unearned" income that is currently taxed by the IRS whether or not it is remitted back to the United States.

Subsidiary   A foreign-based affiliate that is a separately incorporated entity under the host country's law.

Swap   A foreign exchange transaction that combines a spot and a forward contract. More generally, it refers to a financial transaction in which two counterparties agree to exchange streams of payments over time, such as in a currency swap or an interest rate swap.

Swap Rate The difference between spot and forward rates expressed in points (e.g., $0.0001 per pound sterling or DM 0.0001 per dollar).

SWIFT *See* Society for Worldwide Interbank Financial Telecommunications.

Systematic (Nondiversifiable) Risk Marketwide influences that affect all assets to some extent, such as the state of the economy.

Systematic Risk That element of an asset's risk that cannot be eliminated no matter how diversified an investor's portfolio.

Target-Zone Arrangement A monetary system under which countries pledge to maintain their exchange rates within a specific margin around agreed-upon, fixed central exchange rates.

Tariff A tax imposed on imported products. It can be used to raise revenue, to discourage purchase of foreign products, or some combination of the two.

Tax Arbitrage The shifting of gains or losses from one tax jurisdiction to another to profit from differences in tax rates.

Tax Haven A nation with a moderate level of taxation and/or liberal tax incentives for undertaking specific activities such as exporting.

Tax Reform Act of 1986 A 1986 law involving a major overhaul of the U.S. tax system.

Technical Analysis An approach that focuses exclusively on past price and volume movements—while totally ignoring economic and political factors—to forecast future asset prices.

Temporal Method Under this currency translation method, the choice of exchange rate depends on the underlying method of valuation. Assets and liabilities valued at historical cost (market) are translated at the historical rate (current rate).

Term Loan A straight loan, often unsecured, that is made for a fixed period of time, usually 90 days.

Terms of Trade The weighted average of a nation's export prices relative to its import prices.

Time Draft A draft that is payable at some specified future date and as such becomes a useful financing device.

Time Value The excess of an option's value over its intrinsic value.

Total Dollar Return The dollar return on a nondollar investment, which includes the sum of any dividend/interest income, capital gains (losses), and currency gains (losses) on the investment.

Trade Acceptance A draft accepted by a commercial enterprise. *See also* draft.

Trade Draft A draft addressed to a commercial enterprise. *See also* draft.

Transaction Exposure The extent to which a given exchange rate change will change the value of foreign-currency-denominated transactions already entered into.

Transfer Price The price at which one unit of a firm sells goods or services to an affiliated unit.

Translation Exposure *See* accounting exposure.

Treasury Workstation A software package implemented on a computer that treasurers use to run their cash management systems.

Triangular Currency Arbitrage A sequence of foreign exchange transactions, involving three different currencies, that one can use to profit from discrepancies in the different exchange rates.

Unbiased Nature of the Forward Rate (UFR) States that the forward rate should reflect the expected future spot rate on the date of settlement of the forward contract.

Underwriting The act by investment bankers of purchasing securities from issuers for resale to the public.

United Currency Options Market (UCOM) Market set up by the Philadelphia Stock Exchange in which to trade currencies.

Universal Banking Bank practice, especially in Germany, whereby commercial banks perform not only investment banking activities but also take major equity positions in companies.

Unsterilized Intervention Foreign exchange market intervention in which the monetary authorities have not insulated their domestic money supplies from the foreign exchange transactions.

Unsystematic (Diversifiable) Risk   Risks that are specific to a given firm, such as a strike.

Up-and-In Option   An option that comes into existence if and only if the currency strengthens enough to cross a preset barrier.

Up-and-Out Option   An option that is canceled if the underlying currency strengthens beyond the outstrike.

Value-Added Tax   Method of indirect taxation whereby a tax is levied at each stage of production on the value added at that specific stage.

Value Additivity Principle   The principle that the net present value of a set of independent projects is simply the sum of the NPVs of the individual projects.

Value-at-Risk (VAR)   A calculation which allows a financial institution to estimate the maximum amount it might expect to lose in a given time period with a certain probability.

Value Date   The date on which the monies must be paid to the parties involved in a foreign exchange transaction. For spot transactions, it is set as the second working day after the date on which the transaction is concluded.

Value-Dating   Refers to when value (credit) is given for funds transferred between banks.

Virtual Currency Option   A foreign currency option listed on the Philadelphia Stock Exchange which is settled in U.S. dollars rather than in the underlying currency.

Weighted Average Cost of Capital (WACC)   The required return on the funds supplied by investors. It is a weighted average of the costs of the individual component debt and equity funds.

Working Capital   The combination of current assets and current liabilities.

World Bank   *See* International Bank for Reconstruction and Development.

Yankee Bonds   Dollar-denominated foreign bonds sold in the United States.

Yankee Stock Issues   Stock sold by foreign companies to U.S. investors.